Internet Intermediaries and Copyright Law

Internet Intermediaries and Copyright Law

EU and US Perspectives

Stefan Kulk

Wolters Kluwer

Published by:
Kluwer Law International B.V.
PO Box 316
2400 AH Alphen aan den Rijn
The Netherlands
E-mail: international-sales@wolterskluwer.com
Website: lrus.wolterskluwer.com

Sold and distributed in North, Central and South America by:
Wolters Kluwer Legal & Regulatory U.S.
7201 McKinney Circle
Frederick, MD 21704
United States of America
Email: customer.service@wolterskluwer.com

Sold and distributed in all other countries by:
Air Business Subscriptions
Rockwood House
Haywards Heath
West Sussex
RH16 3DH
United Kingdom
Email: international-customerservice@wolterskluwer.com

ISBN 978-94-035-1480-2

e-Book: ISBN 978-94-035-1490-1
web-PDF: ISBN 978-94-035-1500-7

Table of Contents

CHAPTER 1
Introduction

§1.01 INTRODUCTION

Internet intermediaries, such as Internet access providers and search engines, are crucial in our modern information societies.[1] They are the Internet's go-betweens. They enable us to express ourselves, they provide us with access to information, and they allow us to search effectively through the massive amounts of online content. Yet, the increasing prominence of intermediaries in our lives also generates discussions about their social and economic influence.[2] For instance, new issues of privacy and competition law arise with the dominant position of some platforms on markets for searching, social networking, and e-commerce.[3] Furthermore, disinformation and 'filter bubbles' give rise to questions about the plurality of views and opinions that

---

1. Report of the Special Rapporteur on the promotion and protection of the right to freedom of opinion and expression, Frank La Rue, 16 May 2011, A/HRC/17/2, 20: 'Intermediaries play a fundamental role in enabling Internet users to enjoy their right to freedom of expression and access to information.' *Also see*: Rebecca MacKinnon et al., *Fostering Freedom Online* 15 (2014).
2. Recent examples may be the discussions about online disinformation in the European Union (*see* the work of the High Level Group on Fake News and Online Disinformation, https://ec.europa.eu/digital-single-market/en/news/final-report-high-level-expert-group-fake-news-and-online-disinformation (accessed 14 June 2019)) and the US (*see* the work of the US Committee on the Judiciary, *LOCATION CHANGE: Extremist Content and Russian Disinformation Online: Working with Tech to Find Solutions*, https://www.judiciary.senate.gov/meetings/extremist-content-and-russian-disinformation-online-working-with-tech-to-find-solutions (accessed 14 June 2019)). But also a broader discussion about the power of big technology firms, for instance: Farhad Manjoo, *The Upside of Being Ruled by the Five Tech Giants*, The New York Times, www.nytimes.com/2017/11/01/technology/five-tech-giants-upside.html (accessed 4 June 2019); Jonathan Taplin, *Is It Time to Break Up Google*, The New York Times, www.nytimes.com/2017/04/22/opinion/sunday/is-it-time-to-break-up-google.html (accessed 4 June 2019).
3. For example: Maurice Stucke & Alan Grunes, *Big Data and Competition Policy* (2016); Ariel Ezrachi & Maurice E. Stucke, *Virtual Competition* (2016). *Also see*: Bundeskartellamt, Bundeskartellamt prohibits Facebook from combining user data from different sources, https://www.bundeskartellamt.de/SharedDocs/Meldung/EN/Pressemitteilungen/2019/07_02_2019_Facebook.html (accessed 14 June 2019).

social networks may have to promote, as well as the responsibilities of intermediaries to safeguard other democratic values.[4]

The intermediary's role as a facilitator in several economic and social processes allows it to have a shaping effect on online life and the ability to exercise one's communicative freedoms, both positively and negatively. One area where this shaping effect is clearly felt, and possible tension that comes with it, is in the area of copyright protection. Copyright law offers authors control over their intellectual creations and ensures that these authors are rewarded for the use of their materials. It incentivizes creativity by awarding exclusive rights and enables access to copyrighted works by ensuring that certain exceptions are in place. Intermediaries are paramount in this process because they facilitate the dissemination of copyrighted works. Access and hosting providers, for example, offer the basic infrastructure to disseminate music, films, software and other information products, whereas other intermediaries provide the platforms on which content can be advertised and consumed. However, the services of intermediaries can also be used to undermine copyright protection, which has led to discussions about the responsibilities that intermediaries have in copyright enforcement. Access providers, for example, also enable Internet users to share copyrighted materials on peer-to-peer file-sharing networks. Whether the access provider has to block websites, provide identifying information about infringers, or even instal filtering systems to weed out unauthorized materials have been the subject of extensive (academic) debate.[5]

The tension is also felt when looking at the disruptive influence of intermediaries on the business models of the content industries. Here intermediaries have become central actors in the value chain for information products by offering new avenues for distributing and accessing copyrighted works.[6] For instance, news can be accessed directly via a search engine's interface rather than on a newspaper website, and music can easily be streamed via online content platforms rather than bought. These new services have not been met with resounding applause by content creators, which may be attributed to the lack of control that content creators experience and the incompatibility of proven business models with the online reality in which intermediaries play an increasingly prevalent role.

Given the importance of copyright protection and enforcement, and the central role that intermediaries play in our information societies, the liability of intermediaries for infringements should be carefully regulated. The fast-paced technological environment in which intermediaries and copyright owners operate requires that such regulation is future-proof; such regulation must be balanced and flexible. Yet, it is

4. For example: Vian Bakir & Andrew McStay, *Fake News and the Economy of Emotions: Problems, Causes, Solutions*, 6 Digital Journalism 154 (2018); Frederik Zuiderveen Borgesius et al., *Should We Worry about Filter Bubbles?*, 5 Internet Policy Review 1 (2016).
5. For instance: Christina Angelopoulos, *European Intermediary Liability in Copyright: A Tort-Based Analysis* (2016); Martin Husovec, *Injunctions Against Intermediaries in the European Union: Accountable but Not Liable?* (2017); Giancarlo Frosio, *Why keep a Dog and Bark Yourself? From Intermediary Liability to Responsibility*, 26 Oxford International Journal of Law and Information Technology 1 (2018).
6. Jullian Villanueva & Philip Seager, *Marketing in a New Media World* 55 (Mark Rosenberg & Philip Seager eds, 2017).

exactly this environment that also makes it difficult to create future-proof regulation. As the Internet landscape changes and patterns of information use adapt, the effectiveness of rules may be challenged. Legal *uncertainty* may arise about how existing rules are to be interpreted, which may hinder future technological developments and creative processes. Intermediaries presumably become hesitant to offer their services if they are unsure about the liability that they incur.[7] Likewise, if authors and publishers are uncertain about the protection of their creative and entrepreneurial endeavours, they may not produce original content.[8]

§1.02 FOCUS OF THIS BOOK

The central position of Internet intermediaries in the current information ecosystem and the fundamental rights that are involved, combined with the dynamic nature of intermediary technologies and the effect they have on the law, beg the question of how one can devise future-proof EU rules on intermediary liability. In an attempt to answer this question, this book builds on three different pillars that provide support for the recommendations that this book ultimately aims to make.

First, this book maps the current EU legal framework on copyright law and the liability of Internet intermediaries. It will consider the legislation that was adopted by the EU legislator in response to the emerging information society. And it will study subsequent legal developments, such as the case law of the CJEU.

Second, this book critically analyses the current EU legal framework. More specifically, it asks what the framework's strengths and weaknesses are in terms of its 'future-proofness'. Does this legal framework provide sufficient legal certainty to stakeholders, and does it enable a fair balance to be struck between the rights and interests of these stakeholders? As the EU is a multilevel legal order that also leaves certain aspects of intermediary liability to its Member States, this book also takes into consideration the law of two Member States: the Netherlands and Germany.

Finally, to come up with recommendations for devising future-proof EU rules of intermediary liability, this book also delves into the rules of copyright law and intermediary liability in Germany, the Netherlands, and the United States to see what can be learned from the experiences with intermediaries in these legal systems. This book not only considers the actual content of rules in these systems but also considers

7. *Also see*: David Ardia, *Free Speech Savior or Shield for Scoundrels: An Empirical Study of Intermediary Immunity Under Section 230 of the Communications Decency Act*, 43 Loyola of Los Angeles Review 373, 480 (2010), suggesting regarding the liability of intermediaries: 'Without this increased certainty, risk-averse intermediaries would be less willing to facilitate the speech of others and the public would be burdened by their censorship.' Preventing uncertainty about liability was also one of the goals of the liability exemptions – or safe harbours – introduced in the EU and the US (*see* sections §3.04[A] and §6.04[A]). Yet, a complete understanding of the extent to which decisions of intermediaries are actually influenced by exposure to liability requires empirical research into the effects of potential liability on these intermediaries.
8. *Also see:* Ian Hargreaves, *Digital Opportunity: A review of Intellectual Property and Growth* 68 (2011). This assumption is based on theories that see copyrights and other intellectual property rights as incentives to create and innovate. *See* section §2.03[A] for a brief discussion of the justifications for copyright law.

their form and the level at which they are implemented. Hence, it also tries to answer a question that is of a more regulatory nature: how and at what level can intermediary liability best be regulated?

§1.03 METHODOLOGY

A few notes are in order regarding methodology. This book is primarily the product of classical legal research as it studies the content of a particular subdomain of a legal system. It is a descriptive analysis of the texts in legislation and case law in the fields of copyright law and intermediary liability. At times, the book takes a metalegal approach in the sense that it considers questions of how the law develops.[9] It does so in particular with regard to technological developments and the influence that these developments have on the law. It considers the response of legislators to technological developments, especially in the fields of copyright and intermediary liability, and its effect on the law's safeguarding and instrumental functions.

The book's ultimate aim is to provide recommendations. This implies that this research expresses a normative judgment regarding existing law and the desirability of certain changes to it. Essentially, we do not only answer the question of what the law *is* but also what it *ought* to be.[10] Since this study is not merely of a descriptive nature and develops a normative position on the law regarding the liability of intermediaries, the normative angle towards this subject must be clear.

The term 'future-proof' is central to the normative position developed in this book. It captures a subset of values that are deemed important when laying down rules in the domain of copyright law. The selection of these values is a normative choice in itself. Others may prefer to test against other values or weigh these values differently. To offer an insight into how the author came up with these values, Chapter 2 of this book gives an account of the author's thought process. In this chapter, two 'design principles' are articulated which may guide the process of designing a future-proof legal framework on copyright law and intermediary liability.

This book focuses on EU law since the EU has developed an extensive set of rules on copyright and intermediary liability and the EU legislator has been.[11] Both copyright law and intermediary liability are fields of law that have been extensively harmonized

9. Jan Smits, *The Mind and Method of the Legal Academic* 32 (2012), explaining that such research is about 'the question of what is law, in what does the law differ from other sets of rules, why and when it is valid, and how does it develop'.
10. Jan Smits, *The Mind and Method of the Legal Academic* 41 (2012), arguing that while descriptive, empirical, and theoretical approaches to the law are prominent in research, the 'ultimate question of legal science is what the law *ought* to be: the legal discipline reflects upon what it is that individuals, firms, states and other organizations ought to do or ought to refrain from doing'.
11. Case laws of the European Court of Human Rights (ECtHR) on the lability of intermediaries, such as the cases of *Delphi v. Estonia* (ECtHR 16 June 2015, app. no. 64569/09) and *Magyar v. Hungary* (ECtHR 8 November 2016, app. no. 18030/11), fall outside the scope of this research. In these cases, the Court found that the liability on the operators of a news platform for comments from their users was not an infringement of the right of freedom of expression. If the EU legal framework was correctly applied in these cases, these intermediaries would probably be protected by the liability exemptions in the E-Commerce Directive. Moreover, the EU legal

by EU directives. And both fields are also part of the European Commission's broader Digital Single Market Strategy, which aims to remove obstacles to unlock the potential of one digital single EU market.[12] This book also contains chapters on German and Dutch law. These chapters are included for two reasons. First, the laws of these two EU Member States enable us to see how the EU legal framework works out at the Member State level. And second, these legal systems are considered with a view to providing recommendations on devising future-proof intermediary liability rules.

Dutch law on intermediary liability is reviewed for its tendency towards flexible copyright rules.[13] As this book considers the flexibility of the rules on intermediary liability, evaluating Dutch law may be useful. Also, the Dutch experience with fundamental rights in the domain of copyright law may lead to valuable conclusions.[14] German law is included as Germany was a frontrunner in enacting legislation pertaining to intermediary liability. Already in 1997, the German legislator enacted a law, the *Teledienstegesetz* (Teleservices Act), which introduced a set of liability exemptions for intermediaries.[15] At the time, it was considered a leading legislative initiative in the field.[16] Also, later in time, specific laws were introduced to fine-tune the liability of intermediaries, which makes Germany an interesting legal system to study. Moreover, since German copyright law appears to be more author-centric than Dutch copyright law, including German law may offer a different perspective on the role of intermediaries in copyright law.[17]

An important reason for studying American law is its utilitarian approach towards copyright protection. In contrast, the (continental) European *droit d'auteur* tradition focuses on the author's intellectual creations and primarily protects the author's interests.[18] This difference in perspective on why copyrights are protected influences how Internet intermediaries are approached and may therefore lead to interesting conclusions as to how to build a future-proof framework. Moreover, US law

regime appears to have set a higher standard in terms of what can be required from intermediaries than the European Convention on Human Rights. Nevertheless, the case law of the ECtHR on intermediaries opens up new avenues for research on the relationship between the EU legal framework, which includes the EU Charter on Fundamental Rights, and the European Convention on Human Rights.

12. European Commission, *Digital Single Market*, https://perma.cc/5XCC-NTTT (accessed 14 June 2019).
13. Willem Grosheide, *Copyright Issues and the Information Society: Dutch Perspectives*, Electronic Journal of Comparative Law 4, 211 (2002).
14. Yin Harn Lee, *Copyright and Freedom of Expression: A Literature Review*, CREATe Working Paper 2015/04 (2015), signalling that in Netherlands, in contrast to the United Kingdom, Germany, France, and Austria, the courts have acknowledged that the enforcement of copyrights may under certain conditions be in conflict with freedom of expression.
15. BGBl. I 1997 p. 1870.
16. Spindler/Schuster/Hoffmann, TMG Vorb. Rn. 1.
17. German copyright law is based on the creator principle ('*Schöpferprinzip*'). Copyrights are granted to the creator of the work and cannot be transferred to others (Article 29(1) of the German Copyright Act). In a similar vein, German copyright law does not recognize a work made for hire doctrine because the person who created the work should own the rights of that work. Moreover, under German copyright law, the rights protecting the author's moral and exploitation rights are inextricably linked (Dreier/Schulze, UrhG, 4. Aufl. 2013, § 97 Rn. 5).
18. Paul Goldstein & Bernt Hugenholtz, International Copyright: Principles, Law and Practice 14–15 (2010).

contains a rich body of case law on intermediaries and their responsibilities, which enables us to see the effects of particular rules of intermediary liability in practice – at least to the extent that they were invoked in legal disputes.

§1.04 INTERMEDIARY LIABILITY

This book focuses on the liability of Internet intermediaries, which is often referred to as 'intermediary liability'. But what exactly do we mean by this term? For the purpose of this research, intermediary liability is the liability of intermediaries against other private entities.[19] Liability based on criminal or administrative law is outside the scope of this book. The term liability is given a broad meaning here. It does not only entail the liability for damages that may be incurred by intermediaries. The term liability is also used to refer to any legal responsibilities allocated with an intermediary through civil proceedings, such as through injunctions. For instance, if a court orders an Internet access provider to disable access to a particular website, the intermediary is given a legal responsibility – hence the intermediary is liable.

Within the domain of intermediary liability, we will focus on the liability for copyright infringements.[20] This type of liability comes in many shapes and forms. An important distinction that is made here are the types of liability incurred by the intermediary for (1) its own copyright infringements and (2) the infringements of others.[21] First, the Internet intermediary may commit a copyright infringement through its own activities. The intermediary then directly interferes with the copyright owner's exclusive rights. An example may be the copying of parts of articles by a news aggregator. These copies may amount to reproductions under copyright law. If the aggregator is not permitted by the copyright owner to reproduce the content, and no copyright limitations or exceptions apply, the aggregator infringes a copyright and can be held liable as an infringer. The intermediary is then held liable for its own infringements and incurs primary liability in the sense that liability does not in any way depend on the infringements or liability of others.

Second, the intermediary may be liable for the copyright infringements of others, most notably the users of the intermediary service. In this book, this type of liability is referred to as secondary liability.[22] This type of liability is derived from the liability of

19. *Also see:* OECD, The Role of Internet Intermediaries in Advancing Public Policy Objectives (2011).
20. Liability for the infringements of neighbouring rights as such falls outside of the scope of this book.
21. Advocate General Jääskinen also made this distinction in his opinion in *L'Oréal v. eBay*, 9 December 2010, ECLI:EU:C:2010:757, paras 54–55: 'One of the issues in the present case is whether eBay can be held primarily liable for infringements of L'Oreal's trade marks due to the fact that the infringing goods are sold through the electronic market place it hosts. Such primary liability can be eBay's liability over its own infringements or coincide with the liability of the sellers as regards the infringements for which they are responsible. (...) This case also concerns something which I will call "secondary liability": it refers here to the possible liability of an information society service provider for infringements committed by users of the service.'
22. Under US law, secondary liability is part of copyright law itself. The basis for such liability is the 'indirect *infringement*' of a copyright. Still, this type of liability depends on a primary

a primary infringer – for instance, a user uploading copyrighted materials in a peer-to-peer file-sharing network.[23] Tort law or other theories of liability can be used as a basis to hold an intermediary liable for facilitating the copyright infringements of others. But also intermediary liability-specific norms in the domain of copyright law and intellectual property can serve as a basis for, for instance, a duty that is imposed on Internet access providers to prevent their users from downloading infringing materials by blocking a particular website.[24] In both cases, the intermediary is unlikely to infringe a copyright. The intermediary may not even be at fault. But still, the intermediary is given a legal responsibility to stop or prevent the infringements of others.[25]

This distinction between primary and secondary liability has great effect on the liability of intermediaries and what can be required from them with respect to copyright enforcement. The question of whether intermediary activities should (also) amount to primary liability under copyright law is therefore also a matter of policy that is likely to divide stakeholders. This is reflected, for instance, in the heated discussions over the 1996 WIPO Internet Treaty.[26] During those discussions, it was proposed to include the transmission of copyrighted materials by Internet access providers in the scope of the exclusive rights. Under such a rule, access providers would have to prevent infringements by their users in order not to be liable as copyright infringers themselves. Such liability would have resulted in considerable responsibility for Internet access providers to stop infringements by their users. However, transmission by intermediaries was ultimately removed from the scope of the exclusive rights as defined in the WIPO Internet Treaty. The liability of access providers for infringements

---

infringement by another person and is therefore referred to as secondary liability as well. *See*, for instance, the US Supreme Court in *Grokster*: 'Although the Copyright Act does not expressly render anyone liable for infringement committed by another these doctrines of secondary liability emerged from common law principles and are well established in the law' (*Metro-Goldwyn-Mayer Studios Inc. v. Grokster, Ltd.*, 545 U.S. 913, 930 (2005), internal citations omitted). *See also*: Seltzer 2010, p. 177, explaining that 'secondary liability, or intermediary liability, refers to holding one party (the service provider) liable for the acts of another'. *See* section §6.02[D] for an in-depth discussion of secondary liability under US copyright law.

23. For example, Alain Strowel, *Introduction: Peer-to-Peer File Sharing and Secondary Liability in Copyright Law* 1 (Alain Strowel ed., 2009), explaining that secondary liability presupposes a primary infringer; Nicolo Zingales, *Internet Intermediary Liability: Identifying Best Practices for Africa* 4 (2013), referring to secondary liability as the liability 'of intermediaries for the content generated or distributed by their users, and not to the "direct" or "primary" liability for the violation of obligations on the intermediaries themselves'; OECD, *supra* n. 19, at 73, noting that 'secondary liability exists in most legal systems' and that it 'applies liability to an individual or company based on the actions of another party'. Gerald Spindler & Matthias Leistner, 37 *Secondary Copyright Infringement – New Perspectives in Germany and Europe*, IIC 788 (2016) speak of 'secondary copyright *infringement*' but appear to refer to the liability that is derived from the primary infringement of users.
24. For example, under EU copyright law, intermediaries can be ordered to stop providing their services to those who use these services to infringe on copyrights (Article 8(3) of the Copyright Directive). *See* section §3.05[A] for a discussion.
25. Liability may be justified based on the theory that intermediaries are 'least cost avoiders' who can take against infringements at the least cost, *see:* Ronald Mann & Seth Belzley, *The Promise of Intermediary Liability*, 47 William and Mary Law Review 239 (2005).
26. *See* sections §3.03[A][1] and §3.03[B][1][b] for a discussion of these treaties.

then became a matter of secondary liability theories that could still allocate some liability with these intermediaries for the infringements of others.

Another example is the legal status of hyperlinks under copyright law. If a hyperlink refers to copyrighted materials, does that link communicate those materials to the public? In other words, could hyperlinking amount to a copyright infringement? This is of course a legal question. But behind it is also a question of policy that asks whether referring to online materials should be a matter of copyright infringement, or whether it is a matter that is to be solved within the confinements of secondary liability theories.[27] If these interventions are to be considered copyright infringements, then copyright owners generally can rely on strong enforcement measures.[28]

27. A comparison may be drawn with the distinction which is made between so-called property rules and liability rules in law and economics literature (Guido Calabresi & Douglas Melamed, *Property Rules, Liability Rules and Inalienability: One View of the Cathedral*, 85 Harvard Law Review 1089 (1972); Louis Kaplow & Steven Shavell, *Property Rules Versus Liability Rules*, 109 Harvard Law Review 713 (1996); Richard Epstein, *A Clear View of the Cathedral: The Dominance of Property Rules*, 106 The Yale Law Journal 2091 (1997); Henry Smith, *Property and Property Rules*, 79 New York University Law Review 1719 (2004). *Also see:* Henry Smith, *Intellectual Property as Property: Delineating Entitlements in information*, 116 Yale Law Journal 1742, 1745 (2007): 'Property differs from other areas like torts and contracts in its heavier reliance (...) on the exclusion strategy.' *Also see:* Ben Depoorter, *Property Rules, Liability Rules and Patent Market Failure*, 1 Erasmus Law Review 60, 62 (2008): 'The traditional legal emphasis on property rule protection fits well within a general tendency to equate intellectual property law with the law governing property more generally.' Still, some aspects of copyright law are reminiscent of liability rules, such as the compulsory licensing mechanisms and levy systems, which significantly lower the costs of licensing, and loosen the control that copyright owners can exert, *see* for example: Robert Merges, *Contracting into Liability Rules: Intellectual Property Rights and Collective Rights Organizations*, 84 California Law Review 1293 (1996); Kamiel Koelman, *Copyright Law & Economics in the Copyright Directive: Is the Droit D'Auteur Passe?*, International Review of Intellectual Property and Competition Law 603, 611 (2004); G. Hansen & A. Schmidt-Bischoffshausen, *Ökonomische Funktionen von Verwertungsgesellschaften – Kollektive Wahrnehmung im Lichte von Transaktionskosten – und Informationsökonomik*, 56 Gewerblicher Rechtsschutz und Urheberrecht Internationaler Teil 461, 476 (2007).

28. Strong enforcement of copyrights has been secured at the international level through the TRIPS agreement, which requires WTO Members to 'ensure that enforcement procedures (...) are available under their law so as to permit effective action against any act of infringement of intellectual property rights covered by this Agreement'. At the international level and specifically regarding copyright law, the 1996 WIPO Copyright Treaty further adds that technological protection measures implemented by copyright owners also need to be given legal protection. At the EU level, the Enforcement Directive requires that Member States ensure that national judicial authorities can order the provision of information concerning the origin and distribution networks of infringing goods and services, recall infringing goods, and issue injunctions against intermediaries. Furthermore, with regard to the legal costs incurred, Member States should ensure that 'reasonable and proportionate legal costs and other expenses incurred by the successful party shall, as a general rule, be borne by the unsuccessful party, unless equity does not allow this'. The Enforcement Directive in particular required several EU Member States to upgrade their intellectual property enforcement regimes, *see:* Toon Huydecoper, *Nous maintiendrons – de nieuwe 'ricthlijn handhaving'*, Tijdschrift voor Auteurs-, media- & informatierecht 117 (2004); Annette Kur, *The Enforcement Directive – Rough Start, Happy Landing?*, 35 International Review of Industrial Property and Copyright Law 821 (2004).

§1.05 STAKEHOLDERS

The word 'intermediary liability' may signal that only the intermediary is affected by such liability. However, instances of intermediary liability may also affect the interests of other stakeholders. In fact, the issue of intermediary liability is a tripartite issue in which the interests of copyright owners, intermediaries, and users may be in conflict. As a consequence, discussions on intermediary liability often revolve around the relationship between these three stakeholders. Exploring what these interests entail and seeing how these stakeholders interact helps to get a grip on what is at stake when regulating intermediary liability.

[A] Copyright Owners

Copyright owners own the copyrights to copyrighted materials and have an interest in the effective enforcement of their exclusive rights. Under EU law, copyrights must provide a 'high level of protection'.[29] Copyrights are also protected by the fundamental right to property.[30] Moreover, Article 17(2) of the European Charter on Human Rights expressly recognizes the protection of intellectual property as a fundamental right.[31] Yet, this fundamental right is not an absolute right.[32] As Griffiths and McDonagh note: 'it is important that law-makers understand the true scope of Art 17(2) and are not deterred from serving the general interest through misplaced fear of committing a violation of fundamental rights'.[33]

The weight that is attached to the interests of the copyright owner may differ depending on one's opinions regarding copyright law's rationales.[34] If one sees copyright law as a tool to incentivize the socially beneficial creation of original works, then one may put emphasis on economic argumentation in discussions on copyright law.[35] In contrast, a more author-focused perspective on copyright law highlights the

29. Recitals 4 and 9 of the Copyright Directive. *Also see* section §3.03[C].
30. Article 1 of the First Protocol to the European Convention on Human Rights protects property: 'Every natural or legal person is entitled to the peaceful enjoyment of his possessions.' Intellectual property rights are also considered as such possessions, *see:* Aida Grgiæ et al., *The Right to Property under the European Convention on Human Rights* 7 (2007).
31. This provision reads: 'Intellectual property shall be protected.' For a critical opinion on this provision *see*: Christophe Geiger, *Intellectual Property Shall Be Protected!? Article 17 (2) of the Charter of Fundamental Rights of the European Union: A Mysterious Provision with an Unclear Scope*, 31 European Intellectual Property Review 113 (2009).
32. CJEU 24 November 2011, ECLI:EU:C:2011:771, para. 43 (*Scarlet v. Sabam*): 'There is, however, nothing whatsoever in the wording of that provision or in the Court's case-law to suggest that that right is inviolable and must for that reason be absolutely protected.' *Also see*: Draft Charter of Fundamental Rights of the European Union, Note from the Praesidium (CHARTE 4473/00), pp. 19–20.
33. Jonathan Griffiths & Luke McDonagh, '*Fundamental Rights and European Intellectual Property Law – The Case of Art 17(2) of the EU Charter 2012* (Christophe Geiger ed., 2013).
34. For a discussion of the justifications for copyright law, *see* section §2.03[A].
35. For example, Shyamkrishna Balganesh, *Foreseeability and Copyright Incentives*, 122 Harvard Law Review 1569 (2009), arguing that if copyrights are granted to incentivize creation, unforeseeable forms of copying should not be protected by copyright law.

author's inherent right to his creative expressions and is less concerned with incentivizing creation. Depending on the perspective one has on the rationales for copyright protection, the copyright owner's interests and how they are weighed against the interests of the other stakeholders are likely to differ.

In any case, a copyright is a private law entitlement that offers its owner a choice with regard to licensing, and whether and against whom to enforce.[36] This choice may create a grey zone of uses that are technically infringing, but that are nonetheless tolerated by copyright owners for a variety of reasons. According to Wu, 'reasons can include simple laziness or enforcement costs, a desire to create goodwill, or a calculation that the infringement creates an economic complement to the copyrighted work – it actually benefits the owner'.[37] An example of tolerated use may be fan fiction, in which fans of a particular copyrighted work build on that work and its characters to create their own stories. While, technically, these stories could be considered an infringement, copyright owners may nonetheless tolerate the use of their protected materials.[38] Another, more contemporary, example of such tolerated use may be the live streams of players of computer games. They share videos of copyrighted games online, which is tolerated by certain game developers as it may add to the popularity of their games and increase sales.

The enforcement policies of copyright owners, collectives of copyright owners, or the organizations representing them can have a significant influence on how rules of copyright law work in practice. These organizations may take decisions, such as whether to bring actions against individuals, which affect the public and which could be considered as de facto public policy regarding the use of information.

[B] Internet Intermediaries

All forms of online communications and interactions between people and companies on the Internet are facilitated by one or more Internet intermediaries. These intermediaries are service providers who operate their intermediary service for profit. With regard to the regulation of their services, the starting point is that these providers have the 'freedom to conduct a business' as protected by Article 16 of the EU Charter of Fundamental Rights. This right enables 'individual aspirations and expression to flourish, and to promote entrepreneurship and innovation, which in turn is indispensable for sustainable social and economic development'.[39] It places a limit on the EU's regulatory competences and protects businesses from undue state interference in the

36. In some cases, copyright infringement may be sanctioned under criminal law as well, which turns the state into an actor in the enforcement of copyrights. For instance, in the Netherlands, deliberate copyright infringement is considered a crime on the basis of Article 31 of the Dutch Copyright Act.
37. Tim Wu, *Tolerated Use*, 31 Columbia Journal of Law & the Arts 617, 619 (2008).
38. Rebecca Tushnet, *Legal Fictions: Copyright, Fan Fiction, and a New Common Law*, 17 Loyola of Los Angeles Law Review 651, 653 (1997): 'Many entertainment corporations have left fan fiction alone, but a few have attempted and are attempting to stamp out unauthorized use of their proprietary characters.'
39. European Union Agency for Fundamental Rights, Freedom to Conduct a Business: Exploring the Dimensions of a Fundamental Right 4 (2015).

operation of their business.[40] But it also puts the interests of businesses and their owners on a par with the interests of others and serves as a counterweight to their fundamental rights.[41] As we will see later on, the freedom to conduct a business also plays a significant role in determining what duties intermediaries may have vis-à-vis copyright owners under EU law.[42]

Still, the notion of an Internet intermediary is often broader than just the linking capacity suggested by the original meaning of the word 'intermediary'.[43] Newer intermediaries may also provide tools that enable people to find, create, share, or manipulate information on the Internet. One can here think of social networks, content platforms, e-commerce platforms, and search engines (Figure 1). These services build on the information provided by others – including their users – and may add new meaning, value, and functionality to pre-existing content. For example, a video hosting platform is often more than just a storage facility for user-uploaded videos. Such a platform may also provide automatic translation for uploaded videos, categorization, search functionality, and other features that add value to these videos and the service itself.

Figure 1.1 Simplified Overview of Different Types of Intermediaries

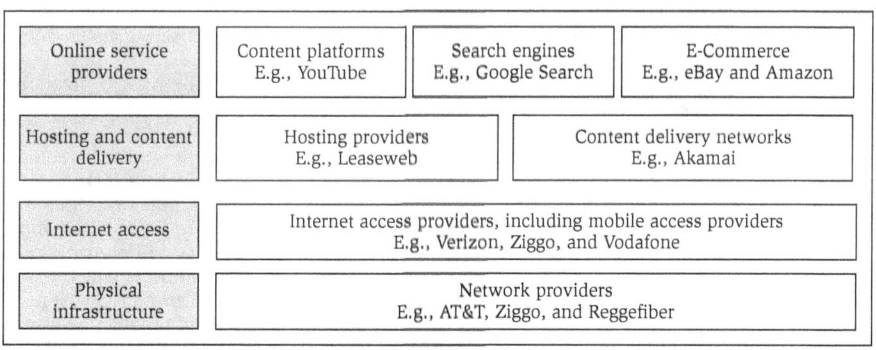

Internet intermediaries can be powerful institutions as they exercise great control over our online communications. As Frank Pasquale puts it: 'intermediaries govern online life'.[44] The decisions that Internet intermediaries make and the policies they adopt have a shaping effect on the Internet, its users, and the information shared on it.[45] Or as

40. Andrea Usai, *The Freedom to Conduct a Business in the EU, Its Limitations and Its Role in the European Legal Order: A New Engine for Deeper and Stronger Economic, Social and Political Integration*, 14 German Law Journal 1867, 1871 (2013).
41. European Union Agency for Fundamental Rights, *supra* n. 39, at 24.
42. *See* section §3.05[D].
43. The Oxford Dictionary defines an intermediary as 'A person who acts as a link between people in order to try and bring about an agreement; a mediator.'
44. Frank Pasquale, *Beyond Innovation and Competition: The Need for Qualified Transparency in Internet Intermediaries*, 104 Northwestern University Law Review 105 (2010).
45. Laura DeNardis, *Hidden Levers of Internet Control*, 15 Journal of Information Communication and Society 720 (2012); Laura DeNardis & Andrea Hackl, *Internet Governance by Social Media*

stated by Frank La Rue, the United Nations Special Rapporteur on freedom of expression: 'given that Internet services are run and maintained by private companies, the private sector has gained unprecedented influence over individuals' right to freedom of expression and access to information'.[46] In a similar vein, Floridi refers to the new technology companies as the 'new grey eminences', or 'the new grey power', controlling online flows of information.[47] Indeed, commercially operating intermediaries have their own political, economic, social, and technological views and interests and may advance those according to their wishes.[48]

Some intermediaries - especially those who provide online platforms - are starting to function more as media companies than as purely 'technological' companies.[49] Due to the essential role that intermediaries play and the considerable power they exert over the flows of information, some intermediaries have attained media-like features.[50] This is also recognized in the revision of the EU Audiovisual Media Services Directive which brings providers of 'video-sharing platforms' within the ambit of EU media regulation.[51] This directive clarifies that these platforms have no editorial

---

Platforms, 39 Telecommunications Policy 761 (2015). *Also see*: Virgilio Almeida, Danilo Doneda & Yasodara Córdova, *Whither Social Media Governance?*, 20 IEEE Internet Computing 82, 82 (2016), noting that social media platforms 'project elements of their intended business model' and that 'the possibilities of individual expression and creativity are often limited not only by technical constraints but by design choices made by the platform itself, reflecting views from the platform controllers and developers'.

46. Report of the Special Rapporteur on the promotion and protection of the right to freedom of opinion and expression, Frank La Rue, 16 May 2011, A/HRC/17/2, 13.
47. Luciano Floridi, *The New Grey Power*, 28 Philosophy & Technology 329 (2015).
48. Twitter, for instance, portrayed itself as a free speech proponent, *see*: Biz Stone, *The Tweets Must Flow*, Twitter, https://blog.twitter.com/2011/tweets-must-flow (accessed June 14). Facebook has at some point banned pictures of women breastfeeding showing a nipple or areola on the basis of its no-nudity policy, *see*: Y. Ibrahim, *The Politics of Image: The Image Economy on Facebook* (Celia Livermore ed., 2012). *Also see*: Online Censorship, https://onlinecensorship.org (accessed June 14) which is a website where users of social media platforms can report the removal of their content or accounts. For more critical analysis, *see*: Tarleton Gillespie, *The Politics of 'Platforms'*, 12 New Media & Society 347, 358 (2010), explaining that some intermediaries frame themselves as 'platforms' to present themselves as neutral actors; and Frank Pasquale, *Platform Neutrality: Enhancing Freedom of Expression in Spheres of Private Power*, 17 Theoretical Inquiries in Law 487, 496 (2016) explaining that 'large technology platforms' strategic, opportunistic, and contradictory self-characterizations take advantage of the siloed nature of legal disputes'.
49. Philip Napoli & Robyn Caplan, *Why Media Insist They're Not Media Companies, Whey They're Wrong, and Why It Matters*, 22 First Monday 1 (2017).
50. Council of Europe, Recommendation CM/Rec(2011) 7 of the Committee of Ministers to member states on a new notion of media, 2: 'A number of "intermediaries" or "auxiliaries", often stemming from the information and communication (ICT) sector, including those serving at the outset as mere hosts or conduits (for example infrastructure, network or platform operators), are essential for digital media's outreach and people's access to them. Services provided by these new actors have become essential pathfinders to information, at times turning the intermediaries or auxiliaries into gatekeepers or into players who assume an active role in mass communication editorial processes. Such services have complemented or, on occasion, partly replaced traditional media actors in respect of those functions. The roles of each actor can easily change or evolve fluidly and seamlessly. Furthermore, some have developed services or applications which have put them in a dominant position on a national or even at a global level.'
51. Directive of the European Parliament and of the Council amending Directive 2010/13/EU on the coordination of certain provisions laid down by law, regulation or administrative action in

responsibility, but it nevertheless recognizes that they determine the organization of content 'by automatic means or algorithms in particular by displaying, tagging and sequencing'.[52]

In particular the practices and policies of larger service providers, such as Google, Facebook, Amazon, Twitter, and others, can have significant effects on how users access information online.[53] The policies of social network intermediaries can, for instance, have significant privacy implications[54] and affect the information disclosed on social networks.[55] Strikingly, research by Jørgensen suggests that these platforms do not always seem to be fully aware of the consequences of their own policies for the protection of human rights, such as the rights to privacy and freedom of expression.[56]

Intermediaries may sometimes have to balance the interests of different user groups and adjust their practices and policies accordingly. Especially if they operate on so-called multisided markets.[57] The multisided nature of an intermediary's service requires that the intermediary must consider the interests of multiple parties and balance those with its own interests to stay viable as a platform.[58] The example of

---

Member States concerning the provision of audiovisual media services (Audiovisual Media Services Directive) in view of changing market realities.

52. Article 1 of the directive.
53. Ira Steven Nathenson, *Super-Intermediaries, Code, Human Rights*, 8 Intercultural Human Rights Law Review 19 (2013).
54. Danah Boyd & Eszter Hargittai, *Facebook Privacy Settings: Who Cares?*, 15 First Monday 1 (2013).
55. For an overview of the literature on one particularly popular social network (Facebook), *see*: Ralf Caers et al., *Facebook: A Literature Review*, 15 New Media & Society 982 (2013). *Also see*: Adam Kramer, Jamie Guillory & Jeffrey T. Hancock, *Experimental Evidence of Massive-Scale Emotional Contagion Through Social Networks*, 24 Proceedings of the National Academy of Sciences of the United States of America 8788 (2014).
56. Rikke Frank Jørgensen, *Framing Human Rights: Exploring Storytelling Within Internet Companies*, 21 Information, Communication & Society 340 (2017): 'The strong belief in the liberating power of technology echoes the United States online freedom agenda, which largely focuses on threats to the free and open internet from repressive governments and pays less attention to the fact that right such as freedom of expression, freedom of information, freedom of association, and so forth are exercized within private platforms – and the boundaries and modalities for these rights and freedoms thus set by companies.'
57. Jean-Charles Rochet & Jean Tirole, *Platform Competition in Two-Sided Markets*, 1 Journal of the European Economic Association 990 (2003); David Evans & Michael Noel, *The Analysis of Mergers That Involve Multisided Platform Businesses*, 4 Journal of Competition Law & Economics 663 (2008); Rupprecht Podszun & Stephan Kreifels, *Digital Platforms and Competition Law*, 5 Journal European Consumers and Market Law 33, 35 (2016). Such markets are also influenced by indirect network effects, where an increase in users on one side of the market (e.g., search engine users) increases the value the product has to users at the other side of the market (e.g., advertisers).
58. Kevin Boudreau & Andrei Hagiu, *Platforms Rules: Multi-sided Platforms as Regulators*, 164-165 (Annabelle Gawer ed., 2008). *Also see*: David Evans, *Governing Bad Behavior by Users of Multi-sided Platforms*, 27 Berkeley Technology Law Journal 1201 (2012), explaining different governance models that platform owners have adopted to regulate behaviour on their platforms. For a recent example of how a platform's policies may have been adjusted to the interests of others: Sapna Maheshwari & Daisuke Wakabayashi, *AT&T and Johnson & Johnson Pull Ads From YouTube*, The New York Times, www.nytimes.com/2017/03/22/business/atampt-and-johnson-amp-johnson-pull-ads-from-youtube-amid-hate-speech-concerns.html (accessed 14 June 2019) And: Julia Kollewe, *Marmite maker Unilever threatens to pull ads from Facebook and Google*, The Guardian, www.theguardian.com/media/2018/feb/12/marmite-unilever-ads-facebook-google accessed 14 June 2019).

search engine services may illustrate that point. A search engine operator generally offers free search services to its users. Revenue is generated at the other side of the search engine market where advertisers pay to display advertisements to those users. If there are no users using the search engine, advertisers will not be willing to advertise with the search engine, which creates an incentive to build a well-functioning search engine. And if there are too much advertisements in the search engine, users may no longer want to use that search engine, which requires the search engine operator to also consider user interests.[59]

Now, the focus in this book will be on intermediaries and their place in the copyright system and the liability they may have for infringements. This latter aspect, the liability issue, may suggest that there is a conflictual relationship between intermediaries and copyright owners. However, that is not necessarily always the case.[60] The intermediary benefits from, and to a certain extent may also be dependent on, the content provided by copyright owners since it may make the intermediary's service more attractive to users and advertisers. Copyright owners, too, can make use of the platforms and social networks provided by intermediaries to distribute and advertise their content.[61] The intermediary's services then facilitate relationships between copyright owners and users.[62]

Moreover, intermediaries and copyright owners may develop a symbiotic relationship. In this respect, Facebook's 'Instant Articles' is a noteworthy initiative.[63] This initiative enables publishers to embed news articles directly into the social network's interface – instead of simply linking to it – and allows publishers to profit from the advertising that is run alongside the articles.[64] This initiative enables Facebook to compete with news-driven platforms such as Twitter; it provides users with a more

59. This theory of course depends on a healthy level of competition on the market for search engine services, which at the user side of the market appears to be limited. *See*: European Commission, 27 June 2017, Press release 'Antitrust: Commission fines Google €2.42 billion for abusing dominance as search engine by giving illegal advantage to own comparison shopping service,' stressing that 'Google's search engine has held very high market shares in all EEA countries, exceeding 90% in most.'
60. *See also*: Niva Elkin-Koren, *After Twenty Years: Revisiting Copyright Liability of Online Intermediaries* (Susy Frankel & Daniel Gervais eds, 2014).
61. Kylie Jarrett, *Beyond Broadcast Yourselftm: The Future of Youtube*, 126 Media International Australia 132 (2008); Jin Kim, *The Institutionalization of YouTube: From User-Generated Content to Professionally Generated Content*, 34 Media Culture & Society 53, 54–56 (2012); Heather McIntosh, *Vevo and the Business of Online Music Video Distribution*, 39 Popular Music and Society 487 (2015).
62. Sonya Yan Song & Steven Wildman, *Evolution of Strategy and Commercial Relationships for Social Media Platforms: The Case of YouTube* (Mike Friedrichsen & Wolfgang Mühl-Benninghaus eds, 2013).
63. *See*: https://perma.cc/8QVP-ZW5N (accessed 14 June 2019).
64. Ravi Somaiya, Mike Isaac & Vindu Goel, *Facebook May Host News Sites* Content, The New York Times, www.nytimes.com/2015/03/24/business/media/facebook-may-host-news-sites-content.html (accessed 14 June 2019). Brian Bergstein, *Facebook's Telltale Heart*, MIT Technology Review, www.technologyreview.com/s/541056/facebooks-telltale-heart/ (accessed 14 June 2019) criticizing Facebook's restrictive policies regarding graphic images and how it could affect the publishing of news through Facebook. Google and Twitter also enable caching of online publications to provide users with a faster online experience on mobile devices: Conor Dougherty & Vindu Goel, *Google, Twitter and Publishers Seek Faster Web*', The New York Times, https://perma.cc/BFQ5-PJ3L (accessed 14 June 2019).

complete platform and enables publishers to monetize their content and connect with users on fast-loading platforms.[65]

Intermediaries and copyright owners may also cooperate to effectively enforce copyrights through private ordering. Private ordering occurs when intermediaries and copyright owners use combinations of private law instruments, such as terms of use, and technology to create a private enforcement regime.[66] Examples include YouTube's Content ID system or Facebook's Rights Manager.[67] In these systems, uploaded content is checked against a database of copyrighted materials. If a match is found, copyright owners are offered a choice as to whether to remove the material, to allow it, or to allow it and share in the advertisement revenues generated by the video.[68] Whether these systems fully satisfy both intermediaries and copyright owners has been a matter of debate.[69] Still, these systems can have a shaping effect on how copyright is enforced and the ways in which users may access online information.[70]

In sum, intermediaries come in many shapes and forms. They offer basic Internet connectivity and allow people to store or transmit information. Other services are performed on top of the Internet's infrastructure and enable people to create, access, share, or manipulate information. As intermediaries play a central role in online communication, they can exert a significant influence on what is communicated online. Internet intermediaries, especially those that offer online platforms to the content of others, may also align their interests with copyright owners. A symbiotic relationship may then develop, which multiplies the potential impact that the practices of intermediaries and copyright owners have on the flows of information. Such a relationship may benefit both intermediaries and copyright, but it may also affect the interests of Internet users.

65. Peter Fernandez, *'Through the Looking Glass: Envisioning New Library Technologies' Educational Trends That Will Impact Library Technology*, 33 Library High Tech News 5 (2016); Mike Ananny, *Networked News Time: How Slow – Or Fast – Do Publics Need News to Be*, Digital Journalism 8 (2016). But *see*: Rasmus Kleis Nielsen & Sarah Anne Ganter, *Dealing with Digital Intermediaries: A Case Study of the Relations Between Publishers and Platforms*, 20 New Media & Society 1600 (2018), highlighting that news media organizations are concerned about editorial identity, access to data, and revenue.
66. Annemarie Bridy, *Graduated Response and the Turn to Private Ordering in Online Copyright Enforcement Litigation*, 89 Oregon Law Review (1) 81, 84 (2010); Benjamin Boroughf, *The Next Great YouTube: Improving Content ID to Foster Creativity, Cooperation and Fair Compensation*, 25 Albany Law Journal of Science and Technology, 95, 104 (2015). Yafit Lev-Aretz, *Copyright Lawmaking and Public Choice: From Legislative Battles to Private Ordering*, 27 Harvard Journal of Law & Technology (1) 203, 2010 (2013), distinguishing between three types of relationships in which private ordering in copyright may take place: (1) the user-industry relationship, (2) the inter-industry relationship, and (3) the cross-industry relationship.
67. For Google's system, *see:* YouTube, *How Content ID Works*, https://perma.cc/HP34-RV5R (accessed 4 June 2019). For Facebook's system, *see:* Facebook, *Rights Manager*, https://perma.cc/SK3V-5VVQ (accessed 14 June 2019).
68. For an in-depth discussion of these systems, *see* section §6.05.
69. F. Moore, *Making YouTube face the music on royalties*, The Guardian, https://perma.cc/E5HX-2JN2 (accessed 14 June 2019).
70. *Also see*: Lucas Hilderbrand, *Youtube: Where Cultural Memory and Copyright Converge*, 61 Film Quarterly 48 (2007).

[C] Users

Users are here considered to be those members of the public who consume copyright-protected content and make use of intermediary services. These services enable users to locate, retrieve, and enjoy online content. Digital technologies have also enabled individuals to more actively participate in the creation and distribution of information.[71] If they create and distribute their own content, such content is often referred to as 'user-generated content', or 'user-created content'.[72] Users may also share materials that they did not produce themselves, or include materials of others in their own content. If such content is copyright-protected, infringement may loom.

The interests of users are protected at different levels in the EU legal system. Users have fundamental rights, such as the right to privacy and data protection, and the right to freedom of expression, including the right to receive and impart information.[73] Copyright law itself does not give users *rights* regarding the use of copyrighted materials. Instead, copyright law is grounded in the need to protect the interests of authors.[74] Still, copyright law also considers the interests of users and the public by stipulating limitations and exceptions and other mechanisms that limit the exclusivity afforded by copyright law.[75]

From the perspective of the copyright owner, a user either lawfully or unlawfully consumes his work. The lawful use of copyrighted materials is generally authorized by the copyright owner or is permitted on the basis of one of copyright law's limitations or exceptions. Users reward the copyright owner either directly through payment or compensate the owner indirectly through systems of collective rights management or other public or semi-public systems that guarantee that the author is remunerated. In the current information ecosystem, users may also 'pay' for content by sharing personal data and exposing themselves to targeted advertising on content platforms.[76]

71. Yochai Benkler, *From Consumers to Users: Shifting the Deeper Structures of Regulation Toward Sustainable Commons and User Access*, 52 Federal Communications Law Journal 561 (2000).
72. OECD, Participative Web and User-Created Content. Web 2.0, Wikis and Social Networking, 9 (2017), defining user-generated content as 'content made publicly available over the Internet, which reflects a certain amount of creative effort, and which is created outside of professional routines and practices'. For a comprehensive study of the phenomenon of user-generated content *see:* IDATE, IViR, TNO, *User-Created-Content: Supporting a participative Information Society* (2008).
73. Articles 7, 8, and 11 of the EU Charter of Fundamental Rights.
74. Thomas Riis & Jens Schovsbo, *Users' Rights: Reconstruction Copyright Policy on Utilitarian Grounds*, 29 European Intellectual Property Review 1 (2007); Tatiana-Tatiana-Eleni Synodinou, *The Lawful User and a Balancing of Interests in European Copyright Law*, 41 International Review of Industrial Property and Copyright Law 819 (2010). *Also see*: Julie Cohen, *The Place of the User in Copyright Law*, 74 Fordham Law Review 347 (2005).
75. *See* section §2.03[B].
76. This new way of paying for online content is also accommodated in the European Commission's proposal for a directive on digital content, which acknowledges that the provision of personal data may serve as a counter-performance for the use of digital services and content: Commission Proposal for a European Parliament and Council Directive on certain aspects concerning contracts for the supply of digital content, COM 2015/634. But *also see* the critical Opinion 4/2017 of the European Data Protection Supervisor.

If people unlawfully consume or share copyrighted materials, the help of intermediaries may be needed to effectively enforce the rights of copyright owners. For instance, it can be hard to hold users of peer-to-peer responsible, or find out who uploaded infringing materials to a video hosting platform. Users can make use of the Internet in relative anonymity. An IP address is generally the only piece of information that connects infringing online activity to a person in the offline world.[77] Access providers can link these IP addresses to a particular subscriber and can thus play a crucial role in identifying Internet users. However, such identification of infringers is again made difficult by privacy-enhancing technologies, such as Virtual Private Networking (VPN) technology, that can obscure or hide the user's identity.[78] The identification of infringers, therefore, remains a difficult task.

Still, intermediaries and their services can serve as 'points of control' in the sense that the intermediary's infrastructure or platform can be put to use to regulate user behaviour.[79] In some cases, intermediaries are urged to intervene in the behaviour of their users or Internet users. A prime example may be a duty that is laid on an access provider to block access to a website offering copyright-infringing materials. Such a measure effectively prevents both the website owner and Internet users from engaging in copyright-infringing activities. As already noted, intermediaries may also privately regulate user behaviour to prevent liability, or as part of an agreement with copyright owners. If user behaviour is regulated by intermediaries, the user's fundamental rights may come into play as well, as interventions by intermediaries can affect the user's ability to communicate freely on the Internet.[80] The user's interests must thus be part of the equation when intermediaries are given responsibilities or take it upon themselves to adopt responsibilities to enforce copyrights.

§1.06 FROM STORAGE AND TRANSMISSION TO CURATION

Part of this book critically analyses the rules regarding the liability of Internet intermediaries and the role of these intermediaries in the copyright system. The development of these rules – as much of copyright law – is spurred by technological advances that alter the ways in which information is produced and used.[81] The EU and US copyright and liability rules that shape the intermediary's role and responsibilities

77. Kevin Bauer, Dirk Grunwald & Douglas Sicker, *The Arms Race in P2P*, the Proceedings of the 37th Research Conference on Communication, Information, and Internet Policy 12 (2009).
78. Bauer, Grunwald & Sicker, *supra* n. 77; Stefan Larsson et al., *Law, norms, piracy and online anonymity Practices of de-identification in the global*, 6 Journal of Research in Interactive Marketing: Special Issue of Digital Piracy 260 (2012); Stefan Larsson, *Conceptions of Copyright in a Digital Context. A Comparison between French and American File-sharers*, Lexis 89 (2014).
79. Jonathan Zittrain, *Internet Points of Control*, 44 Boston College Law Review 653, 687 (2002); Jonathan Zittrain, *A History of Online Gatekeeping*, 19 Harvard Journal of Law and Technology 253, 255 (2006). *Also see*: Jack Balkin, *Old-School/New-School Speech Regulation*, 127 Harvard Law Review 2296 (2014), highlighting that speech is increasingly regulated by focusing on intermediary services.
80. *See* section §3.05[D]. Specifically on website blocking, *see*: Christophe Geiger & Elena Izyumenko, *The Role of Human Rights in Copyright Enforcement Online: Elaborating a Legal Framework for Website Blocking*, 32 American University International Law Review 43 (2016).
81. *See* section §2.02.

in the copyright system were designed and enacted in the late 1990s and early 2000s, at a time that the Internet was adopted by the masses and the technology established itself as a popular communication medium. Later chapters will present an account of how these rules on intermediaries came into being. Nevertheless, an introduction into the technical developments that gave rise to these rules, and subsequent developments, is in order here. Especially since one of the arguments made in this book will be that new technological developments have occurred, which may justify a rethinking of the existing rules and the framework as a whole.

As the Internet emerged in the 1990s, new rules were put in place to modernize copyright law. At the international level, the 1996 WIPO Copyright Treaty (WCT) aimed at clarifying copyright law and making it fit for the digital and connected reality.[82] In the US, the 1998 Digital Millennium Copyright Act updated US copyright law accordingly.[83] On the other side of the Atlantic, in 2001, the EU adopted the Copyright Directive to update and harmonize copyright law.[84] The 2000 E-Commerce Directive had, by then, already introduced rules regarding the liability of intermediaries for unlawful materials and activities of their users.[85]

Internet intermediaries were a new species in the information ecosystem that gained prominence as the Internet became a popular means of communication. They provided communication technologies that did not fit nicely in the contemporaneous information ecology and the copyright regime based on this ecology. For example, would the temporary storage of materials by Internet access providers – also called 'caching' – be relevant under copyright law?[86] And with large-scale infringements of copyrighted materials looming,[87] what responsibilities should intermediaries have in the enforcement of copyrights in the online sphere?[88]

82. WIPO Copyright Treaty, preamble: '*Recognizing* the need to introduce new international rules and clarify the interpretation of certain existing rules in order to provide adequate solutions to the questions raised by new economic, social, cultural and technological developments; *Recognizing* the profound impact of the development and convergence of information and communication technologies on the creation and use of literary and artistic works ... .'
83. *See* section §6.04.
84. Directive 2001/29/EC of the European Parliament and of the Council of 22 May 2001 on the harmonisation of certain aspects of copyright and related rights in the information society (*OJ* 2001, L 167/10). For a discussion, *see* section §3.03.
85. Directive 2000/31/EC of the European Parliament and of the Council of 8 June 2000 on certain legal aspects of information society services, in particular electronic commerce, in the Internal Market (*OJ* 2000, L 178/1). For a discussion, *see* section §3.04[A].
86. Bernt Hugenholtz, *Het Internet: het auteursrecht voorbij? Preadvies* 483 (2000). Caching is the temporary storage of content to make access to that content more efficient.
87. For example, Egbert Dommering, *Copyright Being Washed Away Through the Electronic Sieve. Some Thoughts on the Impending Copyright Crisis by Prof. Egbert Dommering* (P.B. Hugenholtz ed., 1996); Jack Lacy, J.H. Snyder & David Maher, *Music on the Internet and the Intellectual Property Protection Problem*, ISIE '97 Proceeding of the IEEE International Symposium on Industrial Electronics (1997).
88. Commission Communication, 'Follow-up to the Green Paper on copyright and related rights in the information society', COM 1996/438, p. 24: 'the need to tackle the scope and limits of the responsibility of on-line service providers was underlined repeatedly'.

The intermediary activities considered in the late 1990s by the EU and US legislators were mainly the transmission and storage of information by intermediaries.[89] Both legislators adopted special liability exemptions for these intermediaries. The notion underlying these rules appears to be that these intermediaries were 'passive' go-betweens that do not have knowledge of or control over the communicated information. Intermediaries are not to be treated as the publishers of information, who generally *are* aware and therefore are also responsible for the information made public.[90] Moreover, the EU legislator surgically removed the traditional intermediary activities of transmission and storage from the scope of exclusive rights to prevent that early intermediaries would be liable as copyright infringers.[91]

Yet, one of the arguments that this book makes is that the simple distinction between intermediaries who mediate information and publishers who produce information no longer fully captures the current landscape of intermediaries. Modern intermediaries, such as search engines and platforms, employ technologies that go well beyond the transmission and storage of information for others. These uses of new technology challenge the legal terminology used to frame the liability and responsibilities of Internet intermediaries. An important aspect of technologies offered by these modern intermediaries is that they *curate* information.

The curation of information is something that is not a purely passive activity, nor is it typically editorial.[92] But what is it? The primary meanings of the verb 'to curate' is to 'select, organize, and look after the items in (a collection or exhibition)'.[93] It is reminiscent of the term 'curator', which is the term used for a person who is 'a keeper or custodian of a museum or other collection'.[94] When museums are concerned, curation is often seen as the act of selecting, organizing, and looking after the items in a museum's collection or exhibition.[95] A museum curator picks from a broader

89. The US Digital Millennium Copyright Act contains also a safe harbour for 'information location tools'. For a discussion, *see* section §6.04[E].
90. Thibault Verbiest et al., *Study on the Liability of Internet Intermediaries,* CRID 47 (2007): 'In the early days of internet law, discussion arose on analogies to Press law on the grounds that host providers could technically be viewed as "publishers" helping to distribute and disseminate third party content. ... However, today – as far as has been reported – Member States do not generally treat host providers as press publishers, notwithstanding reservations in some specific cases such as those involving operators of discussion forums closely linked to online press publications.'
91. *See* section §3.03[D][1][b].
92. The discussion of the concept of curation depends on earlier research carried out with Tijana Milosevic and Melinda Sebastian, which was conducted as part of a research project at Harvard's Berkman Center for Internet and Society. More information about this research project is available at: Urs Gasser and Wolfgang Schulz, *Governance of Online Intermediaries: Observations From a Series of National Case Studies,* Berkman Klein Center, https://cyber.law.harvard.edu/publications/2015/online_intermediaries (accessed 14 June 2019).
93. Oxford Dictionary.
94. Oxford Dictionary.
95. For instance: Michael Bawaya, *Curation in Crisis,* 317 Science 1025 (2007); Nancy Van House & Elizabeth Churchill, *Technologies of Memory: Key Issues and Critical Perspectives,* 1 Memory Studies 295, 301 (2008): 'librarians, archivists and historians know that preservation requires curation: decisions have to be made about which information is to be preserved and in what formats, as well as methods of capture, representation, presentation and reproduction'. Also in the digital domain, the need for the curation of digital collections of data and information

collection of works certain paintings or other objects that, for instance, illustrate a societal development during a specific period of time, or that puts a painting and its painter into a line of other works of art and artists. Curators take care of collections and develop exhibitions that illustrate a narrative or that deliver a message.[96]

Some Internet intermediaries also perform curatorial functions regarding pre-existing online information. One intermediary that typically curates online information is a search engine. If we would think of the web as a museum's storage or a library's collection of books, then Internet search engines present us, based on our preferences, with relevant pieces from that museum or library. Before search engines like Google's existed, Internet users depended mainly on human-maintained lists covering only a selection of the information available on the web.[97] In contrast, today's search engines instantly provide us with relevant search results and information for any search query.

Social media services, such as Facebook and Twitter, can also be seen as curators of information. They enable individuals to create a public or semi-public profile within the network's system and to articulate a list of other users with whom they share a connection.[98] The photos, status updates, and other sets of information could be seen as 'artefacts', which are automatically ordered, filtered, and made searchable by these social media services. As Hogan writes:

> Everyone can have his or her own exhibit, as long as the relevant information can be displayed with some coherence. Yet it is simply impractical to have a human curator pore over one's social information and devise a unique and relevant exhibit for each person, on demand. Consequently, computers have taken on this role, devising continually more sophisticated ways to curate artefacts.[99]

A key difference with the type of curation done by traditional curators is that curation by Internet intermediaries is done automatically. Intermediary services generally use computer algorithms to curate available information.[100] Algorithms are proceduralized choices by a machine, which may reflect human choices, but which run

---

has been highlighted. Curation may then mean that the information is maintained and that value is added thereto for current and future use, *see:* Nick Beagrie, *Digital Curation for Science, Digital Libraries and Individuals*, 1 The International Journal of Digital Curation 3 (2006).

96. American Alliance of Museums Curators Committee, *Curator Core Competencies*, https://perma.cc/WR7T-GF2X: 'curators are much more than academics who work with collections; they are *information brokers* who, through learned and creative interpretation, create meaningful experiences for people' (emphasis added) (accessed 14 June 2019).
97. With their Google search engine, inventors Sergey Brin and Lawrence Page intended to build a search engine that went beyond a 'human-maintained list' that 'cover popular topics effectively but are subjective, expensive to build and maintain, slow to improve, and cannot cover all esoteric topics' (Sergey Brin & Larry Page, *The Anatomy of a Large-Scale Hypertextual Web Search Engine*, 30 Computer Networks and ISDN Systems 107 (1998)).
98. Dana Boyd & Nicole Ellison, *Social Network Sites: Definition, History, and Scholarship*, 13 Journal of Computer-Mediated Communication 210, 211 (2008).
99. Bernie Hogan, *The Presentation of Self in the Age of Social Media: Distinguishing Performances and Exhibitions Online*, 30 Bulletin of Science Technology Society 377, 381 (2010).
100. The development of these technologies has given rise to a new literature asking who should be liable for these automatic processes and on what basis. For instance: Stavroula Karapapa & Maurizio Borghi, *Search Engine Liability for Autocomplete Suggestions: Personality, Privacy and the Power of the Algorithm*, 23 International Journal of Law and Information Technology

automatically without direct human intervention. Algorithmic curation by intermediaries can also be supported by user input that is fed into the algorithm.[101] These algorithmic processes differ from purely editorial processes in which information is ordered on the basis of subjective choices by experts and organizations such as news media.[102]

Some types of curation of online information by intermediaries require that certain pieces of information are adopted by the intermediary or that copies are made. For example, a social network may copy a few lines from a copyrighted news article to offer a glimpse of what that article is about. A search engine needs to copy the information that is available on the web in order to index it, and it may show a piece of that information in order to render a search result. Likewise, an image search engine must generate a thumbnail image to offer previews of the images that it found on the web. These new types of use of copyrighted materials go beyond storage and simple transmission and do not fit nicely into the categories of intermediary activity as devised in the late 1990s.

§1.07 OVERVIEW

This introductory chapter explained the focus of this book, elaborated on the methodology used, explained the key concepts used in this book, and introduced the relevant stakeholders. The remainder of this book is structured as follows. Chapter 2 explores the concept of a 'future-proof' legal framework and distinguishes two design principles that can contribute to building such a legal framework.

Chapter 3 introduces the current EU legal framework on copyright law and the liability of Internet intermediaries. It describes the most important pieces of EU law that make up the current legal framework: the Copyright Directive and the E-Commerce Directive.[103] It also critically analyses these directives and related case law and

261 (2015); Pieter-Jan Ombelet, Aleksandra Kuczerawy & Peggy Valcke, *Supervising Automated Journalists in the Newsroom: Liability for Algorithmically Produced News Stories*, CiTiP Working Paper 25/2016; Eric Tjong Tjin Tai, *Aansprakelijkheid voor robots en algoritmes*, 14 Nederlands Tijdschrift voor Handelsrecht 123 (2017).

101. For instance: S.B. Liu, *Trends in Distributed Curatorial Technology to Manage Data Deluge in a Networked World*, 11 The European Journal for the Informatics Professional 18 (2010); T. Joachims & F. Radlinski, *Search Engines That Learn from Implicit Feedback*, Computer 34 (2007); Arthur Germain & Jacob Chakareski, *Spotify Me: Facebook-Assisted Automatic Playlist Generation*, IEEE *15th* International Workshop on Multimedia Signal Processing (2013). And: Robert Gehl, *YouTube as Archive: Who Will Curate This Digital Wunderkammer?*, 12 International Journal of Cultural Studies 43, 47 (2009): 'It is in the best interest of any user who uploads a video to choose accurate and search-friendly titles, tags and descriptions, because in YouTube's search algorithms, these terms carry more weight than other factors; neither the popularity of the video nor of the user who uploaded it pushes a video up in the search. These elements are extremely important in the curatorial process, and the users are the ones who decide which are used.'
102. Tarleton Gillespie, *The Relevance of Algorithms* (Tarleton Gillespie, Pablo Boczkowski & Kirsten Foot eds, 2014).
103. Directive 2001/29/EC of the European Parliament and of the Council of 22 May 2001 on the harmonisation of certain aspects of copyright and related rights in the information society (*OJ* 2001, L 167/10). Directive 2000/31/EC of the European Parliament and of the Council of 8

highlights the legal framework's strengths and weaknesses in terms of its 'future-proofness'. This chapter also considers a recent legislative development that has altered the EU legal framework: the Directive on Copyright in the Digital Single Market, or DSM Directive.[104]

Chapters 4 and 5 discuss Dutch and German law on the position of Internet intermediaries under copyright law and the liability that they may have for copyright infringements. These chapters offer insights into how the EU legal framework works out at Member State level and enable an analysis to be made of that overarching-legal framework. The law studied in these chapters also serves as a source of inspiration for providing recommendations.

Chapter 6 on US law explores the role of Internet intermediaries and their liability for infringements under US copyright law. This chapter introduces US copyright law; it rather discusses and zooms in on those elements of US intermediary law that can provide valuable input to our enquiry.

Chapter 7 links and synthesizes the findings of the previous chapters and draws final conclusions.

June 2000 on certain legal aspects of information society services, in particular electronic commerce, in the Internal Market (OJ 2000, L 178/1).

104. Directive (EU) 2019/790 of the European Parliament and of the Council of 17 April 2019 on copyright and related rights in the Digital Single Market and amending Directives 96/9/EC and 2001/29/EC (OJ 2019, L 130).

CHAPTER 2
Principles of Future-Proof Rules

§2.01 INTRODUCTION

What are future-proof rules? The term 'future-proof' is not a traditional legal term, but it is often used to indicate that a regulatory regime or regulatory instrument is not just up-to-date, but that it may also cover and effectively regulate future developments.[1] If applied to a legal framework, the term future-proof could thus mean the framework's ability to offer certainty and to regulate effectively as societal and technological developments occur, while also staying true to legal framework's objectives. This chapter takes a closer look at how this idea of future-proof regulation and legislation can be translated into the domain of copyright law. In order to do so, section §2.02 elaborates on the relationship between copyright law and information technologies. That section will explain that copyright law has generally proven to be susceptible to technological change and that it may not be as future-proof as one might hope. In response to these findings, sections §2.03 and §2.04 put forward two design principles that may contribute to the creation of a future-proof legal framework.

§2.02 COPYRIGHT LAW AND INFORMATION TECHNOLOGY

Developments in copyright law have often gone hand in hand with developments in the field of information technologies. One development in information technology in particular gave rise to rules of copyright law: the invention of the printing press. Copyright laws emerged in the eighteenth and nineteenth century in times of changing economic, social, and technological circumstances. As Mark Rose explains:

> Copyright – the practice of securing marketable rights in texts that are treated as commodities – is a specifically modern institution, the creature of the printing

1. For example, *see:* Madeleine de Cock Buning, *Towards a Future-Proof Framework for the Protection of Minors in European Audiovisual Media*, 10 Utrecht Law Review (5) 9 (2014).

> press, the individualization of authorship in the late Middle Ages and early Renaissance, and the development of the advanced marketplace society in the seventeenth and eighteenth centuries.[2]

Later inventions in the field of information technology, such as photography, the recording of music, and television, have also left their mark on copyright law. It is fair to say that 'copyright law is the child of technology'.[3] Copyright law primarily deals with the exploitation of creative works. As new technologies to exploit and consume copyrighted materials emerge, copyright law is likely to be affected by these technological developments. New information technologies raise questions about the application of existing copyright rules and may spur legislators to change existing rules or to adopt new ones.[4]

The Dutch copyright scholar De Beaufort in his 1932 copyright treatise already highlighted copyright law's susceptibility to technological change. He wrote:

> The development of technology, to the extent that it offers new avenues for the publication and reproduction of works of art and literature, plays a major role in the development of copyright law, and they will likely continue to do so.[5]

De Beaufort referred to technologies such as photography, the recording of music and film, but his words still ring true today. Later inventions, such as television and the Internet, have also had their effect on copyright law. Indeed, what these information technologies have in common is that they provide new avenues for the use and exploitation of protected materials. They required a redefinition of copyright law's subject matter, its exploitation rights, and the limitations of and the exceptions to these rights.

De Cock Buning in her research on the influence of several information technologies on copyright law highlights a similar development.[6] According to De Cock Buning, three stages can be distinguished in the legislative response to a new information technology: (1) rejection, (2) specific protection, and (3) normalization.

[A] An Example: The Recording of Music

In the first stage, protection for new forms of expression and exploitation is often rejected. Doubts arise as to whether and how existing copyright law should be applied to the new technology. For example, in the nineteenth century, when musical works were consumed either on paper or through performances, *recording* music was not considered to be an infringement. The 1886 Berne Convention specifically stated that

2. Mark Rose, *Authors and Owners: The Invention of Copyright* 3 (1993). *Also see:* Ernst Hirsch-Ballin, *Auteursrechtelijke Opstellen* 13 (1970).
3. Paul Goldstein, *Copyright in the New Information Age*, 4 Catholic University Law Review 829 (1991).
4. Madeleine de Cock Buning, *Auteursrecht en informatietechnologie* (1998).
5. Henri de Beaufort, *Auteursrecht* (1932). Own translation, SK.
6. De Cock Buning, *supra* n. 4. In her research, De Cock Buning looked at how different legislators responded to the invention of photography, music recording, computer software, and 'cybernetic creations'.

'the manufacture and sale of instruments for the mechanical reproduction of musical airs in which copyright subsists shall not be considered as constituting an infringement of musical copyright'.[7] This provision can be traced back to interventions by the Swiss delegation, which aimed to protect the Swiss music box industry that always operated without having to worry about the copyrights to the music.[8] Music authors did not protest against this provision in the Berne Convention.[9] Presumably because these new instruments could reproduce only short melodies and did not lend themselves to public performances.[10]

In the second stage, as the new technology is more broadly used and exploited specific legislation is adopted. In this medium term, affected parties set up lobbies and try to push the legislative response in a direction that is beneficial to them. In particular at the European level, the legislative debate on copyright law can be characterized as conflictual, engaging a variety of different interest groups.[11] In the end, compromises are likely to be struck between stakeholders, which are then laid down in legislation giving these compromises ultimate binding power.[12] As legislators address specific frictions between stakeholders that are caused by new information technologies, this new legislation may be tailored to the specific technological change. If that happens, the legislation runs the risk of being *technology-specific*.

Going back to our example of the rise of mechanical recording technology, we indeed see how the influence of different stakeholders caused a technology-specific right to be created. By the early 1900s, a profitable record industry had emerged.[13] With the general adoption of the gramophone, a form of large-scale exploitation arose that could no longer be ignored by music authors. Music authors were ultimately given a share in this industry. Article 13(1) of the 1908 Berne Convention gave authors of musical works a new right specifically pertaining to 'the adaptation of those works to

7. Article 3 of the Final Protocol to the Berne Convention, as reproduced in: Sam Ricketson & Jane Ginsburg, *International Copyright and Neighbouring Rights: The Berne Convention and Beyond appendix 15* (2006).
8. Walter Copinger & James Easton, *The Law of Copyright, in Works of Literature, Art, Architecture, Photography, Music and the Drama: Including Chapters on Mechanical Contrivances and Cinematographs: Together with International and Foreign Copyright, with the Statutes Relating Thereto* 320 (1915): 'This Clause was inserted in the Closing Protocol in the interests of the Swiss manufacturers of musical boxes, which were only capable of reproducing tunes, not words.'
9. Stephen Ladas, *The International Protection of Literary and Artistic Property. Vol I*, 412 (1938): 'At the time the Berne Convention entered into effect, mechanical instruments were known little, and only in such countries as France, Germany and Switzerland. The delegates at the Conference of 1884 were not fully alive to the significance of the provision proposed by Switzerland and inserted in the Final Protocol.'
10. Willem Mak, *Rights Affecting the Manufacture and Use of Gramophone Records*, 23 (1952); Sam Ricketson, *Berne Convention for the Protection of Literary and Artistic Works: 1886–1986*, 69 (1987).
11. Heike Klüver, *Lobbying in the European Union*, 138 (2013).
12. For instance, on industry involvement in drafting US copyright law *see:* Jessica Litman, *Copyright Legislation and Technological Change*, 68 Orgeon Law Review 275 (1989); Cassandra Imfeld & Victoria Ekstrand, *The Music Industry and the Legislative Development of the Digital Millennium Copyright Act's Online Service Provider Provision*, 3 Communication Law and Policy, 3 Communication Law and Policy 291 (2005).
13. Pekka Gronow, *The Record Industry: The Growth of a Mass Medium*, 1 Popular Music 53, 55 (1983).

instruments which can reproduce them mechanically'.[14] Phonogram producers had also successfully lobbied for the protection of their businesses, which resulted in a provision allowing 'reservations and conditions' for this new exclusive right in national law.[15] These provisions on mechanical recording were ultimately a compromise between the phonogram producers who had always freely produced phonograms and the music authors who wanted a piece of the pie as well.[16]

In the third and final stage, the technology-specific rules either disappear or dissolve into general concepts of copyright law. In the case of mechanical recording, the 1967 Stockholm Conference led to the adoption of a general provision concerning the copyright owner's reproduction right.[17] This right included the right to make mechanical recordings. Today, Article 9(3) of the Berne Convention states that 'any sound or visual recording shall be considered as a reproduction for the purposes of this Convention'. This clarification is merely a reminder of the discarded Article 13(1) that once stipulated a separate exclusive right to authorize mechanical reproductions.[18] The adoption of a general reproduction right meant that the specific right regarding mechanical recordings had dissolved into the broader concept of reproduction. With it, a technology-specific rule then disappeared.

The example of mechanical recording shows that, in particular in the medium term, rules were enacted that focused on a given new technology. However, this case of mechanical recording does not stand on its own. In her research, De Cock Buning demonstrated that similar legislative reflexes occurred with the introduction of other technologies, such as photography and computer technologies.[19] All these technologies caused friction between different stakeholders that were active in the markets for copyrighted materials. Some stakeholders called for changes to the law. Legislators

14. Article 13(1) of the 1908 Berne Convention read: 'The authors of musical works shall have the exclusive right of authorizing: (1) the adaptation of those works to instruments which can reproduce them mechanically; (2) the public performance of the said works by means of these instruments.' Reproduced in: Sam Ricketson & Jane Ginsburg, *International Copyright and Neighbouring Rights: The Berne Convention and Beyond appendix 17* (2006).
15. Article 13(1) of the Berne Convention, as reproduced in: Ricketson & Ginsburg, *supra* n. 14.
16. Mak, *supra* n. 9, 24: 'A fierce war of interests was now waged between the authors on one side and the manufacturers on the other, preceding the recognition of the right of mechanical reproduction with the result that in quite a number of cases the provisions in respect of the right of mechanical reproduction are decidedly in the nature of a compromise.' Michael Freegard, *The Berne Convention, Compulsory Licensing and Collecting Societies* 1 Columbia Journal of Law & the Arts 137, 141 (1986): 'In the preparatory documentation prepared by the German government and the International Bureau, concern had been expressed to safeguard the interests of small manufacturers by protecting them both against the risk of "excessive demands" on the part of authors and publishers and against the danger that large manufacturers might gain a monopoly of the right to record successful works. The compromise medicine prescribed to meet these ills, real or imaginary, was the one which is familiar to us today.'
17. Article 9 of the Berne Convention: 'Authors of literary and artistic works protected by this Convention shall have the exclusive right of authorizing the reproduction of these works, in any manner or form.'
18. Records of the Intellectual Property Conference of Stockholm (June 11 to July 14, 1967 Volume II), Report on the Work of Main Committee I, as published in Sam Ricketson & Jane Ginsburg, *International Copyright and Neighbouring Rights: The Berne Convention and Beyond appendix 29* 292 (2006).
19. De Cock Buning, *supra* n. 4.

who answered that call generally did so by laying down technology-specific rules to address particular imbalances.

[B] The Problem with Technology-Specific Rules

An apparent advantage of technology-specific rules is that they offer clear guidance as to what they entail and how they should be applied. Yet, there are also several downsides to using technology-specific rules in legislation. At least three specific problems can be identified that relate to (1) the effectiveness of such rules, (2) the fair balance between the interests of different stakeholders, and (3) their lack of normative guidance in the longer term.

First, as time progresses, and information technology advances, technology-specific rules may become irrelevant.[20] It has been argued that technology-specific rules are to be preferred over technology-neutral rules if the ways in which a new technology may be used are still uncertain. Moreover, technology-specific rules are unlikely to spill over into other fields of activity, thereby reducing the risk of unintended consequences.[21] However, it can also be argued that the *lack* of a spill-over effect is problematic if technological developments render a rule ineffective. Technology-specific rules then produce satisfactory results for a short time only and may not be effective in the longer term. The US experience with the Audio Home Recording Act serves as an example.

The US Audio Home Recording Act of 1992 was introduced at a time when digital recording devices were first sold. These devices enabled perfect copies of a (music) record to be made. Unlike analogue copying, as is done on cassettes, these digital recordings showed no degradation in sound quality as the copy is copied. This new digital audio recording technology had the potential to disrupt the music industry as it enabled large-scale unauthorized copying. In order to prevent that from happening, the US legislator introduced the Audio Home Recording Act, which prohibited the importation, manufacture, or distribution of any 'digital audio recording device' or interface device that does not incorporate copying controls.[22] This act also introduced a royalty payment system for these devices and 'digital audio recording media'.[23]

The 1992 Audio Home Recording Act was the result of negotiations between the music industries and the new consumer electronic industries. US Congress attempted in particular to rebalance the music industry's concerns with the interests of society in having access to the new technology.[24] Yet, not long after the Audio Home Recording Act was adopted, the Internet emerged as a new communication medium. It offered new ways to copy and share music. MP3 compression technology made it possible to download music relatively quickly and to store many music files on a hard drive. In

20. De Cock Buning, *supra* n. 4, at 221–222.
21. Chris Reed, *Taking Sides on Technology Neutrality*, 3 SCRIPT-ed 263 (2007).
22. Section 1002 of the US Copyright Act.
23. Section 1004 of the US Copyright Act.
24. Christine Carlisle, *The Audio Home Recording Act of 1992*, 2 Journal of Intellectual Property Law 335 (1994).

1995, MP3 files containing music and other audio materials started to proliferate on the web.[25] And in 1998, the first portable MP3 players were sold on the market which could play downloaded songs on the go.[26] It did not take long until the question arose whether the Audio Home Recording Act also applied in this new technological context. The answer came with the Ninth Circuit Court of Appeal's decision in *RIAA v. Diamond*.[27]

In *RIAA v. Diamond*, the central question was whether the 'Rio' MP3 player could be considered a 'digital audio recording device' to which the rules of the Audio Home Recording Act applied. Simply put, the Ninth Circuit Court of Appeals held that the act did not apply, which also meant that producers of MP3 players would not have to incorporate copying controls. The Court held that the MP3 player in question did not record music from a 'digital music recording' – which is how the older digital recording devices copied audio files, and to which the Audio Home Recording Act was tailored.[28] The ruling in *RIAA v. Diamond* illustrates how the adoption of Internet and MP3 technology quickly rendered technology-specific legislation ineffective and created new legal uncertainties.[29] As Lichtman and Landes wrote in 2003: '[the Audio Home Recording Act] is unimportant; it carefully regulates a technology that turned out to be an embarrassing commercial flop'.[30]

A second problem is that technology-specific rules do not necessarily strike a fair balance between all the interests that are at stake.[31] As pointed out in the previous section, technology-specific copyright law rules mainly appear to be the result of a negotiation process between different stakeholders. Every legislative reconsideration of copyright law that is spurred by technological change carries a risk that it represents an opportunity for stakeholders to push their agenda. It will encourage rent-seeking by groups who stand to benefit from favourable legislation.[32] Moreover, there is a risk that rules are tailored to the interests of contemporary stakeholders only. The interests of stakeholders who did not have a strong presence, or the interests of future stakeholders, are unlikely to be taken into account.[33] As new stakeholders enter the picture, the

25. Karlheinz Brandenburg, *MP3 and AAC Explained* 1, AES 17th International Conference on High Quality Audio Coding (1999).
26. Karlheinz Brandenburg & Harald Popp, *MPEG Layer-3* 1 (2000).
27. *Recording Industry Association of America v. Diamond Multimedia Systems, Inc.*, 180 F.3d 1072 (9th Cir. 1999).
28. *Recording Industry Association of America v. Diamond Multimedia Systems, Inc.*, *supra* n. 27, at 1076.
29. David Nimmer, *Back from the Future: A Proleptic Review of the Digital Millennium Copyright Act*, 4 Berkeley Technology Law Journal 855, 867 (2001); Aaron Melville, *The Future of the Audio Home Recording Act of 1992: Has it Survived the Millenium Bug?*, 2 Boston University Journal of Science & Technology Law 372 (2001); Ben Depoorter, *Technology and Uncertainty: The Shaping Effect on Copyright Law*, 6 University of Pennsylvania Law Review 1831, 1835 (2009).
30. Douglas Lichtman & William Landes, *Indirect Liability for Copyright Infringement: An Economic Perspective*, 2 Harvard Journal of Law and Technology 395, 401 (2003). *Also see:* Joseph Liu, *Regulatory Copyright*, North Carolina Law Review (1) 87, 145 (2004).
31. *Also see:* Agnieszka Vetulani-Cęgiel, *EU Copyright Law, Lobbying and Transparency of Policy-Making: The Cases of Sound Recordings Term Extension and Orphan Works Provisions*, 2 JIPITEC 146 (2015).
32. Mark Lemley & Dan Burk, *Policy Levers in Patent Law*, 7 Virginia Law Review 1575, 1637 (2003).
33. De Cock Buning, *supra* n. 4.

application of technology-specific rules to these new stakeholders may become cloudy.[34]

And finally, a third problem is that technology-specific rules do not provide sufficient normative guidance in new technological contexts. Courts may struggle to find meaning in those rules. As Litman noted with regard to US copyright law, 'indeed, it is the language tailored to reflect specific factual conditions that gives the courts nothing to work with once the predicate facts have grown outdated'.[35] Courts are then left with little guidance as to how the law should apply in new technological settings. The technology-specific nature of a rule may also obscure the rule's rationales, which makes it more difficult to render decisions that consider the underlying goals of the rule in question.[36] If the legislator does not step in to fill the void, the application of these rules may become unclear and give rise to legal uncertainty among stakeholders. Yet, if the legislator decides to act on this uncertainty, the new rules may again be vulnerable to industry pressure, which may lead to new technology-specific legislation.[37] A patchwork of technology-specific rules may emerge that obstructs the view on copyright law's foundations, making it even more difficult for the courts to interpret a particular rule and to render a desirable decision.[38] This patchwork of technology-specific rules then lacks the theoretical underpinnings that are required to develop coherent and predictable norms.[39]

[C] Towards Future-Proof Rules

All in all, copyright law appears to be particularly susceptible to technological developments. When technological developments occur and the modes of communication change, the business and distribution models of copyright owners and other players on the markets for copyrighted materials may be upset. Legislators may be enticed to adopt technology-specific rules that restore the balance. Although technology-specific rules may have particular advantages, such as their precision, there are also downsides to using these technology-specific rules. The problems with

34. Litman, *supra* n. 12, on the development of the US Digital Millennium Copyright Act: 'Narrow provisions became inapplicable or irrelevant as technology developed, while those interests absent from the meetings of industry representatives encountered significant legal barriers to their activities.'
35. Litman, *supra* n. 12, at 333.
36. Gregory Mandel, *Legal Evolution in Response to Technological Change* 230–231 (Roger Brownsword, Eloise Scotford & Karen Yeung eds, 2017), highlighting the importance of considering a rule's rationale when applying the rule in a new technological context.
37. Depoorter, *supra* n. 29, at 1858, on US copyright law: 'Indeed, there is some consensus among scholars that legislative decision making in copyright law disproportionately reflects the interests of those who are able to organize and lobby Congress most effectively – the entertainment industry. By this account, technological uncertainty might provide another explanation for the amount of legislative activity in copyright law and the consequences thereof.'
38. De Cock Buning, *supra* n. 4, 223.
39. *Also see:* Jacqueline Lipton, *Law of the Intermediated Information Exchange*, 64 Florida Law Review 1337 (2012), arguing specifically regarding intermediary liability that the fact that legislation and case law focus on particular harms prevent the development of a cohesive and predictable set of rules.

technology-specific rules, as identified in the previous section, all highlight a certain lack of 'future-proofness'. These rules provide little normative guidance as technological developments occur. They may also become (less) effective when the patterns of information use change. And they may, especially over time, fail to secure a fair balance between the interests at stake.

One of the goals of this study is to critically analyse the EU legal framework on copyright law and intermediary liability with respect to the legal framework's future-proofness. That begs the question: what aspects should be considered in building a future-proof legal framework? The remainder of this chapter introduces and explains the two design principles that ideally contribute to building a future-proof legal framework specifically in the domain of copyright law. These principles are used to assess the current EU legal framework on copyright law and intermediary liability and serve as a basis for providing recommendations later on in this book.

§2.03 THE FIRST PRINCIPLE: PRESERVING THE COPYRIGHT BALANCE

The first design principle that is put forward in this chapter entails that the legal framework must be able to *preserve* a balance between the interests of copyright owners and other parties affected by copyright and its enforcement. It is argued that copyright law ultimately aims to strike a balance between the interests of copyright owners, on the one hand, and the users of protected material and the public, on the other. As technological circumstances change, the framework should be able to adapt to those circumstances and maintain a balance between the interests at stake. This enables the legal framework to remain true to the objectives of copyright law.

But what exactly are those objectives? There is not one unifying and generally accepted theory that explains the goals of copyright protection or the objectives of copyright law. Copyrights are granted to those who create original works because this is fair, but also to promote creativity. Copyright law also protects the interests of others and the public as a whole, for instance by limiting the scope of copyrights. It is argued here that copyright law ultimately strikes a balance between the interests of copyright owners, the interests of individuals affected by copyrights, and greater societal needs.

In this section, we will first explore the arguments that are generally put forward in favour of copyright protection (section §2.03[A]). After that, we will discuss the mechanisms within copyright law that enable a balance to be struck between the interest of copyright owners and those affected by copyrights and the public as a whole (section §2.03[B]). But copyrights and their enforcement can also be limited by fundamental rights. These fundamental rights then function as 'external' balancing mechanisms (section §2.03[C]). Besides these more structural internal and external balancing mechanisms, we will see that the EU legislator has also adopted fine-grained rules to modulate specific forms of use of copyrighted materials (section §2.03[D]). This 'regulatory' approach towards copyright law too is an illustration of how EU copyright law ultimately aims to balance the interests of the copyright owner with the interests of others, and the general interest. We will end this section by bringing together these insights and highlighting the importance of the legal framework's ability to maintain and preserve a balance in copyright law (section §2.03[E]).

[A] Copyright Law's Justifications

A sense of what copyright law aims to protect can be found in the arguments that are generally put forward in favour of copyright protection. This section presents a brief overview of the different types of arguments that exist to justify copyright protection. Its goal is not to provide a fully fledged analysis of these justifications. This section rather aims to explain that copyright law has many faces and that its justifications are part of a spectrum between author-centred and society-oriented arguments.

In *droit d'auteur* traditions, that are dominant in continental Europe, the author and his intellectual creation are the centrepieces of copyright law. In particular these author-centred theories can be seen as the basis for giving authors not only a bundle of exploitation rights but also moral or personality rights that the authors cannot transfer to others.[40] Some of the theories consider it just and fair to give the creator control over his intellectual creations.[41] Other theories see original works as extensions of the author's personality. There exists a sacred bond between authors and their works, which justifies that these works are protected by a strong property right.[42] Authors are protected against any misappropriation, modification, and unauthorized exploitation of those works.[43] Another justification focuses on the labour that the author put into the creation of his work. Drawing from Locke's labour theory, this justification entails that the author has a natural right over the products of his intellectual labour.[44] This theory can also imply that there is a level of equality between earlier and later authors. Later authors should have access to and be able to build on the works of others just as earlier authors.[45]

There are also theories of copyright law that are more society-oriented. These theories do not just focus on the author's creation, but also highlight his role in society and the importance of creative endeavours for the greater good. In particular, in

40. Neil Netanel, *Copyright Alienability Restrictions and the Enhancement of Author Autonomy: A Normative Evaluation*, 24 Rutgers Law Journal 347, 382 (1993), explaining that 'autonomy inalienabilities under Continental law arise principally from the idea that an author retains a personal connection with her work even if someone else acquires the rights to exploit the work'.
41. Lionel Bently & Brad Sherman, *Intellectual Property Law* 34 (2014).
42. For example, a reference to such a bond can be found in Article 11 of the German Copyright Act: '*Das Urheberrecht schützt den Urheber in seinen geistigen und persönlichen Beziehungen zum Werk und in der Nutzung des Werkes*'.
43. Justin Hughes, *The Philosophy of Intellectual Property*, 77 Georgetown Law Journal 287, 330 (1988), explaining that 'such a justification posits that property provides a unique or especially suitable mechanism for self-actualization, for personal expression, and for dignity and recognition as an individual person'.
44. Hughes, *supra* n. 43, at 287 (1988).
45. Wendy Gordon, *A Property Right in Self-Expression: Equality and Individualism in the Natural Law of Intellectual Property*, 102 Yale Law Journal 1533 (1993). *Also see:* Lior Zemer, *The Making of a New Copyright Lockean*, 29 Harvard Journal of Law & Public Policy 891 (2005). *Also see:* James Boyle, *The Public Domain: Enclosing the Commons of the Mind* 263 (2008), on the importance of the public domain as a 'vital contributor to innovation and culture'.

Anglo-American *copyright* systems, theories of copyright are based on utilitarian arguments and less on the idea that authors deserve inherent protection of their intellectual creations.[46] Under these theories, creativity is rewarded to enhance the creation and dissemination of information and knowledge that benefits society as a whole.[47] Moreover, rewarding authors with exclusive rights to their creations may not only be an incentive to create but also to create *with quality*.[48] Limitations and exceptions to the exclusive rights also play a role in incentivizing the creation of new works.[49] For instance, allowing parody and quotations enables people to build on the work of others and promote new creative processes.[50] Similarly, the limited duration of copyrights creates a public domain of works that are no longer protected, a pool of information and cultural products from which everyone can draw.

Incentive-based argumentation can be found in EU copyright law as well. For example, the Copyright Directive specifies that 'a harmonised legal framework on copyright and related rights (...) will foster substantial investment in creativity and innovation (...)'.[51] Furthermore, the directive 'should seek to promote learning and culture by protecting works and other subject-matter while permitting exceptions or limitations in the public interest for the purpose of education and teaching'.[52] Also, more recently, a utilitarian view on copyright protection can be found in the Collective Rights Management Directive. The first recital of the directive reads as follows:

> The Union Directives which have been adopted in the area of copyright and related rights already provide a high level of protection for rightholders and thereby a framework wherein the exploitation of content protected by those rights can take

46. For example, the 'Intellectual Property clause' in the US Constitution states that 'The Congress shall have power (...) to promote the progress of science and useful arts, by securing for limited Times to Authors and Inventors the exclusive Right to their respective Writings and Discoveries.' That is not to say that US law does not recognize any moral rights. For instance, the 1990 Visual Artists Rights Act (VARA) grants additional rights to authors of works of visual art.
47. A limitation to incentive-based theories is that they focus on economic incentives only. People may be intrinsically motivated to produce creative original works as well, which nuances economic reward as an incentive to create such works, *see:* Diane Leenheer Zimmerman, *Copyrights as Incentives: Did We Just Imagine That,* 12 Theoretical Inquiries in Law 29 (2011).
48. William Landes & Richard Posner, *An Economic Analysis of Copyright Law*, 18 The Journal of Legal Studies 325, 332 (1989), arguing that without copyright, there would only exist an incentive to create 'faddish, ephemeral, and otherwise transitory works'. Regarding the digital and networked environment, the European Commission also suggested that ineffective copyright protection would 'have a negative impact on ... consumers, as these would eventually have less content at their disposal or content of lower quality' (Proposal for a European Parliament and Council Directive on the harmonization of certain aspects of copyright and related rights in the Information Society, COM 1997/628, 7).
49. Christophe Geiger, *Promoting Creativity through Copyright Limitations: Reflections on the Concept of Exclusivity in Copyright Law*, 12 Vanderbilt Journal of Entertainment & Technology Law 515 (2010).
50. Martin Senftleben, *The International Three-Step Test*, JIPITEC (2) 67 (2012).
51. Recital 4 of the Copyright Directive. This focus on incentives may be explained by the limited competences of the EU to regulate in certain areas, in particular also the fact that EU legislation on copyright law is based on Article 144 of the TFEU, which confers on the EU the power to adopt measures which have as their object the establishment and functioning of the internal market.
52. Recital 14 of the Copyright Directive.

place. Those Directives contribute to the development and maintenance of creativity.[53]

Another society-oriented argument for copyright protection highlights the support of ideals of democracy and freedom of expression.[54] Such argumentation is prominent in US thinking about copyright law. For instance, in *Harper & Row Publishers v. Nation Enterprises*, the US Supreme Court stated that: 'the Framers [of the US Constitution] intended copyright itself to be the engine of free expression. By establishing a marketable right to the use of one's expression, copyright supplies the economic incentive to create and disseminate ideas'.[55]

In continental European traditions, freedom of expression as a rationale for protection is less developed. In those traditions, copyrights are generally seen as exceptions to the freedom of expression. Whereas this conflict between copyright protection and freedom of expression has been internalized in rules of US copyright law, in Europe the relationship between the two is viewed as a conflict between two separate legal regimes.[56] This may also explain why the Copyright Directive does not explicitly refer to freedom of expression as a rationale and instead presents it as a distinct concept: 'The proposed harmonisation ... relates to compliance with the fundamental principles of law and especially of property, including intellectual property, and freedom of expression and the public interest.'[57]

Related to the freedom of expression rationale is the idea that copyright law promotes diversity in autonomous views because it frees authors from state influence, as well as from private patronage.[58] The Copyright Directive hints at this argument when it refers to the independence of authors:

> A rigorous, effective system for the protection of copyright and related rights is one of the main ways of ensuring that European cultural creativity and production receive the necessary resources and of safeguarding the independence and dignity of artistic creators and performers.[59]

53. Directive 2014/26/EU of the European Parliament and of the Council of 26 February 2014 on collective management of copyright and related rights and multi-territorial licensing of rights in musical works for online use in the internal market (*OJ* 2014, L 84/72).
54. Neil Netanel, *Copyright and a Democratic Civil Society*, 106 Yale Law Journal 283 (1996); Niva Elkin-Koren, *Cyberlaw and Social Change: A Democratic Approach to Copyright Law in Cyberspace*, 14 Cardozo Arts & Entertainment Law Journal 215 (1996); Pamela Samuelson, *Copyright and Freedom of Expression in Historical Perspective*, 10 Journal of Intellectual Property Law 319 (2003).
55. *Harper & Row Publishers, Inc. v. Nation Enterprises*, 471 U.S. 539, 558 (1985).
56. Michael Birnhack, *Copyrighting Speech: A Trans-Atlantic View* (Paul Torremans ed. 2004); Herman Cohen Jehoram, *Copyright and Freedom of Expression, Abuse of Rights and Standard Chicanery: American and Dutch Approaches*, EIPR 275 (2004).
57. Recital 3 of the Copyright Directive.
58. Herman Cohen Jehoram, *Central Issues of Intellectual Property and Media Law* 25 (1984): 'Copyright guarantees the author a share in the marketing of his works, and as such is a means of securing independence of authors from a Maecenas State or some other rich benefactors, who might well influence in the subsidised. In this sense copyright is one of the oldest means of securing freedom of expression and information.'
59. Recital 11 of the Copyright Directive.

All in all, there does not appear to be a single unifying and generally accepted theory on the rationales for copyright law. Rather, the above discussion demonstrates that there exist different rationales that are part of a spectrum between author-centred and society-oriented argumentation. The perceived primacy of one or more rationales may influence the desired content and application of the rules of copyright law. For example, personality and natural-rights theories can be used in support of strong and long-lasting copyright protection, while incentive-based theories would focus more on the level of encouragement that is necessary to actually incentivize creation. Still, it seems that the protection of copyrights is not exclusively based on the idea that it is fair or just to give authors control over their intellectual creations. Copyright law, at least, seems to exist to advance public policies as well.[60]

[B] Internal Balancing Mechanisms

A closer look at how copyright law works shows that it is the result of a balancing act between the interests of the copyright owners and those affected by copyrights, including the public at large. It balances these interests with respect to (1) the subject matter that is protected, (2) the duration, (3) the scope of the exclusive rights, and (4) the limitations and exceptions to those rights.

First, copyright law gives those who create an exclusive right to their intellectual creations. International treaties ensure that there is genuine protection for every author, wherever he lives or creates.[61] Yet, in order to be protected under copyright law, intellectual creations must generally be 'original'. By laying down this requirement, copyright law essentially draws a line between intellectual creations which may be exclusively exploited by the copyright owner and those creations which are free to use.[62] For instance, the CJEU in its *Infopaq* decision clarified that indeed only the 'author's own intellectual creation' is to be protected under EU copyright law.[63] This criterion presupposes that the author makes free and creative choices.[64] And the more

60. *Also see:* Gillian Davies, *Copyright and the Public Interest*, 173 (1997).
61. *See*, for example, Article 5(1) of the Berne Convention which stipulates that 'authors shall enjoy, in respect of works for which they are protected under this Convention, in countries of the Union other than the country of origin, the rights which their respective laws do now or may hereafter grant to their nationals, as well as the rights specially granted by this Convention'. *Also see:* Zechariah Chafee, *Reflections on the Law of Copyright: I*, 45 Columbia Law Review (4) 503, 506 (1945), highlighting the ideal of international protection: 'Although international copyright seems of little value during the present dislocation of war, it will eventually become more desirable than ever before on account of the growing cultural interdependence of the world and our hopes for a measure of political interdependence after the fighting has ceased.'
62. Bernt Hugenholtz, *Works of Literature, Science and Art* 34 (Bernt Hugenholtz, Antoon Quaedvlieg & Dirk Visser eds, 2012), explaining with regard to Dutch copyright law that 'more than any other instrument in the law on copyright (such as rules on scope, duration, limitations, exceptions and remedies) the notion of a work draws the borderline between intellectual productions that are exclusive to their author(s) and those that may be freely used by all'.
63. CJEU 16 July 2009, ECLI:EU:C:2009:465, para. 37 (*Infopaq International v. Danske Dagblades Forening*).
64. Eleonora Rosati, *Judge-Made EU Copyright Harmonization: The Case of Originality* 187 (2012).

creative choices the author has made, the stronger his copyright will generally be.[65] Features of a work that are dictated by technology or functionality cannot be free creative choices and hence cannot be protected by copyright law.[66] Moreover, copyright can only protect concrete expressions. In general, ideas and styles cannot be the object of copyright protection, which prevents facts and abstract notions from being copyrighted.[67]

Second, looking at their duration, we see that rights are protected for periods that span more than the author's lifetime.[68] But protection is not perpetual. Hence, works that were once protected ultimately become part of the public domain and can be used by everyone. Under EU copyright law, works are protected for the life of the author and for seventy years after his or her death.[69] In the US, the term of protection is seventy years after the author's death as well.[70] The US Constitution also explicitly states that US Congress may adopt rules of copyright law, but that copyrights can be secured for '*limited* times' only.[71]

Third, also the scope of the exclusive rights granted under copyright law reflects a balance between the interests of copyright owners and the interests of others. For instance, the exclusive rights do not cover every type of use of protected materials, but generally only concern the exploitation of these materials. Moreover, the exclusive rights traditionally have no reach in the private sphere. Copyright owners have the exclusive right to communicate works to a public, but this right generally does not include the consumption of works at home with friends and family.[72]

---

65. Daniel Gervais, *Feist Goes Global: A Comparative Analysis of the Notion of Originality in Copyright Law*, 49 Journal of the Copyright Society of the U.S.A. 949, 975: 'If a work contains just a sufficient number of creative choices, then its creativity level (from a copyright perspective) is minimal. Then as the number increases, originality increases proportionally, which in turn may lead to a broader scope of protection.'
66. For example, *see*: CJEU 14 October 2010, ECLI:EU:C:2010:816, paras 48–49; CJEU 4 October 2011, ECLI:EU:C:2011:631, para. 98 (*Football Association Premier League and Others*).
67. De Beaufort, *supra* n. 5, at 66, explaining that copyright law respects the principle that 'thoughts are free'. In the US, this has been explicitly recognized in Section 102 of the Copyright Act. *Also see: Harper & Row Publishers, Inc. v. Nation Enterprises*, 471 U.S. 539 (1985).
68. Recital 12 of the Term Directive: 'In order to establish a high level of protection (...) the term of protection for copyright should be harmonised at 70 years after the death of the author (...)' (Directive 2006/116/EC of the European Parliament and of the Council of 12 December 2006 on the term of protection of copyright and certain related rights (*OJ* 2006, L 382/12)). *Also see* Directive 2011/77/EU of the European Parliament and of the Council of 27 September 2011 amending Directive 2006/116/EC on the term of protection of copyright and certain related rights (*OJ* 2011, L 265/1).), which extended the term of protection for fixations of performances and for phonograms.
69. Article 1(1) of the Copyright Term Directive.
70. Section 302(a) of the US Copyright Act.
71. Article 1 of Section 8, Clause 8 of the US Constitution. In 1998, US Congress extended the term of protection by 20 years by means of the Copyright Term Extension Act (Pub. L. 105–298, §102(b) and (d), 112 Stat. 2827– 2828 (amending 17 U. S. C. §§302, 304). The US Supreme Court in *Eldred v. Ashcroft* held that an extension was not categorically beyond Congress' authority under the US Constitution (537 U.S. 186 (2003)).
72. Natali Helberger & Bernt Hugenholtz, *No Place Like Home for Making a Copy: Private Copying in European Copyright Law and Consumer Law*, 22 Berkeley Technology Law Journal (3) 1061, 1068 (2007).

Fourth, limitations on and exceptions to the exclusive rights are arguably the most prominent means to strike the copyright balance. These limitations and exceptions link back to the values protected by fundamental rights, such as the right to receive and impart information and the right to privacy.[73] One example of an exception safeguarding the right to freedom of expression is the quotation exception, which permits quotations from copyright-protected materials.[74] In recent CJEU case law, we see that the Court explicitly considers fundamental rights in its analysis of the limitations and exceptions. In *Maria Painer vs. Standard Verlags and others*, the CJEU acknowledged that this exception should be viewed in the context of Recital 31 of the Copyright Directive, which requires that a 'fair balance' must be safeguarded between, on the one hand, the rights and interests of authors and, on the other, the rights of users of the protected materials. Specifically regarding that balance, the CJEU noted that the quotation exception 'is intended to strike a fair balance between the right to freedom of expression of users of a work or other protected subject-matter and the reproduction right conferred on authors'.[75]

The private copying exception is an example of an exception that is rooted, at least partly, in the protection of the privacy of users of copyrighted materials.[76] The explanatory memorandum to the Copyright Directive explains that private copying is exempted not only for practical reasons but also to protect the user's privacy:

> The major reason for this exception has been the non-enforceability of the exclusive right in this area in practice as well as the thought that it was not even desirable to try to enforce an exclusive right in this area of private use for reasons of privacy.[77]

Striking a balance between the interests of copyright owners and those who make use of copyrighted materials is key to copyright law. These balancing mechanisms are built into the system of copyright law that, one the one hand, grants exclusive rights, but, on the other hand, also sets limits to what can be protected by copyrights, sets limits on the term of protection, and requires limitations and exceptions to the exclusive rights.

[C] External Balancing by Fundamental Rights

As explained, copyright law has built-in mechanisms to balance different rights and interests. But in Europe, copyrights can also be balanced externally by fundamental rights. One of the fundamental rights recognized in the EU Charter is the right to the

73. Martin Senftleben, *Copyright, Limitations, and the Three-Step Test: An Analysis of the Three-Step Test in International and EC Copyright Law* 22 (2004).
74. Article 5(3)(d) of the Copyright Directive.
75. CJEU 1 December 2011, ECLI:EU:C:2011:798, para. 134 (*Maria Painer*).
76. For an overview of justifications for the private copying exception, *see*: Helberger & Hugenholtz, *supra* n. 72, at 1067–1073.
77. Commission Proposal for a European Parliament and Council Directive on the harmonization of certain aspects of copyright and related rights in the Information Society, COM 1997/628, 16.

protection of intellectual property.[78] This can be seen as an explicit legislative recognition of the fact that copyright deserves protection as a fundamental right. However, such copyright protection also has to compete with the fundamental rights of others.

The balance between these fundamental rights can be struck at two levels within the EU legal order: at the Member State level and the EU level.[79] First, when the interpretation of EU law is concerned, Member States have to make sure that they (and their courts) strike a fair balance between the conflicting fundamental rights. In *Promusicae v. Telefónica de España*, the CJEU was asked whether EU law requires Member States to obligate Internet access providers to release subscriber data to ensure effective copyright protection.[80] After finding that there is no such duty under the relevant directives, the CJEU made clear that EU law does require a consideration of the relevant fundamental rights when Member States implement these directives.[81] In this case, the Court considered the rights to property and to an effective remedy for copyright owners.[82] But it also referred to the right to private life and the right of Internet users to have their data protected.[83] The Court held that Member States in transposing the directives must rely on an interpretation that allows a 'fair balance' to be struck between these fundamental rights.[84]

Second, in *Scarlet v. Sabam*, we see that the CJEU itself interpreted EU law, in particular the relevant directives, in light of the fundamental rights protected by the EU Charter of Fundamental Rights. In this case, the CJEU was asked whether EU law precluded an injunction requiring an Internet access provider to instal a filtering system. In its decision, the CJEU clarified that there is nothing in the Charter, nor in the CJEU's case law, that suggests that the right to intellectual property is 'inviolable and must for that reason be absolutely protected'.[85] In fact, national authorities and their courts must strike 'a fair balance between the protection of copyright and the protection of the fundamental rights of individuals who are affected by such measures'.[86] Instead of leaving it solely to the Member State to determine whether the injunction struck a fair balance, the CJEU itself balanced the fundamental rights in question. The CJEU found that the injunction would result in a serious infringement of the Internet access provider's freedom to conduct a business and that the injunction could also infringe the rights to the protection of personal data and the freedom of expression.[87]

The Court concluded that the injunction would not strike a fair balance:

78. Article 17(2) of the EU Charter on Fundamental Rights.
79. Aurelia Colombi Ciacchi, *Constitutionalization of European Private Law* (Hans Micklitz ed. 2014), speaking of a 'double horizontal effect' of fundamental rights in the EU.
80. CJEU 29 January 2008, ECLI:EU:C:2008:54 (*Promusicae v. Telefónica de España*).
81. *Promusicae v. Telefónica de España*, *supra* n. 80, paras 61–70.
82. Articles 17 and 47 of the Charter.
83. Articles 7 and 8 of the Charter.
84. *Promusicae v. Telefónica de España*, *supra* n. 80, para. 68.
85. CJEU 24 November 2011, ECLI:EU:C:2011:771, para. 43 (*Scarlet v. Sabam*).
86. *Scarlet v. Sabam*, *supra* n. 85, para. 45.
87. *Scarlet v. Sabam*, *supra* n. 85, paras 48–52.

> Consequently, it must be held that, in adopting the injunction requiring the ISP to install the contested filtering system, the national court concerned would not be respecting the requirement that a fair balance be struck between the right to intellectual property, on the one hand, and the freedom to conduct business, the right to protection of personal data and the freedom to receive or impart information, on the other.[88]

While the focus of this book is on EU law, it is noteworthy that the European Court of Human Rights (ECtHR) also recognizes in its case law that copyright law, in particular its enforcement, needs to be balanced with the right to freedom of expression. In its *Ashby Donald* decision, the ECtHR recognized that enforcement measures in principle interfere with Article 10 of the European Convention on Human Rights, which protects the freedom of expression. The ECtHR held that the availability of limitations and exceptions in copyright law cannot prevent that the enforcement of copyrights may be limited on the basis of Article 10 of the Convention.[89] Enforcement measures must meet the test of Article 10(2) of the Convention, which requires that they are prescribed by law, serve a legitimate aim, and be proportionate. As Geiger and Izyumenko note, 'according to the ECtHR, freedom of expression has to be considered as the point of departure, the principle from which copyright law deviates: in this sense, the rule becomes the exception and the exception becomes the rule, challenging the prevailing traditional position in copyright law'.[90]

In sum, copyright law is not only internally balanced but also especially regarding enforcement fundamental rights serve as additional external balancing mechanisms. By recognizing that copyright protection and its enforcement are a fundamental right under the Charter of Fundamental Rights, copyright law protection has undoubtedly attained constitutional status within the EU. At the same time, copyrights and their enforcement have to be balanced with the fundamental rights of others as well.

[D] Copyright Law as a Regulatory Tool

Besides these more structural internal and external balancing mechanisms, we also see that states also use copyright law as a *regulatory* tool to actively guide the flows of information and adjust the balance between the interests of different parties with greater precision. It is the deliberate intervention in the functioning of a particular market by the state to pursue collective goals.[91] It is characterized by a high level of statutory complexity and the allocation of rights and responsibilities in a detailed

88. *Scarlet v. Sabam, supra* n. 85, para. 53.
89. ECtHR 10 January 2013, app. no. 36769/08 (*Ashby Donald v. France*). *Also see:* ECtHr 19 February 2013, app. no 40397/12 (*Neij and Sunde Kolmisoppi v. Sweden*), holding that Article 10 also applies to the means of transmission or reception, which includes the running of a website on which copyright-protected content is shared.
90. Christophe Geiger & Elena Izyumenko, *Copyright on the Human Rights' Trial: Redefining the Boundaries of Exclusivity Through Freedom of Expression*, 45 International Review of Intellectual Property and Competition Law 316, 325 (2014).
91. Robert Baldwin, Martin Cave & Martin Lodge, *Understanding Regulation* 3 (2012), in particular in its meaning as deliberate state influence, 'where regulation has a more broad sense and covers all state actions that are designed to influence business or social behavior'.

manner.[92] Copyright law is then seen as a field of law that regulates the market for copyrighted materials on which copyright owners, publishers, service providers, and other parties are active.[93]

The EU legislator's attempt to promote the digitization of cultural heritage may be an example of how copyright law is used to more actively guide the flows of information. Through new legislation, the EU legislator aimed to make it easier for cultural heritage organizations to digitize and display their collections online. Although national copyright laws often allow archives and libraries to digitize their archives, permission is usually required for content to be displayed online.[94] If the rights in question are not vested in one pair of hands, rights clearance can be a burdensome task.[95] Furthermore, rights clearance may be obstructed if one or more rights owners remain unidentifiable or untraceable – the problem of 'orphan works'.[96] If such works are digitized and communicated to the public, the cultural heritage organization exposes itself to liability for infringements.[97]

By means of the 2012 Orphan Works Directive, the EU legislator aimed to solve the orphan works problem at the EU level. The directive 'targets the *specific* problem of the legal determination of orphan work status and its consequences in terms of the permitted users and permitted uses of works or phonograms considered to be orphan works'.[98] The directive aims to solve this problem by establishing when a work is an orphan work and specifying the conditions under which such a work may be reproduced and made available online. It requires Member States to implement a specific exception to enable the digitization and communication of orphan works to the public subject to the condition that a 'diligent search' for the rightholders has been conducted.[99] In line with the directive, the Office for Harmonization in the Internal Market maintains a database of orphan works that are available at cultural heritage organizations all over Europe.[100] Although the directive does not solve the problem of individual rights clearance,[101] the directive can be seen as an example of the regulatory

92. Liu, *supra* n. 30.
93. Willem Grosheide, *Copyright Law from a User's Perspective: Access Rights for Users*, EIPR 321 (2001).
94. *See* Article 5(2)(c) of the Copyright Directive, which provides an exception to the reproduction right only. *Also see:* Lucie Guibault et al., *Study on the Implementation and Effect in Member States' Laws of Directive 2001/29/EC on the Harmonisation of Certain Aspects of Copyright and Related Rights in the Information Society* (2007).
95. Johan Axhamn, *Cross-Border Extended Collective Licensing: A Solution to Online Dissemination of Europe's Cultural Heritage?*, Research and Advanced Technology for Digital Libraries 501 (2011).
96. Stef van Gompel & Bernt Hugenholtz, *The Orphan Works Problem: The Copyright Conundrum of Digitizing Large-Scale Audiovisual Archives, and How to Solve It*, 8 Popular Communication 61, 62 (2010).
97. Stef van Gompel, *The Orphan Works Chimera and How to Defeat It: A View from Across the Atlantic*, 3 Berkeley Technology Law Journal 1347, 1354 (2012).
98. Recital 3 of the Orphan Works Directive.
99. Article 6 of the Orphan Works Directive.
100. The database is available at: https://euipo.europa.eu/ohimportal/en/web/observatory/orphan-works-database (accessed 14 June 2019).
101. Van Gompel & Hugenholtz, *supra* n. 96; Allard Ringnalda, *Orphan Works, Mass Rights Clearance, and Online Libraries: The Flaws of the Draft Orphan works Directive and Extended Collective Licensing as a Solution* 8 Medien und Recht International 3 (2011).

characteristics of copyright rules which, in this particular example, are aimed at making it easier for cultural heritage organizations to digitize protected materials for the benefit of the broader public.

Another example of a more regulatory approach towards copyright may be the introduction of the legal protection of technological protection measures. This protection was introduced in the EU by means of the Copyright Directive to prevent large-scale copying works.[102] Member States must provide 'adequate legal protection' against the circumvention of technological protection measures.[103] One can here think of technologies that prevent a DVD or other disk from being copied.[104] Or technologies in video game consoles that protect the copyrights in games.[105] To prevent the limitations and exceptions – such as the private copying exception – from losing their effect, the directive also contains provisions that require copyright owners to ensure that users can still benefit from these limitations and exceptions.[106] If copyright owners do not take such measures, Member States must take action to mitigate the negative effects that technological protection measures may have on the user's ability to access the materials in question. In most national implementations, users can appeal to an administrative tribunal if their lawful use is restricted by a technological protection measure.[107] There has been quite some criticism of these rules as they fail to sufficiently protect the interests of users.[108] Still, the introduction of these provisions can be seen as clear government intervention to specifically address the challenges posed by digital copying, while also striking through fine-grained rules a balance between the interests of copyright owners and users.

102. The first part of recital 47 of the Copyright Directive reads: 'Technological development will allow rightholders to make use of technological measures designed to prevent or restrict acts not authorised by the rightholders of any copyright (...) The danger, however, exists that illegal activities might be carried out in order to enable or facilitate the circumvention of the technical protection provided by these measures.' Bernt Hugenholtz, *Het Internet: het auteursrecht voorbij? Preadvies* (1998), signalling this form of protection as the third 'layer' of copyright protection after traditional legal protection and technological protection.
103. Article 6 of the Copyright Directive. It is an implementation of Article 11 of the WIPO Copyright Treaty.
104. Jeffrey Bloom et al., *Copy Protection for DVD Video*, 87 Proceedings of the IEEE, Special Issue on Identification and Protection of Multimedia Information 1267 (1999), discussing efforts by the Motion Picture Association of America (MPAA), the Consumer Electronics Manufacturers Association (CEMA), and members of the computer industry to protect video materials on DVD.
105. CJEU 23 January 2014, ECLI:EU:C:2014:25, para. 37 (*Nintendo v. PC Box and 9Net*).
106. Article 6(4) of the Copyright Directive. Member States, however, are not obligated to take measures to secure the private copying exception.
107. Ian Brown, *The Evolution of Anti-circumvention Law*, 3 International Review of Law, Computers & Technology 239, 248 (2006).
108. For example: *see*: Helberger & Hugenholtz, *supra* n. 72; Marie-Christine Janssens, *The Issue of Exceptions: Reshaping the Keys to the Gates in the Territory of Literary, Musical and Artistic Creation* (Estelle Derclaye ed., 2009).

[E] Preserving the Balance

The need to balance the interests of different stakeholders has been part of copyright law for a long time. Copyright law offers authors of creative works an exclusive right to exploit these works, but it also contains internal balancing mechanisms that recognize the interests of others and the public at large. The rights granted to copyright owners and the enforcement of these rights also need to be balanced with the fundamental rights of others. The previous section also highlighted a perspective on copyright law that sees it, at least certain elements thereof, as specific state interventions to regulate the markets for copyrighted materials and to bring about balanced outcomes.

Since both copyright law and intermediary liability are fields of law that are subject to technological developments, there is a risk that the balance that was once struck may lose its relevance or applicability as new technologies emerge. Technological developments then challenge the balance that legislators ultimately aimed to strike in copyright law. For the EU legal framework on copyright law and the liability of Internet intermediaries to be future-proof, it must be designed in a way that enables it to cope with this challenge. Hence, the legal framework must not only strike a particular balance but also enable a balance *to be preserved* between the interests of copyright owners and other parties affected by copyrights and their enforcement as new technological developments occur.

§2.04 THE SECOND PRINCIPLE: FLEXIBILITY

The second design principle that is put forward here entails that the legal framework should be flexible. This principle requires that there is sufficient room within the legal framework to adapt to new technological circumstances. In the following, we will first consider the benefits of flexibility in the domain of copyright law (section §2.04[A]). However, when striving for flexibility, rules may also end up being less predictable. Therefore, this section also considers how these potentially negative effects of flexible rules can be mitigated. For the legal framework to be future-proof, copyright law's rules must be flexible, but attempts must also be made to improve the predictability of those rules (section §2.04[B]).

[A] Flexible Copyright Law

Flexibility can be attained by legislators not by specifying the precise conditions for the application of a particular rule, but by using open-ended language.[109] Such language has a higher level of 'vagueness', which means that it may be uncertain as to its

109. Lutz-Christian Wolff, Law and Flexibility – Rule of Law Limits of a Rhetorical Silver Bullet, 11 The Journal Jurisprudence 549 (2011).

application to a number of particular aspects.[110] The choice for flexible rules at heart appears to be a choice for more rule-making by the courts. This choice between giving content to a rule *ex ante* or *ex post* has been described in US law and economics literature as a choice between 'rules' and 'standards'.[111] The distinction between the two is 'the extent to which efforts to give content to the law are undertaken before or after individuals act'.[112] Rules specify the content of the law *ex ante*, whereas standards leave more room for interpretation by courts that specify the content of the law *ex post*. If standards are used, the full content of the law is not provided by the legislator, but a part thereof must be found by the courts.[113]

[1] Flexible Protection

Flexible copyright protection may be needed for copyright law to give copyright owners meaningful control over the exploitation of their intellectual creations. For instance, with regard to the object of copyright, using open-ended language enables protection to be offered throughout the spectrum of human creativity.[114] Maintaining an 'open list' of categories of subject matter ensures that types of subject matter that were not foreseen by the legislator are protected as well. In contrast, a closed list specifies only the types of works protected by copyright law, without also offering the flexibility to include new types of works.[115] An open list enables copyright law to keep pace with technological developments and to provide comprehensive protection.[116]

Technological developments may create uncertainty about the protection offered by copyright law. Moreover, sometimes technologies are used by people specifically to undermine copyright protection. For example, the rise and development of peer-to-peer file-sharing technologies can be seen as attempts to avoid legal sanctions and circumvent copyright law.[117] Depoorter describes how, in the US, holding liable the developers of a particular peer-to-peer file-sharing application led to the creation of new software that was outside of copyright law's reach:

---

110. Reed Dickerson, *The Diseases of Legislative Language*, 1 Harvard Journal on Legislation 5, 10 (1964).
111. Louis Kaplow, *Rules Versus Standards: An Economic Analysis*, 42 Duke Law Journal 557, 559 (1992). The distinction between rules and standards is a matter of degree (Louis Kaplow, *Rules Versus Standards: An Economic Analysis*, 3 Duke Law Journal. 557, 561–562 (1992), speaking of 'rule-like' and 'standard-like' advance determinations of legal commands.)
112. Kaplow, *supra* n. 111, at 560.
113. Cass Sunstein, *Problems with Rules*, 83 California Law Review 953, 964 (1995).
114. *Also see*: Chafee, *supra* n. 61, at 504, highlighting 'complete coverage' as one of the principles of copyright law.
115. Anthony Reese, *Copyrightable Subject Matter in the 'Next Great Copyright Act'*, 29 Berkeley Technology Law Journal 1489, 1492 (2014), describing the development from a closed list to a more open list in US copyright law.
116. Tanya Aplin, *Subject Matter* 71 (Estelle Derclaye ed., 2009).
117. Tim Wu, *When Code Isn't Law*, 89 Virginia Law Review 103 (2003). *Also see*: Kathy Bowrey & Matthew Rimmer, *Rip, Mix, Burn: The Politics of Peer to Peer and Copyright Law*, 7 First Monday 1 (2002): 'Developers would seek to outsmart overbearing and unsympathetic regulation. Gnutella, Madster/Aimster, Grokster, Morpheus, KazaA, FreeNet and numerous other peer to peer systems provide different technological frameworks and legal issues. For some the desire was to render law irrelevant and redundant through technological innovation.'

> When the Ninth Circuit in *Napster* established that copyright law implicates developers of centralized peer-to-peer technology by way of contributory liability, developers of file-sharing technology developed decentralized peer-to-peer file-sharing applications that were functionally equivalent to those explicitly prohibited in the *Napster* decision. By removing central servers, which gave rise to contributory liability on behalf of software developers, the developers successfully evaded the legal rule created in *Napster*.[118]

To effectively protect the interests of copyright owners and to prevent that they are left empty-handed as technological developments enable new forms of exploitation, a certain level of flexibility of the protections offered by copyright law is needed. A flexible definition of copyright law's subject matter, and the exclusive rights it grants to copyright owners, enables protection to be offered in new technological contexts. Of course, legislators can amend the law to regulate the use of a new technology. But copyright owners are then dependent on the legislator to redefine the scope of protection. Especially in the European Union context, it can take quite some time to enact new legislation, which may leave copyright owners without effective protection. In contrast, by defining open-ended rules, courts are enabled to consider the copyright owner's interests in concrete cases and offer protection where protection is desirable.

Flexible copyright protection does not only benefit copyright owners but also can help to maintain the copyright balance. For example, Advocate General Trstenjak in her opinion in the *Infopaq* case called for a flexible interpretation of the reproduction right to prevent a chilling effect on innovation:

> In the past, it was easier to define reproduction, given the limited number of methods of reproduction, but with the development of information technology and the possibility of digital reproduction, there are now more possibilities of easier and faster reproduction. *Because reproduction is easier and faster it is necessary, on the one hand, to ensure adequate protection of copyright; that protection must however and on the other hand be flexible enough not to hinder the development or the normal functioning of the new technologies.* In order to reply to the questions referred in the present case, it is necessary to take as a basis an appropriate balance between protection of copyright which is sufficiently high and at the same time sufficiently flexible.[119]

Indeed, flexible copyright protection can work both ways. It might provide protection to copyright owners where there would be no protection if stricter language were used. But flexibility may at the same time prevent overprotection and the hindrance of technological developments since the content of the rule can be tailored to the specifics of a particular new technology.[120]

118. Depoorter, *supra* n. 29, at 1864.
119. Opinion of AG General Trstenjak 12 February 2009, ECLI:EU:C:2009:89, para. 49 (*Infopaq International v. Danske Dagblades Forening*).
120. *Also see:* Christophe Geiger, *Flexibilising Copyright – Remedies to the Privatisation of Information by Copyright Law*, 39 International Review of Intellectual Property and Competition Law 178 (2008).

[2] *Flexible Limitations and Exceptions*

Flexibility in copyright law is often linked to the limitations and exceptions that are available in copyright law.[121] Current EU copyright law provides for a predefined set of limitations and exceptions that Member States may implement in their national laws.[122] Criticism of this regime highlights that there is not enough room to permit socially beneficial uses of protected materials that do not harm the interest of copyright owners, and which were not foreseen by the EU legislator. Hugenholtz and Senftleben discuss several cases in which the lack of flexibility caused national courts to apply 'a variety of – sometimes rather implausible – legal doctrines to create ad hoc legroom in the law of copyright'.[123] They signal that European copyright law is unable to accommodate particular forms of use that are within the scope of the exclusive rights, but which are nonetheless desirable from a social, cultural, or economic perspective.

Flexible limitations and exceptions give courts the room to develop these rules through interpretation and further crystallization. There are several benefits to opening up limitations and exceptions in copyright law. It prevents the need for the legislator to step in and change the law as new technologies emerge that enable socially beneficial uses of copyrighted materials. Flexible exceptions may in particular allow for *unforeseen* uses enabled by new technologies.[124] They also ensure that existing copyright law adequately considers and balances the interests that are at stake.[125] Moreover, flexibility also enables a smooth functioning of the copyright system.[126] In particular in the multilevel jurisdiction that is the European Union, in which a harmonization effort can easily exceed ten years,[127] the importance of a flexible approach to copyright law should not be underestimated.

[B] Predictability

Arguably one of the most important qualities that any legal system offers is a sense of predictability to the actors operating within that system. If legislation is flexible, courts are effectively given a responsibility to interpret these rules and add to the normative content of these rules when disputes arise. These rules are 'open', and their content is

121. *See*, for example, the effort of the Global Network on Copyright User Rights to create a Model Flexible Copyright Exception, available at: http://infojustice.org/flexible-use (accessed 14 June 2019).
122. *See* section §3.03[E].
123. Bernt Hugenholtz & Martin Senftleben, *Fair Use in Europe: In Search of Flexibilities* 10 (2011). *Also see*: Martin Senftleben, *The International Three-Step Test*, JIPITEC (2) 67 (2010); Martin Senftleben, *The Perfect Match – Civil Law Judges and Open-Ended Fair Use Provisions*, 33 American University International Law Review 231 (2017).
124. Rob van der Noll et al., *Flexible Copyright* 24 (2012); Bernt Hugenholtz, *Fair Use in Europe*, 5 Communications of the ACM 26 (2013).
125. Katharina de la Durantaye, *Allgemeine Bildungs- und Wissenschaftsschranke* 196 (2014).
126. Thomas Dreier, *Überlegungen zur Revision des Schrankenkatalogs der Richtlinie 2001/29/EG*, GRUR Int (7–8) 648, 652 (2015).
127. Mireille van Eechoud et al., *Harmonizing European Copyright Law. The Challenges of Better Lawmaking* 298 (2009).

determined depending on the circumstances of a particular case through a process of further concretization by courts.[128]

This may cause a level of unpredictability of these rules, which impedes legal certainty. There thus appears to be tension between striving for flexibility and the need to lay down predictable rules.[129] Flexible rules may not be sufficiently clear and precise for individuals and companies to anticipate the legal implications of their behaviour and that of others. At the same time, it is clear that full predictability cannot be achieved and may in fact also be undesirable in environments subject to technological change.

[1] *Clarity, Consistency, and Unambiguity*

Predictability is closely related to legal certainty, which is one of the general principles of EU law.[130] Of the many material and formal aspects of legal certainty, the requirement that laws and decisions must be definite and clear is arguably the most important for our discussion.[131] EU law should be predictable and clear to those who are subject to it.[132] The CJEU has explained that it is the principle's aim to 'ensure that situations and legal relationships governed by Community law remain foreseeable'.[133] Legal certainty implies that rules 'should be clear and precise, so that individuals may be able to ascertain unequivocally what their rights and obligations are and may take steps accordingly'.[134]

The principle of legal certainty requires a relative level of predictability, not an absolute one. The use of abstract or vague terms does not necessarily conflict with the principle of legal certainty.[135] A certain level of uncertainty in rules is acceptable.[136] The protection afforded by the principle of legal certainty may also differ depending on the rule's implications. If the application of a rule results in financial consequences, the principle may entail that those that are subject to that rule know with precision what

128. Martijn Hesselink, *The Concept of Good Faith* 622 (Arthur Hartkamp et al. eds, 2010).
129. *Also see:* Frederick Schauer, *Playing by the Rules: A Philosophical Examination of Rule-Based Decision-Making in Law and in Life* 140 (1991): 'Although the ability to predict and then rely on the decisions of others has undeniable value when viewed in isolation, decision-making environments can offer predictability only by diminishing their capacity to adapt to a changing future.'
130. CJEU 6 April 1962, ECLI:EU:C:1962:11 (*De Geus en Uitdenbogerd v. Bosch*).
131. Other aspects entail that (1) laws and court decisions must be made public, (2) laws and decisions must be definite and clear, (3) decisions of courts must be binding, (4) limitations on the retroactivity of laws and decisions must be imposed, and (5) legitimate expectations must be protected. *See:* Takis Tridimas, *The General Principles of EU Law* 242-97 (2006).
132. CJEU 12 November 1981, ECLI:EU:C:1981:270, para. 10 (*Amministrazione delle finanze dello Stato v. Srl Meridionale Industria Salumi and others*).
133. CJEU 15 February 1996, ECLI:EU:C:1996:51, para. 20 (*Duff and Others v. Minister for Agriculture and Food, Ireland, and the Attorney General*).
134. CJEU 14 April 2005, ECLI:EU:C:2005:223, para. 31 (*Kingdom of Belgium v. Commission of the European Communities*).
135. CJEU 9 October 2001, ECLI:EU:C:2001:523 (*Kingdom of the Netherlands v. European Parliament and Council of the European Union*).
136. CJEU 14 April 2005, ECLI:EU:C:2005:223, para. 31 (*Kingdom of Belgium v. Commission of the European Communities*).

they are obligated to do or not to do.[137] In the competition law case of *Akzo Nobel Chemicals v. European Commission*, the CJEU stated that 'it must be recalled that legal certainty is a general principle of European Union law which requires in particular that rules involving negative consequences for individuals should be clear and precise and their application predictable for those subject to them'.[138] In contrast, if no negative consequences are expected, exceptions to the principle of legal certainty are more readily accepted.[139]

Looking at what the EU legislator finds important in its own lawmaking, we see the qualities of clarity, consistency, and unambiguity being reflected. By means of the 2016 Interinstitutional Agreement on better lawmaking, the European Parliament, the Council, and the Commission aimed to improve the quality of lawmaking in the EU.[140] In exercising their legislative powers, these institutions recognize that legislation should be, among other things, 'as simple and as clear as possible'.[141] The three legislative institutions also agree that 'Union legislation should be comprehensible and clear' and 'allow citizens, administrations and businesses to easily understand their rights and obligations'.[142]

At face value, flexible rules may seem problematic in terms of the limited legal certainty that such rules provide. If rules of copyright law are unpredictable, these rules may not succeed in providing copyright owners with the protection that they deserve, nor would copyright law create sufficient incentives to authors. Unpredictable copyright rules can also have a negative effect on legitimate uses of copyrighted materials. Risk-averse users who are uncertain about, for instance, the scope of the exclusive rights may not pursue their intended use or apply for licences while they actually do not need such licences.[143] Uncertainty then has a restraining effect on the lawful use of copyrighted materials. Moreover, these licensing practices may change the perception of whether a particular use is permissible and, as such, will influence the development of copyright itself, to the detriment of these lawful uses.[144]

Similarly, intermediaries may be hesitant to roll out new services if they are unsure, or can only be sure after becoming involved in costly legal disputes, as to the liability they might incur.[145] While financially strong intermediaries may be willing to

---

137. Tridimas, *supra* n. 131, at 244–245. The principle has often been applied in cases concerning the payment of taxes, such as customs tariffs.
138. CJEU 14 September 2010, ECLI:EU:C:2010:512, para. 100 (*Akzo Nobel Chemicals Ltd and Akcros Chemicals Ltd v. European Commission*).
139. Henry Schermers & Denis Waelbroeck, *Judicial Protection in the European Union* 118 (2001).
140. Interinstitutional Agreement between the European Parliament, the Council of the European Union and the European Commission on Better Law-Making (*OJ* 2016, L 123/1).
141. Recital 2 of the Interinstitutional Agreement.
142. Paragraph 3 of the Interinstitutional Agreement.
143. Depoorter, *supra* n. 29, at 1850.
144. James Gibson, *Risk Aversion and Rights Accretion in Intellectual Property Law*, 116 Yale Law Journal 882 (2007), making this point with regard to the US fair use doctrine, which takes into consideration the effects of a use on the market. Similarly, Article 5(5) of the Copyright Directive requires that exceptions and limitations be applied in cases which, among other things, 'do not conflict with a normal exploitation of the work'.
145. John Blevins, *Uncertainty as Enforcement Mechanism: The New Expansion of Secondary Copyright Liability to Internet Platforms*, 34 Cardozo Law Review 1821 (2013); David Ardia,

take the risk and test the boundaries of copyright law, smaller intermediaries may not. Unpredictable rules may then hamper competition and innovation. In this respect it is also important to note that under current EU copyright law infringers in principle bear the legal costs and expenses of the copyright owner.[146] Since this raises the financial stakes, the importance of predictability has only grown in the field of intellectual property.

[2] Mitigating Unpredictability

Given the importance of legal certainty, a legal framework on intermediary liability and copyright law should not only be flexible but also sufficiently predictable. At least three different predictability-enhancing elements can be distinguished: (1) consistency in case law, (2) delegation of rule-making power, and (3) the promotion and adoption of private regulation.

[a] Consistency in Case Law

Consistent case law plays an important role in making flexible rules more predictable. A flexible rule can obtain an *ex ante* understanding as court decisions specify the rule over time, adding to the predictability of the rule in particular cases. While an interpretation of the flexible rule by a court in one case may, for that case, be considered as giving meaning to the rule *ex post*, in later cases the interpretation in this earlier case may serve as *ex ante* meaning. Kaplow explains that, 'to the extent laws are promulgated as standards, predictability will be enhanced by precedent to the extent precedent transforms standards into rules'.[147] Court decisions then add normative content to a flexible rule and provide guidance in future situations and cases.[148]

While in civil law systems there is no such thing as binding or persuasive precedent, earlier court decisions undeniably shape a rule's future application. For instance, research suggests that the CJEU's case law, in particular when preliminary references are concerned, can become an important source of law in later decisions.[149] Specifically in the field of copyright law, the CJEU generally refers to its earlier decisions to confirm the position of the court on a point or to distinguish the factual situation from that of previous cases.[150] For instance, the CJEU's case law on the right of communication to the public, which is harmonized in Article 3 of the Copyright

---

Free Speech Savior or Shield for Scoundrels: An Empirical Study of Intermediary Immunity Under Section 230 of the Communications Decency Act, 43 Loyola of Los Angeles Review 373, 485 (2010).

146. Article 14 of the Enforcement Directive.
147. Kaplow, *supra* 112, at 611.
148. Specifically regarding the US fair use standard, *see:* Niva Elkin-Koren & Orit Fischman-Afori, *Rulifying Fair Use*, 59 Arizona Law Review 161 (2017).
149. Mattias Derlén & Johan Lindholm, *Characteristics of Precedent: The Case Law of the European Court of Justice in Three Dimensions*, 16 German Law Journal 1073, 1073–1098 (2015).
150. Marcella Favale, Martin Kretschmer & Paul Torremans, *Is There an EU Copyright Jurisprudence? An Empirical Analysis of the Workings of the European Court of Justice*, 79 Modern Law Review 31 (2016).

Directive, can be seen as an iterative process in which the Court builds on its earlier case law, refines its position, and attempts to consolidate the law.[151]

If there is little or no case law on a particular issue, a flexible rule is unlikely to be predictable. In a similar vein, inconsistency in the application of a flexible rule by the courts detracts from the predictability of the rule. It is therefore also important that the rationales behind the flexible rule are clear so that courts can consider these rationales when further developing the flexible rule. If those rationales are not clear, courts may struggle to consistently apply the rule, thereby diminishing the rule's predictability.

Defining a list of factors that should be considered by courts when applying a flexible rule contributes to the creation of a consistent and predictable body of case law. These factors can be listed in legislation or may be developed by the courts themselves in case law. A list can also be made non-exhaustive, which leaves the development of additional factors to the courts.[152] However, only those factors that truly inform the decision-making process of courts can add to the predictability of the flexible rule.[153] If the list of factors does not contain any normative content, these factors are merely *aspects* that may point courts to relevant facts or circumstances, but that do not offer the courts any direction as to what the outcome of a particular case should be. These factors then are also unlikely to add to the flexible rule's predictability because they do not in any way enable stakeholders to know how the rule applies to them.

A technique that is related to defining factors is the provision of a list of non-exhaustive examples of a particular legal concept. For instance, the Copyright Directive provides for an exception for quotations 'for purposes such as criticism or review (...)'.[154] Ideally, this approach creates a level of flexibility, while also providing stakeholders with a considerable degree of legal certainty as to how the rule is applied in particular cases.[155] It also enables courts to interpret the rule by analogy and to apply it to previously unforeseen fact patterns. At the same time, it must be prevented that stakeholders, when determining their conduct, and courts when applying the law, narrowly interpret the rule by focusing on these examples only.

[b] Delegation

Flexible legal provisions can also be clarified through processes of delegation in which rule-making power is assigned to a lower level of government that can respond to developments in greater detail. Of course, if lower levels of government are given the power to set rules, the democratic legitimacy of those rules may be at issue.[156] At the same time, the legislator can set conditions that must be met by the lower level of government when exercising the rule-making power. The legislator can also reverse

151. Favale, Kretschmer & Torremans, *supra* n. 150, at 60.
152. Sunstein, *supra* 113.
153. Maurits Barendrecht, *Recht als model van rechtvaardigheid. Beschouwingen over vage en scherpe normen, over binding aan het recht en over rechtsvorming* 187 (1992).
154. Article 5(3)(d) of the Copyright Directive.
155. Katharina de la Durantaye, *Allgemeine Bildungs- und Wissenschaftsschranke* 211 (2014).
156. Luc Verhey & Charald Aal, *Delegatie van regelgevende bevoegdheid in Nederland: tijd voor herbezinning*, 32 RegelMaat: Kwartaalblad voor Wetgevingsvraagstukken 241 (2017).

the decision to assign rule-making power if need be. Delegation can also be set up in such a way that the lower level of government can also be held accountable by parliamentary bodies.[157]

An example of delegation in the realm of copyright law is the involvement of the US Librarian of Congress in defining exemptions to the ban on the circumvention of technological protection measures.[158] The US Copyright Act defines the types of use that should be exempted using open-ended language, while leaving it up to the Librarian to exempt specific forms of use.[159] Another example is from Israel, which in 2007 adopted a new Copyright Act that includes an open-ended fair use exception. Under Israeli copyright law, the Minister of Justice may 'make regulations prescribing conditions under which a use shall be deemed a fair use'.[160] While no such regulations have been issued, this form of delegation of rule-making has the potential to make the open-ended rule more predictable, while at the same time maintaining its flexibility.[161]

[c] Private Regulation

Predictability may also be achieved by way of promoting and adopting private regulation in which private actors set rules, which are implemented and enforced entirely or in part by the private actors themselves.[162] Such private regulation includes forms of self- or co-regulatory regimes in which stakeholders fill in the blanks and define, monitor, and enforce rules among themselves within the flexible legal framework.[163] Co-regulatory regimes can be distinguished from self-regulatory regimes by looking at the involvement of the state at one or more levels in the regulatory regime.

---

157. For a discussion of delegation under Dutch law *see*: Philip Eijlander & Wim J.M. Voermans, *Wetgevingsleer* 40 (2000).
158. Section 1201(a) of the US Copyright Act prohibits individuals from circumventing technological protection measures that are in place to effectively control access to a copyrighted work. Section 1201(c) of the US Copyright Act gives the Librarian of Congress the power to lift the prohibition on the circumvention of technological protection measures. It is an experimental regulatory approach to copyright law in which the Librarian of Congress determines the scope of the ban through a triennial administrative rule-making process. For a discussion, *see*: Gabriel Michael, *Politics and Rulemaking at the Copyright Office*, 11 Journal of Information Technology & Politics 64 (2014); Mark Gray, *New Rules for a New Decade: Improving the Copyright Office's Anti-Circumvention Rulemakings*, 29 Berkeley Technology Law Journal 7 (2014).
159. Section 1201(c) of the US Copyright Act also lists factors that the Librarian of Congress should consider.
160. Article 19(c) of the Israeli Copyright Act, available at: www.wipo.int/wipolex/en/text.jsp?file_id=202010 (accessed 14 June 2019). For a discussion of the Israeli fair use rule, *see*: Michael Birnhack, *Judicial Snapshots and Fair Use Theory*, 5 Queen Mary Journal of Intellectual Property 264 (2015).
161. Lital Helman, *Session IV: Fair Use and Other Exceptions*, 40 Columbia Journal of Law & the Arts 395 (2017).
162. *See* Marie-Claire Menting, *Industry Codes of Conduct in a Multi-layered Dutch Private Law* 10 (2016), defining 'private regulation'. *Also see*: Baldwin, Cave & Lodge, *supra* n. 91, at 137, explaining that self-regulation takes place 'when a group of firms or individuals exert control over its own membership and their behaviour'. And *see*: Julia Black, *Decentring Regulation: Understanding the Role Self-Regulation in a 'Post- Regulatory' World*, 54 Current Legal Problems 103, 113 (2001): 'whatever "self"-regulation is, it is not state regulation'.
163. Vassilis Hatzopoulos, *Regulating Services in the European Union* 288 (2012).

Black explains how a collective of persons or bodies can regulate itself. She describes the spectrum of the different forms of regulation as follows:

> (1) mandated self-regulation, in which a collective group, an industry or profession for example, is required or designated by the government to formulate and enforce norms within a framework defined by the government, usually in broad terms; (2) sanctioned self-regulation, in which the collective group itself formulates the regulation, which is then subjected to government approval; (3) coerced self-regulation, in which the industry itself formulates and imposes regulation but in response to threats by the government that if it does not the government will impose statutory regulation; (4) and voluntary self-regulation, where there is no active state involvement, direct or indirect, in promoting or mandating self-regulation.[164]

Black here focuses on the state's relation to the private regulatory effort. She also mentions as factors: the nature of participants, the structure of the regulation, enforcement, and the types of rules.[165] Distinctions between forms of private regulation can also be made along with other lines, such as the legal effect of the form of private regulation in question,[166] the way in which the responsibility to regulate is delegated to private actors,[167] or the levels at which private regulation takes place.[168]

Intellectual property rights provide the basis for the private regulation that accommodates the needs of right owners and other interested parties.[169] In the domain of copyright law, we also see that stakeholders increasingly set rules among themselves with little or no government involvement or oversight. Traditional forms of enforcement through court orders are replaced by private dispute resolution and enforcement mechanisms.[170] These mechanisms are forms of voluntary self-regulation, which are implemented legally through contracts such as Terms of Service, but which can also be built into technology itself.[171] In particular the technologies of intermediaries enable

164. Julia Black, *Constitutionalising Self-Regulation*, 59 The Modern Law Review 24, 27 (1996). Numbering added.
165. Black, *supra* n. 164, at 27–28 (1996).
166. For instance: Tanja Ehnert, *The EU and Nanotechnologies: A Critical Analysis* 46 (2017), considering the extent to which rules are binding.
167. For instance: Mislav Mataija, *Private Regulation and the Internal Market: Sports, Legal Services, and Standard Setting in EU Economic Law* 9 (2016), distinguishing between *ex ante* delegation of responsibility to regulate and *ex post* recognition of regulation.
168. Fabrizio Cafaggi, *Transnational Private Regulation: Regulating Private Regulators* (Sabino Cassese ed., 2016).
169. *Also see* section §1.05[A] on the affordances of copyrights, and section §1.05[B] on private ordering by intermediaries.
170. Graeme Dinwoodie, *Private Ordering and the Creation of International Copyright Norms: The Role of Public Structuring*, 1 Journal of Institutional and Theoretical Economics 161 (2004); Bernt Hugenholtz, *Codes of Conduct and Copyright: Pragmatism v. Principle*, 6 International Review of Intellectual property and Competition Law 635 (2008); Niva Elkin-Koren, *After Twenty Years: Revisiting Copyright Liability of Online Intermediaries* (Susy Frankel & Daniel Gervais eds, 2014); Clement Petersen & Thomas Riis, *Private Enforcement of IP Law by Internet Service Providers: Notice and Action Procedures* (T. Riis ed., 2016).
171. Niva Elkin-Koren, *Governing Access to Users-Generated-Content: The Changing Nature of Private Ordering in Digital Networks* (Eric Brousseau, Meryem Marzouki & Cécile Meadel eds., 2009). And more generally: Lawrence Lessig, *Code and Other Laws of Cyberspace* 89 (1999), explaining how the technological architectures can regulate behaviour. And Corien Prins,

these intermediaries to influence and control interactions between people and thus to privately order the online information ecosystem using their technologies.[172]

When the regulation of technologies is concerned, private regulation can offer certainty to affected parties in efficient rule-setting processes. Private regulation may also help to overcome any jurisdictional issues that are inherent in operating a business online.[173] In addition, private regulation can be adapted to technological changes in a flexible and smooth manner because the rules are set in a more informal setting.[174] Because the rules can be easily changed and updated, more precise language can be used, which adds to the predictability of those rules.

At the same time, private regulation also has serious drawbacks, which include its low level of transparency and the accountability of private actors, its lack of (democratic) legitimacy, and the lack of consideration being given to fundamental rights.[175] Specifically regarding copyright law, private regulation does not necessarily contribute to maintaining the fair balance that rules of copyright law ideally promote.[176] Private regulation in the domain of copyright law can also be the result of opaque negotiation processes, leaving the public effectively out of the discussion.[177] Moreover, not all affected parties, such as the users of copyrighted materials, are necessarily involved in the development of the regime, which does not add to the private regulation's legitimacy.[178]

[C] A Flexible Legal Framework

In discussions about copyright law, the importance of flexibility is often stressed in the context of copyright's limitations and exceptions. Most importantly, such flexibility

---

Normering, regulering en rechtshandhaving door technologie: over de implicaties van techno-regulering voor het privaatrecht, Weekblad voor Privaatrecht, Notariaat en Registratie 1075 (2011), arguing that in Dutch private law little attention has been paid to regulation by technology.

172. *Also see* section §1.06[A] on the central role that intermediaries play in online communications.
173. Agnieszka Janczuk-Gorywoda, *The New Transnational Payment Law and Global Trade: Online Platforms as Providers of Private Legal Orders*, 24 European Review of Private Law 223 (2016), explaining how Paypal's payment system and private legal order has enabled the creation of new international markets.
174. Baldwin, Cave & Lodge, *supra* n. 91, at 140.
175. Eva Lievens & Peggy Valcke, *Regulatory Trends in a Social Media Context* (Monroe Price, Stefaan Verhulst & Libby Morgan eds., 2013). *Also see*: Ian Brown, *Beware Self-Regulation, Index on Censorship* 98 (2010). Christina Angelopoulos, *European Intermediary Liability in Copyright: A Tort-Based Analysis* 78 (2016), concluding that 'States may not delegate their primary obligation to secure the realization of fundamental rights in practice, either to self-regulatory bodies, or to private parties. Genuine, effective exercise of fundamental rights may require positive measures of protection by States authorities, even in the sphere of relations between individuals, or specifically between online intermediaries and their users.'
176. Niva Elkin-Koren, *Copyrights in Cyberspace – Rights Without Laws?*, 73 Chicago Kent Law Review 101 (1998).
177. Yafit Lev-Aretz, *Copyright Lawmaking and Public Choice: From Legislative Battles to Private Ordering*, 27 Harvard Journal of Law & Technology (1) 203 (2013).
178. Clement Petersen & Thomas Riis, *Private Enforcement of IP Law by Internet Service Providers: Notice and Action Procedures* 246 (T. Riis ed., 2016), specifically on the enforcement of intellectual property rights by intermediaries.

enables to accommodate for new forms of information use that were not foreseen by the legislator and to maintain the copyright balance. In order to also effectively protect the interests of copyright owners, a certain level of flexibility towards copyright protection and its enforcement appears to be desirable as well.

Yet, flexibility may also have a negative impact on the legal framework's predictability. As the dissemination of digital content through networks has become such a prevalent aspect of daily life, copyright issues arise throughout our societies and affect both businesses and people. Rules on copyright law and liability for infringements must therefore be as clear and consistent as possible, so that copyright owners, intermediaries, and users are able to know, at least to some extent, how the law applies to them and what they can expect from one another.[179] If rules are not sufficiently clear, they may negatively affect the protection of original works, the use of such works, and the innovative services that enable the communication of such works. It is therefore imperative that, when striving for flexibility, the need for predictable rules is respected as well and attempts are made to mitigate the potential negative effects on predictability.

§2.05 CONCLUSION

In this chapter, we have studied the effects that technological developments can have on copyright law. Especially if a legislator is convinced that a particular technological development warrants legislative intervention, there is a risk that technology-specific rules are adopted. An advantage of such rules is that they are quite precise and provide clear-cut solutions for specific (legal) problems. But a downside is that these rules, over time, may no longer be effective, nor predictable. The legislative 'reflex' to technological developments in copyright law does not appear to contribute to the 'future-proofness' of copyright law. In response to this finding, this chapter developed two design principles that can contribute to the future-proofness of a legal framework on copyright law.

The first principle entails that the legal framework must be able to preserve a balance between the interests of copyright owners and other parties affected by copyright and its enforcement, and as such stay true to its objective. We have seen that technology-specific rules are likely to become irrelevant over time and that they may provide legal certainty for a short time only. Since both copyright law and intermediary liability are fields of law that are subject to technological developments, there is a risk that rules that once struck a particular balance may lose their relevance or applicability. The legal framework must therefore be designed in such a way that enables these challenges to be dealt with and to preserve a balance between the interests of copyright owners, users, and intermediaries, also when technological conditions change.

The second design principle distinguished in this chapter requires that the legal framework should regulate flexibly. This chapter has put forward that such an

179. *Also see*, regarding the need for predictable US copyright law: Maria Pallante, *The Next Great Copyright Act*, 36 Columbia Journal of Law & the Arts 315, 323 (2013).

approach prevents copyright owners from being left empty-handed. But the importance of flexibility has also been stressed in the context of copyright limitations and exceptions. Flexibility may accommodate new forms of the beneficial use of protected materials, which were not anticipated by the legislator. In particular where rules are set at the international or EU level, as is the case with regard to much of copyright law, and the creation and adaption of rules is a time-consuming process, flexibility is all the more important.

Yet, flexibility may also detract from the law's predictability. If rules are predictable, stakeholders are able to know, to some extent, how the law applies to them and their conduct. If uncertainty exists about the application of copyright rules, this uncertainty may have a negative effect on the creation of original works, the use of these works, and the innovative services that enable the communication of such works. Therefore, we must also mitigate the negative effects that flexibility can have on the predictability of rules.

CHAPTER 3

The EU Legal Framework

§3.01 INTRODUCTION

The previous chapter defined two design principles that, if taken into account, can contribute to the 'future-proofness' of a legal framework on copyright law and intermediary liability. These principles highlight the need for a flexible framework that has the ability to preserve a balance between the interests of copyright owners, users, and intermediaries.

The current chapter aims to provide an overview of the current EU legal framework on intermediaries and copyright law. It will also critically analyse the framework to see what its strengths and weaknesses are in terms of its future-proofness. Section §3.02 first provides a brief overview of the EU legislative framework on intermediary liability and introduces the most important legislative instruments. Sections §3.03 to §3.05 explore and analyse the norms that make up the legal framework and identify problem areas with regard to the framework's future-proofness.

§3.02 OVERVIEW OF THE EU LEGAL FRAMEWORK

The focal point of this book is on the EU legal framework on intermediary liability and copyright law, which consists of the whole body of legal sources of EU that are relevant to copyright law, the enforcement of copyrights, and the liability of intermediaries for copyright infringements. This legal framework includes primary EU law, most notably the EU Charter of Fundamental Rights, which protects a set of fundamental rights that are also relevant for questions of copyright enforcement and intermediary liability. The legal framework further comprises of secondary EU law. In particular different directives containing provisions on copyright law, the enforcement of copyrights, as well as on the liability of intermediaries. Finally, also the CJEU's case law, in which the

Court interprets the norms in the aforementioned sources of EU law, is considered to be part of the EU legal framework that is studied and analysed here.

The different legal sources that make up the EU legal framework will not be analysed in isolation. Rather, they are discussed side by side, taking the relevant directives and the provisions therein as the starting point. These directives provide rules that are relevant for both the intermediary's primary and secondary liability for copyright infringements.[1] Most importantly they harmonize rules of copyright law and provides rules on liability specifically for intermediaries. However, there are also matters which these directives leave untouched and that are left to the EU Member States to regulate. Below is a first outline of all these different aspects. A set of four EU directives are important here: the Copyright Directive,[2] the E-Commerce Directive,[3] the Enforcement Directive,[4] and the Directive on Copyright in the Digital Single Market (hereinafter 'DSM Directive').[5] The latter directive was adopted in the spring of 2019 and has significantly altered the EU legal framework by introducing new rules regarding the liability of operators of online platforms and the online use of press publications by intermediaries. This directive is a response to the new ways in which copyrighted materials are produced, distributed, and exploited on the Internet. With the new rules, the EU legislator also aimed to recalibrate the relationship between the producers of copyrighted materials and certain intermediaries who benefit from the availability of such materials.

The EU legal framework is discussed as follows. First, we will consider the rules on primary liability, the cases in which an intermediary may be liable as a copyright infringer. In particular the Copyright Directive is relevant here. It harmonizes to a large extent the rules of copyright law. Among other things, it defines a set of exclusive rights and lists the limitations and exceptions to those rights.[6] These rules are important in particular when determining whether the intermediary itself infringes upon a copyright with its intermediary activities. These rules set the standard for infringement, but they are also relevant when determining the intermediary's possible liability for infringements by others – the intermediary's secondary liability. We will also consider the recently adopted DSM Directive, in particular its rules regarding the online use of press

1. For an explanation of both forms of liability, *see* section §1.04.
2. Directive 2001/29/EC of the European Parliament and of the Council of 22 May 2001 on the harmonisation of certain aspects of copyright and related rights in the information society (*OJ* 2001, L 167/10).
3. Directive 2000/31/EC of the European Parliament and of the Council of 8 June 2000 on certain legal aspects of information society services, in particular electronic commerce, in the Internal Market (*OJ* 2000, L 178/1).
4. Directive 2004/48/EC of the European Parliament and of the Council of 29 April 2004 on the enforcement of intellectual property rights (*OJ* 2004, L 157/45).
5. Directive 2019/790/EU of the European Parliament and of the Council of 17 April 2019 on copyright and related rights in the Digital Single Market and amending Directives 96/9/EC and 2001/29/EC (*OJ* 2019, L130/92).
6. The Copyright Directive distinguishes between the reproduction right (Article 2), the right to communicate to the public (Article 3), and the distribution right (Article 4). For a discussion of the first two rights, *see* sections §3.03[D]. Limitations and exceptions are provided for in Article 5 of the directive. For a discussion of the limitations and exceptions and their interpretation, *see* sections §3.03[C] and §3.03[E].

publications. The directive specifies new exclusive rights for publishers of press publications in relation to the use of these publications by intermediaries.

Second, we will take a look at the liability exemptions in the EU legal framework. The E-Commerce Directive provides for a set of rules specifying the conditions under which intermediaries are *not* to be held liable for the information of others. These liability exemptions protect intermediaries against liability for damages. The types of intermediary activity exempted in the E-Commerce Directive are: 'mere conduit', 'caching', and 'hosting' activities.[7] The directive does not provide rules that determine if and when intermediaries are to be held liable. Hence, the rules in the E-Commerce Directive shape the liability of intermediaries in a negative way only: these rules focus on the absence rather than the presence of certain circumstances giving rise to liability.[8] Importantly, the DSM Directive altered how these liability exemptions apply to online platforms. These service providers are no longer shielded by the hosting liability exemption when copyright infringements are concerned.

Third, the EU legal framework does assume that certain intermediaries have some responsibility for the infringements of others. Most notably by recognizing in all three directives that injunctions may be issued against intermediaries when their services are used by others to infringe.[9] Requirements with regard to these injunctions are set forth in the Copyright Directive and the Enforcement Directive, which harmonize aspects of the enforcement of intellectual property rights.[10] The E-Commerce Directive contains a rule that prohibits injunctions that amount to a general monitoring of the intermediary's service.[11] EU legislation does *not* harmonize the legal basis on which injunctions are issued, nor does it provide guidance as to when they should be issued. The European Commission, however, did take steps to further shape the responsibilities of intermediaries by means of its recommendation on 'measures to effectively tackle illegal content online'.[12] And, specifically regarding online platforms, the DSM Directive has put in place a new liability regime that requires from platforms that they take proactive steps to stop and prevent infringements.

In the following subsections, we will first explore the copyright rules in the EU legal framework as they were laid down in the Copyright Directive and the Directive on Copyright in the Single Market (section §3.03). We will then turn to the E-Commerce Directive's liability exemptions that were put in place to protect intermediaries against liability for the information and activities of others (section §3.04). And finally, we will discuss the way in which the EU legal framework makes sure that intermediaries still

7. Articles 12, 13, and 14 of the E-Commerce Directive. For a discussion of these liability exemptions, *see* section §3.04.
8. For instance, Article 14 of the E-Commerce Directive determines that hosting service providers are not to be held liable if they have no knowledge of infringements.
9. Articles 12(3), 13(2), and 14(3), and recital 45 of the E-Commerce Directive. Article 8(3) and recital 59 of the Copyright Directive. Article 11 and recital 23 of the Enforcement Directive. For a discussion, *see* section §3.05[A].
10. Article 8(3) of the Copyright Directive and Article 3 of the Enforcement Directive. For a discussion, *see* section §3.05[B].
11. Article 15(1) of the E-Commerce Directive. For a discussion, *see* section §3.05.
12. Commission Recommendation on Measures to Effectively Tackle Illegal Content Online, C(2018) 1117.

have some sort of a responsibility for copyright infringements – here the Enforcement Directive and the Directive on Copyright in the Single Market are of importance (section §3.05).

§3.03 COPYRIGHT LAW

In the EU, copyright law is harmonized by a set of ten directives which deal with, among other things, the rental and lending right, the resale of art, satellite broadcasting and cable retransmission, and databases. The 2001 Copyright Directive has been called the 'most horizontal' and comprehensive EU measure that has so far been adopted in the field of copyright law.[13] It harmonizes to a great extent the exclusive rights and the limitations and exceptions to those rights. The 2019 DSM Directive is equally important as it updates the harmonized exclusive rights and list of limitations and exceptions to include and accommodate new forms of information use.

In the following subsections, the EU copyright regime is discussed with a focus on intermediary activities. This is done by first introducing the Copyright Directive (section §3.03[A]) and the DSM Directive (section §3.03[B]). Then two principles that underlie both directives are discussed: the high level of protection that needs to be guaranteed and the fair balance of rights and interests (section §3.03[C]). We then consider the exclusive rights and the limitations and exceptions to those rights as they are defined in the Copyright Directive (sections §3.03[D] and §3.03[E]). After these more general sections, we will take a closer look at how the rules in the directives apply to several intermediary activities (sections §3.03[F] to §3.03[I]).

[A] The 2001 Copyright Directive

The Copyright Directive harmonized copyright law to ensure that EU Member States would uniformly respond to the challenges of new technologies. The need to also update existing copyright law to the emerging information society was clearly felt.

The EU legislator's concern with copyright law dates back to 1988 when the European Commission adopted its Green Paper on 'Copyright Law and the Challenge of Technology'.[14] In this Green Paper, the Commission signalled the rise of a new society in which the production of information goods and services would be paramount.[15] In that society, the importance of copyright protection seemed more important than ever before.[16]

13. Commission Staff Working Paper, The Review of the EC Legal Framework in the Field of Copyright and Related Rights, SEC 2004/995, 3.
14. Commission Green Paper, Copyright and the Challenge of Technology – Copyright Issues Requiring Immediate Action, COM 1988/172.
15. *Commission Green Paper*, *supra* n. 14, at 2: 'A shift has continued in the economic activity of industrialized countries away from the production of goods having the character primarily of staple commodities and towards the production of goods to which considerable value has been added through the application of technology, skill and creativity.'
16. *Commission Green Paper*, *supra* n. 14, at 3: 'The growing economic importance of the industries needing copyright protection against ready misappropriation of their products, particularly by

In the early 1990s, the European Union joined the ranks of many national governments and international organizations that published visionary reports and policy statements on the emerging information society.[17] In its 1993 White Paper on 'Growth, Competitiveness and Employment', the European Commission established that new information and communication technologies dramatically transformed many aspects of economic and social life.[18] The EU aimed to accelerate the development of new 'information highways', with which it meant an early version of the Internet.[19] It is against this background of the emerging information society that the most important EU rules regarding copyright law and intermediary liability were adopted.

The importance of intellectual property for the creation of the information society was also recognized in the 1994 Bangemann Report.[20] Its focus was highly economic and the report was less concerned with the social and cultural aspects of the information society.[21] Describing Europe's creativity and innovation as two of its most important economic assets, the report called for a European response to maintain a high level of intellectual property protection. It suggested a re-examination of existing national and EU legal regimes in order to promote the development of new information products and services. In this regard, in particular 'the ease with which digitised information can be transmitted, manipulated and adapted' required new solutions to protect copyright owners.[22]

In 1994, the European Commission marked the protection of intellectual property and copyright as one of the main areas in need of action.[23] The Commission's first step towards updating copyright law in the EU was the 1995 Green Paper on 'Copyright and related rights in the information society', which set the stage for a consultation process.[24] In the 1996 Follow Up to the Green Paper, the Commission published its proposals to update copyright law.[25]

The European Commission, however, was not the only organization trying to deal with the challenges posed by new Internet technologies. At the international level, the World Intellectual Property Organization (WIPO) was also concerned with the

---

copying, has naturally produced pressure for the modernization of existing copyright protection systems at both national and Community level.'

17. William Melody, *Toward a Framework for Designing Information Society Policies*, Telecommunications Policy (4) 243 (1996).
18. Commission White Paper, Growth, Competitiveness, Employment: The Challenges and Ways Forward into the 21st Century, COM 1993/700, 92.
19. Commission White Paper, *supra* n. 18, at 13–14.
20. M. Bangemann et al., Europe and the Global Information Society. Bangemann report Recommendations to the European Council (1994).
21. Jacques Berleur & Jean-Marc Galand, *ICT Policies of the European Union: From an Information Society to eEurope: Trends and Visions*, 38–40 (Jacques Berleur & Chrisanthi Avgerou eds., 2005).
22. Bangemann, *supra* n. 20, at 22.
23. Commission Communication, 'Europe's Way to the Information Society. An Action Plan', COM 1994/347.
24. Commission Green Paper, 'Copyright and Related Rights in the Information Society', COM 1995/382.
25. Commission Communication, 'Follow-up to the Green Paper on copyright and related rights in the information society', COM 1996/438.

impact of new information technologies on copyright law. This organization is a specialized agency of the United Nations, which administers, among other intellectual property treaties, the Berne Convention for the Protection of Literary and Artistic Work.[26] It was preparing a response to the emerging information society as well.

In 1995, when the European Commission started its consultation, discussions about new WIPO instruments were well underway.[27] In 1996, WIPO's involvement led to the adoption of two new international instruments specifically dealing with the issues raised by digital and networking technologies. These instruments are the WIPO Copyright Treaty and the WIPO Performances and Phonograms Treaty, sometimes collectively referred to as the WIPO Internet Treaties.[28] These instruments were pushed by the European Community and also steered the EU's own legislative efforts in the late 1990s.[29]

The WIPO Copyright Treaty deals with many aspects of copyright law. It specified two new types of copyrightable subject matter: computer software and databases.[30] It also contains provisions on the scope of the distribution right, the rental right, and the right of communication to the public.[31] The Treaty also introduced rules on technological protection measures in order to give copyright owners more control over the digital use of their materials.[32]

These WIPO Internet Treaties had a great influence on the substance of the later EU Copyright Directive. The WIPO Internet Treaties were approved by the European Council on behalf of the EU.[33] And the EU also took on the task of implementing a significant number of the international obligations arising from the WIPO Internet Treaties by means of the Copyright Directive.[34] The recitals to the directive note that the 'Treaties update the international protection for copyright and related rights significantly, not least with regard to the so-called "digital agenda", and improve the means to fight piracy world-wide.'[35]

26. *See*: www.wipo.int/treaties (accessed 14 June 2019).
27. Commission Green Paper, *supra* n. 24, at 81.
28. The WIPO Copyright Treaty is a so-called Special Agreement under the Berne Convention, to which Members of the Union established in the Convention can become party. *See* Article 1 of the WIPO Copyright Treaty and Article 20 of the Berne Convention.
29. Lucie Guibault et al., Study on the Implementation and Effect in Member States' Laws of Directive 2001/29/EC on the Harmonisation of Certain Aspects of Copyright and Related Rights in the Information Society, 4 (2007).
30. Articles 4 and 5 of the WIPO Copyright Treaty.
31. Articles 6 to 8 of the WIPO Copyright Treaty.
32. Article 11 of the WIPO Copyright Treaty provides that 'Contracting Parties shall provide adequate legal protection and effective legal remedies against the circumvention of effective technological measures that are used by authors in connection with the exercise of their rights under this Treaty or the Berne Convention and that restrict acts, in respect of their works, which are not authorized by the authors concerned or permitted by law.'
33. These treaties were approved by the European Council on behalf of the European Community: Council Decision of 16 March 2000 on the approval, on behalf of the European Community, of the WIPO Copyright Treaty and the WIPO Performances and Phonograms Treaty (*OJ* 2000, L 98/6).
34. Commission Proposal for a European Parliament and Council Directive on the harmonization of certain aspects of copyright and related rights in the Information Society, COM 1997/628, 3.
35. Recital 15 of the Copyright Directive.

Developments in information technologies in the late 1990s not only offered both a chance to copyright owners to exploit their works but also posed a danger to their economic interests. Or as Advocate General Trstenjak put it in her 2010 opinion in the *Padawan* case:

> [The Copyright Directive] is the Community legislature's reaction to technological development in information technology, which on the one hand opens up new forms of output and exploitation for rightholders, but on the other hand presents new challenges to the protection of intellectual property in the light of the risk of piracy, counterfeiting and the unauthorised reproduction of works and other subject-matter.[36]

In responding to these technological developments, the EU legislator did not adopt a wait and see approach. It is interesting to note what rapporteur Enrico Boselli of the Legal Affairs and the Internal Market wrote in his recommendations for the European Parliament's second reading of the Copyright Directive. His view illustrates that the European Commission was shooting at a moving target when it drafted the directive:

> In the last three years, the information society has evolved in the direction of ever-more advanced solutions which could scarcely have been imagined in 1997, the year in which the Commission's proposal for a directive was drawn up.[37]

After listing a few of the recent technological developments, Boselli's conclusion was not that the draft legislation should be reconsidered or that the legislator should operate more cautiously.[38] Instead, Boselli concluded that 'it is, therefore, desirable that the directive be adopted as rapidly as possible, since if not it may become prematurely outdated'.[39] Indeed the directive was quickly adopted and transposition would have to take place within a term that only Denmark and Greece were able to meet.[40]

[B] The 2019 Directive on Copyright in the Digital Single Market

In 2015, the European Commission published its plans to foster the 'Digital Single Market', which is a market in which consumers enjoy cross-border access to digital services, which provides a level playing field for companies, and which creates the

36. Opinion of AG Trstenjak 11 May 2010, ECLI:EU:C:2010:264, para. 41 (*Sociedad General de Autores y Editores v. Padawan*).
37. Recommendation for Second Reading on the Council common position for adopting a European Parliament and Council directive on the harmonisation of certain aspects of copyright and related rights in the Information Society, A5-0043/2001, 15.
38. Martin Kretschmer, *Copying the Digital Millennium Copyright Act: European Struggles with Information Control*, 25 (2013).
39. Recommendation for Second Reading on the Council common position for adopting a European Parliament and Council directive on the harmonisation of certain aspects of copyright and related rights in the Information Society, A5-0043/2001, 15.
40. Foundation for Information Policy Research, *Implementing the EU Copyright Directive* (2003).

conditions for a vibrant digital economy and society.[41] Part of the Commission's Digital Single Market strategy was to reduce the difference between national copyright laws and to further harmonize the EU legal framework on copyright law.[42] Legislative proposals were announced regarding several different topics, such as the portability of content, cross-border access to online services, and use of copyrighted materials. A proposal was also announced to clarify the rules on the 'activities of intermediaries in relation to copyright-protected content'.[43]

In its Communication 'Towards a modern, more European copyright framework', the European Commission explained its plans.[44] It expressed concern about whether the EU legal framework on copyright law ensured that the 'value generated by some of the new forms of online content distribution is fairly shared'.[45] The Commission here focused on the role played by online platforms and content aggregation services in the online domain. Part of the problem was the legal uncertainty about if and how the right of communication to the public applied to the types of use by these newer intermediaries. Lack of clarity prevented that copyright owners are in a position to authorize and to be remunerated for use of their materials in the online context.[46] Specifically regarding online platforms, the Commission highlighted that these intermediaries might put forward that they do not communicate works to the public and that they are protected from liability under the rules in the E-Commerce Directive.[47] Therefore, the Commission announced that it would examine whether the exclusive right of communication to the public had to be redefined.[48]

In 2016, the European Commission published its proposal for the Directive on Copyright in the Single Market.[49] The Commission repeated that there was a 'growing concern about the equitable sharing of the value generated by some of the new forms of online content distribution along the value chain'.[50] According to the Commission Staff Working Paper, some intermediaries 'have *de facto* become major actors of online content distribution and have substantial number of users and significant market valuations rightholders are not necessarily able to enter into agreements with them for the use of their content'.[51] The proposed directive contained a provision that would strengthen the position of copyright owners vis-à-vis the operators of content platforms, such as video hosting websites. And it would introduce a new set of exclusive rights for press publishers with regard to the online use of press publications.

41. Jean-Claude Juncker, *Political Guidelines for the next European Commission*, speech given on 22 October 2014 in Strasbourg, available at: https://ec.europa.eu/commission/sites/beta-political/files/juncker-political-guidelines-speech_en.pdf (accessed 14 June 2019).
42. Commission Communication, *A Digital Single Market Strategy for Europe*, COM 2015/192.
43. Commission Communication, *supra* n. 42, at 8.
44. Commission Communication, 'Towards a modern, more European copyright framework', COM 2015/192.
45. Commission Communication, *supra* n. 44, at 9.
46. Commission Communication, *supra* n. 44, at 9.
47. Commission Communication, *supra* n. 44, at 10.
48. Commission Communication, *supra* n. 44, at 10.
49. Commission Proposal for a Directive of the European Parliament and of the Council on copyright in the Digital Single Market, COM 2016/593.
50. Commission Proposal, *supra* n. 49, 7.
51. Commission Staff Working Paper, 'Impact Assessment', SWD 2016/301, 138.

The negotiations between the EU legislative institutions took more than two years. In spring 2019, the European Commission, Council, and Parliament finished their trialogue negotiations. The Parliament approved the compromise text in March 2019. The Council approved the Parliament's position in April 2019, but not unanimously. Three Member States abstained from voting. Italy, Luxembourg, the Netherlands, Poland, Finland, and Sweden voted against the directive.[52] These Member States explained in a joint statement that they support the need for modernization of EU copyright law, but that they did not support the final text of the directive. They stressed that the directive would hinder innovation, rather than promote it; that the directive would negatively impact the competitiveness of the European Digital Single Market; and that it would lead to legal uncertainty for stakeholders and may 'encroach upon EU citizens' rights'.[53] As the directive was nonetheless adopted and has entered into force, Member States will have to implement the directive by 7 June 2021.[54]

[C] A High Level of Protection and a Fair Balance of Rights and Interests

In EU legislation on copyright law, the need for a 'high level of protection' of copyrighted works is a recurring theme.[55] One of the principles in the 2001 Copyright Directive too is that it must ensure a high level of protection to copyright owners. This high level of protection is linked to an instrumental vision on copyright law: the promotion of intellectual creations.[56] In its recitals, it is noted that 'any harmonisation of copyright and related rights must take as a basis a high level of protection, *since such rights are crucial to intellectual creation*'.[57] Also in the DSM Directive it is underlined that changes to EU copyright law were necessary, 'while keeping a high level of protection of copyright and related rights'.[58] Here the high level of protection is also linked to developments in technology that have changed how copyrighted materials are produced, distributed, and exploited.

In interpreting the Copyright Directive, the CJEU has stressed in several of its decisions that the high level of protection is in fact 'the principal objective' of the Copyright Directive.[59] The Court has also used this need for a high level of protection as an interpretative tool in its case law. On numerous occasions, the Court has held that the exclusive rights should be interpreted broadly, specifically with a view to establishing a high level of protection.[60] Similarly, in *Infopaq I*, the CJEU interpreted 'the

52. Voting result, 2016/0280(COD), 8612/19.
53. Statements by Member States, 2016/0280(COD), 7986/19, ADD 1 REV 2.
54. Article 29(1) of the DSM Directive.
55. Sheldon Halpern & Philip Johnson, *Harmonising Copyright Law and Dealing with Dissonance*, 109–110 (2014).
56. *See also*: Halpern & Johnson, *supra* n. 55, at 33.
57. Recital 9 of the Copyright Directive. Emphasis added.
58. Recital 3 of the Directive on Copyright in the Digital Single Market.
59. CJEU 19 November 2015, ECLI:EU:C:2015:764, para. 14 (*SBS Belgium v. Sabam*); CJEU 7 March 2013, ECLI:EU:C:2013:147, para. 21 (*ITV Broadcasting and others v. TVCatchup*); CJEU 4 October 2011, ECLI:EU:C:2011:631, para. 186 (*Football Association Premier League and Others*).
60. This argument was first used by the Court of Justice in *SGAE v. Rafael Hoteles*: CJEU 7 December 2006, ECLI:EU:C:2006:764, para. 42. It was repeated in later decisions, including: *Football*

scope of protection' of a copyrighted work in light of this need for a high level of protection.[61] And in *Stichting de Thuiskopie*, the CJEU held that Member States must ensure that authors actually receive fair compensation for the use of their works with a view to safeguarding a high level of protection.[62]

Whereas the high level of protection underlines the copyright owner's interests in particular, the Copyright Directive also makes clear that these interests must be balanced with the rights and interests of *users* of protected materials. It perhaps does not do so very prominently, but the directive states in recital 31 that:

> A fair balance of rights and interests between the different categories of rightholders, as well as between the different categories of rightholders and users of protected subject-matter must be safeguarded.

This fair-balance recital has also served as an interpretative tool for the CJEU in its copyright case law. In the case of *Hewlett-Packard v. Reprobel*, the Court had to interpret the reprographic and private copying exceptions in Articles 5(2)(a) and (b) of the Copyright Directive.[63] Under these provisions, particular forms of copying are allowed as long as copyright owners receive fair remuneration. On the basis of *inter alia* recital 31, the CJEU found that these systems must not lead to overcompensation by users since it would not be 'compatible with the requirement (...) that a fair balance be safeguarded between the rightholders and the users of protected subject-matter'.[64]

Another example is the case of *Technische Universität Darmstadt v. Eugen Ulmer* on the interpretation of the limitation in Article 5(3)(n).[65] This provision permits Member States to exempt the communication of works on 'dedicated terminals' for the purpose of research or private study. In this case, the CJEU rejected a particularly narrow interpretation of this limitation by referring to the need to strike a fair balance:

> Furthermore, the interpretation proposed by Ulmer is difficult to reconcile with the aim pursued by Article 5(3)(n) of Directive 2001/29, which is to maintain a fair balance between the rights and interests of rightholders, on the one hand, and, on the other hand, users of protected works who wish to communicate them to the public for the purpose of research or private study undertaken by individual members of the public.[66]

Association Premier League and Others, *supra* n. 59, at 186; *ITV Broadcasting and others v. TVCatchup*, *supra* n. 59, at 20; CJEU 31 May 2016, ECLI:EU:C:2016:379, para. 36 (*Reha Training Gesellschaft für Sport- und Unfallrehabilitation v. Gesellschaft für musikalische Aufführungs- und mechanische Vervielfältigungsrechte*); CJEU 8 September 2016, ECLI:EU:C:2016:644, para. 30, *IER* 2016/47, with note by J.M.B. Seignette (*GS Media v. Sanoma Media Netherlands and others*).

61. CJEU 16 July 2009, ECLI:EU:C:2009:465, para. 40 (*Infopaq International v. Danske Dagblades Forening*).
62. CJEU 16 June 2011, ECLI:EU:C:2011:397, paras 32 and 41 (*Stichting de Thuiskopie v. Opus Supplies Deutschland and others*).
63. CJEU 12 November 2015, ECLI:EU:C:2015:750 (*Hewlett-Packard Belgium v. Reprobel*).
64. *Hewlett-Packard Belgium v. Reprobel*, *supra* n. 63, at 85–86.
65. CJEU 11 September 2014, ECLI:EU:C:2014:2196 (*Technische Universität Darmstadt v. Eugen Ulmer*).
66. *Technische Universität Darmstadt v. Eugen Ulmer*, *supra* n. 65, at 31.

The European Commission in its 2015 Communication 'Towards a Modern, more European Copyright Framework' also highlighted the importance of providing a high level of protection *and* striking a fair balance between interests:

> The modernisation of EU copyright rules was first announced in President Juncker's Political Guidelines for the incoming Commission and further outlined in the digital single market strategy. It aims to achieve a wide availability of creative content across the EU, to make sure that EU copyright rules continue to provide a high level of protection for right holders, and to maintain a good balance with other public policy goals, like education, research and innovation, or equal access for persons with disabilities, in the digital environment.[67]

While in *Hewlett-Packard* and *Technische Universität Darmstadt*, the CJEU referred to the fair balance that must be struck specifically in relation to the limitations and exceptions in the Copyright Directive, in *GS Media* the CJEU used the fair-balance formula in interpreting the exclusive right of communication to the public.[68] This case dealt with the question of whether placing a link to unauthorized materials amounts to a communication to the public.[69] In its decision, the Court appears to use the fair-balance formula as a proxy to bring the right to freedom of expression into the equation:

> It follows from recitals 3 and 31 of Directive 2001/29 that the harmonisation effected by it is to maintain, in particular in the electronic environment, a fair balance between, on one hand, the interests of copyright holders and related rights in protecting their intellectual property rights, safeguarded by Article 17(2) of the Charter of Fundamental Rights of the European Union ('the Charter') and, on the other, the protection of the interests and fundamental rights of users of protected objects, in particular their freedom of expression and of information, safeguarded by Article 11 of the Charter, and of the general interest.[70]

The fair-balance formula thus requires that the interests of copyright owners should be weighed against the fundamental rights of those who are affected by those copyrights. In *GS Media*, the CJEU used that balance to come to an interpretation of the exclusive right that respects both the copyright owner's interests and the user's right to freedom of expression.

Also in the DSM Directive the need for a fair balance is highlighted. Recital 6 of that directive explains that the exceptions and the limitations in the directive 'seek to achieve a fair balance between the rights and interests of authors ... and users'. This recital appears to affirm that the exceptions and limitations should be interpreted also with a view to achieving a fair balance.

As we will see, the CJEU has required that a fair balance is struck in cases regarding the responsibilities that intermediaries may have to halt or prevent copyright infringements.[71] More precisely, interpretations of EU law must enable a fair balance to

67. Commission Communication, *supra* n. 44, at 2.
68. *GS Media v. Sanoma Media Netherlands and others*, *supra* n. 60.
69. *Also see* section §3.03[G] on hyperlinking.
70. *GS Media v. Sanoma Media Netherlands and others*, *supra* n. 60, at 31.
71. *See* section §3.05[C] for a discussion of this case law.

be struck between the fundamental rights of the copyright owner, the intermediary, and users. This balance should not be confused with the balance that is discussed in the current section. The balance of interests discussed in the current section is part of EU copyright law itself and may guide the interpretation of exclusive rights and limitations and exceptions to those right. In contrast, the fair balance that is discussed later on in this chapter deals specifically with the necessity to balance fundamental rights in cases of intermediary liability and measures of copyright enforcement more generally.

[D] Exclusive Rights in the Copyright Directive

After discussing the underlying principles of the Copyright Directive, we now turn to the exclusive rights as they are harmonized by the directive. These exclusive rights are studied here to see if and how EU copyright law might apply to intermediary activities. The scope of these rights is also relevant from the perspective of potential secondary liability that intermediaries may incur for the copyright infringements of others.

The Copyright Directive harmonizes three exclusive rights: the reproduction right in Article 2, the right of communication to the public in Article 3, and the distribution right in Article 4. Of those three rights, only the reproduction right and the right of communication to the public are discussed here. Although it is not immediately apparent from Article 4 of the directive, the distribution right applies to material copies only.[72] Internet communication by definition is *immaterial*, and intermediaries facilitating such communication are therefore unlikely to infringe the distribution right.

In contrast, the reproduction right can apply to both material and immaterial copies. For instance, this right applies to the making of paper copies of articles and books (material), but also to making digital copies of material stored online (immaterial). The right of communication to the public applies to immaterial forms of communication only. As we will see, this right applies in cases in which the public is not present at the place where the communication originates, such as making available materials on the web.

A short note on the structure of this section is in order. As will be explained, the reproduction right also applies to reproductions in part and temporary reproductions. Article 5(1) of the Copyright Directive stipulates an exception for temporary reproductions that are essential to particular technological processes. Because this exception is closely related to the reproduction right's broad scope, we will examine this exception in the context of the exclusive right.

[1] The Reproduction Right

The reproduction right is harmonized by Article 2 of the Copyright Directive. This article requires that Member States 'shall provide for the exclusive right to authorise or prohibit direct or indirect, temporary or permanent reproduction by any means and in

72. Recital 28 of the Copyright Directive reads: 'Copyright protection under this Directive includes the exclusive right to control distribution of the work incorporated in a *tangible article*.'

any form, in whole or in part'. By laying down such a broad reproduction right, the EU legislator has succeeded in what had turned out to be impossible to accomplish at the international level.

When the WIPO Copyright Treaty was discussed, the scope of the reproduction right was a hot topic that involved heavy lobbying by different stakeholders.[73] The US pushed for a definition of a reproduction right that would also encompass *temporary* copying. Such a broad exclusive right fitted nicely with their view to give copyright owners the right to control every form of access, viewing or use of their works.[74] Moreover, it would make Internet access providers, who need to temporarily copy materials in order to transmit those materials, strictly liable for the infringements of their users.[75] This approach effectively put intermediaries in a position where they would have to enforce copyright law on their networks in order not to be liable as copyright infringers themselves. In other words, these early intermediaries would be directly liable for infringements by their users.

Questions can be raised about the actual need to update the reproduction right at the international level. The WIPO Copyright Treaty's parent treaty, the Berne Convention, already defined an exclusive reproduction right that was quite flexible. Article 9(1) of the Convention specifies that 'Authors of literary and artistic works protected by this Convention shall have the exclusive right of authorizing the reproduction of these works, in any manner or form.' The words 'in any manner or form' indicate that the provision may also cover digital acts of reproduction, such as electronic and digital storing, and the uploading and downloading of information.[76] Indeed, the Convention aimed to define a lasting reproduction right. The 1978 WIPO Guide to the Berne Convention described the right as encompassing all methods of reproduction now and in the future: 'design, engraving, lithography, offset and all other printing processes, typewriting, photocopying, xerox, mechanical or magnetic recording (discs, cassettes, magnetic tape, films, microfilms, etc.), and all other processes known or yet to be discovered'.[77]

Despite the reproduction right's apparent flexible scope, the Basic Proposal of the WIPO Copyright Treaty included an article providing that the reproduction right would also apply to indirect and temporary reproductions in any manner or form.[78] In a second paragraph, national governments would be permitted to limit the reproduction right in cases where a temporary reproduction would have the sole purpose of making

73. Julie Sheinblatt, *The WIPO Copyright Treaty*, Berkeley Technology Law Journal (1) 535, 450–541 (1998); Mihály Ficsor, *Copyright for the Digital Era: The WIPO Internet Treaties*, Columbia Journal of Law and the Arts (3/4) 197, 203 (1996).
74. Working Group in Intellectual Property Rights, *Intellectual Property and the National Information Infrastructure*, 64–66 (1995). *See* section §6.02[C][1].
75. Pamela Samuelson, *The U.S. Digital Agenda at WIPO*, Virginia Journal of International Law (2) 369, 382–383 (1997).
76. Mihály Ficsor, *The Law of Copyright and the Internet*, 445 (2002), arguing that in the early 1970s it was already a shared point of view that the storage of a work in an electronic memory entails the making of reproductions.
77. World Intellectual Property Organization, Guide to the Berne Convention for the Protection of Literary and Artistic Works, 54 (1978).
78. Article 7 of the Basic WIPO Proposal (WIPO CRNR/DC/4).

the work perceptible or where the reproduction would be of a transient or incidental nature. This limitation would only apply to temporary reproductions made 'in the course of use of the work that is authorized by the author or permitted by law'. This provision aimed to exempt the copies that are necessary to load lawfully acquired copies of works onto their computers. The limitation would not apply to the copies made by network and Internet access providers. These intermediaries would still be held liable for infringements if unauthorized copies travelled through their computer systems.

This wide scope of the reproduction right in the Basic Proposal for the WIPO Copyright Treaty, and the implications it would have for intermediaries, turned out to be one of the most controversial issues during the WIPO diplomatic conference.[79] Delegations could not agree on if and how to exclude temporary reproductions from the scope of the reproduction right.[80] A few countries proposed to delete the provision on the reproduction right altogether.[81] The delegation of Denmark stressed that the reproduction right in Article 9 of the Berne Convention covering reproductions 'in any manner or form' could be applied 'with its normal flexibility'.[82] Telecommunication service providers, Internet access providers, and stakeholders from the fields of education and research, who were afraid of increased exposure to liability, used their influence and were successful in arguing against a broad definition of the reproduction right.[83] The combined efforts of these stakeholders prevented the adoption of an all-encompassing reproduction right that would bring all forms of online communication, including intermediary activities, within the scope of copyright law. The provision on the reproduction right was ultimately deleted, and no other provision regarding the scope of the right of reproduction made it into the adopted version of the WIPO Copyright Treaty.[84]

Now, as already mentioned, the EU legislator *did* lay down a broad reproduction right that also covers temporary reproductions. According to the European Commission, the concept of reproduction had to be reviewed 'in order to determine whether the reproduction right should come into play in the ordinary use (digitization, intermediate copies, downloading into main memory) of the computers and other equipment which characterize the information society'.[85] The Commission noted that 'a substantial degree of uncertainty' existed regarding the acts protected by the reproduction right.[86] Therefore, the Commission proposed to harmonize the reproduction right and to make sure that scanning, uploading, downloading, and other forms of digital reproduction

79. Silke von Lewinski, *Die diplomatische Konferenz der WIPO 1996 zum Urheberrecht und zu verwandten Schutzrechten*, GRUR Int (8/9) 667, 672 (1997).
80. Jorg Reinbothe & Silke von Lewinski, *The WIPO Treaties on Copyright*, 40–41 (2015).
81. Reinbothe & Von Lewinski, *supra* n. 80, at 41.
82. Summary Minutes of Main Committee I, WIPO CRNR/DC/102, 130.
83. Samuelson, *supra* n. 75, at 385–386; Anne Prentice, *Copyright, WIPO and User Interests: Achieving Balance among the Shareholders*, The Journal of Academic Librarianship (4) 309, 310 (1997).
84. Samuelson, *supra* n. 75, at 390.
85. Commission Green Paper, *supra* n. 24, at 52.
86. Commission Communication, *supra* n. 25, at 10.

would be covered by the reproduction right. Temporary acts of reproduction would have to be covered as well.[87]

As is evident from the current wording of Article 2 of the Copyright Directive – 'reproduction by any means and in any form' – the reproduction right applies to both traditional forms of reproduction and digital forms of reproduction. For instance, it applies not only to paper reproductions of a book on paper but also to digital forms of reproduction, such as the uploading, downloading, and storing of digital information.

The reproduction right should be given a broad meaning, in particular with a view to ensuring legal certainty.[88] In its *Infopaq I* decision, the CJEU also held that the reproduction right should be interpreted broadly, specifically to safeguard a high level of protection for copyright owners:

> With respect to the scope of such protection of a work, it follows from recitals 9 to 11 in the preamble to Directive 2001/29 that its main objective is to introduce a high level of protection, in particular for authors to enable them to receive an appropriate reward for the use of their works, including at the time of reproduction of those works, in order to be able to pursue their creative and artistic work.
>
> Similarly, recital 21 in the preamble to Directive 2001/29 requires that the acts covered by the right of reproduction be construed broadly.
>
> That requirement of a broad definition of those acts is, moreover, also to be found in the wording of Article 2 of that directive, which uses expressions such as 'direct or indirect', 'temporary or permanent', 'by any means' and 'in any form'.
>
> Consequently, the protection conferred by Article 2 of Directive 2001/29 must be given a broad interpretation.[89]

By also including temporary reproductions in the definition of the reproduction right, the Copyright Directive takes a literal and technology-oriented approach to the act of reproduction.[90] This conception of the reproduction right brings every act that is *technically* a reproduction within the ambit of the exclusive right. As we will see in the next section, also copies made in the course of intermediary activities can fall within the scope of the exclusive right.

The difficulty with such a technology-oriented reproduction right is that it leaves little room for a more normative perspective on copying. Already in 1995, the European Commission's Legal Advisory Board warned against a purely technical approach towards the act of reproduction:

87. Commission Communication, *supra* n. 25, at 11.
88. Recital 21 of the Copyright Directive: 'This Directive should define the scope of the acts covered by the reproduction right with regard to the different beneficiaries. This should be done in conformity with the acquis communautaire. A broad definition of these acts is needed to ensure legal certainty within the internal market.'
89. *Infopaq International v. Danske Dagblades Forening*, *supra* n. 61, at 40–43.
90. J.-P. Trialle et al., Study on the Application of Directive 2001/29/EC on Copyright and Related Rights in the Information Society (the 'Infosoc Directive'), 120 (2013). *Also see*: Institute for Information Law, The Recasting of Copyright & Related Rights for the Knowledge Economy, 54 (2006): 'The broad scope of the reproduction right also draws in virtually all parties involved in the dissemination and use of protected subject matter, where in the world of physical distribution their roles – especially those of mere carriers – would not have involved restricted acts.'

> In the opinion of the [Legal Advisory Board], in examining (and, possibly, redefining) these rights the European legislator should not focus on technological detail, but follow the normative approach inherent in the realm of copyright and neighbouring rights. The notions of 'reproduction' and 'communication to the public' are only fully understood if they are interpreted not as technical, but as normative (man-made) notions, i.e. they are not in a simple sense descriptive but purpose-oriented and used to define and delimit existing proprietary rights in a sensible and acceptable way. Thus, if the use of a protected work transmitted over a computer network causes (parts of the work) to be intermediately stored, this technical fact does not, in itself, justify the conclusion that an exclusive reproduction right is potentially infringed.[91]

A consequence of this technical approach is that it has become difficult to mitigate any undesirable outcomes of the reproduction right's broad scope. Because there is no room for normativity within the exclusive right itself, courts cannot fine-tune the reproduction right to come to acceptable decisions. Only the EU legislator can make adjustments by providing for limitations and exceptions to permit specific forms of beneficial use.[92]

[a] Reproductions in Part

Article 2 of the Copyright Directive clarifies that reproductions in part are also covered by the reproduction right. Intermediary activities that copy small elements of protected materials may fall within the scope of the reproduction right. For instance, when intermediaries refer to online information, they often reproduce pieces of information to give an impression of that information. Search engines and news aggregators provide snippets of the content they link to. Social networks may also provide outtakes from the content that their users share on the platform.

How much of the work should be reproduced for that work to be reproduced *in part*? The CJEU answered this question in its *Infopaq I* decision. This case centred on Infopaq's media monitoring and analysis business in which it drew up summaries of selected articles from Danish newspapers and other periodicals. Based on the customer's search words, excerpts were provided consisting of the search word and the five words before and after that search word. For instance, from the *Dagbladet Arbejderen* of 4 November 2005, the following phrase was extracted: 'a forthcoming sale of the telecommunications group TDC which is expected to be bought'.[93]

According to the CJEU, for there to be a reproduction in part that is within the scope of the reproduction right, the extract must be 'the expression of the intellectual creation of the author of the work'.[94] The concept of originality is thus key to considering whether a particular outtake should be considered a reproduction in part.[95]

---

91. As reproduced in: Mireille van Eechoud et al., *Harmonizing European Copyright Law. The Challenges of Better Lawmaking*, 87 (2009).
92. *See* section §3.03[E] on limitations and exceptions.
93. *Infopaq International v. Danske Dagblades Forening*, *supra* n. 61.
94. *Infopaq International v. Danske Dagblades Forening*, *supra* n. 61, at 39.
95. This decision had a great impact on EU copyright law as the CJEU effectively harmonized the originality criterion.

In its decision, the CJEU considered that isolated sentences or even certain parts of sentences 'may be suitable for conveying to the reader the originality of a publication such as a newspaper article, by communicating to that reader an element which is, in itself, the expression of the intellectual creation of the author of that article'.[96]

According to the CJEU, the reproduction of eleven consecutive words from an article can thus be a reproduction. That is provided that the reproduction conveys an element of the author's own intellectual creation. Hence, not every unauthorized reproduction of eleven words will infringe the reproduction right. Originality is the primary determinant. Opinions differ as to whether the originality criterion specified by the CJEU sets the bar for infringement too low. The German scholar Leistner notes that 'the *Infopaq* judgment should definitely not be misunderstood in the sense that the CJEU lowered the standard of protection for parts of a work to smaller excerpts of about 11 words'.[97] In contrast, the English scholar Griffiths notes that the fact that copying a short phrase could constitute reproduction seems to have 'maximizing tendencies'.[98]

[b] *Temporary Reproductions*

The Copyright Directive requires Member States to grant copyright owners a reproduction right that covers both temporary and permanent reproductions.[99] With this distinction, the European Commission aimed 'to clarify the fact that in the network environment very different types of reproduction might occur which all constitute acts of reproductions within the meaning of this provision'.[100] Besides long-lived reproductions, also a 'non-visible temporary copy of the work in the working memory of a computer' should be covered by the reproduction right.[101]

To prevent overly broad protection, a mandatory exception for specific temporary reproductions was added in Article 5(1) of the Copyright Directive. This article exempts temporary reproductions that are required for either lawful uses or the transmission of copyrighted material. Article 5(1) reads:

> Temporary acts of reproduction referred to in Article 2, which are transient or incidental [and] an integral and essential part of a technological process and whose sole purpose is to enable:
>
> (a) a transmission in a network between third parties by an intermediary, or
> (b) a lawful use

96. *Infopaq International v. Danske Dagblades Forening, supra* n. 61, at 40–47.
97. Matthias Leistner, *Copyright at the Interface Between EU Law and National Law: Definition of 'Work' and 'Right of Communication to the Public'*, Journal of Intellectual Property Law & Practice (8) 626 (2015).
98. Jonathan Griffiths, *The Role of The Court of Justice in the Development of European Union Copyright Law*, 1106 (Irini Stamatoudi & Paul Torremans eds, 2014).
99. Article 2 of the Copyright Directive.
100. Commission Proposal, *supra* n. 34, at 24–25.
101. Commission Proposal, *supra* n. 34, at 25.

of a work or other subject-matter to be made, and which have no independent economic significance, shall be exempted from the reproduction right provided for in Article 2.

Article 5(1) of the Copyright Directive permits two types of temporary reproduction: (1) temporary reproductions that are necessary to transmit online materials and (2) temporary reproductions that enable a lawful use. Both of these types of temporary copying must also meet the other requirements set in Article 5(1). Before we discuss those requirements, let us first consider these two types of temporary copying.

The first type of temporary copying was included to prevent copies made by network and access providers to transmit materials from falling within the scope of the exclusive reproduction right. In several Member States in the late 1990s, making such reproductions could amount to an infringement of the reproduction right.[102] The European Commission therefore wanted to clarify at the European level that the reproductions made to transmit content would not be covered by the reproduction right.[103] The European Commission's initial proposal contained a relatively broad exception that would exempt 'temporary acts of reproduction which are an integral part of a technological process for the sole purpose of enabling use to be made of a work (...), and having no independent economic significance'.[104] The aim of this exception would be to exclude short-lived reproductions that are 'dictated by technology, but which have no separate economic significance of their own' from the scope of the reproduction right.[105]

However, as the legislative process continued, the exception's wording became more detailed and complex. As Cohen Jehoram would later note with reference to Article 5(1) of the Copyright Directive, 'this convoluted text betrays the intense discussions that have been going on about it'.[106] Within the Council, delegates could not agree whether Article 5(1) should apply to lawful uses only.[107] Moreover, considering that the E-Commerce Directive already provided for a set of liability exemptions, questions were raised about the actual need for an exception.[108] Parliamentary amendments were adopted to address the concerns of copyright owners and intermediaries. To reassure Internet access providers and other intermediaries that they could safely make temporary reproductions to transmit content, an explicit reference was made to the concept of transmission in Article 5(1).[109]

102. C. Kohler & K. Burmeister, *Copyright Liability on the Internet Today in Europe (Germany, France, Italy and the E.U.)*, European Intellectual Property Review (10) 485 (1999).
103. Commission Proposal, *supra* n. 34, at 29: 'Such an obligatory exception at Community level is vital as such short lived reproductions ancillary to the final use of a work will take place in most acts of exploitation of protected subject matter, which will often be of a transnational nature.'
104. Article 5(1) of the Commission Proposal, *supra* n. 34, at 45.
105. Commission Proposal, *supra* n. 34, at 29.
106. Herman Cohen Jehoram, *European Copyright Law – Ever More Horizontal*, IIC – International Review of Intellectual Property and Competition Law (5) 532, 540 (2001).
107. Council Report, 1997/0359, 8647/00, 4.
108. Council Summary of proceedings, 97/0359(COD), 5499/00, 3.
109. Amended proposal for a European Parliament and Council Directive on the harmonisation of certain aspects of copyright and related rights in the Information Society, COM 1999/250.

The second type of temporary reproduction that is permitted by Article 5(1) of the Copyright Directive concerns temporary reproductions that enable *lawful* uses of a work. With this category of temporary reproductions, the EU legislator had in mind in particular the copies made on the computers of users when they browse the Internet and other forms of temporary storage that enable the lawful consumption of copyrighted materials.[110] This type of temporary reproduction focuses on the user of materials and the copies that are made to lawfully experience works.[111] CJEU case law has clarified that lawful uses are not only the types of use permitted by copyright owners but also those uses that cannot be restricted on the basis of copyrights, such as the making of copies that are necessary to receive television broadcasts.[112] The copying of materials in order to make summaries of those materials is a lawful use as well.[113] If materials are temporarily copied to enable *unlawful* uses, Article 5(1) of the Copyright Directive generally does not apply. Such temporary copying must then be permitted by the copyright owner.

A type of use that currently exists in a grey area is the streaming of online materials. Streaming technology is a relatively new means to communicate audiovisual content online that the EU legislator did not consider when the Copyright Directive was drafted and negotiated.[114] Offering an online stream should be considered a communication to the public.[115] But does receiving such a stream amount to an infringement as well? Unlike downloading a song or a movie, the streaming of audiovisual content does not result in a full and permanent copy being made.[116] If one consumes a video stream of, for instance, a football match in a browser, a flow of temporary copies is made in order to display the video. In 2017, the CJEU in *Filmspeler* gave the beginning of an answer in a case about a physical media player on which add-ons were installed

110. Recital 33 of the Copyright Directive.
111. *Also see* on the copying of loaned e-books: Opinion of AG General Szpunar 16 June 2016, ECLI:EU:C:2016:459, para. 58 (*Vereniging Openbare Bibliotheken v. Stichting Leenrecht*): 'In so far as concerns the reproduction made by a user on his computer or any other electronic reading device when downloading a book borrowed from a library, that is, in my opinion, covered by the mandatory exception provided for in Article 5(1) of Directive 2001/29. Indeed, such a reproduction is temporary, since the copy made on the user's equipment will be deleted or deactivated automatically at the end of the loan period. It is also incidental and an integral part of a technological process, that is to say, downloading. Lastly, the only purpose of such a reproduction is to enable a lawful use to be made of the work, namely use in the context of a digital loan. Neither does it have any independent economic significance. Such a reproduction therefore fulfils the conditions listed in Article 5(1) of Directive 2001/29, as interpreted in the case-law of the Court.'
112. *Football Association Premier League and Others*, *supra* n. 59, at 117–172.
113. CJEU 17 January 2012, ECLI:EU:C:2012:16, paras 44–45 (*Infopaq International v. Danske Dagblades Forening*).
114. Opinion of AG General Campos Sánchez-Bordona 8 December 2016, ECLI:EU:C:2016:938, para. 68 (*Stichting Brein v. Jack Frederik Wullems (Filmspeler)*), noting that 'the development of telecommunications (among other factors, the extension of fibre-optic networks which provide very high connection speeds) has meant that illegal downloading onto data carriers – which received a lot of attention until a few years ago – is gradually being superseded, if not replaced, by the reproduction of digital content through streaming, to such a point that this has become one of the most sought-after methods of reproduction'.
115. *ITV Broadcasting and others v. TVCatchup*, *supra* n. 59.
116. Downloading from 'illegal sources' is likely to be considered a form of unauthorized reproduction after the CJEU's *ACI Adam* decision (CJEU 10 April 2014, ECLI:EU:C:2014:254).

that offered access to unauthorized films, series, and live broadcasts. One of the questions asked was whether the users of such a device could be excused on the basis of Article 5(1). On the basis of its earlier hyperlinking case law, discussed below in section §3.03[G], the CJEU gave a fact-specific and nuanced ruling in which the Court considered, among other things, that the player effectively enabled access to materials that were unauthorized. Therefore, the exception could not apply.[117] Since the Court's holdings focus on the offering of a player that was essentially programmed to offer infringing material, it is difficult to determine to what extent other forms of streaming of copyrighted materials, such as streaming a video in one's browser, would be covered by the exception.

Thus far, we have only discussed the two types of temporary copying that are mentioned in Article 5(1) of the Copyright Directive. But Article 5(1) also provides a list of other requirements that must be met for the temporary reproductions to be exempted. Let us take a closer look at these requirements.

Only reproductions that are *transient* or *incidental* are exempted under Article 5(1) of the Copyright Directive. In *Infopaq I*, the CJEU clarified that a reproduction can only be transient if 'its duration is limited to what is necessary for the proper completion of the technological process in question'.[118] Moreover, 'that process must be automated so that it deletes that act automatically, without human intervention, once its function of enabling the completion of such a process has come to an end'.[119] The alternative criterion was clarified by the CJEU in *PRCA*.[120] This decision dealt with the application of Article 5(1) to copies made on a person's computer hard disk and screen while browsing the Internet. The CJEU explained that a reproduction is incidental if 'it neither exists independently of, nor has a purpose independent of, the technological process of which it forms part'.[121]

Another requirement is that the reproduction should not have independent economic significance. If the copy would create additional economic value, a value that goes beyond the use that it enables, the copy would fall outside the scope of Article 5(1) of the Copyright Directive.[122] The rationale of this requirement appears to be that if the temporary copies themselves can be exploited, the exemption should not apply, and permission has to be sought.[123]

For a temporary reproduction to be exempted, it must also be an 'integral and essential part of a technological process'. Legal scholars raised questions early on about the scope of this requirement. For example, Hart wrote that it is by no means clear what

117. CJEU 26 April 2017, ECLI:EU:C:2017:300, paras 69–70 (*Stichting Brein v. Jack Frederik Wullems (Filmspeler)*).
118. *Infopaq International v. Danske Dagblades Forening*, *supra* n. 61, at 64.
119. *Infopaq International v. Danske Dagblades Forening*, *supra* n. 61, at 64.
120. CJEU 5 June 2014, ECLI:EU:C:2014:1195 (*Public Relations Consultants Association v. Newspaper Licensing Agency and others*).
121. *Public Relations Consultants Association v. Newspaper Licensing Agency and others*, *supra* n. 120, at 43.
122. Cf. *Football Association Premier League and Others*, *supra* n. 59, at 174–178.
123. *Also see* recital 33 of the Copyright Directive, which explains that the reproductions should have 'no separate economic value on their own'.

the phrase 'integral and essential part of a technological process' should exclude.[124] In a similar vein, Spindler raised the question of whether 'an integral and essential part of a technological process' means that the temporary reproduction is actually necessary for the operation of a technological process, or that the reproduction is used occasionally and is just linked to the technological process.[125] Hugenholtz pointed out that if the essentiality requirement is taken literally, it would exclude the *caching* that is done by Internet access providers to make transmission more efficient.[126] While such caching is desirable, it is not *essential* to a technological process. A literal interpretation of the provision in Article 5(1) of the Copyright Directive would therefore exclude this form of caching that is beneficial to all Internet users, including copyright owners wanting to exploit their works via the Internet.

The CJEU clarified the essentiality requirement in its 2012 *Infopaq II* order.[127] Advocate General Trstenjak already wrote in her opinion in *Infopaq I* that 'it is not necessary for the act of reproduction to be an indispensable element of a given technological process for it to constitute its integral and essential part'.[128] In its *Infopaq II* order, the CJEU explained that 'this concept also assumes that the completion of the temporary act of reproduction is necessary, in that the technological process concerned could not function correctly and efficiently without that act'.[129] *Efficiency* thus plays a role in making a particular temporary reproduction an *essential* part of a technological process. Therefore, caching by Internet access providers is likely to be covered by the exception.

[2] The Right of Communication to the Public

After discussing the scope of the reproduction right, we now turn to the other exclusive right specified in the Copyright Directive that is relevant to our study: the right of communication to the public. This right is defined in Article 3(1) of the Copyright Directive and is essentially copied from the WIPO Copyright Treaty.[130]

One of the issues that the WIPO Copyright Treaty tried to deal with was the on-demand use of copyrighted materials, which was a new type of use made possible by Internet technologies. Articles 11, 11bis, and 11ter of the Berne Convention already provided for rights regarding public performances, broadcasting, and the recitation of works. Yet, with the rise of individualized communication, in particular via the

124. Michael Hart, *The Copyright in the Information Society Directive: An Overview*, European Intellectual Property Review (2) 58, 59 (2002).
125. Gerald Spindler, *Europäisches Urheberrecht in der Informationgesellschaft*, GRUR (2) 105, 111 (2002).
126. Bernt Hugenholtz, *Brussels Broddelwerk. Recht en Krom in de Auteursrechtrichtlijn*, AMI (2) 2 (2001).
127. *Infopaq International v. Danske Dagblades Forening*, *supra* n. 113.
128. Opinion of AG Trstenjak 12 February 2009, ECLI:EU:C:2009:89, para. 94 (*Infopaq International v. Danske Dagblades Forening*).
129. *Infopaq International v. Danske Dagblades Forening*, *supra* n. 113, at 30.
130. In particular Article 8 of the WIPO Copyright Treaty.

Internet, questions had arisen about the on-demand use of copyrighted materials.[131] Article 8 of the Treaty introduced a right to authorize 'any communication to the public of their works, by wire or wireless means, including the making available to the public of their works in such a way that members of the public may access these works from a place and at a time individually chosen by them'. It aimed to clarify that copyright owners also have control over the communication of their materials over the Internet.

The EU legislator aimed to bring individualized and on-demand forms of the use of copyrighted materials within the scope of copyright protection.[132] Article 3(1) of the Copyright Directive, which defines the exclusive right to communicate to the public, provides that:

> Member States shall provide authors with the exclusive right to authorise or prohibit any communication to the public of their works, by wire or wireless means, including the making available to the public of their works in such a way that members of the public may access them from a place and at a time individually chosen by them.

The exclusive right does not cover typical offline forms of communication. It only applies where copyrighted materials are communicated to a public that is *not present* at the place where the communication originates.[133] For instance, a performance of a classical piece of music in a concert hall is not covered.[134] In *Circul Globus Bucureşti*, the CJEU explained that the Copyright Directive aimed to create a 'general and flexible framework at EU level in order to foster the development of the information society and to adapt and supplement the current law on copyright and related rights in order to respond to technological development, which has created new ways of performing protected works'.[135] According to the Court, the right to communicate to the public is not intended to cover 'conventional' forms of communication to the public, such as the live performance of a work.[136]

Just like the reproduction right, the right of communication to the public is to be widely interpreted. As noted by the CJEU in *Premier League*, 'the concept of communication must be construed broadly, as referring to any transmission of the protected works, irrespective of the technical means or process used'.[137]

The Copyright Directive does not provide a definition of the concept of a communication to the public. However, the CJEU has consistently held that there are two requirements: (1) an act of communication that is directed to (2) a public. The CJEU has held in several cases that an 'individual assessment' is required to answer the

131. Paul Goldstein & Bernt Hugenholtz, *International Copyright: Principles, Law and Practice*, 328 (2010).
132. Commission Green Paper, *supra* n. 24.
133. Recital 23 of the Copyright Directive.
134. Gerard Mom, *Uitvoering in (strikt) besloten kring*, AMI (3) 81, 87 (2010).
135. CJEU 24 November 2011, ECLI:EU:C:2011:772, para. 38 (*Circul Globus Bucureşti v. Uniunea Compozitorilor şi Muzicologilor din România – Asociaţia pentru Drepturi de Autor*).
136. *Circul Globus Bucureşti v. Uniunea Compozitorilor şi Muzicologilor din România – Asociaţia pentru Drepturi de Autor, supra* n. 135, at 39.
137. *Football Association Premier League and Others, supra* n. 59, at 193.

question of whether one makes a communication to the public.[138] To make that assessment, 'account has to be taken of several complementary criteria, which are not autonomous and are interdependent'.[139] Also the goals of the Copyright Directive must be considered.[140]

[a] An Act of Communication

For there to be an act of communication it is sufficient that 'the work is made available to the public in such a way that the persons forming that public may access it'.[141] It is not necessary that these persons actually access the work – offering the *opportunity* to access the work is enough for there to be an act of communication.

Article 3(1) covers both linear forms of communication and non-linear forms of communication. Broadcasting, which requires tuning in by the public, is a form of linear communication. In non-linear forms of communication, individual users may choose when and where they consume the materials, such as a video on YouTube, an online newspaper article, or music on Spotify.

While the *transmission* of a work is covered by the right of communication to the public, the Copyright Directive clarifies in its recitals that the 'mere provision of physical facilities for enabling or making a communication' is not.[142] Here the directive follows the Agreed Statement adopted regarding Article 8 of the WIPO Copyright Treaty.[143] The strong presence of access providers, online service providers, and representatives from the telecommunications industry at the treaty negotiations ensured that merely providing the technologies to access online materials would not be an infringement of the new right of communication to the public.[144] In its recitals, the Copyright Directive also clarifies that merely providing the facilities to communicate cannot lead to an infringement.[145]

138. *Reha Training Gesellschaft für Sport- und Unfallrehabilitation v. Gesellschaft für musikalische Aufführungs-und mechanische Vervielfältigungsrechte, supra* n. 60, at 35; *GS Media v. Sanoma Media Netherlands and others, supra* n. 60, at 33.
139. *Reha Training Gesellschaft für Sport- und Unfallrehabilitation v. Gesellschaft für musikalische Aufführungs-und mechanische Vervielfältigungsrechte, supra* n. 60, at 35; *GS Media v. Sanoma Media Netherlands and others, supra* n. 60, at 34.
140. *SGAE v. Rafael Hoteles, supra* n. 60, at 34, stating that the interpretation of EU law requires consideration not only of the wording of a provision but 'also the context in which it occurs and the objectives pursued by the rules of which it is part' must be considered.
141. *SGAE v. Rafael Hoteles, supra* n. 60, at 43.
142. Recital 27 of the Copyright Directive.
143. Agreed Statement to Article 8 of the WIPO Copyright Treaty. This Agreed Statement clarifies that 'it is understood that the mere provision of physical facilities for enabling or making a communication does not in itself amount to communication within the meaning of this Treaty or the Berne Convention'.
144. Ficsor, *supra* n. 73, at 22.
145. Recital 27 of the Copyright Directive. The European Parliament had requested the introduction of a separate paragraph regarding the provision of physical facilities. Article 3(4) was added thereto in the Amended Proposal (Amended proposal for a European Parliament and Council Directive on the harmonisation of certain aspects of copyright and related rights in the Information Society, COM 1999/250). However, the Council decided that such a clarification was not necessary, for the proposed directive in its recitals already contained a clarification

The right of communication to the public does not therefore apply to the provision of the means to transmit electronic or fibre-optic signals through cables and airwaves by network providers. Nor does it apply to the routing of information through routers, switches, and other networking devices by access providers. As Advocate General Trstenjak noted in the *Del Corso* case:

> I consider that [Article 3(1)] should be construed as meaning that persons who provide players, but do not at the same time control access to copyright works, do not make any communication to the public. This is the case, for example, where televisions or radios are sold or rented or where an internet service provider merely provides access to the internet.[146]

The right of communication to the public is thus unlikely to apply when an intermediary provides basic Internet connectivity to others. However, this right may come into play where newer intermediary activities are concerned, such as the caching of webpages by search engines, linking to information on the Internet, and news search and aggregation. These intermediary activities are discussed separately in sections §3.03[H] and [I].

[b] The Public

For copyrighted materials to be communicated to the public, they must not only be *communicated* but also be communicated to *a public*. The concept of a 'public' is not defined in the Copyright Directive. Nor is it defined at the international level. When the directive was negotiated, it was agreed that it should be left to Member States to define it.[147] Nevertheless, the CJEU has interpreted this concept in a series of cases. In these cases, the CJEU gradually developed quite a detailed and complex understanding of what it means to communicate copyrighted materials to the public.

SGAE v. Rafael Hoteles dealt with the distribution of signals by means of television sets to customers in hotel rooms.[148] In its decision, the CJEU used the WIPO Guide to the Berne Convention as its starting point. This Guide explains that if a copyright owner authorizes the broadcasting of his work, he considers only those users who own the equipment to receive the programme and who view or listen to it

---

regarding the provision of physical facilities (Commission Communication to the European Parliament pursuant to the second subparagraph of Article 251 (2) of the EC Treaty concerning the common position of the Council on the adoption of a Directive of the European Parliament and of the Council on the harmonisation of certain aspects of copyright and related rights in the information Society, SEC/2000/1734). A separate provision regarding physical facilities was not therefore adopted.

146. Opinion of AG Trstenjak 29 June 2011, ECLI:EU:C:2011:431, para. 95 (*SCF Consorzio Fonografici v. Marco Del Corso*).

147. The European Commission considered the definition of the notion of the 'public' to be a matter for national law (Commission Proposal, *supra* n. 34, at 25). *See also* Commission Staff Working Paper, 'The Review of the EC Legal Framework in the Field of Copyright and Related Rights', SEC 2004/995, 15.

148. *SGAE v. Rafael Hoteles*, *supra* n. 60.

personally or in their own private or family circles.[149] If the programme is received and made available to a broader public, the protected materials are communicated to a *new public*. Such communication then requires the copyright owner's permission. Consequently, the CJEU held that the hotel customers, to which the broadcast material was made available, consisted of a new public. Without the hotel owner's intervention, these customers would, in principle, not be able to enjoy the broadcast work.[150] Moreover, the Court considered that the fact that the hotel owner aimed to obtain a benefit from the provision of the televisions was relevant. The Court highlighted that while profit-making is not a decisive factor, it is definitely relevant in determining whether a communication to the public occurred.[151] The basic idea behind the decision is that for there to be a (new) communication to the public, the communication must reach an audience that was not taken into account by the copyright owner when he initially communicated the materials or permitted such communication by others.

The 'new public' criterion was suggested by Advocate General Sharpston in her opinion in *SGAE v. Rafael Hoteles*.[152] However, there is reason to believe that the adoption of this criterion is ill-founded as it appears to be based on a misreading of the 1978 WIPO Guide to the Berne Convention.[153] Both Sharpston and later also the CJEU interpreted the right of communication in light of Article 11bis(1)(ii) of the Berne Convention. This article affords protection against 'any communication to the public by wire or by rebroadcasting of the broadcast of the work, when this communication is made by an organization other than the original one'. According to Sharpston, this other organization criterion had to be interpreted as requiring that a new public would have to be reached by the communication (a 'fresh circle of listeners').[154] Sharpston based this interpretation on the WIPO Guide's notes regarding Article 11bis(1)(iii) of the Berne Convention – and not Article 11bis(1)(ii) of the Berne Convention. The CJEU referred to these notes as well and applied the 'new public' test in this case.[155] It held that the hotel customers formed such a new public as the hotel owner knowingly intervened to give access to a group of people who 'would not, in principle, be able to enjoy the broadcast work'.[156]

Apart from it being based on a misreading of the WIPO Guide, the introduction of this criterion is also problematic as it creates greater uncertainty about the scope of the exclusive right. Instead of focusing on the entity that communicates, the CJEU requires that the much more diffuse group of people that make up the receiving public should be focused upon. In fact, it is for reasons of predictability that the 'new public' criterion

149. World Intellectual Property Organization, Guide to the Berne Convention for the Protection of Literary and Artistic Works (Paris Act, 1971) 68–69 (1978).
150. *SGAE v. Rafael Hoteles, supra* n. 60, at 42.
151. *SGAE v. Rafael Hoteles, supra* n. 60, at 44.
152. Opinion of AG Sharpston 13 July 2006, ECLI:EU:C:2006:479, para. 50 (*Sociedad General de Autores y Editores de España v. Rafael Hoteles*).
153. Bernt Hugenholtz & Sam van Velze, *Communication to a New Public? Three Reasons Why EU Copyright Law Can Do Without a 'New Public'*, IIC (7) 797 (2016).
154. Opinion of AG Sharpston 13 July 2006, ECLI:EU:C:2006:479, para. 50 (*Sociedad General de Autores y Editores de España v. Rafael Hoteles*).
155. *SGAE v. Rafael Hoteles, supra* n. 60, at 41.
156. *SGAE v. Rafael Hoteles, supra* n. 60, at 42.

was rejected during the 1948 Brussels revision of the Berne Convention.[157] The criterion was considered not to be sufficiently clear since any kind of retransmission could be classified as reaching a new audience.[158] Instead the other organization criterion was adopted. It was regarded as a criterion that was easier to apply because the identity of the organization responsible for a retransmission could usually be easily ascertained.

Nevertheless, with the CJEU's decision in *SGAE*, the 'new public' criterion has become and remains central to determining whether the exclusive right to communicate to the public is being infringed. In its later case law, the CJEU further specified this criterion. It gradually developed a set of factors that are relevant in determining whether a new public is reached.

Premier League dealt with a bar owner who showed soccer matches in her bar.[159] The question was whether the bar's customers were a 'new public' and whether permission from the copyright owner was required. In *Premier League*, we see that the CJEU also considered the role of the user – the bar owner – and the economic character of that use. The CJEU held that the customers constituted an additional public that was not considered when the copyright owners authorized the broadcasting of the soccer matches. Hence, showing these matches amounted to a communication to the public, which required the permission of the copyright owner. In this respect, the Court also stated that it was 'not irrelevant' that the matches were shown in order to attract more customers and that the communication was of a profit-making nature.[160]

SCF v. Marco Del Corso dealt with a dentist who played musical works broadcast on the radio in his private dental practice.[161] In this case, the CJEU introduced a formula that further opened up the right of communication to the public. The Court stated that an 'individual approach' was needed to assess whether a communication to the public had taken place.[162] And in making that assessment, account must be taken of several complementary criteria, which are not autonomous and are interdependent. 'Consequently, [these criteria] must be applied individually and in the light of their interaction with one another, given that in different specific situations, they may be met to varying degrees.'[163] Taking into account these criteria, the Court held that the

157. Sam Ricketson, *Berne Convention for the Protection of Literary and Artistic Works: 1886–1986*, 449 (1987).
158. Makeen, *The Controversy of Simultaneous Cable Retransmission to Hotel Rooms under International and European Copyright Laws*, Journal – Copyright Society of The USA (1/2) 59, 63 (2010).
159. *Football Association Premier League and Others, supra* n. 59.
160. *Football Association Premier League and Others, supra* n. 59, at 204–206. However, the CJEU also clarified in *ITV Broadcasting and others v. TVCatchup* that the profit-making aspect does not determine conclusively whether a communication to the public was made (*ITV Broadcasting and others v. TVCatchup, supra* n. 59, at 43).
161. CJEU 15 March 2012, ECLI:EU:C:2012:140 (*Società Consortile Fonografici v. Marco Del Corso*). This case concerned the broadcasting of phonograms which is covered by Article 8(2) of the Rental and Lending Directive. Yet, the CJEU's consideration regarding the communication of these phonograms are equally relevant to the development of the right to communicate to the public in Article 3(1) of the Copyright Directive.
162. *Società Consortile Fonografici v. Marco Del Corso, supra* 161, at 78.
163. *Società Consortile Fonografici v. Marco Del Corso, supra* 161, at 79.

dentist did not make a communication to the public. His communication only reached a 'determinate circle of potential recipients' (the dentist's patients).[164] These patients were not present in the dentist's practice at the same time.[165] And as a final point, the Court noted that the dentist did not turn on the radio in order to attract more customers or to charge a higher price for his treatments. Hence his use was not of a profit-making nature.[166]

An important nuance was added to the doctrine in *ITV v. TVCatchup* - one that offered a novel perspective on the 'new public' criterion. This case dealt with an Internet television broadcasting service that picked up free-to-air television broadcasts and offered them as streaming video on the Internet. These broadcasts were thus made available on the Internet to a group of users who were already licensed to consume these broadcasts via television. Unlike the hotel owner in *SGAE*, the bar owner in *Premier League*, and the dentist in *Del Corso*, TVCatchup used a technology that differed from the technology that was used for the original communication. TVCatchup took works that were originally communicated by terrestrial broadcasting and prepared them for live streaming over the Internet. The CJEU considered that 'each of those two transmissions must be authorised individually and separately by the authors concerned given that each is made under specific technical conditions, using a different means of transmission for the protected works, and each is intended for a public'.[167] Hence, if the specific technical conditions of a transmission are changed, we are dealing with a new transmission, which renders the new public criterion irrelevant. The lesson to be learnt from *ITV v. TVCatchup* is that the new public criterion does not play a role if works are transmitted by different technological means.

The CJEU's case law before *ITV v. TVCatchup* created room for nuanced rulings that considered the role of the use and the nature of that use.[168] *TVCatchup*, however, again emphasizes the importance of the copyright owner's permission - at least to the extent that material is communicated through a different technology.[169] As such, *TVCatchup* enables the right of communication to the public to offer protection if materials are used in new technological contexts.[170] At the same time, this nuanced approach to the new public criterion also raises the question of where exactly to draw the line between certain technologies and when to apply the new public criterion.[171]

Reha Training v. GEMA is the last case that we will discuss here as it nicely illustrates how fact-intensive the CJEU's analysis under the new public criterion can

164. *Società Consortile Fonografici v. Marco Del Corso, supra* 161, at 95.
165. *Società Consortile Fonografici v. Marco Del Corso, supra* 161, at 96.
166. *Società Consortile Fonografici v. Marco Del Corso, supra* 161, at 97-99.
167. *ITV Broadcasting and others v. TVCatchup, supra* n. 59, at 39.
168. Matthias Leistner, *Europe's Copyright Law Decade: Recent Case Law of the European Court of Justice and Policy Perspectives*, Common Market Law Review (2) 559, 569-572 (2014).
169. Matthias Leistner, *Copyright at the Interface Between EU Law and National Law: Definition of 'Work' and 'Right of Communication to the Public'*, Journal of Intellectual Property Law & Practice (8) 626, 632 (2015).
170. Lucie Guibault & João Quintais, *Copyright, Technology and the Exploitation of Audiovisual Works in the EU*, IRIS Plus (4) 1, 14 (2014).
171. Katarzyna Klafkowska-Wasniowska, *Public Communication Right: Towards the Full Harmonisation?*, European Intellectual Property Review (12) 751 (2013).

become.[172] Reha Training operated a rehabilitation centre that offered victims of accidents post-operative treatment on its premises. Patients could watch television in two waiting rooms and a training room. Did Reha communicate the broadcast works to the public? In his analysis of the case, Advocate General Bot acknowledged that the CJEU's case law had not yet provided a comprehensible set of criteria as he spoke 'of an opportunity to reiterate and *clarify* its case-law on this subject'.[173]

In its ruling, the CJEU stated that for there to be a communication to the public, the communication must reach a public that was not taken into account by the copyright owner.[174] The Court also highlighted the 'indispensable role of the user' – which is the person making the communication.[175] That person 'must, in full knowledge of the consequences of its actions, give access to the television broadcast containing the protected work to an additional public'.[176] The Court explained that it had 'already held that the operators of a café-restaurant, a hotel or a spa establishment carry out an act of communication where they intentionally broadcast protected works to their clientele by intentionally distributing a signal by means of television or radio sets which they have installed in their establishment'.[177] According to the Court, the rehabilitation centre had also intentionally broadcast protected materials to its patients. Did the centre also reach a new public by setting up televisions for its patients? Yes, said the Court. It considered that the patients constituted a public that right owners had not taken into account. And, regarding the profit-making nature, it noted that 'the broadcasting of television programmes on television sets, in so far as it is intended to create a diversion for the patients of a rehabilitation centre, such as that at issue in the main proceedings, during their treatment or in the waiting time, constitutes the supply of additional services which, while not having any medical benefit, does have an impact on the establishment's standing and attractiveness, thereby giving it a competitive advantage'.[178] Hence, Reha Training, by showing the TV programmes in its centre, communicated the TV programmes to the public.

What becomes clear from the above discussion of the right of communication to the public is that the CJEU has developed quite a detailed and complex doctrine. Several independent and complementary criteria need to be considered in an individualized assessment. And these criteria may be met to varying degrees depending on the situation. After studying the full body of CJEU case law on the right of communication

172. *Reha Training Gesellschaft für Sport- und Unfallrehabilitation v. Gesellschaft für musikalische Aufführungs-und mechanische Vervielfältigungsrechte, supra* n. 60, at 48.
173. Opinion of AG Bot 23 February 2016, ECLI:EU:C:2016:109, para. 4 (*Reha Training Gesellschaft für Sport-und Unfallrehabilitation v. Gesellschaft für musikalische Aufführungs-und mechanische Vervielfältigungsrechte*).
174. *Reha Training Gesellschaft für Sport- und Unfallrehabilitation v. Gesellschaft für musikalische Aufführungs-und mechanische Vervielfältigungsrechte, supra* n. 60, at 48.
175. *Reha Training Gesellschaft für Sport- und Unfallrehabilitation v. Gesellschaft für musikalische Aufführungs-und mechanische Vervielfältigungsrechte, supra* n. 60, at 46.
176. *Reha Training Gesellschaft für Sport- und Unfallrehabilitation v. Gesellschaft für musikalische Aufführungs-und mechanische Vervielfältigungsrechte, supra* n. 60, at 46.
177. *Reha Training Gesellschaft für Sport- und Unfallrehabilitation v. Gesellschaft für musikalische Aufführungs-und mechanische Vervielfältigungsrechte, supra* n. 60, at 54.
178. *Reha Training Gesellschaft für Sport- und Unfallrehabilitation v. Gesellschaft für musikalische Aufführungs-und mechanische Vervielfältigungsrechte, supra* n. 60, at 48.

to the public, Sirinelli, Benazeraf, and Bensamoun found that the legal concept of a communication to the public consists of sixteen different criteria that in themselves are not easy to comprehend, nor are they applied consistently.[179] Considering also that the CJEU's case law is geared towards specific fact patterns that are only briefly summarized by the Court, they conclude that it is hard to deduce from this case law any guidance with respect to other cases.[180]

[E] Limitations and Exceptions in the Copyright Directive

After discussing the relevant exclusive rights (the reproduction right and the right of communication to the public), we now turn to the limitations and exceptions to those exclusive rights. The approach that the Copyright Directive takes is one of *broad* exclusive rights and *specific* limitations and exceptions to those rights. Article 5 of the Copyright Directive contains an exhaustive list of limitations and exceptions that may be implemented or maintained by Member States. Member States cannot introduce or maintain new limitations and exceptions that are not on this list. The directive also contains one exception that Member States must implement: the exception for temporary copying, which has already been discussed.[181]

While some of the available limitations and exceptions are formulated in more flexible terms than others, they are nonetheless specific in the sense that they focus on particular forms of use,[182] types of users,[183] purposes of the use,[184] or combinations thereof.[185] It is not the aim of this section to provide an overview of the available limitations and exceptions. Rather, the focus is on the method that was chosen by the EU legislator to shape limitations and exceptions at the EU level.

[1] Optional Limitations and Exceptions

As already mentioned, Article 5(1) of the Copyright Directive specifies a mandatory exception regarding temporary reproductions.[186] The implementation of the other limitations and exceptions listed in Article 5(2) and (3) is not mandatory. Member States may choose from the directive's list the limitations and exceptions they wish to implement or maintain. If, however, Member States implement any of these optional limitations and exceptions, they must do so in accordance with the directive. Member

179. Pierre Sirinelli, Josée Benazeraf & Alexandra Bensamoun, Mission: Right of Communication to the Public, High Council for Literary and Artistic Property 18 and 23 (2016).
180. Sirinelli, Benazeraf & Bensamoun, *supra* n. 179, at 21.
181. *See* section §3.03[D][1][b].
182. For example, Article 5(3)(g) allows exemptions for uses during religious celebrations or official celebrations organized by a public authority.
183. For example, Article 5(2)(c) allows an exemption for reproductions made by publicly accessible libraries, educational establishments or museums, or archives.
184. For example, Article 5(3)(a) allows exemptions for the sole purpose of illustration for teaching or scientific research.
185. For example, Article 5(2)(b) allows an exemption for reproductions made by natural persons for certain private uses.
186. *See* section §3.03[D][1][b].

States are then bound by the CJEU's case law and its interpretations of the limitations and exceptions in the directive.[187]

This approach towards the limitations and exceptions shows that while the Copyright Directive aimed to harmonize copyright law, it also leaves room for the different copyright traditions to coexist.[188] As a consequence, Member States have relative freedom to implement the directive in line with their own traditions and values. The downside is that the directive is not very effective in achieving its objective of harmonization.[189] In fact, Member State laws with respect to limitations and exceptions appear to differ significantly.[190]

[2] A Closed List of Limitations and Exceptions

The list of limitations and exceptions in Article 5 of the Copyright Directive is a closed list. As stated in recital 31 of the Directive, it 'provides for an exhaustive enumeration of exceptions and limitations to the reproduction right and the right of communication to the public'. Member States may not introduce or maintain exceptions that are not on the list. Article 5(3)(o) provides for a minor exception to this: it allows Member States to permit 'use in certain other cases of minor importance where exceptions or limitations already exist under national law'.

The closed list makes it difficult for Member States to lay down limitations and exceptions for new forms of use that had not been contemplated when the Copyright Directive was drafted in the late 1990s. As a consequence, the directive may hamper the use of protected materials that falls within the scope of the broad exclusive rights, but for which no limitations or exceptions currently exist in the directive. In this set-up of EU copyright law, the EU legislator must specify the types of use that can be exempted at the Member State level. If a new type of use emerges that has not been considered, and that does not fit within the existing types of limitations and exceptions, only the EU legislator can accommodate that form of use. An example of such use is data mining, through which one can deduce new information from already available data. Under the Copyright Directive, data mining appeared not to be allowed without

187. CJEU 10 April 2014, ECLI:EU:C:2014:254, para. 34 (*ACI Adam and others v. Stichting de Thuiskopie and Stichting Onderhandelingen Thuiskopie vergoeding*): 'It follows that the Member States have the option of introducing the different exceptions provided for in Article 5 of that directive, in accordance with their legal traditions, but that, once they have made the choice of introducing a certain exception, it must be applied coherently, so that it cannot undermine the objectives which Directive 2001/29 pursues with the aim of ensuring the proper functioning of the internal market.'

188. Opinion of AG Trstenjak 11 May 2010, ECLI:EU:C:2010:264, para. 41 (*SGAE v. Padawan*): 'In terms of regulatory policy, Directive 2001/29 represents a compromise, which, despite the declared objective of harmonisation, sufficiently takes into account the differing legal traditions and views in the Member States of the European Union – including in particular the common law concept of copyright and the continental European concept of copyright protection –, for instance by providing for numerous exceptions and allows the Member States considerable flexibility in the transposition of the directive.'

189. Lucie Guibault, *Why Cherry-Picking Never Leads to Harmonisation: The Case of the Limitations on Copyright*, JIPITEC (2) 55, 58 (2010).

190. *See*: https://copyrightexceptions.eu (accessed 14 June 2019).

prior authorization by copyright owners holding the exclusive right to, for instance, the content in databases.

Research highlighting the benefits of data mining technologies go back to at least the mid-1990s.[191] Hargreaves in his 2011 review of UK copyright law explicitly referred to data mining technologies in arguing that a broader non-consumptive exception should be adopted at the EU level.[192] And research by Handke, Guibault, and Vallbé suggests that the directive's inability to accommodate the use of data mining technologies has in fact already impeded the development of data mining technology in the European Union.[193] It took the European Commission until late 2015 to announce that it would consider a legislative proposal in order to allow data mining by public interest research organizations for scientific purposes.[194] In 2016, the Commission published a proposal for the DSM Directive that would indeed introduce a mandatory exception for data mining.[195] The DSM Directive was finally adopted in the spring of 2019 and requires Member States to provide for exceptions for data mining.[196] As the directive will have to be implemented by Member States in 2021, the long process of accommodating data mining in the EU legal order is still not finished yet.

[3] Interpretation of Limitations and Exceptions

The way in which limitations and exceptions are to be interpreted influences their (potential) scope. The Copyright Directive in recital 44 provides guidance on how limitations and exceptions should be interpreted:

> Such exceptions and limitations may not be applied in a way which prejudices the legitimate interests of the rightholder or which conflicts with the normal exploitation of his work or other subject-matter. The provision of such exceptions or limitations by Member States should, in particular, duly reflect the increased economic impact that such exceptions or limitations may have in the context of the new electronic environment. Therefore, the scope of certain exceptions or limitations may have to be even more limited when it comes to certain new uses of copyright works and other subject-matter.

Limitations and exceptions should thus not be applied in a way that prejudices the legitimate interests of copyright owners or that conflicts with the normal exploitation of the copyrighted materials. This principle that is derived from international copyright law – the so-called three-step test – has also been laid down in Article 5(5) of

191. For instance: Ming-Syan Chen, Jiawei Han & Philip Yu, *Data Mining: An Overview from a Database Perspective*, IEEE Transactions on Knowledge and Data Engineering (6) 866 (1996). *Also see* Google Ngram for the term 'data mining', showing that use of the term has increased significantly starting from the early 1990s.
192. Ian Hargreaves, Digital Opportunity. A Review of Intellectual Property and Growth 47 (2011).
193. Christian Handke, Lucie Guibault, Joan-Josep Vallbé, Is Europe Falling Behind in Data Mining? Copyright's Impact on Data Mining in Academic Research (2015).
194. Commission Communication, *supra* n. 44, at 8.
195. Commission Proposal, *supra* n. 49.
196. Articles 3 and 4 of the DSM Directive.

the Copyright Directive.[197] Specifically with regard to new forms of the use of copyrighted materials, the recital highlights that 'the scope of certain exceptions or limitations may have to be even more limited'.

In its case law, the CJEU has also emphasized that limitations and exceptions should be interpreted strictly. The principle of strict interpretation can be traced back to a natural-rights conception of copyright law in which broad and flexible exploitation rights are defined while exceptions are defined restrictively and need to be strictly interpreted.[198] A more utilitarian view of copyright law is likely to find such a restrictive approach to the limitations and exceptions problematic.[199] Together with the exclusive rights, the limitations and exceptions balance the interests of copyright owners and those of others, as well as the public at large. The limitations and exceptions may also contribute to the creation of new works, since they enable the work of others to be built upon. In this respect, the limitations and exceptions and the exclusive rights are equally important and may have to be dealt with in that way.[200]

The principle of the strict interpretation of limitations and exceptions was first recognized by the CJEU in *Infopaq I*.[201] In this case, the Court had to interpret the scope of the mandatory exception in Article 5(1) of the Copyright Directive regarding temporary reproductions. Article 2 of the directive provides for a broad reproduction right that includes temporary reproductions. The exception in Article 5(1) requires that particular reproductions that are dictated by technology should be exempted.[202] According to the CJEU, the exception deviates from the 'general principle' of the protection of copyright owners' rights and therefore the exception needs to be 'interpreted strictly'.[203] In later case law, the CJEU nuanced the principle of a strict interpretation. In these cases, the Court has made clear that, while limitations and exceptions should be interpreted strictly, the purpose of a particular limitation or exception must be considered as well.

197. *See* Articles 9(2) of the Berne Convention, 13 of the Agreement on Trade-related Aspects of Intellectual Property Rights (TRIPS), and 10 of the WIPO Copyright Treaty. For a discussion of this three-step test, *see*: Christophe Geiger, Daniel Gervais & Martin Senftleben, *The Three-Step-Test Revisited: How to Use the Test's Flexibility in National Copyright Law*, American University Law Review (3) 581 (2014); Martin Senftleben, *Copyright, Limitations, and the Three-Step Test: An Analysis of the Three-Step Test in International and EC Copyright Law* (2004).
198. Senftleben 2004, *supra* n. 197, at. 6. For a discussion of the justifications for copyright, *see* section §2.03[A]. *See also* section §5.04[B] on the German interpretation of the limitations and exceptions.
199. For example, *Opinion of European Copyright Society on the EU Copyright Reform Package* (2017), 4–5: 'In our opinion, any forward-looking copyright policy at EU level should reflect not only the economic needs and interests of traditional right holders, but should also be designed in light of a broader and more inclusive ambition to foster cultural production, access to culture and knowledge and technological progress (*see* e.g. art. 3(3) of the TFEU).'
200. Esther Derclaye, *Infopaq International A/S v Danske Dagblades Forening (C-5/08): Wonderful or Worrisome? The Impact of the ECJ Ruling in Infopaq on UK Copyright Law*, European Intellectual Property Review (5) 247, 251 (2010); Alexander Peukert, *The Fundamental Right to (Intellectual) Property* 145 (Christophe Geiger ed. 2015).
201. *Infopaq International v. Danske Dagblades Forening, supra* n. 61.
202. For a discussion of this exception, *see* section §3.03[D][1][b].
203. *Infopaq International v. Danske Dagblades Forening, supra* n. 61, at 64. *Infopaq International v. Danske Dagblades Forening, supra* n. 113, at 27.

The CJEU adopted a more purposive interpretation in *Premier League*.[204] This case dealt with the use of foreign decoding devices to receive satellite broadcasts of soccer matches broadcast in another country. According to the Court, the temporary copies made in memories of satellite decoders and on television screens are within the scope of the reproduction right.[205] In determining whether the exception for temporary copying in Article 5(1) of the Copyright Directive applied, the Court first acknowledged that exceptions must be interpreted strictly. Yet, the Court also held that the interpretation of the exception in Article 5(1) must enable the effectiveness of the exception, which permits that also its purpose is observed.[206] In this regard, the CJEU stated that the exception for temporary reproductions must be interpreted in the light of its purpose of ensuring technological development and the fair balance of rights and interests:

> In accordance with its objective, that exception must allow and ensure the development and operation of new technologies and safeguard a fair balance between the rights and interests of right holders, on the one hand, and of users of protected works who wish to avail themselves of those new technologies, on the other.[207]

The CJEU cleared the way for an interpretation of the exception for temporary reproductions that also considers the effects on technological innovation:

> If the acts at issue were not considered to comply with the conditions set by Article 5(1) of the Copyright Directive, all television viewers using modern sets which, in order to work, need those acts of reproduction to be carried out would be prevented from receiving broadcasts containing broadcast works, in the absence of an authorisation from copyright holders. That would impede, and even paralyse, the actual spread and contribution of new technologies, in disregard of the will of the European Union legislature as expressed in recital 31 in the preamble to the Copyright Directive.[208]

In *Deckmyn*, the CJEU also adopted a more purposive interpretation.[209] This case dealt with the exception in Article 5(3)(k) of the Copyright Directive, which permits the use of copyrighted materials for the purpose of caricature, parody, or pastiche. After reiterating the principle of a strict interpretation, the CJEU noted that the concept of parody must be interpreted also in light of the purpose of the exception.[210] And specifically with regard to that exception, the Court highlighted the exception's importance for the freedom of expression:

> As regards the objective referred to in Article 5(3)(k) of Directive 2001/29, the objectives of that directive in general must be recalled, which include, as is

204. *Football Association Premier League and Others*, *supra* n. 59.
205. *Football Association Premier League and Others*, *supra* n. 59, at 159.
206. *Football Association Premier League and Others*, *supra* n. 59, at 163.
207. *Football Association Premier League and Others*, *supra* n. 59, at 164.
208. *Football Association Premier League and Others*, *supra* n. 59, at 179. *Public Relations Consultants Association v. Newspaper Licensing Agency and others*, *supra* n. 120, at 24.
209. CJEU 3 September 2014, ECLI:EU:C:2014:2132 (*Deckmyn*).
210. *Deckmyn*, *supra* n. 209, at 23.

> apparent from recital 3 in the preamble to that directive, a harmonisation which will help to implement the four freedoms of the internal market and which relates to observance of the fundamental principles of law and especially of property, including intellectual property, and freedom of expression and the public interest. It is not disputed that parody is an appropriate way to express an opinion.[211]

In its interpretation of the exception, the CJEU also referred to the fair balance of rights and interests in recital 31 of the Copyright Directive:

> It follows that the application, in a particular case, of the exception for parody, within the meaning of Article 5(3)(k) of Directive 2001/29, must strike a fair balance between, on the one hand, the interests and rights of persons referred to in Articles 2 and 3 of that directive, and, on the other, the freedom of expression of the user of a protected work who is relying on the exception for parody, within the meaning of Article 5(3)(k).[212]

Although in specific cases the CJEU has adopted a more purposive approach to interpreting the limitations and exceptions in the Copyright Directive, a strict interpretation remains the starting point. In the case of *ACI Adam v. Stichting de Thuiskopie*, the CJEU decided on the scope of the private copying exception in Article 5(2)(b) and its applicability to copies made from unlawful sources.[213] In this 2014 decision, the Court explained that the principle of a strict interpretation applies to all limitations and exceptions in Article 5(2). It stated:

> As regards the scope of those exceptions and limitations, it must be pointed out that, according to the settled case-law of the Court, the provisions of a directive which derogate from a general principle established by that directive must be interpreted strictly (...).
>
> It follows that the different exceptions and limitations provided for in Article 5(2) of [the Copyright Directive] must be interpreted strictly.[214]

In sum, we thus see that the principle of a strict interpretation of limitations and exceptions still stands, but that the CJEU is also willing to adjust the strictness of its interpretation in individual cases in order to strike a fair balance.[215] It is noteworthy that the CJEU has also given weight to the development and operation of new technologies that enable lawful uses. And that it has been willing to consider the objectives of limitations or exceptions in determining their scope.

211. *Deckmyn*, *supra* n. 209, at 25.
212. *Deckmyn*, *supra* n. 209, at 27.
213. *ACI Adam and others v. Stichting de Thuiskopie and Stichting Onderhandelingen Thuiskopie vergoeding*, *supra* n. 187.
214. *ACI Adam and others v. Stichting de Thuiskopie and Stichting Onderhandelingen Thuiskopie vergoeding*, *supra* n. 187, at 23.
215. Martin Senftleben, *Breathing Space for Cloud-Based Business Models – Exploring the Matrix of Copyright Limitations, Safe Harbours and Injunctions*, JIPITEC (2) 87, 93 (2013); Jonathan Griffiths et al., The European Copyright Society's 'Opinion on the judgment of the CJEU in Case C-201/13 Deckmyn', European Intellectual Property Review (3) 127 (2015).

[F] Taking a Closer Look

In the following sections, we will take a closer look at how the set-up of EU copyright law works out specifically with regard to several forms of intermediary activity. We will start by discussing the act of linking, which is one of the basic functions of the web (section §3.03[G]). Under what circumstances can linking be relevant under EU copyright law? Subsequently we will consider a newer form of intermediary activity that had not yet emerged or that was not as visible at the time the Copyright Directive was drafted and negotiated: search engine use of copyrighted materials (section §3.03[H]). Special attention is also paid to the online use of press publications, for which the DSM Directive provides a new set of rules (section §3.03[I]).

[G] Hyperlinking

A hyperlink – or 'link' for short – is essentially a reference to another location on the web or Internet. A link connects pieces of online information and enables people to browse the web. Intermediaries, too, may link to information available elsewhere. For instance, the core functionality of a search engine is that it presents relevant links to other web pages.[216] News search engines may link to articles available online as well. A video hosting platform uses links to refer to other videos available on the platform.

The question of whether linking to online materials is a communication of those materials to the public has been a matter of debate ever since the late 1990s.[217] Yet, debates about the posting of hyperlinks reached a new high when the CJEU was involved in the matter in 2014. In several decisions, the CJEU brought the act of linking to copyrighted materials within the scope of the right of communication to the public. These cases are an illustration of the flexible scope of the right of communication. At the same time, we will see that the Court seems to have conflated primary and secondary liability standards into a single conception of a 'communication to the public'.

In *Svensson*, the CJEU was asked for the first time about the applicability of the right of communication to the public with regard to hyperlinking.[218] The case concerned a Swedish website that offered a customized set of links to freely accessible articles published on other websites, including articles from the *Göteborgs-Posten* newspaper. With a view to ensuring the high level of protection, the CJEU held that 'the provision of clickable links to protected works' is an act of communication.[219]

Does that mean that linking to protected materials requires the permission of the copyright owners under EU law? Well, that depends on whether the linked-to materials were published online with the authorization of the copyright owner. In *Svensson*, the

216. However, we *also see* that search engines increasingly present information that is available on the web on their own pages.
217. For example: Madeleine de Cock Buning & Marike Vermeer, *Hyperlinks en metatags; meeliften in cyberspace*, Computerrecht (4) 166 (1999); Alain Strowel & Nicolas Ide, *Liability with Regard to Hyperlinks*, Columbia Journal of Law & the Arts (4) 403 (2001).
218. CJEU 13 February 2014, ECLI:EU:C:2014:76 (*Nils Svensson and others v. Retriever Sverige*).
219. *Nils Svensson and others v. Retriever Sverige*, *supra* n. 218, at 20.

CJEU explained that since linking is a form of communication that uses the same technical means used for the initial communication – the Internet – this communication must be directed at a new public in order for a link to be a communication *to the public*.[220] The Court held that linking to freely accessible material does not reach a new public and therefore does not constitute a communication to the public. Essentially, if a work has been lawfully made available on the web, it is considered to be communicated to the whole web.[221] However, the Court also stated that if the link is used to circumvent restrictions that were put in place to restrict access, the link *does* reach a new public – the public that did not have access to the website.[222] It is currently unclear what kind of restrictions the Court was hinting at, but it could be that it had in mind content that is protected by a 'paywall' or by means of geo-blocking.[223]

Considering hyperlinking as an act that is relevant under copyright law has always been controversial. Before the CJEU gave its judgment in *Svensson*, the European Copyright Society argued that linking to protected materials does not constitute the transmission of a work and could not therefore be an act of communication.[224] However, the CJEU saw linking as a form of 'making available', which is part of the right of communication to the public and which does not necessarily involve transmission.[225]

Svensson only dealt with links to *authorized* materials that were freely available on the web. After *Svensson*, discussions emerged about the status of links to *unauthorized* materials. This question is also of particular importance for search engines and aggregators who may link to unauthorized content as well.[226] *Svensson* did not address the question of whether linking to unauthorized materials amounts to a communication to the public.[227] Also the CJEU's order in *BestWater*, regarding the embedding of a YouTube video, did not answer this question.[228]

Questions referred to the CJEU by the Dutch Supreme Court in the *GS Media* case offered an opportunity to clarify the issue of linking to unauthorized content.[229] This

220. *Nils Svensson and others v. Retriever Sverige, supra* n. 218, at 24.
221. *Nils Svensson and others v. Retriever Sverige, supra* n. 218, at 27–28.
222. *Nils Svensson and others v. Retriever Sverige, supra* n. 218, at 31.
223. In *C More*, the CJEU could have clarified whether a paywall is a form of access restriction in the sense of *Svensson* (CJEU 26 March 2015, ECLI:EU:C:2015:199 (*C More Entertainment v. Linus Sandberg*)). Unfortunately, the Swedish Supreme Court withdrew its questions related to access restrictions. For the initial question of the Swedish Supreme Court, *see*: http://curia.europa.eu/juris/document/document.jsf?docid=139178 (accessed 14 Jun 2019).
224. Opinion of the European Copyright Society in Svensson, 2–6 (2013).
225. Pekka Savola, *Blocking Injunctions and Website Operators' Liability for Copyright Infringement for User-Generated Links*, European Intellectual Property Review (5) 279, 281 (2014).
226. Marie-Christine Janssens, *De impact van het internet op de sector van het auteursrecht (of is het omgekeerd?) – een analyse aan de hand van de rechtspraak van het Hof van Justitie*, SEW (10) 454, 462 (2014), raising the issue that automated processes are unable to distinguish between authorized and unauthorized materials.
227. Toby Headdon, *An Epilogue to Svensson: The Same Old New Public and the Worms That Didn't Turn*, Journal of Intellectual Property Law & Practice & Practice (8) 662, 668 (2014).
228. Gregor Schmid, *BestWater: Framing No 'Communication to the Public'*, Journal of Intellectual Property Law & Practice (2) 82 (2015); Schmid 2015; Tito Rendas, *How Playboy Photos Compromised EU Copyright Law: The GS Media Judgment*, Journal of Internet Law (5) 11, 12–13 (2017).
229. *GS Media v. Sanoma Media Netherlands and others, supra* n. 60.

case concerned a link to a file containing leaked Playboy pictures that were difficult to find. Some scholars had argued that linking to unauthorized materials should be considered a communication to the public. They put forward that such links are directed at a new public as the copyright owner simply had not given his permission when the materials were first made available on the web.[230] Advocate General Wathelet supported a less expansive application of copyright law and argued that linking should not even be considered an *act of communication*. According to Wathelet, links 'merely facilitate' the finding of works and do not make them available.[231] He argued that copyright owners already had sufficient means to stop online infringements as they are able to apply for injunctions against intermediaries or hold them liable if they knew of the copyright infringements.[232]

However, as became clear from the CJEU's decision in *GS Media*, there appeared to be a third path. The CJEU in *GS Media* stuck to its earlier holding in *Svensson* and again held that a link is an act of communication. Through an individualized assessment, involving 'several complementary criteria, which are not autonomous and are interdependent',[233] the Court considered in particular the user's intervention and the deliberate nature of the intervention, the number of people having access to the materials, and the profit-making nature of the use.

In its decision in *GS Media*, the CJEU tried to strike a balance between the protection of the copyright owner's interests, on the one hand, and the importance of the Internet for the freedom of expression, on the other. The CJEU underlined the importance of the copyright owner's permission that is needed to communicate protected materials to the public. But the Court was also cognizant of the potential restrictive effects on the freedom of expression. In that regard, the Court noted that:

> The internet is in fact of particular importance to freedom of expression and of information, safeguarded by Article 11 of the Charter, and that hyperlinks contribute to its sound operation as well as to the exchange of opinions and information in that network characterised by the availability of immense amounts of information.[234]

The CJEU was also aware that it can be difficult for individuals to determine whether certain linked-to materials are authorized or not. It therefore stated that an individual does not 'as a general rule, intervene in full knowledge of the consequences of his conduct in order to give customers access to a work illegally posted on the internet'.[235] And, 'where the work in question was already available with unrestricted

230. Johan Axhamn, *Hyperlinking: Case C-466/12 Svensson and Others and Its Impact on Swedish Copyright Law, Europarättslig tidskrift* (4) 847, 865 (2015); Alexander Tsoutsanis, *Why Copyright and Linking Can Tango*, Journal of Intellectual Property Law & Practice (6) 495, 507 (2014).
231. Opinion of AG Wathelet 7 April 2016, ECLI:EU:C:2016:644, para. 54 (*Nils Svensson and others v. Retriever Sverige*). Wathelet argued that a link could only be a communication to the public if the link is vital or indispensable in order to benefit from or enjoy copyrighted materials (para. 57).
232. Opinion of AG Wathelet, *supra* n. 231, at 80–87.
233. *GS Media v. Sanoma Media Netherlands and others, supra* n. 60, at 33–34.
234. *GS Media v. Sanoma Media Netherlands and others, supra* n. 60, at 45.
235. *GS Media v. Sanoma Media Netherlands and others, supra* n. 60, at 48.

access on the website to which the hyperlink provides access, all internet users could, in principle, already have access to it even [in, sic] the absence of that intervention'.[236] But, if a person *knew* or *ought to have known* that the link provides access to an unauthorized copy of a work, such a link does amount to a communication to the public.[237] According to the Court, copyright owners can also notify a person about the unauthorized nature of the linked-to materials. Specifically regarding those who post links for profit, the CJEU established a presumption of the awareness of the unauthorized nature of the materials.[238] They are expected to check whether the material has been authorized.

In *GS Media*, the CJEU put to the forefront the knowledge that the linking entity has about the nature of the linked-to materials. Although the newly invented rule aims to balance the interests of copyright owners and Internet users, this rule is also bound to create new uncertainties. It is true that knowledge had always been a factor in the CJEU's case law. Already in 2006, the CJEU in *SGAE* deemed it relevant that the hotel owner intervened 'in *full knowledge* of the consequences of its action' to give access to TV programmes.[239] However, this knowledge referred to a level of awareness that materials would be communicated to the public. It essentially requires considering whether the communication can be attributed to that person. In contrast, the knowledge criterion in *GS Media* focuses on the awareness of the *unauthorized nature of the initial communication*. Hence, whether the person was aware of the fact that someone else communicated the materials without the copyright owner's authorization. According to the CJEU, those who link 'for profit' are presumed to have knowledge about the unauthorized nature. But how does one determine whether links are posted for profit? Should the provision of the link itself be placed for profit? Hence, should the financial gains be connected to people clicking on the link? Or can the profit-making nature of the links be derived from the fact that income is somehow generated with advertisements on the website?[240] And does someone maintaining a personal blog with advertisements fall within the scope of this new rule, or does it only apply to professional media?[241]

---

236. *GS Media v. Sanoma Media Netherlands and others, supra* n. 60, at 48.
237. *GS Media v. Sanoma Media Netherlands and others, supra* n. 60, at 49: 'In contrast, where it is established that such a person knew or ought to have known that the hyperlink he posted provides access to a work illegally placed on the internet, for example owing to the fact that he was notified thereof by the copyright holders, it is necessary to consider that the provision of that link constitutes a 'communication to the public' within the meaning of Article 3(1) of Directive 2001/29.'
238. *GS Media v. Sanoma Media Netherlands and others, supra* n. 60, at 51.
239. *SGAE v. Rafael Hoteles, supra* n. 60, at 42.
240. Roosa Tarkiainen, *Tipping the Scale in GS Media: A Proposal to Restore the Balance Between Rightholders and Internet Users*, Journal of Intellectual Property Law & Practice (6) 502, 506 (2017); Eleonara Rosati, *GS Media and its Implications for the Construction of the Right of Communication to the Public Within EU Copyright Architecture*, Common Market Law Review (4) 1221 (2017).
241. In *The Pirate Bay* the CJEU considered that generating 'considerable income' through advertising was an indication of a profit-making purpose: 'Furthermore, there can be no dispute that the making available and management of an online sharing platform, such as that at issue in the main proceedings, is carried out with the purpose of obtaining profit therefrom, it being

The presumption of knowledge introduced in *GS Media* essentially put in place a duty for professional linkers to check whether linked-to materials are authorized or not. Such checks can be difficult as it is not always clear whether particular material is in fact copyrightable, and if it is, whether any of the limitations and exceptions apply to the use of the materials on the source page. While the knowledge presumption disincentivizes links to clearly infringing materials, it can also have a chilling effect on the dissemination of information of which it is not so clear whether it is infringing or not.[242]

According to Tarkiainen, this duty to check may also imply an obligation to *monitor* the content that is linked to.[243] As web pages and online content can change, a link to a particular location on the web may over time direct people to unauthorized materials. To prevent that one is linking to unauthorized materials, one would have to check the linked-to pages on a regular basis. Alternatively, the provider of the link would have to be able to rebut the presumed knowledge.

With regard to links generated by intermediaries, the decision in *GS Media* gives rise to questions for which there are, as yet, no answers. The liability exemptions in the E-Commerce Directive, which are discussed later on in section §3.04, may not apply because they aim to exempt the storage and transmission of information for others and not the intermediary's own activities.[244] Search engines and other intermediaries generally do not have concrete knowledge of the materials that they link to. It may be argued that these intermediaries link for profit and that knowledge of the infringing nature of the materials must be presumed.[245]

The applicability of the liability exemptions is also relevant in determining how much effort can be expected from these intermediaries to carry out 'the necessary checks to ensure' that they do not link to unauthorized materials. Article 15(1) of the E-Commerce Directive prohibits Member States from imposing on intermediaries a general obligation to monitor. However, strictly speaking, Article 15 only applies to intermediary activities that are covered by the liability exemptions in the directive.[246] Offering search tools and the provision of links are not covered by the directive, and the prohibition on general monitoring may thus not protect search engine activities.[247]

All this is not to say that in fact these intermediaries are to be held liable under the *GS Media* standard. Rather, these questions illustrate how *GS Media* has created new uncertainties, which, at some point, may need to be resolved in procedures at the

clear from the observations submitted to the Court that that platform generates considerable advertising revenues' (CJEU 14 June 2017, ECLI:EU:2017:456, para. 46).

242. *Cf.* section §3.04[G][2] on notice-and-takedown.

243. Tarkiainen, *supra* n. 240, at 506.

244. That is also why the liability of access providers as direct infringers was limited in Article 5(1) of the Copyright Directive, regardless of the E-Commerce Directive that also provided liability exemptions for the transmission and caching of information.

245. *Cf. EuGH*, GRUR 2016, 1152 (1157) – GS Media, with note by A. Ohly, arguing that after *GS Media* there is a pressing need for a liability exemption for search engines in Germany.

246. Article 15(1) of the E-Commerce Directive states that 'Member States shall not impose a general obligation on providers, *when providing the services covered by Articles 12, 13 and 14*, to monitor the information which they transmit or store, nor a general obligation actively to seek facts or circumstances indicating illegal activity.' Emphasis added.

247. *See* section §3.04[D].

Member State level and will ultimately have to be decided upon by the CJEU. It remains to be seen how Member State courts will interpret the knowledge criterion and whether the CJEU will be in a position to clarify some of these aspects to enhance the case law's predictability.[248]

Another, more fundamental issue with *GS Media* relates to the distinction between primary and secondary liability. Primary liability – the liability incurred for a direct infringement of a copyright – has been harmonized by means of the Copyright Directive. For instance, publishing Playboy pictures on a web page is to be assessed on the basis of the Copyright Directive's rules and may lead to an infringement for which one is primarily liable. Secondary liability – the liability incurred for infringements by *others* – was not harmonized by EU legislation.[249] Yet, *GS Media* implies that the right of communication to the public may also apply to those who are not the primary infringers of a copyright. By using the knowledge of someone else's infringement as a factor, the CJEU in *GS Media* essentially incorporated elements of secondary liability in the standard for direct infringement.[250] Secondary liability generally depends on a person's knowledge of or control over an infringement by another party.[251] As such, *GS Media* appears to blur the line between these two forms of liability and effectively harmonizes secondary liability with respect to linking.[252]

The CJEU appears to have continued this line of reasoning also in the context of peer-to-peer file-sharing. In *The Pirate Bay*, the question was whether The Pirate Bay itself communicated protected works to the public by offering a platform to users of peer-to-peer file-sharing networks and indexing and categorizing 'torrent' files.[253] Advocate General Szpunar argued that this case differed from *Svensson* and *GS Media*. With regard to linking, Szpunar spoke of a 'secondary communication of works already accessible on the internet'.[254] According to Szpunar it was clear that the original communications were made on the peer-to-peer network itself and the question was: who makes these works available, The Pirate Bay or its users?[255]

However, in its decision the CJEU did not make such a distinction. In fact, the Court built on *Svensson* and *GS Media* to explain that The Pirate Bay had indeed made an 'act of communication'.[256] The Court was aware that the copyrighted materials were

248. *See* section §5.04[C] for a discussion of how the knowledge presumption introduced in *GS Media* applies to search engines.
249. *See* section §3.04[B].
250. *Also see*: Graeme Dinwoodie, *A Comparative Analysis of the Secondary Liability of Online Service Providers* 15 (2017).
251. *See* section §4.04[B] on Dutch law and section §6.02[D] on US law. The liability exemption for hosting intermediaries in the E-Commerce Directive is also based on the absence of control over and knowledge of unlawful materials (Article 14). This exemption aims to protect intermediaries who store information provided by *others* against liability for copyright infringements and other unlawful activities. For a discussion, *see* section §3.04[G].
252. Martin Senftleben, *Copyright Reform, GS Media and Innovation Climate in the EU – Euphonious Chord or Dissonant Cacophony?*, AMI (5) 130, 132 (2016).
253. CJEU 14 June 2017, ECLI:EU:C:2017:456 (*Stichting Brein v. Ziggo BV and XS4ALL Internet*).
254. Opinion of AG Szpunar 8 February 2017, ECLI:EU:C:2017:99, para. 4 (*Stichting Brein v. Ziggo BV and XS4ALL Internet*).
255. Opinion of AG Szpunar, *supra* n. 254, at 48.
256. *Stichting Brein v. Ziggo BV and XS4ALL Internet*, *supra* n. 253, at 32.

placed online by Internet users. But the Court also considered that the operators of The Pirate Bay 'by making available and managing an online sharing platform such as that at issue in the main proceedings, intervene, with full knowledge of the consequences of their conduct, to provide access to protected works, by indexing on that platform torrent files which allow users of the platform to locate those works and to share them within the context of a peer-to-peer network'.[257] And as such The Pirate Bay played an 'essential role' in making the copyrighted materials available.[258] Moreover, The Pirate Bay could not be considered to be the provider of a 'physical facility' that enabled the communication of copyrighted materials by others.[259]

The Pirate Bay also communicated copyrighted materials *to the public* by making these materials available to the users of the platform.[260] This public was a new public as these users had not been taken into account by the copyright owner.[261] In this respect, the CJEU deemed it to be relevant that The Pirate Bay aimed to obtain a profit from offering the copyrighted materials by selling advertising space on its website.[262] Also The Pirate Bay's knowledge of the infringements was considered by the Court. The Court pointed to several circumstances indicating that The Pirate Bay 'could not be unaware' that it provided access to copyrighted materials without the permission of the copyright owners.[263]

From the perspective of copyright owners, the decisions in *GS Media* and *The Pirate Bay* may represent a welcome development. One of the consequences of these decisions is that the strict EU rules regarding the enforcement of copyrights will also apply in – what we used to think of as – cases of secondary liability. Hence, intellectual property-specific enforcement rules regarding evidence and preserving it, rights of information, the possibility of provisional and precautionary measures, and damages and legal costs all apply in these cases as well. Moreover, copyright owners can also apply for injunctions against intermediaries and require their assistance in the enforcement of their rights.[264] Specifically regarding torrent sharing platforms, *GS Media* will provide an even stronger basis for blocking injunctions against access providers.[265] Yet, with respect to predictability, this CJEU case law has created new uncertainties and appears to cloud the distinction between primary and secondary liability.

[H] Search Engine Indexing and Caching

From linking to materials, we move on to the activities of search engines, in particular indexing and caching of – sometimes – copyrighted materials. Search engines are

257. *Stichting Brein v. Ziggo BV and XS4ALL Internet, supra* n. 253, at 36.
258. *Stichting Brein v. Ziggo BV and XS4ALL Internet, supra* n. 253, at 37.
259. *Stichting Brein v. Ziggo BV and XS4ALL Internet, supra* n. 253, at 38.
260. *Stichting Brein v. Ziggo BV and XS4ALL Internet, supra* n. 253, at 40–43.
261. *Stichting Brein v. Ziggo BV and XS4ALL Internet, supra* n. 253, at 44.
262. *Stichting Brein v. Ziggo BV and XS4ALL Internet, supra* n. 253, at 46.
263. *Stichting Brein v. Ziggo BV and XS4ALL Internet, supra* n. 253, at 45.
264. *See* section §3.05.
265. For example, the Dutch Supreme Court held that the fact that The Pirate Bay itself infringes on copyrights as well is relevant in striking a balance between the different interests (Hoge Raad 13 November 2015, ECLI:NL:HR:2015:3307, para. 5.3.2 (*Brein/Ziggo & XS4ALL*)).

modern-day oracles. They provide us with answers to all questions that we may have. To index and rank information, search engines must make copies of information that is available on the web. These copies are generally reproductions of copyrighted materials. Search engines may also display these copies – also called 'cache' copies – to show their users what the search engine encountered when it indexed the web page.[266] Both the making and the displaying of these copies are discussed and analysed to see to what extent EU copyright law currently accommodates for these types of uses.

First, we will deal with the making of cache copies. The temporary copies that search engines make to index the web are likely to be considered reproductions under Article 2 of the Copyright Directive. A search engine generally offers website owners a possibility to opt out from being indexed and consequently the temporary copying of their materials.[267] However, strictly speaking, making cache copies requires the copyright owner's permission or must be covered by a limitation or exception for the copying to be permitted.

We have seen that Article 5(1) of the Copyright Directive introduced an exception for temporary reproductions.[268] With this exception, the EU legislator aimed to exempt in particular the temporary reproductions made on a user's device when lawfully consuming copyrighted materials and the reproductions made by intermediaries involved in the transmission of copyrighted materials. The temporary reproductions made by search engines, however, serve a different purpose. They enable the search engine to index the web and offer archival functionalities.[269]

Would Article 5(1) of the Copyright Directive apply to the copies that search engines make to index the web? It appears reasonable to assume that a search engine does not enable a 'transmission' between third parties, as it only points people to information that is available on the web.[270] It could be argued that the search engine enables the 'lawful use' of online content by Internet users – which is the other purpose recognized in Article 5(1). Also the search engine's own use – the indexing – could be considered a lawful use.[271] Especially since it is the exception's purpose to strike a fair balance between interests, and to allow and ensure the development and operation of new technologies.[272] Considering that the CJEU has allowed a purposive interpretation of the exception for temporary copying, it can be argued that the temporary copying of copyrighted materials for search engine indexing is indeed permitted under the exception in Article 5(1).

An argument against applying the exception could be that the search engine's business model depends on temporary copying works. Article 5(1) of the Copyright

266. For example, Google also makes available a cache copy for every link on its search engine result pages, *see*: https://perma.cc/L9QX-8XB9 (accessed on 14 June 2019).
267. *See*: www.robotstxt.org (accessed on 14 June 2019).
268. *See* section §3.03[D][1][b].
269. Miquel Peguera, *Copyright Issues Regarding Google Images and Google Cache*, 169 (Aurelio Lopez-Tarruella ed., 2012).
270. *Infopaq International v. Danske Dagblades Forening*, *supra* n. 113, at 41.
271. *Cf. Infopaq International v. Danske Dagblades Forening*, *supra* n. 113, at 44, in which the Court held that the drafting of summaries of newspaper articles by a media monitoring service is not in any way limited by copyright law.
272. *See* section §3.03[D][1][b].

Directive does not apply to reproductions that have independent economic significance. At the same time, economic significance alone is not enough for the non-applicability of Article 5(1). The economic significance should be '*independent*' for Article 5(1) to be *inapplicable*.[273] In that respect, the reproductions made by search engines to index the web may still be permitted. These reproductions themselves appear to have no economic value.

Another argument against the applicability of Article 5(1) of the Copyright Directive may be that the exception only covers temporary copies of *authorized* materials. Following the CJEU's decision in *Filmspeler*, Article 5(1) of the Copyright Directive may not apply to unauthorized copies.[274] In this case, the CJEU held that the reproductions made on a media player that offered links to unauthorized streams could not be considered as reproductions made for a lawful purpose. Therefore, the exception in Article 5(1) of the Copyright Directive did not apply to the reproductions made by the media player. The Court's findings were tailored to the media player offering access to unauthorized materials, so there may still be room to distinguish the type of use in the *Filmspeler* case from search engine indexing.

All in all, there are arguments for and against considering search engine copying as a temporary reproduction in the sense of Article 5(1) of the Copyright Directive. As a consequence, it remains unclear whether the exception for temporary reproductions would apply to the copies that search engines make to index the web, and whether de jure a search engine would need permission to make cache copies of online materials.

Another issue is the *displaying* of cache copies made by search engines. Some search engines display such copies to show the content of the page at the time it was indexed by the search engine. These reproductions may serve an archival function. They also show users where their search terms are located in a particular online document. Can a search engine operator rely on the exception for temporary reproduction in Article 5(1) of the Copyright Directive? If these copies are made and stored for the public to see and use, these copies are no longer transient or incidental. Nor are they essential to a technological process.

Moreover, as these cache copies are also displayed online, the right of communication to the public comes into play as well. It could be argued that the quotation exception in Article 5(2)(d) of the Copyright Directive applies. This article allows for quotations 'for purposes such as criticism or review'. This open-ended language may allow search engine use of online materials and the displaying of cache copies. However, it is questionable whether a full copy of a webpage that is displayed without any context, or minimal context only, can be considered to be a quotation. It seems that under the current Copyright Directive, the displaying of cache copies is likely to interfere with the exclusive right to communicate to the public.

In several EU countries, the inability of EU and national copyright law to accommodate search engine caching has led the courts to permit caching by finding a

273. *Infopaq International v. Danske Dagblades Forening*, *supra* n. 113, at 49.
274. CJEU 26 April 2017, ECLI:EU:C:2017:300 (*Stichting Brein v. Jack Frederik Wullems (Filmspeler)*).

way around copyright law.[275] In this regard, the decision of the Spanish Supreme Court in *Megakini.com v. Google Spain* is remarkable.[276] After finding that no limitations or exceptions applied to Google's provision of a cache copy, the Court came to a surprising conclusion. The Court found that: 'although the exceptions to copyright must be interpreted strictly, neither Art. 31.1 [n]or Art. 40.bis of the [Spanish] Copyright Act exclude the application of the *ius usus inoqui* doctrine in order to allow uses that are innocuous regarding the principles contained within the Copyright Act'.[277] The Spanish Court used this *ius usus inoqui* doctrine to permit Google's use of cache copies, regardless of the fact that its activities were covered by the exclusive rights and no limitations or exceptions applied.

[I] Online Use of Press Publications

The DSM Directive requires Member States to introduce new exclusive rights for press publishers regarding the use of online press publications. This new exclusive right appears to be tailor-made to cover the use of press publications by news search engines, aggregators, and online platforms.

[1] The Press Publisher's Right

News search engines and aggregators provide a service that displays news from different sources on the web. A well-known example of such a service is Google News, which provides an overview of newspapers, blogs, and other materials covering current affairs. These search engines provide links to news articles that are generally accompanied by a short extract from those articles – so-called snippets. Modern platforms and social networks like Twitter and Facebook may also include snippets of the content that is shared by their users to offer a preview of the linked-to content.

We have seen that the CJEU in *Infopaq I* accepted that the reproduction of eleven words from a news article could fall within the scope of the reproduction right. That is provided that the extract conveys the expression of the intellectual creation of the author of the work. Hence, that the extract copies from the work's originality. *Infopaq I* may have the effect that operators of news search engines are held liable for copyright infringements by reproducing and displaying an article's title and extracts from it.[278] In the Belgian *Copiepresse* case, the Brussels Court of Appeal indeed held that Google had

275. Martin Senftleben, *Internet Search Results – A Permissible Quotation?*, Revue Internationale du Droit d'Auteur (1) 3 (2013).
276. Spanish Supreme Court, 3 April 2012, 172/2012 (*Megakini.com v Google Spain*).
277. As translated by: Gemma Alejandre, *Google cache is legal in Spain*, Queen Mary Journal of Intellectual Property (1) 81 (2013).
278. Ed Baden-Powell, *Think Before You Link: Yesterday's News – Today's Copyright Conundrum*, Computer and Telecommunications Law Review (2) 25, 26 (2011); Thomas Hoppner, *Reproduction in Part of Online Articles in the Aftermath of Infopaq (C-5/08): Newspaper Licensing Agency Ltd v Meltwater Holding BV*, European Intellectual Property Review (5) 331, 332 (2011); Raquel Xalabarder, *Google News and Copyright*' (Aurelio Lopez-Tarruella ed., 2012).

reproduced news articles by copying an article's title and first three lines.[279] The Brussels Court considered that the parts that were reproduced generally conveyed essential information. As a consequence, people would no longer read the entire article on the publisher's website.

In recent years, the discussion about the use of journalistic articles by news search engines, aggregators, and platforms intensified. These discussions are spurred by a declining number of news and magazine subscriptions, the difficulty of traditional news publishers to adapt their business models to the online environment, and the great profits that platform and search intermediaries make, primarily through advertising. There were calls for introducing a new and specific exclusive right for press publishers regarding the articles they publish. In Germany, a neighbouring right was introduced the protect the entrepreneurial efforts of press publishers – the '*Leistungsschutzrecht für Presseverleger*'. This new intellectual property right enables press publishers to prohibit search engines and aggregators from making available the articles they publish.[280]

In 2015, the European Parliament rejected the introduction of new rights for press publishers.[281] The European Commission was nevertheless tempted by the idea of offering publishers additional protection. In its 2015 Communication 'Towards a modern, more European copyright framework', the Commission stated that it would 'consider whether any action specific to news aggregators is needed, including intervening on rights'.[282] With its proposal for the DSM Directive, the European Commission aimed to grant press publishers their own exclusive rights regarding the digital use of press publications.[283] The proposal stressed 'the key role press publishers play in terms of investments in and overall contribution to the creation of quality journalistic content'.[284] This new right would strengthen the negotiation position of press publishers and enable them to obtain a fair share of the revenue.[285] Giving these press publishers their own exclusive rights would also make rights management significantly easier for these publishers. They would then no longer have to depend on (obtaining) rights from journalists, photographers, etc. to recoup their investments.

The introduction of a publisher's right gave rise to a great deal of criticism.[286] Many found the Commission's economic rationales for creating a separate intellectual

279. Court of Appeal of Brussels 11 May 2011 (*Google v. Copiepresse*).
280. *See* section §5.05 for a discussion of this exclusive right and its reception. A similar right has been introduced in Spain as well. For a discussion, *see*: R.M. Hilty & V. Moscon, *Protection of Press Publications Concerning Digital Uses* 6 (2017).
281. European Parliament Resolution of 9 July 2015 on the implementation of Directive 2001/29/EC of the European Parliament and of the Council of 22 May 2001 on the harmonisation of certain aspects of copyright and related rights in the information society, A8-0209/2015. The Parliament rejected an amendment hinting at the protection of journalists and press publishers (A8-0209/1).
282. Commission Communication, *supra* n. 44, at 10.
283. Commission Proposal, *supra* n. 49.
284. Commission Communication, 'Promoting a fair, efficient and competitive European copyright-based economy in the Digital Single Market', COM 2016/592, 7.
285. Commission Proposal, *supra* n. 49, at 3.
286. For example, *Academics Against Press Publishers' Right*, available at: https://www.ivir.nl/academics-against-press-publishers-right (accessed 14 June 2019).

property right unconvincing.[287] The Parliamentary Committee on the Internal Market and Consumer Protection also believed that it lacks sufficient justification.[288] Moreover, the Committee noted that the problem that press publishers are facing is actually an enforcement issue. Based on the copyrights that a press publisher has obtained from journalists and photographers, it should already be possible to protect the publisher's interests. It was suggested that creating a presumption of copyright ownership or transfer could make it easier for press publishers to enforce these rights.[289]

Nevertheless, the EU legislator has adopted a somewhat toned-down set of exclusive rights for press publishers regarding the online use of press publications in Article 15 of the DSM Directive. The recitals to the directive highlight the important role that the press play in a pluralistic and democratic society and they stress that publishers should be able to recoup the investments they make.[290] These recitals also link the organizational and financial contribution of press publishers to the need to 'foster the availability of reliable information'.[291] Hence, it appears that the introduction of a press publisher's right is also considered to be helpful in countering online disinformation – or 'fake news'.

The exclusive rights that are to be granted by Member States to press publishers are in fact rights related to the exclusive rights owned by the copyright owner of a press publication.[292] Article 15 of the DSM Directive states that the publishers of press publications should be provided with a reproduction right and a right of making available press publications to the public.[293] Article 15 also provides rules about how the press publisher's right relates to the intellectual property rights of others, including the rights of authors of works that are included in press publications.[294] The focus of the remainder of this section will be on the exclusive rights to be granted, their subject and object, and the duration of these rights.

[2] Publishers

The Commission's original proposal for a new directive said nothing about how the press publisher's rights apply in an international context. It remained silent on where the articles should be published and by who. This changed as the Council added that

287. For example, Martin Kretschmer et al., *The European Commission's Public Consultation on the Role of Publishers in the Copyright Value Chain: A Response by the European Copyright Society*, European Intellectual Property Review (10) 591 (2016); European Policy Centre, Rewarding quality journalism or distorting the Digital Single Market? The case for and against neighbouring rights for press publishers (2017); Hilty & Moscon, *supra* n. 280; Mireille van Eechoud, *A Publisher's Intellectual Property Right. Implications for Freedom of Expression*, Authors and Open Content Policies (2017).
288. European Parliament Committee on the Internal Market and Consumer Protection, Opinion on the proposal for a directive of the European Parliament and of the Council on copyright in the Digital Single Market, 2016/0280(COD), 4.
289. Hilty & Moscon, *supra* n. 280, at 14. Article 5 of the Enforcement Directive.
290. Recital 54 of the DSM Directive.
291. Recital 55 of the DSM Directive.
292. Recital 55 of the DSM Directive.
293. Article 15(1) of the DSM Directive.
294. Article 15(2) and (5) of the DSM Directive.

the protection granted to press publishers should be limited to publishers who are established in a Member State.[295] Based on Article 15(1), the related rights are granted to publishers of press publications 'established in a Member State'. The directive here adds a new touch to the territorial scope of protection in the field of intellectual property by focusing on where a right owner is 'established'. There is no guidance in the directive as to how to determine whether a publisher is established in a Member State. There is a hint in the directive's recitals, which state that only those publishers who 'have their registered office, central administration or principle place of business within the Union' are to be offered protection.[296]

The notion of a 'publisher' in the sense of Article 15 the DSM Directive is closely related to the object of the exclusive rights: the 'press publication'. The recitals in the directive explain that the 'concept of publisher of press publications should be understood as covering service providers, such as news publishers or news agencies, when they publish press publications within the meaning of this directive'.

[3] Press Publications

Press publications are defined in Article 2(4) of the DSM Directive as a 'collection composed mainly of literary works of a journalistic nature'. Hence, it is not so much the articles in a newspaper to which the exclusive rights apply, but it is the collection of such articles that together make up the 'press publication'.[297] This collection should be composed *mainly* of literary works of journalistic nature, but they can also 'include other works or other subject matter'. Hence, also if the article contains photographs, which are not literary works, the article may still be part of a press publication in the sense of Article 2(4) of the directive. The words 'composed mainly' appear to relate only to the type of works included in the press publication – literary works – and not the journalistic nature of those works. This assumption is based on the fact that Article 2(4) explains that the press publication can 'also include other works or other subject matter'. Moreover, the recitals to the directive mention that the concept of a press publication should be defined so 'that it only covers journalistic publications'.[298]

The 'journalistic nature' requirement may give rise to questions about what is covered by the press publisher's rights and what is not. Should we understand 'journalistic' narrowly to prevent an all-encompassing publisher's right that may hamper the dissemination of news? Or should we interpret the term 'journalistic'

295. Proposal for a Directive of the European Parliament and of the Council on Copyright in the Digital Single Market – Update of negotiating mandate, 2016/0280(COD), 5138/19, 102.
296. Article 15(1) and recital 55 of the DSM Directive.
297. *Also see* recital 56 of the DSM Directive.: 'The press publications that should be covered include, for instance, daily newspapers, weekly or monthly magazines of general or special interest, including subscription-based magazines, and news websites.'
298. Recital 56. The directive uses inconsistent language here. In Article 2(4) of the DSM Directive, the journalistic nature refers the nature of the works that are collected in the press publication. In contrast, recital 56 refers to the collection as a whole, the press publication, when it indicates that such publications should be journalistic.

broadly to make sure that investments in all forms are journalism – including citizen journalism – are protected?[299]

There are several criteria that must be met in order for a publication to qualify as a press publication. First, Article 2(4)(a) of the DSM Directive requires that the press publication constitutes an 'individual item within a periodical or regularly updated publication under a single title, such as a newspaper or a general or special interest magazine'. This requirement may cause confusion about what exactly is a press publication, as the directive here appears to refer to a press publication as a single item within a broader publication – such as an article in a newspaper – and not the collection of such articles.

Second, Article 2(4)(b) of the DSM Directive requires that the press publication has the 'purpose of providing the general public with information related to news or other topics'. Publications providing information *related* to news are covered by the definition. Information related to *other* topics is included as well. Magazines covering topics such as literature, technology, religion, sports are likely to be covered. It seems that the publications must be geared towards the general public, to the masses, and not to particular communities with their own norms or business practices, such as academia. Despite lobbying efforts from academic publishers, Article 2(4) of the directive clearly states that 'periodicals that are published for scientific or academic purposes, such as scientific journals, are not press publications for the purposes of this Directive'.[300]

Finally, Article 2(4)(c) of the DSM Directive requires that the press publication is published 'in any media under the initiative, editorial responsibility and control of a service provider'. Traditional print media such as newspapers and magazines clearly meet this requirement. These are also mentioned in Article 2(4)(b) of the directive. Article 2 is silent on *online* sources offering news and other information. Nevertheless, recital 56 of the directive also mentions 'news websites' as an example of press publications that are covered by the definition. Other types of websites, such as personal blogs, are unlikely to be covered by the definition as this recital also states that the protection should not 'apply to websites, such as blogs, that provide information as part of an activity that is not carried out under the initiative, editorial responsibility and control of a service provider, such as a news publisher'. Likewise, intermediaries, such as news search engines and aggregators, are unlikely to meet the requirement of editorial responsibility.

---

299. For example, with regard to the journalistic exception in data protection law, the CJEU has held that 'in order to take account of the importance of the right to freedom of expression in every democratic society, it is necessary, first, to interpret notions relating to that freedom, such as journalism, broadly' (CJEU 16 December 2008, ECLI:EU:C:2008:727, para. 56 (*Tietosuojavaltuutettu v. Satakunnan Markkinapörssi Oy and Satamedia Oy*)).
300. For example, STM, a trade association for academic and professional publishers, has stated in a response to the proposal that it finds the exclusion of scientific publications 'disappointing, unwarranted and potentially discriminatory', available at: https://perma.cc/5GAT-YP9D (accessed 14 June 2019). LERU, the League of European Research Universities, stated in response that 'it would be a black day for Europe if STM's suggested extension of copyright protection were adopted', available at: https://perma.cc/XE6H-384X (accessed 14 June 2019).

[4] Online Use

The rights that are granted to press publishers are a reproduction right and a right of making available press publications. The rights are only provided regarding 'the online use' by information society providers. Hence, the rights of press publishers only apply in an online context and only to the extent that their publications are used by service providers such as search engines, platforms, and other online service providers.

According to Article 15(1) of the DSM Directive, the rights provided 'shall not apply to private or non-commercial uses of press publications by individual users'. This addition appears to be superfluous as the scope of the right is limited to information society service providers, which are providers of service that are normally provided for remuneration.[301]

Recital 58 of the DSM Directive clarifies that the use of press publications can also consist of the use of parts of press publications. Hence, the reproduction of elements from a news article is also within the scope of the press publisher's rights. However, if only a small part is reproduced or made available, the right does not apply. Article 15(1) of the directive states that the rights 'shall not apply in respect of the use of individual words or very short extracts of a press publication'. This raises the question of when exactly an excerpt is short enough to be exonerated or long enough to be within the scope of protection. In Germany, where a press publisher's right already exists, a similar provision about how many words one can use has given rise to great legal uncertainty.[302] Recital 58 may offer some, albeit limited, guidance to courts having to interpret Article 15(1) and its future national counterparts. It highlights the 'massive aggregation' of press publications by information society providers and stresses that 'that the exclusion of very short extracts be interpreted in such a way as not to affect the effectiveness of the rights provided for in this Directive'.

Article 15(1) of the DSM Directive also clarifies that the publisher's rights do not apply to 'acts of hyperlinking'. This provision may give rise to legal uncertainty as well because the directive does not specify what hyperlinking is. Technically speaking, a hyperlink contains a reference to a location on the Internet (a URL). A user can browse to that location by clicking or tapping on an 'anchor', which is a piece of text, picture, or another portion of a web page that activates the hyperlink. The hyperlink can thus also contain pieces of a press publication, such as an article's title or opening lines, or an image. Nevertheless, the statement in Article 15(1) that protection 'shall not apply to hyperlinking' can probably not be interpreted as meaning that including parts of a press publication in a hyperlink is outside the scope of the press publisher's right. That would go against granting press publishers effective protection. But where does hyperlinking end and reproduction in part starts?

The rules in the Copyright Directive regarding limitations and exceptions should equally apply to the rights that are to be granted to publishers.[303] In particular if users share and comment on journalistic content, this type of use may be covered by

301. *See* section §4.04[C] for a discussion of the term 'information society provider'.
302. *See* section §5.05[A].
303. Article 5(3) of the DSM Directive.

quotation or parody exceptions. For instance, if a user includes a link to a news article and copies the title and a few lines from the article to comment on that article on a social network, that use may be covered by the quotation exception as harmonized in Article 5(3) of the Copyright Directive. However, if a social network or other platform includes automatically generated snippets of the linked-to content, these snippets come within the scope of the press publisher's rights. These snippets may also include a title, one or two lines, or a thumbnail of an image that is used in the linked-to article. And these snippets may contextualize the user's comments. Yet, since the platform itself does not use the press publication for purposes of criticism or review, this type of use is probably not covered by the quotation exception.

[5] Duration

According to Article 14(4) of the DSM Directive, the rights to be granted to press publishers expire two years after the press publication is published. The term of protection is to be calculated from the first of January of the year following the date on which the press publication is published. This term of protection is much shorter than the term that was initially proposed by the European Commission. In its proposal for a new directive, the Commission introduced a term of twenty years after the publication of the press publication,[304] which is rather long considering that press publications generally have a much shorter commercial lifespan than other copyrighted materials.[305]

The European Commission also proposed to let the rights have retroactive effect, which would have meant that any service provider who has been making use of press publications in the past must obtain a licence from the press publisher (or a collective management organization) in order not to become liable as an infringer.[306] This retroactive effect was removed in the final version of the DSM Directive. Article 4(2) of the directive explicitly mentions that the exclusive rights 'shall not apply to press publications first published before 6 June 2019' – which is the date the directive entered into force.

§3.04 LIABILITY EXEMPTIONS FOR INTERMEDIARIES

In the previous section, we focused on the circumstances in which an intermediary can be liable as a copyright infringer. In particular we considered how linking, search engine indexing and caching, and the use of press publications can fall within the scope of the exclusive rights granted to the copyright owner. The focus of the current section

304. Article 11(4) of the proposed directive.
305. European Parliament Committee Culture and Education, Opinion on the proposal for a directive of the European Parliament and of the Council on copyright in the Digital Single Market, 2016/0280(COD), 51. In Germany, a similar right was created that expires one year after publication. For a discussion of this '*Leistungsschutzrecht fur Presseverleger*', *see* section §5.05.
306. Article 18(2) of the proposed directive.

will be on another type of liability: the liability that intermediaries may incur *for the infringements of others* – the intermediary's secondary liability.[307] The EU legal framework did not harmonize the basis for such secondary liability. This liability is thus a matter of Member State law. Nevertheless, the E-Commerce Directive harmonizes a set of liability *exemptions* that prevent intermediaries from being liable for the information or activities of others.

This section describes the background to the E-Commerce Directive (section §3.04[A]) and introduces the liability exemptions in the directive (section §3.04[B]). We discuss the first requirement that needs to be met by all intermediaries wanting to benefit from the liability exemptions: they must provide an 'information society service' (section §3.04[C]). We will then go into the requirements that must be met for the specific liability exemptions (sections §3.4[D] to §3.4[G]). The E-Commerce Directive requires that liability exemptions be provided for three types of intermediary activity. First, the exemption for mere conduit activity involves the transmission of information provided by others (section §3.04[E]). This exemption is tailored to the activities of access providers who generally do not have knowledge of or control over the information they transmit. Second, there is an exemption specifically dealing with caching, which is the temporary storage of information to access that information with greater efficiency (section §3.4[F]). And third, there is the hosting liability exemption, which covers the storage of information provided by others (section §3.04[G]). This exemption ensures that liability is exempted to the extent that the intermediary does not have knowledge of the infringement. If the intermediary does obtain such knowledge, it should make sure that the infringing materials in question are removed.

While the E-Commerce Directive requires Member States to limit the liability of intermediaries, the directive also assumes that intermediaries can be given a responsibility to stop or prevent infringements. In a similar vein, the Copyright Directive stipulates that intermediaries *can* be subject to injunctions if their services are used to infringe a copyright.[308] These aspects are not discussed here but are discussed in section §3.05 below. The current section only deals with the liability exemptions in the E-Commerce Directive.

[A] The E-Commerce Directive

The E-Commerce Directive harmonizes certain rules on electronic commerce, such as information requirements, unsolicited commercial communication, and electronic contracts. Its aim is to remove a series of obstacles to cross-border online services and to offer consumers and businesses legal certainty.[309] It was the first EU measure to address several private law aspects of online trade and in that regard it may be considered 'a landmark in Community legislation'.[310]

307. *See* section §1.04 for a discussion of the distinction between primary and secondary liability.
308. Article 8(3) of the Copyright Directive. For a discussion, *see* section §3.05[A].
309. Recital 5 of the E-Commerce Directive.
310. Graham Pearce & Nicholas Platten, *Promoting the Information Society: The EU Directive on Electronic Commerce*, European Law Journal (4), 363, 378 (2000).

In the late 1990s, the European Commission wanted to clarify the legal position of intermediaries at the EU level. On the one hand, the Internet would enable great economic, social, and cultural development. On the other hand, as the Commission noted, 'like any other communication technologies, particularly in the initial stages of their development, the Internet carries an amount of potentially harmful or illegal contents or can be misused as a vehicle for criminal activities'.[311] According to the Commission, the Internet's international and decentralized nature posed a novel problem that was in need of resolution.[312] Instead of focusing on the type of illegal conduct at issue – for instance the infringement of a copyright, publishing defamatory speech, or spreading child pornography – the Commission proposed to deal with these unlawful activities all at once. No specific rules on liability for copyright infringements were to be developed.[313]

The European Commission seemed well aware of the importance of limiting intermediary liability for reasons of free expression and innovation. The European Commission was mindful of the chilling effect that intermediary liability could have on the free flow of information. Intermediaries can be caught in the middle if they are confronted with illegal online conduct. If intermediaries are in doubt about their liability for transmitted or stored information, they may block access or remove information too quickly. Therefore, the Commission thought it was necessary to clarify and limit the liability of access providers and hosting providers in order 'to steer a path between accusations of censorship and exposure to liability'.[314] The potential of further economic growth within the EU presumably played a role as well. One of the driving forces behind the E-Commerce Directive was to offer the legal certainty that was needed to innovate and unlock the economic potential of the Internet.[315]

[B] General Aspects

The basic distinction underlying the E-Commerce Directive's rules on liability is that there are (1) publishers of online information and (2) intermediaries facilitating online communication. The E-Commerce Directive does not provide an exemption for the publishers of online information who generally have knowledge of and control over the published materials.[316] If a newspaper publisher publishes an article containing false information about a person, the exemptions do not apply and Member State law

311. Commission Communication, 'Illegal and Harmful Content on the Internet', COM 1996/487, 3.
312. Commission Communication, *supra* n. 311, at 5.
313. Commission Proposal, *supra* n. 34, at 9, explaining that the Copyright Directive would not contain provisions on liability in general, or on the liability of online intermediaries.
314. Commission Communication, *supra* n. 311, at 12–13.
315. Commission Communication, *supra* n. 311, at 3–4: 'Like in any new and fast-growing industry, legal and regulatory certainty is the conditio sine qua non to foster investments, guarantee the development of a competitive Internet services sector, and ensure the growth of a wider Internet-based economy in Europe.'
316. On the liability of a publisher for the online version of its newspaper and the applicability of national rules on civil liability, *see*: CJEU 11 September 2014, ECLI:EU:C:2014:2209, para. 47–53 (*Sotiris Papasavvas v. O Fileleftheros Dimosia Etairia and others*).

regarding libel may apply. In contrast, an intermediary involved in the transmission or storage of that information should in principle not be held liable for that information.

The rules for establishing the intermediary's liability are not harmonized by the E-Commerce Directive. The directive frames the liability of intermediaries in negative terms as it only provides for a set of conditions under which intermediaries are *not to be held liable*. As a consequence, establishing liability remains a matter of Member State law.[317] Nevertheless, the establishment of liability can become a matter of EU law if at the Member State level liability is imposed which should have been exempted on the basis of the E-Commerce Directive.

The E-Commerce Directive's provisions on liability require Member States to provide intermediaries with a minimum level of protection. Member States may adopt exemptions for intermediary activities that are outside the scope of the directive. For example, the E-Commerce Directive does not provide an exemption for providers of search engines or other information location tools. This, however, does not preclude Member States from introducing such an exemption.[318]

The liability exemptions cover *liability for monetary damages* only. The intermediary cannot be held liable for damages if he satisfies the conditions in the liability exemptions.[319] Any claims regarding the reimbursement of the costs of serving formal notice or court costs incurred in relation to a claim for damages are covered by the liability exemptions as well.[320] Yet, the exemptions do not shield the intermediary from injunctive relief. Nor do they protect against claims for the reimbursement of costs made by a copyright owner to obtain injunctive relief against the intermediary.[321] Hence, the liability exemptions do not completely absolve the intermediary from responsibility for the information that is transmitted or stored for others. In fact, the E-Commerce Directive explicitly leaves open the possibility of injunctions in order to terminate or prevent an infringement.[322] Moreover, Article 8(3) of the Copyright Directive requires that copyright owners should be in a position to apply for an injunction against intermediaries whose services are used by a third party to infringe a copyright.[323]

---

317. CJEU 23 March 2010, ECLI:EU:C:2010:159, para. 107 (*Google France v. Louis Vuitton Malletier*): 'Section 4 [of the E-Commerce Directive] ..., seeks to restrict the situations in which intermediary service providers may be held liable pursuant to the applicable national law. It is therefore in the context of that national law that the conditions under which such liability arises must be sought, it being understood, however, that, by virtue of Section 4 of that directive, certain situations cannot give rise to liability on the part of intermediary service providers.'
318. For a discussion of several national regimes on search engine activities, *see*: Joris van Hoboken, Search Engine Freedom. On the Implications of the Right to Freedom of Expression for the Legal Governance of Web Search Engines 234 (2012).
319. CJEU 15 September 2016, ECLI:EU:C:2016:689, para. 74 (*Mc Fadden v. Sony Music Entertainment Germany*).
320. *Mc Fadden v. Sony Music Entertainment Germany*, *supra* n. 319, at 75.
321. *Mc Fadden v. Sony Music Entertainment Germany*, *supra* n. 319, at 78.
322. Articles 12(3), 13(2), and 14(3) of the E-Commerce Directive.
323. *See also* the third sentence of Article 11 of the Enforcement Directive.

The E-Commerce Directive's liability exemptions do not distinguish between the types of unlawful information or activities but deal with liability horizontally.[324] These exemptions equally apply to any kind of unlawful information or activity – from child pornography to copyright infringement.[325] In this respect, the EU's approach towards intermediary liability differs significantly from the US approach. As is explained in more detail in Chapter 6, the US legislator designed a copyright-specific liability regime by means of the Digital Millennium Copyright Act, which enabled fine-grained copyright-specific rules on liability and the removal of copyright-infringing materials to be laid down.[326]

Intermediaries must meet several requirements to be eligible for the liability exemptions listed in the E-Commerce Directive. All exemptions require that the intermediary provides an 'information society service'. Depending on the specific liability exemption in question, there are other requirements that must be met as well. These requirements are discussed and analysed below.

[C] Information Society Services

First, for any of the liability exemptions to apply, the intermediary must provide an information society service. The definition of an 'information society service' covers any service normally provided for remuneration, at a distance, by means of electronic equipment for the processing and storage of data, at the individual request of a recipient of a service.[327] This broad definition covers the services provided by many intermediaries, such as access providers, hosting providers, search engines, social networks, and content platforms.[328]

The remuneration requirement essentially requires that the intermediary's service represents some sort of economic activity.[329] Access providers and hosting providers are usually remunerated by their users directly – they generally offer their services on the basis of subscription models. Intermediaries operating on top of the Internet's infrastructure, such as video hosting platforms and search engines, usually generate revenue indirectly. They offer multisided platforms that offer their users a

324. Article 1(5)(b) of the E-Commerce Directive appears to signal that the liability exemptions do not protect against liability incurred for infringements of data protection law. Yet, the General Data Protection Regulation (*OJ* 2016, L 119/1) in recital 21 specifies that it 'is without prejudice to the application of [the E-Commerce Directive], in particular of the liability rules of intermediary service providers in Articles 12 to 15 of that Directive'. The interplay between the liability exemptions and the data protection rules thus appears to be in need of further crystallization. *See also*: David Erdos, *Delimiting the Ambit of Responsibility of Intermediary Publishers for Third Party Rights in European Data Protection: Towards a Synthetic Interpretation of the EU acquis* (2017).

325. Christina Angelopoulos & Stijn Smet, *Notice-and-Fair-Balance: How to Reach a Compromise Between Fundamental Rights in European Intermediary Liability*, Journal of Media Law (2) 266 (2016).

326. *See* section §6.04.

327. Article 2(a) and recital 17 of the E-Commerce Directive.

328. Recital 18 of the E-Commerce Directive.

329. Recital 18 of the E-Commerce Directive.

particular service and offer advertisers the possibility to advertise on the platform.[330] These intermediaries should also be considered as providers of information society services, as services that are remunerated indirectly can be information society services as well.[331]

The other requirements that need to be fulfilled – the provision of a service at a distance, by means of electronic equipment for the processing and storage of data, and at the individual request of a recipient of a service – rule out the applicability of the liability exemptions to services that are not at a distance, on-demand, or electronic. A cable television provider, who provides services at a distance and by electronic means, is not an information society provider because these services are not provided on individual request.[332] Nor is a *near*-on-demand video an information society service.[333]

[D] Traditional Intermediary Activities

Intermediaries may benefit from the liability exemptions if they perform 'mere conduit', 'caching', or 'hosting' activities.[334] These activities concern either the transmission or storage of information that is provided by others.

It was not the EU legislator's aim to differentiate between categories of service providers.[335] Instead, the E-Commerce Directive distinguishes between three types of intermediary activity. Yet, it is no coincidence that these three types of activity correspond to the activities of physical network providers, access providers, and Internet hosting providers. These service providers were the main players on the Internet at the time the E-Commerce Directive was negotiated and drafted. There were intermediaries that provided space to publish information – hosting providers – and intermediaries that transmitted information on the Internet – the physical network and access providers (mere conduits). Specifically regarding hosting activities, the European Commission in its proposal for the E-Commerce Directive referred to 'the provision of server space for a company's or an individual's web site, for a BBS, a newsgroup'.[336] Also, the Commission's first report on the application of the E-Commerce Directive highlights that the exemptions were introduced with a view to ensuring 'basic' intermediary services.[337]

330. *See* section §1.05[B] on the multisided nature of some intermediary services.
331. *Sotiris Papasavvas v. O Fileleftheros Dimosia Etairia and others*, *supra* n. 316, at 30. *See also* recital 18 of the E-Commerce Directive.
332. Recital 18 of the E-Commerce Directive.
333. CJEU 2 June 2005, ECLI:EU:C:2005:348, paras 37–39 (*Mediakabel v. Commissariaat voor de Media*), holding that a near-video-on-demand service, which offers a list of films that are broadcast simultaneously at times determined by the provider is not an information society service provider.
334. Articles 12 to 14 of the E-Commerce Directive.
335. Commission Proposal for a European Parliament and Council Directive on certain legal aspects of electronic commerce in the internal market, COM 1998/586, 27.
336. Commission Proposal, *supra* n. 335, at 29.
337. Commission Report, 'First Report on the application of Directive 2000/31/EC of the European Parliament and of the Council of 8 June 2000 on certain legal aspects of information society services, in particular electronic commerce, in the Internal Market (Directive on electronic commerce)', COM 2003/207, 4: 'The provisions on the liability of intermediaries create legal

Research suggests that the liability exemptions have a positive effect on legal certainty as they clarify the liability of these early intermediaries.[338] However, in cases where the liability exemptions do not apply, or in cases in which it is unclear whether they do apply, intermediaries may not be so certain about their liability for infringements.

One type of intermediary activity, which was known at the time, but for which the EU legislator did not provide a liability exemption, is Internet search. The E-Commerce Directive clarifies in its recitals that search engines should be considered as an information society service.[339] The directive also mentions 'providers of hyperlinks and location tool services', but only to stipulate that the need for a proposal concerning the liability of these providers will have to be examined.[340] From this wording, it can be inferred that search engine providers and other service providers offering information location tools are not covered by the intermediary liability regime in the E-Commerce Directive.

In contrast, the two-year older US Digital Millennium Act (DMCA, 1998) does provide for an exemption for 'information location tools', with which the US legislator had in mind providers of directories and early search engines.[341] With regard to the liability of these intermediaries, the DMCA appears to be more forward-looking than the E-Commerce Directive (2000). Why did the EU legislator exclude the issue of search engine liability from the directive? Van Hoboken suggests that since search engine operators were predominantly based in the US, they may not have been involved, or less involved, in the preparation of the E-Commerce Directive.[342] As a consequence their liability was not explicitly addressed in the directive, at least not positively through the adoption of a liability exemption.

In 2011, the European Commission recognized that the introduction of new intermediary services made the application of the liability exemptions a challenging task.[343] Legal uncertainty existed, for instance, with regard to the activities of video hosting platforms and social networks. Unsurprisingly, the views of rightholders, on

---

certainty for intermediary service providers and thus help to ensure the provision of basic intermediary services in the internet.'

338. Copenhagen Economics, Study on the Economic Impact of the Electronic Commerce Directive 16 (2007).
339. Recital 18 of the E-Commerce Directive reads, in part: 'information society services are not solely restricted to services giving rise to on-line contracting but also, in so far as they represent an economic activity, extend to services which are not remunerated by those who receive them, such as those offering on-line information or commercial communications, or those providing tools allowing for search, access and retrieval of data'.
340. Article 21(2) of the E-Commerce Directive.
341. *See* section §6.04[E].
342. Van Hoboken, *supra* n. 318, at 230.
343. Commission Staff Working Paper, 'Online services, including e-commerce, in the Single Market', SEC 2011/1641, 25: 'The main question is to what extent new services that have not been explicitly mentioned in these articles (e.g. because they did not exist at the time of the adoption of the Directive) are intermediary activities in the sense of Articles 12 to 14 and can therefore benefit, in principle, from a liability exemption.'

the one hand, and intermediaries, on the other, differ as to the exemption of these newer intermediary activities.[344]

Although the liability exemptions were not aimed at particular intermediaries, and instead focused on certain intermediary *activities*, it seems that the liability exemptions were made-to-measure early intermediaries, in particular network, access, and traditional hosting providers. These intermediaries have clearly benefited from the liability exemptions. However, the application of the liability exemptions to newer intermediaries, such as search engines, video hosting platforms, and social networks, was less clear. This is particularly evident from the application of the liability exemption for hosting. This exemption is discussed in more detail in section §3.04[G]. But before we discuss the hosting liability exemption, we will first discuss the two other exemptions.

[E] Mere Conduit

Article 12 of the E-Commerce Directive requires that intermediaries acting as a 'mere conduit' are exempted from liability for the information that they transmit and temporarily store. This exemption appears to focus on Internet access providers who typically transmit information from one point to another without having knowledge of or control over that information. In order to transmit information, they may also temporarily store that information.

Intermediaries can benefit from this exemption on condition that (i) they do not initiate the transmission, (ii) do not select the receiver of the transmission, and (iii) do not select or modify the information contained in the transmission. The intermediary's activity should thus be of a 'mere technical, automatic and passive nature' which implies that the intermediary has 'neither knowledge of nor control over the information which is transmitted or stored'.[345] Unlike the hosting liability exemption that is discussed in section §3.04[G], intermediaries qualifying as mere conduits do not need to remove information once they obtain knowledge about infringements occurring on their networks.[346]

Article 12(2) of the E-Commerce Directive clarifies that the exemption also applies to the 'automatic, intermediate and transient storage' that is needed to transmit information. This provision seems to overlap with the limitation for temporary reproductions in Article 5(1) of the Copyright Directive. However, Article 5(1) ensures that intermediaries themselves do not infringe copyrights when they make reproductions to transmit information – it limits their primary liability.[347] Article 12(2) of the E-Commerce Directive clarifies that the temporary storage of unlawful materials – not

344. Commission Staff Working Paper, *supra* n. 343, at 27: 'Some respondents, in particular right holders, asked for the exclusion of several new online activities from the scope of Articles 12–14, whereas others, in particular selling platforms, video sharing sites, social networks and search engines, favoured the inclusion of those activities within the "safe harbour" regime.'
345. Recital 42 of the E-Commerce Directive.
346. *Mc Fadden v. Sony Music Entertainment Germany*, *supra* n. 319.
347. *See* section §3.03[D][1][b] on temporary reproductions.

only copyright-infringing materials – that is transmitted *for others* cannot lead to liability for damages.

[F] Caching

Article 13 applies to 'automatic, intermediate and temporary storage of that information, performed for the sole purpose of making *more efficient the information's onward transmission to other recipients of the service* upon their request'. Article 13 essentially enables caching, which is the duplication of online materials to allow faster information access than if the content had to be retrieved from the original server. Information can then be offered from a location that is closer to the information consumer. And the load on a particular server can be distributed to allow servers to run more efficiently.[348]

There is a long list of conditions that the intermediary needs to fulfil in order to benefit from the exemption: the intermediary should (i) not modify the information; (ii) comply with the conditions on access to the information; (iii) comply with rules regarding the updating of the information, specified in a manner widely recognized and used by industry; (iv) not interfere with the lawful use of technology, widely recognized and used by industry, to obtain data on the use of the information; and (v) act expeditiously to remove or to disable access to the information it has stored upon obtaining actual knowledge of the fact that the information at the initial source of the transmission has been removed from the network, or access to it has been disabled, or that a court or an administrative authority has ordered such removal or disablement.[349]

In contrast to the other exemptions, and despite its many requirements, the caching exemption has not given rise to any case law at the EU level. The absence of case law on caching may suggest that Article 13 of the E-Commerce Directive and its national counterparts are perfectly clear and work well. Alternatively, it could be that these rules on caching are of little practical relevance.[350]

[G] Hosting

Intermediaries that store information so that others can access that information are protected by the liability exemption in Article 14 of the E-Commerce Directive. The directive refers to this activity as 'hosting'. Of the exemptions provided in the directive, this exemption has caused the most discussion and confusion.

To benefit from the hosting exemption, the intermediary should not have actual knowledge of illegal activity or information and must not be aware of facts or

348. For instance, the Social Science Research Network (http://www.ssrn.com) offers publications in its repository through servers of the European Corporate Governance Institute (London), Korea University (Seoul), Stanford Law School (California), and the University of Chicago Booth School of Business (Illinois). These servers 'increase [SSRN's] response capacity and also serve as multiple backups to ensure that SSRN never loses its database of papers', available at: www.ssrn.com/update/general/mjensen.html (accessed 14 June 2019).
349. Article 13(1) of the E-Commerce Directive.
350. *Cf.* section §6.04[D][2] on the US exemption for 'system caching'.

circumstances from which the illegal activity or information is apparent.[351] And if the intermediary obtains such knowledge or awareness, it should act expeditiously to remove or to disable access to the information.[352] On this issue, the hosting liability exemption differs significantly from the mere conduit exemption, which does not require any action by the intermediary in order to be shielded from liability.

The hosting liability exemption cannot apply if 'the recipient of the service is acting under the authority or the control of the provider'.[353] In other words, if the intermediary has control over the person uploading infringing materials, the intermediary cannot benefit from the exemption in Article 14 of the E-Commerce Directive.

[1] Storage for Others

Which intermediaries qualify as hosting providers under Article 14 of the E-Commerce Directive? Hosting is not explicitly defined, but from Article 14 we can deduce that it 'consists of the storage of information provided by a recipient of the service'. Hence, this liability exemption protects the intermediary against liability for information that is provided by the recipients of the service - the intermediary's users. Traditional hosting providers, which offer digital storage space to publish a website, are included in this definition. These providers offer a service that was explicitly considered when the E-Commerce Directive was drafted.[354]

However, as newer forms of intermediary activity emerged, which go beyond the simple storage of information provided by others, the liability exemption for hosting has become harder to apply. A 2006 study by Verbiest, Spindler, Riccio, and Van der Perre signalled that the exemption was not being consistently applied to electronic market places such as eBay.[355] A later study comparing national interpretations of the hosting liability exemption also noted that the concept of 'hosting' does not easily translate to newer forms of intermediary activity:

> Although this criterion may be very suitable for the traditional services for which it was conceived, its weaknesses become apparent when applied to other services, and particularly cloud computing services and other Web 2.0 services where storage is just one aspect of the entire service package.[356]

Case law at the Member State level started to deviate as intermediary services emerged that offered something more than simple hosting, such as search functionality or editing functions.[357]

From 2010 onwards, a small body of CJEU case law emerged, which has shed some light on the activities covered by the hosting liability exemption. *Google France v.*

351. Article 14(1)(a) of the E-Commerce Directive.
352. Article 14(1)(b) of the E-Commerce Directive.
353. Article 14(2) of the E-Commerce Directive.
354. *See* section §3.04[D].
355. Thibault Verbiest et al., *Study on the Liability of Internet Intermediaries* 36 (2007).
356. DLA Piper, EU study on the Legal analysis of a Single Market for the Information Society. New rules for a new age? Chapter 6 - Liability of online intermediaries 16 (2009).
357. DLA Piper 2009, *supra* n. 356, at 16–17.

Louis Vuitton Malletier dealt with trademark-infringing advertisements displayed in Google's search engine.[358] The CJEU clarified that the hosting liability exemption could apply to the advertisement space offered by the search engine. The CJEU considered that in order to benefit from the exemptions in the directive, an intermediary must be 'neutral in the sense that its conduct is merely technical, automatic and passive, pointing to a lack of knowledge or control of the data which it stores'.[359] While Google processes the information provided by advertisers, ranks advertisements, and shows them on the basis of selected keywords, the CJEU found that Google did not have control over or knowledge of the advertisements it stored.

Google France was the first CJEU decision that considered the scope of the hosting liability exemption. It clarified that the exemption also covers forms of non-traditional hosting. Yet, in interpreting the scope of the exemption, the Court held that hosting activities should be of 'a mere technical, automatic and passive nature'.[360] To support this view, the CJEU referred to recital 42 of the E-Commerce Directive. Strictly speaking, recital 42 of the directive only concerns the mere conduit and caching exemptions and not the hosting exemption. Although the recital speaks of the 'exemptions from liability established in this directive', it also contains a clear reference to mere conduit and caching activities.[361] Hosting is addressed in the separate recital 46. In this recital, there is no reference to 'a mere technical, automatic and passive nature'.[362] It thus seems that the CJEU in *Google France* inadvertently limited the scope of the hosting liability exemption.

In the later *L'Oréal v. eBay* case on the liability of a provider of an electronic marketplace, Advocate General Jääskinen expressed his concern about the interpretation of the hosting liability exemption in *Google France*. If recital 42 were to apply to the exemption, 'the objectives of the [E-Commerce Directive] would be seriously endangered and called into question'.[363] Jääskinen also argued that the 'neutrality' criterion would not be the right test:

> Indeed, I would find it surreal that if eBay intervenes and guides the contents of listings in its system with various technical means, it would by that fact be

358. *Google France v. Louis Vuitton Malletier*, *supra* n. 317.
359. *Google France v. Louis Vuitton Malletier*, *supra* n. 317, at 118.
360. *Google France v. Louis Vuitton Malletier*, *supra* n. 317, at 176.
361. Recital 42 of the E-Commerce Directive speaks of activities that are 'limited to the technical process of operating and giving access to a communication network over which information made available by third parties is transmitted or temporarily stored, for the sole purpose of making the transmission more efficient'.
362. Recital 46 of the E-Commerce Directive states that 'in order to benefit from a limitation of liability, the provider of an information society service, consisting of the storage of information, upon obtaining actual knowledge or awareness of illegal activities has to act expeditiously to remove or to disable access to the information concerned; the removal or disabling of access has to be undertaken in the observance of the principle of freedom of expression and of procedures established for this purpose at national level; this Directive does not affect Member States' possibility of establishing specific requirements which must be fulfilled expeditiously prior to the removal or disabling of information'.
363. Opinion of AG Cruz Jääskinen 9 December 2010, ECLI:EU:C:2010:757, para. 142 (*L'Oréal and others v. eBay*).

deprived of the protection of Article 14 regarding storage of information uploaded by the users.[364]

Despite the Advocate General's criticism, the CJEU in *eBay* underlined the neutrality criterion in its decision, albeit in a slightly modified form. The CJEU dropped the 'passive nature' and spoke only of 'merely technical and automatic processing of the data'.[365] This rephrasing of the neutrality criterion put the lack of human intervention at centre stage. Not only traditional hosting that is truly passive is covered by the exemption, but also intermediaries involved in the storage of information and the processing thereof by algorithms and other automatic processes are likely to benefit from the exemption.[366] Regarding the knowledge standard set in Article 14, the CJEU held that the awareness of facts or circumstances indicating unlawful activities or information is to be assessed based on what 'a diligent economic operator should have identified the illegality in question'.[367] Hence, only those intermediaries who operate diligently when they are somehow confronted with unlawful activities or information are shielded by the hosting liability exemption.

In *Sabam v. Netlog*, the CJEU also briefly considered the scope of the hosting liability exemption. In this case, the Court considered the liability of a social network provider for the sharing of copyrighted materials on the network.[368] The main issue in this case was whether the social network could be ordered to instal a filtering system to prevent its users from sharing copyrighted materials. In the case of *Scarlet v. Sabam* – a different case – the CJEU had already held that a similar injunction against an access provider would not be in accordance with EU law.[369] The Court more or less reproduced its findings on filtering from that earlier decision in its later decision in *Sabam v. Netlog*. Specifically regarding the hosting liability exemption, the CJEU held that 'the owner of an online social networking platform – such as Netlog – stores information provided by the users of that platform, relating to their profile, on its servers, and that it is thus a hosting service provider within the meaning of Article 14'.[370] This simple conclusion is somewhat surprising, since the CJEU in its previous decisions appeared to be stricter in its interpretation of the liability exemption for hosting.[371]

364. Opinion of AG Cruz Jaäskinen, *supra* n. 363, at 146.
365. CJEU 12 July 2011, ECLI:EU:C:2011:474, para. 113 (*L'Oréal and others v. eBay*).
366. *Also see*: Patrick van Eecke, *Online service providers and liability: a plea for a balanced approach*, Common Market Law Review (5) 1455, 1483 (2011): 'Indeed, because the ECJ now interprets neutrality as "lack of knowledge", the hosting provider will remain protected when offering tools to upload, categorize, display or search for photos or videos.'
367. *L'Oréal and others v. eBay*, *supra* n. 365 at 120.
368. CJEU 16 February 2012, ECLI:EU:C:2012:85 (*SABAM v. Netlog*).
369. CJEU 24 November 2011, ECLI:EU:C:2011:771 (*Scarlet v. Sabam*). *See* section §3.05[C][3] for a discussion of this decision.
370. *SABAM v. Netlog*, *supra* n. 368, at 27.
371. *Also see*: Natali Helberger & Joris Van Hoboken *(Fast)food for Thoughts: de uitspraak van het Hof van Justitie in de Scarlet/Sabam-zaak*, Nederlands tijdschrift voor Europees recht (2) 72, 82 (2012), suggesting before the CJEU had decided in *Netlog* that social network providers are unlikely to be covered by the hosting liability exemption because they are actively engaged in the content on their networks.

Mc Fadden is the latest decision in which the CJEU has explained the scope of the hosting liability exemption.[372] It did so by clarifying how the exemption for hosting providers relates to the exemption for mere conduits. Regarding the hosting exemption, the Court explained that 'in order to benefit from the exemption from liability laid down in that provision *in favour of* internet website hosts, such hosts must act expeditiously upon obtaining knowledge of illegal information to remove or to disable access to it'.[373] Later on, the CJEU explained that 'the position of an internet website host on the one hand and of a communication network access provider on the other are not similar (...)'.[374] The CJEU specifically referred to 'internet website hosts' to explain which service providers may benefit from the hosting liability exemption, and not the wider group of intermediaries that store and process user-provided information, such as social networks and video hosting websites. These explanatory considerations in *Mc Fadden* should not be taken as a limitation to the scope of the hosting exemption. Yet, the CJEU's reasoning does perhaps show how the conventional meaning of the term 'hosting' – as in website hosting – can lead to strict interpretations of the hosting liability exemption in Article 14 of the E-Commerce Directive.

In sum, it seems that the hosting liability exemption can also apply in case the intermediary does more than simply storing information for others. Curatorial activities related to the storage of information, such as contextualizing and ranking that information, may fall within the scope of the exemption as well and do not preclude protection. Still, the CJEU's case law regarding this exemption is limited and does not yet show a consistent approach towards the interpretation of the hosting liability exemption.

[2] Notice-and-Takedown

For an intermediary to be covered by the hosting liability exemption, it must not have actual knowledge of the illegal activity or information and not be aware of facts or circumstances from which the illegal activity or information is apparent.[375] And once the intermediary obtains such knowledge or awareness, it should act 'expeditiously to remove or to disable access to the information'.[376] The requirement of not having knowledge or awareness about a particular infringement has led to the implementation of so-called notice-and-takedown systems, which place responsibility for finding and signalling unlawful activities on copyright owners. These systems enable copyright owners to notify the intermediary about infringing materials. The intermediary then removes – or 'takes down' – the infringing material.

The EU legal framework does not provide any rules on the modalities of notice-and-takedown systems. Rather, it leaves it to the Member States to lay down

372. *Mc Fadden v. Sony Music Entertainment Germany*, *supra* n. 319.
373. *Mc Fadden v. Sony Music Entertainment Germany*, *supra* n. 319, at 58.
374. *Mc Fadden v. Sony Music Entertainment Germany*, *supra* n. 319, at 60.
375. Article 14(1)(a) of the E-Commerce Directive.
376. Article 14(1)(b) of the E-Commerce Directive.

rules or promote self-regulation.[377] The E-Commerce Directive 'should constitute the appropriate basis for the development of rapid and reliable procedures for removing and disabling access to illegal information'.[378] Of the EU Member States, only Finland has incorporated a statutory notice-and-takedown regime that specifically deals with copyright infringements.[379] Other Member States have left it to intermediaries to come up with their own mechanisms. The Netherlands is one of the few countries in which a code of conduct has been adopted.[380]

The lack of rules on notice-and-takedown can be problematic for at least two reasons. First, there is a risk of the fragmentation of notice-and-takedown regimes.[381] This damages the interests of copyright owners, users, and intermediaries alike. Intermediaries may not be sure what their duties are in order to be protected by the hosting exemption. Copyright owners may have difficulty exercising their rights, since there may be just as many procedures as there are hosting providers. And users, too, can be confronted with a multitude of different notice-and-takedown systems. The plethora of systems may make it more difficult for users to fully understand the intermediary's procedures as well as the options they have to appeal decisions taken by the intermediary to remove their content.

Second, the lack of rules on notice-and-takedown can be problematic from the perspective of the freedom of expression of Internet users. The E-Commerce Directive recognizes in recital 46 that indeed the right to freedom of expression needs to be observed when content is removed. At the same time, the directive incentivizes the removal of materials by exposing the intermediary to liability once it is notified about infringements.

Notice-and-takedown systems put intermediaries in a position where they have to decide about the materials complained of. The intermediary has to consider whether the material is copyrightable, whether it infringes an exclusive right, and whether any of copyright law's limitations and exceptions might apply. In cases of obvious copyright infringement and piracy, it may not be difficult for the intermediary to make the correct decision about removal. However, in less obvious cases of alleged infringement, this can be a daunting task. Intermediaries are likely to stay on the safe side and remove content without a serious consideration of the lawfulness of the notified materials in order to be covered by the liability exemption.[382] In that respect, there is a

---

377. Report from the Commission to the European Parliament, the Council and the European Economic and Social Committee, 'First Report on the application of Directive 2000/31/EC of the European Parliament and of the Council of 8 June 2000 on certain legal aspects of information society services, in particular electronic commerce, in the Internal Market (Directive on electronic commerce)', COM 2003/207, 16.
378. Recital 40 of the E-Commerce Directive.
379. For a discussion of the Finish regime, *see*: Foundation for Cultural Policy Research Cupore, Assessing Copyright and Related Rights Systems. Sanctions and Remedies for Copyright Infringement, Finnish Ministry of Education and Culture, 19 (2013).
380. *See* section §4.05[D][2].
381. Dunja Mijatović, *Freedom of Expression on the Internet* 32 (2010).
382. Rosa Julià-Barceló & Kamiel Koelman, *Intermediary Liability In The E-Commerce Directive: So Far So Good, But It's Not Enough*, Computer Law & Security Report (4) 231 (2000).

risk that notice-and takedown systems have a chilling effect on the free expression of Internet users.[383]

This chilling effect was also recognized by the Committee of Ministers of the Council of Europe, which in 2003 adopted a declaration regarding 'Freedom of communication on the internet'.[384] In this declaration, the Committee stated specifically with regard to intermediary liability that 'due care must be taken to respect the freedom of expression of those who made the information available in the first place, as well as the corresponding right of users to the information'.[385] The commentary on the declaration warns against the deleterious effect on freedom of expression that might occur if intermediaries have to decide about the lawfulness of online materials:

> Questions about whether certain material is illegal are often complicated and best dealt with by the courts. If service providers act too quickly to remove content after a complaint is received, this might be dangerous from the point of view of freedom of expression and information. Perfectly legitimate content might thus be suppressed out of fear of legal liability.[386]

If the intermediary makes an incorrect assessment, any legitimate use of copyrighted materials by users may be hindered. EU law does not provide for any mechanisms that can mitigate the negative effects that notice-and-takedown systems can have on the freedom of expression. For instance, EU law does not prescribe a procedure for counter-notification through which users can reinstate content if they believe that their content has been wrongfully removed by the intermediary.[387] Nor does the current EU legislative framework explicitly require a consideration of the user's interests when notice-and-takedown systems are implemented.

The European Commission has also recognized the problem of legal uncertainty and the fundamental rights issues surrounding notice-and-takedown. In 2012, the European Commission argued that it was necessary to set up a 'horizontal European framework for notice and action procedures'.[388] If it were up to the Commission, a clarification of the removal procedures at the EU level would go hand in hand with strengthening procedures to combat the spreading of unlawful material. With 'action' the Commission here meant not only removal but also additional measures against repeat infringers, as well as proactive and preventive measures.[389]

383. OECD, The Role of Internet Intermediaries in Advancing Public Policy Objectives 20 and 36 (2011); I. Baraliuc, S. Depreeuw, & S. Gutwirth, *Copyright Enforcement in the Digital Age: A Post-ACTA View on the Balancing of Fundamental Rights*, International Journal of Law and Information Technology (1) 92, 103 (2013); Rebecca MacKinnon et al., Fostering Freedom Online 41 (2014).
384. Council of Europe, Declaration adopted by the Committee of Ministers on 28 May 2003, 'Freedom of communication on the Internet'.
385. Council of Europe, *supra* n. 384, principle 6.
386. Council of Europe, *supra* n. 384, explanatory note to principle 6, par 4.
387. US copyright law does provide for such a counter-notification procedure, *see* section §6.04[F][2].
388. Commission Communication, 'A coherent framework for building trust in the Digital Single Market for e-commerce and online services', COM 2011/942, 13.
389. Memorandum of Understanding, 4 May 2011, https://perma.cc/SV5S-2QSZ (accessed 14 June 2019).

The issues identified by the Commission ranged from the requirements that a notification must meet to the time frame within which materials must be removed.[390] Specifically regarding the possibility of counter-notification, the Commission noted that copyright owners and intermediaries were against such a possibility since it would make the procedure 'more burdensome, slower and less effective'.[391] In addition, counter-notification would not be appropriate in the case of manifestly illegal information, such as child pornography.[392] There was a high level of disagreement between intermediaries and copyright owners on how to proceed.[393] Intermediaries felt 'pressurised into taking down content although they are neither able nor authorised to judge its illegality and are liable to face prosecution if they take down content in good faith, but in error'.[394] Copyright owners criticized the costs, complexity, and inefficacy of the notice-and-takedown systems. Moreover, some of them 'suspected that providers of new services not foreseen by the legislators of the [E-Commerce Directive] "hide" behind its liability exemption although it should not apply to them'.[395] Some copyright owners were therefore of the opinion that newer intermediaries, such as video hosting platforms, should not be eligible for the liability exemptions.

Copyright owners argued for a notice-and-*stay*-down procedure, which would require intermediaries not only to remove the content complained of but also to prevent any reappearance.[396] Intermediaries argued that such systems would entail a general obligation to monitor for infringements, which is prohibited under Article 15(1) of the E-Commerce Directive.[397] Moreover, it would create barriers to entering the market for intermediary services, since it requires that intermediaries acquire or develop technologies to proactively combat infringements. In contrast, some intermediaries and civil liberty organizations advocated a notice-and-*notice* procedure, which requires intermediaries to pass on a notification to the user.[398]

In the summer of 2013, it became clear that the European Commission was working on a proposal for a directive on notice-and-*action*.[399] This draft, however, was again withdrawn by the Commission. According to Horten, rightholders in particular

390. Commission Staff Working Paper, 'Online services, including e-commerce, in the Single Market', SEC 2011/1641, 43–47.
391. Commission Staff Working Paper, *supra* n. 390, at 44.
392. Commission Staff Working Paper, *supra* n. 390, at 44.
393. For an overview of the responses, *see*: Aleksandra Kuczerawy, *Intermediary Liability & Freedom of Expression: Recent Developments in the EU Notice & Action Initiative*, Computer Law and Security Review (1) 46 (2015). *Also see*: Trisha Meyer, *The Politics of Online Copyright Enforcement in the EU* (2017).
394. Summary of the results of the Public Consultation on the future of electronic commerce in the Internal Market and the implementation of the Directive on electronic commerce 10, available at: https://perma.cc/HN7A-4LHF (accessed 14 June 2019).
395. Summary of the results of the Public Consultation, *supra* n. 394, at 12.
396. Summary of the results of the Public Consultation, *supra* n. 394, at 12.
397. For a discussion of Article 15(1) of the E-Commerce Directive, *see* section §3.05[B].
398. Summary of the results of the Public Consultation, *supra* n. 394, at 12–13.
399. Letter of Members of the European Parliament, 3 July 2013, available at: https://perma.cc/74HL-4AB8 (accessed 14 June 2019).

were against the adoption of a directive specifying rules on notice-and-action. Most notably, they opposed a provision introducing the possibility of counter-notification.[400]

In late 2015, a new European Commission had taken over and a new consultation started. In its Communication, the Commission noted that it was carrying out a comprehensive assessment of online platforms, which also covered notice-and-action mechanisms.[401] The Commission staff in its Working Document stressed that 'conflicting jurisprudence at national level and the fragmentation of rules on notice-and-action procedures across the EU has a negative impact on legal certainty and predictability, which can hamper innovation and growth'.[402] The Commission acknowledged the concerns of copyright owners who find that current procedures can be slow and complicated. The Commission also noted that 'it is important to avoid unjustified take-downs, as this could adversely affect freedom of expression and the freedom to conduct a business online'.[403]

§3.05 RESPONSIBILITIES OF INTERMEDIARIES

Regardless of the liability exemptions for damages, the EU legal framework presupposes that intermediaries can have a responsibility for stopping or preventing the copyright infringements of others. Notice-and-takedown systems have played an important role in that respect. But, as we will see, the additional responsibilities that intermediaries may have are primarily shaped by injunctions that are issued at the Member State level. Injunctions can be issued against intermediaries to prohibit them from doing something, such as providing access to infringing materials. Mandatory injunctions can also be used to require that the intermediary takes action, such as the implementation of a system to detect copyright infringements.

We will begin this section with a discussion of Article 8(3) of the Copyright Directive, which introduced a rule that copyright owners should be in a position to apply for an injunction against an intermediary if the intermediary's service is used by others for infringements (section §3.05[A]). The EU legal framework does not harmonize the legal basis for such injunctions, but only provides for a set of general requirements that injunctions must meet (section §3.05[B]). The role that the CJEU plays in assessing injunctions against intermediaries for their compatibility with EU law is discussed as well. Fundamental rights have become a crucial element in the CJEU's analysis and as such have a shaping effect on the types of injunctions that can be issued against intermediaries (section §3.05[C]).

Within the EU legal framework, there is also room for self-regulation to enhance copyright enforcement and further shape the responsibilities of intermediaries (section §3.05[D]). Nevertheless, the EU legislator has also shown renewed interest in more

400. Monica Horten, *Notice and action directive to be blocked as EU backs down*, available at: https://perma.cc/5HQF-P3GB (accessed 14 June 2019).
401. Commission Communication, *supra* n. 44, at 11.
402. Commission Staff Working Paper, 'A Digital Single Market Strategy for Europe – Analysis and Evidence', SWD 2015/100, 55–56.
403. Commission Staff Working Paper, *supra* n. 402, at 56.

precisely specifying the responsibilities of intermediaries in the DSM Directive. We will close this section with a discussion of Article 17 of the DSM Directive, which, under certain conditions, would require platforms to implement content identification technologies to prevent infringements (section §3.05[E]).

[A] Intermediaries Whose Services Are Used to Infringe

Article 8(3) of the Copyright Directive requires that copyright owners 'are in a position to apply for an injunction against intermediaries whose services are used by a third party to infringe a copyright'.[404] This provision was added to enable copyright owners to hold intermediaries responsible even if these intermediaries are not involved in the infringement of a copyright.[405]

This possibility of injunctive relief does not depend on the lawfulness of the activities of the intermediary.[406] A knowledge requirement was considered but did not make it into the Copyright Directive.[407] Intermediaries thus do not need to be at fault to be subject to injunctions based on Article 8(3) of the Copyright Directive. For Article 8(3) to apply, it suffices that a copyright infringement by a third party is established and that the intermediary's service was used for that infringement. The rationale behind Article 8(3) of the Copyright Directive appears to be one in which intermediaries are viewed as least cost avoiders: intermediaries can rectify the problem of infringement while incurring the least costs.[408]

The Enforcement Directive contains a provision regarding the responsibility of intermediaries as well. Article 11 of that directive requires that injunctive relief should be available to copyright owners and also requires Member States to 'ensure that rightholders are in a position to apply for an injunction against intermediaries whose services are used by a third party to infringe an intellectual property right'.

[B] Requirements for Injunctions

Specifically regarding injunctions against intermediaries, the Copyright Directive specifies in its recitals that 'the conditions and modalities relating to such injunctions

404. *See also* Article 11 of the Enforcement Directive.
405. Council Report, 1997/0359, 9512/00 ADD 1, 13.
406. Commission Communication 'The common position of the Council on the adoption of a Directive of the European Parliament and of the Council on the harmonisation of certain aspects of copyright and related rights in the information Society', SEC 2000/1734.
407. Council Consolidated Text, 1997/0359, 14238/99, 27.
408. Recital 59 of the Copyright Directive: 'In the digital environment, in particular, the services of intermediaries may increasingly be used by third parties for infringing activities. In many cases such intermediaries are best placed to bring such infringing activities to an end.' *See also*: Ronald Mann & Seth Belzley, *The Promise of Intermediary Liability*, 47 William and Mary Law Review (1) 239 (2005); Matthias Leistner, *Grundlagen und Perspektiven der Haftung für Urheberrechtsverletzungen im Internet*, ZUM (10) 722, 723 (2012). *Also see* section §1.05[B] on the role of intermediaries in regulating user behaviour.

should be left to the national law of the Member States'.[409] Still, the EU legislative framework provides for general requirements that injunctions must meet.

On the basis of Article 8(1) of the Copyright Directive, sanctions and remedies should be 'effective, proportionate and dissuasive'. Article 3 of the Enforcement Directive provides for a more extensive set of criteria and requires that enforcement measures should 'be fair and equitable and shall not be unnecessarily complicated or costly, or entail unreasonable time-limits or unwarranted delays'. Moreover, they should be 'effective, proportionate and dissuasive and shall be applied in such a manner as to avoid the creation of barriers to legitimate trade and to provide for safeguards against their abuse'.

The requirements referred to in both of these articles are fairly wide. The notion of fairness enables many different aspects of a particular enforcement measure to be considered. What is striking is that the user's interests are not explicitly considered, nor do the directives require that these interests should be considered when devising an injunction. However, their interests could be considered as part of the broader requirements of the injunction having to be 'fair' and 'equitable'. And the Enforcement Directive's recitals highlight that it 'respects the fundamental rights and observes the principles recognised in particular by the Charter of Fundamental Rights of the European Union'.[410]

It is not clear whether the requirements in the Enforcement Directive - which deals with intellectual property enforcement in general - were meant to apply in cases of copyright infringement as well. Article 11 of the Enforcement Directive states that right owners should be in a position to apply for an injunction against intermediaries. But it does so 'without prejudice to Article 8(3) of [the Copyright Directive]'. Now, it could be that this phrase only relates to the availability of injunctive relief and not the requirements laid down in other parts of the Copyright Directive. In other words, Article 11 of the Enforcement Directive does not in any way affect the possibility of copyright owners to apply for an injunction stipulated in Article 8(3) of the Copyright Directive. However, Article 2(2) of the Enforcement Directive also states that the directive 'shall be without prejudice to the specific provisions on the *enforcement* of rights and on exceptions contained in Community legislation concerning copyright and rights related to copyright ... in [the Copyright Directive] and, in particular, Articles 2 to 6 and Article 8 thereof'. This could mean that the additional requirements in the Enforcement Directive would not apply if intermediaries are subject to injunctions in cases of copyright infringement. Hence, such injunctions would then not have to be 'fair' and 'equitable' and not 'unnecessarily complicated or costly', etc. From the perspective of a fair balance between the interests of copyright owners, intermediaries, and users, this would be an undesirable conclusion.

The CJEU it its case law regarding copyright enforcement does refer to the requirements in the Enforcement Directive. For instance, in *Scarlet v. Sabam*, the Court held that a requirement to instal a filtering system would be 'contrary to the conditions laid down in Article 3(1) of [The Enforcement Directive], which requires that measures

409. Recital 59 of the Copyright Directive.
410. Recital 32 of the Enforcement Directive.

to ensure the respect of intellectual-property rights should not be unnecessarily complicated or costly'. However, in the more recent case of *The Pirate Bay*, Advocate General Szpunar stated that 'so far as the matters covered by Article 8 of [the Copyright Directive] are concerned, that provision takes precedence over Article 11 of [the Enforcement Directive]'.[411] He did so in order to explain that Article 8(3) of the Copyright Directive is relevant in copyright cases, and not to argue that the Enforcement Directive's stricter requirements would not apply. Still the opinion of Advocate General Szpunar could be an indication that, strictly speaking, injunctions against intermediaries should only be tested against the requirements in the Copyright Directive.

The E-Commerce Directive also sets a limitation on what can be required from intermediaries. Pursuant to Article 15(1) of the E-Commerce Directive, courts cannot impose a general obligation on intermediaries to monitor the information that they transmit or store, nor a general obligation to actively seek facts or circumstances indicating illegal activity. In *Scarlet v. Sabam*, the CJEU assessed an injunction that imposed on an access provider a duty to filter out music files on peer-to-peer networks.[412] The CJEU held that the injunction would be contrary to Article 15(1) of the E-Commerce Directive because it would entail monitoring *all* data from *all* customers for *any* future infringement of intellectual property, and for an *unlimited* time.[413] Likewise, in *Mc Fadden*, the CJEU found that an injunction to monitor the communications of Wi-Fi users would be in conflict with Article 15(1).[414]

The rationale behind this prohibition on general monitoring appears to be of practical nature. General monitoring by intermediaries was deemed to be too great a burden. According to the European Commission, 'general monitoring of millions of sites and web pages would, in practical terms, be impossible and would result in disproportionate burdens on intermediaries and higher costs of access to basic services for users'.[415] The CJEU in *L'Oréal v. eBay* also stated that 'a general monitoring obligation would be incompatible with Article 3 of [the Enforcement Directive], which states that the measures referred to by the directive must be fair and proportionate and must not be excessively costly'.[416]

Unfortunately, the cases of *Scarlet v. Sabam* and *Mc Fadden* are the only opportunities that the CJEU has had to clarify the scope of Article 15 of the E-Commerce Directive. Since both of these types of filtering duties appear to be archetypical general monitoring duties, it remains to be seen how Article 15(1) will apply to more specific monitoring duties. For instance, a filtering system that is specific with respect to the

411. Opinion of AG Szpunar 8 February 2017, ECLI:EU:C:2017:99, para. 56 (*Stichting Brein v. Ziggo BV and XS4ALL Internet*).
412. *Scarlet v. Sabam*, *supra* n. 369.
413. *Scarlet v. Sabam*, *supra* n. 369, at 39–40.
414. *Mc Fadden v. Sony Music Entertainment Germany*, *supra* n. 319, at 87.
415. Report from the Commission to the European Parliament, the Council and the European Economic and Social Committee, 'First Report on the application of Directive 2000/31/EC of the European Parliament and of the Council of 8 June 2000 on certain legal aspects of information society services, in particular electronic commerce, in the Internal Market (Directive on electronic commerce)', COM 2003/207, 12–13.
416. *L'Oréal and others v. eBay*, *supra* n. 365 at 139.

group of persons (e.g., repeat infringers) but general in respect of the monitored content.[417]

[C] A Fair Balance Between Fundamental Rights

A difficulty with the EU directives that shape the intermediary's responsibility is that they do not specify the conditions under which injunctions must be issued by a Member State court. The rules in the Enforcement Directive and the E-Commerce Directive only set the outer boundaries within which injunctions may be issued.[418] Moreover, the requirements in Article 8(3) of the Copyright Directive and Article 11 of the Enforcement Directive use open-ended language and leave a fair amount of room for interpretation and discussion at the Member State level.

The EU Charter of Fundamental Rights, however, plays a key role in shaping the intermediary's responsibility at the EU level. The fundamental rights enshrined in the Charter are used by the CJEU to further specify what can be expected from intermediaries. The CJEU's decision in *Promusicae* was instrumental in recognizing that the field of intermediary liability is at the crossroads of the fundamental rights of copyright owners, intermediaries, and users. Let us take a closer look at *Promusicae* and subsequent CJEU case law.

[1] Promusicae

Promusicae dealt with the release of subscriber data by access providers.[419] These subscribers shared music files in peer-to-peer networks. The release of such identifying data would enable copyright owners to enforce their rights against infringing users.

The CJEU was asked whether EU law requires Member States to oblige access providers to release data about subscribers. The CJEU found that no such obligation exists under secondary EU law. In its reference for a preliminary ruling, the Spanish court had also referred to the fundamental rights to property and effective judicial protection as protected by the EU Charter of Fundamental Rights.[420] Yet, according to the CJEU, another fundamental right had to be considered as well: the subscriber's right to privacy, which is also protected by the Charter.[421] In its ruling, the CJEU came up with a formula requiring that Member States must implement EU law in a way that allows for a fair balance between the relevant fundamental rights:

417. Stefan Kulk & Frederik Zuiderveen Borgesius, *Filtering for Copyright Enforcement in Europe after the Sabam Cases*, European Intellectual Property Review (11) 791, 795 (2012). *Also see* recital 47 of the E-Commerce Directive: 'Member States are prevented from imposing a monitoring obligation on service providers only with respect to obligations of a general nature; this does not concern monitoring obligations in a specific case and, in particular, does not affect orders by national authorities in accordance with national legislation.'
418. Martin Husovec, *Injunctions Against Innocent Third Parties: The Case of Website Blocking*, JIPITEC (2) 116, 117–118 (2012).
419. CJEU 29 January 2008, ECLI:EU:C:2008:54, para. 68 (*Promusicae v. Telefónica de España*).
420. Articles 17 and 47 of the EU Charter of Fundamental Rights.
421. Articles 7 and 8 of the EU Charter of Fundamental Rights.

> The Member States must, when transposing the directives mentioned above, take care to rely on an interpretation of the directives which allows a fair balance to be struck between the various fundamental rights protected by the Community legal order. Further, when implementing the measures transposing those directives, the authorities and courts of the Member States must not only interpret their national law in a manner consistent with those directives but also make sure that they do not rely on an interpretation of them which would be in conflict with those fundamental rights or with the other general principles of Community law, such as the principle of proportionality.[422]

The CJEU left it to the Spanish court to balance the fundamental rights in question and to strike a fair balance between those rights.

[2] Bonnier Audio

Bonnier Audio was a Swedish case that dealt with the release of subscriber data as well. Swedish law explicitly provides for an obligation to release subscriber data in civil procedures.[423] The release of such data could only be ordered if there is clear evidence of an infringement. Moreover, information should only be released if it contributes to an investigation into the infringement of the intellectual property right. And, finally, the release of subscriber data would have to be proportionate. The CJEU was asked whether this Swedish obligation was compatible with EU law. In its decision, the CJEU reiterated that Member States should rely on an interpretation of relevant EU law 'which allows a fair balance to be struck between the various fundamental rights protected by the European Union legal order'.[424]

In contrast to *Promusicae*, the CJEU in *Bonnier Audio* also considered whether Swedish law succeeds in striking that fair balance. According to the CJEU, the Swedish procedure enabled the Swedish courts to weigh the conflicting interests on the basis of the facts of each case, while also taking due account of the requirements of the principle of proportionality. The CJEU therefore concluded that the procedure was likely to ensure 'a fair balance between the protection of intellectual property rights enjoyed by copyright holders and the protection of personal data enjoyed by internet subscribers or users'.[425]

[3] Scarlet

The case of *Scarlet v. Sabam* dealt with a filtering obligation placed on an Internet access provider.[426] Sabam applied for an injunction against the access provider Scarlet in order for the latter to be required to instal a system that would filter out protected materials in peer-to-peer file-sharing traffic. The CJEU held that such filtering amounts

---

422. *Promusicae v. Telefónica de España*, *supra* n. 419, at 68.
423. CJEU 19 April 2012, ECLI:EU:C:2012:219 (*Bonnier Audio and others v. Perfect Communication Sweden*).
424. *Bonnier Audio and others v. Perfect Communication Sweden*, *supra* n. 423, at 57.
425. *Bonnier Audio and others v. Perfect Communication Sweden*, *supra* n. 423, at 60.
426. *Scarlet v. Sabam*, *supra* n. 369.

to a general obligation to monitor that is prohibited by Article 15(1) of the E-Commerce Directive.[427]

Yet, the CJEU also considered the fundamental rights that may be affected by the measure in question. Regarding the right to the protection of intellectual property in Article 17(2) of the EU Charter, the CJEU clarified that this right is not inviolable and that it does not require absolute protection.[428] National authorities and courts must strike 'a fair balance between the protection of copyright and the protection of the fundamental rights of individuals who are affected by such measures'.[429] Instead of leaving it solely to the Belgian court to determine whether the injunction strikes a fair balance, the CJEU balanced the fundamental rights in question.

The CJEU found that the injunction would result in a serious infringement of the access provider's freedom to conduct a business and that it could also infringe the user's rights to the protection of personal data and freedom of expression. The injunction would require the access provider to instal a 'complicated, costly, permanent computer system at its own expense', which was not only a contrary to the requirements in Article 3(1) of the Enforcement Directive but also a 'serious infringement' of the provider's freedom to conduct a business.[430]

With regard to the user's fundamental rights, the CJEU stated that the injunction may infringe the user's right to the protection of personal data in Article 8 of the EU Charter.[431] The user's freedom of expression could also 'potentially' be undermined, since the filtering system would 'not distinguish adequately between unlawful content and lawful content, with the result that its introduction could lead to the blocking of lawful communications'.[432]

While the CJEU's further concretization of the fair-balance requirement should be welcomed, its analysis of fundamental rights seems to be rather cursory, and as such provides little information on how a fair balance should be struck.[433] Moreover, the CJEU only mentioned the user's right to the protection of personal data and not the separate right to respect for one's private life in Article 7 of the Charter. The Court's limited analysis led Griffiths to think that 'the Court's application of the Charter in [*Scarlet v. Sabam*] is little more than window-dressing, functioning primarily to bolster the prior conclusion that the national court's order was incompatible with the requirements of the E-commerce and Enforcement Directives'.[434] Griffiths argued for 'much closer attention to the respective weights of the rights at issue within the framework of established jurisprudence on fundamental rights'.[435]

427. *See* section §3.05[B].
428. *Scarlet v. Sabam, supra* n. 369, at 43.
429. *Scarlet v. Sabam, supra* n. 369, at 45.
430. *Scarlet v. Sabam, supra* n. 369, at 48.
431. *Scarlet v. Sabam, supra* n. 369, at 51.
432. *Scarlet v. Sabam, supra* n. 369, at 52.
433. Kulk & Zuiderveen Borgesius, *supra* n. 417.
434. Jonathan Griffiths, *Constitutionalising or Harmonising? The Court of Justice, the Right to Property and European Copyright Law*, European Law Review (1) 60 (2013).
435. Griffiths, *supra* n. 434, at 60.

[4] UPC Telekabel

In *UPC Telekabel*, the CJEU went into much more detail about how a fair balance should be struck.[436] This Austrian case revolved around an injunction to block the German website *kino.to*, which enabled users to download and stream unauthorized copies of movies. The Austrian Court ordered the access provider to prevent its users from accessing the infringing website. The Austrian Court issued a so-called *Erfolgsverbot*, which is an injunction that requires the addressee to ensure that a particular outcome is prevented.[437] Such an injunction does not specify the measures that should be taken by the addressee in order to comply with it.

After repeating its fair-balance formula, the CJEU identified the relevant fundamental rights: the right to the protection of intellectual property, the freedom to conduct a business, and the Internet user's right to freedom of information.[438] The CJEU found that while the injunction restricted the access provider's freedom to conduct a business, the injunction did not 'infringe the very substance' of this freedom.[439] Although the access provider would be limited in the free use of its resources, it could nevertheless choose a measure that best fits its business practices.[440] Moreover, the injunction did not require unbearable sacrifices to be made and it allowed the access provider to avoid liability by proving that it has taken all 'reasonable measures'.[441]

Regarding the right to the protection of intellectual property, the CJEU found that measures must be sufficiently effective:

> The measures which are taken by the addressee of an injunction, such as that at issue in the main proceedings, when implementing that injunction must be sufficiently effective to ensure genuine protection of the fundamental right at issue, that is to say that they must have the effect of preventing unauthorised access to the protected subject-matter or, at least, of making it difficult to achieve and of seriously discouraging internet users who are using the services of the addressee of that injunction from accessing the subject-matter made available to them in breach of that fundamental right.[442]

Hence, the complete cessation of the infringements is not required for the injunction to strike a fair balance.[443]

---

436. CJEU 27 March 2014, ECLI:EU:C:2014:192 (*UPC Telekabel Wien v. Constantin Film Verleih and Wega Filmproduktionsgesellschaft*).
437. Opinion of AG Cruz Villalón 26 November 2013, ECLI:EU:C:2013:781, para. 60 (*UPC Telekabel Wien v. Constantin Film Verleih and Wega Filmproduktionsgesellschaft*).
438. Articles 17(2), 16, and 11 of the EU Charter of Fundamental Rights.
439. *UPC Telekabel Wien v. Constantin Film Verleih and Wega Filmproduktionsgesellschaft*, *supra* n. 436, at 51.
440. *UPC Telekabel Wien v. Constantin Film Verleih and Wega Filmproduktionsgesellschaft*, *supra* n. 436, at 52.
441. *UPC Telekabel Wien v. Constantin Film Verleih and Wega Filmproduktionsgesellschaft*, *supra* n. 436, at 53.
442. *UPC Telekabel Wien v. Constantin Film Verleih and Wega Filmproduktionsgesellschaft*, *supra* n. 436, at 62.
443. *UPC Telekabel Wien v. Constantin Film Verleih and Wega Filmproduktionsgesellschaft*, *supra* n. 436, at 63.

In choosing a measure, the access provider must ensure 'compliance with the fundamental right of internet users to freedom of information'.[444] The CJEU held that the injunction must be strictly targeted, in the sense that it would have to end copyright infringements. If the measure would affect the user's access to lawful information, the 'provider's interference in the freedom of information of those users would be unjustified in the light of the objective pursued'.[445] Yet, the CJEU's position on the issue of blocking access to legitimate materials does not seem to be completely clear, because in a later paragraph the Court explained that the fair balance of fundamental rights requires that the injunction should not '*unnecessarily* deprive internet users of the possibility of lawfully accessing the information available'.[446] This latter standard appears to allow at least some level of interference with the user's ability to access legitimate materials.

The most striking element of the CJEU's decision is probably that it makes users responsible for ensuring that their right to the freedom of information is respected. According to the CJEU, courts must be able to check whether the interference with the user's right to the freedom of information is justified. If the user's rights are not brought up by the intermediary during the enforcement proceedings, 'the national procedural rules must provide a possibility for internet users to assert their rights before the court once the implementing measures taken by the internet service provider are known'.[447] On this issue, Schellekens noted that 'the effect of the decision of the [CJEU] is that the problem is placed on the shoulders of the parties that are economically least able to defend their interests in court'.[448] Indeed, if users must protect their own fundamental rights, the balance found by the CJEU can become a shaky one if users do not intervene in the proceedings.

[5] Mc Fadden

Mc Fadden is the latest decision in a line on intermediary liability cases.[449] In this case, the CJEU considered the extent to which a provider of free wireless Internet access (Wi-Fi) can be required to take measures against copyright infringements by users. The referring German court had already established that there were only three methods to stop infringements: the intermediary would have to terminate the connection,

444. *UPC Telekabel Wien v. Constantin Film Verleih and Wega Filmproduktionsgesellschaft*, *supra* n. 436, at 55.
445. *UPC Telekabel Wien v. Constantin Film Verleih and Wega Filmproduktionsgesellschaft*, *supra* n. 436, at 56.
446. *UPC Telekabel Wien v. Constantin Film Verleih and Wega Filmproduktionsgesellschaft*, *supra* n. 436, at 63.
447. *UPC Telekabel Wien v. Constantin Film Verleih and Wega Filmproduktionsgesellschaft*, *supra* n. 436, at 57.
448. Maurice Schellekens, *The Internet Access Provider: Unwilling or Unable?*, International Journal of Law and Information Technology (3) 310, 320 (2015).
449. *Mc Fadden v. Sony Music Entertainment Germany*, *supra* n. 319.

password-protect the connection, or monitor the communication of users.[450] All these measures were considered by the CJEU.

With respect to these measures, the CJEU noted that multiple fundamental rights are at issue. On the one hand, the injunction serves the fundamental right to the protection of intellectual property in Article 17(2) of the EU Charter of Fundamental Rights.[451] On the other hand, the injunction places a burden on the access provider and interferes with its right to the freedom to conduct a business as protected by Article 16 of the EU Charter. Also, the user's right to the freedom of information, which is protected by Article 11 of the Charter, is interfered with.[452]

Would the injunction strike a fair balance between the fundamental rights at issue? Regarding the first measure – monitoring user communications – the CJEU noted that such a measure is in conflict with Article 15(1) of the E-Commerce Directive, which prohibits general monitoring duties.[453] Strikingly, the Court did not refer to the fundamental right to privacy and the protection of personal data in Articles 7 and 8 of the EU Charter. If communication is monitored, these fundamental rights are likely to be at issue as well.

Regarding the second measure – termination of the Internet connection by the Wi-Fi provider – the CJEU noted that it would be a 'serious infringement' of the freedom to conduct a business. The CJEU found that such a measure would not strike a fair balance between the fundamental rights at issue:

> As regards, second, the measure consisting in terminating the internet connection completely, it must be found that so doing would cause a serious infringement of the freedom to conduct a business of a person who pursues an economic activity, albeit of a secondary nature, consisting in providing internet access by categorically preventing that provider from pursuing the activity in practice in order to remedy a limited infringement of copyright without considering the adoption of measures less restrictive of that freedom.[454]

The CJEU here also considered the measure's impact on the service provider in relation to the infringement on the right of the copyright owner. This language seems to imply that the interference with the right of the service provider should be proportionate in relation to the copyright infringements.

The third measure – password-protecting the Internet connection – does strike a fair balance between the fundamental rights in question. According to the CJEU, requiring password-protection does not 'damage the essence' of the Wi-Fi provider's right to the freedom to conduct a business, as it requires minimal adjustments to the service.[455] Nor does the measure 'appear to be such as to undermine the essence' of

450. Request for a preliminary ruling from the Landgericht München I (Germany) lodged on 3 November 2014 – Tobias Mc Fadden v Sony Music Entertainment Germany GmbH, question 9 (*OJ* 2015, C 46/18). For a discussion of the liability of Wi-Fi providers under German law, *see* section §5.06[C].
451. *Mc Fadden v. Sony Music Entertainment Germany*, *supra* n. 319, at 91.
452. *Mc Fadden v. Sony Music Entertainment Germany*, *supra* n. 319, at 82.
453. *Mc Fadden v. Sony Music Entertainment Germany*, *supra* n. 319, at 87.
454. *Mc Fadden v. Sony Music Entertainment Germany*, *supra* n. 319, at 88.
455. *Mc Fadden v. Sony Music Entertainment Germany*, *supra* n. 319, at 91.

users' right to information.[456] The measure only requires that users obtain the network's password.

The Court held that access to lawful information would not be affected by a duty to secure one's network. The CJEU reiterated its decision in *UPC Telekabel* that interference with the freedom of information of Internet users would be unjustified if the measure is not strictly targeted. According to the CJEU, the injunction must bring the infringement to an end without affecting the possibility of access to lawful information through the access provider's service.[457] In this light, the CJEU found that securing a network does 'not appear to be capable' of affecting access to lawful information because no websites are blocked by the measure.[458]

Regarding the right to the protection of intellectual property, the CJEU held that injunctions must be sufficiently effective to ensure genuine protection of the fundamental right to the protection of intellectual property. An injunction 'must have the effect of preventing unauthorized access to the protected subject matter or, at least, of making it difficult to achieve and of seriously discouraging internet users who are using the service' to infringe.[459] The CJEU suggested that password-protection may dissuade users from infringing. Yet, the CJEU left this enquiry into the effectiveness of the injunction to the German court:

> The Court finds that a measure consisting in password-protecting an internet connection may dissuade the users of that connection from infringing copyright or related rights, provided that those users are required to reveal their identity in order to obtain the required password and may not therefore act anonymously, a matter which it is for the referring court to ascertain.[460]

As password-protection is the only available measure, the CJEU did find that *not* taking this measure would 'deprive the fundamental right to intellectual property of any protection', which would be 'contrary to idea of a fair balance'.[461] The CJEU stated that 'a measure intended to secure an internet connection by means of a password must be considered to be necessary in order to ensure the effective protection of the fundamental right to protection of intellectual property'.[462]

In the cases discussed above, we see that the CJEU has framed the liability of intermediaries as an issue that involves the fundamental right of copyright owners, intermediaries, and users. The CJEU has moved from simply requiring that a fair balance be struck between these rights, to more concretely specifying how that balance should be struck. The decision in *Mc Fadden* may be considered as the next step in the CJEU's evolutionary path towards a more concrete determination of the content of injunctions. In this decision, the CJEU held that password-protection of a Wi-Fi network is a measure that is *capable* of striking a fair balance. Yet, the CJEU also

456. *Mc Fadden v. Sony Music Entertainment Germany*, *supra* n. 319, at 92.
457. *Mc Fadden v. Sony Music Entertainment Germany*, *supra* n. 319, at 93.
458. *Mc Fadden v. Sony Music Entertainment Germany*, *supra* n. 319, at 94.
459. *Mc Fadden v. Sony Music Entertainment Germany*, *supra* n. 319, at 95.
460. *Mc Fadden v. Sony Music Entertainment Germany*, *supra* n. 319, at 96.
461. *Mc Fadden v. Sony Music Entertainment Germany*, *supra* n. 319, at 98.
462. *Mc Fadden v. Sony Music Entertainment Germany*, *supra* n. 319, at 99.

seemed to suggest that password-protection may be necessary to strike a fair balance if it is the only measure available, in particular with a view to effective copyright enforcement. Hence, *Mc Fadden* suggests that a fair balance of fundamental rights may require that a particular injunction is issued. Admittedly, the CJEU's determinations are coloured by the German court's preliminary questions and the assumption that there were only three measures available. Still, *Mc Fadden* may be an example of how Member State courts can obtain more clarity from the CJEU as to what exactly the fair balance of fundamental rights requires.

[D] Self-Regulation

The previous sections all dealt with formal legal rules that define the intermediary's lability and responsibility for copyright infringements. However, the current EU legal framework also presupposes some level of self-regulation.

We have already seen that in the domain of notice-and-takedown, the EU legislator left room for self-regulation to shape notice-and-takedown procedures.[463] But also more generally, the EU legal framework promotes private regulation. Under both the E-Commerce Directive and the Enforcement Directive, the European Commission and Member States are to encourage the creation of codes of conduct 'by trade, professional and consumer associations or organisations'.[464] These codes are considered to be a supplementary means to strengthen the existing legal framework. As is noted in the recitals to the Enforcement Directive:

> Industry should take an active part in the fight against piracy and counterfeiting. The development of codes of conduct in the circles directly affected is a supplementary means of bolstering the regulatory framework.[465]

The E-Commerce Directive, moreover, 'establishes principles upon which industry agreements and standards can be based'.[466] The E-Commerce Directive also requires that Member States and the European Commission encourage the involvement of consumer organizations when codes of conducts are drafted.[467]

Article 17(b) of the Enforcement Directive requires Member States to encourage 'the submission to the Commission of draft codes of conduct at national and Community level and of any evaluations of the application of these codes of conduct'. In a similar vein, Article 16(d) of the E-Commerce Directive requires that both Member States and the European Commission encourage 'the communication to the Member States and the Commission, by trade, professional and consumer associations or organisations, of their assessment of the application of their codes of conduct and their impact upon practices, habits or customs relating to electronic commerce'. Sharing

463. *See* section §3.04[G][2].
464. Article 16(1) of the E-Commerce Directive and Article 17(a) of the Enforcement Directive. The Enforcement Directive refers only to Member States having to encourage the development of codes of conduct.
465. Recital 29 of the Enforcement Directive.
466. Recital 41 of the E-Commerce Directive.
467. Article 16(a) of the E-Commerce Directive.

experiences with codes of conduct can assist the Commission in evaluating the effectiveness of private regulation. Unfortunately, as of 2015, no codes had been submitted to the Commission, while in fact there were codes of conduct in place at the Member State level.[468] One such example is the Code of Conduct on Notice and Takedown in the Netherlands, which will be discussed in Chapter 4 on Dutch law.[469]

In December 2015, the European Commission announced that it would engage in setting up 'follow-the-money' mechanisms. Such mechanisms should deprive those who infringe intellectual property rights on a commercial scale of their revenue streams. Such mechanisms may, for instance, prevent peer-to-peer file-sharing websites from generating income through advertising. The Commission initially aimed to reach an agreement with stakeholders by the spring of 2016.[470] In its September 2016 Communication, the Commission stated that 'the Commission is fully committed to achieving concrete results in these processes, crucial to combat piracy, and expects that the widest possible range of stakeholders will join them (...)'.[471] In October 2016, a set of basic principles for an agreement were published on the website of the European Commission.[472] In the summer of 2017, an agreement was supposed to be signed during the International IP Enforcement Summit co-organized by the EUIPO, the EU Commission, and the German Ministry of Justice and Consumer Affairs.[473] However, at the time of writing, no voluntary agreements have as yet been signed.

[E] Between Primary Liability and Responsibility: Online Platforms

The DSM Directive contains a provision that will shape online copyright law in the next years to come. By means of Article 17, the EU legislator has tried to strengthen the position of copyright owners vis-à-vis online platforms, such as social networking websites and video hosting websites. Before Article 17 of the DSM Directive entered into force, Article 14 of the E-Commerce Directive required Member States to shield them from liability.[474] These platforms could only be given a responsibility to stop infringements based on the rules in the Copyright Directive and the Enforcement Directive.[475]

Article 17 of DSM Directive completely changes that approach. First, Article 17 essentially requires Member States to render the liability exemption for hosting providers inapplicable to online platforms where it concerns copyright infringement. Second, Article 17 gives an online platform-specific meaning to the right of communication to the public that makes these platforms liable as infringers for the materials that

468. Personal communication with the Commission. Email on file with the author.
469. *See* section §4.05[D][2].
470. Commission Communication, *supra* n. 44, at 11.
471. Commission Communication, *supra* n. 284, at 9.
472. Available at: https://perma.cc/5H9Z-N52E (accessed 14 June 2019).
473. European Commission, DG GROW, minutes of the 6th meeting of the Group of experts on the enforcement of intellectual property rights, 3 April 2017, 2, available at: https://perma.cc/7TTF-X9AU (accessed 14 June 2019).
474. On Article 14 of the E-Commerce Directive, *see* section §3.04[G].
475. *See* section §3.05[A].

are made available on their platforms. These platforms will therefore have to obtain licences from copyright owners for the copyrighted materials uploaded their users. And third, by defining how these platforms may escape liability, Article 17 of the directive also specifies the responsibility that online platforms have for preventing the uploading of unauthorized materials. In the following sections, Article 17 is analysed in more detail.

[1] Towards Greater Responsibility

When the Commission published its proposal for the DSM Directive, it noted that there was 'growing concern about the equitable sharing of the value generated by some of the new forms of online content distribution along the value chain. Right holders report difficulties faced when seeking to authorise and be fairly remunerated for the use of their content online'.[476] Certain intermediaries offer the public access to a great amount of copyrighted materials and create revenue by selling advertisements, whereas copyright owners receive little to no remuneration. As noted in the European Commission Staff Working Paper:

> While some of the providers of these services have de facto become major actors of online content distribution and have substantial number of users and significant market valuations rightholders are not necessarily able to enter into agreements with them for the use of their content. This affects rightholders' possibility to determine whether, and under which conditions, their content is made available on the services and to get an appropriate remuneration for it.[477]

The European Commission proposed that these intermediaries would have to 'take measures to ensure the functioning of agreements concluded with rightholders for the use of their works or other subject-matter or to prevent the availability on their services of works or other subject-matter identified by rightholders through the cooperation with the service providers'.[478] The proposal also explicitly mentioned 'effective content recognition technologies' as an example of a measure that would have to be implemented. The measures envisioned in the proposal are reminiscent of the system that Google has voluntarily put in place for its video hosting platform YouTube. Google's 'Content ID' system identifies uploaded materials and informs copyright owners about the use of copyrighted content. The Content ID system gives copyright owners a choice as to whether they want to remove or allow the materials.[479] Yet, the European Commission aimed to take content identification one step further by requiring platform operators to work together with copyright owners and by implying that these intermediaries should also acquire licences for copyrighted materials featured on their platforms.

---

476. Commission Proposal, *supra* n. 49, at 7.
477. Commission Staff Working Paper, 'Impact Assessment', SWD 2016/301, 138.
478. Article 13 of Commission Proposal, *supra* n. 49.
479. *See* section §6.05[B] for a discussion of Google's Content ID programme.

The proposal and subsequent versions of the directive led to a great deal of discussion and criticism.[480] Under the regime of the E-Commerce Directive, these intermediaries could only be held liable once they obtained knowledge of the infringing materials on their platforms. This led to the advent of notice-and-takedown regimes in which intermediaries only remove materials after they have been uploaded and flagged as infringing. The proposal, however, would require platforms like YouTube and Facebook to strike licensing deals with copyright owners and use content identification technologies to *proactively* remove unlicensed materials before they would be made public on their platform.

The proposal was not completely clear as to what the consequences would be of not removing unlicensed materials. On the one hand, it suggested that the activities of online platforms could come within the scope of the right of communication to the public.[481] On the other hand, it appeared to treat these online platforms more as intermediaries that are used by others to communicate works to the public and that only have a responsibility to assist copyright owners in enforcing their rights.[482] In the adopted version of the DSM Directive, Article 17 does clearly indicate that online platforms can, under certain conditions, be considered as infringers if they make copyrighted materials available by users. An online platform needs to obtain an authorization from the copyright owner for the user-uploaded materials. If no authorization is granted to the platform, the platform is *in principle* liable for making available the unlicensed materials to the public. If, however, the online platform has essentially done its best to obtain a licence and to proactively remove unlicensed materials, the platform may still escape liability.

[2] Online Content-Sharing Service Providers

Article 17 of the DSM Directive does not apply to all online platforms, but only to specific 'online content-sharing service providers'. The goal of the directive is to only target the type of platforms 'that play an important role on the online content market by competing with other online content services, such as online audio and video streaming services, for the same audiences'.[483] An example of such a platform is YouTube, which competes with music services like Spotify, but which did not have to

480. For instance: Felipe Romero-Moreno, *'Notice and Staydown' and Social Media: Amending Article 13 of the Proposed Directive on Copyright*, International Review of Law, Computers & Technology (2) 187 (2019); Martin Senftleben et al., *The Recommendation on Measures to Safeguard Fundamental Rights and the Open Internet in the Framework of the EU Copyright Reform*, European Intellectual Property Review (3) 149 (2018). *Also see*: https://saveyourinternet.eu/ (accessed 14 June 2019).

481. Article 13(1) of the Commission Proposal, *supra* n. 49, spoke of 'service providers that (...) *provide to the public access* to large amounts of works' and it required that these service providers 'take measures to ensure the functioning of *agreements* concluded with rightholders *for the use of their works*'.

482. Article 13(1) of the Commission Proposal, *supra* n. 49, mentioned that the service providers should take measures to 'prevent the availability on their services of works or other subject-matter identified by rightholders through the cooperation with the service providers'.

483. Recital 62 of the DSM Directive.

pay for licences, as it was protected by the liability exemptions of the E-Commerce Directive.

According to Article 2(6) of the DSM Directive, an online content-sharing service provider is a 'provider of an information society service of which the main or one of the main purposes is to store and give the public access to a large amount of copyright-protected works or other protected subject matter uploaded by its users, which it organises and promotes for profit-making purposes'. There are several aspects to this definition that require clarification.

This definition imports the notion of an 'information society service provider'. As explained in section §3.04[C], such a provider offers a service at a distance, by electronic means and at the individual request of a recipient of services. An information society service is 'normally provided for remuneration'. Although users do not have to pay for services like YouTube and Facebook, the definition of an information society service providers also covers services that are remunerated indirectly.[484] The definition of an online content-sharing service provider itself also contains a reference to the revenue that must be generated. As per the definition in Article 2(5), the service provider must 'organise' and 'promote' the user-uploaded and copyrighted materials for profit-making purposes. Hence, there is a double reference to the revenue that must be generated by the online content-sharing service provider.

The online content-sharing service provider must have as its main purpose, or one of its main purposes to 'store and give the public access to a large amount of copyright protected works or other protected subject-matter uploaded by its users which it organises and promotes for profit-making purposes'. The reference to user-uploaded materials brings in service providers that are typically referred to as platforms. They host and 'give access to' materials that are shared by their users. If the service provider also offers some of its own original content – such as YouTube, as part of its YouTube Premium plan – the service provider may still be covered by Article 17, since the service provider will still have as its 'main purpose' or 'one of its main purposes' that it stores and gives access to materials uploaded by users. It is questionable whether a social network provider like Facebook that allows its users to upload materials to its platform can be considered an online content-sharing service provider. Does it have as its main purpose or one of its main purposes to give access to large amounts of copyrighted works if it also hosts and give access to status updates, photos, and videos that are created by its users? Cloud storage services like Dropbox appear to be outside the scope of the definition as they allow users to upload content for their own use and they do not have as their primary purpose to give the public access to large amounts of copyright-protected content.[485] Moreover, these service providers generally do not organize or promote content that is uploaded by their users.

While Article 17 of the DSM Directive clearly only applies to service providers offering access to copyrighted materials for profit, the EU legislator felt the need to specifically mention several types of non-profit service providers in the directive. Article 2(6) of the directive highlights that 'not-for-profit online encyclopedias' and

484. *Stichting Brein v. Ziggo BV and XS4ALL Internet*, *supra* n. 253.
485. *Also see* recital 62 of the DSM Directive.

'not-for-profit educational and scientific repositories' are not to be considered online content-sharing service providers. Article 2(6) also specifies that open-source software-developing-and-sharing platforms are excluded from the definition.

A question that may arise is how Article 17 of the DSM Directive relates to existing CJEU case law. In *The Pirate Bay*, the Court held that the operator of a peer-to-peer file-sharing platform communicates to the public the works that are shared by its users.[486] Are operators of peer-to-peer file-sharing platforms covered by the definition of an online content-sharing service provider in Article 2(6) of the directive? That would of course go against the aims of Article 17 of the directive, which clearly targets legitimate platforms and also offers them an opportunity to escape liability if they meet certain requirements. While operators of peer-to-peer file-sharing platforms may give public access to large amounts of copyrighted materials, these operators generally do not *store* the content that is shared among users. They thus appear to be outside of the definition of an online content-sharing service in the sense of Article 2(6) of the directive. The recitals of the directive also provide an indication that Article 17 only applies to legitimate platforms and not to the operators of peer-to-peer file-sharing platforms. Recital 62 states that 'in order to ensure a high level of copyright protection, the liability exemption mechanism provided for in this Directive should not apply to service providers the main purpose of which is to engage in or to facilitate copyright piracy'. The CJEU's case law regarding operators of peer-to-peer file-sharing platforms and other facilitators of large-scale copyright infringements thus still stands.

Now, for a service provider to be covered by Article 17 of the DSM Directive, the amount of stored and made available copyrighted materials must also be large. Whether an amount of materials is large enough is to be determined on 'a case-by-case basis' and by looking at a 'combination of elements, such as the audience of the service and the number of files of copyright-protected content uploaded by the users of the services'.[487] It is not clear whether this criterion relates to an absolute amount of copyrighted materials (the total amount of copyrighted materials on the platform must be large) or a relative amount of copyrighted materials (a large part of the materials available on the platform must be copyrighted). As mentioned, also the audience of the platform is relevant in determining whether there is a large amount of copyrighted materials available on the platform. Consideration of this factor could lead to an interpretation in which a service provider offering a large amount of copyrighted materials to a small number of users is not covered by Article 17.

[3] A Communication to the Public

Article 17 of the DSM Directive takes as its starting point that online platforms communicate to the public the copyrighted materials that are uploaded by their users. These platforms therefore need to obtain authorization from the copyright owners of

486. *See* section §3.03[G].
487. Recital 63 of the DSM Directive.

those materials.[488] This significantly strengthens the position of the copyright owner vis-à-vis the platform as the latter can be held liable for infringements if no authorization is obtained. Licensing agreements will have to be struck between platforms and copyrights owners for the copyrighted music, series, films, and other audiovisual content that is made available by the platforms. This means that platforms will have to get involved in rights clearance. Senftleben notes that 'collecting societies seem natural partners in the development of the required umbrella solution', but he also notes that without full-coverage of all relevant rights throughout the European Union, it will be difficult for platforms to fulfil their rights clearance tasks.[489] Platforms then run the risk of being held liable as infringers if they do not proactively remove unlicensed user-uploaded materials.

Importantly, Article 17(2) of the DSM Directive requires Member States to provide that these licensing agreements also cover the user's communication to the public. Yet, the directive states that only the activities of users who are not 'acting on a commercial basis' or 'where their activity does not generate significant revenues' are covered by these licences. Platforms and copyright owners are of course free to agree on more inclusive licences. Article 17(2) of the directive essentially only sets a minimum standard as to what user activities are considered to be included.

As to the application of the hosting liability exemption in Article 14 of the E-Commerce Directive, Article 17(3) of the DSM Directive clearly states that this exemption does not apply if the platform communicates materials to the public in the sense of Article 17 of the directive. Hence, as Member States implement Article 17 of the DSM Directive, copyright-specific liability regimes for platforms will emerge and exist next to the general liability regimes based on Article 14 of the E-Commerce Directive. The liability of platforms for non-copyright related infringements of the law, such as defamation, should still be limited by Member States based on Article 14 of the E-Commerce Directive.[490]

[4] Liability Exemption

If a platform did not manage to obtain authorization, i.e., to strike a licensing deal, for content that is made available on the platform, the platform is in principle liable as an infringer. Article 17(4) of the DSM Directive requires that the liability of the platform is limited if it demonstrates that it has met the following three criteria. (1) The platform should have made 'best efforts' to obtain an authorization.[491] (2) The platform should have 'made, in accordance with high industry standards of professional diligence, best efforts to ensure the unavailability of specific works and other subject matter for which the rightholders have provided the service providers with the relevant and necessary

488. Article 17(1) of the DSM Directive.
489. Martin Senftleben, *User-Generated Content – Towards a New Use Privilege in EU Copyright Law* (Tanya Aplin ed., 2019).
490. Article 17(3), final sentence, of the DSM Directive. *Also see* recital 65 of the DSM Directive: 'That should not affect the application of Article 14(1) of Directive 2000/31/EC to such service providers for purposes falling outside the scope of this Directive.'
491. Article 17(4)(a) of the DSM Directive.

information'.[492] And, (3) the platform should have 'acted expeditiously, upon receiving a sufficiently substantiated notice from the rightholders, to disable access to, or to remove from their websites, the notified works or other subject matter, and made best efforts to prevent their future uploads'.[493] In essence, the platform should thus be able to demonstrate that it has done its best to strike licensing deals, to remove materials for which they have not obtained licences and it is informed about, and to implement a notice-and-*stay-down* procedure for materials that it has not proactively removed.

Article 17 of the DSM Directive does not require that the platform proactively removes or make unavailable any copyrighted materials. It can only be held liable for the availability of unlawful materials for which the intermediary has received the 'relevant and necessary information'.[494] Article 17 thus requires a level of cooperation between copyright owners and platforms. Copyright owners should provide platforms with information about the copyrighted materials that should be made unavailable. They should, for instance, provide the platform with relevant metadata about the copyrighted materials and media files to enable the platform to recognize the copyrighted materials in user-uploads. Only these materials need to be made unavailable. In turn, online platforms should inform copyright owners about the 'functioning of their practices' and share information about the use of licensed materials.[495]

While the European Commission's proposal for the DSM Directive mentioned the use of 'effective content recognition technologies', Article 17(4) of the DSM Directive leaves open how platforms should ensure the unavailability of unlicensed materials. While this offers less certainty to platforms, it also offers flexibility to determine the responsibility of platforms as technology progresses.[496] According to Article 17(5) of the DSM Directive, the platform's responsibility is to be determined 'in light of the principle of proportionality', and considering among other things 'the type, the audience and the size of the service and the type of works or other subject matter uploaded by the users of the service' and the 'the availability of suitable and effective means and their cost for service providers'. Recital 66 also highlights that the responsibility may change depending on the platform, the content in question, and the means available to remove unlicensed materials:

492. Article 17(4)(b) of the DSM Directive.
493. Article 17(4)(c) of the DSM Directive.
494. Recital 66: 'If unauthorised works and other subject matter become available despite the best efforts made in cooperation with rightholders, as required by this Directive, the online content-sharing service providers should be liable in relation to the specific works and other subject matter for which they have received the relevant and necessary information from rightholders, unless those providers demonstrate that they have made their best efforts in accordance with high industry standards of professional diligence.'
495. Article 8 of the DSM Directive.
496. Indeed, the Committee on the Internal Market and Consumer Protection noted that the provision in the European Commission's preproposal is 'technologically specific'. *See*: European Parliament Committee on the Internal Market and Consumer Protection, Opinion on the on the proposal for a directive of the European Parliament and of the Council on copyright in the Digital Single Market, 2016/0280(COD), 4. The Committee also noted that 'the market may react by simply changing technical processes or designing new business models that defy this outlined mode of categorisation' (5).

> For the purposes of that assessment, a number of elements should be considered, such as the size of the service, the evolving state of the art as regards existing means, including potential future developments, to avoid the availability of different types of content and the cost of such means for the services. Different means to avoid the availability of unauthorised copyright-protected content could be appropriate and proportionate depending on the type of content, and, therefore, it cannot be excluded that in some cases availability of unauthorised content can only be avoided upon notification of rightholders. Any steps taken by service providers should be effective with regard to the objectives pursued but should not go beyond what is necessary to achieve the objective of avoiding and discontinuing the availability of unauthorised works and other subject matter.

Still, the use of content identification technologies is likely to be required as such technologies are already available on the market and implemented by platforms like Google and Facebook. How advanced these systems should be remains to be seen and may also change over time as technology progresses. If there will be no clarity as what is expected from platforms, there is a risk that platforms may stay on the safe side and implement filters that are too strict. Moreover, there is a risk that content identification technologies make mistakes. Lester and Pachamanova point out that the use of algorithms for copyright enforcement can also lead to 'false positives', where uploaded materials are incorrectly matched to copyrighted materials.[497] Such false positives can be triggered by errors in the algorithms or the quality of the data that the algorithm uses to match materials.[498] There then is a risk that non-infringing content will be deleted, which is problematic from the perspective of the user's right to freedom of expression.

In that regard, Article 17(8) of the DSM Directive states that 'the application of this Article shall not lead to any general monitoring obligation'. This requirement is reminiscent of the prohibition on general monitoring in Article 15 of the E-Commerce, the exact contents of which remain vague.[499] Unfortunately, the DSM Directive does not provide guidance on what constitutes 'general monitoring'. At first sight, requiring platforms to proactively remove or make unavailable unlicensed materials may seem to be at odds with the requirement in Article 17(8). However, as Article 17(4) requires platforms to remove or make unavailable materials for which the copyright owner has provided information, the platform's responsibility should, in the EU legislator's view, probably not be seen as requiring general monitoring. While all user-uploads need to be checked for unlicensed materials, the monitoring is still specific as to the materials that need to be removed or made unavailable based on the copyright owner's request and subsequent provided information.

The Commission's proposal for the DSM Directive made little mention the user's rights and interests. The focus of the initial provision was on the relationship between

497 Toni Lester & Dessislava Pachamanova, *The Dilemma: Making Content ID Algorithms More Conducive to Fostering Innovative Fair Use in Music Creation*, UCLA Entertainment Law Review (1) 51 (2017).
498. Lester & Pachamanova, *supra* n. 510, at 61–64.
499. *See* section §5.05[B].

intermediaries and copyright owners.[500] That changed with the version of Article 17 as adopted in the DSM Directive, which does contain clear references to the user's rights and interests. Still, it is questionable whether the rights and interests of users, in particular their right to freedom of expression, are sufficiently protected.

Article 17(7) of the DSM Directive requires that 'the cooperation between online content-sharing service providers and rightholders shall not result in the prevention of the availability of works or other subject matter uploaded by users, which do not infringe copyright and related rights, including where such works or other subject matter are covered by an exception or limitation'. Moreover, Article 17(9) states that the directive 'shall in no way affect legitimate uses, such as uses under exceptions or limitations provided for in Union law'. Member States have an important role to play here. Recital 66 adds that: 'steps taken by such service providers should, therefore, not affect users who are using the online content-sharing services in order to lawfully upload and access information on such services'. The language used in these provisions and recital is strict: there can be no disabling access to or removal of lawful materials. Yet, it is not clear what the consequences are if content identification technologies, or other measures, lead to the removal of lawful materials. Is the use of these technologies in that case disproportionate or ineffective, and can implementation of these technologies as a result not be required from online platforms?[501] This seems to go against the purpose of Article 17, which by requiring complaints mechanisms also indicates that some degree of removal of legitimate materials is accepted as long as there is a possibility for users to issue a complaint. As such, the provisions in Article 17(7) and 17(9) appear to be more of a starting point than an absolute requirement.

The DSM Directive specifies what is required from Member States with respect to the protection of the user's rights and interests in the second part of Article 17(7). It requires Member States to ensure that users of online platforms will be able to rely on the quotation and parody exceptions, which are exceptions that guarantee freedom of expression.[502] Article 17(7) does not specify *how* Member States should ensure that legitimate uses are not removed and that users can rely on the quotation and parody exceptions. Are specific legislative measures necessary, or is taking part in the stakeholder meetings and steering discussions towards user protection sufficient?

500. *See* Article 13 of the Commission Proposal, *supra* n. 49. *Also see*: European Parliament Committee on the Internal Market and Consumer Protection, Opinion on the on the proposal for a directive of the European Parliament and of the Council on copyright in the Digital Single Market, 2016/0280(COD), 43.

501. Article 17(5) of the DSM Directive: 'In determining whether the service provider has complied with its obligations under paragraph 4, and in light of the principle of proportionality, the following elements, among others, shall be taken into account: (a) the type, the audience and the size of the service and the type of works or other subject matter uploaded by the users of the service; and (b) the availability of suitable and effective means and their cost for service providers.'

502. Recital 70 of the DSM Directive: 'Users should be allowed to upload and make available content generated by users for the specific purposes of quotation, criticism, review, caricature, parody or pastiche. That is particularly important for the purposes of striking a balance between the fundamental rights laid down in the Charter of Fundamental Rights of the European Union ('the Charter'), in particular the freedom of expression and the freedom of the arts, and the right to property, including intellectual property.'

There is also no guidance as to *what* measures Member States should take to protect the user's freedom of expression. Should users, for instance, be able to indicate that their use contains quotations or is a parody, and should platforms be extra careful to filter out these uses? Should content identification technologies be audited, and their use monitored? While the directive is relatively clear on the copyright owner's position and the platform's responsibilities, the directive lacks such clarity when it comes to the instructions given to Member States regarding the protection of the rights and interests of users.

It could very well be that no concrete legislative Member State measures are necessary to protect the user's rights and interests, as Article 17(10) of the DSM Directive also calls on the European Commission to organize, in cooperation with Member States, stakeholder dialogues to discuss best practices for the cooperation between online platforms and copyright owners.[503] Moreover, the European Commission will, after consulting platforms, copyright owners, and users' organizations, and taking into account the outcomes of the stakeholder dialogues, issue 'guidance' on how Article 17 should be applied. During these dialogues, attention should be paid to the 'the need to balance fundamental rights and of the use of exceptions and limitations'.

Article 17(9) of the DSM Directive contains a remarkable provision that appears to speak directly to online platforms: 'online content-sharing service providers shall inform their users in their terms and conditions that they can use works and other subject matter under exceptions or limitations to copyright and related rights provided for in Union law'. As directives only bind Member States, this provision should probably be interpreted as meaning that Member States should ensure that online platforms adopt their terms and conditions accordingly. The content of the provision is equally remarkable. Article 17(9) appears to introduce an information duty. Yet, as that information should be provided as part of the online platform's terms and conditions, it may also create a contractual right for users to use copyrighted materials on the platform in line with available limitations or exceptions. And not just the limitations and exceptions that are available in Member State law; Article 17(9) speaks of 'exceptions or limitations (...) provided for in Union law'. Of course, for users to be able to rely on a particular exception or limitation vis-à-vis the copyright owner, the exception or limitation needs to be available in Member State law. Nevertheless, having a contractual obligation towards users could incentivize online platforms to devise content identification and removal systems that respect limitations and exceptions. It also opens the door to contractual remedies in case materials are unjustly removed.

Regarding content that has been made unavailable or removed, the DSM Directive does provide concrete rules that strengthen the user's position. These provisions only become relevant after the user-uploaded materials have been made unavailable or removed. Article 17(9) of the DSM Directive requires Member States to provide that online platforms put in place 'an effective and expeditious complaint and redress mechanism' for users 'in the event of disputes over the disabling of access to,

503. According to recital 71, these stakeholder dialogues should commence 'as soon as possible after the date of entry into force of this Directive'.

or the removal of, works or other subject matter uploaded by them'. Article 17(9) of the DSM Directive also lists a set of requirements that the mechanisms should meet:

> Complaints submitted under the mechanism (...) shall be processed without undue delay, and decisions to disable access to or remove uploaded content shall be subject to human review. Member States shall also ensure that out-of-court redress mechanisms are available for the settlement of disputes. Such mechanisms shall enable disputes to be settled impartially and shall not deprive the user of the legal protection afforded by national law, without prejudice to the rights of users to have recourse to efficient judicial remedies. In particular, Member States shall ensure that users have access to a court or another relevant judicial authority to assert the use of an exception or limitation to copyright and related rights.

Besides the procedural rights that are to be given to users, Article 17(9) also mentions that decisions to disable access to or remove content should be '*be subject to human review*'. Hence, while access to content may be removed through automated processes, complaints of users relating to such removals cannot be dealt with entirely by automated decision-making processes.[504]

Questions have been asked about whether obligating online platforms to use content identification technologies to filter out infringing materials is in line with the CJEU's case law regarding the fair balance between fundamental rights.[505] Strictly speaking, Article 17 in the DSM Directive does not introduce a clear obligation to implement such technologies. Rather, it leaves open the possibility that platforms may have a duty to implement content identification technologies if no licensing deals are struck and offers a set of open-ended criteria for determining when that is the case. What may be expected from a platform differs from platform to platform and may even differ based on the type of copyrighted materials in question.[506] Nevertheless, on the basis of the CJEU decisions in *Scarlet v. Sabam* and *Mc Fadden*, we can deduce the elements that are relevant in determining whether Article 17, and Member State legislation that implements it, strikes a fair balance.[507] Whether or not a fair balance is

504. *Cf.* Article 22 of the General Data Protection Regulation (GDPR), which gives data subjects 'the right not to be subject to a decision based solely on automated processing, including profiling, which produces legal effects concerning him or her or similarly significantly affects him or her'. Article 17(9) of the DSM Directive is to be considered a *lex specialis*. Any limitations in Article 22 of the GDPR should therefore not apply in cases of removal of user-uploaded content in the sense of Article 17 of the DSM Directive.
505. For instance, Christina Angelopoulos, On Online Platforms and the Commission's New Proposal for a Directive on Copyright in the Digital Single Market 39 (2017). *Also see*: Felipe Romero-Moreno, *'Notice and staydown' and Social Media: Amending Article 13 of the Proposed Directive on Copyright, International Review of Law*, Computers & Technology (2) 187 (2019). UN Special Rapporteur on the promotion and protection of the right to freedom of opinion and expression also expressed his concerns about the use of filtering technologies: Press release of The Office of the High Commissioner for Human Rights, 11 March 2019, available at: https://www.ohchr.org/en/NewsEvents/Pages/DisplayNews.aspx?NewsID=24298&LangID=E (accessed 14 June 2019).
506. Recital 66: 'Different means to avoid the availability of unauthorised copyright-protected content could be appropriate and proportionate depending on the type of content, and, therefore, it cannot be excluded that in some cases availability of unauthorised content can only be avoided upon notification of rightholders.'
507. *See* sections §3.05[C][3] and §3.05[C][5] for an analysis of these decisions.

struck with a duty to implement content identification technologies may depend on aspects such as the costs that are involved (and how they are shared),[508] the effectiveness of the system,[509] the ability of copyright owners to have effective recourse against infringements,[510] the personal data that is processed,[511] the extent to which legitimate content may be blocked,[512] and the possibilities for users to dispute the decisions of intermediaries and copyright owners.[513] All these elements have to be considered and weighed by Member States in their implementation of Article 17, but also by their courts, and possibly the CJEU if it is confronted with cases in which a concrete duty to implement content identification technologies or other duty is imposed on a platform. In particular, the aspect that relates to the extent to which legitimate materials may be blocked by content identification technologies and whether the user's rights and interests are sufficiently protected are likely to become a point of contention in the future as Member States implement Article 17.

[5] Newer Online Platforms

Not all providers of online platforms that qualify as online content-sharing service providers need to implement the measures in Article 17(4) of the DSM Directive. To protect newer online platforms, Article 17(6) exempts platforms that 'available to the public in the Union for less than three years and which have an annual turnover below EUR 10 million'. These platforms only need to make best efforts to obtain licences and follow a notice-and-takedown regime. Hence, these platforms do not need to take proactive measures to ensure that unlicensed materials are made unavailable on their platforms.

These smaller platforms should implement a notice-and-*stay*-down procedure and thus prevent further uploads of the removed materials if their 'average number of monthly unique visitors ... exceeds 5 million, calculated on the basis of the previous calendar year'. Hence, if a newer online platform attracts a large audience, the platform's responsibility is also increased. While the notion of 'monthly unique visitors' may seem like an objective standard, it is not clear who or what accounts as a 'visitor'. Are crawlers, bots and other agents visitors as well? Moreover, it can be hard to determine which visitors are actually unique.[514] This criterion is therefore likely to cause evidential problems if it is not further specified.

508. *Scarlet v. Sabam*, *supra* n. 369, at 48.
509. *Scarlet v. Sabam*, *supra* n. 369, at 63.
510. *Mc Fadden v. Sony Music Entertainment Germany*, *supra* n. 319, at 96.
511. *Scarlet v. Sabam*, *supra* n. 369, at 51.
512. *Scarlet v. Sabam*, *supra* n. 369, at 55–56.
513. *Scarlet v. Sabam*, *supra* n. 369, at 57.
514. Max Fomitchev-Zamilov, *How Google Analytics and Conventional Cookie Tracking Techniques Overestimate Unique Visitors*, Proceedings of the 19th International Conference on World Wide Web, WWW 2010, Raleigh, North Carolina, USA, April 26–30 (2010).

§3.06 CONCLUSION

The 2001 Copyright Directive and the 2000 E-Commerce Directive were drafted at a time when the Internet and its many applications were still evolving. Digitization of information and the introduction of networking technologies spurred the EU legislator to adopt rules in the field of copyright law and intermediary liability. The EU legislator did not adopt a wait and see approach but tackled these issues head-on. This EU legislation aimed to regulate the activities of Internet intermediaries, which were still a new group of players in the information ecosystem. Whereas the Copyright Directive harmonizes issues of copyright law specifically regarding the emerging information society, the E-Commerce Directive provides rules concerning, among other things, the liability of Internet intermediaries.

The technological state of affairs has since changed. Search engines have become the primary means to find information online. Content platforms, such as video hosting websites, enable people to upload, watch, discuss, or otherwise interact with audiovisual content. Social networks enable people to share all sorts of information with one another. The activities of these intermediaries go beyond the mere storage and transmission of others. These developments have challenged the predictability of the EU legal framework and its ability to preserve a balance between the interests of copyright owners, intermediaries, and users. Specifically regarding platforms and aggregators, the DSM Directive aims to establish a new balance by introducing new exclusive rights for press publishers and by introducing a new and specific liability regime for platforms.

[A] Copyright Law

One of the issues with the current EU legal framework is that there is a risk that innovative uses, including beneficial intermediary uses, may end up in the nets of copyright law. In the current set-up of EU copyright law, *broad* exclusive rights are defined that need to be interpreted *broadly* to secure a high level of protection. Member States may only implement the limitations and exceptions that are listed in the Copyright Directive. There may still be some room within the limitations and exceptions to allow for a flexible interpretation. However, as these limitations and exceptions must in principle be interpreted strictly, the space for such a flexible interpretation is unlikely to be fully utilized. This issue – the inability of the Copyright Directive to accommodate new uses – is a cause for concern and solving this issue will be one of the goals in the remainder of this research.

This chapter has also analysed Article 15 of the DSM Directive, which introduces new exclusive rights for press publishers. It tries to readjust the EU rules of copyright law to reflect changes in the way people access information online through new intermediary services.[515] The EU legislator's efforts here seem to be driven by a willingness to support press organizations that are having difficulties in adjusting to the

515. Commission Proposal, *supra* n. 49.

online environment. However, in this chapter we have questioned the necessity for such a new intellectual property right. Moreover, given the uncertainties that exist regarding the scope and application of this new right, there is a chance that it will have a chilling effect on curatorial uses by online platforms.[516]

[B] Liability Exemptions

The liability exemptions in the E-Commerce Directive, just as the rules in the Copyright Directive, are reminiscent of a time when the Internet landscape mainly consisted of publishers of information and intermediaries who stored or transmitted information for others. The exemptions offer traditional intermediaries legal certainty about their liability. However, especially in relation to the hosting liability exemption, it is clear that the E-Commerce Directive framework does not fully capture the current Internet ecosystem in which intermediaries may also offer curatorial functions that create order in, categorize, contextualize, or otherwise give additional meaning to pre-existing information.

The provisions in the E-Commerce Directive were a compromise between intermediaries and those who are affected by unlawful online materials and activities. On the one hand, these provisions limit the liability of intermediaries. On the other hand, intermediaries still have a responsibility to take action against infringements. Intermediaries that store information for others ('hosting') are incentivized to adopt systems through which people can send them notifications of infringement. However, as such notice-and-takedown systems incentivize the removal of materials, these systems can have a chilling effect on the freedom of expression.[517] Moreover, the lack of procedural rules regarding notice-and-takedown has paved the way for legal fragmentation in notice-and-takedown systems and legal regimes.

[C] Responsibilities of Intermediaries

With respect to the intermediary's responsibility for infringements, the current EU legal framework offers an open-ended set of rules. The responsibility of intermediaries is primarily shaped by injunctions that require intermediaries to cooperate in the enforcement of copyrights.[518] It has enabled courts to determine the responsibilities of intermediaries in concrete cases. Injunctions are sought by copyright owners at the Member State level according to Member State law. As injunctions against intermediaries must meet the requirements set by the EU legal framework, Member State courts may refer questions to the CJEU to enquire whether a particular form of injunctive relief complies with these requirements. By answering these questions, the CJEU either

516. In section §5.05 of this book, we consider the German right for press publishers (*Leistungsschutzrecht für Presseverleger*) in order to draw lessons from the German experience with this new intellectual property right.
517. *See* section §3.04[G][2].
518. Article 8(3) of the Copyright Directive.

agrees with or rejects the injunction that is devised at the Member State level.[519] For instance, after the CJEU's decision in *UPC Telekabel*, we know that access providers may be ordered to block a website offering infringing materials.[520] And after *Scarlet v. Sabam*, we know that access providers cannot be compelled to instal a specific system that filters Internet traffic for music shared on peer-to-peer networks.[521]

The CJEU's case law on intermediaries has been instrumental in recognizing the user's interests.[522] At times, the CJEU's analysis of fundamental rights has seemed to be somewhat minimalistic, as it has not provided a fully fledged analysis of these rights, nor has it always seemed to apply all relevant fundamental rights. Although the CJEU in earlier case law on intermediary liability only required that *a fair balance* be struck between the relevant fundamental rights, we see that the Court's later case law progressed towards more concretely defining what such a fair balance entails and what can be expected from intermediaries.[523] As such, the CJEU's case law has also added to the predictability of an otherwise hollow legal framework. Still, questions can be asked about whether this CJEU process of the concretization of the types of injunctions that may be issued is the most efficient way to create a predictable legal framework.

With the DSM Directive, the EU legislator takes a new approach and offers more concrete rules on one particular type of intermediary: the online platform. Article 17 of the directive is an attempt to resolve the friction that the rise of online platforms produced. It is a specific and complex provision to solve a contemporary problem, but it also leaves room to further develop and fill in the responsibility of online platforms. The approach that is taken effectively requires copyright owners and intermediaries to work together to implement enforcement measures. These stakeholders, together with the European Commission and Member States, will have to flesh out those measures in agreements and best practices. This offers flexibility, but it also creates a risk that the user's rights and interests are not sufficiently protected. Member States and the European Commission are made responsible for ensuring that the rights and interests of users, including their right to freedom of expression, are protected. Whether Article 17 strikes a fair balance between all relevant interests and rights will therefore greatly depend on what will come out of the stakeholder dialogues, the European Commission's guidance, and Member State initiatives.

519. *Also see*: *Mc Fadden v. Sony Music Entertainment Germany*, *supra* n. 319, at 98, in which the CJEU explicitly used the term 'rejected'.
520. *See* section §3.05[C][4].
521. *See* section §3.05[C][3].
522. *See* section §3.05[C].
523. *See* section §3.05[C][5].

CHAPTER 4

Intermediary Liability in the Netherlands

§4.01 INTRODUCTION

The goal of the current chapter on Dutch law – and the next chapter on German law – is to see how the EU legal framework works out at the Member State level. The current chapter also aims to see what can be learned from the Dutch approach towards the issue of intermediary liability. This chapter first offers a brief overview of Dutch law on intermediary liability (section §4.02). We continue with a discussion of Dutch copyright law and how it may apply to intermediary activities (section §4.03). This part analyses the scope of the exclusive rights and the exceptions and limitations to those rights, as well as the role that fundamental rights play as external limitations on copyright law.

If an intermediary does not itself infringe a copyright, the intermediary may be liable for the infringements of others (secondary liability). In the Dutch legal system, tort law has played an important role in allocating liability for the facilitation of infringements by others. We will explore how Dutch tort law has enabled copyright owners to take action against those who facilitate infringements (section §4.04). We will then consider the liability exemptions that were introduced in Dutch law following the E-Commerce Directive (section §4.05). This chapter ends with an analysis of the responsibilities that intermediaries may have regardless of these liability exemptions (section §4.06).

§4.02 OVERVIEW

In general, an intermediary can be held liable for its own copyright infringements under Dutch copyright law, for a violation of a duty of care under Dutch tort law, and under the intermediary-specific provision in Article 26d of the Dutch Copyright Act (*Auteurswet*). A copyright is infringed if someone, without the permission of the copyright owner, uses the protected material in way that interferes with the exclusive exploitation rights granted to the copyright owner in the Dutch Copyright Act.

The intermediary's secondary liability for the infringements of others is shaped by Dutch tort law and Article 26d of the Dutch Copyright Act. Tortious liability is determined on the basis of Article 6:162 of the Dutch Civil Code (*Burgerlijk Wetboek*). Generally, intermediaries which structurally facilitate the infringements of others can be liable under Dutch tort law for violating a duty of care. Article 26d of the Dutch Copyright Act offers copyright owners the possibility to apply for injunctions against an intermediary if the intermediary's service is used for infringements. Injunctions can be issued on the basis of Article 26d of the Dutch Copyright Act regardless of the intermediary being at fault.

§4.03 COPYRIGHT LAW

Dutch copyright law is enshrined in the Dutch Copyright Act (*Auteurswet*). This law was first adopted in 1912, but it has been amended and updated many times since.[1] In 2004 it was amended to implement the EU Copyright Directive.[2] In the current section, we will explore how Dutch copyright law may apply to intermediary activities. We will also consider how Dutch copyright law has been influenced by the relevant EU directives.

Dutch copyright law grants copyright owners two exclusive rights (section §4.03[A]). The exclusive rights granted to copyright owners are limited by a list of limitations and exceptions in the Dutch Copyright Act (section §4.03[B]). Our analysis will focus on the quotation exception in Dutch copyright law, which enables Dutch courts to consider and permit curatorial forms of use by intermediaries. The fundamental rights recognized in the European Convention on Human Rights have also been used by Dutch courts to further limit the enforcement of copyrights. The role that these fundamental rights play is discussed in this section as well (section §4.03[C]).

[A] Exclusive Rights

Dutch copyright law grants the copyright owner two exclusive rights—both are discussed here (section §4.03[A][1]). Special attention will be paid to how the Dutch legislator implemented the exception for temporary reproductions of Article 5(1) of the Copyright Directive (section §4.03[A][2]). This section also touches upon the Agreed Statement to the WIPO Copyright Treaty that clarifies that the provision of physical facilities cannot amount to a communication to the public. In Dutch law, this Agreed

1. For a list of changes to the Dutch Copyright Act, *see:* http://wetten.overheid.nl/BWBR0001886 (accessed 14 June 2019).
2. Wet van 6 juli 2004 tot aanpassing van de Auteurswet 1912, de Wet op de naburige rechten en de Databankenwet ter uitvoering van richtlijn nr. 2001/29/EG van het Europees Parlement en de Raad van de Europese Unie van 22 mei 2001 betreffende de harmonisatie van bepaalde aspecten van het auteursrecht en de naburige rechten in de informatiemaatschappij (PbEG L 167), Stb. 2004, 336. An unofficial translation of the Dutch Copyright Act by Mireille van Eechoud is available at: www.ivir.nl/syscontent/pdfs/119.pdf (accessed 14 June 2019).

Statement has served as an interpretative tool to distinguish between liability as a copyright infringer and potential secondary liability for the infringement of others (section §4.03[A][3]).

[1] Broad Exclusive Rights

In contrast to international and EU copyright law, Dutch copyright law 'only' provides for two exclusive exploitation rights: the reproduction right ('*verveelvoudigingsrecht*') and the right to communicate works to the public ('*openbaarmakingsrecht*').[3] These rights do cover the full spectrum of exclusive rights recognized at both the international and EU levels.

The Dutch reproduction right covers the literal copying of a work but also making adaptations of a work, such as translations and dramatizations.[4] The Dutch reproduction right is thus broader than the reproduction right recognized in the EU Copyright Directive, which only covers literal reproductions.[5] Likewise, the Dutch right to communicate works to the public includes all forms of communication covered in the directive. But the Dutch exclusive right also encompasses the public performance of works[6] and the distribution of physical copies of works.[7] Rental and lending are covered by the Dutch right to communicate to the public as well.[8]

The two exclusive rights that are granted to copyright owners are part of an open system of rights that can evolve as technological and societal developments occur. There is no definition of the reproduction right in the Dutch Copyright Act, other than that it *includes* translation, the arrangement of music, cinematographic adaptation or dramatization, and generally any partial or total adaptation or imitation in a modified form, which cannot be regarded as a new, original work.[9] There is also no definition of the right to communicate to the public in Dutch copyright law. Article 12 of the Dutch Copyright Act lists the types of uses that amount to a communication to the public, but the list is not exhaustive. The Dutch legislator has always aimed at giving this exclusive right a broad meaning and has refrained from defining it in the Dutch Copyright Act.[10] When the Copyright Directive harmonized the right of communication to the public,

3. Article 1 of the Dutch Copyright Act.
4. These rights are recognized as separate rights in the Berne Convention in respectively Articles 9(1), 12, and 8.
5. Mireille van Eechoud, *Adapting the Work* 166 (Mireille van Eechoud ed., 2014), explaining that while it is generally accepted among scholars that the adaptation right is currently not harmonized, Article 2 of the Copyright Directive does lend itself to a broad interpretation that may include 'all types of copying, borrowing and reworking'.
6. Article 12(1)(4) of the Dutch Copyright Act.
7. The distribution right was first recognized as a separate right in: Hoge Raad 18 December 1953, *NJ* 1954, 258 (*Polak/De Muinck*). It was codified in Article 12(1)(2) of the Dutch Copyright Act. The Copyright Directive harmonizes that right in Article 4(1).
8. Article 12(1)(3) of the Dutch Copyright Act.
9. Article 13 of the Dutch Copyright Act. *Also see:* Article 14 of the Dutch Copyright Act regarding the recording of works.
10. *Kamerstukken II* 1911/12, 227, 3, para. 4 (MvT). *Also see:* Dirk Visser, *Openbaar maken: Communication to the Public* 228 (Bernt Hugenholtz, Antoon Quaedvlieg & Dirk Visser eds, 2012).

the Dutch legislator saw no reason to change the Dutch Copyright Act on this issue.[11] According to the Dutch legislator, the scope of the Dutch right to communicate to the public was broad enough to cover also the new forms of use which the Copyright Directive aimed to regulate.[12]

[2] Temporary Reproductions

As explained in the previous chapter, the EU legislator developed a technical approach to the reproduction right.[13] Article 2 of the Copyright Directive essentially aimed to make sure that every act of the reproduction of copyrighted materials would be covered by the reproduction right. Article 5(1) of the Copyright Directive requires Member States to implement an exception for temporary reproductions, in particular the reproductions made by access providers to transmit copyrighted materials.

This technical approach towards the reproduction right posed a problem for the Dutch legislator. In Dutch copyright law, the reproduction right had always been approached normatively. A normative approach allows the courts to decide, on a case-by-case basis, whether a particular activity should be qualified as a reproduction in a legal sense. Hence, under Dutch copyright law, not every act that is technically a reproduction would automatically fall within the scope of the exclusive reproduction right. When the Copyright Directive had to be implemented into Dutch law, the Dutch legislator saw no need to clarify that temporary reproductions would be covered by the Dutch reproduction right as well. According to the Dutch legislator, the Dutch exclusive right was already able to cover such acts.[14] The Dutch legislator actively refrained from specifying that temporary reproductions are covered by the reproduction right as it wanted to maintain a normative approach towards this exclusive right.

The Dutch legislator did introduce an exception for temporary reproductions, as required by Article 5(1) of the Copyright Directive, in Article 13a of the Dutch Copyright Act.[15] The exception permits the making of temporary reproductions by access providers to transmit online content. Strictly speaking, Article 13a of the Dutch Copyright Act does not define an *exception*.[16] Instead, it removes certain temporary reproductions from the scope of the reproduction right and clarifies that these reproductions are not covered by the reproduction right in the first place.[17] If the Dutch legislator had provided for an exception, it would have acknowledged that these

11. Article 3(1) of the Copyright Directive. For a discussion, *see* section §3.03[b]2.
12. *Kamerstukken II* 2001/2002, 28 482, 3, p. 14 (MvT). *Also see:* Commissie Auteursrecht, *Advies over de uitvoering van de EG-richtlijn auteursrecht en naburige rechten in de informatiemaatschappij* 8 (2001), advising against the adoption of a separate right to make works available online in order to maintain the flexibility of the Dutch right to communicate to the public.
13. *See* section §3.03[D][1].
14. *Kamerstukken II* 2001/2002, 28 482, 3, p. 37 (MvT).
15. Article 13a of the Dutch Copyright Act.
16. Cyril Van der Net, *Artikel 13a Aw (technische en functionele kopieen)*, AMI (5) 168, 169 (2005).
17. *Kamerstukken II* 2001/2002, 28 482, 3, p. 38 (MvT). *Also see:* Commissie Auteursrecht, *supra* n. 12, at 7, advising the Dutch government to implement Article 5(1) of the Copyright Directive not as a limitation, but as part of the scope of the reproduction right.

temporary reproductions would normally fall within the scope of the reproduction right and that would go against the normative approach towards the reproduction right in Dutch copyright law.[18]

Article 13a of the Dutch Copyright Act on temporary reproductions lists the same requirements as are laid down in Article 5(1) of the Copyright Directive. Article 13a of the Dutch Copyright Act aims to exempt not only the reproductions that are needed to 'transmit messages in a network by an internet access provider' but also the copies in computer memories that are needed to project protected materials on a computer screen.[19]

One Dutch court case shows how a normative conception of the reproduction right may enable a more flexible approach towards the exception for temporary copying. In *Zoekallehuizen.nl*, the Arnhem Court of Appeal extended the scope of Article 13a of the Dutch Copyright Act to also include search engine indexing.[20] The case of *Zoekallehuizen.nl* dealt with a search engine that indexed the websites of real estate agents and that stored in a database the first few lines of the description, the price, the address, and a picture of the real estate object as advertised on the websites of these agents. The Court held that this type of use was covered by Article 13a since its aim was to extract data from those pages. While the Court did not explicitly state so, it must have considered the extraction of data to be a lawful use and the copying of data to extract that data as a use that is dictated by technology.[21]

The findings in *Zoekallehuizen.nl* regarding a special purpose search engine may also apply to general-purpose search engines which make temporary copies of websites in order to index and refer to these websites in search results.[22] However, it should be noted that Article 13a of the Dutch Copyright Act (and also Article 5(1) of the Copyright Directive) only apply if reproduction rights are at issue. The display of snippets or cache copies by search engines is not covered by the exemption. Yet, as we will see, the Dutch quotation exception may still permit such use of copyrighted materials in a search engine.[23]

[3] Provision of 'Physical Facilities'

In line with the Agreed Statement to Article 8 of the WIPO Copyright Treaty, the Copyright Directive in its recitals clarifies that the provision of physical facilities for enabling or making a communication is not considered a communication to the

18. *Also see*: Herman Cohen Jehoram, *Nu de gevolgen van trouw en ontrouw aan de Auteursrechtrichtlijn voor fair use, tijdelijke reproductie en driestappentoets*, AMI (5) 153 (2005).
19. *Kamerstukken II* 2001/2002, 28 482, 3, p. 38 (MvT).
20. Gerechtshof Arnhem 4 June 2006, ECLI:NL:GHARN:2006:AY0089 (*Zoekallehuizen.nl*).
21. *Also see:* Gerechtshof Arnhem 24 June 2008, ECLI:NL:GHARN:2008:BG1062 (*Openbareverkopen.nl*), concerning a webpage that copied real estate advertisements from a competing website.
22. CJEU 17 January 2012, ECLI:EU:C:2012:16 (*Infopaq International v. Danske Dagblades Forening*) *Also see:* Commissie Auteursrecht, Advies aan de Staatssecretaris van Veiligheid en Justitie over de mogelijkheden van het invoeren van een flexibel systeem van beperkingen op het auteursrecht. Deel 2: Zoekmachines en andere probleemgebieden 9 (2013).
23. *See* section §4.03[B][2].

public.[24] Hence, merely providing the technologies to access online materials cannot amount to a copyright infringement. In the explanatory memorandum to the Dutch law implementing the Copyright Directive, the Dutch legislator also stated that the Dutch right to communicate to the public does not cover the mere provision of physical facilities.[25]

The examples given in the memorandum indicate that the Dutch legislator had a literal understanding of the term 'physical'. The memorandum speaks of 'the creation of a network of cables by digging holes in which the cables are put' and 'the provision of a set of monitors in a "consulting space."'[26] There is no mention of Internet access in the memorandum, but there is reason to believe that under EU copyright law the provision of Internet access should be considered as the provision of such physical facilities as well.[27]

Can intermediaries that provide their services on top of the Internet's physical infrastructure also be considered as providers of physical facilities? Strictly speaking, these intermediaries do not provide *physical* facilities to their users. Their services are immaterial and do not involve the provision of a physical network of cables or networking devices.[28] Nevertheless, in Dutch case law, we see that the Agreed Statement has also been applied to service providers which offer their users a platform on which to share information. While these service providers may have been liable for facilitating infringements by others, these service providers could therefore not be held liable as copyright infringers. As such, the Agreed Statement has served as an interpretative tool to distinguish copyright infringements from the tortious liability that the provider may have for facilitating the infringements of others.

In the *Mininova* case, which dealt with the liability of a provider of a torrent sharing platform, the Utrecht District Court held that the torrent sharing platform did not communicate to the public the works shared by its users.[29] With reference to the Agreed Statement, the Court considered that the torrent platform merely facilitated the exchange of files between its users and therefore did not itself infringe any copyrights.[30] In another case that dealt with the liability of the co-founders of The Pirate Bay for copyright infringement, the torrent sharing platform was considered a provider of physical facilities as well.[31] Both the operators of Mininova and The Pirate Bay were not liable as copyright infringers for the copyrighted materials shared by their users. Instead, their liability was assessed based on a secondary liability standard. Both of these cases were decided in 2009, long before the CJEU's decisions in *GS Media* and *The*

24. Recital 27 of the Copyright Directive. For a discussion, *see* section §3.03[D][2][a].
25. *Kamerstukken II* 2001/2002, 28 482, 3, pp. 13–14 (MvT).
26. *Kamerstukken II* 2001/2002, 28 482, 3, p. 14 (MvT).
27. *See* section §3.03[D][2][a].
28. That is not to say that their services do not depend on such physical facilities.
29. Rechtbank Utrecht 26 August 2009, ECLI:NL:RBUTR:2009:BJ6008 (*Brein/Mininova*).
30. Brein/Mininova, *supra* n. 29, at para. 4.7 (Brein/Mininova).
31. Rechtbank Amsterdam 22 October 2009, ECLI:NL:RBAMS:2009:BK1067, para. 5.6 (*The Pirate Bay*).

Pirate Bay.[32] It is safe to say that these Dutch decisions are no longer compatible with these CJEU's decisions. Under current EU copyright law, the activities of the operators of these platforms would probably amount to copyright infringement.

Also, the Leeuwarden Court of Appeal in a 2012 case on the online market platform Marktplaats and its responsibility for copyright-infringing images in advertisements decided that the platform provided physical facilities to its users.[33] The Court held that the platform was an intermediary in the sense of the hosting liability exemption of Article 14 of the E-Commerce Directive. It only provided physical facilities and thus did not communicate copyrighted works to the public.[34]

In conclusion, we see that the Dutch courts have not limited their interpretation to the exact wording, literal meaning, or the specific factual situations for which the temporary reproduction and physical facilities exemptions were drafted. Especially the exemption regarding the provision of physical facilities has been used by Dutch courts as a tool to distinguish between primary and secondary liability. Those who offer such physical facilities do not infringe copyrights themselves, but may still be secondarily liable for infringements by their users. However, after the CJEU's decisions in *GS Media* and *The Pirate Bay*, this line of argumentation is no longer viable – those who knowingly facilitate the infringements of others must now be considered as copyright infringers as well.[35]

[B] Limitations and Exceptions

Dutch copyright law follows the Continental European copyright tradition in the sense that it provides for broadly defined exclusive exploitation rights and a predefined set of limitations and exceptions to those rights. Nevertheless, the Dutch legislator has shown a willingness to adopt flexible limitations and exceptions. Dutch case law also displays an inclination towards a flexible interpretation of limitations and exceptions.

This section highlights a development in Dutch case law towards the flexibilization of limitations and exceptions and discusses the effects that the Copyright Directive has on that development (section §4.03[B][1]). Attention is also paid to the quotation exception in Dutch copyright law and the way in which it enables the Dutch courts to consider new forms of curatorial use by intermediaries (section §4.03[B][2]).

---

32. CJEU 8 September 2016, ECLI:EU:C:2016:644 (*GS Media v. Sanoma Media Netherlands and others*); CJEU 14 June 2017, ECLI:EU:2017:456 (*Stichting Brein v. Ziggo BV and XS4ALL Internet*). For a discussion of these cases, *see* section §3.03[G].
33. Gerechtshof Leeuwarden 22 May 2012, ECLI:NL:GHLEE:2012:BW6296 (*Stokke/Marktplaats*).
34. *Stokke/Marktplaats*, *supra* n. 33, at para. 6.2.
35. *See* section §3.03[D][1]. *See* for an example of how the CJEU's decision in *The Pirate Bay* is applied: Gerechtshof Den Bosch 17 October 2017, ECLI:NL:GHSHE:2017:4524.

[1] Room for New Exceptions? Dior v. Evora

The decision of the Dutch Supreme Court in *Dior v. Evora* plays an important role in the flexibilization of the exceptions and limitations in Dutch copyright law.[36] In *Dior v. Evora*, the Dutch Supreme Court held that the existing catalogue of limitations and exceptions could be opened up by acknowledging that it is possible to permit forms of use that were not considered by the Dutch legislator.

Dior v. Evora dealt with the owner of a drugstore chain, Evora, who sold Dior parallel imports without being one of Dior's exclusive retailers. Evora advertised Dior perfume products in its brochures using pictures of the perfume bottles and their boxes. Concerned about its reputation and wanting to block the sale of its products by Evora, Dior argued that Evora had committed a copyright infringement by using pictures of the copyrighted designs of perfume bottles and boxes.

The Dutch Supreme Court's decision in *Dior v. Evora* breaks with a tradition of defining strict limitations and exceptions in statutory copyright law.[37] The Court essentially ruled that one can advertise what one is selling, even if that requires using images of copyrighted designs of the product. The Court based its finding on the idea that, underlying these limitations and exceptions, there is a balance between the interests of copyright owners and the interests of others and the public at large. In particular, if a limitation has not been considered by the Dutch legislator and that limitation fits within the existing copyright system, then copyright protection may be limited. As such, the Court's findings could enable the 'gaps in the limitation infrastructure' to be filled.[38]

Yet, the Dutch Supreme Court decided in *Dior v. Evora* before the adoption of the EU Copyright Directive. As Member States may only implement limitations and exceptions enumerated in that directive, the flexibility created in *Dior v. Evora* now appears to be incompatible with EU law.[39] Moreover, *Dior v. Evora* has not given rise to any new case law that makes use of this flexibility. Part of *Dior v. Evora*'s limited practical effect may also be attributed to the introduction of a more flexible statutory quotation exception.

[2] Quotation Exception and Search Engine Use

At the time the EU Member States negotiated the Copyright Directive, the Dutch government argued for a fair use type of exception that would enable courts to allow

36. Hoge Raad 20 October 1995, ECLI:NL:HR:1995:ZC1845 (*Dior/Evora*).
37. Martin Senftleben, *Comparative Approaches to Fair Use: An Important Impulse for Reforms in EU Copyright Law* 63 (Graeme Dinwoodie ed., 2013).
38. Martin Senftleben, *The Perfect Match – Civil Law Judges and Open-Ended Fair Use Provisions*, 33 American University International Law Review 231 (2017).
39. Christiaan Alberdingk Thijm, *Fair Use: het auteursrechtelijk evenwicht hersteld*, AMI (9) 145, 147 (1998). Herman Cohen Jehoram, *Implementatie van de Auteursrechtrichtlijn: De stille strijd tegen een spookrijder*, 34 Nederlands Juristenblad 1690, 1693 (2002). Madeleine de Cock Buning, *Auteursrecht en informatievrijheid: over de beperkte toepassing van artikel 10 EVRM*, Mediaforum (4) 157, 165.

forms of use that were not considered by the legislator. Neither the European Commission nor any of the other EU Member States supported the adoption of such a fair use rule in the Copyright Directive.[40]

Nevertheless, the Dutch legislator opted for an approach that would implement the directive with as much flexibility as possible.[41] The result of this Dutch exercise shows that there may be more flexibility within the closed list of the Copyright Directive than one might expect. Although the directive provides a closed list of implementable limitations and exceptions, it does so without specifying the precise conditions under which they should be available. For instance, Article 5(3)(d) of the directive permits Member States to implement an exception for quotations. This provision does not limit the purposes for which a quotation exception may be adopted. Rather it speaks of 'quotations for purposes *such as* criticism or review'. Likewise, the parody exception in Article 5(3)(k) mentions only that exceptions may be provided for 'use for the purpose of caricature, parody or pastiche', without further limiting the conditions in which a parody exception may be applicable, or defining the concepts used in the directive.

When the Dutch legislator implemented the Copyright Directive, the existing quotation exception in Dutch copyright law was flexibilized.[42] Before Article 15a of the Dutch Copyright Act was changed, the exception only applied to quotations for the purposes of an announcement, review, polemic or scientific treatise. Under the current Article 15a of the Dutch Copyright Act, quotations are permitted if they quote from the work in an announcement, review, polemic or scientific treatise or an expression 'with a similar purpose'. This change implied a loosening of the context requirement, which required that the reproduction must be connected to the context in which it is used. According to the Dutch legislator, this would also clarify that one could quote images, sounds, and in certain circumstances also a whole work.[43]

For a quotation to be permissible under Dutch copyright law, the quoted work must be lawfully communicated to the public.[44] Furthermore, the quotation must be 'in accordance with what social custom regards as reasonably acceptable'.[45] Here the Dutch legislator opted to import a duty of care-like rule into the quotation exception. Also, the amount and size of the quoted parts should be justified by the quotation's purpose.[46] The author's moral rights must be observed as well.[47] And finally, the source, including the author's name, must be indicated to the extent that this is reasonably possible.[48]

As the Dutch quotation exception is expressed in broad and open-ended terms, the exception enables courts to also permit the use of protected works in curatorial

40. *Kamerstukken II* 1999/2000, 26 538, 2, p. 21.
41. *Kamerstukken II* 2001/2002, 28 482, 3, p. 17.
42. Dirk Visser, *De Auteurswet gewijzigd: Artikel 15 Aw (citaatrecht)*, AMI (4) 132 (2005).
43. *Kamerstukken II* 2002/2003, 28 482, 3, p. 40 (MvT).
44. Article 15(1)(1) of the Dutch Copyright Act.
45. Article 15(1)(2) of the Dutch Copyright Act.
46. Article 15(1)(2) of the Dutch Copyright Act.
47. Article 15(1)(3) of the Dutch Copyright Act.
48. Article 15(1)(4) of the Dutch Copyright Act.

technologies. Search engine use of copyrighted materials is an example of a type of use that appears to be permitted under the flexible quotation exception.[49] One Dutch court decision in particular supports the stance that the quotation exception also applies to the use of protected materials by dedicated search engines.[50] *Zoekallehuizen.nl* dealt with the use of information about real estate objects by a search engine.[51] In this case, the Arnhem Court of Appeal considered whether the copying of an address, a price, and a few sentences from the object's description amounted to a permissible quotation. The Court attached little weight to the context requirement and explained that the quotation exception also covers quotations that are not used for a critique or a review. According to the Court, the dedicated search engine had the same goal as the real estate agents, which was making the object visible to potential buyers. This fact played a decisive role in the Court's ruling. The search engine enabled users to find the agents' websites by providing relevant information and referring users to these websites.

The Dutch Copyright Commission, which consists of copyright law experts who advise the Dutch legislator on copyright issues, raised the possibility of explicitly referring to search engine use in Article 15a of the Dutch Copyright Act.[52] A downside recognized by the Commission is that an explicit reference to technologies could diminish the exception's flexibility. Indeed, adding an example of a contemporary technology might create uncertainty about the provision's applicability to future technologies. Discussions might arise about whether a particular new technology should be considered a search technology in the sense of the exception. Moreover, since discussions are then likely to focus on technological aspects, attention may be shifted away from the normative questions at hand. Keeping the exception open prevents a focus on technological aspects and enables courts to consider a particular use in light of the underlying goal of the exception. In that respect, the *Zoekallehuizen.nl* decision is an example of how a Dutch court has used the flexibility of the quotation exception to give a well-reasoned decision that does not consider technicalities, but which is grounded in the exception's purpose.

A question that is still open is whether this high level of flexibility of the Dutch quotation exception is in conformity with EU law. The EU 'template' for a quotation exception also uses open-ended language and seems to leave some room for Member States to make their own policy decisions.[53] Article 5(3)(d) of the Copyright Directive allows quotations for 'purposes *such as* criticism or review' and requires that they are made 'in accordance with fair practice'.

Yet, in *Maria Painer*, Advocate General Trstenjak of the CJEU expressed a narrow understanding of the purposes covered by the quotation exception: 'There must (...) be a material reference back to the quoted work in the form of a description, commentary

49. Commissie Auteursrecht, *supra* n. 22.
50. Martin Senftleben, *Internet Search Results – A Permissible Quotation?*, Revue Internationale du Droit d'Auteur (1) 3 (2013).
51. *Zoekallehuizen.nl*, *supra* n. 20. Regarding the copying of headlines by an aggregator, *see:* Rechtbank Rotterdam 22 August 2000, ECLI:NL:RBROT:2000:AA6826 (*Kranten.com*).
52. Commissie Auteursrecht, *supra* n. 22.
53. Bernt Hugenholtz & Martin Senftleben, *Fair Use in Europe: In Search of Flexibilities* (2011).

or analysis. The quotation must therefore be a basis for discussion.'[54] The CJEU remained silent concerning the purposes covered by the quotation exception in the Copyright Directive.[55] It reiterated that limitations and exceptions must be interpreted strictly since they are a derogation from the general rule of copyright protection.[56] But the CJEU also highlighted that the interpretation of the quotation exception must 'enable the effectiveness of the exception thereby established to be safeguarded and its purpose to be observed'.[57] In this regard, the CJEU stated that the quotation exception is 'intended to strike a fair balance between the right to freedom of expression of users of a work or other protected subject-matter and the reproduction right conferred on authors'.[58]

All in all, the Dutch legislator flexibilized the quotation exception to enable it to also cover new forms of information usage. We know that it covers search engine use and that it has the potential to accommodate other information location tools. Seeing such use as a 'quotation' may be a departure from the classical meaning of the word, as promoted by Advocate General Trstenjak. But it may also enable courts to permit curatorial forms of use that were not considered or anticipated by the legislator.[59]

[C] External Limitation by Fundamental Rights

As explained in Chapter 2, recent ECtHR and CJEU case law recognizes that fundamental rights can serve as external balancing mechanisms and limit how copyrights are enforced. In the Netherlands, the fundamental rights in the European Convention on Human Rights were used as external balancing mechanisms much earlier. Already in 1995, the Dutch Supreme Court in *Dior v. Evora* recognized that fundamental rights, and the right to the freedom of expression in particular, can externally balance copyright protection.[60] In later case law, the Dutch lower courts also recognized that, under certain conditions, a copyright should not be enforced if such enforcement is in conflict with the right to the freedom of expression.

There is an important difference between the CJEU's case law and Dutch case law on the relationship between fundamental rights and copyright law. Thus far, the CJEU's case law has concerned specific enforcement measures, especially in relation to intermediaries and their duty to stop and prevent infringements. If such a measure, for instance a filtering system, does not strike a fair balance between the relevant fundamental rights, such a measure cannot be pursued. Hence, the CJEU recognized that fundamental rights can stand in the way of specific measures of copyright enforcement.[61] In contrast, in Dutch case law, we see that fundamental rights may

54. Opinion of AG Trstenjak 12 April 2011, ECLI:EU:C:2011:239, para. 210 (*Maria Painer*).
55. CJEU 1 December 2011, ECLI:EU:C:2011:798, para. 123 (*Maria Painer*).
56. *See* section §3.03[E][3] for a discussion of this principle of strict interpretation.
57. *Maria Painer*, *supra* n. 54, para. 133.
58. *Maria Painer*, *supra* n. 54, para. 134.
59. *See also*: Martin Senftleben, *Quotations, Parody and Fair Use* 360 (Bernt Hugenholtz, Antoon Quaedvlieg & Dirk Visser eds, 2012).
60. Dior/Evora, *supra* n. 36.
61. *See* section §3.05[C].

stand in the way of the enforcement of a copyright altogether. The copyright owner cannot then invoke his exclusive rights because it would interfere with a fundamental right.

Dutch case law has focused on the relationship between copyright law and the freedom of expression as well as the ability of the latter to override the former (section §4.03[C][1]). However, a recent lower court decision shows how also other fundamental rights, in particular those in the EU Charter of Fundamental Rights, can accommodate the use of new technologies (section §4.03[C][2]).

[1] Freedom of Expression

The Dutch courts have not always given freedom of expression claims much consideration. In two separate decisions in 1984 and 1994, the Dutch Supreme Court had held that copyrights and their enforcement were justified interferences in the freedom of expression.[62] There seemed to be no room to consider whether the protection afforded by a copyright was in conformity with Article 10 of the European Convention on Human Rights. A change came in 1995 when the Dutch Supreme Court delivered its judgment in the *Dior v. Evora* case.[63] The Court acknowledged that copyright protection could be cast aside by the right to the freedom of expression.[64] While the Court noted that Dior's right to copyright protection did not give way to Evora's right to the freedom of expression in this particular case, the Court did recognize that copyright protection may be limited by the right to the freedom of expression.

The 1994 *Boogschutter* decision of the Amsterdam District Court was a first signal that the tide was changing and that copyright protection should also be seen in light of the right to the freedom of expression.[65] The Dutch newspaper *de Volkskrant* had published an interview featuring a picture of the interviewee posing next to a copyrighted sculpture. The District Court of Amsterdam held that none of the available limitations – including the old quotation right – applied.[66] But the Court's analysis did not stop there. The Court also considered whether the enforcement of the exclusive rights pertaining to the sculpture was proportionate in the sense of Article 10 of the European Convention on Human Rights. Hence, the Court examined whether the interference with the newspaper's right to the freedom of expression was justified in order to protect the interests of the copyright owner in question. While the Court held that there was no infringement of the newspaper's right to the freedom of expression, it nevertheless considered Article 10 of the European Convention on Human Rights to

62. Hoge Raad 14 January 1983, ECLI:NL:PHR:1983:AG4520 (*Kabelpiraten*); Hoge Raad 24 December 1994, ECLI:NL:HR:1993:ZC1201 (*Draadomroepinrichtingen*). *See also*: Bernt Hugenholtz, *Auteursrecht contra informatievrijheid in Europa* 8 (Wouter Hins & Aernout Nieuwenhuis eds., 2003); De Cock Buning, *supra* n. 39, at 162; Herman Cohen Jehoram, *De Enstra-tapes: een zeldzame botsing tussen auteursrechten en informatievrijheid*, NJB 329 (2009).
63. Dior/Evora, *supra* n. 36.
64. For an in-depth discussion of this case, *see* section §4.03[B][1].
65. Rechtbank Amsterdam 19 January 1994, ECLI:NL:RBAMS:1994:AK2254 (*Volkskrant/Stichting Beeldrecht*).
66. *Volkskrant/Stichting Beeldrecht*, *supra* n. 65. According to the Court, the quoted work was not part of an announcement, review, or polemic or scientific treatise.

assess whether the rights granted by copyright law could be invoked in this particular case.

In the limited case law that there is on copyright and the freedom of expression, the 2003 *Scientology* decision of the Court of Appeal of The Hague stands out.[67] It is the only case in which Article 10 of the European Convention on Human Rights actually cast aside the enforcement of a copyright. The publicist Karin Spaink had uploaded secret teachings of the Scientology organization to her home page. As these secret texts had not been lawfully published, the quotation right of Article 15a of the Dutch Copyright Act did not apply to Spaink's publication of the materials. However, since Spaink's aim was to expose Scientology and its practices, the Court held that the publication of the materials was protected by Article 10 of the European Convention on Human Rights and that publication could not be prohibited on the basis of copyright law. The Court was cognizant of the importance that this information could be communicated and received freely. It took into consideration that Scientology rejected democratic values, tried to exert power over its members, and prevented any discussion about the organization's practices by concealing its teachings. Also given the non-commercial nature of the use of the materials, the Court held that the enforcement of Scientology's copyright would violate the right to freedom of expression.

In its considerations, the Court of Appeal of The Hague took Article 10 of the European Convention on Human Rights as its starting point.[68] The Court thus seemed to put the fundamental right of freedom of expression first and looked at copyright protection as a private law exception to that fundamental right. Yet, contemporary conceptions of the relationship between copyright law and the freedom of expression highlight that copyright protection is a fundamental right as well. As such, the right to freedom of expression and other fundamental rights have to compete with this fundamental right to the protection of intellectual property and a 'fair balance' must be struck between these rights.

Twenty years after its 1995 decision in *Dior v. Evora*, the Dutch Supreme Court was given another opportunity to address the tension between copyright law and the freedom of expression.[69] In *GS Media*, the Court underlined that whenever an argument is made against the enforcement of a copyright by appealing to a fundamental right, courts need to consider whether these fundamental rights stand in the way of enforcement.[70] Although it is primarily the legislator's prerogative to balance between the different fundamental rights in its copyright legislation, the Dutch Supreme Court held that the Dutch courts have a duty to investigate whether the invoked fundamental right is not unduly interfered with. The Dutch Supreme Court thus not only accepted the legislator's primacy over copyright law and its built-in balancing mechanisms but also recognized that in particular cases an external balancing by fundamental rights might be required.

67. Gerechtshof Den Haag 4 September 2003, ECLI:NL:GHSGR:2003:AI5638 (*Scientology*).
68. Scientology, *supra* n. 67.
69. Dior/Evora, *supra* n. 36.
70. Hoge Raad 13 November 2015, ECLI:NL:HR:2015:3307 (*Brein/Ziggo & XS4ALL*).

Proportionality is key in assessing whether an enforcement measure is compatible with fundamental rights.[71] The Dutch Supreme Court was mindful of the CJEU's decision in *Scarlet v. Sabam* and *UPC Telekabel*, in which the CJEU underlined that Member States must interpret EU law in a way that strikes a fair balance between the fundamental rights at issue.[72] But the Dutch Supreme Court also considered the decision of the European Court of Human Rights in *Ashby Donald*, which requires that enforcement measures must serve a 'pressing social need' and be proportionate for them not to infringe the right to the freedom of expression.[73] According to the Dutch Supreme Court, the question of whether the freedom of expression should prevail depends on the circumstances of the case, including the nature of the expression in question. In this context, the Dutch Supreme Court noted that commercial speech generally deserves less protection than speech relating to public affairs.[74]

A question that arises is how an external balancing by fundamental rights relates to the closed list of limitations and exceptions in the Copyright Directive.[75] One could argue that there is no place for an external limitation of the copyright owner's rights by fundamental rights as the Copyright Directive provides an exhaustive list of (internal) limitations and exceptions. The CJEU itself has referred to the fundamental rights recognized in the EU Charter in several decisions relating to copyright. However, the CJEU has only done so within the context of an existing limitation or exception by using these fundamental rights as a basis for a particular interpretation of a limitation or exception.[76] A distinction should probably be made between Member State interpretations that remain within the confines of the limitations and exceptions enumerated in the Copyright Directive and interpretations that go beyond these existing limitations and exceptions. If the latter is the case, a Member State court enters muddy waters by introducing a de facto new limitation or exception that is not listed in Article 5 of the Copyright Directive. Compatibility with EU law then depends on the CJEU's willingness to accept that the fundamental rights protected in the Charter can have an overriding (external) effect on the enforcement of a copyright. Here tensions may also arise regarding a Member State's obligations under the European Convention on Human Rights.[77] Future CJEU decisions in the cases of *Funke Medien*, *Pelham*, and *Spiegel Online* on the flexibility of the limitations and exceptions in the Copyright

71. *Brein/Ziggo & XS4ALL*, *supra* n. 70, at para. 5.2.5.
72. CJEU 24 November 2011, ECLI:EU:C:2011:771 (*Scarlet v. Sabam*); CJEU 27 March 2014, ECLI:EU:C:2014:192 (*UPC Telekabel Wien v. Constantin Film Verleih and Wega Filmproduktionsgesellschaft*).
73. ECtHR 10 January 2013, app. no. 36769/08 (*Ashby Donald v. France*).
74. *Brein/Ziggo & XS4ALL*, *supra* n. 70, at para. 5.2.6.
75. *Also see:* De Cock Buning, *supra* n. 39, at 165.
76. *See* section §3.03[E].
77. Advocate General Verkade noted in 2005 that although EU law obligates Member State legislators not to implement other limitations and exceptions in their copyright laws, the Copyright Directive cannot prevent Article 10 of the European Convention on Human Rights from playing its role in copyright-related disputes (16 December 2005, ECLI:NL:PHR:2005:AT2056, para. 6.9).

Directive and the role that fundamental rights can play will hopefully offer valuable input as to what is possible under Dutch law in that respect.[78]

It can be argued that the consideration of fundamental rights may add to the unpredictability of copyright infringement analysis. In response to the *Scientology* decision, Quaedvlieg argued that the use of 'additional correction mechanisms' should be limited to exceptional cases only.[79] Legal certainty suffers if courts see Article 10 of the European Convention on Human Rights as a carte blanche to readjust copyright law. Moreover, if Article 10 of the European Convention on Human Rights is used as a balancing mechanism that functions alongside copyright law's statutory limitations and exceptions, it may be uncertain whether a particular use is lawful, even after applying the rules of copyright law.

Indeed, the consideration of fundamental rights may have a negative effect on predictability. By using flexible concepts to determine the law, the law is generally determined *ex post* by the courts, which detracts from the law's predictability. However, as has been argued in Chapter 2, case law can also provide an *ex ante* understanding and add to the predictability of the law in general.[80] For example, the Dutch Supreme Court's decision in *GS Media* clarified that the right to freedom of expression does not cast aside copyright protection and enforcement in exceptional cases only. A factor that is important in determining whether the freedom of expression should prevail over copyright enforcement is its contribution to public discourse. And, in this respect, we also know that the commercial use of protected works is less likely to be protected by the freedom of expression.[81]

Admittedly, the Dutch Supreme Court has not often been in a position to clarify the relationship between copyright protection and the freedom of expression and to generate greater predictability. At the same time, the Dutch Supreme Court's reasoning in *GS Media* depended heavily on international developments, in particular, the decisions of the CJEU in *Scarlet v. Sabam* and *UPC Telekabel* and the European Court of Human Rights in *Ashby Donald*, which were decided in respectively 2011, 2012, and 2013.[82] After the Supreme Court's decision in *GS Media*, fundamental rights-based arguments against the enforcement of copyrights might surge, giving courts the opportunity to further develop criteria and provide more guidance.

In conclusion, the Dutch Supreme Court's decision in *GS Media* represents an important change in thinking about the relationship between copyright law and the freedom of expression and other fundamental rights in the Netherlands. This change in thinking is directly attributable to the CJEU's case law on intermediary liability and the need to strike a fair balance between the fundamental rights at issue. In line with this

78. *See* the references to the CJEU in the cases of *Funke Medien* (C-469/17), *Pelham* (C-476/17), and *Spiegel Online* (C-516/17).
79. Gerechtshof Den Haag 4 September 2003, ECLI:NL:GHSGR:2003:AI5638, *BIE* 2004, 57, with note by Antoon Quaedvlieg (*Scientology*). *Also see:* Antoon Quaedvlieg, *Een modern citaatrecht belemmert niet de uitingsvrijheid*, AMI 197 (2006).
80. *See* section §2.04[B][3].
81. Council of Europe, Internet: case-law of the European Court of Human Rights, 17 (2015).
82. *Scarlet v. Sabam*, *supra* n. 72; *UPC Telekabel Wien v. Constantin Film Verleih and Wega Filmproduktionsgesellschaft*, *supra* n. 72; *Ashby Donald v. France*, *supra* n. 73.

case law, the Dutch Supreme Court has recognized that copyright protection is a fundamental right which is on an equal footing with the freedom of expression and other fundamental rights. This approach no longer sees copyright and its enforcement as a private law matter that is generally considered to be a justified interference with the freedom of expression. Instead copyright protection is levelled with other fundamental rights and may also collide with these fundamental rights. This places the potential conflict of copyright protection with other fundamental rights at the forefront. It is now clear from the outset that under Dutch law, copyright enforcement is an integral part of a broader fundamental rights framework. As such, fundamental rights contribute to maintaining the copyright balance: they enable courts to consider the effects of a copyright on the interests of others, including the broader public, and to strike a fair balance between these interests.

[2] Fundamental Rights and New Technologies

Thus far, we have focused on the role of fundamental rights as an external balancing mechanism. Yet, consideration of fundamental rights can also enhance the flexibility of the copyright system. It may even enable courts to consider new technological uses and to permit them, even if there is no limitation or exception that covers such use. There is one Dutch court case that illustrates this point: the 2015 *Anne Frank diaries* case.[83] In this case, the Amsterdam District Court used the freedom of the arts and sciences, as protected by Article 13 of the EU Charter of Fundamental Rights, to permit a text analysis of Anne Frank's diaries by researchers.

The *Anne Frank diaries* case revolved around reproductions of the Anne Frank diaries that were made by the Dutch Anne Frank Foundation in cooperation with the Royal Netherlands Academy of Arts and Sciences. These organizations already owned facsimile copies of the diaries but decided to create so-called XML-TEI files of these copies for research purposes. XML-TEI files contain structured data and are used in linguistic studies to analyse texts. The Swiss Anne Frank Fund holding the copyrights to Anne Frank's works argued that its rights had been infringed. The Court considered, among other limitations and exceptions, the quotation exception and the private copying exception in Articles 15a and 16a of the Dutch Copyright Act. None of them applied. The Court referred to the Dutch Supreme Court's decision in *GS Media* to justify its consideration of fundamental rights in this case. And in that context, after considering that the copies were necessary for carrying out textual analyses and the limited impact that such unauthorized copying would have, the Court held that the 'freedom of science' outweighed copyright enforcement. The Court thus balanced copyright protection with the fundamental right protected in Article 13 of the EU Charter of Fundamental Rights.

Although there was no exception in Dutch copyright law that allows for reproduction for purposes of text analysis, the Dutch District Court essentially permitted its

83. Rechtbank Amsterdam 23 December 2015, ECLI:NL:RBAMS:2015:9312 (*Anne Frank-Fonds/Anne Frank Stichting*).

use in light of the freedom of science. By elevating the discussion about copyright enforcement to the level of conflicting fundamental rights, it created space to take into account the effects that copyright enforcement would have on the interests of the researchers and the public's interest in science. In doing so, the Court was able to accommodate the use of a beneficial new information processing technology that had not been considered by the Dutch legislator.

§4.04 SECONDARY LIABILITY

After discussing how copyright law may apply to intermediaries and other useful technologies, we now turn to the issue of secondary liability: the cases in which an intermediary may be liable for an infringement by others.[84] This section explains how Dutch tort law offers an open-ended basis for liability when someone violates a duty of care (section §4.04[A]). As the Internet was used to disseminate copyright-infringing materials, discussions emerged about whether Internet intermediaries were to be held directly liable under copyright infringement theory or on the basis of this general duty of care in Dutch tort law. We will see that Dutch tort law has always offered copyright owners an additional level of protection by enabling them to go after those who facilitate the infringements of others, for instance by operating a peer-to-peer file-sharing platform or linking to infringing materials (section §4.04[B]). However, the CJEU decisions in *GS Media* and *The Pirate Bay* require that this 'Dutch approach' towards secondary liability will have to reflect that such facilitation amounts to copyright infringement in itself.[85] After these decisions, much of what used to be in the domain of Dutch tort law's duty of care will now have to be considered through a copyright lens (section §4.04[C]).

[A] The General Duty of Care

With respect to intermediaries and their liability, the relevance of Dutch tort law ('*onrechtmatige daad*') is not so much in its ability to serve as a basis for obligations to pay damages. Their liability for damages is limited under Article 6:196c of the Dutch Copyright Act, which implements the liability exemptions in the E-Commerce Directive.[86] Rather, Dutch tort law can serve as a basis for *injunctions* against intermediaries because those who commit a tort can be ordered to do something or stop doing something in relation to the tortious conduct.[87] Such injunctions are generally available if someone acts or will act tortiously and the claimant has a sufficient interest in the claim.[88]

Article 6:162 of the Dutch Civil Code (*Burgerlijk Wetboek, BW*) provides the basis for tortious liability under Dutch law. Article 6:162(1) provides that 'a person who

84. For a discussion of the concept of secondary liability, *see* section §1.04.
85. *See* section §3.03[G].
86. *See* section §4.05.
87. Article 3:296(2) of the Dutch Civil Code.
88. GS Onrechtmatige daad II.1.2.1.2.1 (Deurvorst).

commits an unlawful act toward another which can be imputed to him, must repair the damage the other person suffers as a consequence thereof'.[89] Article 6:162(2) provides for three categories of unlawful acts that need to be repaired. The first category of unlawful acts is that of an infringement of a subjective right – such as a copyright.[90] The second category consists of acts or omissions that violate a statutory duty. For instance, if a rule of unfair competition is violated and a competitor of the tortfeasor suffers damage from this violation, that damage may have to be repaired. The third category relates to acts or omissions that violate a rule of unwritten law pertaining to proper social conduct. This category will be referred to as a violation of the general duty of care.[91]

A (direct) infringement of a copyright falls into the first category since it is a right that is granted to copyright owners by Dutch copyright law.[92] A breach of a copyright leads to *eo ipso* unlawfulness. Liability does not depend on whether the infringer acted negligently; the infringement will be imputed to him. As the Dutch Supreme Court stated: 'if someone, without being entitled to do so, uses a good, to which another holds an exclusive right, and therefore infringes that exclusive right, he then acts unlawfully against the rightholder if there is no justification for the infringement'.[93] Damages usually consist of the profits that would be gained if a licence to use the copyrighted work would have been concluded between the copyright owner and the infringer.[94]

However, when intermediaries are concerned, the third category of unlawful acts is much more relevant: the violation of the general duty of care. This category of unlawful acts was recognized by the Supreme Court in 1919 in the landmark case of *Lindenbaum Cohen*.[95] It came at a time when the Netherlands was developing its own industry and the need was felt to more flexibly protect against unfair competition.[96] In

89. Translation by Jaap Spier, *The Netherlands. Wrongfulness in the Dutch Context* 87 (Francesco Donato Busnelli ed., 1998).
90. GS Onrechtmatige daad, artikel 162 Boek 6 BW, aant. 7 (Jansen).
91. In Dutch case law and literature this category is often referred to as conduct that violates '*de maatschappelijke zorgvuldigheid*'. I use the term 'general duty of care' to refer to this category of torts, not as a broader legal notion that underlies the law of obligations (*see*, for instance: Eric Tjong Tjin Tai, *Zorgplichten en zorgethiek* (2006). When I speak of a 'duty of care' (leaving out 'general'), I mean a specific duty that has been developed by the courts under the 'general duty of care'.
92. Titia Deurvorst, *Schadevergoeding, voldoening van een redelijke gebruiksvergoeding en winstafdracht bij inbreuk op intellectuele eigendomsrechten* 15 (1994). Other examples of such rights include the right to privacy, bodily integrity, or a property right.
93. Hoge Raad 12 March 2004, ECLI:NL:HR:2004:AN8483 (*XS4ALL/Ab.fab*). This case dealt with the Internet service provider XS4ALL's right to its computer capacity, bandwidth, and customer base, in a case of email spamming. Own translation.
94. Titia Deurvorst, *Schadevergoeding en proceskostenveroordeling bij inbreuk op auteursrecht*, AMI (3) 85, 86 (2012); Arnoud Engelfriet, *Schadevergoeding bij online auteursrecht- inbreuk: stand van zaken 2015*, AMI (5) 125 (2015).
95. Hoge Raad 31 January 1919, *NJ* 1919, 161 (*Lindenbaum/Cohen*).
96. For a comprehensive analysis of the development of this category in Dutch tort law, *see:* Gerrit van Maanen, *Onrechtmatige daad. Aspekten van de ontwikkeling van een omstreden leerstuk* (1986) and Gerrit van Maanen, *De Zutphense juffrouw en de ontrouwe bediende van Lindenbaum* (1995). For an overview of the discussions on the introduction of an open category of unlawful acts, *see:* Feer Verkade, *100 jaar 'Oneerlijke concurrentie' in Nederland*

this decision, the Dutch Supreme Court accepted that acts or omissions that violate *morals* or the *care* that can be expected in society regarding another person or his goods could constitute unlawful acts. The general duty of care as a basis for imposing tortious liability can thus be traced back to a willingness to create a more open system of liability that is able to keep up with social and economic developments. This openness of the tort law system enables social practices and norms to be incorporated and provides for sanctions when persons fail to take sufficient care.[97]

The general duty of care has enabled courts to develop specific duties of care that apply in particular scenarios.[98] In defining a duty of care, courts may build on international, EU, and Dutch law regarding conduct that is related to the conduct in question, but also general principles of law, customs, codes of conduct, and previous case law.[99] Some of the duties developed under Article 6:162 of the Dutch Civil Code are fairly detailed, which implies that they hardly fit the facts of other cases and certainly not perfectly.[100] Other duties have a more general application, such as the duty of care developed by the Dutch Supreme Court in the 1965 *Kelderluik* decision.[101] In this case, the Dutch Supreme Court considered the liability of a delivery man for the damage suffered by a person who fell into a cellar hatch (*kelderluik*), which the delivery man had left open. In this decision, the Dutch Supreme Court developed factors to assess whether sufficient care has been taken. These factors, which have come to be known as the *Kelderluik* factors, are now used as a starting point to determine whether the general duty of care has been breached specifically in cases concerning dangerous situations.[102]

[B] Facilitation of an Infringement

If an intermediary does not commit a copyright infringement itself, that intermediary may still be held liable for the infringements of others on the basis of the general duty of care in Dutch tort law. Courts must, however, take due account of how the application of the general duty of care relates to the rules of copyright law. A court

– *Molengraaff en de onbetamelijke mededinging*, Bijblad Industriële Eigendom (7) 155, 156. Mention must also be made here of Molengraaff's 1887 seminal article on the lack of available actions against passing off trademarks: Willem Molengraaff, *De 'oneerlijke concurrentie' voor het forum van den Nederlandschen rechter*, Rechtsgeleerd Magazijn (1) 373 (1887).

97. Eric Tjong Tjin Tai, *Zorg, Privaatrecht en publiekrecht: van ondersteuning naar handhaving, en terug*, Recht der Werkelijkheid (3) 6, 10 (2010).
98. For a categorized overview, *see:* Asser/Hartkamp & Sieburgh 6-IV* 58–73. Examples of the discussed duties of care deal with unfair competition, abuse of market power, professional misconduct, banks, directors, etc.
99. Asser/Hartkamp & Sieburgh 6-IV 76.
100. Asser/Hartkamp & Sieburgh 6-IV* 57. An example of such a very specific duty of care can be found in the Hoge Raad 8 January 1982, ECLI:NL:HR:1982:AG4306 (*Natronloog*). In this decision, the Dutch Supreme Court constructed a very specific duty of care regarding the placement of a dangerous liquid as garbage to be collected.
101. Hoge Raad 5 November 1965, ECLI:NL:HR:1965:AB7079 (*Kelderluik*).
102. Gerrit Van Maanen, David Townend & Almaz Teffera, *The Dutch 'Cellar Hatch' Judgment as a Landmark Case for Tort Law in Europe: A Brief Comparison with English, French and German Law with a Law and Economics Flavour*, 5 European Review of Private Law 871 (2008).

cannot consider certain activities to be a violation of the general duty of care if those activities are expressly allowed by copyright law, such as through an exception. Yet, if particular activities harm the copyright owner and those activities are not expressly permitted under copyright law, Dutch copyright law does not generally preclude the protection of the copyright owner's interests by tort law.[103] It has long been established that under certain conditions, the facilitation of the copyright infringements of others can amount to a violation of the general duty of care and as such lead to liability under tort law. In its 1965 decision in *Buma v. De Vries*, the Dutch Supreme Court held that a bar owner had violated a duty of care by not stopping his musicians from engaging in unauthorized performances of musical works.[104] The Court considered that the bar owner had been notified about the infringements taking place in his establishment and that he had control over the musicians. The bar owner thus had knowledge of the infringements and control over those who infringed.

The first steps towards seeing the activities of intermediaries as a matter of secondary liability were set in the 1996 *Scientology v. XS4ALL* case. This decision gained a great deal of attention worldwide and is believed to have served as inspiration for the liability in the E-Commerce Directive.[105] It dealt with the liability of access and hosting providers for storing and transmitting copyright-infringing materials. Scientology argued that the access and hosting providers were liable as copyright infringers. In summary proceedings, the District Court of The Hague made the fundamental decision not to consider the responsibility of these intermediaries under copyright law. The Court held that access providers and hosting providers only provide the technological facilities to make information available.[106] While the intermediaries were off the hook as far as copyright infringement was concerned, the Dutch court did recognize that they could still be liable for violating the general duty of care in Dutch tort law. Yet, liability could then only be incurred if the intermediary had obtained knowledge of the infringement, for instance because it had been notified thereof.[107]

With the rise of peer-to-peer file-sharing software and networks, discussions emerged about the liability of those who offer such software and networks, but also on the liability of intermediaries for the infringement of their users. Early discussions in the literature revolved around the question of whether the Dutch Supreme Court's

103. Jaap Spoor, Feer Verkade & Dirk Visser, *Auteursrecht. Auteursrecht, naburige rechten en databankenrecht* 404 (2011).
104. Hoge Raad 8 March 1957 (*Buma/De Vries*).
105. Gerechtshof Den Haag 4 September 2003, ECLI:NL:GHSGR:2003:AI5638 (*Scientology/XS4all and others*).
106. Vzr. Rechtbank Den Haag 12 March 1996, *AMI* 1996–5 (*Scientology/XS4all and others*). For an unofficial English translation, *see:* https://kspaink.home.xs4all.nl/cos/verd1eng.html (accessed 14 June 2019). Confirmed in: Rechtbank Amsterdam 9 June 1999, ECLI:NL:RBSGR:1999:AA1039 (*Scientology/XS4all and others*). And upheld in: Gerechtshof Den Haag 4 September 2003, ECLI:NL:GHSGR:2003:AI5638 (*Scientology/XS4all and others*).
107. Rechtbank Amsterdam 9 June 1999, ECLI:NL:RBSGR:1999:AA1039, para. 16.

decision in the so-called *Cable Pirates* case also applied to online communication.[108] In this decision, the Dutch Supreme Court held the operator of a broadcast system liable for a 'secondary' communication to the public of materials broadcast by cable pirates.[109] Seignette argued that the reasoning in the *Cable Pirates* decision should also apply to intermediary services that facilitate online peer-to-peer file-sharing of protected materials.[110] In contrast, Dommering argued that the liability of intermediaries should be considered on the basis of the general duty of care in tort law. According to Dommering, intermediaries should not be strictly liable for infringements under copyright law. Instead their involvement should be assessed based on culpability.[111] Likewise, Visser argued that the Supreme Court should have never held the cable organization liable for copyright infringement in the first place and instead should have used the general duty of care as a basis to consider the organization's liability. According to Visser, the liability of intermediaries should also be approached using the 'flexible' norms in tort law.[112]

In later case law, questions of intermediary liability were indeed generally dealt within the context of tort law's general duty of care. On the whole, general-purpose intermediaries were never held liable for the infringements of their users. Yet, in several decisions, the Dutch courts have held that only those providers who *systematically* and *structurally* facilitate copyright infringements can be liable for violating a duty of care. Courts have taken different factors into account to establish such a systematical and structural facilitation of copyright infringements.[113] They include objective or subjective knowledge of the infringements,[114] the intensity of the infringements,[115]

108. Kabelpiraten, *supra* n. 62.
109. These pirates used weak close-range transmitters to transmit broadcasts of pirated movies directly into the reception system of the Amsterdam cable television organization KTA. Since KTA could not be considered a part of the organization that was responsible for the initial transmission of the broadcasts by the cable pirates, KTA secondarily communicated the pirated movies to the public. KTA thus committed a copyright infringement. The fact that KTA failed to prevent the use of its equipment by others was essential to this finding.
110. Jacqueline Seignette, *Napster en de controle van de rechthebbende over de distributie van zijn werk*, AMI (2) 29 (2001).
111. Egbert Dommering, *De Auteursrechtelijke aansprakelijkheid van intermediars* 79 (Dirk Visser ed., 1998).
112. Dirk Visser, *'Napsteren', 'Gnutellen' en de afwezigheid van legale muziek op Internet*, Computerrecht (3) 131 (2001).
113. In particular with regard to the list of factors, De Vries noted that there exists uncertainty about the set of factors developed to determine when one 'systematically and structurally' facilitates the infringements as there is no one conclusive list of factors that need to be considered to establish such facilitation (Caroline de Vries, *Subjectieve verwijtbaarheid. Een toets om de aansprakelijkheid van internettussenpersonen voor het faciliteren van auteursrechtinbreuken te beoordelen*, AMI (1) 1, 3 (2012)). *Also see:* Bart van der Sloot, *De verantwoordelijkheid voorbij: de ISP op de stoel van de rechter*, Tijdschrift voor Internetrecht (5) 136 (2011).
114. Gerechtshof Amsterdam 16 March 2010, ECLI:NL:GHAMS:2010:BL7920, para. 3.10 (*ShareConnector*). For a discussion about objective and subjective standards *see:* De Vries, *supra* n. 113.
115. For instance: Gerechtshof Den Haag 15 November 2010, ECLI:NL:GHSGR:2010:BO3980, para. 6.3 (*FTD/Eyeworks*), considering that 80% to 96% of the entertainment files on Usenet that FTD linked to were unauthorized.

the profits earned,[116] and the interventions one makes to enable users to find certain works.[117]

The *Zoekmp3.nl* case offers an example of how these factors may play out.[118] This case dealt with the liability of an operator of a dedicated MP3 search engine. Since the operator knew that the search engine would 'systematically and structurally' refer to unauthorized MP3 files, the operator was liable for violating the general duty of care.[119] General search engines, such as Google's, are unlikely to be covered by this criterion, since they may incidentally refer to infringing materials, and not 'systematically and structurally' as was the case in the *Zoekmp3.nl* case.

Another example may be the 2009 *Mininova* case, which dealt with the liability of a torrent platform, and in which the Amsterdam District Court held that the platform provider itself did not commit a copyright infringement.[120] The Court stated that the simple fact that the platform offered an opportunity for others to infringe is not itself sufficient to conclude that the provider communicated the infringing materials to the public.[121] The platform, however, did act tortiously by facilitating, inducing, and profiting from the infringements of its users.

Linking to copyrighted material too has long been considered irrelevant under Dutch copyright law. While clicking on a link and downloading the linked-to materials may amount to a reproduction, offering a link itself is not a reproduction.[122] In the late 1990s, some scholars argued that a link to copyrighted material should be considered a communication to the public.[123] However, most legal scholars agreed that linking to copyrighted materials should not constitute a communication to the public.[124] Hyperlinks were to be compared to footnotes, which only referred to information that is available elsewhere. If hyperlinks were to be considered a communication to the public, the consequence would be that every link, in principle, would require the permission of the copyright owner of the linked-to materials. This would mean the end of the Internet as a space of interconnected information.

116. Gerechtshof Amsterdam 15 June 2006, ECLI:NL:GHAMS:2006:AX7579, para. 4.14 (*ZoekMP3*); Vzr. Rechtbank Den Haag 22 March 2011, ECLI:NL:RBSGR:2011:BS8763, para. 4.33 (*Premier League/MyP2P*). Although structurally and systematically facilitating copyright infringement as a hobby has also been considered a violation of a duty of care: *ShareConnector, supra* n. 114.
117. For instance: Rechtbank Haarlem 28 September 2011, HA ZA 09-2443, para. 4.23 (*FTD/Brein*), holding that FTD, by offering a forum and categorizing links to files on Usenet, made it easier to find the unauthorized files.
118. *ZoekMP3, supra* n. 116.
119. *ZoekMP3, supra* n. 116, at para. 4.11.
120. Brein/Mininova, *supra* n. 29 (Brein/Mininova).
121. Brein/Mininova, *supra* n. 29, at para. 4.4 (Brein/Mininova).
122. Madeleine de Cock Buning & Marike Vermeer, *Hyperlinks en metatags; meeliften in cyberspace*, Computerrecht (4) 166 (1999); Spoor, Verkade & Visser, *supra* n. 103.
123. Maurice H.M. Schellekens & Gijsbert Brunt, *Auteursrecht in Digiworld* (Wolter Wefers Bettink ed., 1996); Gijsbert Brunt, *Is de hyperlink, hyper link*, IT en Recht (1) 1 (1997).
124. Dirk Visser, *The Economic Rights Involved: Report on the Netherlands* (Marcel Dellebeke ed., 1997). Bernt Hugenholtz, Het Internet: het auteursrecht voorbij? Preadvies 8 (1998); Remy Chavannes, *Hype of echt link: de hyperlinkaansprakelijkheid van informatieaanbieders, internetaanbieders en zoekmachines*, JAVI (1) 2 (2003).

In Dutch case law, linking was generally considered *not* to be a communication of the linked-to materials to the public.[125] Also in cases concerning more indirect 'links', through which files may be located on a peer-to-peer file-sharing network, Dutch courts have held that there is no communication to the public.[126] The entities linking to such files generally do not store the files they link to, nor do they play a role in the transmission of those files. Instead, they could be liable for the structural facilitation of the infringements of their users.

Primary liability for infringements may come into play if the intermediary manually edits or categorizes the content that is uploaded by others to its platform. Moving erotic videos to a special 'xxx' category on the platform was one of the factors that led a Dutch District Court to believe that the video hosting provider communicated those videos to the public.[127] Another example may be the active moderation done by forum moderators, which has led a Dutch court to conclude that the owner of the forum was liable for the infringing materials posted to the forum.[128]

[C] The Influence of *The Pirate Bay* and *GS Media*

The CJEU's decision in *The Pirate Bay* is bound to have extensive consequences for the Dutch approach towards secondary liability in peer-to-peer file-sharing cases.[129] In this decision, the CJEU de facto harmonized the standard to assess secondary liability for peer-to-peer file-sharing.[130] In *The Pirate Bay*, the CJEU held that the operator of such a platform is liable as a copyright infringer with regard to the materials communicated on the BitTorrent file-sharing network. As a consequence, the Dutch courts can no longer apply their duty of care analysis to those who operate peer-to-peer file-sharing platforms, which enabled culpability to be considered, i.e., the involvement of the person in the infringement of another.

Instead, they must consider whether the exclusive right to communicate to the public has been infringed based on the factors that the CJEU developed in its case law on the right of communication to the public. Dutch courts will now have to look at the facilitation of infringements through a copyright law lens, which is something they had in fact rejected due to its strict liability nature. What is striking in that respect is that the CJEU in its case law has also softened the edges of the copyright infringement standard, at least with respect to cases involving the facilitation of infringements. The two perspectives thus seem to converge. The facilitation of copyright infringements must

125. Dirk Visser, *Openbaar maken met ketchup*, AMI (2) 41, 49 (2013).
126. *Brein/Mininova*, *supra* n. 29 (*Brein/Mininova*). Gerechtshof Den Bosch 12 January 2010, ECLI:NL:GHSHE:2010:BM9205, para. 4.98 (*C More/MyP2P*); Rechtbank Den Haag 5 January 2007, *Computerrecht* 2007, 46 (*Brein/KPN*); Vzr. Rechtbank Amsterdam 2009, KG ZA 09-1809 WT/RV, para. 5.6, *AMI* 2010, 2 (*Neij c.s./Brein*); Rechtbank Den Haag 2012, 412217 / HA ZA 12-153, para. 4.4 (*Brein/XSNetworks*); *ShareConnector*, *supra* n. 114; *FTD/Eyeworks*, *supra* n. 115.
127. Rechtbank Amsterdam 24 November 2010, ECLI:NL:RBAMS:2010:BP6880, para. 4.21 (*Kim Holland/123video*).
128. Rechtbank Den Haag 16 January 2013, IEPT20130116 (*Dijkstra/Brandweerforum*).
129. *GS Media v. Sanoma Media Netherlands and others*, *supra* n. 32.
130. *See* section §3.03[G].

no longer be assessed on the basis of the general duty of care in Dutch tort law. Instead, such facilitation has become an issue of copyright law. Yet, an assessment of whether an infringement has occurred, more specifically the infringement of the right of communication to the public, requires consideration of the role that facilitators play and the knowledge they have of the infringements of others. In that sense, culpability now appears to play a role under the infringement standard in EU copyright law as well.

Still, the above is not an admission that nothing will change. From the perspective of copyright owners, the CJEU's decision in *The Pirate Bay* may be a welcome extension of (Dutch) copyright law. The enforcement mechanisms that are only available in intellectual property cases will be available regarding facilitators of infringements as well. It will also be easier to involve intermediaries in the enforcement against the providers of such platforms.[131] Article 26d of the Dutch Copyright Act enables the courts to order intermediaries to stop providing their service to *infringers*.[132] It does not apply in cases of violations of the general duty of care in Dutch tort law.[133] Hence, by extending the scope of the exclusive right to communicate works to the public, the responsibilities that intermediaries have may be extended as well.

Just as with the facilitation of peer-to-peer file-sharing, the CJEU's decisions in *Svensson* and *GS Media* require a change in the Dutch way of thinking about hyperlinks.[134] After these decisions, links to unauthorized materials must, under certain circumstances, be considered a communication to the public. As the Dutch Supreme Court's Advocate General Van Peursem noted in the Dutch proceedings in the *GS Media* case: *Svensson* has turned Dutch copyright law 'on its head'.[135] After these decisions, the act of linking to unauthorized materials will have to be considered by the Dutch courts under copyright norms. Moreover, this issue has become an issue of EU copyright law.

§4.05 LIABILITY EXEMPTIONS FOR INTERMEDIARIES

The liability exemptions introduced in the E-Commerce Directive were implemented in Article 6:196c of the Dutch Civil Code. This section first deals with some general aspects of the Dutch implementation of the liability (section §4.05[A]). We will then discuss the mere conduit activity, caching, and hosting liability exemptions in the Dutch Civil Code (sections §4.05[B] to §4.05[D]).

131. The rules in the Enforcement Directive and its Dutch implementation will now apply. For example, the Dutch Supreme Court has held that the fact that The Pirate Bay itself infringes on copyrights as well is relevant in striking a balance between the different interests (*Brein/Ziggo & XS4ALL*, *supra* n. 70, at para. 5.3.2).
132. *See* section §4.06.
133. For instance: *FTD/Eyeworks*, *supra* n. 115.
134. CJEU 13 February 2014, ECLI:EU:C:2014:76 (*Nils Svensson and others v. Retriever Sverige*); *GS Media v. Sanoma Media Netherlands and others*, *supra* n. 32. *See* section §3.03[G] for a discussion of these decisions.
135. Opinion of AG Van Peursem 9 January 2015, ECLI:NL:PHR:2015:7, para. 2.3.16 (*GS Media v. Sanoma and others*).

As explained in the previous chapter on the EU legal framework, the hosting liability exemption in the E-Commerce Directive incentivizes the adoption of notice-and-takedown systems by intermediaries. While the Dutch legislator did not adopt a statutory regime on notice-and-takedown, the Dutch government promoted a self-regulatory regime. The Code of Conduct on Notice and Takedown that was the result of this effort is also discussed here (§4.05[D][2]).

[A] General Aspects

In the years preceding the adoption of the E-Commerce Directive, the Dutch government contemplated the possibility of laying down a statutory regime for the liability of intermediaries, in particular Internet access providers, for unlawful online activities and information. Nevertheless, the Dutch government considered that tort law, and its open-ended wording of the general duty of care, would be sufficient to determine the liability and responsibilities of intermediaries in the online environment.[136] When the E-Commerce Directive was drafted, the Dutch government objected against the adoption of liability exemptions: 'the proposed rules on liability do not fit in the balanced and technology-independent system of Dutch private and criminal law'.[137]

The E-Commerce Directive nonetheless introduced liability exemptions, which had to be implemented by the Dutch legislator. These liability exemptions were implemented in Article 6:196c of the Dutch Civil Code. This article is part of a broader section on tort law in the Dutch Civil Code. In line with the E-Commerce Directive, the applicability of the liability exemptions depends on the intermediary being a provider of information society services.[138] Article 6:196c sets out the conditions under which intermediaries are not to be held liable for damages. If an intermediary fails to meet the requirements determined in Article 6:196c, liability is not automatically incurred. Liability then has to be based on the general rules of tort law.[139]

Article 6:196c of the Dutch Civil Code follows the distinction made in the E-Commerce Directive between mere conduit activity, caching, and hosting. Article 6:196c, however, does not explicitly refer to these activities by the name they were given in the E-Commerce Directive. Instead, Article 6:196c contains descriptions of these activities. For instance, Article 6:196c(4) speaks of a service that consists of the storage of information provided by and at the request of others, and thereby implements the hosting liability exemption in Article 14 of the E-Commerce Directive.

In line with the Copyright Directive and the Enforcement Directive, intermediaries may still have a responsibility to act to stop or prevent infringements, or otherwise assist copyright owners in the enforcement of their rights.[140] Article 6:196c(5) of the Dutch Civil Code expressly states that the exemptions do not stand in the way of

136. Wetgeving voor de elektronische snelweg, Kamerstukken II 1997-1998, 25 880, nr. 2, p. 6, and 66.
137. Verslag van een Notaoverleg, *Kamerstukken II* 1998-1999, 25 880, nr. 5, p. 14.
138. Article 3:15d(3) of the Dutch Civil Code provides a definition of the term information society provider.
139. MvT, *Kamerstukken II* 2001-2002, 28 197, nr. 3, p. 47.
140. *See* section §3.05.

injunctions. The exemptions thus only protect the intermediary from liability for damages and not against injunctive relief.[141] The responsibilities that the intermediary may have are discussed in section §4.06.

[B] Mere Conduit

According to Article 6:196c(1) of the Dutch Civil Code, intermediaries that transmit materials provided by others, or that provide access to a communication network, are not liable for the materials that they transmit. Article 6:196c(2) also exempts the temporary storage that is necessary to transmit the materials. These provisions implement Article 12(1) and (2) of the E-Commerce Directive.

With these provisions, the Dutch legislator had in mind access providers which provide basic Internet connectivity and which enable people to send and receive information online. These providers generally do not have knowledge of the materials that they transmit or temporarily store in cache memories.[142] Even if the access provider has acquired such knowledge (for instance, through a notification), the provider cannot be held liable for the transmitted materials.[143] If, however, the intermediary wilfully cooperates with its users in unlawful activities, the intermediary is no longer shielded from liability for damages.[144]

For intermediaries to benefit from the mere conduit exemption, they must not have initiated the transmission of the materials. They should also not have decided to whom the materials are transmitted to. Nor should the intermediary have selected or changed the transmitted materials. Encryption of data and other technical measures that do not alter the materials as such do not deprive access providers of the mere conduit exemption.[145]

This exemption has not given rise to any case law that deals with its scope or the requirements for non-liability. It seems clear that under Dutch law, access providers cannot be held liable for damages when others commit copyright infringements while using their service. As to the responsibilities that these intermediaries may still have, such as the obligation to block particular websites, there is less certainty.[146]

[C] Caching

The liability exemption for caching in Article 13 of the E-Commerce Directive has been implemented in Article 6:196c(3) of the Dutch Civil Code. There is a long list of conditions that the intermediary needs to fulfil in order to benefit from the exemption: the intermediary must (i) not modify the information; (ii) comply with conditions on access to the information; (iii) comply with rules regarding the updating of the

141. Stokke/Marktplaats, *supra* n. 33.
142. MvT, *Kamerstukken II* 2001-2002, 28 197, nr. 3, p. 47.
143. MvT, *Kamerstukken II* 2001-2002, 28 197, nr. 3, p. 47.
144. MvT, *Kamerstukken II* 2001-2002, 28 197, nr. 3, p. 48.
145. MvT, *Kamerstukken II* 2001-2002, 28 197, nr. 3, p. 47.
146. *See* section §4.06[A][2].

information, specified in a manner that is widely recognized and used by industry; (iv) not interfere with the lawful use of technology, that is widely recognized and used by industry, to obtain data on the use of the information; and (v) must act expeditiously to remove or to disable access to the information it has stored upon obtaining actual knowledge of the fact that the information at the initial source of the transmission has been removed from the network, or access to it has been disabled, or that a court or an administrative authority has ordered such removal or disablement.

The liability of caching providers has never been at issue, nor has it led to any case law in the Netherlands. Specifically regarding the liability of caching intermediaries for copyright infringements, this exemption seems to be of little relevance. This exemption has been put in place not to shield against liability towards third parties, but to protect against liability towards the person who has provided the cached materials.[147] Hence, it concerns the potential liability of an intermediary vis-à-vis the person whose materials are cached and not of others who may be harmed by the temporary storage of those materials.

[D] Hosting

Article 6:196c(4) of the Dutch Civil Code provides that an intermediary which stores for others materials provided by others is not liable for those materials. This provision implements the hosting liability exemption of Article 14 of the E-Commerce Directive. The Dutch legislator primarily had in mind traditional hosting services, which consist of the provision of storage space that is needed to publish a website. In the explanatory memorandum to the law implementing the directive, the government spoke of 'the disk space that [the intermediary] makes available'.[148] The liability exemption would also apply to the information shared by users in chat services.[149]

In contrast to the liability exemption for mere conduit activity and caching, knowledge of the unlawful nature of the materials does play a role in the applicability of this liability exemption. An intermediary wanting to benefit from the hosting exemption should not have any knowledge of the unlawful activity or information. And in the case of a claim for damages, the intermediary also should not have known about the unlawful activity or information. If the intermediary knew or reasonably should have known about the unlawful activity or information in question, the intermediary should promptly remove the information or prevent access to it. According to the Dutch legislator, an intermediary acquires knowledge about the unlawful nature of information or activity when the intermediary is notified thereof.[150] The legislator also endorsed a rule that had developed in the case law entailing that only notices of which their accuracy cannot be reasonably doubted can constitute knowledge in sense of the

147. MvT, *Kamerstukken II* 2001-2002, 28 197, nr. 3, p. 48.
148. MvT, *Kamerstukken II* 2001-2002, 28 197, nr. 3, p. 49. *Also see*: Tina van der Linden, *Het is niet goed of het deugt niet: De juridische positie van internet tussenpersonen is onbevredigend!*, Tijdschrift voor Internetrecht (1) 4, 6 (2014).
149. *Kamerstukken I* 2003/04, 28 197, nr. C, p. 4.
150. MvT, *Kamerstukken II* 2001-2002, 28 197, nr. 3, p. 49.

liability exemption.[151] Notices cannot reasonably be doubted if they are given by a court, or if the information or activity in question is manifestly unlawful.[152] General knowledge that infringements are committed on the intermediary's platform does not suffice as knowledge under Article 6:196c(4) of the Dutch Civil Code. Nor does the law require from intermediaries that they actively search for infringements.[153]

In practice, it is more likely that an intermediary is confronted with an infringement notice by a copyright owner than a court order declaring that the stored information amounts to a copyright infringement. The question arises when, exactly, a notice can lead to the conclusion that the stored materials are manifestly unlawful. The answer to this question of course depends on the circumstances of a particular case.[154] In concrete situations, it can be difficult for an intermediary to assess whether the materials that it stores are manifestly unlawful.[155] Making available online a Hollywood blockbuster movie before it has even been released for distribution seems like a manifest copyright infringement. However, other forms of use of copyrighted material may not be such clear infringements.

When the intermediary knows or reasonably should know about the unlawfulness of the materials on its servers, it should promptly act to remove the unlawful materials. How promptly? That is a question that cannot be answered with great precision either. Removal should take place within a 'reasonable term' so that the intermediary can contact the person who has provided the materials and take action.[156] Dutch law currently does not provide any guidelines on this issue. Nevertheless, waiting several years to remove a torrent sharing website that structurally facilitated copyright infringements cannot be considered prompt removal.[157] The passage of several months before infringing content is removed is not quick enough either, even if the hosting provider receives many removal requests.[158] In a case concerning Google's blogging platform Blogger, the Den Bosch Court of Appeal held that replying to a takedown notice within one month seemed to be reasonable.[159]

151. MvT, *Kamerstukken II* 2001-2002, 28 197, nr. 3, p. 49.
152. MvT, *Kamerstukken II* 2001-2002, 28 197, nr. 3, p. 49. *Also see:* Gerechtshof Amsterdam 7 November 2002, ECLI:NL:GHAMS:2002:AF0091, paras 4.8–4.9 (*XS4ALL/Deutsche Bahn*), holding that a hosting provider should ask for more information when it is not clear, based on the notice, that the information is unlawful; Rechtbank Haarlem 14 May 2008, ECLI:NL:RBHAA:2008:BD1446, para. 4.8 (*A-Group*), holding that the fact that the Dutch government notified the unlawful content creates knowledge or awareness that the content is unlawful. *Also see:* Maurice Schellekens, *Aansprakelijkheid van internetaanbieders* 203 (2001).
153. *Stokke/Marktplaats*, *supra* n. 33, at para. 5.14.
154. Christiaan Alberdingk Thijm, *Wat is de zorgplicht van Hyves, XS4ALL en Marktplaats?*Ars Aequi (7/8) 573, 577 (2008).
155. A.P. de Wit, *De civielrechtelijke aansprakelijkheid van internetproviders (Deel I)*, Tijdschrift voor Internetrecht (2) 37, 40 (2009).
156. MvT, *Kamerstukken II* 2001-2002, 28 197, nr. 3, p. 50.
157. Rechtbank Den Haag 2012, 412217 / HA ZA 12-153 (*Brein/XSNetworks*).
158. Rechtbank Den Haag 1 November 2013, IEPT20131101 (*Eksmo/Ecatel*).
159. Gerechtshof Den Bosch 6 October 2015, ECLI:NL:GHSHE:2015:3904 (*Blogger*).

[1] Storage for Others

Recent Dutch case law signals that Dutch courts take 'storage for others' not as traditional web hosting only. For instance, a blogging platform on which users may set up and publish a blog must be considered as an exempted hosting service.[160] The provision of an early social network that enabled people to create their own profile pages has been considered hosting in the sense of the hosting exemption as well.[161]

Nevertheless, there is also one decision from 2009 in which a Dutch court displayed a particularly narrow understanding of the liability exemption for hosting providers. In a case about the torrent file-sharing platform Mininova and its liability for infringements, the Utrecht District Court considered that the hosting liability exemption was meant for *web hosting* activities only, and not for 'individual website owners'. The Court based this finding on the European Commission's 'First Report on the application of the E-Commerce Directive'.[162] In this 2003 report, the Commission touched upon the prohibition of general monitoring duties in Article 15 of the directive and explained that this prohibition is important 'as general monitoring of millions of sites and web pages would, in practical terms, be impossible'.[163] From this statement, the Dutch Court inferred that it was the European legislator's intention to exempt only traditional hosting service providers which host many webpages and not the operators of individual web pages. It thus seems that the technology-specific explanation of the European Commission resulted in the Dutch Court narrowly interpreting the liability exemption. It must be noted that this case was decided before the CJEU gave its ruling in the *Google France* case, which clarified that the exemption does apply not only to traditional hosting but also to websites offering a platform to others.[164]

The liability exemption for hosting may also apply to forums or message boards on which users may post information. However, if these providers moderate or otherwise check the content that is uploaded by users, Dutch courts have held that these providers are no longer protected by the exemption as they have actively engaged with user-provided content.[165] Also, determining who has access to the forum and using the forum for one's own activities can lead to the exemption being lost.[166] Here it thus seems that passivity and not removing unlawful materials until a concrete notice

160. Vzr. Rechtbank Den Haag 23 September 2015, ECLI:NL:RBDHA:2015:11276, para. 4.4 (*Verborgen camera*).
161. Vzr. Rechtbank Arnhem 10 January 2008, ECLI:NL:RBARN:2008:BC2736, para. 4.18 (*Hyves*).
162. Commission Report on the application of Directive 2000/31/EC of the European Parliament and of the Council of 8 June 2000 on certain legal aspects of information society services, in particular electronic commerce, in the Internal Market (Directive on electronic commerce), COM 2003/702.
163. Commission Report, *supra* n. 162, at para. 72.
164. CJEU 23 March 2010, ECLI:EU:C:2010:159 (*Google France v. Louis Vuitton Malletier*). For a discussion of this decision, *see* section §3.04[G][1].
165. For instance: Vzr. Rechtbank Amsterdam 12 March 2009, ECLI:NL:RBAMS:2009.BH7529 (*internetoplichting.nl*), Vzr. Rechtbank Noord-Nederland 3 July 2013, ECLI:NL:RBNNE:2013:3992 (*waldnet.nl*). *Also see* on a video hosting platform: *Kim Holland/123video*, *supra* n. 127.
166. Vzr. Rechtbank Amsterdam 1 November 2007, ECLI:NL:RBAMS:2007:BB6926 (*Stichting Martijn*).

is received is a better strategy than actively trying to monitor for such unlawful materials. Those who take responsibility for their platforms thus seem to be 'punished' with losing the liability exemption. Several commentators have pointed to this undesirable consequence of the liability exemption's focus on the passivity of the intermediary.[167]

The hosting liability exemption also applies to an online market platform, such as the Dutch website 'Marktplaats'. In a case concerning the platform's liability, the Leeuwarden Court of Appeal heavily relied on the CJEU's decision in *L'Oréal v. eBay* and held that the Dutch platform is protected as a hosting service provider against liability for infringements by its users.[168] The Dutch Court considered that the fact that Marktplaats proactively checked advertisements for unlawful material did not detract from the applicability of the hosting liability exemption. The intermediary's neutral position was not harmed by removing advertisements after receiving a notice, or by monitoring its platform for unlawful and unwanted information. According to the Court, the E-Commerce Directive's liability regime effectively requires the removal of materials. The directive also allows for specific monitoring duties. If, according to the Court, the removal of material would result in an intermediary losing the protection offered by the liability exemption, this would go against the broader system in the E-Commerce Directive. Hence, the Court concluded that the online market platform's removal and the monitoring of user-provided content did not deprive it of protection.

The automatic nature of the processing of the stored information is a decisive factor in the applicability of the hosting liability exemption. Editing submitted texts and scanning and uploading photos can deprive a service provider of protection by the liability exemption.[169] A question that remains is whether the exemption applies to processing that does not directly involve human interaction, but that is done by algorithms that nevertheless represent human choices. Human intervention in the algorithm has led at least one Dutch court to decide that the operator of the website in question could not be protected by the hosting liability exemption. In this case, dealing with infringing materials that were placed on a platform for user-provided news articles, the Court held that the algorithm was programmed in a way that reflected decisions regarding which articles would be placed on the front page.[170] The Court also deemed it to be relevant that there was additional software available that would enable the algorithm to make distinctions between infringing and non-infringing materials, which would prevent infringing materials from being promoted to the front page. The operator of the website had not made use of this software because it was too expensive.

---

167. Van der Linden, *supra* n. 148; Arnoud Engelfriet, *Naar een passend beschermingsregime voor forumbeheerders en bloggers*, Tijdschrift voor Internetrecht (3) 77 (2009); Lodder in his note to Gerechtshof Leeuwarden 22 May 2012, ECLI:NL:GHLEE:2012:BW6296, CR 2015, 155. On this subject, the European Commission has highlighted in its 2017 communication on 'Tackling Illegal Content Online' that voluntary and proactive measures should not lead to the loss of the liability exemption (COM 2017/555, pp. 11–12).
168. CJEU 12 July 2011, ECLI:EU:C:2011:474 (*L'Oréal and others v. eBay*).
169. For instance: Rechtbank Den Bosch 11 January 2006, ECLI:NL:RBSHE:2006:AU9504 (*Pevry Press*).
170. Rechtbank Amsterdam 18 December 2013, HA EXPL 13-176 (*De Nieuwe Krant*).

The position of search engines is not specifically addressed in Dutch law and is assessed on the basis of general rules of tort law.[171] It is unlikely that the hosting liability exemption would apply to these providers as search engines do not store information at the request of others. Instead, they refer to information that is available elsewhere. In this sense, there is also a broader uncertainty as to the liability position of intermediaries providing curatorial functions with copyrighted materials. Especially if they actively engage with available information through algorithms, which may jeopardize their 'neutrality' or 'passiveness'.[172]

Specifically regarding content hosting platform, Dutch law will have to be adapted to reflect the stricter liability regime in Article 17 of the DSM Directive.[173] The liability exemption in Article 6:196c(4) of the Dutch Civil Code can then no longer apply to these platforms. The Netherlands will have to implement the stricter liability regime by 7 June 2021.[174]

[2] Notice-and-Takedown

As has been noted in Chapter 3, the E-Commerce Directive incentivizes the adoption of notice-and-takedown systems by intermediaries.[175] The Dutch implementation of this exemption also promotes the adoption of such systems. At least one Dutch court has held that the availability of an efficient notice-and-takedown system is sufficient to meet the liability exemption's requirement of prompt removal.[176] At the same time, if a notice-and-takedown system is in place, copyright owners are still allowed to contact the intermediary by other means in order to alert that intermediary.[177] In other words, copyright owners are not obliged to use the notice-and-takedown system to notify the intermediary of infringing materials.

It has also been noted in Chapter 3 that notice-and-takedown systems can be problematic from the perspective of the freedom of expression of Internet users.[178] Since non-removal exposes the intermediary to liability, the incentive to remove may be greater than the incentive to leave the content in place. The Dutch legislator acknowledged that a hosting service provider might have to choose between two evils. On the one hand, the provider risks liability for the unlawful information or activities;

171. Joris van Hoboken, *De aansprakelijkheid van zoekmachines. Uitzondering zonder regels of regels zonder uitzondering?*, Computerrecht (1) 15 (2008); Leonie Siemerink, *IE(-rechten), P2P en ISP: handhaving van auteursrechten op internet nog mogelijk?*, Maandblad voor Vermogensrecht (7/8) 179, 181 (2008).
172. Gerechtshof Amsterdam 7 March 2017, ECLI:NL:GHAMS:2017:739 (*Skyscanner/Stiching Reclame Code*). *Also see:* Veerle van Druenen, *De verantwoordelijkheid van vergelijkingssites*, Computerrecht (1) 14, 20 (2016).
173. Directive (EU) 2019/790 of the European Parliament and of the Council of 17 April 2019 on copyright and related rights in the Digital Single Market and amending Directives 96/9/EC and 2001/29/EC (OJ 2019, L 130/91). *See* section §3.05[E].
174. Article 29(1) of the DSM Directive.
175. *See* section §3.04[G][2].
176. Gerechtshof Amsterdam 19 August 2014, ECLI:NL:GHAMS:2014:3435, para. 3.4.10, *Computerrecht* 2014/181, with note by Maurice H.M. Schellekens (*NSE/Brein*).
177. *Blogger, supra* n. 159.
178. *See* section §3.04[G][2].

on the other hand, the provider has a contractual duty to provide a service to its client. Yet, the legislator did not consider this to be an insurmountable problem because deletion or the prevention of access is only required when there are no reasonable doubts as to the unlawfulness of the materials.[179]

Interestingly, the Dutch legislator hinted at the possibility of obtaining an indemnification from the notifying person regarding the liability that might arise vis-à-vis the person who has provided the allegedly unlawful information.[180] Such indemnifications would incentivize those who notify to carefully consider whether sending a takedown notice is appropriate. However, without any legal obligations or other incentives to agree upon such indemnifications, it is unlikely that copyright owners and other entities with an interest in the enforcement of copyrights would actually indemnify the intermediary in the case of an erroneous removal.[181]

Dutch law contains no provisions on the removal of information by intermediaries. This 'gap' in the law has created uncertainties regarding the procedure that is to be followed, the conditions under which materials have to be removed, and the timing of such removal. The 2008 'Code of Conduct on Notice and Takedown' aimed to fill this gap and provides for a procedure for notice-and-takedown. The code of conduct was created by the *Nationale Infrastructuur ter bestrijding van Cybercrime* (NICC – National Infrastructure to fight Cybercrime), the Dutch government, businesses and interest groups.[182] It is currently administered by the *Platform voor de InformatieSamenleving* (ECP – Platform for the InformationSociety), which is an independent platform for businesses, Dutch government organizations, and interest groups, and that aims to foster the use of information technologies in Dutch society.[183]

The code of conduct applies to any kind of unlawful online information or activity and mixes elements of a notice-and-takedown and a notice-and-notice system. In essence, the code requires endorsing parties to take down materials that are manifestly unlawful. If the materials are not manifestly unlawful, the intermediary is required to inform the person that filed the notice and give an explanation. If the intermediary is not able to assess the lawfulness of the materials, the content provider is to be informed about the notice and is requested to contact the person that filed the notice. These parties then need to come to an agreement without the intermediary's involvement.[184]

The code prescribes the information that the person notifying an intermediary must provide to that intermediary:

- the contact details of the notifying person;
- information that is needed by the intermediary to assess the materials, which includes at least the URL at which that information can be found;

179. MvT, *Kamerstukken II* 2001-2002, 28 197, nr. 3, p. 49. *See* section §4.05[D] for a discussion.
180. MvT, *Kamerstukken II* 2001-2002, 28 197, nr. 3, p. 50.
181. *Also see: XS4ALL/Deutsche Bahn, supra* n. 152, holding that the hosting provider in question could not require an indemnification before the removal of the contested content.
182. The code is available at: http://www.ecp-epn.nl/sites/default/files/GedragscodeNTD-NL.pdf (accessed 14 June 2019). An English version is available at: http://www.ecp-epn.nl/sites/default/files/NTD_Gedragscode_Engels.pdf (accessed 14 June 2019).
183. https://ecp.nl (accessed 14 June 2019).
184. Article 6 of the Code of Conduct.

- an explanation about why the materials are unlawful.[185]

According to the code, the intermediary may request an indemnification from the person sending the notice against potential claims of the person whose materials are removed.[186] The voluntary nature of both the code and in particular also this provision turn the indemnification into a mere possibility only.

Another aspect that the code leaves unregulated is the promptness of the removal. While the code prescribes that intermediaries share information about their removal procedure and the terms within which notices are dealt with, the code provides no rules on timing.[187] The explanatory memorandum to the code does mention that a term of five working days would be reasonable if the materials are not manifestly unlawful. If the materials are manifestly unlawful, intermediaries are expected to quickly remove these materials.

Endorsement of the code is voluntary. According to the explanatory memorandum to the code, 'there can be no formal enforcement in the case of noncompliance'.[188] Nevertheless, self-regulatory codes can be used as normative input by courts in proceedings based on open norms such as the general duty of care in Dutch tort law.[189] It is then imperative for courts to assess the extent to which a code actually represents the norms of a particular group, and whether the interests of others who are affected by the code are sufficiently considered.[190]

There is no formal list of members adhering to the code of conduct. Parties that are known to endorse the code of conduct are listed on the ECP's website.[191] Not only the Internet access provider KPN, the Dutch Hosting Service Provider Association, NLKabel (an association of cable network providers) but also service providers such as Google and Marktplaats/eBay have endorsed the code. Brein, which represents the entertainment industry, and the anti-counterfeiting organization SNB-react endorse the code as well. The Dutch civil liberties organization Bits of Freedom participated in the setting up of the code of conduct[192] but is not listed as a party that supports the code.

---

185. Article 4 of the Code of Conduct.
186. Article 4(d) of the Code of Conduct.
187. Article 3(a) of the Code of Conduct.
188. Code of Conduct, p. 7.
189. Ivo Giesen, *Alternatieve regelgeving en privaatrecht* 68 (2007). Also, the Dutch Supreme Court in *Achmea/Rijnberg* considered the contents of a code of conduct to determine whether an insurance company had breached the right to privacy of an insured person (Hoge Raad 18 April 2014, ECLI:NL:HR:2014:942). *See* on this decision: Marie-Claire Menting, *(R)Evolutie in het privaatrecht? Enkele beschouwingen over de rol van private regelgeving en de invloed van het EVRM naar aanleiding van HR Achmea/Rijnberg*, Nederlands Tijdschrift voor Burgerlijk Recht (4) 104 (2015).
190. In one case, the Rotterdam District Court held that a municipal archive could not require a copyright owner to first notify the archive about infringements in accordance with the code of conduct. According to the Court, the archive could not be considered an intermediary in the sense of Article 6:196c of the Dutch Civil Code (Rechtbank Amsterdam 2014, ECLI:NL:RBAMS:2014:6959, para. 4.24 (*Pictoright/Gemeente Rotterdam*)).
191. For a list of endorsements, *see:* https://ecp.nl/activiteiten/werkgroep-notice-and-takedown (accessed 14 June 2019).
192. *Kamerstukken II* 2003/04, 28 197, nr. 15, p. 4.

The extent to which the code of conduct is actually adopted by intermediaries is not clear. The code requires that intermediaries using the code must make themselves known.[193] Yet, there seems to be no clear duty in the code to communicate to users that the intermediary adheres to the code. Google, which is listed as an endorsing party, does not mention the code of conduct but states that it follows the US DMCA procedure.[194] A 2013 draft response of the Dutch government to the European Commission Green Paper 'Preparing for a Fully Converged Audiovisual World: Growth, Creation and Values' states that the procedure in the code of conduct is used by 90% of the Dutch Internet services market.[195] Yet that number certainly cannot be accounted for or further quantified. In contrast, research conducted in 2012 by the Dutch civil liberties organization Bits of Freedom into a sample of the removal policies of web hosting providers suggests that the code is all but universally adopted among hosting providers.[196]

While the self-regulatory code is a flexible means to lay down a procedure for notice-and-take-down, the above also shows that such self-regulatory mechanisms can be lacking in transparency. The code does not enable transparency as to its use and users. It does not require any transparency about requests that intermediaries receive, nor does it promote openness about the reasons why materials have been removed (e.g., copyright infringement) and the frequency of removal. Such transparency would make it possible for the government, civil society, and academia to keep an eye on removal processes, to assess its effectiveness, and to determine whether the code actually strikes a fair balance between the interests of different stakeholders.

§4.06 RESPONSIBILITIES OF INTERMEDIARIES

Regardless of the liability exemptions in Article 6:196c of the Dutch Civil Code, intermediaries can be subject to court orders that require them to assist copyright owners in the enforcement of their rights. Article 6:196c(5) of the Dutch Civil Code expressly leaves open this possibility of injunctive relief.

In this section, we will discuss the possibility for copyright owners to request Dutch courts to issue an injunction against intermediaries when their services are used to infringe a copyright (section §4.06[A]). And we will consider another duty that has developed independently from the EU legal framework, which is the duty to release identifying information about alleged infringers (section §4.06[B]).

193. Article 7(a) of the Code of Conduct.

194. *See* 'Veelgestelde vragen over het auteursrecht', https://perma.cc/TXZ5-32H3 (accessed 14 June 2019).

195. Technische informatie over de publicatie Nederlandse concept-reactie op het groenboek 'voorbereiding op een volledig geconvergeerde audiovisuele wereld', Vergaderjaar 2012–2013 Bijlage bij Kamerstuk 22112 nr. 1659.

196. Bits of Freedom, *Overgeleverd aan willekeur* (2013). This research concerned the notice-and-takedown procedure of ten selected hosting providers.

[A] Intermediaries Whose Services Are Used to Infringe

Article 8(3) of the Copyright Directive requires Member States to 'ensure that rightholders are in a position to apply for an injunction against intermediaries whose services are used by a third party to infringe a copyright or related right'. This provision was not explicitly implemented into Dutch law. According to the Dutch legislator, injunctions could already be issued against intermediaries on the basis of Dutch tort law.[197]

However, a separate copyright-specific basis for injunctions against intermediaries was added to the Dutch Copyright Act in 2007. Article 26d of the Dutch Copyright Act implements Article 11 of the Enforcement Directive, which requires that right owners are in a position to apply for an injunction against intermediaries whose services are used to infringe their intellectual property rights. The introduction of Article 26d in the Dutch Copyright Act significantly increased the possibilities for copyright owners to enforce their rights with the help of intermediaries. It enables intermediaries to be held accountable without them being at fault. This responsibility of the intermediary is not grounded in tort law and its general duty of care.[198] Rather it serves as an independent legal basis to require assistance from intermediaries in the enforcement of copyrights.

Article 26d of the Dutch Copyright Act offers a legal basis to require a hosting provider to terminate a hosting agreement and to remove infringing materials.[199] Such an order has been deemed appropriate in particular when the copyright infringer cannot be reached or has refused to remove the infringing materials.[200] But it may also apply to access providers which can be required to stop providing access to web pages containing infringing materials.[201]

In determining whether the requested injunction should be issued, Dutch courts have to take into account the degree in which the intermediary is involved in the infringement and the proportionality between the court order and the loss or damage that is suffered by the intermediary as a consequence thereof.[202] Although there appears to be no rule of subsidiarity in Article 26d of the Dutch Copyright Act, the explanatory memorandum states that Article 26d only applies when the copyright owner has no other means to redress the infringement.[203] If the copyright owner is in a position to sue the infringer as well, then the court should reject the request for an injunction against the intermediary.[204] Injunctions based on Article 26d must also meet the requirements set in the Copyright Directive and the Enforcement Directive. In line

197. *Kamerstukken II*, 2001/02, 28 482, nr. 3, p. 36 (MvT).
198. *NSE/Brein*, *supra* n. 176, at para. 3.6.8.
199. Eksmo/Ecatel, *supra* n. 158.
200. For example: Vzr. Rechtbank Den Haag 17 August 2016, ECLI:NL:RBDHA:2016:9605, para. 4.4 (*04stream.com*).
201. *See* sections §3.05[A] and §4.06[A][2].
202. MvT, *Kamerstukken II* 2005-2005, 30 392, nr. 3, p. 26.
203. MvT, *Kamerstukken II* 2005-2005, 30 392, nr. 3, p. 26.
204. MvT, *Kamerstukken II* 2005-2005, 30 392, nr. 3, p. 26.

with the CJEU's case law, Dutch courts must also make sure that injunctions strike a fair balance between the fundamental rights that are at issue.[205]

The Dutch legislator failed to explicitly implement Article 15(1) of the E-Commerce Directive, which prohibits general monitoring duties. It seems that the Dutch legislator considered Article 15(1) primarily as an instruction to Member State legislatures and disregarded the fact that courts too can be in a position to issue injunctions that amount to a general duty to monitor.[206] Nevertheless, after the CJEU's decision in *Scarlet v. Sabam*, in which the CJEU held that an injunction requiring filtering for infringing music files would amount to an impermissible general duty to monitor, it is clear that Dutch courts are bound by the prohibition in Article 15(1) as well.[207]

The CJEU's decisions in *GS Media* and *The Pirate Bay* are likely to widen the applicability of Article 26d of the Copyright Act. Strictly speaking, Article 26d of the Dutch Copyright Act only applies to services that are used for copyright *infringements*,[208] and not the structural facilitation of infringements for which one could have been liable under tort law's general duty of care.[209] Yet, after *GS Media* and *The Pirate Bay*, also the facilitation of another's infringement can be an infringement of the exclusive right of communication to the public and thus a copyright infringement. It will therefore become easier for copyright owners to claim assistance from intermediaries on the basis of Article 26d with regard to those who facilitate infringements, such as the operators of peer-to-peer file-sharing platforms.

[1] Filtering

No Dutch courts have yet required an intermediary to filter for infringing materials. In the earlier-mentioned *Marktplaats* decision, the Leeuwarden Court of Appeal considered a filtering system that would quarantine potentially infringing materials on the basis of a keyword filter, after which a manual check would take place to see if the materials actually infringe.[210] According to the Court, Article 15 of the E-Commerce Directive, prohibiting general monitoring duties, did not stand in the way of ordering the e-commerce platform to instal the filter system. The filter would not involve the surveillance of all users for illegal materials. Instead, the system would only filter out materials meeting particular criteria, which would then be manually checked, while

---

205. *See* section §3.05[C] on this fair balance. For instance, in the *Marktplaats* case, the Leeuwarden Court of Appeal underlined that Dutch courts, when interpreting Article 26d of the Dutch Copyright Act, must consider the aim of the Enforcement Directive, while also making sure that a fair balance is struck between the rights and interests of stakeholders (*Stokke/Marktplaats*, *supra* n. 33, at para. 7.13).
206. Tweede Kamer, vergaderjaar 2001–2002, 28 197, nr. 3, p. 27.
207. *Scarlet v. Sabam*, *supra* n. 72. For a confirmation, *see: NSE/Brein*, *supra* n. 176.
208. MvT, *Kamerstukken II* 2005-2005, 30 392, nr. 3, p. 26.
209. For an example of non-infringement and therefore the non-applicability of Article 26d of the Dutch Copyright Act, *see:* Rechtbank Den Haag 2 November 2011, ECLI:NL:RBSGR:2011:BU3223, para. 4.34 (*Real Networks*). *Also see: FTD/Eyeworks*, *supra* n. 115, at para. 6.8.
210. Stokke/Marktplaats, *supra* n. 33.

the rest of the materials provided by users would not be checked.[211] Still, the Court denied the injunction because the filtering system would be costly, while the enforcement costs of copyright owners decreased only marginally. Moreover, there was a chance that legitimate advertisements would be quarantined as well. Some advertisers would then have to wait longer for their advertisements to be published. This would make Marktplaats a less popular online market platform and would create a barrier to legitimate trade.

While no filtering duties have been imposed on intermediaries in the Netherlands yet, Article 17 of the DSM Directive opens the door to duties that require from online platforms that they implement technologies to recognize and remove copyrighted materials in user-uploaded materials.[212] As such, Article 17 of the DSM Directive will have a great impact on what can be expected from online platforms under future Dutch law.

[2] Blocking Websites

The question of whether access providers can be ordered to block websites containing infringing materials has been a hot topic of debate. In the Netherlands, the focus has been on the website of The Pirate Bay, which offers users a platform for sharing torrent-files. These torrent-files can be used to download files on the BitTorrent peer-to-peer file-sharing network.

In 2010, Brein started proceedings against a group of access providers and claimed that these intermediaries should block access to The Pirate Bay.[213] In these proceedings, the focus was primarily on the effectiveness of the injunction in question. As the District Court of The Hague had ordered the access providers to block access to The Pirate Bay, data could be collected about the effects that such an injunction has on user-infringements.[214] In 2014, the Court of Appeal considered that the blockade had been evaded by users as they used proxy-services to reach The Pirate Bay and to visit other torrent websites.[215] According to the Court of Appeal, the blockade was therefore ineffective. Although the injunction would be easy to implement and would cost almost nothing, the Court of Appeal nevertheless considered it an interference with the freedom to conduct a business. The access providers would be limited in their choice as to how they want to run their business. Given the ineffectiveness of the blockade and its inability to contribute to the protection of intellectual property rights, the Court held, based on the principle of proportionality, that the injunction would be an unjustified interference in the freedom to conduct a business. In this context, the Court also considered that Brein's focus on just one torrent website, which Brein considered a 'test case', did not detract from the ineffectiveness of the blockade.

211. *Stokke/Marktplaats*, *supra* n. 33, at para. 8.2.
212. *See* section §3.05[E].
213. Rechtbank Den Haag 11 January 2012, ECLI:NL:RBSGR:2012:BV0549, para. 1.1 (*Brein/Ziggo & XS4ALL*).
214. Rechtbank Den Haag 11 January 2012, ECLI:NL:RBSGR:2012:BV0549 (*Brein/Ziggo & XS4ALL*).
215. Gerechtshof Den Haag 28 January 2014, ECLI:NL:GHDHA:2014:88 (*Brein/Ziggo & XS4ALL*).

The case reached the Dutch Supreme Court, which gave its ruling in late 2015.[216] The Dutch Supreme Court held that the Court of Appeal had not applied the right standard regarding the effectiveness of the blockade.[217] Following the CJEU's 2014 decision in *UPC Telekabel*, the Dutch Supreme Court explained that the circumvention of a blockade does not by definition render the blockade ineffective.[218] Also, there was no need to claim that the websites of other torrent platforms had to be blocked for the blockade of The Pirate Bay to be effective.[219]

The Dutch Supreme Court referred questions to the CJEU with regard to the scope of the right of communication to the public. In essence, the Dutch Supreme Court asked whether The Pirate Bay itself communicated to the public the works shared on the peer-to-peer networks. If that was the case, there would be a stronger basis for a blockade on the basis of Article 26d of the Dutch Copyright Act. The answers came in 2017 when the CJEU held that The Pirate Bay indeed itself infringes copyrights as well.[220]

The CJEU's decision in *The Pirate Bay* has increased the chances of Brein obtaining a blocking injunction against Internet access providers in the Netherlands. Yet, the final verdict on the issue of website blocking is unlikely to be issued anytime soon. The Dutch Supreme Court had already ruled that the Court of Appeal had not applied the right effectiveness test. The chances are that the Dutch Supreme Court will require the Court of Appeal to assess the blocking injunction under the standard set in *UPC Telekabel*.[221] Because the Court of Appeal's decision was primarily concerned with the effectiveness of the blocking injunction, the decision did not deal with the freedom of expression aspects that must be considered as well. Blocking a platform like The Pirate Bay may have the effect that some legitimate materials that are shared through this platform and the materials on the platform's website itself are blocked as well. The CJEU's position on this issue of overblocking in *UPC Telekabel* is not completely clear.[222] On the one hand, the Court expressed in quite absolutist terms that no legitimate materials can be blocked. On the other hand, the Court expressed that a blockade must '*not unnecessarily*' deprive Internet users of access to lawful materials, which seems to imply a test of proportionality.[223] It could well be that questions have to be referred to the CJEU once again in order to clarify the extent to which blocking legitimate materials plays in the overall analysis of blocking injunctions.

Parallel to these legal proceedings, the Dutch Ministry of Justice has facilitated dialogues between copyright owners and access providers to discuss the possibilities of

216. Brein/Ziggo & XS4ALL, *supra* n. 70.
217. *Brein/Ziggo & XS4ALL*, *supra* n. 70, at para. 4.4.2.
218. *Brein/Ziggo & XS4ALL*, *supra* n. 70, at paras 4.4.2–4.4.6. *See* section §3.05[C][4] for a discussion of *UPC Telekabel*.
219. *Brein/Ziggo & XS4ALL*, *supra* n. 70, at para. 4.4.3.
220. *Stichting Brein v. Ziggo BV and XS4ALL Internet*, *supra* n. 32. For a discussion of this decision, *see* section §3.03[D][1].
221. *UPC Telekabel Wien v. Constantin Film Verleih and Wega Filmproduktionsgesellschaft*, *supra* n. 72.
222. *See* section §3.05[C][4].
223. *UPC Telekabel Wien v. Constantin Film Verleih and Wega Filmproduktionsgesellschaft*, *supra* n. 72.

improving access to licensed materials and educating the public about downloading from (il)legal sources.[224] In January 2017, copyright owners from the audiovisual sector launched a website and an app to direct consumers to outlets where they can watch films legally, such as on Netflix.[225] These copyright owners also started a media campaign to promote this new platform. Access providers have offered to promote the website and the apps in their communications with their customers. The initial costs of developing and promoting the platform amounted to EUR 600,000. The Dutch Ministry of Education, Culture and Science has granted a subsidy of EUR 100,000 and the access providers have pledged a further EUR 25,000. It remains to be seen what the effects of this educational campaign will be.

Although the above initiative appears to be the beginning of a meaningful cooperation between copyright owners and access providers, these stakeholders have not come to an agreement with respect to the enforcement of copyrights.[226] Both groups are still involved in legal proceedings, including the proceedings concerning The Pirate Bay, which does not appear to foster a cooperative mindset. Moreover, both groups of stakeholders have indicated that they also wanted to wait for the developments at the EU level, most notably the revision of the 2004 Enforcement Directive.

In sum, proceedings on the duty of access providers to block access to The Pirate Bay are still ongoing. After eight years of court proceedings, it could well be that it may still take some time until we have a definitive answer as to whether Dutch access providers should block access to peer-to-peer file-sharing platforms. Attempts to bring copyright owners and access providers together to discuss enforcement possibilities have thus far yielded little effect. It appears that as long as it is unclear whether access providers have a duty to block access to torrent sharing platforms, Dutch stakeholders are unwilling to come to an agreement.

[B] Information Duties

Intermediaries, in particular access and hosting providers, may be in a position where they are the only ones that are capable of knowing the identity of a copyright infringer.[227] Obtaining information from them about the people that have used their services can be valuable to copyright owners wanting to enforce their rights.

Article 8(1)(c) of the Enforcement Directive requires Member States to enable copyright owners to obtain information about those who infringe copyrights from persons 'providing on a commercial scale services used in infringing activities'. These persons may include intermediaries whose services are used to commit an infringement. This article has been implemented into Dutch law in Article 28(9) of the Dutch

224. *Kamerstukken II*, 2016–2017, nr. 29 838, nr. 89.
225. This platform is available at: www.film.nl (accessed 14 June 2019).
226. In contrast, in Belgium, the Belgian Entertainment Association and a group of access providers work together and have started a court procedure in order for the access providers to be obliged to block a list of infringing websites. *See: 'L'industrie du film et de l'internet ensemble contre la piraterie'*, L'Echo 1 March 2018, https://perma.cc/2C75-BCBJ (accessed 14 June 2019).
227. *Also see* section §1.05[C] on the intermediary's ability to identify users.

Copyright Act and enables the courts to order intermediaries to provide identifying information about infringers.

Dutch case law also recognizes the possibility of requiring information about *alleged* infringers. This duty was confirmed in the 2005 Dutch Supreme Court decision in *Lycos v. Pessers*, a case dealing with a stamp collector who had been accused of fraud on a website hosted by Lycos.[228] After trying to contact the website owner, Pessers approached the hosting provider and requested identifying information about the website owner. The hosting provider refused to hand over the information. In its decision, the Dutch Supreme Court upheld that a hosting provider can violate a duty of care by not releasing identifying information about a website owner. Whether that duty is violated depends on the circumstances of the case.[229] The circumstances that need to be taken into account are the likelihood that the published information is unlawful, the interests of the harmed person, and the unavailability of less intrusive alternatives to identify the person in question. Also, the interests of the harmed person, the service provider, and the unidentified person must be weighed.

This form of liability is not based on the intermediary's involvement in the unlawful activities of others; it is rather based on the notion that intermediaries are often the only entities that are able to identify wrongdoers on the Internet. Intermediaries do not have a duty to actively inform other parties harmed by unlawful online conduct – that may imply a general duty to monitor. But if the intermediary is asked to identify an alleged wrongdoer, the intermediary may have a duty to release identifying information in a specific case.

The Dutch Supreme Court's decision in *Lycos v. Pessers* and the factors it developed in this decision have become a standard that is also applied in cases of copyright infringement. This duty may also apply when a third party does not infringe a copyright but nevertheless acts unlawfully by facilitating the infringements of others.[230] Of course, if there is no such infringement or facilitation thereof, there can be no duty to release information.[231] While *Lycos v. Pessers* concerned a hosting service provider, the standard set by the Dutch Supreme Court also applies to access providers which provide access to self-hosted infringing materials.[232] This seems reasonable and in line with the principle of subsidiarity that underlies *Lycos v. Pessers*, as in such cases only access providers can identify infringers. Also, a provider that hosts Usenet newsgroups has been ordered to identify users who posted copyrighted materials.[233]

The standard set in *Lycos v. Pessers* effectively requires that intermediaries assess the lawfulness of the information in question and the interests that are at stake when

228. Hoge Raad 25 November 2005, ECLI:NL:HR:2005:AU4019, para. 3.1 (*Lycos/Pessers*).
229. *Lycos/Pessers*, *supra* n. 228, at para. 5.2.2.
230. For example: Gerechtshof Amsterdam 3 July 2008, ECLI:NL:GHAMS:2008:BD6223 (*Leaseweb*).
231. For example: Vzr. Rechtbank Midden-Nederland 16 December 2015, ECLI:NL:RBMNE:2015:8974 (*Brein/Ziggo Blogger*, *supra* n. 159.
232. Rechtbank Den Haag 5 January 2007, *Computerrecht* 2007, 46 (*Brein/KPN*). *See* critically: Remy Chavannes, *Brein/KPN: het gevaar van een bagatel?*, Mediaforum (10) 174 (2007).
233. Vzr. Rechtbank Amsterdam 26 April 2017, ECLI:NL:RBAMS:2017:4038, para. 4.5 (*XS News/Abavia*). *Also see:* Vzr. Rechtbank Oost-Brabant 12 December 2016, ECLI:NL:RBOBR:2016:6846 (*Brein/Amazing Webshops*), highlighting also the scale of the infringements as a factor in assessing whether identifying data has to be released.

they are requested to release information about a customer.[234] The *alleged* copyright infringer or facilitator of infringements, who has a fundamental right to privacy and the freedom of expression, does not play a role in summary proceedings based on *Lycos v. Pessers*. Hence, a consideration of the interests and (fundamental) rights of customers depends on the intermediary's commitment to its customers and the intermediary's willingness to defend its customers in court.

In 2011, when the Dutch government presented an overview of its copyright law policies, it stated that it had plans to lay down a duty to release identifying information in statutory law. The government stated that identifying information should only be released in the case of large-scale infringements. The government also wanted to codify the factors developed by the Dutch Supreme Court in *Lycos v. Pessers*.[235] This would solidify the duty of care developed under tort law and give it a statutory basis in Dutch copyright law. This desire never materialized, however, which means that the Dutch Supreme Court's decision in *Lycos v Pessers* remains the starting point in cases on the release of identifying information about alleged infringers.[236]

CJEU case law, in particular the decisions in *Promusicae* and *Bonnier Audio*, revived discussions about the duty to release information about alleged infringers and its validity under EU law.[237] Dommering argued that the standard in *Lycos v. Pessers* no longer suffices.[238] In its case law, the CJEU has clarified that Member States must ensure that they interpret EU law in a way that allows for 'a fair balance' to be struck between the fundamental rights at issue. In *Lycos v. Pessers*, the Dutch Supreme Court may not have sufficiently considered those fundamental rights. A related issue is whether the duty to release data, and the weighing of interests that is based on the general duty of care in Dutch tort law, is a law that is sufficiently accessible and foreseeable. Article 15(1) of the ePrivacy Directive allows Member States to adopt '*legislative* measures' to restrict the scope of the rights and obligations in the directive.[239] Moreover, Article 8(2) of the European Convention on Human Rights requires that interferences with the right to respect for private and family life are 'in accordance

234. Remy Chavannes, *Effectief procederen tegen anonieme internetgebruikers*, Nederlands Juristenblad (29) 1 (2007); Bart van der Sloot, *De verantwoordelijkheid voorbij: de ISP op de stoel van de rechter*, Tijdschrift voor Internetrecht (5) 136 (2011).
235. *Kamerstukken II*, 2011(-2012), nr. 29 838, nr. 30, p. 38.
236. Vragen van het lid Verhoeven (D66) aan de Minister van Veiligheid en Justitie over het beboeten van illegale downloads en de vrijheid van het internet (ingezonden 4 december 2015). Antwoord van Minister Van der Steur (Veiligheid en Justitie) (ontvangen 18 december 2015). 2015–2016, aanhangselnummer 930.
237. CJEU 29 January 2008, ECLI:EU:C:2008:54 (*Promusicae v. Telefónica de España*); CJEU 19 April 2012, ECLI:EU:C:2012:219 (*Bonnier Audio and others v. Perfect Communication Sweden*).
238. Egbert Dommering, *De zaak Scarlet/Sabam. Naar een horizontale integratie van het auteursrecht*, AMI (2) 49 (2011); Sil Kingma, *De botsing tussen IE- en privacyrechten*, Privacy & Informatie (4) 170 (2012). *Cf*: Siemerink, *supra* n. 171, arguing that the *Promusicae* decision brought nothing new.
239. On this issue at least one Dutch lower court has held that Dutch tort law provides a sufficient legal basis to limit the rights in the ePrivacy Directive: Rechtbank Amsterdam 26 April 2017, ECLI:NL:RBAMS:2017:4038, para. 4.5 (*XS News/Abavia*).

with the law,' which requires, among other things, that such interferences must be foreseeable.[240]

§4.07 CONCLUSION

The aim of this chapter was to see how the EU legal framework on the liability of intermediaries works out at the Member State level, in particular with a view to assessing the 'future-proofness' of this framework. Besides being an element in the evaluation of the EU legal framework, this chapter also aimed to learn lessons from the Dutch experience with intermediary liability.

This chapter has highlighted the Dutch legislator's inclination towards flexible provisions of copyright law and intermediary liability. The Dutch courts, too, have displayed a willingness to interpret Dutch copyright law flexibly in order to accommodate new types of use that were not considered by the legislator. But this chapter has also shown that the EU legal framework's inflexibility may stand in the way of such flexible rules and interpretations at the Member State level. We have seen that the opening up of the list of limitations and exceptions in *Dior v. Evora* may be in conflict with the closed list of limitations and exceptions in the Copyright Directive.[241] Also, the use of fundamental rights as external balancing mechanisms creates tension with the Copyright Directive's and the CJEU's strict approach towards limitations and exceptions.

We also saw how the Dutch legislator struggled with the Copyright Directive's technical approach towards the reproduction right. Under that approach, everything that is technically a reproduction is also a reproduction in the legal sense.[242] In contrast, Dutch copyright law had always approached the concept of reproduction normatively, which enabled courts to take into account the facts and circumstances of a particular case and come to acceptable rulings, without the need for specific legislative interventions.

The CJEU's case law on the need to strike a fair balance between conflicting fundamental rights in cases of copyright enforcement appears to have a positive effect on Dutch law, in particular its ability to let courts balance the interests of relevant stakeholders.[243] This case law, combined with the Dutch Supreme Court's decision in *GS Media*, has reinvigorated the role that fundamental rights play in determining enforcement measures.

There may also be something to learn from the Dutch experience with fundamental rights and copyright law. Thus far, the CJEU's 'fair-balance' case law has focused on the enforcement of copyrights with the help of intermediaries only. Depending on the qualities of the *specific* enforcement measure in question and its

240. In cases in which Article 28(9) of the Dutch Copyright Act applies, this provision is likely to offer a sufficient legal basis for interference with the right to privacy. *See: 04stream.com, supra* n. 200.
241. *Dior/Evora, supra* n. 36. *See* section §4.03[B][1] for a discussion of this decision.
242. *See* section §3.03[D][1].
243. *See* section §3.05[C] on that CJEU case law. *Brein/Ziggo & XS4ALL, supra* n. 70.

effect on fundamental rights, the measure may or may not be permitted under EU law. Yet, under Dutch law, fundamental rights can stand in the way of enforcing a copyright *altogether*.[244] If such enforcement produces a result that is undesirable from the perspective of, for instance, the right to the freedom of expression, the copyright cannot be enforced. In the *Anne Frank Diaries* case, we saw that the freedom of science, protected in Article 13 of the EU Charter, enabled a Dutch court to put copyright enforcement to one side in order to accommodate new text-analysis technologies for scientific purposes.[245] This case is an example of how the consideration of fundamental rights may also offer the flexibility to accommodate new technological uses.

In the domain of secondary liability, we saw that the general duty of care in Dutch tort law has long offered an extra layer of protection that complemented copyright law's exclusive rights. It has enabled those who systematically and structurally facilitate the infringements of others to be held liable. The general duty of care operated alongside copyright law and the intermediary-specific provision in Article 26d of the Dutch Copyright Act. It has enabled copyright owners to protect their rights as piracy took new shapes and forms and these other specific rules had no reach. Yet, since the CJEU's case law in *GS Media* and *The Pirate Bay*, it now appears that also the facilitation of the infringements of others can under certain conditions be considered a copyright infringement as well.[246] These decisions have reiterated the relevance of the intermediary-specific provision in Article 26d and have made it easier to involve intermediaries in the enforcement against those who – essentially – facilitate the infringements of others.

From the perspective of the creation of a predictable set of responsibilities, injunctions based on a duty of care may be preferable to the rules introduced in Article 26d of the Dutch Copyright Act and Article 8(3) of the Copyright Directive. The latter type of rules only indicates that there is a responsibility, without in any way specifying the normative concepts on which that responsibility is based. They are accompanied by general requirements that injunctions must meet, but they only set the outer boundaries. They say little about the circumstances under which injunctions should indeed be issued by a court.[247] In contrast, injunctions based on a general duty of care require that courts consider the role of the intermediary in the infringement and give positive arguments as to why there is responsibility. This approach towards the intermediary's liability enables courts to develop a normative framework, a set of factors, or factual conditions, to assess the responsibility of an intermediary in a given case. The duty to release information about users by intermediaries, that has been developed by the Supreme Court in *Lycos v. Pessers*, is a clear example of that.

The need for predictable rules may require that the responsibilities of intermediaries for the infringements of others are defined more concretely in legislation. But such rules may not be technology-neutral and may become obsolete as technology

244. *See* section §4.03[C].
245. Anne Frank-Fonds/Anne Frank Stichting, *supra* n. 83.
246. *GS Media v. Sanoma Media Netherlands and others*, *supra* n. 32; *Stichting Brein v. Ziggo BV and XS4ALL Internet*, *supra* n. 32. *See* section §3.03[G] for a discussion of these decisions.
247. *See* section §3.05.

progresses. A middle ground could be the use of co-regulatory instruments through which concrete responsibilities are defined, but which can be adapted if need be. The Dutch experience of organizing stakeholder dialogues shows that it can be difficult to come to agreements if the legal duties that intermediaries have vis-à-vis copyright owners have not yet fully crystalized into concrete obligations.[248] In contrast, the Dutch voluntary Code of Conduct on Notice and Takedown shows that if there is a clear duty to remove materials, stakeholders may be willing to come to an agreement with respect to the procedural implementation of that duty.[249] Although this code is a flexible means of regulation, it does not necessarily enable the copyright balance to be maintained. In that respect, it is imperative that the Dutch government safeguards user interests and that it promotes transparency about the use and workings of the code.

248. *See* section §4.06[A][2].
249. *See* section §4.05[D][2] for a discussion of this code of conduct.

CHAPTER 5

Intermediary Liability in Germany

§5.01 INTRODUCTION

The current chapter investigates the effects of the EU legal framework on German law and identifies where the EU legal framework may have restrained or encouraged future-proof regulation. In addition, this chapter draws lessons from the German experience with intermediary liability.

We will begin by providing a brief overview of how German law deals with liability for infringements (section §5.02). We will consider a distinction that is made in German law between the intermediary's 'own information' and information that is provided by others (section §5.03). If an intermediary makes use of copyrighted materials that must be considered as the intermediary's own information, there is a risk that the intermediary is directly liable for its own infringements (section §5.04). News search engines and aggregators may in particular also be liable for infringements of the neighbouring right for press publishers when they copy from press publications (section §5.05).

This chapter will also discuss the cases in which the intermediary's liability is limited (section §5.06). Regardless of these exemptions, intermediaries may still have responsibilities to stop or prevent infringements. These responsibilities and the legal basis for such responsibilities are discussed as well (section §5.07).

§5.02 OVERVIEW

Simply put, under German law an intermediary can be held liable either for its own copyright infringement or through the application of the judge-made *Störerhaftung* doctrine. A copyright is infringed if someone, without permission from the author, uses the protected material in a way that interferes with the exclusive exploitation rights granted to the copyright owner.[1] While theoretically an infringement of a copyright is considered a tort under Article 823 of the German Civil Code (*Bürgerliches Gesetzbuch*), infringements of copyrights are dealt with under the German Copyright Act.[2]

Article 97(1) of the German Copyright Act (*Urheberrechtsgesetz*) provides the basis for injunctive relief against copyright infringers.[3] Anyone who infringes a copyright can be ordered to terminate that infringement. If there is a risk of a repeat infringement, the infringer can be required to cease and desist further infringements. A potential infringer who has not yet infringed can also be subject to injunctions. Preventive injunctions may be issued against those who have infringed and who may infringe again, but also those who have not yet infringed but are likely to do so in the future. Article 97(2) of the German Copyright Act enables copyright owners to claim compensation for damage caused by the copyright infringement.

An intermediary can also be liable under the doctrine of *Störerhaftung* if the intermediary contributed to the infringement of another party. Traditionally, *Störerhaftung* is a form of nuisance liability that has its origins in property law and that has been extended into the fields of copyright law and trademark law. As intermediaries cannot easily be held liable for their own copyright infringements, *Störerhaftung* is the most prominent means of holding intermediaries liable in Germany.[4]

§5.03 OWN INFORMATION AND THE INFORMATION OF OTHERS

German law on the liability of intermediaries makes a principal distinction between liability for one's own information and non-liability for the information of others. This distinction stems from the 1997 Teleservices Act (*Teledienstegesetz*) and thus predates the liability regime set in the E-Commerce Directive.[5] It was maintained in the 2007 Telemedia Act (*Telemediengesetz*).

1. Dreier/Schulze, UrhG, 5. Aufl. 2015, § 97 Rn. 5.
2. Basil Markesinis & Hannes Unberath, *The German Law of Tort: A Comparative Treatise* 14 (2002). Intermediaries can theoretically be liable as joint tortfeasors if others commit an infringement through their services. Pursuant to Article 830(1) of the German Civil Code, if two or more persons cause damage through a jointly committed tort, then all of those persons are jointly liable. Also, those who participate in a tort by instigating a tort or being an accessory to a tort are liable as joint tortfeasors (Article 830(2) of the German Civil Code). These forms of participation require intent as an element for liability (MüKoBGB/Wagner BGB § 830 Rn. 27-30). According to the German Federal Court of Justice, participation requires at least a conditional intent, which entails an awareness of a specific infringement (*BGH*, GRUR 2004, 860 (863) – Internetversteigerung I). The automatic nature of the services provided by intermediaries generally precludes such awareness (*BGH*, GRUR 2007, 708 (710) – Internetversteigerung II. *Also see*: Thomas Hoeren & Silviya Yankova, *The Liability of Internet Intermediaries – The German Perspective*, IIC (5) 501, 503 (2012). Moreover, a general awareness of infringements is not enough to establish intent (Internetversteigerung II, *supra* n. 2). Only when an intermediary blatantly promotes infringements have German courts held these providers liable as joint tortfeasors, for example: *LG München I*, ZUM-RD 2016, 392 – Sharehosting.
3. For an English translation of the German Copyright Act, *see*: http://www.gesetze-im-internet.de/englisch_urhg (accessed 14 June 2019).
4. Matthias Leistner, *Structural Aspects of Secondary (Provider) Liability in Europe*, Journal of Intellectual Property Law & Practice (1) 75, 78 (2014); Matthias Leistner, *Reformbedarf im materiellen Urheberrecht: Online-Plattformen und Aggregatoren*, ZUM (7) 580, 583–584 (2016).
5. Begr. des RegE, BT-Drs. 13/7385, p. 20.

This distinction between one's own information and the information of others separates content providers who are fully liable for the information they publish, from intermediary service providers who only store or transmit the information of others and whose liability is limited. Still, an intermediary can become liable for information that was initially provided by others if the intermediary makes that information its own. The liability exemptions then have no effect, and the intermediary can be held liable for the information on the basis of, for instance, a copyright infringement.

The liability exemptions are discussed in more detail in section §5.06. Because the distinction between the intermediary's own information and the information of others is crucial to understanding the conditions under which an intermediary may be liable for infringements, the current section first clarifies this distinction. In this section, we will discuss the types of information that are considered the intermediary's own information (section §5.03[A]). We will also explore how an intermediary may adopt the information of others as its own (section §5.03[B]). The liability exemptions in the Telemedia Act only apply if the intermediary processes information that is provided by others. This type of information is discussed as well (section §5.03[C]).

[A] The Intermediary's Own Information

Article 7(1) of the Telemedia Act provides that 'service providers are responsible for their own information, that they make available for use, according to the general laws'.[6] A news website publishing defamatory statements is fully liable for that information because it makes its own information available. In contrast, intermediaries generally do not make their own information available. They offer access to information that is provided by others.

Intermediaries which perform curatorial activities using the information of others can be liable for the information they add to the pre-existing information.[7] This information is then considered to be the intermediary's own information for which the intermediary can be fully liable. The information provided by a search engine's autocomplete function serves as an example. If a search engine user enters keywords into the search engine's input field, this function automatically suggests additional keywords or alternative queries.[8] The German Federal Court of Justice (*Bundesgerichtshof*) considered such information as the search engine operator's own information ('*eigenen Inhalt*') in the sense of Article 7(1) of the Telemedia Act.[9] However, this does not mean that the search engine is liable. It only means that the search engine's conduct is not covered by the liability exemptions and that it *can* be liable on the basis of other laws. The Telemedia Act itself does not provide for a basis for liability.

6. Own translation.
7. For a discussion of the term 'curation', *see* section §1.06.
8. For an overview of German law on search engine liability for autocomplete suggestions, *see*: Stavroula Karapapa & Maurizio Borghi, *Search Engine Liability for Autocomplete Suggestions: Personality, Privacy and the Power of the Algorithm*, International Journal of Law and Information Technology (3) 261 (2015).
9. *BGH*, ZUM 2013, 550 (552) – Suchergänzungsvorschläge in Internetsuchmaschine.

[B] Adopting the Information of Others

Information that was initially provided by someone else can become the intermediary's own information if the intermediary makes the user-provided content its own ('*zu eigen machen*').[10] The German Federal Court of Justice clarified this concept of making information one's own in a case concerning photos published on the recipe website *Chefkoch.de*.[11] The website published recipes and photos of dishes that were provided by users of the website. Some of these users had taken photos from *Marions-kochbuch.de* and uploaded these to *Chefkoch.de*. The question before the Court was whether the operator of *Chefkoch.de* had infringed Marion's copyrights by publishing these user-provided photos.

The German Federal Court of Justice held that the operator of *Chefkoch.de* had made the uploaded content its own and could thus be held liable for copyright infringement.[12] The Court considered that the operator exercised editorial control over published recipes and photos. Moreover, the user-provided content was, what the Court called, the 'editorial core' of the website.[13] The Court also deemed the website's terms and conditions to be relevant. These mentioned that the operator would exercise editorial control and also stipulated a licence for reproductions of the user-provided content. Furthermore, the operator offered the recipes to third parties for further commercial use. The Court also deemed it relevant that the recipe pages included the website's logos, which would be even larger if the recipes were printed on paper.

The German Federal Court of Justice rejected the argument that it was clear to the website's visitors that the recipes were provided by other users. While the names of users who submitted these recipes were mentioned on the page, the Court argued that in light of the editorial control and the website's overall presentation, the operator insufficiently distanced itself from the published content. The operator was not considered to be an intermediary and the published content thus had to be considered as the operator's own information in the sense of Article 7(1) of the Telemedia Act. As mentioned, the Telemedia Act does not provide rules on establishing liability for the service provider's own information. According to Article 7(1), liability is to be established according to other laws that do provide a basis for liability.[14] In the case of *Marions-kochbuch.de*, the Court held that the website operator had infringed the reproduction rights on the photographs in question and that it was liable for the infringements.[15]

User-provided materials thus become the intermediary's own if the intermediary makes editorial choices regarding those materials. The rise of the algorithmic processing of information has made that criterion more difficult to apply. Should such information be considered one's own information because the algorithm that produces

10. Begr. des RegE, BT-Drs. 13/7385, p. 19.
11. *BGH*, GRUR 2010, 616 – marions-kochbuch.de.
12. *BGH*, GRUR 2010, 616 (618–619) – marions-kochbuch.de.
13. *BGH*, GRUR 2010, 616 (618–619) – marions-kochbuch.de.
14. Article 7(1) of the Telemedia Act. *Also see*: *BGH*, MMR 2007, 518 (518) – Meinungsäußerung im Internetforum.
15. *BGH*, GRUR 2010, 616 (619–620) – marions-kochbuch.de.

the information reflects human choices? Here we touch upon the grey area between editing information, for which one is fully liable, and classic intermediary activity consisting of the mere storage and transmission of information that is generally exempted.

As a rule, intermediaries that make the information of others available through automated processes do not make that information their own.[16] Also, an intermediary like YouTube, which supports the materials uploaded by its users with additional functionalities, and makes a profit from its platform through advertising, does not make the user-uploaded videos its own and thus cannot be held liable as an infringer.[17]

Yet, if an algorithm makes choices about what information is displayed and what information is not, the intermediary utilizing the algorithm may make that information its own. A 2016 decision by the Berlin Regional Court regarding Amazon's liability for infringements illustrates that point.[18] Amazon on its shopping platform not only sells its own products but also hosts offers by third-party sellers. These sellers uploaded information, such as product pictures, into Amazon's system. Based on this information, Amazon's algorithm then generated a product detail page for the product. If multiple pictures were uploaded for a particular product, the algorithm made a selection of which pictures to publish on the product page.

The perfume maker Davidoff argued that Amazon had infringed its copyrights by displaying unauthorized copies of pictures of one of its perfumes. The Berlin Regional Court held that Amazon was liable as an infringer for infringing pictures on its shopping platform.[19] According to the Court, Amazon had intervened in the autonomy of the sellers, who may have selected other non-infringing pictures. The fact that Amazon's process was automated and that staff members were not aware of the infringing pictures did not detract from this conclusion. Instead of allowing staff members to decide on which pictures to display, Amazon designed an algorithm that incorporated its selection criteria. This algorithm represented a form of human intervention in the selection and display of information for which Amazon could be held liable as an infringer.

Hence, it is not only the manual editing of user-provided materials that can give rise to liability for those materials as one's 'own information'. Also, the automatic processes that put together user-provided materials can reflect human decision-making for which an intermediary can be held liable. Depending on the extent to which the algorithm expresses concrete human choices regarding the materials, an intermediary may assert control over those materials. Such materials then become the intermediary's information for which it can be fully liable. This subfield of law - the liability for copyright infringements 'made' by algorithms - is still developing in Germany and has not yet led to conclusive decisions by the German Federal Court of Justice.[20]

16. Internetversteigerung I, *supra* n 2, at 862.
17. *OLG Hamburg*, MMR 2016, 269 - Störerhaftung von YouTube, with note by H. Frey.
18. *LG Berlin*, MMR 2016, 624 - Amazon.
19. *LG Berlin*, MMR 2016, 624 - Amazon.
20. Matthias Berberich, *Zwischenstand zur Haftung von Plattformbetreibern als Intermediäre bei der Werkverwertung*, GRUR-Prax 269, 270 (2017). *Also see* section §4.05[D][1] on the applicability of the Dutch liability exemptions to the algorithmic processing of information.

[C] Liability Exemptions for the Information of Others

The previous sections have discussed the concept of one's own information and how intermediaries may make user-provided information their own. Yet, intermediaries may also process information that is provided by others (*'fremde Information'*). If an intermediary stores or transmits such information, it is generally not liable for that information.

The Telemedia Act provides for three liability exemptions that protect the intermediary from liability for damages. The provisions in the Telemedia Act do not provide the basis for liability. They rather determine the conditions under which particular intermediaries cannot be liable.[21] The liability exemptions thus have a filtering function.[22] Consequently, cases dealing with the liability of an intermediary often start with the applicability of the exemptions for a particular intermediary activity. These liability exemptions are discussed separately in section §5.06.

§5.04 COPYRIGHT LAW

Intermediaries can be liable if the infringing materials have to be considered as the intermediary's own information or if it has adopted those materials as its own information. For there to be a copyright infringement, the intermediary must have infringed one of the exclusive rights granted to the copyright owner.[23] In this section, we will discuss these exclusive rights (section §5.04[A]) and the limitations and exceptions to those rights (section §5.04[B]). We will then explore the application of German copyright law to two forms of intermediary activity: linking to other materials (section §5.04[C]) and the use of images by image search engines (section §5.04[D]).

[A] Exclusive Rights

German copyright law is author-centric and is based on the creator principle (*'Schöpferprinzip'*). Pursuant to Article 7 of the German Copyright Act, 'the author is the creator of the work'. The German Copyright Act grants him a copyright that he cannot transfer to others.[24] This reinforces the idea that in German Copyright law, the author is the central actor. If a person other than the author wants to make use of the protected materials, then that person needs to acquire the rights from the author.[25] Although,

21. *BGH*, MMR 2007, 518 – Meinungsäußerung im Internetforum.
22. Begr. des RegE, BT-Drs. 14/6098, p. 23.
23. Under German Copyright law, the rights protecting the author's moral and exploitation rights are inextricably linked (Dreier/Schulze, UrhG, 4. Aufl. 2013, § 97 Rn. 5). The author's moral rights play a marginal role in discussions on the online use of copyright-protected materials, and they are therefore omitted from the discussion in this chapter. (Thomas Dreier & Matthias Leistner, *Urheberrecht im Internet: die Forschungsheraus forderungen*, GRUR (9) 881, 886 (2013), explaining that in the context of the Internet, moral rights play a role in particular when collaborative creation is concerned.)
24. Article 29(1) of the German Copyright Act.
25. Article 29(2) of the German Copyright Act.

strictly speaking, only the author of a work should be referred to as a copyright owner, for reasons of simplicity the term copyright owner is used to indicate the person or entity holding any or all of the economic exclusive rights in a copyrighted work.

Article 15 of the German Copyright Act provides for a catalogue of exclusive exploitation rights that are granted to the copyright owner. On the one hand, Article 15(1) grants the right to exploit works in material forms ('*Werk in körperlicher Form zu verwerten*'). This broader right includes other exploitation rights that are also specified in the German Copyright Act. In a similar vein, Article 15(2) defines a broad right of the immaterial communication of works to the public ('*unkörperlicher Form öffentlich wiederzugeben*'). This right also consists of, but is not limited to, a set of rights specified in the German Copyright Act.[26]

In implementing the Copyright Directive, some alterations were made to the catalogue of exploitation rights in the German Copyright Act. A right to make available ('*Recht der öffentlichen Zugänglichmachung*') was added by means of Article 19a of the German Copyright Act. It grants the copyright owner the exclusive right to 'make the work available to the public, either by wire or wireless means, in such a manner that members of the public may access it from a place and at a time individually chosen by them'. A work is made available to the public 'if it is intended for a plurality of members of the public'.[27] In defining this right, the German legislator remained close to the text of Article 3(1) of the Copyright Directive. The legislator considered it to be a technology-neutral right that would not only apply in online settings.[28]

Article 2 of the Copyright Directive introduced a broad reproduction right that also applies to temporary reproductions. The German legislator also wanted to make that clear in the definition of the reproduction right. Therefore Article 16 of the German Copyright Act specifies that the reproduction right also covers temporary reproductions.

[B] Limitations and Exceptions

German Copyright law provides for a statutory list of limitations and exceptions in Section VI of the German Copyright Act. Following the adoption of the Copyright Directive, the German legislator did not make extensive use of the possibility to introduce new limitations and exceptions. A specific exception was added to improve access to protected materials by disabled people.[29] An exception was also added regarding the use of work for educational and research purposes.[30] A fair amount of existing limitations and exceptions were altered to reflect the fact that they also applied in the digital and connected environment. For example, it was added to Article 48 of the German Copyright Act that this exception for the use of materials relating to current

26. Begr. des RegE, BT-Drs. 15/38, p. 17.
27. Article 15(3) of the German Copyright Act.
28. Begr. des RegE, BT-Drs. 15/38, p. 17.
29. Article 45a of the German Copyright Act.
30. Article 52a of the German Copyright Act.

affairs in public speeches also applies to 'other data carriers which mainly record current events'.

German Copyright law also provides an exception for temporary reproductions ('*Vorübergehende Vervielfältigungshandlungen*'). Article 44a of the German Copyright Act provides that certain temporary acts of reproduction are outside the scope of the reproduction right. This Article closely resembles the wording of Article 5(1) of the Copyright Directive, the only mandatory exception in the directive.

For a reproduction to be considered a temporary act of reproduction, it must be transient or incidental and constitute an integral and essential part of a technical process. Furthermore, the reproduction's sole purpose should be either to enable a transmission in a network between third parties by an intermediary or a lawful use.[31] And finally, the reproduction should not have independent economic significance. The exception in Article 44a of the German Copyright Act is unlikely to apply to other intermediaries than network and access providers. German case law underlines that the limitation for temporary reproductions for this first purpose – the purpose of enabling a transmission in a network – has been put in place for these intermediaries only.[32]

[C] Linking

The question of whether linking to freely available materials can amount to copyright infringement was answered early on by the German Federal Court of Justice in *Paperboy*.[33] In this 2003 decision, the Court held that linking to copyrighted materials does not interfere with the copyright owner's exclusive right to reproduction, nor its right of communication to the public. Deep linking, which bypasses the homepage of a website, also did not amount to an infringement. The Court considered that a person who posts a link to copyrighted materials merely refers to those materials. The German Federal Court was aware of the importance that hyperlinks have for the freedom of information: 'Without the use of search services and their use of hyperlinks (even in the form of deep-links), the valuable use of the vast amounts of information on the World Wide Web would practically be impossible.'[34]

In *Session ID*, the German Federal Court of Justice decided on a link that bypassed access restrictions.[35] The technical measure at issue in *Session ID* made sure that only users with a particular identifier – a 'session ID' – had access to the copyright-protected map. This identifier was assigned to users on the website's homepage. Deep linking to

31. A temporary reproduction made to transmit content on the Internet does not necessarily have to enable a lawful use (Dreier/Schulze, UrhG, 4. Aufl. 2013, § 7 Rn. 7).
32. *LG Berlin*, GRUR-RR 2004, 228 (231) – Unzulässigkeit der Versendung von Presseartikeln per E-Mail und Fax. For a critique, *see*: Stefan Haupt & Loy Ullmann, *Der Fax- und E-Mail-Versand sind in der Informationsgesellschaft verboten*, ZUM (1) 46 (2005). *Also see BGH*, GRUR 2010, 628 (630) – Vorschaubilder I, holding that the exception did not apply to the display of thumbnail images in a search engine because these reproductions had an independent economic significance.
33. *BGH*, ZUM 2003, 855 – Paperboy.
34. *BGH*, ZUM 2003, 855 (860) – Paperboy. Own translation.
35. *BGH*, MMR 2011, 47 – Session-ID.

the maps meant that this technical measure would be bypassed and that access would be provided to people who did not have access to the work. Therefore, the German Federal Court of Justice held that the link in question made that work available to the public.[36] This decision appears to be in line with the later CJEU decision in *Svensson*, in which the CJEU also held that the circumvention of access restriction measures could lead to an infringement.[37]

After *Paperboy* and *Svensson*, the question arose whether linking to unauthorized materials should be assessed any differently.[38] This question was still open after the CJEU's decision in *Svensson* and its *BestWater* order.[39] Did *Svensson* mean that links to unauthorized materials reach a new public because they were not considered by the copyright owner?[40] According to Jani and Leenen, this would have far-reaching consequences and cause legal uncertainty as one cannot always know with certainty whether online material is authorized or unauthorized.[41] Leistner argued that in order to solve this problem, the liability exemptions in the Telemedia Act might have to be analogously applied in order to provide clarity to intermediaries.[42]

In its decision in *Die Realität II*, which was the continuation of the *BestWater* case, the German Federal Court of Justice interpreted the CJEU's case law as meaning that linking to unauthorized materials would amount to an infringement.[43] The German Court argued that linking to unauthorized materials indeed reaches a 'new public' as such links make the material available to a public that the copyright owner did not have in mind when he authorized the publication.

Die Realität II was not well received by German scholars as it brought any link to unauthorized materials within the ambit of the right to communicate to the public. According to Leistner, the decision could create a chilling effect on Internet communication.[44] Spindler wrote that while this decision by the German Federal Court of Justice is in line with the CJEU's case law, its consequences for online communication and the use of hyperlinks, including use by search engines, were immeasurable.[45] The German Federal Court of Justice in *Die Realität II* interpreted the CJEU's decision in *Svensson* as meaning that any link to unauthorized materials amounts to a communication to the public as such a link reaches a public that was not considered by the

36. *BGH*, MMR 2011, 47 (48) – Session-ID.
37. CJEU 13 February 2014, ECLI:EU:C:2014:76 (*Nils Svensson and others v. Retriever Sverige*). For a discussion, see section §3.03[G].
38. Stefanie Fuchs & Thomas Farkas, *Kann der EUGH dem Paperboy das (Best)Water reichen?*, ZUM (2) 110 (2015).
39. CJEU 13 February 2014, ECLI:EU:C:2014:76 (*Nils Svensson and others v. Retriever Sverige*); CJEU 21 October 2014, ECLI:EU:C:2014:2315 (*BestWater*).
40. *See* section §3.03[G].
41. *EuGH*, GRUR 2014, 360 – Svensson, with note by O. Jani and F. Leenen. *Also see*: Joachim Sternberg, *Die Rechtsprechung des EuGH und des BGH zum Urheberrecht und zu den verwandten Schutzrechten im Jahre 2014*, GRUR (3) 205, 210 (2015).
42. Matthias Leistner, *Urheberrecht an der Schnittstelle zwischen Unionsrecht und nationalem Recht*, GRUR (12) 1145, 1154 (2014).
43. *BGH*, GRUR 2016, 171 – Die Realität II.
44. Matthias Leistner, *Reformbedarf im materiellen Urheberrecht: Online-Plattformen und Aggregatoren*, ZUM (7) 580, 582 (2016).
45. Gerald Spindler, *Das Ende der Links: Framing und Hyperlinks auf rechtswidrige Inhalte als eigenständige Veröffentlichung?*, GRUR 157, 157 (2016).

copyright owner. However, the CJEU in *GS Media* introduced a much more nuanced rule that appears to do more justice to the positive effects that linking has on the freedom of expression.

The decision of the German Federal Court of Justice in *Die Realität II* appears to be in conflict with the more recent CJEU decision in *GS Media*.[46] The CJEU's decision implies that linking to unauthorized material does not under all conditions lead to infringement.[47] Knowledge of the unauthorized nature of the linked-to materials has become the key criterion to determine whether such linking amounts to a communication to the public. Those who link to unauthorized materials for profit are assumed to have knowledge of the unauthorized nature of the materials.

GS Media has been welcomed by German scholars because it effectively takes the rough edges off the liability for links to unauthorized materials. According to Leistner, *GS Media* offers a realistic and pragmatic perspective on linking, that also considers the importance of links for online freedom of expression.[48] Ohly highlights that the CJEU in *GS Media* moved away from a more technical and 'schematic' conception of the right of communication to the public, to a more functional and economically oriented conception of this exclusive right. According to Ohly, it enables a normative approach to the right of communication, which can be adapted to rapidly changing online markets.[49]

Criticism of the decision focuses on the uncertainties that *GS Media* creates. Leistner points out that the decision blurs the distinction between copyright infringement, *Störerhaftung*, and other theories of secondary liability.[50] Grünberger makes a similar point. He argues that the CJEU blurred the liability for infringement in Article 3(1) of the Copyright Directive, with the measures and sanctions in Article 8 of that directive.[51] Ohly argues that the decision is reminiscent of the E-Commerce Directive's liability exemption for hosting in the sense that non-liability revolves around the absence of knowledge. Ohly finds this a sensible approach, but he also argues that it would be more appropriate to deal with the issue of linking to unauthorized materials in the context of the rules on intermediary liability and not in copyright law.[52]

German scholars have also expressed their discontent with the knowledge presumption introduced in *GS Media*. For instance, Leistner argues that it is not clear what level of knowledge is required to satisfy the standard.[53] Schmidt-Wudy argues that it is unclear when one links for profit.[54] In that regard, Abrar asks whether it is enough that the website is maintained for profit, or whether the placement of the links

46. *EuGH*, EuZW 2016, 785 (789) – GS Media, with note by F. Schmidt-Wudy.
47. CJEU 8 September 2016, ECLI:EU:C:2016:644, *IER* 2016/47 (*GS Media v. Sanoma Media Netherlands and others*). *See* section §3.03[G] for a discussion of the decision.
48. *EuGH*, ZUM 2016, 980 (981) – GS Media, with note by M. Leistner.
49. *EuGH*, GRUR 2016, 1152 (1157–1158) – GS Media, with note by A. Ohly.
50. *EuGH*, ZUM 2016, 980 (982) – GS Media, with note by M. Leistner. *Also see*: *EuGH*, EuZW 2016, 785 (789–790) – GS Media, with note by F. Schmidt-Wudy.
51. Michael Grünberger, *Zugangsregeln bei Verlinkungen auf rechtswidrig zugänglich gemachte Werke*, ZUM (11) 905, 918 (2016).
52. *EuGH*, GRUR 2016, 1152 (1157) – GS Media, with note by A. Ohly.
53. *EuGH*, ZUM 2016, 980 (983) – GS Media, with note by M. Leistner.
54. *EuGH*, EuZW 2016, 785 (790) – GS Media, with note by F. Schmidt-Wudy.

should be done for profit.[55] Ohly raises a related point. The CJEU requires that those who link to make a profit can be expected to carry out 'necessary checks' to ensure that they do not link to unauthorized materials.[56] Ohly argues that it can be difficult, also for those who link for profit, to assess whether particular online materials are in fact unauthorized. This uncertainty could have a chilling effect on people's willingness to link online information.[57]

The CJEU's decision in *GS Media* could also have a major impact on search engines that link to unauthorized materials.[58] One of the questions that remains is whether the knowledge presumption also applies to these intermediaries and whether that means that they would have to check the materials they refer to.

In its 2017 decision in *AOL.de*, the German Federal Court of Justice held that it did not.[59] This case dealt with AOL's Internet portal which incorporated Google's image search engine. This search engine linked to erotic images that were published without the copyright owner's consent. The German Federal Court of Justice held that *GS Media*'s knowledge presumption did not apply to search engines and the search functionalities offered by AOL. The Court referred to the freedom of expression protected in Article 11 of the EU Charter of Fundamental Rights and highlighted the importance of hyperlinks for making information accessible.[60] Specifically regarding search engines, the Court noted that the information location tools offered by search engines play an important role in enabling the flows of information.[61] Without search engines, the use of online information would be practically impossible.[62]

According to the German Federal Court of Justice, the CJEU did not consider the special role of search engines when it defined its knowledge presumption.[63] In contrast to individuals who may deliberately link to infringing materials, search engines automatically generate links and cannot differentiate between authorized and unauthorized materials.[64] Search engines cannot therefore be expected to check the materials they link to. If the knowledge presumption would apply to them, search engine services would be at risk as their operators would be exposed to liability for numerous infringements.[65] Hence, the German Federal Court of Justice held that even though search engines offer a service for profit, knowledge of an infringement cannot be assumed.[66] Instead, the Court held that a search engine operator can only be liable

55. *EuGH*, GRUR-Prax 2016, 450 – GS Media, with note by S. Abrar.
56. *GS Media v. Sanoma Media Netherlands and others*, *supra* n. 47, at par 51.
57. *EuGH*, GRUR 2016, 1152 (1157) – GS Media, with note by A. Ohly.
58. *Cf. EuGH*, GRUR 2016, 1152 (1157) – GS Media, with note by A. Ohly, arguing that after *GS Media* there is a pressing need for a liability exemption for search engines in Germany.
59. BGH, I ZR 11/16 – AOL.de. This decision has not yet been reported and is available via: http://juris.bundesgerichtshof.de.
60. AOL.de, *supra* n. 59, at par 55.
61. AOL.de, *supra* n. 59, at par 56.
62. AOL.de, *supra* n. 59, at par 55.
63. AOL.de, *supra* n. 59, at par 60.
64. AOL.de, *supra* n. 59, at par 61.
65. AOL.de, *supra* n. 59, at par 62.
66. AOL.de, *supra* n. 59, at par 63.

as an infringer if the search engine operator knew or should have known about the unauthorized nature of the link.[67]

[D] Image Search

One intermediary activity in particular gave rise to discussions about the flexibility of the limitations and exceptions in German copyright law: image search.[68] Image search engines use thumbnail images to offer their users a preview of the images found on the web. In two decisions, *Vorschaubilder I* and *II*, the German Federal Court of Justice ruled on the liability of the providers of such search engines for copyright infringements.[69] In these decisions, we see that the Court struggled with the limited flexibility of the available limitations and exceptions in German copyright law. In the *Vorschaubilder* decisions, the Court acknowledged that the use of thumbnails by a search engine is covered by the copyright owner's exclusive rights and that none of the available limitations or exceptions applied. In an attempt to prevent that image search would be obstructed by copyright law, the Court in *Vorschaubilder I* came up with a novel theory to allow the use of images available on the web.

In *Vorschaubilder I*, the German Federal Court of Justice qualified the thumbnail images as reproductions in the sense of Article 16(2) of the German Copyright Act. Displaying such images also amounted to a communication to the public in the sense of Article 19a of the German Copyright Act. The quotation exception could not apply because there was no contextual connection between the 'quoted' images and the originals. The thumbnail images only enabled access to the original. The Court explicitly rejected the argument that a broad interpretation of the quotation exception was needed in light of technological developments enabling new forms of information dissemination.[70] Neither the Internet user's right to freedom of expression and communication nor the search engine operator's freedom to conduct a business could change that conclusion.[71] The Court made it very clear that there is no room in German copyright law to consider general public interest arguments.[72]

---

67. AOL.de, *supra* n. 59, at par 63.
68. Gerald Spindler, *Bildersuchmaschinen, Schranken und konkludente Einwilligung im Urheberrecht Besprechung der BGH-Entscheidung 'Vorschaubilder'*, GRUR (9) 785 (2010); Ansgar Ohly, *Zwölf Thesen zur Einwilligung im Internet*, GRUR (10) 983, 992 (2012); Gerald Spindler in his note to BGH, MMR 2012, 383 – Vorschaubilder II; Thomas Dreier & Matthias Leistner, *Urheberrecht im Internet: die Forschungsheraus forderungen*, GRUR (9) 881, 890 (2013). And in anticipation of Vorschaubilder I: Britta Heymann & Georg Nolte, *Blockiert das Urheberrecht sinnvolle Informationsdienste? Zur rechtlichen Beurteilung der Bildersuche*, K&R (12) 759 (2009). Nolte and Wimmers also took issue with the closed list of limitations and exceptions in the Copyright Directive which does not permit use by valuable information services that do not harm the interests of copyright owners (Georg Nolte & Jörg Wimmers, *Wer stört? Gedanken zur Haftung von Intermediären im Internet – von praktischer Konkordanz, richtigen Anreizen und offenen Fragen*, GRUR-Beil. (1) 58, 68 (2014)).
69. Vorschaubilder I, *supra* n. 32; *BGH*, GRUR 2012, 602 – Vorschaubilder II.
70. Vorschaubilder I, *supra* n. 32, at 630.
71. Vorschaubilder I, *supra* n. 32, at 630.
72. Vorschaubilder I, *supra* n. 32, at 630.

Nevertheless, the German Federal Court of Justice held that the search engine operator's use of the thumbnail images was lawful because the operator had reason to believe that the copyright owner had implicitly consented to the use of his work. The copyright owner had not made use of the opportunity to exclude his website from the search engine's index. In fact, the copyright owner had implemented measures to be indexed by search engines. According to the Court, the search engine operator therefore had reason to believe that it could use the images for normal use in an image search engine. This 'belief' was objectively construed, as the Court considered that it was irrelevant whether the search engine operator actually believed that the copyright owner had consented to the use.

This implicit consent is limited to those situations in which the *copyright owner* has placed the works online. The German Federal Court of Justice noted in an obiter dictum that the consent theory does not apply when a third party has published an image without the copyright owner's permission. According to the Court, consent can be revoked by implementing technical measures that prevent a search engine from accessing the website. Moreover, the consent theory does not cover situations in which the original images have been removed from the website. Hence, when a copyright owner deletes the images from his website, the search engine operator should also remove the thumbnail images from its result pages in order not to infringe the copyright owner's exclusive rights.

In *Vorschaubilder II*, the German Federal Court of Justice significantly extended the scope of its implied consent theory. It held that consent could also be inferred from the publication of images by an authorized third party.[73] By authorizing third parties to communicate those images on the Internet, the copyright owner also authorizes these third parties to (implicitly) consent to use by an image search engine.[74] While the Court in *Vorschaubilder I* explicitly denied that implicit consent extended to images published without the copyright owner's permission, the Court in *Vorschaubilder II* held otherwise. In this second case, the Court held that also unauthorized images are covered by the consent theory. The Court here considered that search engines are unable to distinguish between images that have been published with the copyright owner's authorization and images that have been published without such authorization.

German scholars welcomed the outcome of the *Vorschaubilder* cases.[75] The German Federal Court of Justice was praised for providing useful search technology with an unambiguous and solid legal basis.[76] However, criticism focused on the *way in which* the Court 'legalized' image search. For instance, Spindler argued that the Court's use of the concept of consent highlights the lack of an open-ended copyright limitation

73. Vorschaubilder II, *supra* n. 69, at 604.
74. Vorschaubilder II, *supra* n. 69.
75. For example, Matthias Leistner, *The German Federal Supreme Court's Judgment on Google's Image Search – A Topical Example of the 'Limitations' of the European Approach to Exceptions and Limitations*, IIC (4) 417, 434 (2011), Winfried Bullinger & Katharina Garbers-von Boehm, *Google -Bildersuche: Schlichte Einwilligung des Urhebers als Lösung?*, GRUR-Prax (12) 257 (2010), calling Vorschaubilder I one of the most important copyright decisions in the past few years.
76. For example, Nadine Klass, *Neue Internettechnologien und das Urheberrecht: Die schlichte Einwilligung als Rettungsanker?*, ZUM (1) 1, 3 (2013).

that enables the interests of copyright owners, search engine operators, and the general public to be balanced.[77] According to Klass, the consent theory conflicts with modern copyright law thinking which balances the adoption of new technological developments with granting copyright owners appropriate control over their works.[78] Indeed, inferring consent for reuse from the availability of online materials runs counter to the idea that copyright owners decide on if and how their works are used. Moreover, Ohly explained that the Court's construction depends on a chain of individual licences and rights that overstretches the concept of consent.[79] In a similar vein, Klass argued that there is no basis in private law to derive consent for a particular use from unauthorized uses by third parties. Klass contended that this objectified and generalized construction of implied consent departs from consent doctrine in German private law.[80]

§5.05 NEIGHBOURING RIGHT FOR PRESS PUBLISHERS

In Germany, the rise of news search engines, such as Google News, led to the adoption of a novel and specific right protecting the interests of press publishers. In 2013, a neighbouring right was introduced to protect the entrepreneurial efforts of these publishers – the '*Leistungsschutzrecht für Presseverleger*'. This new intellectual property right enables press publishers to prohibit search engines and aggregators from making available their press products. In the DSM Directive, a similar neighbouring right for press publishers has been adopted.[81] The German experience provides valuable insights into how such a right might work in practice. This section first explains the workings of the German neighbouring right for press publishers (section §5.05[A]). We will then consider how this right was received and what there is to learn from the German experience with this right (section §5.05[B]).

[A] A Neighbouring Right for Press Publishers

The first steps towards a neighbouring right for press publishers were taken in 2009 when the German coalition parties wanted to introduce a new intellectual property right to 'enhance the protection of press products on the Internet'.[82] Press publishers had lobbied for such a right and demanded a 'fair share' of the profits made by big

77. Spindler, *supra* n. 68, at 791.
78. Klass, *supra* n. 76, at 9–10.
79. Ohly, *supra* n. 68, at 989.
80. Klass, *supra* n. 76, at 7.
81. Article 15 of the DSM Directive. *See* section §3.03[I] for a discussion. *See* section §3.03[D][3].
82. Koaltionsvertrag CDU, CSU und FDP, 'Wachstum. Bildung. Zusammenhalt', available at: https://perma.cc/TLR3-8NPN (accessed 14 June 2019). Own translation.

technology companies.[83] In 2012, Chancellor Merkel delivered a speech at the Newspaper Congress of the Federal Association of German Newspaper Publishers (*Bundesverbandes Deutscher Zeitungsverleger*).[84] After celebrating the Internet's interactivity and information-sharing abilities, Merkel raised the difficult position that press publishers found themselves in. She ascertained that the government had not forgotten its promise to update German copyright law. 'Problematic are so-called news aggregators which are based in part on the work of publishers without rewarding them,' Merkel said.[85]

Indeed, the German government had not forgotten about press publishers. In June 2012, the German Ministry of Justice had prepared a bill to amend the German Copyright Act.[86] It would introduce a new exclusive right for press publishers to make press publications publicly available on the Internet for commercial purposes. This bill intended to rebalance the economic interests of press publishers and those who commercially use press publications.[87] Publishing *links* to press products would not be within the scope of this new right, nor would the bill affect the possibility to cite from a press product.[88]

While this first version mentioned the use of press publications on the Internet, a later version of the bill focused on the use made by news search engines and aggregators.[89] Especially these service providers made use of press productions for their own benefit.[90] Other users, such as bloggers, law firms, or private users, would not be affected by the exclusive right.

In March 2013, the neighbouring right for press publishers was enshrined in the German Copyright Act.[91] Protection is granted for a year from the moment the press product is published.[92] The press publisher is given its own exclusive right; the right is independent of the rights granted to the author of a press article. In that sense, the right is similar to the neighbouring rights granted to phonogram producers for their

83. Georg Nolte, *Zur Forderung der Presseverleger nach Einführung eines speziellen Leistungsschutzrechts. Eine kritische Auseinandersetzung*, Zeitschrift für Geistiges Eigentum (2) 165 (2010).
84. 'Rede von Bundeskanzlerin Angela Merkel anlässlich des Zeitungskongresses des Bundesverbandes Deutscher Zeitungsverleger e.V.', available at: https://perma.cc/Q4A3-CSDL (accessed 14 June 2019).
85. 'Rede von Bundeskanzlerin Angela Merkel anlässlich des Zeitungskongresses des Bundesverbandes Deutscher Zeitungsverleger e.V.', *supra* n. 84. Own translation.
86. Referentenentwurf des Bundesmisteriunms der Justitz, Entwurf eines Siebenten Gesetzes zur Änderung des Urheberrechtsgesetzes, 13 June 2012, available at: https://perma.cc/G6QW-D2FN (accessed 14 June 2019).
87. Referentenentwurf, *supra* n. 86, at 6.
88. Referentenentwurf, *supra* n. 86, at 6.
89. Malte Stieper, *Das Leistungsschutzrecht für Presseverleger nach dem Regierungsentwurf zum 7. UrhRÄndG*, ZUM (1) 10, 12 (2013).
90. Begr. des RegE, BT-Drs. 17/11470, p. 6.
91. Thomas Melcher, *Bundestag verabschiedet Leistungsschutzrecht*, MMR-Aktuell (5) 343382 (2013).
92. Article 87g(2) of the German Copyright Act.

recordings of copyrighted works, which do not protect the original work itself but the entrepreneurial efforts in the production of such a work.[93]

Pursuant to Article 87f(2) of the German Copyright Act, a press product is the editorial and technical fixation of journalistic contributions that are part of a published periodical bearing a single title. Article 87f(2) explains that such journalistic contributions include articles and illustrations which serve to provide information, form opinion, or entertain. Article 87f(1) gives press publishers the exclusive right to make articles or parts thereof available to the public. The concept of 'making available' was derived from Article 19a of the German Copyright Act, which grants copyright owners a general right to make their works available online.[94] This right effectively enables press publishers to prohibit the use of their press products by news search engines and aggregators. It puts them in a position to license these products and to require remuneration for their entrepreneurial efforts. Not all the money should end up in the pockets of the press publishers as Article 87h of the German Copyright Act provides that authors are entitled to a fair share of the remuneration as well.

Article 87(f) of the German Copyright Act applies to commercial use only. Press publications covered by this exclusive right can be used by others for non-commercial purposes. Article 87g(4) specifically states that this limitation of the right's scope does not apply to search engines: 'It shall be permissible to make press products or parts thereof available to the public unless this is done by commercial operators of search engines or commercial operators of services which edit the content.' Therefore, the right's scope is effectively limited to search engine and aggregator use, which makes it quite a narrow and technology-specific right.[95]

The publisher's right applies not only to full press articles but also to parts thereof. Also small parts, or snippets, are protected.[96] Yet, the right does not cover individual words or the smallest of text excerpts.[97] This limitation on the scope of this right was a response to criticism that the right would afford overbroad protection.[98] If the smallest parts of a press product would be protected, the exclusive right would go beyond what is normally protected by copyright law.[99]

News search engines and aggregators may therefore still generate snippets for articles they are linking to without the press publisher's permission. How many words

93. Begr. des RegE, BT-Drs. 17/11470, p. 8. *Also see*: Robert Schweizer, *Schutz der Leistungen von Presse und Journalisten*, ZUM (1) 7, 8 (2010); Gerald Spindler, *Die Reform des Urheberrecht*, NJW (35) 2550 (2014).
94. Spindler/Schuster/Hoffmann, UrhG § 87f Rn. 11.
95. Stieper, *supra* n. 89, at 16.
96. Begr. des RegE, BT-Drs. 17/11470, p. 8.
97. Article 87f(1) of the German Copyright Act: 'The producer of a press product (the publishers of newspapers and magazines) shall have the exclusive right to make the press product or parts thereof available to the public for commercial purposes, unless it consists of individual words or very short text excerpts.'
98. Hans-Peter Kunz-Hallstein & Michael Loschelder, *Stellungnahme der GRUR zur Anhörung des BMJ am 28. 6. 2010 zum Thema 'Leistungsschutzrecht für Verleger'*, GRUR (9) 808, 809 (2010); Hans-Peter Kunz-Hallstein & Michael Loschelder, *Stellungnahme des Fachausschusses Urheber- und Verlagsrecht der GRUR zum Regierungsentwurf eines Siebenten Gesetzes zur Änderung des Urheberrechtsgesetzes (Leistungsschutzrecht für Presseverleger)*, GRUR (3) 268 (2013).
99. Stieper, *supra* n. 89, at 16.

or characters they may use is unclear. The German legislator has not explained how short 'very short text excerpts' are. Here there is therefore significant room for courts to further develop the scope of protection.[100] In light of the *Vorschaubilder* decision, Kahl argued that 250 characters – the amount that has long been used by Google in its Google News products – should be allowed.[101] Schippan, who took the CJEU's decision in *Infopaq I* as an example, argued for an interpretation allowing up to five or eight words.[102] The board of arbitration of the German Patent and Trademark Office in arbitration proceedings between Google and the collecting society VG Media recommended a maximum of seven words, excluding search words.[103] The Munich Higher Regional Court has held that using more than twenty-five words is using too much.[104] Several years after the introduction of the publisher's right, there appears to be, as yet, no final and definitive limit as to the number of words or characters that can be used.

[B] Lessons from Germany

Although there is consensus that journalistic pieces deserve protection from unauthorized use, the neighbouring right does not appear to be the right way forward as it does not seem to achieve its goals. While acknowledging that the press needs sufficient economic foundations to operate, German scholars have argued that the introduction of a press publisher's right does not seem to have helped the press. In fact, even some publishers see the right as backwards-looking and are opposed to the publisher's right.[105]

Although the German legislator stated that the publisher's right would not affect the online flow of information,[106] German scholars have argued that the retrievability of news and other information could be endangered by the new exclusive right.[107] Effectively, the right requires that the operators of news search engines and aggregators obtain permission from all press publishers. This is an indeterminate administrative task which may persuade operators of news search engines and aggregators to stop

100. Artur-Axel Wandtke, *Zum Leistungsschutzrecht der Presseverleger und dem Beteiligungsanspruch der Urheber*, ZUM (11) 847 (2014); Jonas Kahl, *Wen betrifft das Leistungsschutzrecht für Presseverleger? 'Kleinste Textausschnitte' vor dem Hintergrund der BGH-Rechtsprechung*, MMR (6) 348 (2013).
101. Jonas Kahl, *Wen betrifft das Leistungsschutzrecht für Presseverleger? 'Kleinste Textausschnitte' vor dem Hintergrund der BGH-Rechtsprechung*, MMR (6) 348 (2013).
102. Martin Schippan, *Der Schutz von kurzen Textwerken im digitalen Zeitalter*, ZUM (5) 358, 372 (2013).
103. Deutsches Patent- und Markenamt, 'Ergänzung zum Hinweis vom 24.09.2015 – Schiedsstelle nach dem Gesetz über die Wahrnehmung von Urheberrechten und verwandten Schutzrechten entscheidet über 'Tarif Presseverleger', available at: https://perma.cc/L9LL-SFVX.
104. *OLG München*, GRUR-RR 2017, 89 – Kein Vollgas.
105. *See*: http://mediapublishers.eu (accessed 14 June 2019).
106. Begr. des RegE, BT-Drs. 17/11470, pp. 6–8.
107. For instance: Max-Planck-Institut für Immaterialgüter- und Wettbewerbsrecht, Stellungnahme zum Gesetzesentwurf für eine Ergänzung des Urheberrechtsgesetzes durch ein Leistungsschutzrecht für Verleger 2 (2012).

indexing because they have to obtain permission from many different publishers.[108] The payment of a licence fee can in particular be problematic for smaller search engines and aggregators and may as such hamper innovation in the field of information retrieval.[109] In fact, legislation in Spain, which requires news aggregators to pay a licence fee, led Google to close its news service there and to remove Spanish publishers from its index.[110] Research into the Spanish situation has indicated that traffic to news websites significantly dropped and that smaller independent titles and innovative projects have been affected the most.[111]

Thus far, the German neighbouring right for press publishers has not had its intended effect of strengthening the economic position of the press. On the contrary, the new legislation has resulted in Google adopting an opt-in model for the indexation of news, instead of the opt-out model it had always used. This change significantly lowered the retrievability of German news and caused a significant drop in traffic to news websites. In response to Google's policy change, the collecting society VG Media submitted a complaint to the German Competition Authority (*Bundeskartellamt*) arguing that Google abused its dominant market position. The Authority did not start a procedure against Google as VG Media's complaint was insufficient to support the strong initial suspicion that is needed for an abuse of dominance procedure.[112] The Authority considered that VG Media had not first tried to solve the issue directly with Google. Moreover, the fact that Google did not want to pay for a licence fee was not sufficient to suspect any abuse of a dominant position.[113] In order to still remain visible on Google News, VG Media decided to give Google a free licence to use their press products *under protest*. VG Media publishers were 'forced to take this unusual step due to the overwhelming market power of Google'.[114]

It can be argued that the problem that the German legislator tried to solve was not so much a copyright issue, but rather an unfair competition law issue.[115] The German legislator, however, opted to introduce a new intellectual property right specifically protecting press publishers against the use of their products by search engines and

108. Max-Planck-Institut für Immaterialgüter- und Wettbewerbsrecht, Stellungnahme zum Gesetzesentwurf für eine Ergänzung des Urheberrechtsgesetzes durch ein Leistungsschutzrecht für Verleger 5 (2012).
109. Verband der Deutschen Internetwirtschaft, *Leistungsschutzrecht für Presseverleger* 2 (2014). Available at: https://perma.cc/VD2V-BDFS (accessed 14 June 2019).
110. Google Europe, *An update on Google News in Spain*, 11 December 2014, https://perma.cc/268U-QJFF (accessed 14 June 2019).
111. AEEPP, Informe económico del impacto del Nuevo Artículo 32.2 de la LPI (NERA para la AEEPP), 9 July 2015, https://perma.cc/M5CD-96PA (accessed 14 June 2019).
112. Bundeskartellamt, Complaint by VG Media not sufficient to institute formal abuse of dominance proceedings against Google, 22 August 2014, https://perma.cc/N8FZ-XWHP (accessed 14 June 2019).
113. Bundeskartellamt, *supra* n. 112.
114. VG Media, Pressemitteilung Google lehnt 'Waffenruhe' ab – Presseverlage beugen sich Druck Googles und lassen VG Media Gratiseinwilligung für Rechtenutzung erteilen, 22 October 2014, https://perma.cc/CUT7-6SE2 (accessed 14 June 2019).
115. Wandtke, *supra* n. 100, at 848.

aggregators and pushed aside the option of applying general rules of unfair competition.[116] Similarly, it can be argued that if investments in press products are to be protected, it would have made more sense to create a right that is infringed if the commercial exploitation of the original is hampered by the other product.[117] Instead, the German legislator decided to create a neighbouring right that specifically addresses the relation between press publishers and news search engines and aggregators in quite specific terms.

Moreover, it can be argued that German and EU copyright law already provided the tools to qualify use by news search engines. The CJEU's decision in *Infopaq I* had already opened the door – to the extent that it was not already open – for the protection of short pieces of text.[118] Provided that press publishers acquire the necessary rights from their authors, the reproduction right could serve as a basis for claims against search engines and aggregators. At the other end of the spectrum, the German Federal Court of Justice in its *Vorschaubilder* cases ruled that those who share their works online consent to the normal use of their work by search engines.[119] This line of reasoning could also be applied to press articles made available online without any restrictions.[120] Although these cases do not by themselves provide a definitive answer to all issues surrounding news search engines and aggregators, they do show that the pieces to solve the press publication puzzle might have already been available in German and European copyright law.[121]

Questions were also raised about the applicability of the consent theory, developed by the German Federal Court of Justice in the *Vorschaubilder* decisions, to the neighbouring right for press publishers.[122] If this consent theory is to be applied analogously, news search engines could argue that press publishers consent to search engine use by making available press publications online. If that argument holds true, then the neighbouring right for press publishers would prove to be an empty shell, at least to the extent that this use can be qualified as normal search engine use.[123] That would imply that the German legislator has designed a law that has no or a very limited effect, which would again argue against such an interpretation.[124] It is more likely that the new statutory regime on press publications precludes the application of the consent

116. Jürgen Ensthaler & Harald Blanz, *Leistungsschutzrecht für Presseverleger. Notwendiger Schutz von Presseverlagen im Internet oder systemwidriger Eingriff in die Informationsfreiheit?*, GRUR (11) 1104, 1105 (2012).
117. Ansgar Ohly, *Urheberrecht in der digitalen Welt – Brauchen wir neue Regelungen zum Urheberrecht und zu dessen Durchsetzung?*, NJW-Beilage (2) 47, 48 (2014).
118. CJEU 16 July 2009, ECLI:EU:C:2009:465 (*Infopaq International v. Danske Dagblades Forening*).
119. *See* section §5.04[D] for a discussion of these cases.
120. Stieper, *supra* n. 89, at 16.
121. Schippan, *supra* n. 102, at 365.
122. *See* section §5.04[D].
123. Karl-Nikolaus Peifer, *Leistungsschutzrecht für Presseverleger – 'Zombie im Paragrafen-Dschungel' oder Retter in der Not?*, GRUR-Prax (7) 149 (2013); Till Kreutzer, *Das Leistungsschutzrecht für Presseverleger im Lichte der BGH-Rechtsprechung zu Vorschaubildern Was bleibt am Ende übrig?*, MMR (8) 512 (2014). *Also see*: Stefan Koroch, *Das Leistungsschutzrecht für Presseverleger auf dem Weg von Berlin nach Brüssel*, GRUR (2) 127, 129 (2017).
124. Spindler/Schuster/Hoffmann, UrhG § 87f Rn. 13.

theory to news search engines and aggregators.[125] Still, it shows that a very specific legislative intervention, that is instigated by contemporary frictions between press publishers and news search engines, can cause problems with respect to the coherence of copyright law.

What can we learn from the German experience? All in all, the German neighbouring right for press publishers is an example of a right that was introduced to specifically settle friction between press publishers and search engines and aggregators. Apart from its technology-specific nature, there is much to be said against the adoption of a new intellectual property right for press publishers. In Germany, this right has created significant legal uncertainty regarding its application. It seems to have a negative impact on the free flow of information. And it was rather unnecessary as German and EU copyright law already provided the necessary tools to deal with the use of press articles by search engines and aggregators.

§5.06 LIABILITY EXEMPTIONS FOR INTERMEDIARIES

Already in 1997, before the E-Commerce Directive was adopted, Germany had introduced a set of liability exemptions in the Teleservices Act (*Teledienstegesetz*).[126] It was considered to be a leading legislative initiative in Europe.[127] In 2001, it was replaced by the 2001 Telemedia Act ('*Telemediengesetz*'). Article 3 of the Telemedia Act provides for rules on the responsibilities of Internet intermediaries and a set of liability exemptions.

Before discussing these liability exemptions, we will first consider general aspects of the Telemedia Act's provisions on the liability of intermediaries (section §5.06[A]). We will then consider the different liability exemptions (sections §5.06[B] to §5.06[E]). Attention is also paid to the liability of those who offer *wireless* Internet connections, as the German legislator introduced a special liability regime regarding these service providers (section §5.06[C]).

[A] General Aspects

The liability exemptions in the Telemedia Act apply to service providers, which are defined as natural or legal persons offering their own or third-party 'telemedia services'.[128] This definition is rather broad and covers many types of Internet services, including those provided by Internet intermediaries.[129]

The intermediary activities exempted from liability are the transmission (mere conduit activities), caching, and storage of information. There is no liability exemption for search engine providers which refer to the information of others. An analogous

125. Martin Hossenfelder, *Die Nachrichtendarstellung in Suchmaschinen nach der Einführung des Leistungsschutzrechts für Presseverleger*, ZUM (5) 374, 376–377 (2013).
126. BGBl. I 1997 p. 1870.
127. Spindler/Schuster/Hoffmann, TMG Vorb. Rn. 1.
128. Article 2 of the Telemedia Act.
129. Spindler/Schuster/Hoffmann, TMG § 2 Rn. 2-5.

application of the existing safe harbours seems to be excluded.[130] In a 2006 decision, the Regional Court of Berlin held that the liability of a search engine has been consciously left unregulated by the German legislator.[131]

The liability exemptions only protect the intermediary against claims for damages. Intermediaries can still be subject to injunctive relief.[132] The Telemedia Act itself does not provide the basis for claims against intermediaries to stop or prevent copyright infringements. Rather, such claims must be based on copyright law or the *Störerhaftung* doctrine.[133] A provider of, for instance, an online market platform may, regardless of its status as a hosting service provider under Article 10 of the Telemedia Act, can still be subject to injunctive relief based on *Störerhaftung*.[134]

The Telemedia Act sets two general limits to the type of injunctions that can be issued against intermediaries. First, intermediaries cannot be obliged to monitor the materials they transmit or store, nor to look for factors that indicate unlawful activities.[135] Nevertheless, more specific monitoring duties may still be imposed.[136] Second, the secrecy of communications, as protected by Article 88 of the *Telekommunikationsgesetzes* (Telecommunications Act), must be respected.[137]

[B] Mere Conduit

Article 8 of the Telemedia Act is an almost literal implementation of Article 12(1) and (2) of the E-Commerce Directive, which require Member States to exempt the liability of intermediaries offering mere conduit activities.[138] Article 8 of the Telemedia Act exempts intermediaries that automatically transmit information in a communication network without conscious intervention in that communication.[139] The provision covers both the transmission of the information of others – or 'routing' – and the provision of access to a network through which information can be transmitted.[140] The exemption also covers the automatic temporary storage, or caching, that is necessary to transmit data.[141] An intermediary that collaborates with users in unlawful activities cannot benefit from the liability exemption for mere conduits.[142] On this issue, the Telemedia Act is more explicit than the E-Commerce Directive, which only mentions something of the same tenor in its recitals.[143]

130. Spindler/Schuster/Hoffmann, TMG Vorb. Rn. 37-39.
131. *LG Berlin*, ZUM 2006, 461 (461) – Admin C.
132. Article 7(2) second sentence of the Telemedia Act.
133. *See* section §5.07[A] for a discussion of the *Störerhaftung* doctrine.
134. Internetversteigerung I, *supra* n. 2, at 862–863; Internetversteigerung II, *supra* n. 2, at 710.
135. Article 7(2) second sentence of the Telemedia Act.
136. Spindler/Schuster/Hoffmann, TMG § 10 Rn. 4. *Also see* section §5.07[A] on specific monitoring duties.
137. Article 7(2) third sentence of the Telemedia Act.
138. Münchener Kommentar zum StGB (2010), § 8 TMG Rn 1.
139. Spindler/Schuster/Hoffmann, TMG § 8 Rn. 1.
140. Spindler/Schuster/Hoffmann, TMG § 8 Rn. 16.
141. Article 8(2) of the Telemedia Act.
142. Article 8(1) second sentence of the Telemedia Act.
143. Recital 44 of the E-Commerce Directive.

In order for an intermediary to qualify under the mere conduit safe harbour, the intermediary should fulfil the three requirements laid down in Article 8(1) of the Telemedia Act. These requirements are an almost literal implementation of the requirements set in Article 12 of the E-Commerce Directive. First, the intermediary should not have initiated the transmission. Second, the intermediary should not have selected the recipient of the transmission. And third, the intermediary should not have selected or modified the transmitted information. If, for instance, an intermediary does modify the transmitted information, then it runs the risk of being held liable for the information as its own information.[144] These three cumulative requirements aim to ensure that intermediaries exempted under Article 8 of the Telemedia Act are really just *mere* conduits that are in no way involved with the content of the transmitted information.[145]

[C] Wireless Internet Access

In Germany, there has long been uncertainty about the liability of those who offer *wireless* Internet access (Wi-Fi). As a consequence, the availability of Wi-Fi in hotels, cafes, and other establishments appears to lag behind in comparison to other industrial countries.[146] These providers run the risk of being held liable under the *Störerhaftung* doctrine if their connection is used by others for infringements. To escape liability, these providers must implement measures to prevent that their users – for example, hotel and cafe guests – use the Internet connection for infringing activities, such as downloading copyrighted music from peer-to-peer file-sharing networks.

[1] Störerhaftung

The uncertainty surrounding the liability of providers of wireless Internet access has its roots in the 2010 German Federal Court of Justice decision in *Sommer unseres Lebens*.[147] In this decision, the Court held that an individual person who does not use the built-in security measures of a wireless router could be liable as a *Störer* if a third party uses the connection to share copyrighted music in a peer-to-peer file-sharing network.[148] Under the *Störerhaftung* doctrine, that person must take reasonable measures to prevent infringements. In this regard, the Court also held that it was not unreasonable to require protection measures against unauthorized use of a person's network.[149] To prevent infringements, the person in question had to limit access to the network with a long and secure password.[150]

144. Begr. des RegE, BT-Drs. 14/6098, p. 24.
145. Spindler/Schuster/Hoffmann, TMG § 8 Rn. 21.
146. Verband der Deutschen Internetwirtschaft, Verbreitung und Nutzbarkeit von WLAN, WLAN-zuganspunkten Sowie öffentlicher Hotspots in Deutschland 11 (2014).
147. *BGH*, GRUR 2010, 633 – Sommer unseres Lebens, with note by F. Stang and S. Hühner.
148. *BGH*, GRUR 2010, 633 – Sommer unseres Lebens, with note by F. Stang and S. Hühner.
149. *BGH*, GRUR 2010, 633 (634) – Sommer unseres Lebens, with note by F. Stang and S. Hühner.
150. *BGH*, GRUR 2010, 633 (636) – Sommer unseres Lebens, with note by F. Stang and S. Hühner.

The German Federal Court of Justice also considered the liability exemptions in the Telemedia Act. Confusingly, it held that the liability exemption in Article 10 of the Telemedia Act for *hosting service providers* did not apply. Yet, as noted by the German scholars Leible and Jahn, if sharing one's Internet access over a Wi-Fi network would be covered by any of the liability exemptions in the Telemedia Act, an assessment under the mere conduit exemption would have been more appropriate.[151]

The German Federal Court of Justice saw no problem in requiring individuals to secure their networks with a password as it was also in their own interest to limit the access of third parties to their networks. This line of argumentation was criticized by Nenninger who argued that the Court had unduly mixed the individual's own interests into a discussion on the reasonableness of measures to prevent copyright infringements.[152] Likewise, Leible and Jahn argued that it is incorrect to equate one's fault 'against' oneself with a fault against another.[153] Also from a technological perspective, the Court's argument appears to be flawed. As Mantz noted: the openness of the wireless network does not necessarily impair the security of one's data on a computer.[154] In other words, it is not necessarily in the interest of the individual to lock his wireless network.

It was uncertain whether the decisions of the German Federal Court of Justice in *Sommer unseres Lebens* also applied to commercially operating parties providing wireless Internet access either as a stand-alone service or as part of their business, such as the access provided by cafes and hotels. These providers wilfully open their wireless networks, which detracts from the argument that it would be in their own interest to secure their networks.[155] Another argument against an analogous application of *Sommer unseres Lebens* to these Wi-Fi providers is that these providers offer Internet access as part of their business model. In *Sommer unseres Lebens*, which dealt with the liability of an individual, the Court considered that there was no business model that would be endangered by requiring preventive measures. In contrast, if commercially operating providers are required to take measures to prevent infringements, business models could be at stake. That would mean that commercially operating providers could not be required to take measures, or that such measures should at least be limited.[156]

No clear position on the liability of these commercially operating providers has arisen from later lower court decisions.[157] For example, the Regional Court of Hamburg decided that the owner of an Internet cafe could be held liable as a *Störer* for users sharing copyrighted music files.[158] According to the Court, the owner could have prevented the copyright infringement by blocking the ports on the router used for

151. *BGH*, LMK 2010, 306719 – Sommer unseres Lebens, with note by S. Leible and D. Jahn.
152. *BGH*, NJW 2010, 2061 – Sommer unseres Lebens, with note by K. Nenninger.
153. *BGH*, LMK 2010, 306719 – Sommer unseres Lebens, with note by S. Leible and D. Jahn.
154. *BGH*, MMR 2010, 565 (569) – Sommer unseres Lebens, with note by R. Mantz.
155. *BGH*, MMR 2010, 565 (570) – Sommer unseres Lebens, with note by R. Mantz.
156. *BGH*, NJW 2010, 2061 (2064) – Sommer unseres Lebens, with note by K. Nenninger.
157. Frank Füglein & Pascal Lagardère, *Technik, die begeistert? Rechtsprechung, die erschreckt? Die Probleme der Hoteliers und der Störerhaftung*, MMR-Aktuell (2) 341464 (2013); Thomas Hoeren, *WLAN – Haftung – A Never Ending Story?*, ZRP (3) 72, 75 (2014).
158. *LG Hamburg*, BeckRS 2011, 3015 – Internet-Cafe.

peer-to-peer file-sharing. In contrast, the Regional Court of Frankfurt am Main held, regarding a wireless network in a hotel, that informing guests of their duties under statutory legal rules was enough.[159]

[2] The Legislator Steps In

The German legislator wanted to resolve the legal uncertainty surrounding the responsibilities of Wi-Fi providers. The governing political parties CDU, CSU, and SPD in their 2013 *Koalitionsvertrag* agreed that the providers of wireless networks would have to be exempted from liability.[160] With a view to improving the availability of Wi-Fi in Germany, the German Federal Government published a bill that would clarify the liability of providers of wireless Internet access.[161] With this bill, the government aimed to bring these service providers within the scope of the mere conduit liability exemption in Article 8 of the Telemedia Act.[162] But the bill also provided that these providers must take appropriate measures to prevent any abuse of their networks.

These legislative intentions were paralleled by decisions of the German lower courts that held that commercial providers of wireless Internet access are protected against liability under the mere conduit liability exemption. For instance, the Regional Court of Hamburg made clear that the provision of Internet access to hotel guests is covered by Article 8 of the Telemedia Act.[163] Moreover, in 2014, the Regional Court of Munich I in the *Mc Fadden* case had referred questions to the CJEU specifically regarding the applicability of the mere conduit exemption to providers of wireless Internet connections.[164] There was thus a risk that the government's initiative would become untenable and obsolete once the CJEU would answer these preliminary questions.[165]

The German government's bill would clarify that those who offer wireless Internet access would be exempted from *Störerhaftung* if they implemented reasonable measures to prevent infringements. The government's bill prescribed the measures that providers would have to implement in order for their liability to be exempted. First, these providers could only give access to users who declared that they would not use the connection for unlawful activities. Second, these providers would have to make

159. *LG Frankfurt*, MMR 2011, 401 (402) – Filesharing-Abmahnung.
160. 'Deutschlands Zukunft gestalten', Koalitionsvertrag zwischen CDU, CSU und SPD, 48: 'Rechtssicherheit für WLAN-Betreiber ist dringend geboten, etwa durch Klarstellung der Haftungsregelungen (Analog zu Accessprovidern)'.
161. Die Bundesregierung, Digitale Agenda 2014 – 2017, 15: 'Wir werden die Verbreitung und Verfügbarkeit von mobilem Internet über WLAN verbessern. Dabei werden wir darauf achten, dass die IT-Sicherheit gewahrt bleibt und keine neuen Einfallstore für anonyme Kriminalität entstehen'.
162. Available at: www.bmwi.de/BMWi/Redaktion/PDF/S-T/telemedienaenderungsgesetz, property = pdf,bereich = bmwi2012,sprache = de,rwb = true.pdf (accessed 14 June 2019).
163. *AG Hamburg*, BeckRS 2014, 15011 – Hotel. *Cf. AG Berlin-Charlottenburg*, BeckRS 2015, 2858 – Freifunk.
164. *LG München I*, BeckRS 2014 2014, 18492 – Mc Fadden.
165. Reto Mantz & Thomas Sassenberg, *Verantwortlichkeit des Access-Providers auf dem europäischen Prüfstand Neun Fragen an den EuGH zu Haftungsprivilegierung, Unterlassungsanspruch und Prüfpflichten des WLAN-Betreibers*, MMR (2) 85, 90 (2015).

sure that their Internet connections could not be used without their authorization. No specific measures were prescribed for reasons of technology neutrality. Instead the bill spoke of appropriate security measures (*'angemessene Sicherungsmaßnahme'*). Protecting access to the network with 'WPA2 standards' and voluntary user registration were mentioned as examples in the explanatory memorandum to the bill.

The German Senate (*Bundesrat*) criticized the bill for its reference to 'appropriate security measures'.[166] According to the Senate, this requirement would again be in need of interpretation by the courts and would not provide the desired legal clarity. The Senate was of the opinion that the bill would have to be amended in order to clarify that the providers of wireless access providers are covered by the liability exemptions, without requiring any measures from them. This would be a de facto abolition of *Störerhaftung* for wireless access providers.[167]

In March 2016, CJEU Advocate General Szpunar gave his opinion in the earlier-mentioned *Mc Fadden* case. Szpunar made short shrift of the obligation to secure one's wireless network. According to Szpunar, such an obligation could potentially undermine the business models of businesses offering Internet access in their establishments.[168] The security measures would require that the identity of users and their data would have to be stored.[169] While telecommunications providers have such a duty, Szpunar saw in this a burden which was simply too heavy for the owners of a bar, hotel, or cafe. Moreover, 'conferring an active, preventative role on intermediary service providers would be inconsistent with their particular status which is protected under [the E-Commerce Directive]'.[170] As a final point, the Advocate General expressed his doubts about the effectiveness of the measure and hence the appropriateness and the proportionality of the measure. The measure would not strike a fair balance between the right to the protection of intellectual property and the freedom to conduct a business.[171]

[3] The Legislator Steps in Once Again

The opinion of Advocate General Szpunar put a bomb under the German government's bill. A revised and dramatically simplified version of the original bill was passed in July 2016.[172] It introduced a new paragraph in Article 8 of the Telemedia Act, which clarified that the liability exemptions in Article 8 also applied to service providers that offer their users wireless Internet access. The explanatory memorandum clarifies that the measures to prevent infringements had been removed as they were incompatible

166. Bundesrat, Drucksache 440/1/15.
167. Gerald Spindler, *Sperrverfügungen gegen Access-Provider – Klarheit aus Karlsruhe?*, GRUR (5) 451, 459–460 (2016).
168. Opinion of AG Szpunar 16 March 2016, ECLI:EU:C:2016:170, para. 139 (*Mc Fadden v. Sony Music Entertainment Germany*).
169. Opinion of AG Szpunar, *supra* n. 168, at para. 140.
170. Opinion of AG Szpunar, *supra* n. 168, at para. 144.
171. Opinion of AG Szpunar, *supra* n. 168, at para. 147.
172. Bundesgesetzblatt Jahrgang 2016 Teil I Nr. 36, ausgegeben am 26.07.2016, Seite 1766; Zweites Gesetz zur Änderung des Telemediengesetzes.

with EU law and did not contribute to creating more legal certainty.[173] Effectively, the new law thus only clarified that the providers of wireless Internet access cannot be liable for damages. Their potential liability as *Störers* was not affected by the new law.

After the law was adopted in July 2016, the CJEU delivered its judgment in the *Mc Fadden* case in September 2016. Surprisingly, and unlike Advocate General Szpunar, the CJEU held that providers can be required to protect their networks with a password in order to prevent users from engaging in infringing activities.[174] The CJEU only considered password-protection of the network and not the implementation of security protocols that the German legislator initially suggested.[175] The CJEU was also unclear about what level of identification can be required from users for them to be given Internet access. In this regard, it is unlikely that the CJEU's decision in *Mc Fadden* would settle the discussions about what exactly can be required from Wi-Fi providers.

Even though there existed a clear willingness to promote the adoption of wireless Internet access, the *Störerhaftung* doctrine still unabatedly applied to these providers. Since *Mc Fadden*, we know that providers *can* be required to protect Internet access with a password. Yet, there was still no definitive answer as to what could be expected from these providers.

[4] The Legislator Steps in Yet Again

In March 2017, the German government made another attempt to clarify the liability of wireless access providers. It introduced a new law that was adopted by the German Bundestag in July 2017.[176] This law effectively removes *Störerhaftung* for wireless access providers. It added a provision to Article 8 of the Telemedia Act clarifying that providers of wireless Internet access can no longer be subject to injunctive relief, nor can they be liable to pay costs in the case of warnings.[177] Specifically with regard to the providers of wireless Internet access, the new law clarifies that these providers do not have a duty to register their users and they cannot be required to restrict access to their networks with a password.[178]

This new law also codifies a duty to block access to infringing websites. It specifies that such duties can only be imposed by the courts.[179] Providers of wireless access can be ordered to block access to webpages if their networks are used to infringe intellectual property rights.[180] In doing so, the new law prevents copyright owners from

173. Begr. des RegE, BT-Drs. 18/6745.
174. CJEU 15 September 2016, ECLI:EU:C:2016:689 (*Mc Fadden v. Sony Music Entertainment Germany*). *See* section §3.05[C][5] for a discussion of this case.
175. Reto Mantz, *EuGH-Entscheidung zur Haftung beim Betrieb eines WLANs – McFadden (C-484/14) – oder: Kein guter Tag*, 15 September 2016, www.offenenetze.de/2016/09/15/eugh-entscheidung-zur-haftung-beim-betrieb-eines-wlans-mcfadden-c-48414-oder-kein-guter-tag/ (accessed 14 June 2019).
176. Begr. des RegE, BT-Drs. 18/6745.
177. New Article 8(1) of the Telemedia Act.
178. New Article 8(4) of the Telemedia Act.
179. New Article 7(3) of the Telemedia Act.
180. New Article 7(4) of the Telemedia Act.

ending up without having any recourse against infringements.[181] The duty to block must be reasonable and proportionate and may not lead to 'overblocking'.[182] A duty to block can only exist if there is no other possibility for rightholders to stop infringements. Hence, a copyright owner must first try to take action against the actual infringer – for example, a torrent sharing platform – or a hosting provider. In this respect, the new law captures what the German Federal Court of Justice had already held regarding blocking injunctions against access providers.[183]

Moreover, rightholders must bear the costs for obtaining such a blockade as these service providers cannot be obliged to reimburse such costs. With this rule, the German legislator aims to prevent the situation that these service providers, who do not themselves infringe on any rights, would have to pay costs, which could again hamper them in offering Wi-Fi access.[184]

This change to the Telemedia Act is likely to resolve much of the legal uncertainty that exists regarding the responsibilities of the providers of wireless Internet access. All forms of responsibility are ruled out, except for the duty to block access to copyright-infringing websites. The new law codifies a rule that providers of wireless access should only be ordered to block access if other attempts to stop the infringements have failed. The method that providers must use to block access is not clearly defined, though, and must be determined on the basis of the facts and circumstances of a particular case. In this regard, the German legislator mentioned the blocking of a particular website, but also closing certain ports on a router to prevent peer-to-peer file-sharing.[185]

These changes to the Telemedia Act are a novelty: for the first time the responsibility that a particular service provider may bear is defined in *statutory* law. In that sense, the new law moves away from an approach in which the responsibility of an intermediary is defined using open-ended statutory language and in which courts must further define that responsibility. The German legislator has explicitly taken over this task from the German courts, which had been unable to create a coherent and predictable body of case law.[186] The new law only deals with providers of *wireless Internet access*. The responsibilities that access providers have are not defined by this new law. The duties that these providers may have are still a matter that is to be decided by the German courts. The liability of those who share a *wired* Internet connection is also not covered by this law. In that sense, this new *statutory* definition of the responsibilities seems to be specifically driven by the legislator's wish to promote Wi-Fi in Germany and to resolve the uncertainties that exist regarding the responsibilities of these providers in particular.

181. Begr. des RegE, BT-Drs. 18/6745, p. 11–12.
182. Begr. des RegE, BT-Drs. 18/6745, p. 12.
183. *BGH*, GRUR 2016, 268 – goldesel.to. *See* section §5.07[C][2] for a discussion of this decision.
184. Begr. des RegE, BT-Drs. 18/6745, p. 12.
185. Begr. des RegE, BT-Drs. 18/6745, p. 12.
186. Begr. des RegE, BT-Drs. 18/6745, p. 10.

[D] Caching

After discussing the liability exemption for mere conduit activities in Article 8 of the Telemedia Act, we will now touch upon the exemption that was put in place to protect intermediaries who cache information. Article 9 of the Telemedia Act contains a liability exemption regarding the automatic temporary storage of information in order to make access to that information more efficient. Just as the liability exemption for mere conduits, the caching exemption is an almost literal implementation of Article 13(1) and (2) of the E-Commerce Directive.

Caching as exempted under Article 9 of the Telemedia Act is different from the automatic temporary storage exempted under the mere conduit exemption in Article 8 of the Telemedia Act. For the mere conduit exemption to apply, the temporary storage may only serve the purpose of *enabling a transmission*, as is done for instance by Internet access providers. In contrast, the type of caching exempted under Article 9 should be done in order to make the transmission of information *more efficient*. An example of such caching is the temporary storage of an often accessed website by a service provider to enable others to access more efficiently.[187]

The liability exemption for caching applies if five requirements are met. First, the provider should not modify the information. Second, it should comply with the conditions on access to the information. Third, the provider should comply with the rules regarding the updating of the information, as specified in a manner that is widely recognized and used by industry. Fourth, the provider should not interfere with the lawful use of technology, as widely recognized and used by industry, to obtain data on the use of the information. And, fifth, the provider should act expeditiously to remove or to disable access to the information it has stored upon obtaining knowledge of the fact that the information at the initial source of the transmission has been removed from the network, or access to it has been disabled, or that a court or an administrative authority has ordered such removal or disablement.

The caching exemption does not apply to providers of 'mirror' servers or websites.[188] These mirrors provide copies of information that is available elsewhere and as such serve as alternative sources for that information. They can be used to provide reliable access to the information or may serve as a backup. They may also serve as backups of websites to which access has been blocked, for instance for reasons of copyright infringement. This functionality extends beyond simply making the transmission of the information of others more efficient.

The caching exemption does not apply to search engines offering 'cache' versions of indexed websites.[189] These copies enable search engine users to see the contents of a particular website at the time the search engine crawled the website. It may help these users to see why a particular website showed up in the search results. These copies may also serve an archival or backup function. However, because these copies

187. Spindler/Schuster/Hoffmann, TMG § 9 Rn. 10.
188. Spindler/Schuster/Hoffmann, TMG § 8 Rn. 10.
189. Ulrich Sieber & Marc Liesching, *Die Verantwortlichkeit der Suchmaschinenbetreiber nach dem Telemediengesetz*, MMR-Beil. (8) 1, 27–28 (2007).

do not solely make access to the information more efficient and these copies are not temporary, the liability exemption for caching does not apply to the 'cache' copies provided by search engines.[190]

[E] Storage of Information

Article 10 of the Telemedia Act contains a liability exemption for the storage of information ('*Speicherung von Informationen*'). This provision implements Article 14 of the E-Commerce Directive which limits the liability of service providers which host content for their users.

While the liability exemption for hosting was drafted with traditional website hosting services in mind, the scope of the exemption has been widened to cover service providers that store the information of others in the broadest sense of the term. For instance, the liability exemption also protects providers of chat services and forums.[191] Also service providers that offer people a platform to publish their blogs are covered by the hosting service provider.[192]

The exemption also applies to video hosting platforms. The Hamburg Higher Regional Court in a decision regarding the video hosting platform YouTube explained that this intermediary is 'in its basic structure' a hosting provider.[193] The Court relied on the CJEU's decision in *Sabam v. Netlog*, in which the CJEU held that also a social network provider can be a hosting provider.[194] According to the Hamburg Court, the structural difference between a classic hosting provider and a video platform should not in principle lead to different legal treatment. The Court recognized that the video hosting platform differs from traditional hosting in the sense that the platform is not just a place to which users upload videos. Moreover, users cannot again download their content from the platform. Nevertheless, the platform enables users to make materials available to other users. The information exchange *between* users is paramount on YouTube. According to the Court, YouTube thus stored the materials for others and could therefore rely on the hosting liability exemption.

In order to benefit from the liability exemption for hosting, the intermediary should not have knowledge of the unlawful activity or information. When a claim for damages is concerned, the intermediary should also not know of any facts or circumstances from which the unlawful activity or information is apparent. If the intermediary acquires such information, it should expeditiously remove the materials or disable access thereto. The knowledge that must be absent is subjective knowledge about a concrete copyright infringement.[195] Objective knowledge (*Kennenmüssen*)

190. For the same reasons the liability exemption in Article 8(2) of the Telemedia Act does not apply.
191. Spindler/Schuster/Hoffmann, TMG § 9 Rn. 13.
192. *BGH*, MMR 2012, 124 – Blogger.
193. *OLG Hamburg*, MMR 2016, 269 – Störerhaftung von YouTube, with note by H. Frey.
194. CJEU 16 February 2012, ECLI:EU:C:2012:85 (*Netlog*).
195. Spindler/Schuster/Hoffmann, TMG § 10 Rn. 18. *Also see*: *BGH*, GRUR 2004, 74 – Rassistische Hetze.

does not amount to such knowledge.[196] Also a general knowledge of infringements cannot amount to knowledge under Article 10 of the Telemedia Act.[197]

If an intermediary acquires knowledge about a particular infringement, it should expeditiously act to remove the materials or disable access thereto. Article 5(2) of the 1997 Teleservices Act – the predecessor of Article 10 of the Telemedia Act – did not specifically require that materials be removed or access to them be disabled, but spoke of preventing the use of the materials to the extent that is technically possible and reasonable. Although the current Telemedia Act does not explicitly require that removal should be reasonable and technically feasible, the German legislator made clear that these requirements still apply in its explanatory memorandum to the Telemedia Act.[198]

Just as in the Netherlands, the liability regime in the Telemedia Act in practice leads to notice-and-takedown systems.[199] Such systems enable copyright owners to notify intermediaries of infringing materials. Yet, as we will see, in Germany, intermediaries may even have a duty to monitor their service to prevent further infringements – so-called notice-and-*stay-down*.[200]

Whether or not a notice suffices, and which procedure should be followed, is solely based on case law. In *Stiftparfum*, the German Federal Court of Justice clarified that a notice must be concrete enough for the intermediary to determine, without any difficulty, that there is an infringement. Such a notice should not require a detailed legal or factual verification.[201] In another case, the Court prescribed quite a detailed procedure regarding how hosting service providers must respond to notices specifically regarding defamatory materials.[202] The host provider, when it receives a notice, must forward the notice to the alleged defamer who is then given an opportunity to respond. If no response is received, the provider must assume that the notice is accurate and remove the defaming material. However, if the author denies the legitimacy of the notice, the provider must then inform the person affected and, if necessary, require further proof that substantiates the infringement.[203]

§5.07 RESPONSIBILITIES OF INTERMEDIARIES

Regardless of the liability exemptions in the Telemedia Act, intermediaries can be given a responsibility to stop or prevent infringements by others. This section discusses the legal bases for allocating such responsibilities. The most prominent legal basis is the *Störerhaftung* doctrine, which can be used to require intermediaries to take measures to stop or prevent infringements (section §5.07[A]). This doctrine is not only the basis

196. Rassistische Hetze, *supra* n. 195, at 75.
197. Spindler/Schuster/Hoffmann, TMG § 10 Rn. 19.
198. Begr. des RegE, BT-Drs. 14/6098, p. 25.
199. Hoeren/Sieber/Holznagel, Multimedia-Recht, 21.1 Rn 89.
200. *See* section §5.07[B].
201. *BGH*, GRUR 2011, 1038 – Stiftparfum.
202. *BGH*, MMR 2012, 124 – Blogger para. 27.
203. *Also see*: *LG Nürnberg-Fürth*, ZUM 2013, 70 – Haftung eines Hostproviders für persönlichkeitsrechtsverletzende Äußerung.

for monitoring duties (section §5.07[B]) but also the blocking of websites by access providers (section §5.07[C]). Besides the *Störerhaftung* doctrine, German copyright law also provides for a separate statutory legal basis to identify an infringer (section §5.07[D]).

[A] *Störerhaftung*

While intermediaries cannot be generally liable as infringers or participants in the infringements of others, the *Störerhaftung* doctrine offers copyright owners a legal basis to still require from intermediaries that they take responsibility for the infringements of others. An important limitation to the *Störerhaftung* doctrine is that it cannot be a basis for a claim for damages.[204] *Störerhaftung* only provides a basis for injunctions.[205]

The *Störerhaftung* doctrine does not have its roots in German tort law but is based on an analogous application of Articles 862 and 1004 of the German Civil Code on interference with someone else's assets or property.[206] When the Copyright Directive and the Enforcement Directive had to be transposed into German law, the German legislator was of the opinion that the *Störerhaftung* provided sufficient possibilities to require assistance from intermediaries. The legislator explicitly refrained from codifying the doctrine as it would be difficult to define. The legislator preferred to allow the doctrine to develop through court decisions on a case-by-case basis.

When does the *Störerhaftung* doctrine apply? In its *Möbelklassiker* decision, the German Federal Court of Justice recognized that one can be liable as a *Störer* by contributing to bringing about another's copyright infringement in a willing and adequately causal manner.[207] A person's contribution may also consist of supporting or exploiting another's infringement as long as that person had the legal possibility to prevent the infringement.[208] Hence, for an intermediary to be liable as a *Störer*, its service must have at least contributed to the infringement, there must be an 'adequately causal link' between the service and the infringement, and the intermediary should be in a position to prevent the infringement.

The German Federal Court of Justice's decision in *Kopierläden*, on the liability of a copy shop owner for unauthorized copying, provides some clarity on this concept of an adequately causal contribution.[209] The Court considered that it is decisive whether, from an objective point of view, the infringing use is not completely unlikely and can reasonably be expected by the owner of the equipment. The causal connection was not precluded by the fact that these others had infringed independently from the owner of

204. *BGH*, GRUR 2002, 618 (619) – Meißner Dekor.
205. Internetversteigerung II, *supra* n 2, at 711.
206. Meißner Dekor, *supra* n. 204. For an overview, see: Matthias Leistner, *Störerhaftung und mittelbare Schutzrechtsverletzung*, GRUR-Beil. (1) 1 (2010); Ansgar Ohly, *Die Verantwortlichkeit von Intermediären*, ZUM (4) 308 (2015).
207. *BGH*, GRUR 1999, 418 – Möbelklassiker.
208. Möbelklassiker, *supra* n. 207, at 419.
209. *BGH*, GRUR 1984, 54 (55) – Kopierläden.

the equipment.[210] The requirement of an adequately causal contribution is therefore a rather broad connection that can easily be established.

Yet, in order to prevent that every causal contribution leads to liability under *Störerhaftung*, the German courts have limited the doctrine's scope by also requiring that a reasonable duty to inspect (*'Prüfungspflicht'*) must have been violated.[211] In *Möbelklassiker*, the German Federal Court of Justice explained specifically regarding copyright infringements that *Störerhaftung* should not disproportionately affect those who are not infringers.[212] The application of the *Störerhaftung* doctrine to parties other than the primary copyright infringer therefore requires that a duty to inspect has been violated.[213] Or, as the former president of the First Civil Chamber of the German Federal Court of Justice Joachim Bornkamm noted: 'nobody shall be held liable as an interferer (*Störer*) if it would be unreasonable to burden him with a duty to examine whether or not his behaviour could interfere with the (intellectual) property of a third person'.[214] Hence, the liability of an intermediary for copyright infringements under *Störerhaftung* is limited to the extent that the intermediary had a reasonable duty to inspect.

The question of whether, and to what extent, these inspection duties are reasonable depends on the circumstances of a particular case.[215] In determining what can be reasonably expected from an intermediary, the function and tasks of the intermediary, as well as the infringer's own responsibility, are taken into account.[216] Another factor is the extent to which measures are technically feasible. In its *Internetversteigerung II* decision, the German Federal Court of Justice held that an online auction platform could only be obligated to implement measures to the extent that the operator would be technically able to implement them.[217]

Whether or not the intermediary provides a service for profit, or in contrast, offers a service in the public interest without pursuing a profit, is relevant as well.[218] Also the extent to which a particular duty would be in conflict with a business model is taken into account. While in *Internetversteigerung I*, the Federal Court of Justice would only attach *Störerhaftung* to the operator of the online auction platform after it became aware of the infringement, the Federal Court of Justice in *Sommer unseres Lebens* did not require such an awareness.[219] An individual sharing his Internet access with others does not need to know about the infringements of others for the *Störerhaftung* doctrine to apply. According to the Federal Court of Justice this difference is justified by the fact

210. Kopierläden, *supra* n. 209, at 55.
211. Andreas Walter, *Zivilrechtliche Störerhaftung*, 9 JA 658, 660 (2012).
212. Möbelklassiker, *supra* n. 207, at 419–420.
213. Möbelklassiker, *supra* n. 207, at 419.
214. Joachim Bornkamm, *E-Commerce Directive vs. IP Rights Enforcement. Legal Balance Achieved?*, GRUR Int (8/9) 642, 643 (2007).
215. Möbelklassiker, *supra* n. 207, at 420. *Also see*: Internetversteigerung II, *supra* n. 2.
216. *BGH*, GRUR 2014, 657 (659) – BearShare.
217. Internetversteigerung II, *supra* n. 2. *Also see*: *BGH*, GRUR 2010, 633 (735) – Sommer unseres Lebens, with note by F. Stang and S. Hühner.
218. *BGH*, GRUR 2004, 619 (621) – kurt-biedenkopf.de.
219. Internetversteigerung I, *supra* n. 2; *BGH*, GRUR 2010, 633 – Sommer unseres Lebens, with note by F. Stang and S. Hühner.

that there was no business model at stake that would be endangered by imposing preventive inspection duties.

In sum, when Internet intermediaries are concerned, we can distinguish three requirements for the *Störerhaftung* doctrine to apply.[220] First, the intermediary must have made a wilful and adequate causal contribution to the infringing activities of a third party. This requirement is generally satisfied rather easily. Second, the intermediary should have had the possibility to stop the infringements. Third, the intermediary should have infringed a reasonable duty to inspect. Whether a duty is reasonable depends on the facts and circumstances of the case. To see how *Störerhaftung* can be applied to intermediaries, we will now consider two types of injunctions which have been issued against intermediaries: monitoring duties and duties to block access to infringing websites.

[B] Monitoring Duties

Although general duties to monitor for copyright infringements are out of the question, the German courts have nevertheless accepted profound duties requiring intermediaries not only to stop a particular infringement but also to prevent future infringements. Here German law therefore goes beyond notice-and-takedown and requires from particular intermediaries that the infringing materials must also stay down. As the intermediary is more closely involved in the infringements of its users, the level of monitoring that is required increases. *Störerhaftung* can also be a basis for filtering duties. Such duties are not undisputed among German scholars. Questions have been raised about how these duties relate to Article 15 of the E-Commerce Directive, which prohibits a general duty to monitor,[221] and the fair balance between fundamental rights.[222]

In *Internetversteigerung I*, the Federal Court of Justice recognized that an online auction platform should not just remove specific infringing offers on its platform but that the operator should also take precautions to make sure that no similar trademark infringements take place.[223] The operator could, for example, specifically monitor for offers of low-priced 'Rolex' watches. In *Jugendgefährdende Medien bei eBay*, the Federal Court of Justice gave a more detailed explanation of the level of prevention required.[224] While it cannot be expected that the operator inspects all offers for infringements before they are published on the platform, the operator does have a duty to prevent similar infringements in the future. Hence, the monitoring duty concerns not only offers of the same item by the same infringer but also offers of that same item by

220. Leistner, *supra* n. 4, at 78; Ohly, *supra* n. 206.
221. Jan B. Nordemann, *Liability for Copyright Infringements on the Internet: Host Providers (Content Providers) The German Approach*, JIPITEC 37 (1) 46 (2011).
222. For instance: Leistner, *supra* n. 4, at 79; Graziana Kastl, Filter – Fluch oder Segen? Möglichkeiten und Grenzen von Filtertechnologien zur Verhinderung von Rechtsverletzungen, GRUR (7) 671 (2016).
223. Internetversteigerung I, *supra* n. 2, at 864.
224. *BGH*, GRUR 2007, 890 – Jugendgefährdende Medien bei eBay.

other users. This is to prevent users from simply making repeated offers of the infringing goods by registering themselves under a different name.[225]

This level of monitoring can also be expected from intermediaries to prevent copyright infringements. *Alone in the Dark* dealt with the file hosting service RapidShare.[226] In this 2012 case, the German Federal Court of Justice held that RapidShare had to instal a word-filter to retrieve and delete the infringing materials, even if such filtering cannot fully eliminate all infringements. To prevent the removal of lawful materials, RapidShare had to manually check the removed files. While it could not be ruled out that lawful materials would still be removed, the Court held that such removals must be accepted in order to effectively protect copyrights.

In a 2013 decision again concerning RapidShare, the German Federal Court of Justice upheld an even stricter duty.[227] According to the Court, extensive duties are appropriate if a service is particularly prone to infringements ('*Gefahrengeneigtheit*'). In this case, the Court considered that while RapidShare's business model was not based on infringements by its users, RapidShare's actions nevertheless increased the risk of infringements. For example, the service could be used anonymously, which increased the attractiveness of the service for illegal uses. There were also files that had been downloaded around 100,000 times, which, according to the Court, was only possible because these files contained highly attractive infringing materials. The Federal Court of Justice held that RapidShare had a duty to comprehensively observe the market regarding all 4,815 music files in question. RapidShare had to monitor its service using search engines such as those provided by Google, Facebook, or Twitter, to see whether there were any links to its file hosting platform indicating the illegality of the uploaded files.

Extensive monitoring duties have also been imposed on video hosting platforms. In *GEMA v. YouTube*, the Hamburg Higher Regional Court ordered YouTube to use its Content ID system to actively prevent new uploads of videos containing particular musical works.[228] YouTube initially put in place its Content ID system to monitor uploaded content and to give copyright owners a choice as to whether they would like to remove the content or share in the advertising profits. In this decision, the Court obliged YouTube to use the Content ID system also to actively prevent infringements. According to the Court, such monitoring is generally not considered to be a violation of the prohibition on general monitoring duties as it requires monitoring for specific infringements only.[229] After this decision, YouTube obtained a licence from GEMA for the use of music on the platform.[230]

225. Jugendgefährdende Medien bei eBay, *supra* n. 224, at 894.
226. *BGH*, GRUR 2013, 370 – Alone in the Dark.
227. *BGH*, IIC 2014, 716 – RapidShare III.
228. *OLG Hamburg*, MMR 2016, 269 – Störerhaftung von YouTube, with note by H. Frey.
229. *OLG Hamburg*, MMR 2016, 269 (277) – Störerhaftung von YouTube, with note by H. Frey.
230. Pia Lorenz & Constantin Baron van Lijnden, '*Die Gema war bereit, praktisch jeden Preis zu akzeptieren*', *Legal Tribune Online*, 4 November 2016, https://perma.cc/7L4V-KGKP (accessed 14 June 2019).

[C] Blocking Websites

The *Störerhaftung* doctrine has also served as a basis for holding access providers responsible for infringements by their users.[231] Blocking a website can be an effective means to prevent access to websites that facilitate copyright infringements. One may think of blocking websites that offer movies and series for downloading, or that offer streams of live soccer matches.

The CJEU's decision in *UPC Telekabel*, in which the Court did not rule against blocking orders per se, revived German debates about the extent to which such orders can be reasonable under the *Störerhaftung* doctrine.[232] In two parallel proceedings, website blocking was considered by the German Federal Court of Justice after two different German Higher Regional Courts. In December 2015, the German Federal Court of Justice delivered its judgments in both cases. Both cases are discussed below.

[1] 3dl.am

The *3dl.am* case dealt with a website that offered links to unauthorized copies of musical works stored with file hosting websites.[233] The Hamburg Higher Regional Court held that the access provider had no duty to block the website in question. The Court was concerned about the impact that such a blockade would have on the fundamental rights of access providers and users. In this respect, the Court also considered that such a duty could lead to the overblocking of legitimate materials. The Court was also concerned about the secrecy of telecommunications, as protected by Article 10 of the German Basic Law ('*Grundgesetz*') and Article 88 of the German Telecommunications Act. The latter does protect not only the content of telecommunications but also the metadata relating to those communications, such as IP addresses, URLs, and domain names. As there was no statutory basis for the use of these data, the Hamburg Higher Regional Court rejected the injunction to block.

---

231. Matthias Leistner & Karina Grisse, *Sperrverfügungen gegen Access – Provider im Rahmen der Störerhaftung (Teil 1)*, GRUR (1) 19, 19–20 (2015); Joachim Sternberg, *Die Rechtsprechung des EuGH und des BGH zum Urheberrecht und zu den verwandten Schutzrechten im Jahre 2014*, GRUR (3) 205, 216 (2015).
232. Gerald Spindler, *Zivilrechtliche Sperrverfügungen gegen Access Provider nach dem EuGH-Urteil 'UPC Telekabel'*, GRUR (9) 826 (2014); Arian Nazari-Khanachayi, *Access-Provider als urheberrechtliche Schnittstelle im Internet. Europarechtliche Vorgaben im Hinblick auf Zugangserschwerungsverfügungen und Lösungsansätze für das deutsche Recht de lege ferenda*, GRUR (2) 115 (2015); Leistner & Grisse, *supra* n. 231; Matthias Leistner & Karina Grisse, *Sperrverfügungen gegen Access – Provider im Rahmen der Störerhaftung (Teil 2)*, GRUR (2) 105 (2015); Christian Czychowski & Jan B. Nordemann, *Die Entwicklung der unter- und obergerichtlichen Rechtsprechung zum Urheberrecht im Jahr 2014*, GRUR-RR (5) 185 (2015).
233. *OLG Hamburg*, GRUR-RR 2014, 140 (146) – 3dl.am.

[2] Goldesel.to

The Cologne Higher Regional Court had to decide on a similar case. *Goldesel.to* offered links to copyrighted materials available on peer-to-peer file-sharing networks.[234] In contrast to the Hamburg Court, the Cologne Court in *goldesel.to* held that DNS and IP blocking obligations are not in conflict with the secrecy of telecommunications. The Cologne Court explained that an Internet access provider would not obtain more information on the communications than the provider already had.[235] Therefore blocking injunctions do not infringe the right of secrecy of telecommunications.

In contrast to the Hamburg Court in *3dl.am*, the Cologne Court in *goldesel.to* also had the CJEU's decision in *UPC Telekabel* to work with. In this decision, the CJEU had held that EU law and the fundamental rights protected in the EU Charter do not preclude blocking injunctions. Thus, while the Hamburg court had ruled against the permissibility of blocking, the CJEU in *UPC Telekabel* did not rule out the possibility of such injunctions. According to the Cologne Court, part of the answer to these seemingly opposing points of view on blocking injunctions lay in the relationship between EU law and German law. In principle, German law should be interpreted in conformity with EU law. Yet, in line with the *ELOG* and *Quelle* decisions of the CJEU, the obligation to interpret Member State law in conformity with EU law cannot be a basis for interpreting Member State *contra legem*.[236] Therefore, the Cologne Court, in assessing whether blocking orders are within the scope of the *Störerhaftung* doctrine, also considered German law, including the fundamental rights enshrined in the German Basic Law.

The Cologne Court was not convinced that economically reasonable measures were available. Also, if such measures would be available, the Court argued that the consideration of other factors would still lead to the conclusion that the blocking injunction was not reasonable. The Court here in particular referred to the risk that legitimate content would be blocked and the blockade's limited effectiveness.[237]

[3] *The German Federal Court of Justice on These Cases*

Both the *3dl.am* and the *goldesel.to* cases reached the German Federal Court of Justice. In both cases, the Court clarified, also with reference to relevant EU law provisions and the CJEU's decision in *UPC Telekabel*, that access providers can be liable as *Störers* as they adequately and causally contribute to infringements by third parties. However, in both cases, the Court also confirmed that the blocking injunctions in question would be unreasonable.

The German Federal Court of Justice based these decisions on the blocking order's lack of subsidiarity. While the Court admitted that *Störerhaftung* in principle

234. *OLG Köln*, GRUR 2014, 1081 (1087–1089) - goldesel.to.
235. Leistner & Grisse, *supra* n. 231, at 23–24.
236. CJEU 5 July 2006, ECLI:EU:C:2006:443 (*ELOG*); CJEU 17 April 2008, ECLI:EU:C:2008:231 (*Quelle*).
237. *OLG Köln*, GRUR 2014, 1081 (1095) - goldesel.to.

does not require subsidiarity, the Court noted specifically regarding access providers that the rightholder should first try to approach the infringer or hosting service provider in question.[238] Here the Court considered in particular the legitimacy and neutrality of the access provider's business model. For reasons of proportionality, access providers can only have a duty to block a website if actions against the website owner or the hosting service provider have failed. The Court set a high standard as to the efforts that rightholders must make before a blocking injunction may be issued.[239] The question is whether this requirement of subsidiarity holds true if it is put to the EU law test.[240] In his opinion in *UPC Telekabel*, Advocate General Cruz Villalón already noted that the copyright owner 'must, as a matter of priority, so far as is possible, claim directly against the operators of the illegal website or their [hosting service provider]'.[241] The CJEU, however, did not explicitly confirm the existence of such a requirement of subsidiarity.

In *3dl.am*, the infringer in question had submitted a false address to the domain registrar. As a consequence, the letters that the right owner sent had not reached the infringer. In this regard, the German Federal Court of Justice noted that the rightholder should have been aware of the infringer's attempt to conceal his identity and that it must make reasonable efforts to determine the identity of the infringer.[242] In *goldesel.to*, the Court noted, regarding the unidentified operator of the website, that the right owner should take all reasonable measures to reveal the infringer.[243] Such measures include private investigations by a detective or other companies offering the investigation of unauthorized online materials. Also, public investigative authorities could become involved by filing a complaint about the infringements.

In both decisions, the German Federal Court of Justice also assessed whether a fair balance had been struck between the fundamental rights of the affected parties. In the *3dl.am* case, the Federal Court of Justice considered that the Hamburg Higher Regional had not adequately considered the fundamental rights in question. This should come as no surprise since the *UPC Telekabel* decision that requires such a balancing had not yet been rendered by the CJEU.

In both decisions, the German Federal Court of Justice raised the question of the extent to which also nationally protected fundamental rights must be considered. As Article 8(3) of the Copyright Directive and Article 11 of the Enforcement Directive leave the modalities of injunctions to the Member States, the Court held that there is room for the consideration of German fundamental rights. Hence, the Court may also consider fundamental rights that are not included in the EU Charter, such as the right to information and the right to self-determination in Articles 1 and 2(1) of the German Basic Law.

238. *BGH*, GRUR 2016, 268 – goldesel.to, para. 82. *BGH*, GRUR-RS 2016, 1908 – 3dl.am, para. 69.
239. Franz Hofmann, *Störerhaftung von Access-Providern für Urheberrechtsverletzungen Dritter*, NJW (11) 769, 771 (2016).
240. Hofmann, *supra* n. 239, at 771.
241. Opinion of AG Cruz Villalón 26 November 2013, ECLI:EU:C:2013:781, para. 107 (*UPC Telekabel Wien v. Constantin Film Verleih and Wega Filmproduktionsgesellschaft*).
242. *BGH*, GRUR-RS 2016, 1908 – 3dl.am, para. 73.
243. *BGH*, GRUR 2016, 268 – goldesel.to, para. 87.

In light of the fair balance of fundamental rights, the German Federal Court of Justice in both decisions considered the problem of overblocking legitimate materials. Here the Court reiterated the CJEU's considerations in *UPC Telekabel* that measures must be strictly targeted. And that these measures must serve to bring the infringement to an end without thereby affecting the access of users to lawful information. In *goldesel.to*, the Court noted that, in order for an infringer not to give the opportunity to hide behind the availability of lawful materials, a blockade may also be reasonable if it blocks legitimate content. However, that only holds true if a small amount of legitimate material is blocked. How much legitimate material may be blocked does not become clear from the Court's decision. On this issue, there is still some uncertainty.[244]

UPC Telekabel requires that users should be able to assert their rights when they learn of the blocking measures.[245] In this respect, the German Federal Court of Justice noted that users might exercise their rights against the access provider on the basis of the contract between them.[246] The question here arises whether the contractual basis that exists between access providers and subscribers is sufficient to address fundamental rights issues.[247] Problematic are also reseller constructions where users may not have a contractual relationship with the access provider that is subject to the injunction.[248]

In both decisions, the right to the secrecy of communications as protected by Article 10(1) of the German Basic Law was considered by the German Federal Court of Justice. A right that the CJEU did not bring into the equation in its fair balance of fundamental rights in *UPC Telekabel.*[249] The German Federal Court of Justice held that this right was not interfered with as it applies to private communications between concrete parties and not to public communications. It may be argued that from a technical perspective, communications between a user and the server offering the website could be qualified as communication between individuals. Nevertheless, this interpretation seems to be sound, given the aim of Article 10(1) of the Basic Law to protect private communications.[250]

On its effectiveness, the German Federal Court of Justice held that the blockade did not need to reduce peer-to-peer file-sharing on the Internet as a whole. Rather, the effectiveness of the blockade had to be assessed in relation to the effects on the blocked website. Otherwise, the copyright owner would be rendered defenceless to the

244. *BGH*, MRR 2016, 180 (187) – Störerhaftung des Access - Providers, with note by M. Finger and T. Conraths.
245. *See* section §3.05[C][4].
246. *BGH*, GRUR 2016, 268 – goldesel.to, para. 57. *BGH*, GRUR-RS 2016, 1908 – 3dl.am, para. 46.
247. Matthias Leistner, *Reformbedarf im materiellen Urheberrecht: Online-Plattformen und Aggregatoren*, ZUM (7) 580, 585 (2016); Franz Hofmann, *Störerhaftung von Access-Providern für Urheberrechtsverletzungen Dritter*, NJW (11) 769, 771 (2016).
248. Joerg Heidrich & Britta Heymann, *Die Büchse der Pandora erneut geöffnet: Der BGH und Websperren Eine kritische Analyse der Rechtsprechung zu Internetsperren durch Access-Provider*, MMR (6) 370, 373 (2016).
249. Gerald Spindler, *Zivilrechtliche Sperrverfügungen gegen Access Provider nach dem EuGH-Urteil 'UPC Telekabel'*, GRUR (9) 826, 830 (2014). The CJEU only considered the user's right to freedom of expression as protected by Article 11 of the EU Charter of Fundamental Rights.
250. Gerald Spindler, *Sperrverfügungen gegen Access-Provider – Klarheit aus Karlsruhe?*, GRUR (5) 451, 456 (2016).

mass-infringements on the Internet. Also, the fact that the blockade may be circumvented does not detract from a blockade being a reasonable measure.

In sum, the German Federal Court of Justice in principle permits blocking injunctions.[251] The Court confirmed that the *Störerhaftung* doctrine provides a sufficient basis for such injunctions.[252] A nuance that was added by the Court is its considerations regarding subsidiarity. While neither the *Störerhaftung* doctrine nor EU law requires that one should first go after the principal infringer or the hosting provider, the German Federal Court of Justice did introduce such a requirement regarding blocking injunctions.

[D] Information Duties

Article 101 of the German Copyright Act grants copyright owners a right to information. This right initially related to *infringers* only. Following the Enforcement Directive, this right has been broadened and now includes information relating to third parties as well.[253]

Article 101 can also apply to intermediaries, such as Internet access providers who have identifying information about their subscribers.[254] In most cases, only the IP address of an infringer is known. Generally speaking, the Internet access provider that assigned that IP address is able to identify the infringer. On the basis of Article 101 of the German Copyright Act, Internet access providers may have to give copyright owners a helping hand by identifying a person behind a particular IP address. Whether the intermediary has a duty to hand over information about an infringer does not depend on the intermediary's liability under copyright law or *Störerhaftung*. Article 101 provides an independent legal basis for the release of information.

Article 101 of the German Copyright Act specifies the copyright owner's right to information in great detail. Here German law significantly differs from Dutch law, in which such a duty was recognized and developed by the Dutch courts using tort law.[255] Article 101(1) of the German Copyright Act provides that anyone who infringes a copyright on a commercial scale can be required to provide information about the origin and distribution networks of the infringing materials. Also, a service provider whose service is used for an infringement can be obliged to provide the copyright owner with the statutorily prescribed types of information.[256]

These types of information that must be provided are enumerated in an exhaustive list. The German legislator's arguments for creating an exhaustive list were

251. Heidrich & Heymann, *supra* n. 247.
252. In January 2018, a first blockade has indeed been ordered in a case concerning a streaming website: LG München I, Az. 7 0 17752/17 – kinox.to. This decision has not yet been reported but is available at: https://perma.cc/FLC4-6BZ6.
253. BT-Drs. 64/07, p. 67. *Also see*: Dieter Frey & Matthias Rudolph, *EU-Richtlinie zur Durchsetzung der Rechte des geistigen Eigentums*, 7 ZUM 522, 525 (2004).
254. Dreier/Schulze, UrhG, § 101 Rn. 10.
255. *See* section §4.06[B].
256. Article 101(2)(3) of the German Copyright Act.

twofold.[257] First, the list prevents those having to provide the information from being required to conduct extensive research. This relates to the more general limitation laid down in Article 101(4) of the German Copyright Act, which provides that claims for information are precluded if the claim is disproportionate.[258] By specifying the information that needs to be provided, the legal certainty of those obliged to provide that information is secured. Second, the list prevents disputes arising on what information has to be provided. This ideally turns the provision of information into an expeditious process.

Although Article 101 of the German Copyright Act limits the right to information to infringers who infringe 'on a commercial scale', the German Federal Court of Justice has held that it can apply to smaller infringements as well.[259] This has opened the door to the identification of individuals who occasionally download protected materials, for instance on peer-to-peer file-sharing networks.

Intermediaries can be required to provide information in the case of a manifest infringement.[260] An infringement is manifestly infringing if it is so clear that an incorrect decision, and thereby an unjustifiable burden on the defendant, is hardly possible.[261] Whether an infringement is manifest is an objective test, which means that the infringement must be obvious from the perspective of an objective, reasonable observer.[262] Unlike the *Störerhaftung* doctrine, an intermediary's duty to provide information does not depend on a violation of any inspection duties.[263]

If the infringement is not manifest, there can be no obligation to provide information. This may be the case if it is not completely clear whether particular conduct should be considered to be an infringement. The streaming of unauthorized videos serves as an example. As it is not (yet) clear whether the streaming of unauthorized materials amounts to an infringement, an access provider cannot be required to provide information about people who stream unauthorized materials.[264] Also, if there are doubts about whether a particular IP address is correct, the access provider cannot be ordered to release identifying information about the person behind that IP address.[265] Of course, if there is no infringement at all, there can also be no obligation to provide information.[266]

Specifically regarding the provision of telecommunication metadata, Article 101(9) of the German Copyright Act provides that the providers of telecommunication

257. Begr. des RegE, BT-Drs. 11/4792, p. 31.
258. Begr. des RegE, BT-Drs. 11/4792, pp. 31–32.
259. *BGH*, GRUR 2012, 1026 (1028) – Alles kann besser werden.
260. Gerald Spindler, *Der Auskunftsanspruch gegen Verletzer und Dritte im Urheberrecht nach neuem Recht*, ZUM (8/9) 640, 643 (2008).
261. Begr. des RegE, BT-Drs. 11/4792, p. 32.
262. Spindler/Schuster/Hoffmann, UrhG § 101 Rn. 19. Dreier/Schulze, UrhG, § 101 Rn. 19.
263. Dreier/Schulze, UrhG, § 101 Rn. 11.
264. For instance: *LG Köln*, MMR 2014, 196 – Redtube.
265. For instance: *OLG Köln*, ZUM 2011, 421 – IP-Adressen, dealing with a request for information that mentioned the same IP address multiple times, while the Internet access provider dynamically assigned IP addresses.
266. For instance: *OLG Köln*, MMR 2014, 134 – Gewaltpornografie. In this case Article 101 did not apply because the video in question infringed the prohibition of violent pornography and therefore was not awarded copyright protection.

services can be required to provide the necessary information only after a court has permitted the use of the metadata. Metadata are data collected, processed, or used to provide a telecommunications service. For instance, data concerning the date and time of a particular communication are metadata. In particular, when Internet access providers have to identify a user that is behind a so-called dynamic IP address – an IP address that changes from time to time – these providers have to examine metadata.[267] In such cases, information about a subscriber can only be released after a court has allowed the use of the metadata.[268] Whenever the IP addresses in question are static IP addresses – IP addresses that do not change – no metadata needs to be examined by the Internet access provider.[269] No prior court order is needed for the release of subscriber data in such cases.

Combined with the copyright owner's possibility to send infringers a warning letter, the right to information has brought about what some have called a warning industry ('*Abmahn-Industrie*').[270] In this 'industry', thousands of Internet users are identified through a single court order and are sent settlement proposals.[271] A copyright owner may require reimbursements of costs, including the costs for the services of a lawyer.[272] A risk of this system may be that users are not sufficiently protected against unfounded claims. In particular cases where the copyrighted materials constituted pornographic videos, people are more likely to settle with a copyright owner in order to quickly get rid of a potentially embarrassing problem.[273]

§5.08 CONCLUSION

The German legislator obediently implemented the Copyright Directive. Regarding the scope of the reproduction right it was clarified that this right also applies to temporary reproductions. A broad right of making work available was also added to the German Copyright Act. Also in Germany we see that, as a consequence of the exclusive right's elasticity, it is not always clear how it should be applied. German case law regarding linking to online material illustrates that the CJEU's decisions on this issue do not always lead to predictable outcomes. Just as in the Netherlands, the CJEU's decision in *GS Media* requires German courts, including the German Federal Court of Justice, to reconsider their hyperlinking case law.[274] Future German case law will have to reflect

267. *BGH*, GRUR 2012, 1026 (1030) – Alles kann besser werden.
268. There is of course a clear relation to the secrecy of telecommunications protected in Article 10 of the German Basic Law. Article 101(10) therefore also explicitly qualifies the obligation to provide such information as a limitation to this fundamental right.
269. *BVerfG*, NJW 2012, 1419 (1422).
270. Martin Hohlweck, *'Even Heaven Cries' – Eine rechtliche Zwischenbilanz von Filesharing-Verfahren*, GRUR (10) 940 (2014). *Also see*: Thomas Dreier & Matthias Leistner, *Urheberrecht im Internet: die Forschungsheraus forderungen*, GRUR (9) 881, 893–894 (2013).
271. Article 97a(1) of the German Copyright Act requires copyright owners to notify infringers before starting court proceedings and to give infringers an opportunity to settle.
272. Article 97a(3) of the German Copyright Act.
273. Sandra Schmitz, *The RedTube Copyright Infringement Affair in Germany: Shame on Who?*, International Review of Law, Computers & Technology (1) 33 (2015).
274. *GS Media v. Sanoma Media Netherlands and others, supra* n. 47.

the knowledge criterion introduced by the CJEU in this decision. German scholars have rightly pointed out that *GS Media* is unlikely to have laid down a predictable rule as it creates new uncertainties about its application and that it clouded the distinction between primary liability for infringements and secondary liability for the infringements of others.[275]

With regard to the limitations and exceptions in German copyright law, the German legislator chose to update the existing limitations and exceptions to the emerging information society. The German legislator, however, did not flexibilize any of the limitations and exceptions, as was the case in the Netherlands.[276] This may be explained by Germany's strong copyright tradition and its conception of limitations and exceptions as derogations from the general rule of copyright protection.

The effects of German copyright law's inflexibility are demonstrated by the *Vorschaubilder* decisions of the Federal Court of Justice regarding the use of thumbnail versions of images in an image search engine.[277] They illustrate how the Court was unable to permit this technologically new form of information processing within the framework of German copyright law. The Court found a way around German copyright law's tight grip by introducing a novel – and much-criticized – theory of consent through which copyright owners are considered to have consented to search engine use.[278] What we may learn from this case is that if copyright law itself does not enable a fair balance to be struck between the relevant interests, the courts may find a way around it by using or even introducing new legal constructs that are foreign to copyright law. From the perspective of the copyright balance, these interpretations of the law must be welcomed. Yet, from the perspective of predictability, it must be noted that they do not contribute to the creation of a coherent copyright law.

In Germany, the rise of video hosting platforms, as well as news search engines and aggregators, has created tensions between the intermediaries offering these new services and the owners of copyrights. At multiple levels in the German legal system, we see a willingness to address this friction and the use of the law as a steering mechanism to more effectively protect the interests of copyright owners. The German courts have acknowledged that, in particular, video hosting platforms can have a duty not only to remove content but also to monitor for further infringing materials.[279] On this issue, German law shows similarities to the liability regime introduced in the DSM Directive. Still, the German monitoring duties are based on *Störerhaftung*, and not an infringement of a copyright, as is the case under the DSM Directive.[280]

The introduction of a novel neighbouring right for press publishers is another attempt to address the friction between copyright owners and intermediaries. However, this appears to be an example of a technology-specific response to the emergence of news search engines and aggregators. The German legislator attempted to rebalance by using quite detailed statutory language. However, this new legislation gave rise to

275. *See* section §5.04[C].
276. *See* section §4.03[B] on the Dutch approach towards limitations and exceptions.
277. Vorschaubilder I, *supra* n. 32; Vorschaubilder I, *supra* n. 69.
278. *See* section §5.04[D].
279. *See* section §5.07[B].
280. *See* section §3.05[E].

greater uncertainty, may have limited access to news, and does not necessarily strengthen the press. The EU legislator is also considering whether to introduce a neighbouring right for press publishers to protect the investments of press publishers in press products. Yet, the German experience with this new neighbouring right is an indication that the introduction of such a right is unlikely to produce the desired effects.

With regard to the responsibilities that intermediaries may have for the infringements of others, the judge-made *Störerhaftung* doctrine has proven to be a flexible tool to determine the responsibilities of both traditional and newer intermediaries. It has attained features that are reminiscent of a duty of care. This criterion of reasonableness enables the German courts to take into account a host of different factors and to allocate responsibility only to the extent that it is reasonable. Duties can be tailored to the intermediary in question and the context in which the intermediary operates. Moreover, the doctrine's flexibility also enables it to easily adapt to European developments in the field of intermediary liability.[281] The development of the German case law on blocking injunctions is a testament to that.[282]

The flexibility that is needed for copyright owners to effectively enforce their rights also requires a coherent body of case law with authoritative decisions by the German Federal Court of Justice or the European Court of Justice.[283] Otherwise that flexibility may create too much uncertainty for intermediaries and users. The German experience with liability for Wi-Fi shows that if no such case law develops, legal uncertainty can have a limiting effect on the innovative use of technology.

281. *Also see*: Matthias Leistner, *Grundlagen und Perspektiven der Haftung für Urheberrechtsverletzungen im Internet*, ZUM (10) 722 (2012).
282. *See* section §5.07[C]. *Also see*: Leistner & Grisse, *supra* n. 231, at 106.
283. *Also see*: Matthias Leistner, Leistner, *supra* n. 4, at 79–80; Ohly, *supra* n. 206, at 313.

CHAPTER 6

Intermediary Liability in the United States

§6.01 INTRODUCTION

The previous chapters mapped the EU legal framework on intermediary liability and considered how that framework works out at the national level in the Netherlands and Germany. In this chapter, we will consider the US law on the topic of intermediary liability. The aim of this chapter is to draw lessons that may be valuable for improving the EU legal framework. This chapter does not aim to provide a comprehensive overview of the US law on the subject, it rather discusses and zooms in on those elements of US law that are relevant for the intermediary's liability for copyright infringements, especially from an EU perspective.

Three aspects of the US legal system are discussed in this chapter: the fair use doctrine in US copyright law, the safe harbours (liability exemptions), and self-regulation and private ordering. To fully understand and appreciate these different aspects, this chapter will first offer a brief overview of US copyright law and its application to intermediaries (section §6.02).

The fair use doctrine is discussed in this chapter because it is an open-ended exception that is unfamiliar to EU law (section §6.03). After that, we will turn to the liability exemptions in US copyright law and its detailed regime on notice-and-takedown systems (section §6.04). And finally, we will consider self-regulatory efforts and private ordering in the US (section §6.05). Special attention is paid to Google's use of the Content ID system and the implications of this content identification technology, in particular for users.

§6.02 FOUNDATIONS

This section lays the foundations for our discussion of US intermediary liability. It briefly explains how and why US copyright law protects copyrights (section §6.02[A]). We will also cover an important distinction that is made in US copyright law: the distinction between direct copyright infringement and indirect copyright infringement (section §6.02[B]).

Someone *directly* infringes a copyright by infringing on the copyright owner's exclusive rights. Those who are involved in the infringements of others may commit an *indirect* infringement and be secondarily liable. When the first Internet intermediaries emerged, discussions centred on whether these intermediaries should be primarily liable as direct infringers for the materials that they stored and transmitted, or whether they should only be liable under indirect infringement theories. This development is discussed as well (section §6.02[C]). We will close this section by exploring these indirect infringement theories and their relevance in the Internet context (section §6.02[D]).

[A] US Copyright Law

A discussion on US copyright law should start with the US Constitution: Article 1 of Section 8, Clause 8 of the US Constitution grants the US Congress the authority to enact copyright law statutes 'to promote the Progress of Science'. More precisely, Congress may enact such laws 'by securing for limited Times to Authors and Inventors the exclusive Right to their respective Writings and Discoveries'. This clause in the US Constitution provides the legal basis for laws on copyright, in particular also the US Copyright Act.

This clause also reveals US copyright law's utilitarian objective. This objective sets a limit on how and to what extent the US Congress may grant rights to copyright owners. Or as the Supreme Court put it in *Goldstein v. California* in 1973:

> The clause thus describes both the objective which Congress may seek and the means to achieve it. The objective is to promote the progress of science and the arts. ... To accomplish its purpose, Congress may grant to authors the exclusive right to the fruits of their respective works.[1]

The US Copyright Act grants copyright owners a set of exclusive rights. These rights include a reproduction right,[2] a right to prepare derivative works,[3] a distribution right,[4] a performance right,[5] and a right of public display.[6] These exclusive rights are expressed using broad terms that are not directly linked to particular technologies. Section 106(1) of the US Copyright Act defines the reproduction right. The reproduction right goes hand in hand with the distribution right that is defined in Section 106(3) of

1. *Goldstein v. California*, 412 U.S. 546, 555 (1973). Fromer has argued that it is better to consider the promotion of science and the useful arts as the part of the clause that defines Congress' power (Jeanne Fromer, 61 *The Intellectual Property Clause's External Limitations*, Duke Law Journal (7) 1329, 1332 (2012)). *Cf.* Edward Walterscheid, *To Promote the Progress of Science and Useful Arts: The Anatomy of a Congressional Power*, 2 IDEA – The Journal of Law and Technology (1) 1 (2003).
2. Section 106(1) of the US Copyright Act.
3. Section 106(2) of the US Copyright Act.
4. Section 106(3) of the US Copyright Act.
5. Section 106(4) of the US Copyright Act.
6. Section 106(5) of the US Copyright Act.

the US Copyright Act. The distribution right is the exclusive right 'to distribute copies or phonorecords of the copyrighted work to the public by sale or other transfer of ownership, or by rental, lease, or lending'. Whereas the reproduction right enables copyright owners to sue those who *reproduce* works without authorization, the distribution right enables copyright owners to also sue those who distribute unauthorized copies.

The US Copyright Act provides for a list of statutory limitations and exceptions. For instance, there is a limitation regarding copies made by libraries and archives.[7] Another example is the limitation of the performance and display rights when work is used for teaching purposes in classrooms.[8] In this chapter, the focus will be on another exception: the fair use doctrine that is laid down in Section 107 of the US Copyright Act. European commentators have heralded it as a flexible legal instrument that enables courts to decide on a case-by-case basis whether to accommodate a particular new and unforeseen use of copyrighted materials.[9] In section §6.03, we will zoom in on this fair use doctrine and see what there is to learn regarding its flexibility, specifically also in relation to the use of works by intermediaries.

[B] The Distinction Between Direct and Indirect Infringement

In discussions on the liability of intermediaries, an infringement of an exclusive right is sometimes referred to as a *direct* infringement in order to distinguish it from forms of *indirect* infringements: contributory or vicarious infringements. Judge Richard Posner for the Seventh Circuit explained that these direct infringements should merely be called 'infringements' because the law, for instance, also does not speak of 'direct negligence' versus 'contributory negligence'.[10] In the same vein, in this chapter the term 'infringement' is reserved for infringements of the exclusive rights granted to copyright owners.[11] The term 'indirect infringement' is used in relation to the doctrines of contributory and vicarious infringement. The liability that is incurred for such indirect infringements is referred to as 'secondary liability'.

Under US copyright law, two forms of indirect infringement are recognized: contributory copyright infringement and vicarious copyright infringement.[12] These forms of indirect infringement cannot as such be found in the US Copyright Act; they are rather based on common law principles.[13] As the US Supreme Court explained in its seminal decision in *Sony Corp. of America v. Universal City Studios*:

---

7. Section 108 of the US Copyright Act.
8. Section 108(1) of the US Copyright Act.
9. For instance, Christiaan Alberdingk Thijm, *Fair Use: het auteursrechtelijk evenwicht hersteld*, AMI (9) 145 (1998); Martin Senftleben, *The International Three-Step Test*, JIPITEC (2) 67 (2010).; Martin Senftleben, *Breathing Space for Cloud-Based Business Models – Exploring the Matrix of Copyright Limitations, Safe Harbours and Injunctions*, JIPITEC (2) 87 (2013); Bernt Hugenholtz, *Fair Use in Europe*, Communications of the ACM (5) 26 (2013).
10. *Flava Works, Inc. v. Gunter*, 689 F.3d 754, 760 (7th Cir. 2012).
11. On some occasions, the term 'direct infringement' may still be used to more clearly distinguish it from indirect infringements.
12. For a discussion, *see* section §6.02[D].
13. *Metro-Goldwyn-Mayer Studios Inc. v. Grokster, Ltd.*, 545 U.S. 913, 930 (2005).

> The absence of such express language in the copyright statute does not preclude the imposition of liability for copyright infringements on certain parties who have not themselves engaged in the infringing activity. For vicarious liability is imposed in virtually all areas of the law, and the concept of contributory infringement is merely a species of the broader problem of identifying the circumstances in which it is just to hold one individual accountable for the actions of another.[14]

For an indirect infringement to exist, another entity should have directly infringed the copyright. Secondary liability thus depends on the existence of a direct infringement.[15] Copyright owners alleging an indirect infringement will therefore have to assert and demonstrate that a primary infringement has been committed as well. A failure to fulfil this basic requirement for an indirect infringement has the effect that the copyright owner's claim will fail.[16] A mere indication that an intermediary's service is used for infringements, without demonstrating that such infringements have actually taken place, is not enough for an indirect infringement.[17] The *Sony* case mentioned above serves as an example.[18] In *Sony*, the US Supreme Court assessed Sony's liability for copies made with its - at the time - revolutionary Betamax video recorder. The Court held that making copies of television programmes in order to view them at a later time was a fair use.[19] Hence, the users of Sony's apparatus did not infringe and therefore Sony could not be held liable as a contributory infringer.

The concepts of a direct infringement and an indirect infringement complement each other in giving copyright owners control over whether, how, and by whom their works are used. As Goldstein points out, digital and networking technologies have made it possible for the selection and performance of copyrighted works to be shifted from public places, such as bookstores and television stations, to the private sphere of the home and the workplace.[20] These technologies have rendered physical borders almost meaningless, which makes it harder for copyright owners to enforce their rights. Secondary liability for infringements makes that enforcement more effective as it enables a range of different parties that are part of the chain of communications between the provider and the user of copyrighted materials to be held liable.

Claims of indirect infringement have often been successful in cases against entities facilitating peer-to-peer file-sharing.[21] The courts deciding these cases have justified the application of secondary liability theories by referring to the practical problem of having to go after the actual (direct) infringers. In *Metro-Goldwyn-Mayer*

14. *Sony Corp. of America v. Universal City Studios, Inc.*, 464 U.S. 417, 435 (1984).
15. *Matthew Bender & Co., Inc. v. West Pub. Co.*, 158 F.3d 693, 706 (2d Cir. 1998); *A&M Records, Inc. v. Napster*, Inc., 239 F.3d 1004, 1013 (9th Cir. 2001); *Perfect 10, Inc. v. Amazon.com, Inc.*, 508 F.3d 1147 (9th Cir. 2007); *Flava Works, Inc. v. Gunter, supra* n. 10, at 758.
16. For example: *Newborn v. Yahoo!, Inc.*, 391 F.Supp.2d 181, 187 (Dist. Court, D.D.C. 2005).
17. For example: *Arista Records, Inc. v. Mp3Board, Inc.*, 2002 WL 1997918, 3 (Dist. Court, S.D.N.Y. 2002).
18. *Sony Corp. of America v. Universal City Studios, Inc., supra* n. 14.
19. A fair use is use that is permitted under US copyright law. For a discussion of the fair use doctrine, *see* section §6.03.
20. Paul Goldstein, *Goldstein on Copyright* 8:2 (2013).
21. For instance: *A&M Records, Inc. v. Napster*, supra n. 15; In re: Aimster Copyright Litigation, 334 F.3d 643 (7th Cir. 2003); *Metro-Goldwyn-Mayer Studios Inc. v. Grokster, Ltd., supra* n. 13.

Studios. v. Grokster, on the liability of Grokster for providing peer-to-peer file-sharing software, the US Supreme Court noted:

> When a widely shared service or product is used to commit infringement, it may be impossible to enforce rights in the protected work effectively against all direct infringers, the only practical alternative being to go against the distributor of the copying device for secondary liability on a theory of contributory or vicarious infringement.[22]

Or, in the words of Judge Posner, 'recognizing the impracticability or futility of a copyright owner's suing a multitude of individual infringers the law allows a copyright holder to sue a contributor to the infringement instead, in effect as an aider and abettor'.[23]

[C] From Direct Infringement to Secondary Liability

In the US, the rise of Internet intermediaries initially blurred the boundaries between primary and secondary liability. Just as in the EU, the use of copyrighted materials in the networked environment raised questions about the role and liability of intermediaries under copyright law.[24] This section highlights how the US courts and the US government initially looked at intermediary activities through a direct infringement lens (section §6.02[C][1]). That changed with the 1995 *Netcom* decision, which recalibrated infringement theory and rejected the view that intermediaries can be liable as direct infringers (section §6.02[C][2] and [3]).[25]

[1] Initial Case Law

In the 1990s, questions arose about the liability of one of the first intermediary service providers: the Bulletin Board System (BBS) provider. A BBS was a computer system running special software that allowed its users to connect to their telephone lines and to perform certain functions on the computer system.[26] Users could upload to and download data from the system, read news from the system, or send messages to each other. Initially, these BBSs were closed systems: members of a BBS only had access to the services and information on that particular BBS. Later on, BBSs themselves were connected, which extended the network and made it easier to communicate information through different systems. These BBSs were a precursor of the current global Internet and represented a new and revolutionary means to communicate digital information.

The 1993 case of *Playboy Enterprises v. Frena* dealt with the liability of a BBS operator for making available Playboy pictures that were uploaded to the BBS by its

22. *Metro-Goldwyn-Mayer Studios Inc. v. Grokster, Ltd.*, *supra* n. 13, at 929–930.
23. In re: Aimster Copyright Litigation, *supra* n. 21, at 645.
24. *See* section §3.02[A].
25. *Religious Technology Center v. Netcom On-Line Communication Services, Inc.*, 907 F.Supp. 1361 (Dist. Court, N.D. Cal. 1995).
26. Although I speak of BBSs as something from the past, there are still a few BBSs online.

users.[27] A Florida District Court held that the operator had violated Playboy's distribution rights by supplying 'a product containing unauthorized copies of a copyrighted work'.[28] Also the display rights of Playboy had been infringed by the operator. The fact that the operator was unaware of the infringements on his BBS, the Court deemed to be irrelevant:

> There is irrefutable evidence of direct copyright infringement in this case. It does not matter that [the operator] may have been unaware of the copyright infringement. Intent to infringe is not needed to find copyright infringement. Intent or knowledge is not an element of infringement, and thus even an innocent infringer is liable for infringement … .[29]

We see a similar line of reasoning in the 1994 case of *Sega Enterprises v. MAPHIA*, regarding a BBS provider who hosted unauthorized copies of SEGA computer games. According to the California District Court, SEGA demonstrated probable success with its prima facie direct infringement claim as SEGA established that unauthorized copies of its games were uploaded to the BBS with the knowledge of one of the operators of the BBS.[30]

This approach of holding these early online service providers liable as copyright infringers was endorsed by the Working Group on Intellectual Property Rights in 1995. This Working Group was formed by the Clinton Administration to study the application and effectiveness of intellectual property rules in relation to 'the National Information Infrastructure' - the Internet.[31] The Working Group rejected the argument that the liability of intermediaries would have to be lowered. Although the Working Group acknowledged that these service providers process a great deal of data that are not easily reviewed, the Working Group argued that these service providers were not alone in this position:

> Likewise, book sellers, record stores, newsstands and computer software retailers cannot possibly read all the books, listen to all the records, review all the newspapers and magazines or analyze all the computer programs that pass through their establishments for possible infringements. Yet, they may be held strictly liable as distributors if the works or copies they deal in are infringing.[32]

This analysis of the liability of early intermediaries made these intermediaries analogous to the publishers of information which can be liable as direct infringers for the materials they distribute.

27. *Playboy Enterprises, Inc. v. Frena*, 839 F.Supp. 1552 (Dist. Court, M.D. Fla. 1993).
28. *Playboy Enterprises, Inc. v. Frena*, *supra* n. 27, at 1556.
29. *Playboy Enterprises, Inc. v. Frena*, *supra* n. 27, at 1559.
30. *Sega Enterprises Ltd v. MAPHIA*, 857 F.Supp. 679, 686 (Dist. Court, N.D. Cal. 1994).
31. Working Group in Intellectual Property Rights, *Intellectual Property and the National Information Infrastructure*, Information Infrastructure Task Force 120 (1995).
32. Working Group in Intellectual Property Rights, *supra* n. 31, at 116.

[2] The Netcom Decision: Shifting the Focus from Copying to the Copier

A turnaround came with a California District Court's decision in *Religious Technology Center v. Netcom*.[33] In this case on the liability of another BBS provider, the Court in its direct infringement analysis shifted the focus from the act of copying to the person responsible for that copying. *Netcom* dealt with the liability of a BBS operator and an Internet access provider that provided the BBS with an Internet connection. A former member of the Scientology movement had posted portions of the organization's work in a BBS newsgroup for a discussion on and a criticism of Scientology.

The District Court held that copies had been made on the servers of the BBS provider and the Internet access provider. However, the Court also held that these service providers were not directly liable for such copying, as these service providers had not taken 'affirmative action that directly resulted in the copying of (...) works other than by installing and maintaining a system whereby software automatically forwards messages received from subscribers onto the Usenet, and temporarily stores copies on its system'.[34] Hence, although copies were made, the Court held that *Netcom* was not causing the copies to be made.

The District Court also considered the practical consequences of holding these providers liable as copyright infringers. Such a decision would make every service provider liable for the content they transmit. While the Court recognized that copyright infringement results in strict liability, the Court held that 'there should still be some element of volition or causation which is lacking where a defendant's system is merely used to create a copy by a third party'.[35] With regard to the distribution and display rights, the Court noted that it 'is not entirely convinced that the mere possession of a digital copy on a BBS that is accessible to some members of the public constitutes direct infringement by the BBS operator', and that 'such a holding suffers from the same problem of causation as the reproduction argument'.[36]

In *Netcom*, the Court analogized these early intermediaries with the owners of a copy shop who also provided the means to copy, but who do not push the 'green button' to start the copying process. This decision shifted the focus from the copy to the copier. As the Second Circuit Court of Appeals in *Cartoon Network v. CSC Holdings* would indicate in 2008, the relevant question is: 'who made this copy?'[37] As such, *Netcom* departed from the rigid application of the concept of copying endorsed by earlier courts and the Working Group on Intellectual Property Rights and provided a more normative and functional perspective on the activities of intermediaries.

33. *Religious Technology Center v. Netcom On-Line Communication Services*, Inc., *supra* n. 25.
34. *Religious Technology Center v. Netcom On-Line Communication Services*, Inc., *supra* n. 25, at 1368.
35. *Religious Technology Center v. Netcom On-Line Communication Services*, Inc., *supra* n. 25, at 1370.
36. *Religious Technology Center v. Netcom On-Line Communication Services, Inc.*, *supra* n. 25, at 1372.
37. *Cartoon Network LP, LLLP v. CSC Holdings, Inc.*, 536 F.3d 121, 130 (2nd Cir. 2008).

[3] Extending Netcom *to Other Intermediaries*

Netcom's requirement of volitional conduct was adopted in later case law involving other and more modern intermediaries. The requirement made its way into cases dealing with the liability of hosting service providers that hosted the infringing content of others. These hosting providers did not cause the copies to be made, but merely provided the means by which to copy, distribute, or display copyrighted works.[38] The case of *CoStar v. LoopNet* offers an example of how the volitional conduct criterion is applied to a platform for user-provided content. This case dealt with the liability of the real estate listing service LoopNet.[39] The Fourth Circuit Court held that:

> When a customer duplicates an infringing work, the owner of the copy machine is not considered a direct infringer. Similarly, an ISP who owns an electronic facility that responds automatically to users' input is not a direct infringer.[40]

When it comes to the liability of online service providers that are involved in the hosting of newsgroups and the providers of file lockers, case law initially provided somewhat divergent outcomes. The Third Circuit Court in *Parker v. Google* relied on *LoopNet* in a case concerning Google's liability as a Usenet provider for the copies of e-books posted to Google's servers.[41] Google could be compared to the owner of a copying machine and was not liable as an infringer for the copies on its servers.[42] In contrast, a New York District Court held in *Arista Records LLC v. Usenet.com* that the Usenet provider was liable as an infringer because the provider offered dedicated servers to MP3 files and increased the retention for newsgroups containing music files.[43] According to the Court, the provider's ability to block certain users and activities by automated filtering and manual review amounted to volitional conduct.

In *Capital Records v. MP3tunes* regarding an MP3 search engine that enabled users to store files in digital personal lockers, a New York District Court considered that MP3tunes knew that many of the songs were infringing because they were recognizable as copyrighted works. Capitol Records' allegations were 'plausible [and] suggest volitional conduct'.[44] In *Perfect 10 v. Megaupload*, a California District Court saw volitional conduct in Megaupload's creation of distinct websites for certain types of content (e.g., megaporn.com and megavideo.com), encouragement and payments for the uploading of popular media, payments to others who maintain a catalogue of

38. *Marobie-FL, Inc. v. National Ass'n of Fire Equip. Distributors and Northwest Nexus*, 983 F.Supp. 1167, 1178 (Dist. Court, N.D. Ill. E.D. 1997); *Rosen v. Hosting Services, Inc.*, 771 F.Supp.2d 1219, 1222 (Dist. Court, C.D. Cal. 2010). *Also see*: *Field v. Google, Inc.*, 412 F.Supp.2d 1106, 1115 (Dist. Court, D. Nev. 2006). *Cf. Playboy Enterprises, Inc. v. Webbworld, Inc.*, 991 F. Supp. 543, 552 (Dist. Court, N.D. Tex. 1997).
39. *CoStar Group, Inc. v. LoopNet, Inc.*, 373 F.3d 544 (4th Cir. 2004).
40. *CoStar Group, Inc. v. LoopNet, Inc.*, *supra* n. 39, at 550. *Cf. Perfect 10, Inc. v. Amazon.com, supra* n. 15, at 1160, n. 6, involving Google, in its capacity of an image search engine, itself making thumbnail copies of the images for use in its search engine, which the Ninth Circuit qualified as initiating the making of a copy.
41. *Parker v. Google*, 42 Fed.Appx. 833, 836–837 (3rd Cir. 2007).
42. *Parker v. Google*, *supra* n. 41, at 836–837.
43. *Arista Records LLC v. Usenet.com*, 633 F.Supp.2d 124 (Dist. Court, S.D.N.Y. 2009).
44. *Capitol Records, Inc. v. MP3tunes, LLC*, 2009 WL 3364036, 3 (Dist. Court, S.D.N.Y. 2009).

available files, and its plausible awareness of the ongoing, rampant infringements taking place on its websites.[45] Another Californian District Court, deciding on the liability of a service provider which enabled users to convert music to ringtones, disregarded the volitional requirement altogether. The Court stated that 'no Ninth Circuit case has adopted this volitional conduct requirement' and 'in light of the fact that copyright infringement is a strict liability offense, the Court is not inclined to adopt a volitional conduct requirement without clear instruction from the Ninth Circuit'.[46]

However, from 2011 onwards a renaissance in the volitional conduct requirement occurred. First in *Disney v. Hotfile*, on another file locker service provider, a Florida District Court defined *Netcom* as 'the standard in cases alleging that an internet company is infringing a plaintiff's copyright'.[47] And with reference to 'a great weight of authority', the Court pointed out that 'the law is clear that Hotfile and Mr. Titov are not liable for direct copyright infringement because they own and manage internet facilities that allow others to upload and download copyrighted material'.[48] The Court also considered *Capitol Records, Inc. v MP3tunes*, and *Arista Records LLC v. Usenet* but held that these decisions were unconvincing, as they ignored the language of *Netcom* and other cases following *Netcom*.[49] According to the Court, these cases had to be decided on the basis of secondary liability theories.

Another Californian District Court in *Perfect 10. v. Giganews*, in dealing with the liability of a Usenet provider, made short shrift of earlier decisions holding that volitional conduct was not a requirement for an infringement.[50] The District Court did 'not interpret the Ninth Circuit's silence on the so-called "volitional conduct requirement" as disapproval' of the requirement.[51] Indeed, in 2017, the Ninth Circuit Court of Appeals, in a case concerning another Usenet provider, confirmed that 'volitional conduct' is an element of a direct copyright infringement. This decision will likely settle discussions on the volitional conduct requirement, at least in the Ninth Circuit.

Now, the concept of 'volitional conduct' can be confusing. It can be taken as meaning intentional conduct, but intent is not a requirement for infringement. Therefore, it is better to understand the concept as meaning that the infringement in question can be attributed to the person held liable. In *Cartoon Network*, the Second Circuit Court justified its application of the volitional conduct requirement because 'the purpose of any causation-based liability doctrine is to identify the actor (or actors) whose conduct has been so significant and important a cause that he or she should be

45. *Perfect 10, Inc. v. Megaupload Limited*, 2011 WL 3203117 (Dist. Court, S.D. Cal. 2011).
46. *Arista Records LLC v. Myxer, Inc.*, 2011 WL 11660773, 14 (Dist. Court, C.D.Cal. 2011).
47. *Disney Enterprises, Inc. v. Hotfile Corp.*, 798 F.Supp.2d 1303, 1307 (Dist. Court, S.D. Fla. 2011).
48. *Disney Enterprises, Inc. v. Hotfile Corp.*, *supra* n. 47, at 1308.
49. *Disney Enterprises, Inc. v. Hotfile Corp.*, *supra* n. 47, at 1309: 'I nonetheless believe that these cases were not correctly decided. ... First, Arista Records held that a policy encouraging infringement coupled with an ability – but refusal – to stop the massive infringement gave rise to a volitional act. But this conclusion ignores the language of *Netcom* and other cases following *Netcom*. ... Second, Capitol Records, for its part, had no analysis and simply cited *Arista Records* and *Russ Hardenburgh* as authority for its holding.'
50. *Perfect 10, Inc. v. Giganews, Inc.*, 2013 WL 2109963 (Dist. Court, C.D. Cal. 2013).
51. *Perfect 10, Inc. v. Giganews, Inc.*, *supra* n. 50, at 7.

legally responsible'.[52] In 2017, the Ninth Circuit Court of Appeals in *Perfect 10 v. Giganews* gave a similar explanation:

> We wish to emphasize that the word 'volition' in this context does not really mean an 'act of willing or choosing' or an 'act of deciding,' which is how the dictionary defines the term. Rather, as used by the court in [*Netcom*] it 'simply stands for the unremarkable proposition that proximate causation historically underlines copyright infringement liability no less than other torts.'[53]

In sum, the volition requirement adopted by US courts in cases concerning Internet intermediaries has enabled a functional perspective on their activities. The requirement is also an important tool in distinguishing between strict liability for direct infringements, and forms of secondary liability for indirect infringements. As we will see in the next section, these later forms of liability take into account the intermediary's knowledge of or control over the infringements of others. This enables courts to consider the intermediary's actual involvement in the copyright infringements of others and to fine-tune the intermediary's liability accordingly.

[D] Secondary Liability

The *Netcom* court did not want to adopt a rule 'that could lead to the liability of countless parties whose role in the infringement is nothing more than setting up and operating a system that is necessary for the functioning of the Internet'.[54] Nevertheless, intermediaries are not completely relieved from liability as they may still be liable under secondary liability theories.[55] As the *Netcom* court noted: 'Netcom is not free from liability just because it did not directly infringe plaintiffs' works; it may still be liable as a contributory infringer.'[56] Or as the Fourth Circuit Court put it in *CoStar v. LoopNet*: the absence of a direct infringement 'does not mean that a manufacturer or owner of machines used for copyright violations could not have some indirect liability, such as contributory or vicarious liability'.[57]

Under US law, intermediaries may thus still be held liable for a vicarious or contributory infringement of a copyright. The requirements for such liability have been developed by the courts. Both forms are briefly discussed here. Special attention is paid to the inducement theory that was introduced by the US Supreme Court in *Grokster*.[58] This theory has enabled copyright owners to hold accountable those parties who purposefully induce the infringements of others, for instance by operating peer-to-peer file-sharing platforms.

52. *Cartoon Network LP, LLLP v. CSC Holdings, Inc.*, 536 F.3d 121, 130 (2nd Cir. 2008). Internal citation omitted.
53. *Perfect 10, Inc. v. Giganews, Inc.*, 847 F.3d 657, 666 (9th Cir. 2017). Internal citations omitted.
54. *Religious Technology Center v. Netcom On-Line Communication Services, Inc.*, *supra* n. 25, at 1373.
55. For a discussion of the difference between direct and indirect infringement, *see* section §6.02[B].
56. *Religious Technology Center v. Netcom On-Line Communication Services, Inc.*, *supra* n. 25, at 1373.
57. *CoStar Group, Inc. v. LoopNet, Inc.*, *supra* n. 39, at 549.
58. *Metro-Goldwyn-Mayer Studios Inc. v. Grokster*, Ltd., *supra* n. 13.

[1] Vicarious Infringement

Vicarious liability for copyright infringement is based on the principles of *respondeat superior*, a legal doctrine that holds an employer or principal legally responsible for the wrongful acts of an employee or agent if such acts occur within the scope of the employment or agency. In contrast to contributory liability, this type of liability does not depend on knowledge but is based on control over and financial interest in the infringement of another person.

The Second Circuit Court in its 1963 decision in *Shapiro v. Green Company* explained that because of the 'open-ended terminology' used in the 1909 Copyright Act, 'courts have had to trace, case by case, a pattern of business relationships which would render one person liable for the infringing conduct of another'.[59] In deciding on the liability of an owner of a chain of stores for a concessionaire selling unauthorized bootleg records, the Court applied the doctrine of *respondeat superior* that is normally used in employer-employee relationships:

> When the right and ability to supervise coalesce with an obvious and direct financial interest in the exploitation of copyrighted materials – even in the absence of actual knowledge that the copyright monopoly is being impaired ... – the purposes of copyright law may be best effectuated by the imposition of liability upon the beneficiary of that exploitation.[60]

The rationale behind vicarious liability is that it places responsibility on those who are in a position to effectively police the conduct of others.[61] Another textbook example of the extension of vicarious liability into the area of copyright law is *Gershwin Publishing v. Columbia Artists Management*.[62] In this case, the Second Circuit Court held Columbia Artists Management vicariously liable for the infringing conduct of artists who performed songs without the authorization of Gershwin. The Court articulated its test for vicarious liability: 'even in the absence of an employer-employee relationship one may be vicariously liable if he has the right and ability to supervise the infringing activity and also has a direct financial interest in such activities'.[63]

[2] Contributory Infringement

The classic definition of contributory copyright infringement entails that 'one who, with knowledge of the infringing activity, induces, causes or materially contributes to the infringing conduct of another, may be held liable as a "contributory" infringer'.[64]

---

59. *Shapiro, Bernstein & Co. v. HL Green Company*, 316 F. 2d 304, 307 (2nd Cir. 1963).
60. *Shapiro, Bernstein & Co. v. HL Green Company*, *supra* n. 59, at 307.
61. *Shapiro, Bernstein & Co. v. HL Green Company*, *supra* n. 59, at 308: 'For much the same reasons, the imposition of vicarious liability in the case before us cannot be deemed unduly harsh or unfair. Green has the power to police carefully the conduct of its concessionaire Jalen, our judgment will simply encourage it to do so, thus placing responsibility where it can and should be effectively exercised.'
62. *Gershwin Publishing Corp. v. Columbia Artists Management, Inc.*, 443 F.2d 1159 (2nd Cir. 1971).
63. *Gershwin Publishing Corp. v. Columbia Artists Management, Inc.*, *supra* n. 62, at 1162.
64. *Gershwin Publishing Corp. v. Columbia Artists Management, Inc.*, *supra* n. 62, at 1162.

There are thus three types of conduct that can give rise to contributory infringement: inducing, causing, or materially contributing to another's infringement. Under this standard, several courts have held contributors to a copyright infringement liable as contributory infringers. For instance, a video rental store that allowed its customers to view videos in its store was held contributorily liable for these infringing public performances.[65] Also, the operator of a flea market was held contributorily liable for sales of infringing merchandise by vendors to whom it rented space and provided support services.[66]

The classic definition of contributory infringement has been 'refined' by the Ninth Circuit Court 'in the context of cyberspace to determine when contributory liability can be imposed on a provider of Internet access or services'.[67] In its 2001 *Napster* decision, the Ninth Circuit Court held Napster contributorily liable for infringements by users of its peer-to-peer file-sharing software under the standard 'that if a computer system operator learns of specific infringing material available on his system and fails to purge such material from the system, the operator knows of and contributes to direct infringement'.[68] Intermediaries, such as access providers and video hosting providers, are unlikely to be held liable as contributory infringers as they generally lack specific knowledge of infringements.[69] Those intermediaries who remain '*willfully* blind' to infringements can nevertheless be contributory infringers.[70]

One specific form of contributory infringement is the inducement of another's infringement. In *Metro-Goldwyn-Mayer Studios v. Grokster*, the US Supreme Court explained that 'one who distributes a device with the object of promoting its use to infringe copyright, as shown by clear expression or other affirmative steps taken to foster infringement, is liable for the resulting acts of infringement by third parties'.[71] This inducement theory is used to hold liable those who may not have knowledge of or control over specific infringements, but who nevertheless aim to enable or encourage others to infringe copyrights. Although in *Grokster*, the US Supreme Court spoke of devices and products when it enunciated its inducement theory, the theory also applies to those providing services that are used to infringe copyrights. Not only can the providers of peer-to-peer file-sharing software be held liable under the inducement theory[72] but also those who provide services such as the trackers that are needed for file-sharing over the BitTorrent protocol.[73]

65. *Columbia Pictures Indus., Inc. v. Aveco, Inc.*, 800 F.2d 59 (3rd Cir. 1986).
66. *Fonovisa, Inc. v. Cherry Auction, Inc.*, 76 F.3d 259 (9th Cir. 1996).
67. *Perfect 10, Inc. v. Amazon.com, supra* n. 15, at 1171.
68. *A&M Records, Inc. v. Napster, supra* 15, at 1021.
69. *UMG Recordings, Inc. v. Veoh Networks*, 667 F. 3d 1022 (9th Cir. 2011); *Viacom International, Inc. v. Youtube*, Inc., 676 F.3d 19 (2nd Cir. 2012); *Luvdarts, LLC v. AT & T Mobility, LLC*, 710 F.3d 1068 (9th Cir. 2013).
70. *Viacom International, Inc. v. Youtube, Inc., supra* n. 69, at 35.
71. *Metro-Goldwyn-Mayer Studios Inc. v. Grokster, Ltd., supra* n. 13, at 936–937.
72. *Arista Records LLC v. Lime Group LLC*, 784 F.Supp.2d 398 (Dist. Court, S.D.N.Y. 2011).
73. *Columbia Pictures Industries, Inc. v. Fung*, 710 F.3d 1020, 1033 (9th Cir. 2013): 'one can infringe a copyright through culpable actions resulting in the impermissible reproduction of copyrighted expression, whether those actions involve making available a device or product or providing some service used in accomplishing the infringement'.

The 1998 Digital Millennium Copyright (DMCA), which aimed to update US copyright law for the digital and networked age, was adopted before peer-to-peer file-sharing emerged in the US. The DMCA offers copyright owners little in their attempts to stop and prevent file-sharing.[74] Therefore, the inducement theory that was developed by the US Supreme Court in *Grokster* was crucial for copyright owners to hold accountable those who offer peer-to-peer file-sharing software and platforms. The theory is particularly relevant in the context of decentralized peer-to-peer file-sharing in which the distributor of the file-sharing software has no knowledge (important for other forms of contributory liability) or control (crucial for vicarious liability) of the use of the software or system. As such, the inducement theory developed in *Grokster* filled a gap in the protection offered to copyright owners.[75] In the words of the then US Register of Copyrights Pallante, 'courts have picked up where Congress left off'.[76]

§6.03 FAIR USE

The previous section introduced some of the core concepts that are relevant to the intermediary's liability for copyright infringements. We distinguished the primary liability for direct infringement and secondary liability for the infringements of others. In this section, we will take a closer look at a doctrine that limits primary liability: the fair use doctrine. Fair use limits the reach of US copyright law's exclusive rights. It is an open-ended exception that exists alongside more concrete limitations and exceptions in US copyright law. In this section, we will explore the workings of the fair use doctrine and consider how it may apply to intermediaries making use of copyrighted materials.

Under US law, the fair use doctrine is relevant for determining the liability of intermediaries for several reasons. First, the doctrine may prevent an intermediary from itself infringing a copyright. Intermediaries that use the protected materials of others in their intermediary activities may benefit from the fair use exception, especially if such use is 'transformative'.[77] Second, the fair use doctrine may remove the basis for the intermediary's secondary liability. If the user of the intermediary's service does not infringe, the intermediary cannot be secondarily liable.[78] Third, the fair use doctrine is relevant for determining whether an intermediary should remove materials when it is notified about an infringement.[79]

Before going into the content of the fair use doctrine, in this section we will first consider the fair use doctrine's roots (section §6.03[A]). Although the fair use exception is an open-ended exception, the doctrine does provide for a set of factors that courts need to take into account when assessing whether a particular use is fair. These

74. For a discussion of the DMCA, in particular the safe harbour regime that it introduced, *see* section §6.04.
75. Alfred Yen, *Torts and the Construction of Inducement and Contributory Liability in Amazon and Visa*, 34 Columbia Journal of Law & the Arts (4) 513, 515 (2009).
76. Maria Pallante, *The Next Great Copyright Act*, 36 Columbia Journal of Law & the Arts (3) 315, 322 (2013).
77. For a discussion of transformativeness, *see*: section §6.03[B][1].
78. *See* section §6.02[B].
79. *See* section §6.04[F][3].

different factors and how they apply to intermediary activities are discussed as well (section §6.03[B]). This book has contended that rules on copyright law should be flexible, but it also recognizes the need for sufficiently predictable rules.[80] In that regard, we will also consider the effects that the fair use doctrine – which appears to be a flexible copyright exception – has on copyright law's predictability (section §6.03[C]).

[A] Common Law Origins

The fair use doctrine existed long before it was statutorily recognized by Congress in the 1976 Copyright Act. It is a judge-made concept that has long been in the exclusive domain of judges and the courts.[81] Already in 1841, in *Folsom v. Marsh*, Justice Story expressed the essence of the fair use doctrine and its methodology:

> The question, then, is, whether this is a justifiable use of the original materials, such as the law recognizes as no infringement of the copyright of the plaintiffs. (...) In short, we must often, in deciding questions of this sort, look to the nature and objects of the selections made, the quantity and value of the materials used, and the degree in which the use may prejudice the sale, or diminish the profits, or supersede the objects, of the original work. Many mixed ingredients enter into the discussion of such questions.[82]

As we will see in section §6.03[B], the factors distilled from earlier case law by Justice Story are still relevant today. In 1976, these factors were codified in Section 107 of the US Copyright Act. Courts must consider these factors in their fair use analyses.

The fair use doctrine was incorporated in the Copyright Act by the 1976 revision. At the time, there was much resistance against any statutory specification of the doctrine. The Library of Congress had appointed a group of copyright experts who considered, among other things, whether a statutory provision concerning fair use should be introduced in US law. While there was no objection against a mere affirmation of the fair use doctrine, the majority of the experts opposed codification that would define or otherwise contextualize the concept of fair use.[83] Schulman noted that the fair use doctrine 'derives its vitality from its adaptability to conditions not only as they exist today but to new conditions which result from technological and other developments'.[84] The doctrine allowed for fine distinctions to be made between different types of uses in the past and would do so in the future. In the words of Schulman, 'any attempt to confine the doctrine in a straitjacket by enumeration would destroy its vitality and its ability to accommodate itself to all conditions and those as yet

80. *See* section §2.04[B].
81. Leon Yankwich, *What Is Fair Use*, 22 University of Chicago Law Review (1) 203 (1945). Pierre N. Leval, *Nimmer Lecture: Fair Use Rescued*, 44 UCLA Law Review (5) 1449, 1451 (1997).
82. *Folsom v. Marsh*, 9 F. Cas. 342 (Circ. Court, D. Mass. 1841).
83. Alan Latman, *Fair Use of Copyrighted Works, in U.S. Copyright Law Revision, Study no. 14*, 86th Cong., 2nd Sess. 18 (Senate Judiciary Comm. Print 1960), 39–44.
84. John Schulman, *Fair Use and the Revision of the Copyright Act*, 53 Iowa Law Review 832, 837 (1967).

unforeseen'.[85] Melville Nimmer was not against statutory recognition, but warned that such recognition should be done in general terms, without any specific enumeration of particular instances of fair use. Nimmer noted that 'such specific enumeration would be undesirable because it would lead to a mechanical and rigid application of a concept which, by its very nature, is dependent upon a weighting of delicate factors in a given factual situation'.[86] Brown called it an 'abdication of responsibility to ignore the subject [of fair use] in the statute', 'yet the history of statutory attempts in this country, and the examples from abroad, suggest great difficulties in specifying the scope of fair use for particular situations'.[87] In his view, statutory recognition would add nothing to the law as it stood. Furthermore, 'there will always be new situations and new uses arising, so that a detailed statute, even if it gave some present guidance to the courts, would be certain to fall behind the times'.[88]

As the fair use doctrine was incorporated into the 1976 Copyright Act, the US legislator was well aware of the importance of maintaining the fair use doctrine's flexibility. The House Reports to the 1976 Copyright Act underline the need for flexibility in times of rapid technological change and the role that courts play in furthering the fair use doctrine.[89] Furthermore, these House Reports highlight that Section 107 intended 'to restate the present judicial doctrine of fair use, not to change, narrow, or enlarge it in any way'.[90]

[B] The Fair Use Factors

The fair use doctrine is an 'equitable rule of reason' of which no general definition is possible.[91] Or, in the words of the US Supreme Court in *Campbell v. Acuff-Rose Music*, this analysis 'is not to be simplified with bright-line rules, for the statute, like the doctrine it recognizes, calls for case-by-case analysis'.[92] Article 107 of the US Copyright Act does offer guidance to the courts when they have to make a fair use analysis. Section 107 provides several examples of the purposes for which a work may be used: criticism, comment, news reporting, teaching (including multiple copies for classroom use), scholarship, and research. These are only examples, and they are not the only purposes that are recognized in the fair use doctrine.[93]

Article 107 of the US Copyright Act also lists a set of factors that courts must consider. These factors are:

---

85. John Schulman, *Fair Use and the Revision of the Copyright Act*, 53 Iowa Law Review 832, 837 (1967).
86. Latman, *supra* n. 83, at 42.
87. Latman, *supra* n. 83, at 41.
88. Latman, *supra* n. 83, at 42.
89. H.R. Rep. No. 94-1476, *supra*, at 65–66 (1976).
90. H.R. Rep. No. 94-1476, 66 (1976); H.R. Rep. No 94–473, 63 (1975).
91. H.R. Rep. No. 94-1476, at 65–66. Cited in: *Sony Corp. of America v. Universal City Studios, Inc.*, *supra* n. 14, at 448, n. 30.
92. *Campbell v. Acuff-Rose Music, Inc.*, 510 U.S. 569, 577 (1994).
93. Section 107 of the Copyright Act: 'for purposes such as criticism, comment, news reporting, teaching (including multiple copies for classroom use), scholarship, or research, is not an infringement of copyright'.

1. the purpose and character of the use, including whether such use is of a commercial nature or is for non-profit educational purposes;
2. the nature of the copyrighted work;
3. the amount and substantiality of the portion used in relation to the copyrighted work as a whole; and
4. the effect of the use upon the potential market for or value of the copyrighted work.

US Courts need to take these factors into account, but they can also consider others. Section 107 of the US Copyright Act speaks of factors that 'shall [be] include[d]'. Moreover, the US Supreme Court has underlined that these statutory factors should not be dealt with in isolation. These factors need to be explored in each other's context, 'and the results weighed together, in light of the purposes of copyright'.[94]

[1] First Factor: Purpose and Character of the Use

The first factor that courts must consider is 'the purpose and character of the use, including whether such use is of a commercial nature or is for nonprofit educational purposes'. In 1994 the US Supreme Court noted in *Campbell v. Acuff-Rose Music, Inc.* that 'the enquiry here may be guided by the examples given in the preamble to [Section] 107, looking to whether the use is for criticism, or comment, or news reporting, and the like'.[95] The analysis is not however limited to just checking whether a particular purpose of a use is generally within the scope of Section 107 of the US Copyright Act. Rather, the analysis should take into account the separate elements, such as individual passages, and ask whether these are functional to the claimed purpose of the use.[96]

Two subfactors can be distinguished: the commerciality and the 'transformativeness' of the use. This latter subfactor has proven to be particularly relevant when intermediaries use copyrighted materials for curatorial purposes. Hence, when they use materials to create order in, categorize, contextualize, or otherwise give additional meaning to those materials.[97]

First, concerning commerciality: it is important to note that the commerciality of a use does not mean the end of a fair use defence, nor is a commercial use presumptively unfair.[98] In its *Sony v. Universal* decision in 1984, the Supreme Court

94. *Campbell v. Acuff-Rose Music, Inc.*, *supra* n. 92, at 578.
95. *Campbell v. Acuff-Rose Music, Inc.*, *supra* n. 92, at 578–579.
96. Pierre Leval, *Toward a Fair Use Standard*, 103 Harvard Law Review (5) 1105 (1990). In this article, Judge Laval shared his experience with the fair use doctrine and how the Court of Appeals' disagreement with two of his decisions as a District Court judge provoked him to rethink fair use and its application.
97. For an explanation of the concept of curation, *see* section §1.06.
98. Nor is a non-profit use presumptively fair: H.R. Rep. 2237, 89th Cong. 2d Sess. 66 (1966); H.R. Rep. No. 83, at 37. *Also see*: William Patry, *Patry on Copyright* (2014), describing that the addition of 'non-profit educational purposes' to the first fair use factor was the outcome of a political process in which a small concession was granted to an interest group of educators recognizing that their type of use could be fair under appropriate circumstances.

suggested that when a certain use is for a commercial or profit-making purpose, such use would presumably be unfair.[99] After Justice Brennan in 1985 in *Harper & Row Publishers v. Nation Enterprises* criticized the Supreme Court's stance towards commerciality,[100] in 1994 the Supreme Court in *Campbell v. Acuff-Rose Music* made clear that commerciality is only one factor to be weighed among others in the context of the use.[101] Leval, a senior judge at the Second Circuit Court of Appeals, considered this decision to be the 'rescue of fair use' as it recognized that every fair use factor is to be understood within a broader context, considering also the objectives of copyright law.[102]

Second, the subfactor of transformativeness was introduced by the US Supreme Court in *Campbell v. Acuff-Rose Music*.[103] A use of a work is transformative if it does not just supplant the original, but 'instead adds something new, with a further purpose or different character, altering the first with new expression, meaning, or message'.[104] While the transformativeness of a use is not a prerequisite for fair use, the US Supreme Court in *Campbell* did point out that transformative works 'lie at the heart of the doctrine's guarantee of breathing space within the confines of copyright, and the more transformative the new work, the less will be the significance of other factors, like commercialism, that may weigh against a finding of fair use'.[105] According to Netanel, *Campbell* represented a shift in thinking about the fair use doctrine. It removed the focus from the market for materials and the question of whether the copyright owner would have consented to the use and put emphasis on the question of whether the work was used for a different expressive purpose.[106]

---

99. *Sony Corp. of America v. Universal City Studios, Inc.*, *supra* n. 14, at 451: 'Thus, although every commercial use of copyrighted material is presumptively an unfair exploitation of the monopoly privilege that belongs to the owner of the copyright, noncommercial uses are a different matter.' Admittedly, in *Sony Corp. of America v. Universal City Studios, Inc.*, *supra* n. 14, at 448–449, the Supreme Court noted: 'Although not conclusive, the first factor requires that "the commercial or nonprofit character of an activity" be weighed in any fair use decision.' *Also see*: Patry, *supra* n. 98, at 10:16.
100. *Harper & Row Publishers, Inc. v. Nation Enterprises*, 471 U.S. 539, 592 (1985) (Brennan, J., dissenting): 'Many uses [Section] 107] lists as paradigmatic examples of fair use, including criticism, comment, and news reporting, are generally conducted for profit in this country, a fact of which Congress was obviously aware when it enacted [Section] 107. To negate any argument favoring fair use based on news reporting or criticism because that reporting or criticism was published for profit is to render meaningless the congressional imprimatur placed on such uses.'
101. *Campbell v. Acuff-Rose Music, Inc.*, *supra* n. 92, at 585. The Supreme Court gave an example of the importance of the context of the use: 'The use ... of a copyrighted work to advertise a product, even in parody, will be entitled to less indulgence under the first factor of the fair use enquiry than the sale of a parody for its own sake, let alone one performed a single time by students in school.' (*Campbell v. Acuff-Rose Music, Inc.*, *supra* n. 92, at 585).
102. Pierre Leval, *Campbell v. Acuff-Rose: Justice Souter's Rescue of Fair Use*, Cardozo Arts & Entertainment Law Journal (1) 19, 22 (1994).
103. Paul Goldstein, *supra* n. 20, at 12:32: 'In *Campbell v. Acuff-Rose Music, Inc.*, the United States Supreme Court added an important gloss to section 107's first factor in the course of considering whether the defendant's parody was a fair use of the plaintiff's song.'
104. *Campbell v. Acuff-Rose Music, Inc.*, *supra* n. 92, at 579.
105. *Campbell v. Acuff-Rose Music, Inc.*, *supra* n. 92, at 579.
106. Neil Netanel, *Making sense of fair use*, 15 Lewis & Clark Law Review 715 (2011).

According to Samuelson, several types of transformative use can be distinguished.[107] First, there is use that involves the transformation of a particular expression from a pre-existing work in order to provide a critical commentary, such as the parody in *Campbell.* Second, there are what Samuelson calls 'conventional productive uses', such as a quotation by a biographer or historian in order to make a point about the author's temperament. And third, there is the use of the work for a *different purpose* than the original. If intermediaries use copyrighted materials with such a different purpose, their use may be covered by the fair use doctrine in particular with a view to this third type of transformative use.[108]

Intermediaries that make use of protected materials to enable their users to locate online information can benefit from the fair use exception.[109] That is provided that the intermediary enhances access to the materials, without superseding the original materials. In *Kelly v. Arriba Soft*, the Ninth Circuit Court held that image search engines which copy and display images found on the web do not infringe any copyrights. Instead their use is covered by the fair use doctrine.[110] The Court held that the thumbnail copies that search engines make and display in their search results are transformative uses. According to the Court, such uses do 'not stifle artistic creativity because they are not used for illustrative or artistic purposes and therefore do not supplant the need for the originals. In addition, they benefit the public by enhancing information-gathering techniques on the internet'.[111] In *Perfect 10 v. Amazon*, regarding Google's image search engine, the Ninth Circuit Court considered that Google's advertising programme, and thus its commerciality, did not tip the balance in favour of the copyright owner. Instead, given the public utility of Google's image search engine, the Court concluded 'that the transformative nature of Google's use is more significant than any incidental superseding use or the minor commercial aspects of Google's search engine and website'.[112]

A similar line of reasoning was followed in the Second Circuit Court of Appeals' decision in the *Google Books* case.[113] Google had scanned – without asking for

107. Pamela Samuelson, *Unbundling Fair Uses*, 77 Fordham Law Review (5) 2537, 2548 (2009); Pamela Samuelson, *Possible Futures of Fair Use*, 90 Washington Law Review (2) 815, 826 (2015).
108. Pamela Samuelson, *Possible Futures of Fair Use*, Washington Law Review (2) 815, 833 (2015). *Cf.*: Jane Ginsburg, *Fair Use for Free, or Permitted-But-Paid?*, 29 Berkeley Technology Law Journal (3) 1383 (2014).
109. *Also see*: James Grimmelmann, *Speech Engines*, Minnesota Law Review (3) 868, 937 (2014).
110. *Kelly v. Arriba Soft Corp.*, 336 F.3d 811 (9th Cir. 2003).
111. *Kelly v. Arriba Soft Corp.*, *supra* n. 110, at 820.
112. *Perfect 10, Inc. v. Amazon.com, supra* n. 15, at 1167. *Also see*: *Perfect 10, Inc. v. Yandex N.V.*, 2013 WL 4777189, 5 (Dist. Court, N.D. Cal. 2013): 'Yandex's thumbnail versions served a different function than Perfect 10's use: improving access to information on the Internet versus artistic expression' (internal citations omitted). And: *Fox News Network, LLC v. TVEyes, Inc.*, 43 F. Supp. 3d 379, 393 (Dist. Court, S.D.N.Y. 2014), on a TV and radio monitoring service: 'I find that TVEyes' search engine together with its display of result clips is transformative, and serves a new and different function from the original work and is not a substitute for it. In making this finding, I am guided by the Second Circuit's determination that databases that convert copyrighted works into a research tool to further learning are transformative' (internal citations omitted).
113. *The Authors Guild v. Google, Inc.*, 804 F.3d 202 (2nd Cir. Court 2015).

permission – more than twenty million books and made them partly available on its Google Books website. The Google Books service enables users to search through the included books. The Google Books search function also provides snippets displaying where the search terms were found in the book. A brief description of the book is presented as well. The Second Circuit Court considered that the purpose of copying the original books was to make available information about those books and to permit searchers to find books containing particular terms. According to the Court, this use was transformative. The snippets only added to the transformative nature of the use as they show the user 'just enough context surrounding the searched term to help her evaluate whether the book falls within the scope of her interest'.[114] Although Google's service is a free service, and Google does not display advertisements on its service, the copyright owners contended that Google had an overall profit motivation. However, according to the Court, because of Google's 'highly convincing transformative purpose', this overall profit motivation could not detract from the conclusion that Google's use was in fact fair.[115] The Court also stated that '[m]any of the most universally accepted forms of fair use, such as news reporting and commentary, quotation in historical or analytic books, reviews of books, and performances, as well as parody, are all normally done commercially for profit'.[116]

Making cache copies and displaying them in a search engine can be covered by the fair use doctrine as well. In *Field v. Google*, the Nevada District Court acknowledged that the display of cache copies by search engines is transformative, as such copies provide users with access to content if the original page is inaccessible, they allow users to detect changes in particular pages, and they help to understand the response to the search query because the search terms are highlighted in the copies. The Court concluded on the first factor: 'because Google serves different and socially important purposes in offering access to copyrighted works through 'Cached' links and does not merely supersede the objectives of the original creations, the Court concludes that Google's alleged copying and distribution of Field's Web pages containing copyrighted works was transformative'.[117]

[2] Second Factor: Nature of the Copyrighted Work

The second factor that needs to be considered by courts is the 'nature of the copyrighted work'. This factor considers whether the work being used is highly creative or original. If that is the case, this factor weighs against fair use because 'some works are closer to the core of intended copyright protection than others'.[118] In essence, this factor is a manifestation of the idea/expression dichotomy, which

114. *The Authors Guild v. Google, Inc., supra* n. 113, at 218.
115. *The Authors Guild v. Google, Inc., supra* n. 113, at 218.
116. *The Authors Guild v. Google, Inc., supra* n. 113, at 218.
117. *Field v. Google, Inc., supra* n. 38, at 1119.
118. *Campbell v. Acuff-Rose Music, Inc., supra* n. 92, at 586.

recognizes that copyright protects creative expressions and not the underlying ideas of facts.[119]

This factor may be of relevance when intermediaries are involved in the dissemination of more factual works. As with all other factors of fair use, the second-factor analysis should not take place in isolation, but rather in the context of the other factors and the use in general. The District Court in *The Associated Press v. Meltwater* held regarding a news aggregator that 'AP's articles are news stories and therefore more vulnerable to application of the fair use defense than works of fiction.'[120] Nevertheless, the Court in its aggregate assessment of all factors rejected Meltwater's fair use defence for a lack of transformativeness. By the same token, the use of creative works does not rule out a successful fair use defence. In the earlier discussed image search cases, the copied works were creative in nature and the second factor weighed against fair use. Nevertheless, the Ninth Circuit Court held these uses to be fair, in particular because the purpose of the use was transformative in nature.[121]

Another element that is important in the second-factor analysis is the question of whether the used work has been published. This element takes into account the author's right to control the first publication of his work. Section 107 of the US Copyright Act clarifies that 'the fact that a work is unpublished shall not itself bar a finding of fair use if such finding is made upon consideration of [the fair use-factors]'. Nevertheless, the US Supreme Court in *Harper & Row* held that the scope of fair use is narrower with respect to unpublished works.[122]

[3] Third Factor: The Amount and Substantiality of the Portion Used

The third factor that must be considered is the amount and substantiality of the portion used. Under this factor, courts should examine the proportionality of the copied parts of a work. Works that are copied in their entirety run the risk of supplanting the original work.[123] Nevertheless, if such copying is done for a transformative purpose, the use can still be fair. In fact, in the Internet context, making full copies of materials is often necessary. As Leval noted:

119. *Feist Publications, Inc. v. Rural Telephone Service Co., Inc.*, 499 U.S. 340, 347–349 (1991).
120. *The Associated Press v. Meltwater U.S. Holdings, Inc.*, 931 F.Supp.2d 537 (Dist. Court, S.D.N.Y 2013). Internal citations omitted.
121. *Kelly v. Arriba Soft Corp.*, *supra* n. 110, at 820; *Perfect 10, Inc. v. Amazon.com*, *supra* n. 15, at 1167.
122. *Harper & Row Publishers, Inc. v. Nation Enterprises*, *supra* n. 100, at 564: 'While even substantial quotations might qualify as fair use in a review of a published work or a news account of a speech that had been delivered to the public or disseminated to the press ... the author's right to control the first public appearance of his expression weighs against such use of the work before its release.'
123. *Campbell v. Acuff-Rose Music, Inc.*, *supra* n. 92, at 587, holding that verbatim copying 'may reveal a dearth of a transformative character or purpose under the first factor, or a greater likelihood of market harm under the fourth; a work composed primarily of an original, particularly its heart, with little added or changed, is more likely to be a superseding use, fulfilling demand for the original'.

> In the digital age, the need for ability to make complete unchanged copies without liability has soared. Numerous well-reasoned court decisions have found a fair-use home for complete digital copies that transformatively expand knowledge about the works without interfering with the legitimate entitlements or incentives of the authors of the works.[124]

Or as the Ninth Circuit Court considered in *Kelly v. Arriba Soft*, regarding image search:

> It was necessary for Arriba to copy the entire image to allow users to recognize the image and decide whether to pursue more information about the image or the originating web site. If Arriba only copied part of the image, it would be more difficult to identify it, thereby reducing the usefulness of the visual search engine.[125]

The third factor does not just consider the quantity of the portion that is used; it also takes into account the quality and the importance of the used portion. For instance, in *Harper & Row*, the Nation had taken only 300 words out of President Ford's memoirs. However, the US Supreme Court qualified that part as 'the heart of the book', the part that was the most newsworthy and important in licensing for publication.[126] A similar argument was advanced in *Meltwater*: by taking the lede from AP's articles, Meltwater took the 'sentence that takes significant journalistic skill to craft' while 'there is no other single sentence from an AP story that is as consistently important from article to article'.[127]

[4] Fourth Factor: Effect of the Use upon the Potential Market

The fourth fair use factor brings the economic harm caused to the copyright owner into the equation. Courts must consider the effect of the use upon the potential market for or the value of the copyrighted work and derivative works.[128] Positive effects on the potential market for or the value of the work may also be taken into account. If an intermediary's use has a positive effect on the market for or the value of the work, then the fourth factor may weigh in favour of finding fair use.

There is a clear relationship between the first (commerciality and transformativeness) and fourth factor (effect on the market). The US Supreme Court explained in *Campbell* how the assessment under one factor may influence the outcome under the other:

> When a commercial use amounts to mere duplication of the entirety of an original, it clearly supersedes the objects, of the original and serves as a market replacement for it, making it likely that cognizable market harm to the original will occur. But

124. Pierre N. Leval, *Campbell as Fair Use Blueprint*, 90 Washington Law Review (2) 597 (2015).
125. *Kelly v. Arriba Soft Corp.*, *supra* n. 110, at 821. The Ninth Circuit Court held that this third factor neither weighed for nor against either party.
126. *Harper & Row Publishers, Inc. v. Nation Enterprises*, *supra* n. 100, at 568.
127. *The Associated Press v. Meltwater U.S. Holdings, Inc.*, *supra* n. 120. A lede is the opening sentence or paragraph of a news article, summarizing the most important aspects of the story.
128. *Harper & Row Publishers, Inc. v. Nation Enterprises*, *supra* n. 100, at 568.

> when, on the contrary, the second use is transformative, market substitution is at least less certain, and market harm may not be so readily inferred.[129]

The cases of *Associated Press v. Meltwater* and *Perfect 10 v. Google* appear to be each other's opposites and serve as an example of the relationship between the first and fourth factor. Meltwater's use supplanted the original works: 'through its use of AP content and refusal to pay a licensing fee, Meltwater has obtained an unfair commercial advantage in the marketplace and directly harmed the creator of expressive content protected by the Copyright Act'.[130] In contrast, Google's use of materials in its search engine was considered highly transformative, 'and so market harm cannot be presumed'.[131]

[C] Flexibility and Predictability

The fair use doctrine offers great flexibility to the courts to determine the facts and circumstances of a case in light of US copyright law's overall objective of promoting the progress of science and the useful arts. As the Supreme Court noted in *Stewart v. Abend*:

> At common law, the property of the author (...) in his intellectual creation was absolute until he voluntarily parted with the same. The fair use doctrine, which is incorporated into the 1976 Act, evolved in response to this absolute rule. *The doctrine is an equitable rule of reason, which permits courts to avoid rigid application of the copyright statute when, on occasion, it would stifle the very creativity which that law is designed to foster.*[132]

Or as noted by the Second Circuit Court of Appeals in *Bill Graham Archives v. Dorling Kindersley*:

> The ultimate test of fair use is whether the copyright law's goal of promoting the Progress of Science and useful Arts would be better served by allowing the use than by preventing it.[133]

As already explained, Section 107 of the US Copyright Act provides a set of factors that courts must determine, but these are not the only factors that the courts may consider, nor does the Copyright Act ascribe them with a particular importance. The consideration of the transformative nature of a use in particular has enabled courts to allow socially beneficial intermediary uses of materials. The Ninth Circuit Court in *Perfect 10 v. Amazon* underlined that flexibility:

> We conclude that the significantly transformative nature of Google's search engine, particularly in light of its public benefit, outweighs Google's superseding and commercial uses of the thumbnails in this case. In reaching this conclusion,

129. *Campbell v. Acuff-Rose Music, Inc., supra* n. 92, at 591. Internal citations omitted.
130. *The Associated Press v. Meltwater U.S. Holdings, Inc., supra* n. 120.
131. *Perfect 10, Inc. v. Amazon.com, supra* n. 15.
132. *Stewart et al. v. Abend, DBA Authors Research Co.*, 495 U.S. 207, 236 (1990). Internal citations omitted. Emphasis added.
133. *Bill Graham Archives v. Dorling Kindersley Ltd.*, 448 F. 3d 605, 608 (2nd Cir. 2006).

> we note the importance of analyzing fair use flexibly in light of new circumstances.[134]

Does that flexibility come at a price? Yes, says Ginsburg, 'of course, any rule that privileges flexibility necessarily produces unpredictability. The greater the former, the greater also the latter'.[135] And Goldstein notes that 'no copyright doctrine is less determinate than fair use'.[136] Given this unpredictability and considering the sanctions in the case of infringements, people may be more likely to acquire a licence from the copyright owner than to depend on the fair use doctrine.[137]

According to David Nimmer, the fair use factors have not contributed to making the doctrine any more predictable.[138] He states:

> Courts tend first to make a judgment that the ultimate disposition is fair use or unfair use, and then align the four factors to fit that result as best they can. At base, therefore, the four factors fail to drive the analysis, but rather serve as convenient pegs on which to hang antecedent conclusion.[139]

Leval, however, argues that bright-line rules applied to complex circumstances are likely to produce unjustifiable results.[140] Moreover, he questions whether there is a better alternative:

> A bright-line rule that would either place unreasonable restraints on the creativity of secondary users, or unreasonably diminish the protection of original authors, would not be an improvement. Deploring a test's vagueness is easy. Much more difficult is to come up with a clear test that would provide better, or at least acceptable, results. So far as I am aware, none have been suggested.[141]

Moreover, Leval does not agree with the proposition that fair use has been wildly unpredictable:

> While some cases involve very difficult exercises of line drawing, on the whole, I believe the great majority of circuit-level opinions since *Campbell* have been well justified and reasonably predictable.[142]

Two empirical studies on the interpretation of the fair use doctrine by the courts indeed suggest that the fair use doctrine is more predictable, and less arbitrary, than some of its critics have argued. Beebe studied over 300 fair use court cases that were decided between 1978 and 2005 and looked at how the fair use factors were applied. In

134. *Perfect 10, Inc. v. Amazon.com, supra* n. 15, at 1066.
135. Jane Ginsburg, *Fair Use for Free, or Permitted-But-Paid?*, 29 Berkeley Technology Law Journal (3) 1383 (2014).
136. Goldstein, *supra* n. 20, at 12:2. *Also see*: Paul Goldstein, *Fair use in context*, 31 Columbia Journal of Law & the Arts (4) 433 (2008).
137. James Gibson, *Risk Aversion and Rights Accretion in Intellectual Property Law*, 116 Yale Law Journal 882, 890–891 (2007).
138. David Nimmer, *'Fairest of Them All' and Other Fairy Tales of Fair Use*, 66 Law and Contemporary Problems (1-2) 263 (2003).
139. Nimmer, *supra* n. 138, at 281.
140. Leval, *supra* n. 124.
141. Leval, *supra* n. 124.
142. Leval, *supra* n. 124.

contrast to what Nimmer had argued, Beebe's analysis shows that judges actually use the fair use factors to determine the outcome of the analysis:

> Rather than make a fair use determination first and then 'align the four factors to fit that result as best they can,' courts appeared quite willing to call the factor outcomes as they saw them, even when those outcomes did not support the overall test outcome.[143]

Beebe also found that the first and fourth fair use factors are the most important factors of a fair use analysis.[144] Regarding the first factor, which considers the purpose and character of the use, Beebe's study demonstrates that 95.3 % of the 148 decisions that found that this factor disfavoured fair use, also eventually found no fair use. And 90.2 % of the opinions that did find that the first factor favoured fair use, eventually also found fair use.[145]

Sag also conducted an empirical study on the workings of the fair use doctrine. His study is based on a dataset consisting of more than 280 fair use cases decided by US District Courts between 1978 and 2011. Sag's research demonstrates that the extent to which a work is transformative, in the sense that it makes a new work out of an old work, is a 'robust predictor of a finding of fair use'.[146] The results of his study also confirm 'the significance of the statutory factor that addresses "the amount and substantiality" of the defendant's unauthorized use of the plaintiff's work'.[147] Partial copying weighs in favour of finding a fair use. But Sag also notes that 'technologies that rely on digital processing of entire copyrighted works, such as Internet search engines and plagiarism detection software, nonetheless present a very strong case for fair use'.[148] Sag concludes:

> Standards are not necessarily more unpredictable than rules, nor is flexibility the same thing as unpredictability. The evidence presented in this Article suggests that fair use is not nearly so incoherent or unpredictable as is conventionally assumed.[149]

Samuelson argues that the fair use doctrine is both more coherent and more predictable than many have argued once one recognizes that fair use cases tend to fall into common patterns, or what Samuelson calls 'policy-relevant clusters'.[150] Within those clusters, the fair use doctrine operates reasonably predictably. One of the clusters recognized by Samuelson is the 'unforeseen uses'. The fair use doctrine is a balancing mechanism that enables questions posed by new technologies or other developments that were not contemplated by the US legislator to be addressed. The policy underlying the cases within this cluster include the promotion of competition and innovation in

143. Barton Beebe, *An Empirical Study of U.S. Copyright Fair Use Opinions, 1978-2005*, 156 University of Pennsylvania Law Review (3) 549, 34 (2008).
144. Beebe, *supra* n. 143, at 31.
145. Beebe, *supra* n. 143, at 41.
146. Matthew Sag, 73 *Predicting Fair Use*, Ohio State Law Journal (1) 47, 58 and 84 (2012).
147. Sag, *supra* n. 146, at 84.
148. Sag, *supra* n. 146, at 84–85.
149. Sag, *supra* n. 146, at 84–85.
150. Samuelson, *supra* n. 107, at 2541.

complementary technology industries, furthering the privacy and autonomy of users, and promoting enhanced access to information. Regarding this last sub-cluster, Samuelson identifies several factors that are based on case law. These factors consider whether the use facilitates better access to publicly available materials, whether the information access tool makes searches more efficient and effective, whether the copying is necessary to facilitate better access, whether transaction costs for seeking and obtaining permission cannot readily be formed, and finally, whether the information access tool supersedes or supplants the market for the copyright owner's work.

Samuelson concludes with advice to those criticizing the fair use doctrine due to its unpredictability:

> Judges and commentators should stop wringing their hands about how troublesome fair use law is and look instead for common patterns in the fair use case law upon which to build a more predictable body of fair use law. Analyzing fair uses in light of cases previously decided within the same policy cluster will make fair use more rule-like without a concomitant loss in its utility as a flexible standard for balancing a wide range of interests in a wide variety of situations.[151]

Samuelson's research corresponds with the idea that case law can deduce a concrete set of rules from a general standard.[152] Case law then offers greater *ex ante* predictability to the flexible standard. Of course, for a 'policy-cluster' to emerge, there needs to be sufficient case law that interprets and applies the doctrine within that cluster. If such case law does not emerge, the standard of course cannot offer that predictability.[153]

All in all, there is a reason to believe that the fair use doctrine is more predictable than some of its critics have argued. Nevertheless, to the extent that the doctrine may still be unpredictable, it may be possible to mitigate some of that unpredictability. US scholars came up with several solutions to make the fair use doctrine more transparent. Some of them suggest that the US Copyright Office should be involved.[154] For instance, Liu has suggested that the US Copyright Office could be given the authority to develop fair use guidelines or to create new exceptions.[155] Carrol has suggested the establishment of a 'Fair Use Board' within the Copyright Office that gives advisory opinions on whether particular uses are fair.[156] One concrete action that the Copyright Office has taken to make fair use more predictable is the establishment of a fair use index.[157] This searchable database of fair use cases aims to 'make the principles and application of fair use more accessible and understandable to the public by presenting a searchable

151. Samuelson, *supra* n. 107, at 2621.
152. *See* section §2.04[B][3] on mitigating unpredictability.
153. *See also*, in that regard, section §5.06[C] on the German experience with the liability of Wi-Fi providers under the *Störerhaftung* doctrine.
154. The US Copyright Office is a separate federal department within the US Library of Congress and is given specific statutory authorities. *See* Chapter 7 of the US Copyright Act.
155. Joseph Liu, *Regulatory Copyright*, 83 North Carolina Law Review (1) 87, 87 (2010).
156. Michael Carroll, *Fixing Fair Use*, 85 North Carolina Law Review (4) 1089 (2007).
157. Available at: www.copyright.gov/fair-use/fair-index.html (accessed on 14 June 2019).

database of court opinions, including by category and type of use (e.g., music, internet/digitization, parody)'.[158]

Another solution is the articulation of best practices in a dialogical process between users and copyright experts.[159] These best practices translate the principles of fair use into the vocabulary and experiences of a particular community and make fair use more understandable and less abstract.[160] For instance, under the lead of Jaszi and Aufderheide, a 'Set of Principles in Fair Use for Journalism' were created.[161] Principles are given, such as that 'fair use applies when journalists use copyrighted material as documentation, to validate, prove, support, or document a proposition'. And limitations to the principle are expressed as well: 'the journalist should take as much as is reasonably appropriate to enable the news consumer to assess validity of a journalist's assertions and interpretations'. Another example is the fair use guide for non-fiction authors developed by Authors Alliance[162] or the 'Code of Best Practices in Fair Use for Academic and Research Libraries' of the Association of Research Libraries.[163]

Rotham suggests that a limitation to these fair use best practices may be that they are generally based on the input of users – such as journalists – and that they do not take into account the input that copyright owners may have.[164] The inclusion of the input of copyright owners may be required to come to widely supported and balanced best practices.

§6.04 SAFE HARBOURS

In the previous section, we dealt with the fair use doctrine, which limits the intermediary's liability for its own infringements. Uses that are fair cannot be considered a copyright infringement. Still, intermediaries may be liable for the infringements of others, especially if others use their services to infringe copyrights. Just as in the EU, US law provides for a set of liability exemptions – or 'safe harbours'.

In the late 1990s, when the Internet emerged as a new information and communication technology and the first cases on the liability of online service providers were decided, the Digital Millennium Copyright Act (DMCA) was drafted by US Congress.[165] The 1998 DMCA implemented the WIPO Copyright Treaty and aimed to update US copyright law and make it ready for the new 'digital millennium'. With this act, the US

158. Available at: www.copyright.gov/fair-use/index.html (accessed on 14 June 2019).
159. Patricia Aufderheide & Aram Sinnreich, *Documentarians, Fair Use and Free Expression: Changes in Copyright Attitudes and Actions with Access to Best Practices*, 19 Information, Communication & Society (2) 178 (2016).
160. Anthony Falzone & Jennifer Urban, *Demystifying Fair Use: The Gift of the Center for Social Media Statements of Best Practices*, 57 Journal of the Copyright Society of the U.S.A. (3) 337, 342 (2010).
161. Available at: http://cmsimpact.org/code/set-principles-fair-use-journalism (accessed on 14 June 2019).
162. Available at: www.authorsalliance.org/resources/fair-use (accessed on 14 June 2019).
163. Available at: http://www.arl.org/focus-areas/copyright-ip/fair-use/code-of-best-practices (accessed on 14 June 2019).
164. Jennifer Rothman, *Best Intentions: Reconsidering Best Practices Statements in the Context of Fair Use and Copyright Law*, 57 Journal of the Copyright Society of the U.S.A. (3) 371 (2010).
165. H.R. Rep. No. 105-551, pt. 2, at 21 (1998).

legislator aimed to balance the interests of copyright owners, intermediaries, and users in a way that would 'foster the continued development of electronic commerce and the growth of the Internet'.[166]

Importantly, the DMCA also introduced a set of copyright-specific rules regarding the liability of intermediaries for infringements. Section 512 of the US Copyright Act created safe harbours 'for certain common activities of service providers'. They differ from the liability exemptions prescribed by EU law in the sense that they are copyright-specific.[167] Hence, they only apply to cases of copyright infringement.[168] Section 512 also provides for a detailed notice-and-takedown regime. Moreover, Section 512 puts in place particular safeguards that aim to prevent the abuse of notice-and-takedown systems.

This section first provides a brief overview of the history of the safe harbours in the US Copyright Act (section §6.04[A]). These safe harbours were primarily the result of a bargaining process between copyright owners and early Internet intermediaries. We will then discuss how these safe harbours limit the liability of intermediaries and how they relate to secondary liability theories (section §6.04[B]). There is a set of general requirements that intermediaries must meet in order to qualify for the safe harbours. These requirements are discussed as well (section §6.04[C]).

We will then consider the four types of intermediary activity that are exempted by the safe harbour regime: 'transitory digital network communications', 'system caching', 'information residing on systems or networks at direction of users', and 'information location tools' (section §6.04[D]). The latter three safe harbours require intermediaries to remove infringing materials once they are notified about them through notice-and-takedown systems. The statutory notice-and-takedown regime of Section 512 of the US Copyright Act is discussed as well (section §6.04[E]). This section ends with a brief overview of the steps that have been taken towards reforming the notice-and-takedown regime in US copyright law (section §6.04[F]).

[A] The Digital Millennium Copyright Act

The 1998 Digital Millennium Copyright Act (DMCA) laid down a special liability regime for intermediaries. The US legislator aimed to create incentives for intermediaries and copyright owners to work together and to deal with online infringements, while also offering more certainty to intermediaries regarding their liability. Before the introduction of the safe harbours, case law regarding the intermediary's liability for third-party information was inconsistent.[169] There was a genuine risk that these intermediaries would be held contributorily or vicariously liable for the infringing materials they

166. H.R. Rep. No. 551, pt. 2 (1998).
167. *See* section §3.04 for a discussion of the liability exemptions under EU law.
168. Section 230 of the Communications Decency Act (CDA) provides for a safe harbour in respect of other unlawful activities.
169. Michelle Ravn, *Navigating Terra Incognita: Why the Digital Millennium Copyright Act Was Needed to Chart the Course of Online Service Provider Liability for Copyright Infringement*, Ohio State Law Journal (2) 755 (1999).

passed along.[170] Legal certainty as to their liability would enable them to attract the substantial investments necessary to continue the expansion and upgrading of the Internet and services delivered over the global computer network. At the other end of the spectrum, copyright owners feared the effects that digitized and networked communication would have on the enforcement of their copyrights. They wanted effective legal protection mechanisms to quickly redress copyright infringements. Effective copyright protection was at stake, and the need was felt to create incentives for intermediaries to cooperate in the fight against unauthorized use of copyrighted materials.

The liability exemptions in the DMCA were ultimately the result of a bargaining process involving primarily the copyright industries, on the one hand, and new early Internet intermediaries, on the other.[171] Litman describes the expedience of which the DMCA and its liability regime are a product:

> Telephone companies, commercial Internet service providers, libraries, and schools insisted that an agreement setting up a safe harbor for online service providers was a precondition to the enactment of implementing legislation. Content owners, however resisted linking the expansion in digital copyright with relief for Internet service providers. Not only were the two subjects legally unrelated, they argued, but content owner's only meaningful weapon against online pirates was their ability to use the risk of strict liability (liability imposed regardless of fault) for subscribers' copyright infringement to persuade Internet service providers to assist their enforcement efforts. It soon became clear to content owners, however, that the legislation could not move without a solution to the problem of Internet service provider liability.[172]

The issue of intermediary liability was hotly debated. It took several years before copyright owners and intermediaries reached a consensus.[173] Importantly for copyright owners, the rules in the DMCA created an incentive for service providers to cooperate in the fight against unauthorized use of copyrighted works. In particular, the notice-and-takedown regime would enable copyright owners to combat infringing uses of their materials. From the perspective of the intermediaries, the rules would shield them from liability for copyright infringements. In the eyes of the US legislator, this compromise would effectively not only protect copyrights but also promote the development of Internet services.[174]

In retrospect, the objective of providing intermediaries with legal certainty and promoting the development of the Internet appears to have been achieved by the safe

170. David Nimmer, *Brains and Other Paraphernalia of the Digital Age*, Harvard Journal of Law & Technology (1) 1–34 (1996).
171. Cassandra Imfeld & Victoria Ekstrand, The Music Industry and the Legislative Development of the Digital Millennium Copyright Act's online service provider provision, 3 Communication Law and Policy 291 (2005).
172. Jessica Litman, *Digital Copyright*, 134–135 (2006).
173. House floor debate on H.R. 2281, the Digital Millennium Copyright Act (Aug. 4, 1998), statement by congressman Goodlatte who lead the negotiations on the liability of intermediary service providers.
174. S. Rep. No. 105-190, at 8 (1998).

harbours. Chander writes that the introduction of these safe harbours was crucial to creating a thriving high-tech sector in the US:

> [The safe harbours] achieved a modus vivendi between northern and southern California – where Silicon Valley would banish repeat offenders and take down material if requested by the copyright owner, often based in Hollywood. By performing these duties diligently, Silicon Valley enterprises generally managed to avoid liability for the widespread copyright infringement that still occurred through their systems. While some have legitimately criticized [the safe harbours] for leading firms to take down material too quickly for fear of jeopardizing their safe harbor, [the safe harbours] marked a significant accomplishment for Silicon Valley in creating rules that allowed Web 2.0 enterprises to flourish without either excessive copyright management costs or high liability risks.[175]

The effective protection of copyrights seems to have been achieved only to the extent that materials are stored by intermediaries which are subject to the notice-and-takedown regime in Section 512 of the Copyright Act. The DMCA did not have a clear answer to the rise of peer-to-peer file-sharing that developed after the DMCA was adopted.[176] In such systems, information is stored by users, and not by intermediaries, which makes tackling infringements more difficult. In that respect, case law's development of inducement as a form of contributory liability has offered copyright owners greater protection. This liability theory has enabled copyright owners to hold accountable those who produce the software and maintain the platforms that are used for file-sharing.[177]

[B] Limited Remedies

Section 512 of the US Copyright Act does not itself provide the basis for liability, nor does it define the requirements for establishing liability. Section 512 only provides immunity from monetary damages and injunctive relief for qualified online service providers. The US legislator aimed to leave the law on secondary liability doctrines in its evolving state and create a set of exemptions for certain common activities of service providers.[178] Moreover, the safe harbours do not imply that an intermediary is liable for conduct that is outside the scope of the safe harbours, nor does it affect other possible defences against an infringement, such as fair use.[179] Such liability is to be determined on the basis of (other) principles of law.

175. Anupam Chander, *How Law Made Silicon Valley*, Emory Law Journal (3) 639, 661–662 (2014). *Also see*: Edward Lee, *Decoding the DMCA Safe Harbors*, Columbia Journal of Law & the Arts (3) 233 (2009).
176. Tim Wu, *When Code Isn't Law*, Virginia Law Review (4) 103, 160 (2003).
177. *See* section §6.02[D][2].
178. S. Rep. No. 105-190, Report of the Senate Judiciary Committee on S. 2037, the Digital Millennium Copyright Act (May 6, 1998), 19.
179. Section 512(l) DMCA: 'The failure of a service provider's conduct to qualify for limitation of liability under this section shall not bear adversely upon the consideration of a defense by the service provider that the service provider's conduct is not infringing under this title or any other

The liability exemptions only affect the remedies that may be applicable if liability is established.[180] As the Ninth Circuit Court put it:

> The DMCA did not simply rewrite copyright law for the on-line world. (...) Claims against service providers for direct, contributory, or vicarious copyright infringement, therefore, are generally evaluated just as they would be in the non-online world.[181]

The Fourth Circuit Court of Appeals offered more clarity as to the relation of the safe harbours with existing doctrines:

> Thus the DMCA was intended not to change the 'evolving' doctrines on ISP liability for copyright infringement, which included *Netcom* and *Frena*, but to offer a certain safe harbor for ISPs. Courts were left free to continue to construe the Copyright Act in deciding the scope and nature of prima facie liability. The legislative 'compromise' repeatedly invoked by CoStar and its amici was that Congress would not end the debate by importing and fixing copyright infringement liability in the form articulated by *Netcom*, but rather would provide a limited safe harbor immediately necessary to ISPs, and allow the courts to continue defining what constitutes a prima facie case of copyright infringement against an ISP.[182]

The safe harbours protect the intermediary against monetary relief: 'damages, costs, attorneys' fees, and any other form of monetary payment'.[183] The possibility of injunctions or other equitable relief is also limited, but not in an absolute sense.[184] Depending on the safe harbour in question, the types of injunctions are limited. Intermediaries offering hosting, caching, and information location tools can be ordered to stop providing access to infringing materials on an online site or the intermediary's system or network.[185] That intermediary can also be required to stop providing access to a subscriber or account holder engaging in infringing activity.[186] Other forms of injunctive relief are possible as well, provided that such injunctions are necessary to stop or prevent infringements at a particular online location and such relief is the least burdensome for the intermediary among the forms of relief that are comparably effective for that purpose.[187]

Intermediaries involved in mere conduit activities can be ordered to stop 'providing access to a subscriber or account holder of the service provider's system or network who is using the provider's service to engage in infringing activity and is identified in the order, by terminating the accounts of the subscriber or account holder

---

defense.' For example: *Io Group, Inc. v. Veoh Networks, Inc.*, 586 F. Supp. 2d 1132, 1142 (Dist. Court, N.D. Cal. 2008): 'the safe harbor provisions are not exclusive of any other defense an accused infringer might have'.

180. For example: *Perfect 10, Inc. v. Cybernet Ventures, Inc.*, 213 F.Supp.2d 1146, 1179 (Dist. Court, C.D. Cal. 2002): 'Section 512 does not affect the elements of copyright liability. Instead, it affects the remedies available for any infringement which might be found.'
181. *Ellison v. Robertson*, 357 F.3d 1072, 1077 (9th Cir. 2004).
182. *CoStar Group, Inc. v. LoopNet, Inc.*, *supra* n. 39, at 554.
183. Section 512(k)(2) of the US Copyright Act.
184. Or: non-monetary remedies.
185. Section 512(j)(1)(a)(i) of the US Copyright Act.
186. Section 512(j)(1)(a)(ii) of the US Copyright Act.
187. Section 512(j)(1)(a)(iii) of the US Copyright Act.

that are specified in the order'.[188] These intermediaries can also be ordered to stop providing access, by taking reasonable steps specified in the order to block access, to a specific, identified, online location outside the United States.[189]

The possibility of injunctive relief against service providers qualifying for the safe harbours appears to be little used. As noted in the 2013 Green Paper of the Department of Commerce Internet Policy Task Force, 'indeed, there are no reported cases in the U.S. courts in which an injunction has been granted against a service provider that qualifies for a DMCA safe harbor'.[190] To obtain such injunctions, the copyright owner needs a basis for liability. However, as intermediaries are unlikely to be liable as direct or indirect infringers, injunctions against intermediaries appear to be a theoretical possibility only.

Section 512(h) of the US Copyright Act provides that intermediaries can be subpoenaed to identify alleged infringers. This provision only applies to intermediaries that are subject to the notice-and-takedown regime. The District of Columbia Circuit Court of Appeals explained that with this provision the US legislator had in mind 'bulletin board services (BBSs) and file transfer protocol (FTP) sites'.[191] Hence, Section 512(h) is tailored to infringers who make use of hosting services to share infringing materials.

However, with the rise of peer-to-peer file-sharing networks and platforms, users share infringing materials without the need for any hosting. The only intermediary that can identify such infringers is the access provider. Indeed, two different Courts of Appeals have held that Section 512(h) does not apply when the identities of peer-to-peer file sharers are requested from access providers.[192] The District of Columbia Circuit Court understood the consequences of such a decision, but also realized that it could not go against statutory copyright law:

> We are not unsympathetic either to the RIAA's concern regarding the widespread infringement of its members' copyrights, or to the need for legal tools to protect those rights. It is not the province of the courts, however, to rewrite the DMCA in order to make it fit a new and unforeseen internet architecture, no matter how damaging that development has been to the music industry or threatens being to the motion picture and software industries.[193]

Here we can witness how a technology-specific provision in the US Copyright Act fails to effectively address peer-to-peer file-sharing.[194] The DMCA's rules were tailored to a technological configuration in which infringing materials are shared via hosting

188. Section 512(j)(1)(b)(i) of the US Copyright Act.
189. Section 512(j)(1)(b)(ii) of the US Copyright Act.
190. Department of Commerce Internet Policy Task Force, Green Paper on Copyright Policy, Creativity, and Innovation in the Digital Economy 50 (2013).
191. *Recording Industry Ass'n of America, Inc. v. Verizon Internet Services, Inc.*, 351 F.3d 1229 (D.C. Cir. 2003).
192. *Recording Industry Ass'n of America, Inc. v. Verizon Internet Services, Inc.*, *supra* n. 191; In re: Charter Communications, Inc., 393 F.3d 771 (8th Cir. 2005).
193. *Recording Industry Ass'n of America, Inc. v. Verizon Internet Services, Inc.*, *supra* n. 191. *Also see*: In re: Charter Communications, Inc., *supra* n. 192, at 777.
194. Niva Elkin-Koren, *Making Technology Visible: Liability of Internet Service Providers for Peer-to-Peer Traffic*, New York University Journal of Legislation and Public Policy (9) 15 (2005).

services and not the decentralized peer-to-peer architecture in which users share materials from their own devices. Fortunately for copyright owners, US federal procedural law does enable them to identify infringers through subpoenas as well.[195] In that respect, it appears that these general rules of civil procedure have offered copyright owners a more effective means to identify infringers than the regime in the US Copyright Act.

[C] General Requirements

For an intermediary to be shielded against liability, it must meet a set of general requirements in Section 512 of the US Copyright Act. First, the intermediary must be a 'service provider' within the meaning of Section 512(k) of the US Copyright Act. The definition of a service provider differs depending on the type of activity in question. For mere conduit activities, a service provider is defined as 'an entity offering the transmission, routing, or providing of connections for digital online communications, between or among points specified by a user, of material of the user's choosing, without modification to the content of the material as sent or received'.[196] This definition covers intermediaries acting as conduits or passive carriers for online communications, which are 'communications over interactive computer networks, such as the Internet'.[197] Hosting a website, for instance, is not covered by the definition in Section 512(k)(1)(a).[198]

The definition of a 'service provider' is broader for the other types of intermediary activities. The definition then includes the entity described above but also 'a provider of online services of network access, or the operator of facilities therefore'.[199] This category of service providers covers a wide range of providers. Courts have considered the operators of the e-commerce platforms eBay[200] and Amazon,[201] a humour website,[202] and video hosting platforms[203] to be service providers. Also, the provider of an age-verification system for websites containing pornographic materials was deemed to

195. Federal Rule of Civil Procedure 45.
196. Section 512(k)(1)(A) of the US Copyright Act.
197. H.R. Rep. No. 105-551(II), at 63–64. *Also see*: *UMG Recordings, Inc. v. Veoh Networks*, *supra* n. 69, at 1035: 'The narrower definition that applies exclusively to § 512(a), which governs conduit-only functions, expressly excludes service providers that "modif[y] the content of the material as sent or received."'
198. H.R. Rep. No. 105-551(II), at 63–64.
199. Section 512(k)(1)(B) of the US Copyright Act.
200. *Hendrickson v. eBay, Inc.*, 165 F.Supp.2d 1082, 1088 (Dist. Court, C.D. Cal. 2001): 'eBay clearly meets the DMCA's broad definition of online "service provider."'
201. *Corbis Corp. v. Amazon. com, Inc.*, 351 F. Supp. 2d 1090, 1100 (Dist. Court, W.D. Wash. 2004): 'Amazon operates web sites, provides retail and third party selling services to Internet users, and maintains computers to govern access to its web sites. These activities fall squarely within the broad scope of the § 512(k)(1)(B) definition.'
202. *Obodai v. Demand Media, Inc.*, 2012 WL 2189740, 3 (Dist. Court, S.D.N.Y. 2012), affirmed in 522 Fed.Appx. 41 (2nd. Cir. 2013).
203. *Viacom International, Inc. v. Youtube, Inc.*, *supra* n. 69, at 27.

be a service provider,[204] and even the providers of peer-to-peer file-sharing services are covered by the definition.[205] However, that does not mean that the providers of file-sharing services are actually protected by the safe harbours. They are generally unable to clear the many other hurdles in Section 512 of the US Copyright Act.

The second requirement is that the intermediary must have reasonably implemented a repeat infringer policy that aims to terminate the service for users who repeatedly infringe.[206] The US courts, however, have not consistently interpreted this requirement. The exact purport of this requirement therefore remains unclear.[207]

Third, the intermediary should accommodate and not interfere with standard technical measures.[208] Thus far, this requirement has not had any practical meaning.[209] Technologies would have to be developed 'pursuant to a broad consensus of copyright owners and service providers in an open, fair, voluntary, multi-industry standards process', be 'available to any person on reasonable and nondiscriminatory terms', and not 'impose substantial costs on service providers or substantial burdens on their systems or networks'.[210] The US legislator urged copyright owners and intermediaries to develop technologies to detect and prevent infringements, yet the provision was given 'no teeth' to actually ensure that such standards are developed.[211]

[D] The Four Safe Harbours

If an intermediary fulfils the general requirements, the intermediary may qualify under one of the four safe harbours in Section 512 of the US Copyright Act. The safe harbours apply to four different types of intermediary activity and all come with their own requirements. There is a safe harbour for 'transitory digital network communications' (section §6.04[D][1]), 'system caching' (section §6.04[D][2]), 'information residing on systems or networks and direction of users' (section §6.04[D][3]), and 'information location tools' (section §6.04[D][4]).

204. *Perfect 10, Inc. v. Cybernet Ventures, Inc.*, 213 F.Supp.2d 1146, 1175 (Dist. Court, C.D. Cal. 2002): 'Although there appears to be uniform agreement that the definition is broad, or at least broader than the definition of 512(k)(1)(A) concerning conduit-type services, the Court has found no discussion of this definition's limits.'
205. *In re: Aimster Copyright Litigation, supra* n. 21, 655: 'Although the Act was not passed with Napster-type services in mind, the definition of Internet service provider is broad ... and, as the district judge ruled, Aimster fits it.'
206. Section 512(i)(1)(A) of the US Copyright Act.
207. Department of Commerce Internet Policy Task Force, Green Paper on Copyright Policy, Creativity, and Innovation in the Digital Economy 59–60 (2013).
208. Section 512(i)(1)(B) of the US Copyright Act.
209. Lauren Gallo, *The (Im)Possibility of Standard Technical Measures for UGC Websites*, Columbia Journal of Law & the Arts (2) 283, 300 (2010).
210. Section 512(i)(2) of the US Copyright Act.
211. David Nimmer, *Back from the Future: A Proleptic Review of the Digital Millennium Copyright Act*, 16 Berkeley Technology Law Journal (4) 855, 865 (2001).

[1] Transitory Digital Network Communications

The safe harbour in Section 512(a) of the US Copyright Act applies to 'transitory digital network communications'. A service provider that qualifies under this safe harbour will not be liable for copyright infringement by reason of the 'provider's transmitting, routing, or providing of connections for, material through a system or network controlled or operated by or for the service provider, or by reason of the intermediate and transient storage of that material in the course of such transmitting, routing, or providing connections'.[212] With this safe harbour, the US legislator had in mind those intermediaries that act as 'mere conduits' for the transmission of content provided by others.[213]

Besides the earlier-mentioned general requirements that the mere conduit intermediary must meet, the intermediary must also satisfy a set of specific conditions to qualify under this safe harbour. First, the transmission of the material should be initiated by or at the direction of a person other than the service provider.[214] This means that the intermediary can still be held fully liable for material that it transmits on its own initiative. Second, the transmission, routing, provision of connections, or storage should be carried out through an automatic technical process without a selection of the material by the service provider.[215] This requirement reflects the lack of editorial control by the intermediary.[216] The intermediary should thus in no way determine what material is sent, and its conduct should be limited to the automatic and technical process of responding to a command or request by, for example, a user, an 'Internet location tool', or another network.[217]

Third, the intermediary should not select the recipients of the material.[218] The intermediary should thus act as a conduit for communications between one person and another. Fourth, the intermediary should transmit the material through its system or network without modifying the content of the material.[219]

Specifically regarding intermediate or transient storage by an intermediary, there is another (fifth) condition that needs to be fulfilled. The intermediary should make no copies of the materials in the course of such intermediate or transient storage that are maintained on the system or network in a manner that is ordinarily accessible to anyone other than the anticipated recipients.[220] Those copies should also not be

212. Section 512(a) of the US Copyright Act.
213. *In re: Charter Communications, Inc., supra* n. 192, at 755: 'The first safe harbor, under § 512(a), limits the liability of ISPs when they do nothing more than transmit, route, or provide connections for copyrighted material – that is, when the ISP is a mere conduit for the transmission.' *Also see: UMG Recordings, Inc. v. Veoh Networks, Inc.*, 667 F.3d 1022 (9th Cir. 2011), n. 10, distinguishing the Section 512(c) safe harbour from the Section 512(a) safe harbour.
214. Section 512(a)(1) of the US Copyright Act.
215. Section 512(a)(2) of the US Copyright Act.
216. H.R. Rep. No. 105-551(II), p. 51.
217. S. Rept. 105-190, Report of the Senate Judiciary Committee on S. 2037, the Digital Millennium Copyright Act (May 6, 1998), 42.
218. Section 512(a)(3) of the US Copyright Act.
219. Section 512(a)(5) of the US Copyright Act.
220. Section 512(a)(4) of the US Copyright Act.

maintained on the system or network in a manner that is ordinarily accessible to such anticipated recipients for a longer period than is reasonably necessary for the transmission, routing, or provision of connections.

[2] System Caching

Section 512(b) of the US Copyright Act provides a second safe harbour for what is called 'system caching'. System caching is a type of temporary storage that is different from the temporary storage discussed in the previous section. System caching is temporary storage that takes place in order to increase network performance and to reduce network congestion. This type of storage thus makes the transmission of information more efficient. For instance, an intermediary that performs system caching may store the content of a popular website on its servers, in order to relieve other servers.

US scholars have raised questions about the practical relevance of the system caching safe harbour. Seltzer wrote that 'it is unclear whether the caching provision has been of use to anyone'.[221] In a similar vein, Urban and Quilter have recommended that the use of this provision requires further study and argue that 'if it is consistently unused or misapplied, then [Section] 512(b) might safely be repealed'.[222]

To be shielded from liability under this safe harbour, the materials that are stored should be made available online by a person other than the intermediary.[223] Furthermore, the materials should be transmitted by the person who made the information available online, to another person, at the direction of that first person.[224] In other words, if the intermediary decides, on its own initiative, to temporarily store materials to make the transmission of those materials more efficient, the intermediary cannot benefit from the safe harbour.

Intermediaries wanting to benefit from the system caching safe harbour must also implement a notice-and-takedown system.[225] The intermediary must also meet the countless number of additional requirements in Section 512(b)(2) of the Copyright Act.[226] These requirements are not reproduced here.

221. Wendy Seltzer, *Free Speech Unmoored in Copyright's Safe Harbor: Chilling Effects on the DMCA on the First Amendment*, 24 Harvard Journal of Law & Technology (1) 171, 202 (2010).
222. Jennifer Urban & Laura Quilter, *Efficient process or 'Chilling Effects'? Takedown Notices under Section 512 of the Digital Millenium Copyright Act*, 22 Santa Clara Computer & High Technology Law Journal (4) 621, 690 (2005).
223. Section 512(b)(1)(A) of the US Copyright Act.
224. Section 512(b)(1)(B) of the US Copyright Act.
225. The statutory regime regarding notice-and-takedown is discussed in section §6.04[E].
226. Section 512(b)(2) of the US Copyright Act.

[3] *Information Residing on Systems or Networks at the Direction of Users*

The third safe harbour in Section 512(c) of the US Copyright Act covers 'information residing on systems or networks at direction of users'.[227] This safe harbour protects against liability for materials that are stored for others. Unlike the mere conduit safe harbour in Section 512(a), this safe harbour brings elements of knowledge, control, and financial interest into the equation. Intermediaries wanting to benefit from this safe harbour must implement a notice-and-takedown system.[228]

With the 512(c) safe harbour, the US legislator had in mind traditional hosting, but also the provision of server space for a chat room or other forums in which material may be posted by users.[229] The US Courts have rejected a narrow understanding of this safe harbour and clarified that it also applies to the facilitation of access to the stored materials. Two decisions from two different Courts of Appeals on the liability of video hosting platforms indicate that the 512(c) safe harbour should be understood to also cover the automated processing of the materials stored by these intermediaries.

In *Veoh*, the Ninth Circuit Court held that the activities of a video hosting provider regarding user-provided materials are covered by the 512(c) safe harbour.[230] This case centred on Veoh, a former video hosting platform. When a video was uploaded to Veoh, several automated processes took place that facilitated the sharing of the video, such as breaking down the video into smaller pieces and the conversion of the video to popular file formats. UMG contended that the creation of chunked and converted video files was beyond the concept of storage. 'The thrust of UMG's argument seems to be that web hosts do not undertake the sorts of accessibility-facilitating functions that Veoh does,' the Court summarized.[231] In contrast, the Court held that the safe harbour does not only cover the storage of materials but also covers the provision of access to those materials, for that access is implied in the safe harbour:

> The reason one has a website is so that others may view it. As amici note, these access activities define web hosting – if the web host only stored information for a single user, it would be more aptly described as an online back-up service.[232]

The Ninth Circuit Court also considered that the US legislator did not expressly limit the safe harbour's scope to traditional web hosting services only. Instead, the US legislator used more oblique language by limiting liability to service providers for copyright infringement of a copyright 'by reason of the storage'.

In *Viacom v. YouTube*, the Second Circuit Court considered whether the liability of the video hosting platform YouTube was limited under Section 512(c) of the US

227. 17 USC Section 512(c).
228. This statutory regime is discussed in the separate section §6.04[E].
229. S. Rept. 105-190, Report of the Senate Judiciary Committee on S. 2037, the Digital Millennium Copyright Act (May 6, 1998), 43.
230. *UMG Recordings, Inc. v. Veoh Networks*, *supra* n. 69.
231. *UMG Recordings, Inc. v. Veoh Networks*, *supra* n. 69, at 1018.
232. *UMG Recordings, Inc. v. Veoh Networks*, *supra* n. 69, at 1018.

Copyright Act.[233] In its decision, the Second Circuit relied to a great extent on the reasoning of the Ninth Circuit in *Veoh*:

> Two of the software functions challenged here – transcoding and playback – were expressly considered by our sister Circuit in *[Veoh]*, which held that liability arising from these functions occurred 'by reason of the storage at the direction of a user.'[234]

In *Viacom v. YouTube*, the Second Circuit Court also considered the question of whether a software algorithm to identify related videos is done 'by reason of the storage at the direction of a user'. The Court held that the algorithm is closely related to and follows from the storage itself and that the function is narrowly directed towards providing access to material stored at the direction of users. The Court here took into account that the algorithm was fully automated and operates solely in response to user input, without the involvement of YouTube employees.

These two decisions clarify that the provision of automated services aimed at the provision of access, or even the promotion of access as in *Viacom v. YouTube*, is covered by the safe harbour in Section 512(c) of the US Copyright Act.

[a] Knowledge

Section 512(c) of the US Copyright Act only protects 'innocent' intermediaries that do not have actual or constructive knowledge of infringements taking place.[235] If the intermediary becomes aware that its service is used to infringe, and it does not act upon that awareness, the intermediary loses its innocence and can no longer rely on this safe harbour. With this knowledge requirement, the US legislator ensured that intermediaries would not be burdened with a duty to actively monitor for infringing material,[236] while also making sure that they cannot deliberately turn a blind eye to infringements.[237]

The intermediary must not have actual knowledge that the material or the activity using the material is infringing.[238] Hence, the question is whether the intermediary subjectively knew of specific infringements.[239] In the absence of such actual knowledge, the intermediary must also not be 'aware of facts or circumstances from which infringing activity is apparent', which is often referred to as 'red-flag knowledge'.[240] In contrast to the actual knowledge requirement, this type of knowledge does have an

233. *Viacom International, Inc. v. Youtube, Inc.*, *supra* n. 69.
234. *Viacom International, Inc. v. Youtube, Inc.*, *supra* n. 69, at 30.
235. H.R. Conf. Rep. No. 105-796, p 72 (1998).
236. *Also see* Section 512(m)(1) of the US Copyright Act.
237. H.R. Rep. 105-551, p 53; S. Rep. 105-190, p 44.
238. Section 512(c)(1)(A)(i) of the Copyright Act.
239. *Viacom International, Inc. v. Youtube, Inc.*, *supra* n. 69, at 31: 'In other words, the actual knowledge provision turns on whether the provider actually or "subjectively" knew of specific infringement, while the red flag provision turns on whether the provider was subjectively aware of facts that would have made the specific infringement "objectively" obvious to a reasonable person.' *Also see*: *Columbia Pictures Industries, Inc. v. Fung*, *supra* n. 73, at 1043.
240. Section 512(c)(1)(A)(ii) of the Copyright Act.

objective element. The red-flag provision revolves around the question of whether the provider was *subjectively* aware of facts that would have made the specific infringement *objectively* obvious to a reasonable person.[241] If the intermediary obtains actual or red-flag knowledge, for instance through a notification, the intermediary should act 'expeditiously to remove, or disable access to, the material'.[242]

[b] Financial Benefit and the Right and Ability to Control

Furthermore, the intermediary should not 'receive a financial benefit directly attributable to the infringing activity, in a case in which the service provider has the right and ability to control such activity'.[243] With respect to this requirement, the US legislator directed the courts not to adopt a formalistic approach, but rather a common sense and fact-based approach that focuses on where the financial benefits emanate from:

> In general, a service provider conducting a legitimate business would not be considered to receive a 'financial benefit directly attributable to the infringing activity' where the infringer makes the same kind of payment as non-infringing users of the provider's service. Thus, receiving a one-time set-up fee and flat periodic payments for service from a person engaging in infringing activities would not constitute receiving a 'financial benefit directly attributable to the infringing activity.' ... It would however, include any such fees where the value of the service lies in providing access to infringing material.[244]

Hence, the fact that the intermediary is paid for its services does not lead to the safe harbour defence being lost. Only if the financial benefits are linked to the infringements can the intermediary no longer rely on the safe harbour defence in Article 512(c) of the US Copyright Act.

[4] Information Location Tools

Section 512(d) of the US Copyright Act limits the liability of intermediaries for infringements 'by reason of the provider referring or linking users to an online location containing infringing material or infringing activity, by using information location tools, including a directory, index, reference, pointer, or hypertext link, if the service provider'. With this safe harbour, the US legislator had in mind search engines and their precursors which created a directory of the Internet.[245] Linking to infringing

241. S. Rept. 105-190, Report of the Senate Judiciary Committee on S. 2037, the Digital Millennium Copyright Act (May 6, 1998), 43. *Also see*: *Viacom International, Inc. v. Youtube, Inc.*, *supra* n. 69, at 31.
242. Sections 512(c)(1)(A)(iii) and 512(c)(1)(C) of the Copyright Act. For example: *Rosen v. Global Net Access, LLC*, 2014 WL 2803752 (Dist. Court, C.D. Cal. 2014): 'By removing the infringing material some two months later, GNAX failed to act expeditiously.'
243. Section 512(c)(1)(B) of the US Copyright Act.
244. S. Rept. 105-190, Report of the Senate Judiciary Committee on S. 2037, the Digital Millennium Copyright Act (May 6, 1998), 44.
245. *See*: H.R. Rep. 105-551(II), 58, identifying Yahoo! as an example.

materials, as is done by today's general-purpose search engines, thus cannot lead to liability for damages.

The requirements to qualify under this safe harbour mirror those of Section 512(c) of the US Copyright Act. For limiting its liability, the intermediary should 'not have actual knowledge that the material or activity is infringing'.[246] And in the absence of such actual knowledge, it should not be aware of 'facts or circumstances from which infringing activity is apparent'.[247] Once the online service provider obtains such knowledge or awareness, it should act 'expeditiously to remove, or disable access to, the material'.[248] The online service provider should furthermore not 'receive a financial benefit directly attributable to the infringing activity, in a case in which the service provider has the right and ability to control such activity'.[249]

The notice-and-takedown regime in Section 512(c) of the US Copyright Act equally applies to intermediaries wanting to benefit from the safe harbour for information location tools.[250]

[E] Notice-and-Takedown

For intermediaries to be covered by the safe harbours in Section 512(b), (c), or (d) of the US Copyright Act – caching, hosting, and information location tools – they must 'upon notification of claimed infringement' respond 'expeditiously to remove, or disable access to, the material that is claimed to be infringing or to be the subject of infringing activity'.[251] Furthermore, an intermediary needs to have a designated agent to receive such notifications.[252] On its website, the intermediary needs to publish the 'the name, address, phone number, and electronic mail address of the agent',[253] and 'other contact information which the Register of the Copyrights may deem appropriate'.[254] This information also needs to be provided to the US Copyright Office,[255] which on its website offers a directory of so-called DMCA agents.[256]

The intermediary is not liable for the good-faith removal of materials 'claimed to be infringing or based on facts or circumstances from which infringing activity is apparent',[257] even if those materials are ultimately not found to be infringing. The intermediary must take reasonable steps to promptly notify the user who posted the materials and must also comply with the statutory counter-notification procedure.[258] This procedure is discussed below in section §6.04[E][2].

246. Section 512(d)(1)(A) of the US Copyright Act.
247. Section 512(d)(1)(B) of the US Copyright Act.
248. Section 512(d)(1)(C) of the US Copyright Act.
249. Section 512(d)(2) of the US Copyright Act.
250. Section 512(d)(3) of the US Copyright Act.
251. Section 512(c)(1)(C) of the US Copyright Act.
252. Section 512(c)(2) of the US Copyright Act.
253. Section 512(c)(2)(A) of the US Copyright Act.
254. Section 512(c)(2)(B) of the US Copyright Act.
255. Section 512(c)(2) of the US Copyright Act.
256. *See*: https://dmca.copyright.gov/osp/ (accessed on 14 June 2019).
257. Section 512(g)(1) of the US Copyright Act.
258. Section 512(g)(2) of the US Copyright Act.

[1] Notice Requirements

For a notice to be effective, the notice needs to be a written communication to the DMCA agent of the service provider, 'including substantially the following':

- A physical or electronic signature of a person authorized to act on behalf of the owner of an exclusive right that is allegedly infringed.
- Identification of the copyrighted work claimed to have been infringed, or, if multiple copyrighted works at a single online site are covered by a single notification, a representative list of such works at that site.
- Identification of the material that is claimed to be infringing or to be the subject of infringing activity and that is to be removed or access to which is to be disabled, and information reasonably sufficient to permit the service provider to locate the material.
- Information reasonably sufficient to permit the service provider to contact the complaining party, such as an address, telephone number, and, if available, an electronic mail address at which the complaining party may be contacted.
- A statement that the complaining party has a good faith belief that use of the material in the manner complained of is not authorized by the copyright owner, its agent, or the law.
- A statement that the information in the notification is accurate, and under penalty of perjury, that the complaining party is authorized to act on behalf of the owner of an exclusive right that is allegedly infringed.[259]

A notification that fails to 'comply substantially' with the requirements cannot be considered to be actual knowledge or an awareness of facts or circumstances from which the infringement is apparent.[260] For instance, the lack of a statement attesting to good faith and a statement attesting to the fact that the information in the notification is accurate, and the complaining party is authorized to act on behalf of the owner of a copyright owner may render a notification invalid under Section 512(c)(3) of the Copyright Act.[261] Also, the fact that the intermediary has not provided the Copyright Office with information about its DMCA agent may lead to disqualification under the 512(c) safe harbour.[262]

The requirements listed in Section 512(c)(3)(A)(i) of the US Copyright Act should be 'substantially complied' with. But what does that mean? There is very limited case law on this issue. And the case law that actually exists does not show a consistent interpretation of the requirements.

In *ALS Scan v. RemarQ Communities*, the Fourth Circuit Court explained that 'in the spirit of achieving a balance between the responsibilities of the service provider and

259. *Section* 512(c)(3)(A)(i) to (vi) of the US Copyright Act.
260. Section 512(c)(3)(B)(i) of the US Copyright Act.
261. *Hendrickson v. eBay, Inc.*, *supra* n. 200, at 1089–1090.
262. *Perfect 10, Inc. v. RapidShare A.G.*, *CASE NO.* 09-CV-2596 H (WMC), 12–13 (Dist. Court, S.D. Cal. 2010): 'The language of the DMCA clearly states that a service provider can take advantage of the safe harbor only if the service provider has given the Copyright Office specific information regarding its designated agent. ... Accordingly, the Court concludes that, until RapidShare provides the required information to the Copyright Office, RapidShare may not take advantage of the protections afforded by this section of the DMCA.'

the copyright owner, the DMCA requires that a copyright owner put the service provider on notice in a detailed manner but allows notice by means that comport with the prescribed format only "substantially," rather than perfectly'.[263] In this case, the copyright owner directed the newsgroup service provider to two newsgroups that contained erotic images. The copyright owner asserted that virtually all images in those groups were his and referred to two webpages where the service provider could find images of the copyright owner's nude models. Moreover, the copyright owner argued that the images in the newsgroup could be identified as those of the copyright owner because these images included his name and a copyright symbol next to it. This combination of information was deemed to be sufficient by the Fourth Circuit Court: 'We believe that with this information, [the copyright owner] substantially complied with the notification requirement of providing a representative list of infringing material as well as information reasonably sufficient to enable [the service provider] to locate the infringing material.'[264]

Similarly, in *Hendrickson v. eBay*, a California District Court acknowledged that there might be instances where a notification does not need to provide specific items on a webpage:

> For example, if a movie studio advised eBay that all listings offering to sell a new movie (e.g., 'Planet X,') that has not yet been released in VHS or DVD format are unlawful, eBay could easily search its website using the title 'Planet X' and identify the offensive listings.[265]

However, as eBay could not determine whether the movie in question was an authorized copy or not, Hendrickson had to specify item numbers of eBay listings for eBay to be sufficiently notified about the infringements.

Empirical research suggests that the invalidity of notices represents a real problem. Research by Urban and Quilter in 2005 into a set of notices collected by the Lumen project shows that 'at least a third of notices contain at least one of the major categories of flaws'.[266] In these cases, either substantive legal questions could be raised about the underlying copyright claim or the notice itself did not comply with statutory requirements. For instance, there were notices that concerned materials that were not copyrightable, or notices were sent by persons who did not own the copyright.[267]

In their 2016 study, Urban, Karaganis, and Schofield found that a high percentage of the notices sent to Google in relation to its search engine were automated.[268] These researchers wrote that almost one-third of automated removal requests were problematic:

263. *ALS Scan, Inc. v. RemarQ Communities, Inc.*, 239 F.3d 619, 625 (4th Cir. 2001).
264. *ALS Scan, Inc. v. RemarQ Communities, Inc.*, *supra* n. 263, at 625.
265. *Hendrickson v. eBay, Inc.*, *supra* n. 200, at 1090.
266. Urban & Quilter, *supra* n. 222, at 666. The Lumen database is available at: https://www.lumendatabase.org (accessed 14 June 2019).
267. Urban & Quilter, *supra* n. 222, at 667 and 672.
268. Jennifer Urban, Joe Karaganis & Brianna Schofield, *Notice and Takedown in Everyday Practice* 96 (2016).

> Despite the efforts of some major senders to limit algorithmic mistakes, nearly a third of requests presented serious questions about their validity. Potential fair use defenses and outright mistargeting of materials that do not match the [allegedly infringed work] are most concerning, followed closely by substantive problems with identifying the [allegedly infringed work] and [allegedly infringing material].[269]

[2] Counter-Notification

Section 512(g) of the US Copyright Act provides for a counter-notification procedure that enables users whose content has been removed to request that the content be restored. For the intermediary not to be liable for the *removal* of allegedly infringing materials, the intermediary must comply with the counter-notification procedure in Section 512(g) of the US Copyright Act. Section 512 thus creates an incentive for the intermediary to enable such counter-notification and to allow for the reposting of content.

A counter-notification is a 'written communication' that is sent to the DMCA agent of the intermediary. It must 'substantially' include the following information:

- A physical or electronic signature of the subscriber.
- Identification of the material that has been removed or to which access has been disabled and the location at which the material appeared before it was removed or access to it was disabled.
- A statement under penalty of perjury that the subscriber has a good faith belief that the material was removed or disabled as a result of mistake or misidentification of the material to be removed or disabled.
- The subscriber's name, address, and telephone number, and a statement that the subscriber consents to the jurisdiction of Federal District Court for the judicial district in which the address is located, or if the subscriber's address is outside of the United States, for any judicial district in which the service provider may be found, and that the subscriber will accept service of process from the person who provided notification (...) or an agent of such person.[270]

When the intermediary receives a counter-notice, it must promptly send a copy of the counter-notification to the copyright owner who sent the takedown notice. Search engine providers are generally not required to forward such notices, as these intermediaries have no relationship with the owners of the websites included in the search results.[271] The intermediary must also inform the copyright owner that it will replace the removed materials in ten working days.[272] The intermediary must then replace the materials in not less than ten, but not more than fourteen working days following the receipt of the counter-notice.[273] However, there is no such duty if the intermediary receives a notice that the copyright owner has filed an action seeking a court order to

269. Urban, Karaganis & Schofield, *supra* n. 268, at 96–97.
270. *Section* 512(g)(3)(A) to (D) of the US Copyright Act.
271. Urban, Karaganis & Schofield, *supra* n. 268, at 44.
272. Section 512(g)(2)(B) of the US Copyright Act.
273. Section 512(g)(2)(C) of the US Copyright Act.

restrain the alleged infringer from engaging in infringing activity relating to the materials on the intermediary's system or network.[274] In other words, in order to prevent the material from being reinstated, the copyright owner must commence court proceedings against the alleged infringer.

It is questionable whether people actually make use of the counter-notification procedure. The earlier-mentioned 2005 study by Urban and Quilter indicates that while one-third of the notifications were seriously flawed, in only a very few cases was a counter-notification filed.[275] Also, the 2016 study by Urban, Karaganis, and Schofield suggests that the counter-notification procedure is scarcely used:

> Only one respondent among both service providers and rightsholders reported receiving more than a handful per year. Many – including some large services handling thousands of notices per year – reported receiving none.[276]

Their research also suggests that users generally do not have sufficient knowledge of copyright law and have little capacity to assess or to take the risks of filing a counter-notice.[277] Another problem is that users may not even know about the removal of the materials. When the removal of search results is concerned, there is no duty to contact the website owners. As these website owners generally do not know about the removal of their content from the search results, they are unlikely to request that the search results be restored.

[3] Good Faith, Accuracy, and Misrepresentation

For a takedown notice to be valid, it must include a statement that the notifying party believes, in good faith, that the materials are unauthorized.[278] The notification should further contain a statement that the notice is accurate and that the notifying party is authorized to act on behalf of the copyright owner.[279] These requirements are related to Section 512(f) of the US Copyright Act, which states that if a party knowingly misrepresents that material or an activity is infringing, or that material or an activity was removed or disabled by mistake or misidentification, that party shall be liable for the damages caused by such misrepresentations. If, for instance, the copyright owner or another person on his behalf knowingly files a false takedown notice with an intermediary, that person is liable for the damages arising from the removal of those materials.

There are not many examples of misrepresentations reported in case law. One example is the case of *Online Policy Group v. Diebold* regarding the taking down of an

274. Section 512(g)(2)(C) of the US Copyright Act.
275. Urban & Quilter, *supra* n. 222, at 679.
276. Urban, Karaganis & Schofield, *supra* n. 268, at 44.
277. Urban, Karaganis & Schofield, *supra* n. 268, at 44. *Also see*: Emily Asp, *Section 512 of the Digital Millennium Copyright Act: User Experience and User Frustration*, 103 Iowa Law Review (2) 751 (2018), arguing for greater public awareness of copyright law and the procedures to remove online materials.
278. Section 512(c)(3)(A)(v) of the US Copyright Act.
279. Section 512(c)(3)(A)(vi) of the US Copyright Act.

email archive containing compromising information on the functioning of voting machines produced by Diebold.[280] A link to this archive was placed on a news website. Diebold had filed a takedown notice with the hosting service provider. But the hosting service provider alleged that Diebold's claim was an express material misrepresentation of copyright infringement. The California District Court considered that the publication was a fair use and that Diebold was liable for misrepresentation:

> Diebold knowingly materially misrepresented that Plaintiffs infringed Diebold's copyright interest, at least with respect to the portions of the email archive clearly subject to the fair use exception. No reasonable copyright holder could have believed that the portions of the email archive discussing possible technical problems with Diebold's voting machines were protected by copyright, and there is no genuine issue of fact that Diebold knew – and indeed that it specifically intended – that its letters to OPG and Swarthmore would result in prevention of publication of that content.[281]

The California District Court based its decision on the constructive knowledge of the copyright owner. However, in the more recent case of *Rossi v. Motion Pictures*, the Ninth Circuit Court explained that misrepresentation under Section 512(f) of the Copyright Act requires *actual* knowledge of misrepresentation on the part of the copyright owner: 'A copyright owner cannot be liable simply because an unknowing mistake is made, even if the copyright owner acted unreasonably in making the mistake.'[282] *Rossi* thus significantly raised the standard for a claim of material misrepresentation.[283] It is probably the case that this standard will only be met if a person intentionally sends takedown notices containing false infringement allegations.[284]

A somewhat positive development is the 2016 Ninth Circuit Court's decision in *Lenz v. Universal*.[285] This case dealt with a twenty-nine-second YouTube video by Lenz of her two young children dancing to the song 'Let's Go Crazy' by Prince.[286] As mentioned, a person filing a notice must add a statement that he 'has a good faith belief that use of the material in the manner complained of is not authorized by the copyright owner, its agent, or the law'.[287] According to the Court, fair use is a form of use that is 'authorized by...the law'.[288] Therefore, before sending a takedown notice copyright owners must consider whether the use in question is a fair use. Yet, just as in *Rossi*, the Court held that the copyright owner can still rely on his own subjective beliefs

280. *Online Policy Group v. Diebold, Inc.*, 337 F.Supp.2d 1195 (Dist. Court, N.D.Cal. 2004).
281. *Online Policy Group v. Diebold, Inc.*, *supra* n. 280, at 1204.
282. *Rossi v. Motion Picture Association of America, Inc.*, 391 F.3d 1000, 1005 (9th Cir. 2004).
283. Seltzer, *supra* n. 221, at 224–225, arguing that the reach of Section 512(f) of the US Copyright Act is limited.
284. For example: *Curtis v. Shinsachi Pharmaceutical, Inc.*, case no.2:14-cv-00591-ODW(SSx) (Dist. Court, C.D. Cal. 2014).
285. *Lenz v. Universal Music Corp.*, 801 F.3d 1126 (9th Cir. 2015).
286. The video is still available at: www.youtube.com/watch?v = N1KfJHFWlhQ (accessed 14 June 2019).
287. Section 512(c)(3)(A)(v) of the US Copyright Act.
288. *Lenz v. Universal Music Corp.*, *supra* n. 285, at 1132.

regarding the use in question.[289] Hence, if a copyright owner believes that the use amounts to an infringement, and not to fair use, there can be no misrepresentation.

This US experience with a statutory notice-and-takedown procedure may be relevant for our enquiry into the 'future-proofness' of the EU legal framework on intermediary liability. In Chapter 3, it was explained that a notice-and-takedown system could have a chilling effect on free expression. Intermediaries may remove information without serious consideration of the facts and circumstances of a particular use. There are also no safeguards in place to prevent abuses of notice-and-takedown systems.[290]

While the US statutory notice-and-takedown regime in Section 512 of the US copyright Act, at face value, seems to offer a better-balanced regime, the US regime still has its flaws.[291] The US safe harbour regime does not appear to be able to prevent abuses of the notice-and-takedown systems.[292] For instance, research by the Center for Democracy & Technology illustrates that these systems have been used for illegitimately taking down political speeches during election cycles.[293] Moreover, we have seen that the counter-notice procedure, which could prevent mistakes and abuses, appears to be scarcely used. Also, the rule in Section 512(f) that sanctions a misrepresentation of infringements does not appear to provide sufficient protection against false notifications.[294]

[F] Possible Reforms

With respect to the enforcement of copyrights, there is reason to believe that the notice-and-takedown regime prescribed by the US Copyright Act is an effective means to remove infringing materials that are hosted online. The regime has been widely adopted. About 110,200 entities have registered with the US Copyright Office.[295] Many infringing materials have been removed. For instance, in its transparency report, Google reports that since March 2011, it has removed 2.89 billion URLs from its search results in response to requests to remove copyright-infringing material.[296] Google has

289. *Lenz v. Universal Music Corp.*, *supra* n. 285, at 1142.
290. *See* section §3.04[G][2]. For an US perspective, *see*: Urban & Quilter, *supra* n. 222; Mark Lemley, *Rationalizing Internet Safe Harbors*, 6 Journal on Telecommunications & High Technology Law (1) 101, 113 (2007); Seltzer, *supra* n. 221.
291. *Also see*: Daniel Seng, '*Who Watches the Watchmen?' An Empirical Analysis of Errors in DMCA Takedown Notices*, available at: https://papers.ssrn.com/sol3/papers.cfm?abstract_id=256 3202 (accessed 14 June 2019).
292. *See*, for instance, the 'DMCA Hall of Shame' that is maintained by the Electronic Frontier Foundation, available at: www.eff.org/takedowns (accessed 14 June 2019).
293. Center for Democracy and Technology, Campaign Takedown Troubles: How meritless copyright claims threaten online political speech (2010).
294. *Also see*: Rebecca Tushnet, *Fair Use's Unfinished Business*, 15 Chicago-Kent Journal of Intellectual Property (2) 399 (2016).
295. Own calculations based on the database available at: www.copyright.gov/onlinesp/list/a_agents.html (accessed 14 June 2019).
296. *See*: www.google.com/transparencyreport/removals/copyright/?hl=en#glance (accessed 14 June 2019).

also set up a 'trusted submitter programme' that automates and scales the notification process for easier notification by parties administering many copyrights.[297]

Nevertheless, the previous section has also highlighted some issues with the US notice-and-takedown regime that are problematic especially from the user's perspective. But also from the copyright owner's perspective, the notice-and-takedown regime may not offer satisfactory results in terms of the enforcement of their rights. For instance, notice-and-takedown systems cannot prevent peer-to-peer file-sharing or the storage of infringing material in so-called file lockers.[298] Moreover, as the sharing of information on the Internet has only increased, these systems only seem to work well for institutional copyright owners that have the resources to continuously monitor for infringing materials and intermediaries that have the resources to process large amounts of notices.[299] In that respect, questions are also raised about whether the burdens of notice-and-takedown are fairly shared between copyright owners and intermediaries.[300]

The safe harbour provisions are on the radar of the US Congress, which is currently considering whether to reform the US Copyright Act. Moreover, in July 2015, the US Copyright Office commenced a study into the impact and effectiveness of the safe harbour provisions. In response to a request for public comments it received over 92,000 written comments.[301] No concrete steps towards reform have as yet been taken.

§6.05 PRIVATE REGULATION

The US government has supported several initiatives by intermediaries and copyright owners who have tried to combat infringements outside the courtroom. One such example is the Copyright Alert System.[302] This system is a voluntary agreement between copyright owners and a group of Internet access providers who, by alerting users, try to put a halt to peer-to-peer file-sharing. This voluntary agreement was set up with the help of the Intellectual Property Enforcement Coordinator who is part of the US government.[303] Another example is the 'List of Good, Bad, and Situational Practices'

297. *See*: www.uspto.gov/ip/global/copyrights/Google.pdf (accessed 14 June 2019).
298. Department of Commerce Internet Policy Task Force, Green Paper on Copyright Policy, Creativity, and Innovation in the Digital Economy 54 (2013).
299. Department of Commerce Internet Policy Task Force, *supra* n. 298, at 56.
300. Pallante, in her capacity as the US Register of Copyrights, wrote in 2013: 'The section 512 safe harbors in particular have generated more than their fair share of litigation on issues such as eligibility for the safe harbor, inducement and monitoring. Some of these issues were imaginable at the time at the time of their enactment, and others were not. There are other concerns that go more generally to the question of whether the burdens of notice and takedown are fairly shared between copyright owners and intermediaries' (Maria Pallante, *The Next Great Copyright Act*, 36 Columbia Journal of Law & the Arts (3) 315, 329 (2013)).
301. Available at: www.regulations.gov/docketBrowser?rpp = 25&so = ASC&sb = title&po = 0&dct = PS&D = COLC-2015-0013&refD = COLC-2015-0013-0002 (accessed 14 June 2019).
302. *See*: www.copyrightinformation.org/the-copyright-alert-system (accessed 14 June 2019).
303. *See*: www.mpaa.org/wp-content/uploads/2015/10/IPEC-Strategic-Plan-10.16.15.pdf (accessed 14 June 2019). For a critical discussion, *see*: Ben Depoorter & Alain Van Hiel, *Copyright Alert Enforcement: Six Strikes and Privacy Harms*, 39 Columbia Journal of Law and the Arts (2)

for notice-and-takedown developed by the DMCA Notice and Takedown System multistakeholder forum under the leadership of the US Department of Commerce.[304]

Apart from the statutory regime for notice-and-takedown, and these government initiatives, some intermediaries have implemented policies and mechanisms either on their own initiative or in cooperation with copyright owners. A plausible reason for why intermediaries and copyright owners may come together and set their own rules may be the unwillingness, or the incapability, of the legislator to address a particular issue. Bridy describes how, in the US, copyright owners have become more willing to cooperate with access providers because attempts to combat peer-to-peer file-sharing at the legislative and legal fronts have been unsuccessful:

> On the lobbying front, rights owners pressed for – and won – greater statutory protection of copyrights and stiffer penalties for infringement. On the litigation front, they sued – and beat – both the purveyors and the users of disruptive technologies for copying and distributing digital content, most notably P2P software. None of these efforts, however, made much of a dent in the prodigious volume of illegally traded files. Hence, the emerging belief among rights owners is that the time is ripe for a strategic shift away from public law and litigation, toward partnerships with internet service providers (ISPs) and an enforcement regime that operates on Internet users through a combination of technology and private law mechanisms, such as standardized terms of service and acceptable use policies.[305]

This section analyses one of these purely private initiatives: Google's Content ID programme, which is a programme that utilizes content identification technologies to give copyright owners more control over the use of their materials on the video hosting platform YouTube.[306] We will discuss the Content ID programme in particular because, in the proposal for a Directive on Copyright in the Digital Single Market, the European Commission mentions content identification technology as a measure that online platforms may have to implement.[307] Also, Content ID presumably is a system that many Internet users have encountered, given YouTube's prominence in the domain of Internet video.

Google's system works separately from the notice-and-takedown regime introduced by the DMCA and has been called a 'DMCA Plus' system. Such a system has 'moved beyond reactive automation to proactive methods, filtering, for example, that go beyond the DMCA framework of requirements'.[308] With Content ID, Google takes responsibility for spotting unauthorized materials – a task that the DMCA originally

233 (2015). Menell offers a more positive account: Peter Menell, *Design for Symbiosis*, Communications of the ACM (5) 30 (2012).

304. *See*: www.uspto.gov/sites/default/files/documents/DMCA_Good_Bad_and_Situational_Practices_Document-FINAL.pdf (accessed 14 June 2019). On the Multistakeholder Forum: www.uspto.gov/learning-and-resources/ip-policy/copyright/multistakeholder-forum-dmca-notice-and-takedown-system (accessed 14 June 2019).

305. Annemarie Bridy, *Graduated Response and the Turn to Private Ordering in Online Copyright Enforcement Litigation*, 89 Oregon Law Review 81 (2010).

306. For an in-depth discussion of the workings of Content ID, *see*: Adam Holland et al., *NOC Online Intermediaries Case Studies Series: Intermediary Liability in the United States* 31 (2015).

307. *See* section §3.05[E].

308. Urban, Karaganis & Schofield, *supra* n. 268.

assigned to copyright owners. More than 5,000 rightsholder partners currently use Content ID to manage their copyrights on YouTube for free.[309]

It has been suggested that licensing agreements with content providers, such as Sony and Warner, required Google to implement technologies to prevent unauthorized uses.[310] Yet, it has also been suggested that Google's Content ID programme gives Google a competitive edge over other video hosting platforms.[311] It makes YouTube an attractive platform for users, as it enables the uploading of content that includes copyrighted materials. The intermediary may also become more attractive to copyright owners who become more willing to share their materials on the platform, or to license the use of their work

Content ID is in essence a fingerprinting system that automatically identifies uploaded materials. For each reference file that is shared by copyright owners, Google creates a 'hash' – a unique digital identifier. As of October 2016, Google had over 50 million reference files in its database, which means that it is able to recognize the copyrighted materials stored in those files.[312] Every video that is uploaded is checked against this database by an algorithm that compares the data pattern encoded in the hash with the data in the uploaded video file.

If a match is found, copyright owners are given a choice as to whether they want to allow or block the use of the material.[313] Blocking means that the video is blocked either worldwide or only for certain countries. It is also possible to block access to the video from particular devices, applications, or websites on which the matched content may also be available. Another option is to 'mute' the video, which removes the sound from the video. This option is relevant in particular if the video contains copyrighted music. A copyright owner can also choose to allow access to the video, and if he wants to, he can also monetize it by running ads against the video.

The Content ID system not only checks videos uploaded on YouTube but also checks its live streams.[314] If Content ID identifies copyrighted materials, the live stream may be terminated. If the user wants to dispute the system's match, for instance because the user had a licence to use the content or the system had misidentified materials, then that can only be done through the dispute process after the stream has been terminated.[315]

If the content of a YouTube user is matched, the user receives a 'Content ID claim'.[316] The YouTube user can acknowledge the claim and accept the copyright owner's decision regarding the video. If the claim relates to music used in the video, the user can either remove the music or swap the music for free-to-use music. In case the

309. Cédric Manara, *Remuneration for the Use of Works. Exclusivity vs. Other Approaches*, 367 (Silke Von Lewinski ed., 2017).
310. Candace Lombardi, *YouTube cuts three content deals*, *CNET*, 9 October 2006, https://perma.cc/9HR7-S3SH (accessed 14 June 2019).
311. Urban, Karaganis & Schofield, *supra* n. 268, at 95.
312. YouTube Statistics, available at: https://perma.cc/T6DK-NX2M S3SH (accessed 14 June 2019).
313. YouTube Help pages, available at: https://perma.cc/BMD3-JUUZ (accessed 14 June 2019).
314. YouTube Help pages, available at: https://perma.cc/R4AH-ZU7G (accessed 14 June 2019).
315. YouTube Help pages, available at: https://perma.cc/R4AH-ZU7G (accessed 14 June 2019).
316. YouTube Help pages, available at: https://perma.cc/DYB2-EB8F (accessed 14 June 2019).

music used is in fact a song cover, participants in the partner programme may be able to share advertising revenue with the music publisher.

A user can dispute the claim if he believes that the claim is invalid. For instance, because the user makes fair use of matched materials, or the user has acquired a licence. Copyright owners then have thirty days to respond to the dispute.[317] If the copyright owner does not respond to the dispute, the claim will expire. Within those thirty days, the copyright owner has two options: he either releases the claim or upholds it. The claim is released if the copyright owner agrees with the user. If the copyright owner does not agree with the user, the copyright owner can uphold the claim. If the YouTube user believes that the claim was mistakenly upheld, he can appeal the decision with the copyright owner. However, as the Content ID System operates in parallel with the statutory DMCA notice-and-takedown regime, a copyright owner can still choose to take down the video with a takedown notice. This moves the claim away from the Content ID system and brings it within the DMCA notice-and-takedown regime.

While the Content ID programme offers an effective means to deal with infringing content on YouTube, US scholars have also pointed out that the programme is problematic from the perspective of the fair use of works.[318] The system itself is unable to distinguish between lawful and unlawful uses and may thus enable copyright owners to block, mute, or monetize material that they should not have any control over in the first place.[319] It has also been noted that the option for copyright owners to monetize a video disregards the creative endeavours that users may have put into that video. In that respect, Soha and McDowell note:

> The logic of Content ID naturalizes a system in which users are forced to bend to not only the structure of YouTube but additionally to the will of corporate rights holders, allowing their creative contributions to be controlled because of the inclusion, however small or inadvertent, of a copyrighted work.[320]

Lester and Pachamanova point out that the use of algorithms for copyright enforcement can also lead to 'false positives', where uploaded materials are incorrectly

317. YouTube Help pages, available at: https://perma.cc/VW3Z-JSEH (accessed 14 June 2019).
318. Maayan Perel & Niva Elkin-Koren, *Accountability in Algorithmic Copyright Enforcement*, 19 Stanford Technology Law Review (3) 473 (2016); Niva Elkin-Koren, *Fair Use by Design*, 64 UCLA Law Review (5) 1083 (2017), arguing for 'fair use by design'. Indeed, algorithms could also be trained to recognize fair uses and adjust decisions accordingly. For instance, if a use is presumed to be fair, the barriers to the removal of materials could be heightened.
319. Taylor Bartholomew, *The Death of Fair Use in Cyberspace: YouTube and the Problem with Content ID*, 13 Duke Law & Technology Review (1) 66 (2015); Benjamin Boroughf, *The Next Great YouTube: Improving Content ID to Foster Creativity, Cooperation and Fair Compensation*, 25 Albany Law Journal of Science and Technology (1) 95, 108 (2015); Toni Lester & Dessislava Pachamanova, *The Dilemma: Making Content ID Algorithms More Conducive to Fostering Innovative Fair Use in Music Creation*, UCLA Entertainment Law Review (1) 51 (2017). An example of such a fair use may be so-called let's play videos in which people share their experiences with computer games, *see*: Ivan Taylor, *Video Games, Fair Use and the Internet: The Plight of the Let's Play*, University of Illinois Journal of Law, Technology & Policy (1) 247 (2015).
320. Soha & Mcdowell 2016.

matched to copyrighted materials.[321] Such false positives can be triggered by errors in the algorithms or the quality of the data that the algorithm uses to match materials.[322] They advocate more transparency about the workings of the identification algorithms and oversight by the US Copyright Office.[323]

Because the programme is a private system that comes before the DMCA's notice-and-takedown procedure, there is also a risk that the safeguards put in place to protect users are simply circumvented. While copyright owners can always fall back on the statutory notice-and-takedown regime to enforce their rights when they do not want to take part in the Content ID system, users have no such choice, nor can they exert an influence on the design of the system. Users depend on Google to create a fair system based on due process.[324]

Google, with its Content ID system, appears to have adopted a role for itself that is similar to a collective management organization, but without there being any checks on its practices. Through its system, Google offers a transactional service between users and copyright owners and also provides remuneration to a large group of copyright owners through its shared advertising.[325] Similar to collective management, the copyright owner informs Google about his works. This information is then used by Google to match uploaded content with the copyrighted works of the copyright owner. However, Google clearly differs from a collective management organization in the sense that it does not necessarily fully operate in the interests of copyright owners or its users, as it must also think of its own interests as a for-profit intermediary. Moreover, there are no rules in place that require transparency about the workings of systems and algorithms. Furthermore, there is no supervisory authority that monitors Google's activities, nor is there any known representation of copyright owners or users.

§6.06 CONCLUSION

This chapter aimed to answer the question of what there is to learn from the US experience with respect to regulating intermediary liability in a future-proof way. All of the singular points that have been made in this chapter will not be repeated here. Instead, this conclusion provides a high-level analysis of the US system and presents the main points.

Let us first look at the intermediary's liability for direct infringements. Just as in the EU, the rise of digital and networking technologies raised questions about whether and how to apply copyright law to the transmission and storage carried out by

321. Toni Lester & Dessislava Pachamanova, *The Dilemma: Making Content ID Algorithms More Conducive to Fostering Innovative Fair Use in Music Creation*, UCLA Entertainment Law Review (1) 51 (2017).
322. Lester & Pachamanova, *supra* n. 321, at 61–64.
323. Lester & Pachamanova, *supra* n. 321, at 66–72.
324. Google does appear to be willing to actively protect the fair use of materials on YouTube, *see*: https://perma.cc/V9LG-WPNZ (accessed 14 June 2019).
325. Michael W. Carroll, *A Realist Approach to Copyright Law's Formalities*, Berkeley Technology Law Journal (3) 1511, 1527 (2013); Nicholas T. DeLisa, *You(Tube), Me, and Content ID: Paving the Way for Compulsory Synchronization Licensing on User-Generated Content Platforms*, Brooklyn Law Review (3) 1275 (2013).

intermediaries. In the EU legal framework, this problem was solved by introducing a specific carveout from the reproduction right for temporary reproductions that enable a lawful use or that enable a transmission.[326] In contrast, US courts took a step back and solved the issue by asking: did the intermediary cause the copy to be made?[327] This has allowed for a more purposive and functional approach towards the liability of intermediaries as direct infringers. Volition as a requirement for direct infringement has proven to be relevant not only in cases concerning traditional intermediaries but also in cases where more modern intermediaries process user-provided materials.[328]

With regard to the limitations and exceptions in US copyright law, the fair use doctrine stands out as a flexible tool that enables courts to consider new forms of use that the US legislator has not (yet) considered.[329] Any future intermediary activities that put existing information into context and that enhance its accessibility can be considered by the US courts and permitted if they contribute to attaining US copyright law's goals. Innovative curatorial forms of use of protected materials that do not hamper exploitation by copyright owners, such as image search and caching functionalities of search engines, have been accommodated by the fair use doctrine. As we have seen, in Germany, the Federal Court of Justice contrived a much-criticized consent theory to allow use by image search engines.[330] In the US, the fair use doctrine enabled this problem to be resolved within the domain of copyright law, without compromising the private law notion of consent, or causing confusion about the scope of such a theory and its application to other forms of use.[331]

It is important to note here that US copyright law is based primarily on utilitarian grounds.[332] This utilitarian purpose also informs the fair use doctrine, its factors, and its interpretation by the courts. The fair use analysis focuses on the effects that the use has on the market for a work and the benefits of such use for the general public. In contrast, EU copyright law is grounded, at least in part, also in author-centric theories which favour strong exclusive rights and narrow limitations and exceptions.[333] An open-ended limitation does not appear to fit well in that tradition.

The US experience with fair use shows that a flexible exception does not need to be unpredictable.[334] Copyright scholars can play a role in mitigating unpredictability by defining, together with stakeholders, the best practices in a particular sector regarding particular forms of use. An independent regulatory body can also provide clarity by providing more concrete rules that are tailored to specific forms of use, by mediating between stakeholders, or by informing the public about the application of the limitation. Arguably, case law plays the most important role in specifying the content of a flexible limitation and making it more predictable. It raises the question of whether the

---

326. *See* section §3.03[D][1].
327. *See* section §6.02[C][2].
328. *See* section §6.02[C][3].
329. *See* section §6.03.
330. *See* section §5.04[D].
331. *See* section §5.04[D]. For an alternative solution within the copyright domain, *see* the Dutch interpretation of the quotation exception in section §4.03[B][2].
332. *See* section §6.02[A].
333. *See* section §3.03[C].
334. *See* section §6.03[C].

current set-up of EU copyright law would be able to produce sufficient case law to develop a European 'fair use doctrine'. Another problem is that the current EU copyright law does not advance one relatively clear and coherent theory on what EU copyright law aims to accomplish. Unlike in the US, there is thus no clear principle that can guide court decisions.

Let us move away from the intermediary's liability for copyright infringement and focus on the safe harbours that protect intermediaries from secondary liability. Two points can be made with regard to the scope of the US safe harbours that are relevant to our enquiry. First, unlike the EU hosting liability exemption, its US counterpart does not require 'neutrality' or 'passivity'. Instead, the US safe harbour focuses primarily on the knowledge or control that must be absent. Of course, these requirements may result in uncertainties as to their application. Yet, that uncertainty is not caused by a legislative focus on 1990s Internet technologies in the definition of the intermediary activity, as was the case in the EU.[335] Instead, the open definition of the US hosting safe harbour and its interpretation by the US courts have enabled it to more naturally cover intermediary services that enhance access to user-provided materials.

The second point relates to the safe harbour that was put in place for information location tools. Although the E-Commerce Directive and its liability exemptions are of a later date, the EU legislator did not consider the position of search engines. The US legislator did introduce a safe harbour that protects search engines and other information location tools against liability for the information that they refer to.[336] Since the CJEU has ruled that linking to unauthorized materials can amount to copyright infringement, questions may arise about the application of copyright law to search engines.[337] In that respect, it appears that the US safe harbour for search engines offers these intermediaries much more legal certainty regarding their liability for search results.

The US safe harbours for hosting and information location tools are only available to intermediaries that implement the statutorily prescribed notice-and-takedown system. We have seen in the chapter on EU law that the lack of such procedural rules may lead to fragmentation and an insufficient consideration of the user's interests and his communicative freedoms.[338] While the procedural rules regarding notice-and-takedown in US copyright law may have prevented the fragmentation of notice-and-takedown systems, the US experience also shows that they have not been very successful in safeguarding the user's rights and interests. By implementing a counter-notification procedure and a rule regarding the misrepresentation of an infringement, the US legislator was cognizant of the chilling effects that notice-and-takedown may have. Nevertheless, the counter-notification procedure seems to be little used.[339] And the standard for misrepresentation is set too high to create an incentive to file takedown requests with greater care.[340] Procedural rules are therefore not a panacea for the

335. *See* sections §3.04[D] and §3.04[G][1].
336. Section 512(d) of the US Copyright Act. *See* section §6.04[D][4].
337. *See* section §3.03[G].
338. *See* section §3.04[G][2].
339. *See* section §6.04[E][2].
340. *See* section §6.04[E][3].

problems that arise with notice-and-takedown systems. They must be strict enough to prevent abuse and create appropriate incentives to file (automatic) takedown notifications with care.

Regarding the responsibilities that intermediaries may have to stop or prevent infringements by others, it is striking that the rules put in place by the US legislator in response to the emergence of the Internet are less flexible than those in the EU legal framework. US law leaves little room to allocate responsibility with intermediaries for copyright infringements.[341] The removal of infringing materials stored with intermediaries is the only real form of relief that is available to copyright owners under the DMCA. While the DMCA provides a legal basis to require hosting service providers to identify infringers, the technology-specific language used in Section 512(h) of the US Copyright Act prevents access providers from being ordered to identify subscribers involved in peer-to-peer file-sharing.[342]

In the US, the deal that was struck between the content industries and early intermediaries in the late 1990s still defines, to a great extent, the legal duties that intermediaries and copyright owners have today. While the notice-and-takedown regime has enabled copyright owners to act against infringing materials stored with intermediaries, the regime seems to be reaching its limits with regard to its effectiveness.[343] Questions can also be raised about its suitability in the current technological set-up in which algorithms are used to both send and evaluate complaints about infringements.[344]

Still, the development of the intermediary's responsibility for copyright infringements in the US has not come to a complete standstill. Innovation in the enforcement of copyrights, and the role that intermediaries play in that enforcement, has occurred outside the Internet-specific legislative framework devised by the US legislator. General rules of civil procedure have enabled individual file sharers to be identified by access providers.[345] The US Supreme Court's interpretation of contributory liability and its inducement theory have enabled copyright owners to take action against those who promote infringements by others by offering file-sharing software and platforms.[346]

Self-regulatory initiatives in which intermediaries and copyright owners cooperate under the guidance of the US government have also unfolded.[347] Innovative enforcement mechanisms are also being developed privately by intermediaries, either with or without the cooperation of copyright owners. However, the lack of public oversight, the non-involvement of users, and the potential conflict with the balance that copyright law aims to establish are matters of concern.

341. *See* section §6.04[B].
342. *See* section §6.04[B].
343. *See* section §6.04[F].
344. *See* section §6.04[F].
345. *See* section §6.04[B].
346. *See* section §6.02[D][2].
347. *See* section §6.05.

Chapter 7
Conclusion

§7.01 INTRODUCTION

This book dealt with Internet intermediaries and their liability for copyright infringements. It focused on EU law in the area of copyright law, copyright enforcement, and intermediary liability. The question posed at the beginning of this book was whether that body of law – the EU legal framework – is future-proof, and if it is not, how can it be improved to make it more future-proof. This final chapter answers this central question by building on and synthesizing the findings of the previous chapters.

In the following sections, we will first briefly restate the importance of future-proof regulation and recall the two design principles that can contribute to the creation of a future-proof legal framework (section §7.02). The section that follows provides an outline of the current EU legal framework and the different elements that it consists of (section §7.03). We will then take a closer look at these elements and consider their 'future-proofness' (section §7.04). Where, on the basis of this research, concrete suggestions can be made to improve the future-proofness of the legal framework, those suggestions are made separately (section §7.05). The final conclusion will offer a more general view on the liability of intermediaries and copyright law (section §7.06).

§7.02 'FUTURE-PROOFNESS'

Internet intermediaries come in many shapes and sizes, but what they have in common is that their technologies enable or enhance online forms of communication and interactions between people, businesses, or other entities.[1] Early Internet intermediaries, such as access and hosting providers, offered the basic infrastructure for Internet connectivity. As technology progressed, newer intermediaries emerged as well. These

1. *See* section §1.06[B] for a discussion of what intermediaries are and the role that they play in the information ecosystem.

intermediaries, such as providers of search engines, video hosting platforms, and social networks, also offer services that are used by people to create or manipulate, share, or find information on the Internet. In particular, these newer intermediaries may also curate online information; they categorize, contextualize, or otherwise give additional meaning to existing content. As such, they enhance public access to online information.[2]

A central theme in this book has been how technological change may affect the instrumental and safeguarding functions of the law.[3] Technological developments can result in legal uncertainty and render the law ineffective. Ideally, a future-proof legal framework can accommodate these technological developments, while also offering sufficient legal certainty.

This thesis put forward two design principles for the creation of a future-proof legal framework.[4] These principles serve as the starting point for assessing whether the current EU legal framework is future-proof. The first design principle relates to the goals of copyright law. Copyright law ultimately aims to strike a balance between the interests of copyright owners and other parties affected by copyrights and their enforcement.[5] That balance ('the copyright balance') must be maintained as technological developments create new avenues for the exploitation and use of information. The first design principle therefore requires that a future-proof legal framework must be able *to preserve* a balance between the interests of all the stakeholders that are affected by copyrights and their enforcement.[6]

The second design principle relates to the framework's ability to accommodate technological developments. It demands that the legal framework is flexible. In fast-paced technological environments, such as the Internet, flexible copyright protection is necessary to effectively protect the interests of copyright owners.[7] Flexibility also enables the accommodation of new information processing technologies and new forms of use of copyrighted materials.[8] However, flexibility should not lead to an unpredictable legal framework. The legal framework should offer copyright owners, intermediaries, and users sufficient normative guidance for them to know what their legal rights and responsibilities are.[9] Without legal certainty, copyright law may not be an incentive to create, and intermediaries may not innovate. Hence, while flexibility contributes to the creation of a future-proof legal framework, measures should also be taken to mitigate any negative effects on the framework's predictability.

2. *See* section §1.07 for a discussion of the concept of curation.
3. *See* section §2.02 for a discussion of the relationship between copyright law and information technologies.
4. *See* sections §2.03 and §2.04.
5. *See* section §2.03[A].
6. *See* section §2.03 for a more in-depth analysis.
7. *See* section §2.04[A][1].
8. *See* section §2.04[A][2].
9. *See* section §2.04[B][2] on the importance of predictable copyright law.

§7.03 THE CURRENT EU LEGAL FRAMEWORK IN A NUTSHELL

The EU legal framework that has been analysed here consists of the whole body of legal sources of EU law that are relevant to copyright law, the enforcement of copyrights, and the liability of intermediaries for copyright infringements. It includes both primary EU law and secondary EU law. Also, the CJEU's case law on intermediaries is considered to be part of the EU legal framework. Any relevant recommendations given by the European Commission or other EU institutions were included in this study as well. This book took the relevant directives and provisions therein as its starting point for discussion of the EU legal framework. They are the Copyright Directive,[10] the E-Commerce Directive,[11] and the Enforcement Directive.[12] The 2019 Directive on Copyright in the Digital Single Market (DSM Directive) was also studied.[13]

First, the Copyright Directive harmonizes, among other things, the exclusive rights that are granted to the copyright owner and the limitations and exceptions to those rights. These rules were adopted in response to the emerging information society and aimed to prevent copyrights from being undermined by the rise of the global Internet.[14] The rules in the Copyright Directive are relevant when determining whether the intermediary itself infringes a copyright through its intermediary activities – hence whether the intermediary is liable as an infringer. The transmission and hosting of copyrighted materials are generally not considered to be infringements.[15] Intermediaries which provide infrastructure and basic services for Internet communication, such as access and hosting providers, are thus unlikely to be liable as copyright infringers. However, if intermediaries reproduce or communicate copyrighted materials to the public, they can be liable for infringements if their use is not authorized by the copyright owner or the law. Specifically, regarding the use of online press publications by intermediaries, the DSM Directive requires Member States to introduce a new set of intellectual property rights for publishers of these press publications.[16]

Second, the EU legal framework provides rules that exempt certain intermediaries from liability – the so-called safe harbours. The E-Commerce Directive provides rules on when intermediaries are *not* to be held liable for the information they transmit

10. Directive 2001/29/EC of the European Parliament and of the Council of 22 May 2001 on the harmonisation of certain aspects of copyright and related rights in the information society (*OJ* 2001, L 167/10).
11. Directive 2000/31/EC of the European Parliament and of the Council of 8 June 2000 on certain legal aspects of information society services, in particular electronic commerce, in the Internal Market (*OJ* 2000, L 178/1).
12. Directive 2004/48/EC of the European Parliament and of the Council of 29 April 2004 on the enforcement of intellectual property rights (*OJ* 2004, L 157/45). *See* section §3.03 on EU copyright law.
13. Directive 2019/790/EU of the European Parliament and of the Council of 17 April 2019 on copyright and related rights in the Digital Single Market and amending Directives 96/9/EC and 2001/29/EC (*OJ* 2019, L130/92).
14. *See* section §3.03[A].
15. *See* section §3.03[D][1] on the reproduction right, and section §3.03[D][2] on the right of communication to the public.
16. *See* section §3.03[I].

or store for others.[17] These rules touch upon the intermediary's secondary liability – its liability for the infringements of other parties, such as its users.[18] Under the E-Commerce Directive's liability regime, intermediaries cannot be liable for damages arising from the transmission or storage of information for others. Hence, if someone uses his Internet connection to download or upload infringing materials, the access provider transmitting those materials cannot be liable for damages caused by those infringements.[19] Intermediaries that host information for others must, simply put, not have knowledge of the infringements for them to be exempt from liability.[20] If these intermediaries do become aware of infringements, they must remove the infringing materials. This liability regime for hosting has led to the introduction of so-called notice-and-takedown systems through which copyright owners can notify intermediaries about infringements.[21]

Third, regardless of the liability exemptions, the EU legal framework assumes that intermediaries can still be held responsible for the infringements of others through injunctions.[22] Such injunctions must meet the requirements laid down in the Copyright Directive and the Enforcement Directive. Measures must be effective, proportionate, and dissuasive. Moreover, they must be fair and equitable and should not be unnecessarily complicated or costly, or entail unreasonable time limits or unwarranted delays. In addition, the E-Commerce Directive prohibits general monitoring duties to ensure that intermediaries are not too heavily burdened and in order to protect the freedom of expression.[23] Specifically regarding the responsibility of online platforms, Article 17 of the DSM Directive offers more concrete rules.[24]

§7.04 IS THE CURRENT LEGAL FRAMEWORK FUTURE-PROOF?

Is this EU legal framework on intermediaries and copyright law future-proof? While the legal framework certainly has elements which contribute to its 'future-proofness', there are also elements which diminish its future-proofness. On the whole, the legal framework therefore does not appear to be fully future-proof. The aim of the next few sections is to highlight those elements in the EU legal framework that are problematic.

17. *See* section §3.04 on the liability exemptions.
18. Secondary liability is the liability of the intermediary for the copyright infringements of others. An intermediary can be liable as an infringer for its own infringements as well – this liability is referred to as the primary liability of an intermediary. *See* section §1.05 on the concept of intermediary liability and the distinction between primary and secondary liability.
19. *See* section §3.04[E] on the mere conduit liability exemption.
20. *See* section §3.04[G] on the hosting liability exemption.
21. *See* section §3.04[G][2] on notice-and-takedown.
22. *See* section §3.05[A] on injunctions.
23. Article 15 of the E-Commerce Directive. *See* section §3.05[B] for a discussion.
24. *See* section §3.04[D].

[A] The Flexible Nature of the Right of Communication to the Public

In the domain of exclusive rights, we see that the right of communication to the public appears to be quite flexible and that it has been able to offer protection in new technological settings.[25] Unlike the reproduction right, the right of communication is not centred on a technology-oriented activity – the reproduction of copyrighted materials.[26] Instead, it is contingent on the technology-neutral concept of communication. It focuses on the enabling role of the entity communicating materials to the public by considering different factors, such as the level of intervention, the nature of the use, and the public receiving the materials. This leaves room for a purposive interpretation of the exclusive right and allows the protection offered to copyright owners to be fine-tuned to new technological circumstances.

Nevertheless, the flexible nature of the right of communication to the public and the CJEU's seemingly inconsistent interpretation of this exclusive right has also led to legal uncertainty. The CJEU's hyperlinking case law currently leaves questions about the knowledge standard that it introduced for links to unauthorized materials. This may also create uncertainties for intermediaries, which automatically post or refer to online information.[27]

The flexible nature of the right of communication to the public has enabled it to expand to situations that were normally covered by secondary liability standards in Member State law, such as the German *Störerhaftung* doctrine or Dutch tort law.[28] The CJEU's decisions in *GS Media* and *The Pirate Bay* impose primary liability – liability for infringing a copyright – for copyright infringements that are essentially committed by others.[29] The exclusive right of communication to the public can now also apply in cases where another has initially, or also, communicated the material to the public. From the perspective of copyright owners, *GS Media* and *The Pirate Bay* probably represent a welcome shift in EU copyright law. One of the consequences of these decisions is that cases that were traditionally in the unharmonized domain of secondary liability are now a matter of EU copyright law. This makes it easier to enforce copyrights throughout the EU, as there is now a single standard that applies. The strict rules of enforcement that only apply to infringements of intellectual property rights now apply as well.

Yet, this incorporation of secondary liability standards in the right of communication to the public also leads to doctrinal uncertainties. Over time, CJEU may maintain one indivisible concept of communication to the public that applies equally to those who initially communicate materials and those who link to those materials or otherwise facilitate access to them. By using the different factors recognized by the

25. *See* section §3.03[D][2].
26. *See* section §3.03[D][1] for an analysis of the technology-specific nature of the reproduction right.
27. *See* section §3.03[H] for a discussion of hyperlinking under EU law.
28. *See* section §4.04[B] on Dutch law and section §5.04[C] on German law.
29. CJEU 8 September 2016, ECLI:EU:C:2016:644 (*GS Media v. Sanoma Media Netherlands and others*). CJEU 14 June 2017, ECLI:EU:C:2017:456 (*Stichting Brein v. Ziggo BV and XS4ALL Internet*).

CJEU to determine whether a communication to the public has occurred, distinctions can be made between different types of infringements. Different clusters of infringements may then emerge. Alternatively, the CJEU could develop separate theories of direct and indirect infringement, similar to US copyright law.[30] These indirect infringements do not lead to strict liability, but hinge on subjective elements, such as the knowledge of and control over the infringements of others.[31] The advantage of such an approach is that these forms of indirect infringement are clearly separate legal concepts that can develop independently and as such lower the risk of the exclusive right becoming a convoluted legal concept that is hard to grasp and apply.

A recent EU legislative intervention may add to the convolution of the concept of the communication to the public. Article 17 of the DSM Directive gives a platform-specific meaning to the right of communication to the public. It makes online platforms liable as infringers for the materials that are made available on these platforms. These platforms will therefore have to obtain licences from copyright owners for the copyrighted materials that are uploaded by their users. Yet, by defining how these platforms may escape liability, Article 17 of the directive also specifies the responsibility that online platforms have for preventing the uploading of unauthorized materials. The question of whether in a concrete case a platform can be held liable will depend on the circumstances of the case and may even differ depending on the type of copyrighted materials in question. Article 17 implements aspects of a duty of care and combines it with primary liability for infringements. As such, the distinction between secondary liability and primary liability is fading, and the right to communicate to the public may become the end point in which all questions of online copyright law converge.

[B] Static Limitations and Exceptions

The exclusive rights harmonized by the legal framework offer broad and flexible protection that can cover new forms of exploitation, such as the facilitation of peer-to-peer file-sharing and the streaming of copyrighted materials. This enables the legal framework to be adapted through court decisions when technological changes call for this. In contrast, Member States can only adopt limitations and exceptions that are provided for in EU Copyright law.[32] Any new forms of the beneficial use of information that do not conflict with the copyright owner's interest can therefore only be accommodated by new EU legislation. This has led to a situation where the combination of exclusive rights could expand, be adapted, and remain relevant as technology progresses without the need for legislative intervention, while at the same time the body of available limitations and exceptions has remained relatively static.

This becomes particularly clear when we consider the reproduction right that was harmonized in the Copyright Directive. It applies to everything that is technically a reproduction and enables copyright owners to control every copy that is made, both

30. *See* section §6.02 for a discussion of how these theories came into being.
31. *See* section §6.02[D].
32. *See* section §3.03[E][2] on the closed list of limitations and exceptions.

transient and permanent. This technical approach to the reproduction right creates tensions in the digital realm where technologies often require that reproductions are made in order for these technologies to function. Curatorial technologies, such as search, also require that copies are made for the information to be categorized, contextualized, or otherwise given additional meaning. While the reproduction right offers broad protection, there is little room in the Copyright Directive to permit these beneficial reproductions. The directive offers one technology-specific exception that was specifically introduced to exempt temporary copies made by traditional intermediaries offering basic Internet connectivity.[33] But this technology-specific exception in unlikely to exempt newer intermediary activities that also depend on the reproduction of materials, such as the making and displaying of cache copies in a search engine, or generating preview images.[34]

While the broad scope of the exclusive rights enables copyright protection to be extended to new technological settings without the need for legislative intervention, there appears to be less flexibility within the EU legal framework to rebalance or adapt when limitations and exceptions are concerned. This legislation could lead to a situation of *one-sided* flexibility that can lead to an imbalance between the rights and interests of copyright owners, on the one hand, and those of intermediaries and users, on the other.

Still, courts can play an important role in flexibilizing copyright law by broadly interpreting existing limitations and exceptions. For example, the Dutch experience with the quotation exception shows that this exception could be interpreted in such a way that it would enable curatorial uses by intermediaries that depend on the reproduction and display of copyrighted materials.[35] It remains to be seen how the CJEU would deal with such curatorial uses. On the one hand, extensive interpretation of the exception may be contradicted by the CJEU's doctrine of the strict interpretation of copyright limitations and exceptions. The CJEU has held in several decisions that limitations and exceptions are 'derogations' from the principle of copyright protection and that they must therefore be interpreted strictly.[36] At the same time, the CJEU also appears willing to adjust the strictness of its interpretation in individual cases in order to strike a fair balance between the interests of affected parties.[37] In particular in *Premier League*, the CJEU has also given weight to the development and operation of new technologies that enable lawful uses.[38] And in *GS Media*, the CJEU brought the right to freedom of expression into the equation to prevent that every type of link could be considered a communication to the public.[39] In particular these two decisions may

33. Article 5(1) of the Copyright Directive. *See* section §3.03[D][1][b] for a discussion.
34. *See* section §3.03[H]. On image search *see* in particular also section §5.04[D] regarding German copyright law.
35. *See* section §4.03[B][2].
36. *See* section §3.03[E][3] for a discussion of the CJEU's doctrine of strict interpretation.
37. *See* section §3.03[C] on the fair balance in EU copyright law, and section §3.03[E][3] on the CJEU's interpretation of limitations and exceptions.
38. CJEU 4 October 2011, ECLI:EU:C:2011:631 (*Football Association Premier League and Others*).
39. *GS Media v. Sanoma Media Netherlands and others, supra* n. 29. *See also* section §3.03[G].

indicate that the CJEU, in any future cases dealing with curatorial uses, could interpret relevant limitations and exceptions in a flexible manner.

[C] Liability Exemptions and Notice-and-Takedown

Thus far, we have essentially discussed those elements in the EU legal framework that are relevant to the intermediary's potential primary liability as a copyright infringer. But intermediaries can also be secondarily liable for infringements *by others*, most notably their users.

In order to prevent intermediaries from being liable for damages for the information that they process, the E-Commerce Directive provides for a set of liability exemptions.[40] These liability exemptions are likely to have contributed to the promotion of investments in the Internet's infrastructure as they provide Internet access providers and hosting providers with a relatively clear limitation of their liability for the content they transmit or store. Internet access providers are shielded from liability for damages in any case, whereas hosting providers – which are closer to the source of information – can only be liable if they obtain knowledge about infringing materials and refrain from acting upon that knowledge.

The terms used in the liability exemptions – mere conduit activities, caching, and hosting – are reminiscent of the Internet and the web as it was conceived in the late 1990s.[41] This was the time when the web was no more than a collection of static web pages that were stored by hosting providers and transmitted by access providers. Current Internet technologies enable people without programming knowledge to share and manipulate information, to buy and sell goods and services online, and to interact with others in a much more dynamic environment. The intermediaries enabling these interactions may not be as passive or neutral as the intermediaries of the old online world, but they nonetheless provide services that make information more accessible without having actual knowledge of the information that they process.

New types of intermediary activity, which go beyond the simple storage of information for others, could not easily be fitted into these, in retrospect, limited conceptions of intermediary activity as defined in the liability exemptions. Strikingly, the EU legislator effectively left search engine activities out of the liability regime.[42] Also other types of useful ordering of and giving meaning to existing information by intermediaries initially appeared to be outside the scope of the liability exemptions. To the extent that the CJEU did apply the liability exemption to these newer services, the court's interpretations were not obvious, nor were they based on thorough reasoning. On balance, the liability exemptions as they were adopted in the E-Commerce Directive suffer from a lack of flexibility. They may have promoted the development of the Internet's infrastructure, but they score low in predictive value in newer technological contexts.

---

40. *See* section §3.04 for a discussion of these liability exemptions.
41. *See* section §3.04[E].
42. The older US Digital Millennium Copyright Act does provide a liability exemption for 'information location tools', *see* section §6.04[E].

One feature of the *hosting* liability exemption may also have negatively impacted the copyright balance. The liability regime for hosting presupposes that hosting service providers remove infringing materials when they obtain knowledge of these materials. This regime effectively incentivized intermediaries to adopt notice-and-takedown systems, which enable intermediaries to be notified about infringing materials. These systems have long been at the core of the responsibility that intermediaries bear in the enforcement of copyrights. In the past two decades, these notice-and-takedown systems were embedded in the design of many intermediary business models.

Strikingly, the EU legal framework has long had little effect on how these notice-and-takedown regimes were operated. In particular the lack of procedural rules has created legal uncertainty and caused fragmentation as there may be just as many procedures as there are intermediaries in the EU. Moreover, the current regime did not promote that sufficient safeguards are built into notice-and-takedown systems to protect users whose materials may be removed. There are, for instance, no safeguards that protect against abuses of such systems, nor did the framework require that users can have their content reinstated in the case of unjustified removal.[43] Article 17 of the DSM Directive may change that. It requires online platforms and copyright owners to work together to prevent that unlicensed materials are made available. Unlike any provisions in earlier directives, Article 17 of the DSM Directive requires that Member States ensure that complaint and redress mechanisms are available to allow users to dispute the platform's removal decisions. Moreover, Article 17 requires the European Commission, together with Member States, to organize stakeholder dialogues to discuss best practices. The European Commission will also issue guidance on how Article 17 is to be applied.

[D] Flexible Responsibility

Although intermediaries may not be liable for damages when others use their services to share infringing materials, intermediaries may nevertheless have a responsibility to stop or prevent infringements from taking place.[44] This research has highlighted that there are essentially two ways in which intermediaries may take responsibility for the infringements taking place. The current EU legal framework enables intermediaries to be coerced to stop or prevent infringements from taking place through injunctions. But intermediaries may also take responsibility themselves, either on their own or in direct cooperation with copyright owners.[45]

Simply put, under the Copyright Directive and Enforcement Directive, intermediaries *can* be held legally responsible for the infringements of others as long as the measures taken are reasonable. Actual injunctions are based on Member State law, such as the German *Störerhaftung* doctrine or the copyright-specific norms in Dutch

43. *See* section §3.04[G][2] for an analysis of notice-and-takedown under EU law. *Also see* section §4.05[D][2] on the Dutch experience with notice-and-takedown. *Also see* section §6.04[F] on the safeguards put in place in US copyright law.
44. *See* section §3.05.
45. *See* section §6.05 in particular on the US experience with intermediaries and private ordering.

copyright law.[46] The openness of EU law towards the responsibilities of intermediaries has enabled the development of different forms of injunctive relief at the Member State level. It has given both the CJEU and the Member State courts the room to gradually define the emerging and developing relationship between intermediaries and copyright owners, and to shape the duties that the former has towards the latter. In particular where a new technology enables infringements, the EU legal framework provides the possibility to redefine the intermediary's responsibility and allows for new enforcement methods.[47]

Although the Copyright Directive and the Enforcement Directive offer flexible rules on the intermediary's responsibilities, they do not offer any normative guidance as to what the actual duties of an intermediary should be in a given case. These directives only set the outer boundaries within which injunctions against intermediaries *can* be issued. They determine no rules on how, when, and under what conditions injunctions should be issued against which intermediaries. This lack of normative guidance has been mitigated, to a certain extent, by the CJEU's case law on the responsibilities of intermediaries and its use of the EU Charter of Fundamental Rights.[48]

In this case law, the CJEU recognized that the fundamental rights of all stakeholders, including those of users, need to be considered and balanced. If a court requires an intermediary to implement a certain measure, the fundamental rights of the user, such as the right to privacy and the freedom of expression, need to be taken into account. In its case law, the CJEU has moved from simply requiring that a balance between fundamental rights be struck by the Member State court in *Promusicae* and *Bonnier Audio*, to more concretely defining how that balance has to be struck in *Scarlet* and *UPC Telekabel*.[49] The CJEU's decision in *Mc Fadden*, in which the CJEU suggested that a particular injunction may be issued, could be seen as the next evolutionary step towards even more concrete guidance by the court with respect to the responsibilities of intermediaries.[50]

In the current set-up of the EU legal framework, appropriate forms of injunctive relief are thus developed 'bottom-up'. Copyright owners request them at the Member State level on the basis of national liability theories. Member States' courts decide on such requests and may issue, for instance, an injunction requiring an intermediary to block a website offering infringing materials. If the Member State court is in doubt as to the injunction's compatibility with EU law, it may refer questions to the CJEU. The CJEU may then either agree with or reject a particular form of injunctive relief by

46. *See* section §5.07 on German law, and section §4.06 on Dutch law.
47. In that respect, EU law is much more flexible than US law. *See* section §6.04[B] for a discussion on injunctions under US law.
48. *See* section §3.05[C] on this case law.
49. CJEU 29 January 2008, ECLI:EU:C:2008:54, *IER* 2008, 44 (*Promusicae v. Telefónica de España*); CJEU 19 April 2012, ECLI:EU:C:2012:219 (*Bonnier Audio and others v. Perfect Communication Sweden*); CJEU 24 November 2011, ECLI:EU:C:2011:771 (*Scarlet v. Sabam*); CJEU 27 March 2014, ECLI:EU:C:2014:192 (*UPC Telekabel Wien v. Constantin Film Verleih and Wega Filmproduktionsgesellschaft*). For a discussion of these decisions, *see* sections §3.05[C][1] to §3.05[C][4].
50. CJEU 15 September 2016, ECLI:EU:C:2016:689 (*Mc Fadden v. Sony Music Entertainment Germany*). For a discussion of this decision, *see* section §3.05[C][5].

considering, among other things, the fundamental rights at issue. This process essentially creates a catalogue of EU law-proof injunctions that can be issued against intermediaries. For instance, after *UPC Telekabel* we know that injunctions to block a website are in principle permitted under EU law.[51] And the CJEU's decision in *Scarlet v. Sabam* clarified that an access provider generally cannot be ordered to filter out copyright-infringing materials.[52]

This process of 'finding' appropriate forms of injunctive relief is a rather time-consuming process that does not produce definitive answers as to whether a particular form of injunctive relief in a concrete case can and must be issued.[53] Nor does it produce guidance on the modalities of specific injunctions. For instance, with regard to blocking injunctions, there is no guidance on who should bear the costs for the blockade, the blocking technology to be used, the extent to which legitimate information may be blocked, the procedures to be followed in order to update or change the domain addresses or the IP addresses which are to be blocked, etc.

All this does not necessarily mean that the current EU legal framework is *too flexible*. The problem with the framework is that it offers flexibility without providing the normative tools to develop and fine-tune the responsibilities of intermediaries. It creates a catalogue of types of injunctions that *can* be issued, but it offers little to synthesize these responsibilities or their modalities in concrete cases. As such, the Copyright Directive and the Enforcement Directive are unlikely to produce a predictable set of responsibilities that intermediaries have vis-à-vis copyright owners in the EU.

[E] The Rights and Interests of the User

Another issue with the current set-up of the EU legal framework is that stakeholders may increasingly determine the responsibilities and modalities among themselves. Especially now that a catalogue of appropriate injunctions is starting to emerge, stakeholders can take a particular measure – for example, blocking a website – as their starting point and come to an agreement about how to implement it. Courts may only be involved if there are disputes between stakeholders on modalities – for example, the procedure to add domain names to the blockade. Where the rights of users are involved, these users essentially depend on the intermediaries and copyright owners to consider their interests when implementing such measures. Or users depend on the possibility given to them (or digital civil rights organizations) in their Member State to start proceedings. In any case, consideration of the user's interest is probably not an intrinsic property of the decision-making process by copyright owners and intermediaries.

This book has also highlighted how intermediaries may take responsibilities upon themselves, either on their own initiative or in cooperation with copyright

51. *UPC Telekabel Wien v. Constantin Film Verleih and Wega Filmproduktionsgesellschaft*, *supra* n. 49.
52. *Scarlet v. Sabam*, *supra* n. 49.
53. *See* sections §4.06[A][2] and §5.07[C] on blocking orders in the Netherlands and Germany.

owners, without there being any kind of legal duty to implement a particular measure. Primary examples are Google's Content ID system and Facebook's Rights Manager, which rely on contracts with copyright owners and content identification technologies to scan and regulate uploaded materials.[54] They are driven by the self-interest motive to offer attractive and content-rich platforms and the need for partnerships with copyright owners. These systems offer an extra layer of protection that is established by rules of contract law and the use of technology. While they offer innovative tools that can contribute to the effective enforcement of copyrights, they do not necessarily strike a fair balance between all the rights and interests that are at stake. These systems offer little insight into how they work, which makes it difficult to assess the impact that they actually have on the copyright balance. They may also insufficiently consider the interests of users, who depend on the willingness of the intermediary to establish sufficient (procedural) safeguards. For instance, mechanisms to protect the fair use of materials and the ability to challenge decisions made by an intermediary or copyright owner.

Until Article 17 of the DSM Directive was introduced, the EU legal framework did not have any control over these forms of 'private ordering' in which online platforms and copyright owners determine, among themselves, the enforcement policies for the Internet. Given the effects that private ordering can have on the balance of rights and interests, this inability to regulate these private practices is worrisome. It also shows that flexibility alone is not enough to create and maintain the copyright balance.

§7.05 TOWARDS A FUTURE-PROOF LEGAL FRAMEWORK: SUGGESTIONS FOR IMPROVEMENT

What can be done to improve the legal framework's 'future-proofness'? Two specific problems stand out which, by building on the research in this book, may be solved. They are the lack of flexibility in the set-up of EU copyright law, especially where the limitations and exceptions in the Copyright Directive are concerned, and the framework's inability to keep a grip on private ordering and to redress any imbalances in enforcement methods, especially those forms of private ordering that are not covered by Article 17 of the DSM Directive.

[A] Flexible Limitations and Exceptions

We have seen that the Copyright Directive broadly defines the applicable exclusive rights, of which in particular the right of communication to the public allows courts to consider new forms of information use and to adjust copyright protection to new technological conditions. In contrast, the Copyright Directive itself offers little flexibility with respect to limitations and exceptions. The CJEU's purposive interpretation of

54. *See* section §6.05 for an analysis of Google's Content ID programme. In Germany, one court has ordered Google to use its Content ID programme to prevent new infringements, *see* section §5.07[B].

existing limitations and exceptions, already mitigates some of the Copyright Directive's inflexibility. Still, two other methods may further enhance the legal framework's flexibility: (1) external balancing by fundamental rights and (2) the introduction of a European fair use doctrine.

[1] External Balancing by Fundamental Rights

Consideration of fundamental rights can be used as a tool to interpret existing limitations and exceptions with greater flexibility. The CJEU has already used the 'fair-balance' requirement in EU copyright law as a vehicle to internalize fundamental rights considerations when interpreting existing limitations and exceptions, or the scope of the exclusive rights. *Deckmyn* and *Painer* are examples of how the CJEU used the fundamental rights in the EU Charter to interpret existing limitations and exceptions.[55] In *GS Media*, the CJEU even interpreted the scope of the exclusive right in relation to the right to the freedom of expression that is promoted by sharing information via hyperlinks.[56] Both cases are examples of how fundamental rights are used to interpret existing concepts in copyright law. These fundamental rights then internally balance copyright law and its enforcement.[57] If curatorial activities by intermediaries are concerned, the CJEU and Member State courts may too, by referring to fundamental rights, opt for a less restrictive interpretation of the exclusive rights or a flexible interpretation of the limitations and exceptions in EU copyright law. For instance, if the intermediary activity in question advances public access to works without harming the interests of copyright owners. As such, fundamental rights could be used to balance copyright law internally by considering the available limitations and exceptions within the context of those fundamental rights.

An even greater level of flexibility could be achieved by permitting fundamental rights to *externally* balance copyright law and its enforcement. Here, fundamental rights could rule out copyright enforcement where none of the available limitations or exceptions apply.[58] The Dutch *Anne Frank diaries* decision is noteworthy because it shows how the freedom of the arts and sciences as protected by the Article 13 of the EU Charter on Fundamental Rights may enable materials to be copied for data mining purposes.[59] It brings to the fore how fundamental rights, especially those that highlight the importance of the free flow of information, can act as a counterweight to copyright protection and effectively permit the use of copyrighted materials in innovative information processing technologies.[60] Fundamental rights are then not only used as

55. CJEU 3 September 2014, ECLI:EU:C:2014:2132 (*Deckmyn*). *See* section §3.03[E][3] for a discussion. CJEU 1 December 2011, ECLI:EU:C:2011:798, para. 134 (*Maria Painer*). *See* section §2.03[B] for a discussion.
56. *GS Media v. Sanoma Media Netherlands and others, supra* n. 29, at 45. *See* section §3.03[D][1] for a discussion.
57. *See* section §2.03[B] and section §2.03[C] on internal and external balancing.
58. *See* in particular section §4.03[C] on external balancing of copyright law in the Netherlands.
59. Rechtbank Amsterdam 23 December 2015, ECLI:NL:RBAMS:2015:9312 (*Anne Frank-Fonds/Anne Frank Stichting*).
60. *See* section §4.03[C][2].

input when interpreting notions within copyright law but also serve as external and independent legal concepts that can put copyright enforcement to one side if need be.[61] Such an approach may offer flexibility where existing limitations and exceptions have no reach. Future CJEU decisions in the cases of *Funke Medien*, *Pelham*, and *Spiegel Online* on the flexibility of the limitations and exceptions in the Copyright Directive, and the role that fundamental rights can play, will hopefully offer clarification as to what is possible under EU Copyright law.[62]

From the perspective of flexibility and the copyright balance, both internal and external balancing by fundamental rights are beneficial. However, from the perspective of predictability, internal and external balancing may not produce optimal results. Internal balancing by fundamental rights may make copyright infringement less predictable because it imports external values, with independent meaning, into copyright law. Where fundamental rights serve as external limitations, it may be uncertain whether a particular use is lawful or an infringement even after applying rules of copyright law. Fundamental rights then add an extra external layer of conceptual vagueness to copyright law's rules and may make it more difficult for stakeholders to take informed decisions.

Assuming that a certain level of conceptual vagueness is needed to make copyright law flexible, it may be better to explicitly internalize that flexibility and make it part of copyright law itself. While internalizing such flexibility does not mitigate the potential negative effects that flexibility may have on the predictability of rules of copyright law, it does more clearly communicate that in copyright law the lines are not always clear. It will presumably also make it easier to introduce copyright-specific supporting measures to increase predictability. That brings us to the second path to flexibilization.

[2] Fair Use

A second method to flexibilize EU copyright law is the introduction of an open-ended exception to EU copyright law that is modelled after the US fair use doctrine.[63] This essentially requires the EU legislator to acknowledge that copyright law requires a safety valve that explicitly leaves room to the courts to develop copyright as technology progresses. As such, the legal framework's flexibility would no longer be dependent on the CJEU's willingness to interpret existing limitations and exceptions extensively. And, in case there is no related limitation or exception in place, no lengthy legislative procedures would be necessary to accommodate new and beneficial intermediary uses of copyrighted materials.

An EU fair use doctrine could function as a flexible shell surrounding the current body of limitations and exceptions and can accommodate new forms of use that were not contemplated by the EU legislator. It would authorize courts to consider new forms

61. *See* section §2.03[C].
62. *See* the references to the CJEU in the cases of *Funke Medien* (C-469/17), *Pelham* (C-476/17), and *Spiegel Online* (C-516/17).
63. *See* section §6.03 for a discussion of the US fair use doctrine.

of use and either permit or prohibit them on the basis of a balancing test. Such an open-ended exception also enables the development of a clearly demarcated body of fair use case law that would become an integral part of EU copyright law.

To increase the predictability of an EU rule on fair use, the rule would have to be accompanied by a set of factors that guide courts' interpretations. Inspired by the US fair use doctrine, a factor recognizing the 'transformativeness' of the use could enable beneficial intermediary uses of copyrighted materials to be permitted. This subfactor has enabled the US courts to accommodate curatorial uses that put existing information into context and that enhances its accessibility, such as the display of images in image search, and the making of cache copies.[64]

With flexibility may come uncertainty. The lack of predictability is also one of the most prominent points of criticism of the US fair use doctrine. Yet, several studies suggest that the US fair use doctrine is more predictable and less arbitrary than its critics have argued.[65] Moreover, the US experience with its fair use doctrine shows that there are methods that increase the open-ended exception's predictability. For instance, US academics have contributed to the adoption of best practices for journalism, poetry, libraries, etc. and have helped by making information available about the application of the doctrine more generally. Another method to increase predictability could be the involvement of a regulatory body that has the authority to develop guidelines or create specific exceptions.[66]

Simply introducing an EU rule on fair use would probably not lead to satisfactory results. Such an open-ended exception also requires a relatively clear and coherent theory on what EU copyright law ultimately aims to accomplish. These aims can promote consistent case law. Moreover, it is questionable whether the current configuration of EU copyright law enables the production of enough and sufficiently consistent case law that would make the open-ended exception predictable. In that configuration, Member States' courts apply their own harmonized copyright laws, which may lead to diverging case law. Uncertainties about the application of the open-ended exception can then only be cleared up by the CJEU through preliminary rulings. Introduction of an EU rule on fair use would therefore also require greater harmonization of EU copyright law.

Of the two discussed paths towards greater flexibility, the introduction of a fair use doctrine is undoubtedly the most far-reaching option. The introduction of an open-ended exception appears to go against the EU's current approach of defining specific limitations and exceptions. Especially if the transformative nature of a use would be a factor in the infringement analysis, the adoption of a fair use rule would also require a shift in continental European thinking about the role of copyright in society, which not only underlines the intrinsic protection of the author's intellectual creations but also recognizes copyright law's utilitarian nature. As such, an EU rule on fair use

64. *See* section §6.03[B][1].
65. *See* section §6.03[C] on the fair use doctrine's flexibility, its predictability, and the means to increase predictability.
66. Akin maybe to how the US Copyright Office is given the authority to adopt exemptions from the prohibition on the circumvention of technological protection measures, *see* section §2.04[B][3].

is probably the least feasible flexibilization of EU copyright law. Yet, a fair use rule would probably offer the flexibility that is needed to maintain the copyright balance and make it fit for purpose not just now, but in the years to come. Finally, if it is supported by measures to increase its predictability, it would be truly future-proof.

[B] From Private Ordering to Co-regulation

Let us now move away from EU copyright law and focus once again on the responsibilities that intermediaries may have for the infringements of others – the intermediary's secondary liability. As has been pointed out, injunctions have become the primary means to allocate responsibility to intermediaries for the infringements of others. A positive aspect of the current legal framework is its ability to gradually develop the responsibilities of intermediaries, and the room it leaves for new forms of injunctive relief as technological conditions change. This flexibility is essential to the effective enforcement of copyrights.

Yet, a point of criticism concerning the current EU legal framework is that it does not offer the normative guidance to determine whether a particular injunction should be issued, nor does it provide guidance on its modalities. It has also been highlighted that the current legal framework leaves too much room for intermediaries and copyright owners to make private arrangements and to effectively regulate the use of Internet services. The latter can be problematic with a view to protecting the rights and interests of Internet users.

The starting point for the solutions presented here is to maintain the flexibility offered by the framework and to suggest ways in which its predictability can be enhanced, and the balance preserved. There are essentially two ways in which the framework could be improved: (1) adopting new legislation or (2) supporting the current legal framework with co-regulatory efforts.

[1] Codification and Specification

One option would be to complement the current EU legal framework by codifying appropriate forms of injunctive relief and laying down specific norms regarding their modalities. It would leave the current framework's flexibility untouched and add new legislation on accepted forms of injunctive relief. Such an approach would effectively take the norm-setting out of the hands of the courts and stakeholders and ideally enables the proactive regulation of the responsibilities of intermediaries. This approach would also enable the legislator to explicitly consider the user's rights and interests and build in safeguards.

However, if these responsibilities and their modalities are laid down in the law in all their specifications, there is a risk that this law will become outdated when new technologies enable forms of enforcement, or infringers find new ways to infringe.[67]

67. *See* section §2.02[B] on the pitfalls of technology-specific legislation. *Also see* section §6.04[B] on the US experience with the Digital Millennium Copyright Act.

The German experience with the codification of the responsibilities of providers of wireless Internet access (Wi-Fi) shows how difficult it can be to define norms on responsibility in legislation that offer sufficient legal certainty but that are also sufficiently flexible if technological conditions change.[68]

[2] Co-regulation

A better option would be to leave the legal framework's openness intact, to make use of its flexibility to devise new forms of injunctive relief when technological conditions change, and to support it with co-regulatory efforts. Now that certain prototype measures – for example, blocking infringing websites – have been considered to strike a fair balance between the fundamental rights at issue, the EU or its Member States should actively bring the different stakeholders together and guide the process of laying co-regulatory regimes on these accepted forms of intermediary responsibility. Considering that courts can still impose certain measures or modalities based on the open norm of responsibility, there may also be a willingness among stakeholders to work together and come to agreements.[69] The advantage of such co-regulatory initiatives is that they enable the regulation of the modalities of a particular form of responsibility in a flexible manner. Codes or agreements can be amended and updated more easily than legislation.

Co-regulation requires the active involvement of a governmental body to ensure that these initiatives are transparent, and to guarantee that the rights and interests of users are sufficiently considered and protected. For instance, by stipulating and shaping the instruments that enable users to dispute any decisions made by an intermediary (such as a counter-notice procedure), or by setting certain standards with regard to decision-making by intermediaries, or by introducing liability for the misrepresentation of infringements.[70]

Promoting co-regulation should also be considered to make pure private ordering mechanisms regulatable. Co-regulation can help to protect basic principles, such as the protection of fundamental rights, the need for transparency, and a fair consideration of the rights and interests of all affected parties. Specifically regarding copyright law, co-regulation enables governments to prevent that stronger stakeholders – intermediaries and copyright owners – make agreements that undermine the copyright balance. This book is in principle in favour of the *approach* that the EU legislator takes with Article 17 of the DSM Directive. It requires content platforms and copyright owners to work together to implement enforcement mechanisms, such as content identification technologies, and it requires from the European Commission and Member States that they guide this process and ensure that sufficient safeguards are in place. This model of co-regulation is a novelty in the domain of online copyright law. It could be seen as

68. *See* section §5.06[C].
69. The Code of Conduct on Notice and Takedown is an example of that, *see* section §4.05[D][2]. However, if it is not yet clear whether an intermediary has a responsibility at all, agreements are unlikely to be struck. *See* section §4.06[A][2] on blocking injunctions in the Netherlands.
70. *See* section §6.04[F] for US experiences with certain (statutory) safeguards.

an attempt to formalize the private ordering by copyright owners and intermediaries. Nevertheless, doubts have been expressed about whether Article 17 of the DSM Directive sufficiently safeguards the interests of users. Much will depend on the efforts of the European Commission and Member States to ensure that the practices of online platforms and copyright owners will indeed respect the copyright balance.

§7.06 CONCLUSION

The position of intermediaries in the copyright system and their liability for the infringements of others is a complex issue. It is impossible to offer one easy and quick fix for problems encountered by copyright owners, intermediaries, and users. Still, it may be possible to provide a general vision on how questions relating to intermediaries and technology can more generally be solved. In a legal framework that is subject to technological change, it appears that the way forward towards a future-proof legal framework is to broaden it and make it flexible, not to narrow it by adopting (technology-)specific legislation that codifies the technological state of affairs. Case law plays an important part in developing and adapting norms. Where open norms require further specification, co-regulation and the involvement of regulatory bodies need to be considered, instead of legislative interventions.

We have seen that if the framework is not sufficiently flexible to accommodate new technologies, or if it does not strike a fair balance between the interests at stake, courts may find a way around this. Limitations and exceptions are no longer strictly interpreted, but also their purpose is considered. General notions in private law are used either to counter the limiting effect that copyrights may have on the free flow of information or to afford copyright owners with additional protection. Courts consider fundamental rights to bring a balance to the copyright system. That judicial creativity must be harnessed and put to use within copyright law. Exclusive rights should be approached normatively. Liability standards must remain open. And a European fair use doctrine must be considered to enable copyright law to adapt as new (intermediary) technologies emerge.

We have also seen that the rules of copyright law and liability discussed here do not operate in a vacuum but are part of an ecosystem that is governed by contracts and technologies. In that ecosystem copyright owners and intermediaries can exert a great deal of influence on the information that flows through them. Their private ordering mechanisms can have a limiting effect on the communicative freedoms of Internet users. A future-proof legal framework requires a perspective on copyright law that is beyond a purely private law conception of copyrights. Maintaining the copyright balance and safeguarding fundamental rights cannot be left to market forces alone but requires a more regulatory approach towards copyrights and their enforcement. An approach that actively strives for balance.

Bibliography

Christiaan Alberdingk Thijm, *Fair Use: het auteursrechtelijk evenwicht hersteld*, AMI (9) 145 (1998).

Christiaan Alberdingk Thijm, *Wat is de zorgplicht van Hyves, XS4ALL en Marktplaats?* Ars Aequi (7/8) 573 (2008).

Virgilio Almeida, Danilo Doneda & Yasodara Córdova, *Whither Social Media Governance?*, 20 IEEE Internet Computing 82 (2016).

Christina Angelopoulos, *European Intermediary Liability in Copyright: A Tort-Based Analysis* (2016).

Christina Angelopoulos & Stijn Smet, *Notice-and-Fair-Balance: How to Reach a Compromise Between Fundamental Rights in European Intermediary Liability*, Journal of Media Law (2) 266 (2016).

Mike Ananny, *Networked News Time. How Slow – Or Fast – Do Publics Need News to Be*, Digital Journalism 8 (2016).

Tanya Aplin, *Subject Matter* (Estelle Derclaye ed., 2009).

David Ardia, *Free Speech Savior or Shield for Scoundrels: An Empirical Study of Intermediary Immunity Under Section 230 of the Communications Decency Act*, 43 Loyola of Los Angeles Review 373 (2010).

Emily Asp, *Section 512 of the Digital Millennium Copyright Act: User Experience and User Frustration*, 103 Iowa Law Review (2) 751 (2018).

Patricia Aufderheide & Aram Sinnreich, *Documentarians, Fair Use and Free Expression: Changes in Copyright Attitudes and Actions with Access to Best Practices*, 19 Information, Communication & Society (2) 178 (2016).

Johan Axhamn, *Cross-Border Extended Collective Licensing: A Solution to Online Dissemination of Europe's Cultural Heritage?*, Research and Advanced Technology for Digital Libraries 501 (2011).

Johan Axhamn, *Hyperlinking: Case C-466/12 Svensson and Others and Its Impact on Swedish Copyright Law*, *Europarättslig tidskrift* (4) 847 (2015).

Ed Baden-Powell, *Think Before You Link: Yesterday's News – Today's Copyright Conundrum*, Computer and Telecommunications Law Review (2) 25 (2011).

Vian Bakir & Andrew McStay, *Fake News and the Economy of Emotions. Problems, Causes, Solutions*, 6 Digital Journalism 154 (2018).

Robert Baldwin, Martin Cave & Martin Lodge, *Understanding Regulation* 3 (2012).

Shyamkrishna Balganesh, *Foreseeability and Copyright Incentives*, 122 Harvard Law Review 1569 (2009).

Jack Balkin, *Old-School/New-School Speech Regulation*, 127 Harvard Law Review 2296 (2014).

I. Baraliuc, S. Depreeuw, & S. Gutwirth, *Copyright Enforcement in the Digital Age: A Post-ACTA View on the Balancing of Fundamental Rights*, International Journal of Law and Information Technology (1) 92 (2013).

Maurits Barendrecht, *Recht als model van rechtvaardigheid. Beschouwingen over vage en scherpe normen, over binding aan het recht en over rechtsvorming* 187 (1992).

Taylor Bartholomew, *The Death of Fair Use in Cyberspace: YouTube and the Problem with Content ID*, 13 Duke Law & Technology Review (1) 66 (2015).

Kevin Bauer, Dirk Grunwald & Douglas Sicker, *The Arms Race in P2P*, the Proceedings of the 37th Research Conference on Communication, Information, and Internet Policy 12 (2009).

Michael Bawaya, *Curation in Crisis*, 317 Science 1025 (2007).

Nick Beagrie, *Digital Curation for Science, Digital Libraries and Individuals*, 1 The International Journal of Digital Curation 3 (2006).

Henri de Beaufort, *Auteursrecht* (1932).

Barton Beebe, *An Empirical Study of U.S. Copyright Fair Use Opinions, 1978-2005*, 156 University of Pennsylvania Law Review (3) 549, 34 (2008).

Yochai Benkler, *From Consumers to Users: Shifting the Deeper Structures of Regulation Toward Sustainable Commons and User Access*, 52 Federal Communications Law Journal 561 (2000).

Lionel Bently & Brad Sherman, *Intellectual Property Law* (2014).

Matthias Berberich, *Zwischenstand zur Haftung von Plattformbetreibern als Intermediäre bei der Werkverwertung*, GRUR-Prax 269 (2017).

Jacques Berleur & Jean-Marc Galand, *ICT Policies of the European Union: From an Information Society to eEurope: Trends and Visions* (Jacques Berleur & Chrisanthi Avgerou eds., 2005).

Michael Birnhack, *Copyrighting Speech: A Trans-Atlantic View* (Paul Torremans ed. 2004).

Michael Birnhack, *Judicial Snapshots and Fair Use Theory*, 5 Queen Mary Journal of Intellectual Property 264 (2015).

Julia Black, *Constitutionalising Self-Regulation*, 59 The Modern Law Review 24 (1996).

Julia Black, *Decentring Regulation: Understanding the Role Self-Regulation in a 'Post-Regulatory' World*, 54 Current Legal Problems 103 (2001).

John Blevins, *Uncertainty as Enforcement Mechanism: The New Expansion of Secondary Copyright Liability to Internet Platforms*, 34 Cardozo Law Review 1821 (2013).

Jeffrey Bloom et al., *Copy Protection for DVD Video*, 87 Proceedings of the IEEE, Special Issue on Identification and Protection of Multimedia Information 1267 (1999).

Joachim Bornkamm, *E-Commerce Directive vs. IP Rights Enforcement. Legal Balance Achieved?*, GRUR Int (8/9) 642 (2007).

Benjamin Boroughf, *The Next Great YouTube: Improving Content ID to Foster Creativity, Cooperation and Fair Compensation*, 25 Albany Law Journal of Science and Technology (1) 95 (2015).

Kevin Boudreau & Andrei Hagiu, *Platforms Rules: Multi-sided Platforms as Regulators*, 164-165 (Annabelle Gawer ed., 2008).

Kathy Bowrey & Matthew Rimmer, *Rip, Mix, Burn: The Politics of Peer to Peer and Copyright Law*, 7 First Monday 1 (2002).

Dana Boyd & Nicole Ellison, *Social Network Sites: Definition, History, and Scholarship*, 13 Journal of Computer-Mediated Communication 210, 211 (2008).

Danah Boyd & Eszter Hargittai, *Facebook Privacy Settings: Who Cares?*, 15 First Monday 1 (2013).

James Boyle, *The Public Domain: Enclosing the Commons of the Mind* (2008).

Karlheinz Brandenburg, *MP3 and AAC Explained* 1, AES 17th International Conference on High Quality Audio Coding (1999).

Annemarie Bridy, *Graduated Response and the Turn to Private Ordering in Online Copyright Enforcement Litigation*, 89 Oregon Law Review (1) 81 (2010).

Sergey Brin & Larry Page, *The Anatomy of a Large-Scale Hypertextual Web Search Engine*, 30 Computer Networks and ISDN Systems 107 (1998).

Ian Brown, *The Evolution of Anti-circumvention Law*, 3 International Review of Law, Computers & Technology 239 (2006).

Ian Brown, *Beware Self-Regulation, Index on Censorship* 98 (2010).

Gijsbert Brunt, *Is de hyperlink, hyper link*, IT en Recht (1) 1 (1997).

Winfried Bullinger & Katharina Garbers-von Boehm, *Google -Bildersuche: Schlichte Einwilligung des Urhebers als Lösung?*, GRUR-Prax (12) 257 (2010).

Ralf Caers et al., *Facebook: A Literature Review*, 15 New Media & Society 982 (2013).

Fabrizio Cafaggi, *Transnational Private Regulation: Regulating Private Regulators* (Sabino Cassese ed., 2016).

Guido Calabresi & Douglas Melamed, *Property Rules, Liability Rules and Inalienability: One View of the Cathedral*, 85 Harvard Law Review 1089 (1972).

Christine Carlisle, *The Audio Home Recording Act of 1992*, 2 Journal of Intellectual Property Law 335 (1994).

Michael Carroll, *Fixing Fair Use*, 85 North Carolina Law Review (4) 1089 (2007).

Michael Carroll, *A Realist Approach to Copyright Law's Formalities*, Berkeley Technology Law Journal (3) 1511 (2013).

Zechariah Chafee, *Reflections on the Law of Copyright: I*, 45 Columbia Law Review (4) 503 (1945).

Anupam Chander, *How Law Made Silicon Valley*, Emory Law Journal (3) 639 (2014).

Remy Chavannes, *Hype of echt link: de hyperlinkaansprakelijkheid van informatieaanbieders, internetaanbieders en zoekmachines*, JAVI (1) 2 (2003).

Remy Chavannes, *Effectief procederen tegen anonieme internetgebruikers*, Nederlands Juristenblad (29) 1 (2007).

Remy Chavannes, *Brein/KPN: het gevaar van een bagatel?*, Mediaforum (10) 174 (2007).

Ming-Syan Chen, Jiawei Han & Philip Yu, *Data Mining: An Overview from a Database Perspective*, IEEE Transactions on Knowledge and Data Engineering (6) 866 (1996).

Madeleine de Cock Buning, *Auteursrecht en informatietechnologie* (1998).

Madeleine de Cock Buning, *Auteursrecht en informatievrijheid: over de beperkte toepassing van artikel 10 EVRM*, Mediaforum (4) 157 (2005).

Madeleine de Cock Buning, *Towards a Future-Proof Framework for the Protection of Minors in European Audiovisual Media*, 10 Utrecht Law Review (5) 9 (2014).

Madeleine de Cock Buning & Marike Vermeer, *Hyperlinks en metatags; meeliften in cyberspace*, Computerrecht (4) 166 (1999).

Julie Cohen, *The Place of the User in Copyright Law*, 74 Fordham Law Review 347 (2005).

Herman Cohen Jehoram, *Central Issues of Intellectual Property and Media Law* (1984).

Herman Cohen Jehoram, *European Copyright Law – Ever More Horizontal*, IIC – International Review of Intellectual Property and Competition Law (5) 532 (2001).

Herman Cohen Jehoram, *Implementatie van de Auteursrechtrichtlijn: De stille strijd tegen een spookrijder*, 34 Nederlands Juristenblad 1690 (2002).

Herman Cohen Jehoram, *Copyright and Freedom of Expression, Abuse of Rights and Standard Chicanery: American and Dutch Approaches*, EIPR 275 (2004).

Herman Cohen Jehoram, *Nu de gevolgen van trouw en ontrouw aan de Auteursrechtrichtlijn voor fair use, tijdelijke reproductie en driestappentoets*, AMI (5) 153 (2005).

Herman Cohen Jehoram, *De Enstra-tapes: een zeldzame botsing tussen auteursrechten en informatievrijheid*, NJB 329 (2009).

Aurelia Colombi Ciacchi, *Constitutionalization of European Private Law* (Hans Micklitz ed. 2014).

Walter Copinger & James Easton, *The Law of Copyright, in Works of Literature, Art, Architecture, Photography, Music and the Drama: Including Chapters on Mechanical Contrivances and Cinematographs: Together with International and Foreign Copyright, with the Statutes Relating Thereto* (1915).

Christian Czychowski & Jan B. Nordemann, *Die Entwicklung der unter- und obergerichtlichen Rechtsprechung zum Urheberrecht im Jahr 2014*, GRUR-RR (5) 185 (2015).

Gillian Davies, *Copyright and the Public Interest* 173 (1997).

Nicholas T. DeLisa, *You(Tube), Me, and Content ID: Paving the Way for Compulsory Synchronization Licensing on User-Generated Content Platforms*, Brooklyn Law Review (3) 1275 (2013).

Laura DeNardis, *Hidden Levers of Internet Control*, 15 Journal of Information Communication and Society 720 (2012).

Laura DeNardis & Andrea Hackl, *Internet Governance by Social Media Platforms*, 39 Telecommunications Policy 761 (2015).

Ben Depoorter, *Property Rules, Liability Rules and Patent Market Failure*, 1 Erasmus Law Review 60 (2008).

Ben Depoorter, *Technology and Uncertainty: The Shaping Effect on Copyright Law*, 157 University of Pennsylvania Law Review 1831 (2009).

Ben Depoorter & Alain Van Hiel, *Copyright Alert Enforcement: Six Strikes and Privacy Harms*, 39 Columbia Journal of Law and the Arts (2) 233 (2015).

Esther Derclaye, *Infopaq International A/S v Danske Dagblades Forening (C-5/08): Wonderful or Worrisome? The Impact of the ECJ Ruling in Infopaq on UK Copyright Law*, European Intellectual Property Review (5) 247 (2010).

Mattias Derlén & Johan Lindholm, *Characteristics of Precedent: The Case Law of the European Court of Justice in Three Dimensions*, 16 German Law Journal 1073 (2015).

Titia Deurvorst, *Schadevergoeding, voldoening van een redelijke gebruiksvergoeding en winstafdracht bij inbreuk op intellectuele eigendomsrechten* 15 (1994).

Titia Deurvorst, *Schadevergoeding en proceskostenveroordeling bij inbreuk op auteursrecht*, AMI (3) 85 (2012).

Reed Dickerson, *The Diseases of Legislative Language*, 1 Harvard Journal on Legislation 5 (1964).

Graeme Dinwoodie, *Private Ordering and the Creation of International Copyright Norms: The Role of Public Structuring*, 1 Journal of Institutional and Theoretical Economics 161 (2004).

Graeme Dinwoodie, *A Comparative Analysis of the Secondary Liability of Online Service Providers* 15 (2017).

Egbert Dommering, *Copyright Being Washed Away Through the Electronic Sieve. Some Thoughts on the Impending Copyright Crisis by Prof. Egbert Dommering* (Bernt Hugenholtz ed., 1996).

Egbert Dommering, *De Auteursrechtelijke aansprakelijkheid van intermediars* 79 (Dirk Visser ed., 1998).

Egbert Dommering, *De zaak Scarlet/Sabam. Naar een horizontale integratie van het auteursrecht*, AMI (2) 49 (2011);

Thomas Dreier, *Überlegungen zur Revision des Schrankenkatalogs der Richtlinie 2001/29/EG*, GRUR Int (7-8) 648 (2015).

Thomas Dreier & Matthias Leistner, *Urheberrecht im Internet: die Forschungsheraus forderungen*, GRUR (9) 881 (2013).

Veerle van Druenen, *De verantwoordelijkheid van vergelijkingssites*, Computerrecht (1) 14 (2016).

Katharina de la Durantaye, *Allgemeine Bildungs- und Wissenschaftsschranke* 196 (2014).

Mireille van Eechoud, *Adapting the Work* (Mireille van Eechoud ed., 2014).

Mireille van Eechoud et al., *Harmonizing European Copyright Law. The Challenges of Better Lawmaking* 298 (2009).

Philip Eijlander & Wim J. M. Voermans, *Wetgevingsleer* (2000).

Tanja Ehnert, *The EU and Nanotechnologies: A Critical Analysis* 46 (2017).

Niva Elkin-Koren, *Cyberlaw and Social Change: A Democratic Approach to Copyright Law in Cyberspace*, 14 Cardozo Arts & Entertainment Law Journal 215 (1996).

Niva Elkin-Koren, *Copyrights in Cyberspace – Rights Without Laws?*, 73 Chicago Kent Law Review 101 (1998).

Niva Elkin-Koren, *Making Technology Visible: Liability of Internet Service Providers for Peer-to-Peer Traffic*, New York University Journal of Legislation and Public Policy (9) 15 (2005).

Niva Elkin-Koren, *Governing Access to Users-Generated-Content: The Changing Nature of Private Ordering in Digital Networks* (Eric Brousseau, Meryem Marzouki & Cécile Meadel eds, 2009).

Niva Elkin-Koren, *After Twenty Years: Revisiting Copyright Liability of Online Intermediaries* (Susy Frankel & Daniel Gervais eds., 2014).

Niva Elkin-Koren, *Fair Use by Design*, 64 UCLA Law Review (5) 1083 (2017).

Niva Elkin-Koren & Orit Fischman-Afori, *Rulifying Fair Use*, 59 Arizona Law Review 161 (2017).

Arnoud Engelfriet, *Naar een passend beschermingsregime voor forumbeheerders en bloggers*, Tijdschrift voor Internetrecht (3) 77 (2009).

Arnoud Engelfriet, *Schadevergoeding bij online auteursrecht- inbreuk: stand van zaken 2015*, AMI (5) 125 (2015).

Jürgen Ensthaler & Harald Blanz, *Leistungsschutzrecht für Presseverleger. Notwendiger Schutz von Presseverlagen im Internet oder systemwidriger Eingriff in die Informationsfreiheit?*, GRUR (11) 1104 (2012).

Richard Epstein, *A Clear View of the Cathedral: The Dominance of Property Rules*, 106 The Yale Law Journal 2091 (1997).

David Evans, *Governing Bad Behavior by Users of Multi-sided Platforms*, 27 Berkeley Technology Law Journal 1201 (2012).

David Evans & Michael Noel, *The Analysis of Mergers That Involve Multisided Platform Businesses*, 4 Journal of Competition Law & Economics 663 (2008).

Ariel Ezrachi & Maurice E. Stucke, *Virtual Competition* (2016).

Anthony Falzone & Jennifer Urban, *Demystifying Fair Use: The Gift of the Center for Social Media Statements of Best Practices*, 57 Journal of the Copyright Society of the U.S.A. (3) 337 (2010).

Marcella Favale, Martin Kretschmer & Paul Torremans, *Is There an EU Copyright Jurisprudence? An Empirical Analysis of the Workings of the European Court of Justice*, 79 Modern Law Review 31 (2016).

Peter Fernandez, *'Through the Looking Glass: Envisioning New Library Technologies' Educational Trends That Will Impact Library Technology*, 33 Library High Tech News 5 (2016).

Mihály Ficsor, *Copyright for the Digital Era: The WIPO Internet Treaties*, Columbia Journal of Law and the Arts (3/4) 197 (1996).

Mihály Ficsor, *The Law of Copyright and the Internet* (2002).

Luciano Floridi, *The New Grey Power*, 28 Philosophy & Technology 329 (2015).

Max Fomitchev-Zamilov, *How Google Analytics and Conventional Cookie Tracking Techniques Overestimate Unique Visitors*, Proceedings of the 19th International Conference on World Wide Web, WWW 2010, Raleigh, North Carolina, USA, April 26-30 (2010).

Michael Freegard, *The Berne Convention, Compulsory Licensing and Collecting Societies* 1 Columbia Journal of Law & the Arts 137 (1986).

Dieter Frey & Matthias Rudolph, *EU-Richtlinie zur Durchsetzung der Rechte des geistigen Eigentums*, 7 ZUM 522 (2004).

Jeanne Fromer, 61 *The Intellectual Property Clause's External Limitations*, Duke Law Journal (7) 1329 (2012).

Giancarlo Frosio, *Why Keep a Dog and Bark Yourself? From Intermediary Liability to Responsibility*, 26 Oxford International Journal of Law and Information Technology 1 (2018).

Stefanie Fuchs & Thomas Farkas, *Kann der EUGH dem Paperboy das (Best)Water reichen?*, ZUM (2) 110 (2015).

Frank Füglein & Pascal Lagardère, *Technik, die begeistert? Rechtsprechung, die erschreckt? Die Probleme der Hoteliers und der Störerhaftung*, MMR-Aktuell (2) 341464 (2013).

Lauren Gallo, *The (Im)Possibility of Standard Technical Measures for UGC Websites*, Columbia Journal of Law & the Arts (2) 283 (2010).

Christophe Geiger, *Flexibilising Copyright – Remedies to the Privatisation of Information by Copyright Law*, 39 International Review of Intellectual Property and Competition Law 178 (2008).

Christophe Geiger, *Intellectual Property Shall Be Protected!? Article 17 (2) of the Charter of Fundamental Rights of the European Union: a Mysterious Provision with an Unclear Scope*, 31 European Intellectual Property Review 113 (2009).

Christophe Geiger, *Promoting Creativity Through Copyright Limitations: Reflections on the Concept of Exclusivity in Copyright Law*, 12 Vanderbilt Journal of Entertainment & Technology Law 515 (2010).

Christophe Geiger, Daniel Gervais & Martin Senftleben, *The Three-Step-Test Revisited: How to Use the Test's Flexibility in National Copyright Law*, American University Law Review (3) 581 (2014).

Christophe Geiger & Elena Izyumenko, *Copyright on the Human Rights' Trial: Redefining the Boundaries of Exclusivity Through Freedom of Expression*, 45 International Review of Intellectual Property and Competition Law 316 (2014).

Robert Gehl, *YouTube as Archive: Who Will Curate This Digital Wunderkammer?*, 12 International Journal of Cultural Studies 43, 47 (2009).

Arthur Germain & Jacob Chakareski, *Spotify Me: Facebook-Assisted Automatic Playlist Generation*, IEEE 15th International Workshop on Multimedia Signal Processing (2013).

Daniel Gervais, *Feist Goes Global: A Comparative Analysis of the Notion of Originality in Copyright Law*, 49 Journal of the Copyright Society of the U.S.A. 949 (2002).

James Gibson, *Risk Aversion and Rights Accretion in Intellectual Property Law*, 116 Yale Law Journal 882 (2007).

Ivo Giesen, *Alternatieve regelgeving en privaatrecht* (2007).

Tarleton Gillespie, *The Politics of 'Platforms'*, 12 New Media & Society 347 (2010).

Tarleton Gillespie, *The Relevance of Algorithms* (Tarleton Gillespie, Pablo Boczkowski & Kirsten Foot, eds 2014).

Jane Ginsburg, *Fair Use for Free, or Permitted-but-Paid?*, 29 Berkeley Technology Law Journal (3) 1383 (2014).

Paul Goldstein, *Copyright in the New Information Age*, 4 Catholic University Law Review 829 (1991).

Paul Goldstein, *Fair use in context*, 31 Columbia Journal of Law & the Arts (4) 433 (2008).

Paul Goldstein & Bernt Hugenholtz, *International Copyright: Principles, Law and Practice* (2010).

Stef van Gompel, *The Orphan Works Chimera and How to Defeat It: A View from Across the Atlantic*, 3 Berkeley Technology Law Journal 1347 (2012).

Stef van Gompel & Bernt Hugenholtz, *The Orphan Works Problem: The Copyright Conundrum of Digitizing Large-Scale Audiovisual Archives, and How to Solve It*, 8 Popular Communication 61 (2010).

Wendy Gordon, *A Property Right in Self-Expression: Equality and Individualism in the Natural Law of Intellectual Property*, 102 Yale Law Journal 1533 (1993).

Mark Gray, *New Rules for a New Decade: Improving the Copyright Office's Anti-Circumvention Rulemakings*, 29 Berkeley Technology Law Journal 7 (2014).

Aida Grgiæ et al., *The Right to Property under the European Convention on Human Rights* 7 (2007).

James Grimmelmann, *Speech Engines*, Minnesota Law Review (3) 868, 937 (2014).

Pekka Gronow, *The Record Industry: The Growth of a Mass Medium*, 1 Popular Music 53 (1983).

Willem Grosheide, *Copyright Law from a User's Perspective: Access Rights for Users*, EIPR 321 (2001).

Willem Grosheide, *Copyright Issues and the Information Society: Dutch Perspectives*, Electronic Journal of Comparative Law 4 (2002).

Jonathan Griffiths, *Constitutionalising or Harmonising? The Court of Justice, the Right to Property and European Copyright Law*, European Law Review (1) 60 (2013).

Jonathan Griffiths, *The Role of the Court of Justice in the Development of European Union Copyright Law* (Irini Stamatoudi & Paul Torremans eds, 2014).

Jonathan Griffiths & Luke McDonagh, *Fundamental Rights and European Intellectual Property Law – The Case of Art 17(2) of the EU Charter 2012* (Christophe Geiger ed., 2013).

Jonathan Griffiths et al., *The European Copyright Society's 'Opinion on the Judgment of the CJEU in Case C-201/13 Deckmyn'*, European Intellectual Property Review (3) 127 (2015).

Michael Grünberger, *Zugangsregeln bei Verlinkungen auf rechtswidrig zugänglich gemachte Werke*, ZUM (11) 905 (2016).

Lucie Guibault, *Why Cherry-Picking Never Leads to Harmonisation: The Case of the Limitations on Copyright*, JIPITEC (2) 55 (2010).

Lucie Guibault & João Quintais, *Copyright, Technology and the Exploitation of Audio-visual Works in the EU*, IRIS Plus (4) 1 (2014).

Sheldon Halpern & Philip Johnson, *Harmonising Copyright Law and Dealing with Dissonance* (2014).

G. Hansen & A. Schmidt-Bischoffshausen, *Ökonomische Funktionen von Verwertungsgesellschaften – Kollektive Wahrnehmung im Lichte von Transaktionskosten –*

und Informationsökonomik, 56 Gewerblicher Rechtsschutz und Urheberrecht Internationaler Teil 461 (2007).

Michael Hart, *The Copyright in the Information Society Directive: An Overview*, European Intellectual Property Review (2) 58 (2002).

Vassilis Hatzopoulos, *Regulating Services in the European Union* 288 (2012).

Stefan Haupt & Loy Ullmann, *Der Fax- und E-Mail-Versand sind in der Informationsgesellschaft verboten*, ZUM (1) 46 (2005).

Toby Headdon, *An Epilogue to Svensson: The Same Old New Public and the Worms That Didn't Turn*, Journal of Intellectual Property Law & Practice & Practice (8) 662 (2014).

Joerg Heidrich & Britta Heymann, *Die Büchse der Pandora erneut geöffnet: Der BGH und Websperren Eine kritische Analyse der Rechtsprechung zu Internetsperren durch Access-Provider*, MMR (6) 370 (2016).

Natali Helberger & Joris Van Hoboken, *(Fast)food for Thoughts: de uitspraak van het Hof van Justitie in de Scarlet/Sabam-zaak*, Nederlands tijdschrift voor Europees recht (2) 72 (2012).

Natali Helberger & Bernt Hugenholtz, *No Place Like Home for Making a Copy: Private Copying in European Copyright Law and Consumer Law*, 22 Berkeley Technology Law Journal (3) 1061 (2007).

Lital Helman, *Session IV: Fair Use and Other Exceptions*, 40 Columbia Journal of Law & the Arts 395 (2017).

Martijn Hesselink, *The Concept of Good Faith* 622 (Arthur Hartkamp et al. eds, 2010).

Britta Heymann & Georg Nolte, *Blockiert das Urheberrecht sinnvolle Informationsdienste? Zur rechtlichen Beurteilung der Bildersuche*, K&R (12) 759 (2009).

Lucas Hilderbrand, *YouTube: Where Cultural Memory and Copyright Converge*, 61 Film Quarterly 48 (2007).

Ernst Hirsch-Ballin, *Auteursrechtelijke Opstellen* (1970).

Joris van Hoboken, *De aansprakelijkheid van zoekmachines. Uitzondering zonder regels of regels zonder uitzondering?*, Computerrecht (1) 15 (2008).

Thomas Hoeren, *WLAN – Haftung – A Never Ending Story?*, ZRP (3) 72 (2014).

Thomas Hoeren & Silviya Yankova, *The Liability of Internet Intermediaries – The German Perspective*, IIC (5) 501 (2012).

Franz Hofmann, *Störerhaftung von Access-Providern für Urheberrechtsverletzungen Dritter*, NJW (11) 769 (2016).

Bernie Hogan, *The Presentation of Self in the Age of Social Media: Distinguishing Performances and Exhibitions Online*, 30 Bulletin of Science Technology Society 377 (2010).

Martin Hohlweck, *'Even Heaven Cries' – Eine rechtliche Zwischenbilanz von Filesharing-Verfahren*, GRUR (10) 940 (2014).

Thomas Hoppner, *Reproduction in Part of Online Articles in the Aftermath of Infopaq (C-5/08): Newspaper Licensing Agency Ltd v Meltwater Holding BV*, European Intellectual Property Review (5) 331 (2011).

Martin Hossenfelder, *Die Nachrichtendarstellung in Suchmaschinen nach der Einführung des Leistungsschutzrechts für Presseverleger*, ZUM (5) 374 (2013).

Bernt Hugenholtz, *Brussels Broddelwerk. Recht en Krom in de Auteursrechtrichtlijn*, AMI (2) 2 (2001).

Bernt Hugenholtz, *Auteursrecht contra informatievrijheid in Europa* (Wouter Hins & Aernout Nieuwenhuis eds, 2003).

Bernt Hugenholtz, *Codes of Conduct and Copyright: Pragmatism v. Principle*, 6 International Review of Intellectual Property and Competition Law 635 (2008).

Bernt Hugenholtz, *Works of Literature, Science and Art* 34 (Bernt Hugenholtz, Antoon Quaedvlieg & Dirk Visser eds, 2012).

Bernt Hugenholtz, *Fair Use in Europe*, 5 Communications of the ACM 26 (2013).

Bernt Hugenholtz & Martin Senftleben, *Fair Use in Europe: In Search of Flexibilities* (2011).

Bernt Hugenholtz & Sam van Velze, *Communication to a New Public? Three Reasons Why EU Copyright Law Can Do Without a 'New Public'*, IIC (7) 797 (2016).

Justin Hughes, *The Philosophy of Intellectual Property*, 77 Georgetown Law Journal 287 (1988).

Martin Husovec, *Injunctions Against Innocent Third Parties: The Case of Website Blocking*, JIPITEC (2) 116 (2012).

Martin Husovec, *Injunctions Against Intermediaries in the European Union: Accountable but Not Liable?* (2017).

Toon Huydecoper, *Nous maintiendrons – de nieuwe 'ricthlijn handhaving'*, Tijdschrift voor Auteurs-, media- & informatierecht 117 (2004).

Y. Ibrahim, *The Politics of Image: The Image Economy on Facebook* (Celia Livermore ed., 2012).

Cassandra Imfeld & Victoria Ekstrand, *The Music Industry and the Legislative Development of the Digital Millennium Copyright Act's Online Service Provider Provision*, 3 Communication Law and Policy 291 (2005).

Agnieszka Janczuk-Gorywoda, *The New Transnational Payment Law and Global Trade: Online Platforms as Providers of Private Legal Orders*, 24 European Review of Private Law 223 (2016).

Marie-Christine Janssens, *The Issue of Exceptions: Reshaping the Keys to the Gates in the Territory of Literary, Musical and Artistic Creation* (Estelle Derclaye ed., 2009).

Marie-Christine Janssens, *De impact van het internet op de sector van het auteursrecht (of is het omgekeerd?) – een analyse aan de hand van de rechtspraak van het Hof van Justitie*, SEW (10) 454 (2014).

Kylie Jarrett, *Beyond Broadcast Yourself^{tm}: The Future of YouTube*, 126 Media International Australia 132 (2008).

T. Joachims & F. Radlinski, *Search Engines That Learn from Implicit Feedback, Computer* 34 (2007).

Rikke Frank Jørgensen, *Framing Human Rights: Exploring Storytelling Within Internet Companies*, 21 Information, Communication & Society 340 (2017).

Rosa Julià-Barceló & Kamiel Koelman, *Intermediary Liability in the E-Commerce Directive: So Far So Good, but It's Not Enough*, Computer Law & Security Report (4) 231 (2000).

Jonas Kahl, *Wen betrifft das Leistungsschutzrecht für Presseverleger? 'Kleinste Textausschnitte' vor dem Hintergrund der BGH-Rechtsprechung*, MMR (6) 348 (2013).

Louis Kaplow, *Rules Versus Standards: An Economic Analysis*, 42 Duke Law Journal 557 (1992).

Louis Kaplow & Steven Shavell, *Property Rules Versus Liability Rules*, 109 Harvard Law Review 713 (1996).

Stavroula Karapapa & Maurizio Borghi, *Search Engine Liability for Autocomplete Suggestions: Personality, Privacy and the Power of the Algorithm*, 23 International Journal of Law and Information Technology 261 (2015).

Jin Kim, *The Institutionalization of YouTube: From User-Generated Content to Professionally Generated Content*, 34 Media Culture & Society 53 (2012).

Sil Kingma, *De botsing tussen IE- en privacyrechten*, Privacy & Informatie (4) 170 (2012).

Katarzyna Klafkowska-Wasniowska, *Public Communication Right: Towards the Full Harmonisation?*, European Intellectual Property Review (12) 751 (2013).

Nadine Klass, *Neue Internettechnologien und das Urheberrecht: Die schlichte Einwilligung als Rettungsanker?*, ZUM (1) 1 (2013).

Rasmus Kleis Nielsen & Sarah Anne Ganter, *Dealing with Digital Intermediaries: A Case Study of the Relations Between Publishers and Platforms*, 20 New Media & Society 1600 (2018).

Heike Klüver, *Lobbying in the European Union* (2013).

Kamiel Koelman, *Copyright Law & Economics in the Copyright Directive: Is the Droit D'Auteur Passe?*, International Review of Intellectual Property and Competition Law 603 (2004).

C. Kohler & K. Burmeister, *Copyright Liability on the Internet Today in Europe (Germany, France, Italy and the E.U.)*, European Intellectual Property Review (10) 485 (1999).

Stefan Koroch, *Das Leistungsschutzrecht für Presseverleger auf dem Weg von Berlin nach Brüssel*, GRUR (2) 127 (2017).

Adam Kramer, Jamie Guillory & Jeffrey T. Hancock, *Experimental Evidence of Massive-Scale Emotional Contagion Through Social Networks*, 24 Proceedings of the National Academy of Sciences of the United States of America 8788 (2014).

Martin Kretschmer, *Copying the Digital Millennium Copyright Act: European Struggles with Information Control* (2013).

Martin Kretschmer et al., *The European Commission's Public Consultation on the Role of Publishers in the Copyright Value Chain: A Response by the European Copyright Society*, European Intellectual Property Review (10) 591 (2016).

Till Kreutzer, *Das Leistungsschutzrecht für Presseverleger im Lichte der BGH-Rechtsprechung zu Vorschaubildern Was bleibt am Ende übrig?*, MMR (8) 512 (2014).

Aleksandra Kuczerawy, *Intermediary Liability & Freedom of Expression: Recent Developments in the EU Notice & Action Initiative*, Computer Law and Security Review (1) 46 (2015).

Stefan Kulk & Frederik Zuiderveen Borgesius, *Filtering for Copyright Enforcement in Europe after the Sabam Cases*, European Intellectual Property Review (11) 791 (2012).

Hans-Peter Kunz-Hallstein & Michael Loschelder, *Stellungnahme der GRUR zur Anhörung des BMJ am 28. 6. 2010 zum Thema 'Leistungsschutzrecht für Verleger'*, GRUR (9) 808 (2010).

Hans-Peter Kunz-Hallstein & Michael Loschelder, *Stellungnahme des Fachausschusses Urheber- und Verlagsrecht der GRUR zum Regierungsentwurf eines Siebenten Gesetzes zur Änderung des Urheberrechtsgesetzes (Leistungsschutzrecht für Presseverleger)*, GRUR (3) 268 (2013).

Annette Kur, *The Enforcement Directive – Rough Start, Happy Landing?*, 35 International Review of Industrial Property and Copyright Law 821 (2004).

Jack Lacy, J.H. Snyder & David Maher, *Music on the Internet and the Intellectual Property Protection Problem*, ISIE '97 Proceeding of the IEEE International Symposium on Industrial Electronics (1997).

Stephen Ladas, *The International Protection of Literary and Artistic Property. Vol I* (1938).

William Landes & Richard Posner, *An Economic Analysis of Copyright Law*, 18 The Journal of Legal Studies 325 (1989).

Stefan Larsson et al., *Law, norms, piracy and online anonymity Practices of de-identification in the global*, 6 Journal of Research in Interactive Marketing: Special Issue of Digital Piracy 260 (2012).

Stefan Larsson, *Conceptions of Copyright in a Digital Context. A Comparison between French and American File-sharers*, Lexis 89 (2014).

Edward Lee, *Decoding the DMCA Safe Harbors*, Columbia Journal of Law & the Arts (3) 233 (2009).

Yin Harn Lee, *Copyright and Freedom of Expression: A Literature Review* CREATe Working Paper 2015/04 (2015).

Diane Leenheer Zimmerman, *Copyrights as Incentives: Did We Just Imagine That*, 12 Theoretical Inquiries in Law 29 (2011).

Matthias Leistner, *Störerhaftung und mittelbare Schutzrechtsverletzung*, GRUR-Beil. (1) 1 (2010).

Matthias Leistner, *The German Federal Supreme Court's Judgment on Google's Image Search – A Topical Example of the 'Limitations' of the European Approach to Exceptions and Limitations*, IIC (4) 417 (2011).

Matthias Leistner, *Grundlagen und Perspektiven der Haftung für Urheberrechtsverletzungen im Internet*, ZUM (10) 722 (2012).

Matthias Leistner, *Structural Aspects of Secondary (Provider) Liability in Europe*, Journal of Intellectual Property Law & Practice (1) 75 (2014).

Matthias Leistner, *Europe's Copyright Law Decade: Recent Case Law of the European Court of Justice and Policy Perspectives*, Common Market Law Review (2) 559 (2014).

Matthias Leistner, *Urheberrecht an der Schnittstelle zwischen Unionsrecht und nationalem Recht*, GRUR (12) 1145 (2014).

Matthias Leistner, *Copyright at the Interface Between EU Law and National Law: Definition of 'Work' and 'Right of Communication to the Public'*, Journal of Intellectual Property Law & Practice (8) 626 (2015).

Matthias Leistner, *Reformbedarf im materiellen Urheberrecht: Online-Plattformen und Aggregatoren*, ZUM (7) 580 (2016).

Matthias Leistner & Karina Grisse, *Sperrverfügungen gegen Access – Provider im Rahmen der Störerhaftung (Teil 1)*, GRUR (1) 19 (2015).

Matthias Leistner & Karina Grisse, *Sperrverfügungen gegen Access – Provider im Rahmen der Störerhaftung (Teil 2)*, GRUR (2) 105 (2015).

Mark Lemley, *Rationalizing Internet Safe Harbors*, 6 Journal on Telecommunications & High Technology Law (1) 101 (2007).

Mark Lemley & Dan Burk, *Policy Levers in Patent Law*, 7 Virginia Law Review 1575 (2003).

Lawrence Lessig, *Code and Other Laws of Cyberspace* 89 (1999).

Toni Lester & Dessislava Pachamanova, *The Dilemma: Making Content ID Algorithms More Conducive to Fostering Innovative Fair Use in Music Creation*, UCLA Entertainment Law Review (1) 51 (2017).

Yafit Lev-Aretz, *Copyright Lawmaking and Public Choice: From Legislative Battles to Private Ordering*, 27 Harvard Journal of Law & Technology (1) 203 (2013).

Pierre Leval, *Toward a Fair Use Standard*, 103 Harvard Law Review (5) 1105 (1990).

Pierre N. Leval, *Nimmer Lecture: Fair Use Rescued*, 44 UCLA Law Review (5) 1449 (1997).

Pierre Leval, *Campbell as Fair Use Blueprint*, 2 Washington Law Review 597 (2015).

Silke von Lewinski, *Die diplomatische Konferenz der WIPO 1996 zum Urheberrecht und zu verwandten Schutzrechten*, GRUR Int (8/9) 667 (1997).

Douglas Lichtman & William Landes, *Indirect Liability for Copyright Infringement: An Economic Perspective*, 2 Harvard Journal of Law and Technology 395 (2003).

Eva Lievens & Peggy Valcke, *Regulatory Trends in a Social Media Context* (Monroe Price, Stefaan Verhulst & Libby Morgan eds., 2013).

Tina van der Linden, *Het is niet goed of het deugt niet: De juridische positie van internet tussenpersonen is onbevredigend!*, Tijdschrift voor Internetrecht (1) 4 (2014).

Jessica Litman, *Copyright Legislation and Technological Change*, 68 Orgeon Law Review 275 (1989).

Jessica Litman, *Digital Copyright* (2006).

Jacqueline Lipton, *Law of the Intermediated Information Exchange*, 64 Florida Law Review 1337 (2012).

Joseph Liu, *Regulatory Copyright*, 83 North Carolina Law Review (1) 87 (2004).

S.B. Liu, *Trends in Distributed Curatorial Technology to Manage Data Deluge in a Networked World*, 11 The European Journal for the Informatics Professional 18 (2010).

Gerrit van Maanen, *Onrechtmatige daad. Aspekten van de ontwikkeling van een omstreden leerstuk* (1986).

Gerrit van Maanen, *De Zutphense juffrouw en de ontrouwe bediende van Lindenbaum* (1995).

Gerrit Van Maanen, David Townend & Almaz Teffera, *The Dutch 'Cellar Hatch' Judgment as a Landmark Case for Tort Law in Europe: A Brief Comparison with English, French and German Law with a Law and Economics Flavour*, 5 European Review of Private Law 871 (2008).

Rebecca MacKinnon et al., *Fostering Freedom Online* (2014).

Willem Mak, *Rights Affecting the Manufacture and Use of Gramophone Records* (1952).

Makeen Makeen, *The Controversy of Simultaneous Cable Retransmission to Hotel Rooms under International and European Copyright Laws*, Journal - Copyright Society of The USA (1/2) 59 (2010).

Cédric Manara, *Remuneration for the Use of Works. Exclusivity vs. Other Approaches*, 367 (Silke Von Lewinski ed., 2017).

Gregory Mandel, *Legal Evolution in Response to Technological Change* (Roger Brownsword, Eloise Scotford & Karen Yeung eds, 2017).

Ronald Mann & Seth Belzley, *The Promise of Intermediary Liability*, 47 William and Mary Law Review 239 (2005).

Reto Mantz & Thomas Sassenberg, *Verantwortlichkeit des Access-Providers auf dem europäischen Prüfstand Neun Fragen an den EuGH zu Haftungsprivilegierung, Unterlassungsanspruch und Prüfpflichten des WLAN-Betreibers*, MMR (2) 85 (2015).

Basil Markesinis & Hannes Unberath, *The German Law of Tort: A Comparative Treatise* 14 (2002).

Mislav Mataija, *Private Regulation and the Internal Market: Sports, Legal Services, and Standard Setting in EU Economic Law* 9 (2016).

Heather McIntosh, *Vevo and the Business of Online Music Video Distribution*, 39 Popular Music and Society 487 (2015).

Thomas Melcher, *Bundestag verabschiedet Leistungsschutzrecht*, MMR-Aktuell (5) 343382 (2013).

William Melody, *Toward a Framework for Designing Information Society Policies*, Telecommunications Policy (4) 243 (1996).

Aaron Melville, *The Future of the Audio Home Recording Act of 1992: Has it Survived the Millenium Bug?*, 2 Boston University Journal of Science & Technology Law 372 (2001).

Peter Menell, *Design for Symbiosis*, Communications of the ACM (5) 30 (2012).

Marie-Claire Menting, *(R)Evolutie in het privaatrecht? Enkele beschouwingen over de rol van private regelgeving en de invloed van het EVRM naar aanleiding van HR Achmea/Rijnberg*, Nederlands Tijdschrift voor Burgerlijk Recht (4) 104 (2015).

Marie-Claire Menting, *Industry Codes of Conduct in a Multi-layered Dutch Private Law* 10 (2016).

Robert Merges, *Contracting into Liability Rules: Intellectual Property Rights and Collective Rights Organizations*, 84 California Law Review 1293 (1996).

Trisha Meyer, *The Politics of Online Copyright Enforcement in the EU* (2017).

Gabriel Michael, *Politics and Rulemaking at the Copyright Office*, 11 Journal of Information Technology & Politics 64 (2014).

Dunja Mijatović, *Freedom of Expression on the Internet* 32 (2010).

Gerard Mom, *Uitvoering in (strikt) besloten kring*, AMI (3) 81 (2010).

Philip Napoli & Robyn Caplan, *Why Media Insist They're Not Media Companies, Whey They're Wrong, and Why It Matters*, 22 First Monday 1 (2017).

Ira Steven Nathenson, *Super-Intermediaries, Code, Human Rights*, 8 Intercultural Human Rights Law Review 19 (2013).

Arian Nazari-Khanachayi, *Access-Provider als urheberrechtliche Schnittstelle im Internet. Europarechtliche Vorgaben im Hinblick auf Zugangserschwerungsverfügungen und Lösungsansätze für das deutsche Recht de lege ferenda*, GRUR (2) 115 (2015).

Cyril van der Net, *Artikel 13a Aw (technische en functionele kopieen)*, AMI (5) 168 (2005).

Neil Netanel, *Copyright Alienability Restrictions and the Enhancement of Author Autonomy: A Normative Evaluation*, 24 Rutgers Law Journal 347 (1993).

Neil Netanel, *Copyright and a Democratic Civil Society*, 106 Yale Law Journal 283 (1996).

Neil Netanel, *Making Sense of Fair Use*, 15 Lewis & Clark Law Review (2) 715 (2011).

David Nimmer, *Brains and Other Paraphernalia of the Digital Age*, Harvard Journal of Law & Technology (1) 1 (1996).

David Nimmer, *Back from the Future: A Proleptic Review of the Digital Millennium Copyright Act*, 16 Berkeley Technology Law Journal (4) 855 (2001).

David Nimmer, *'Fairest of Them All' and Other Fairy Tales of Fair Use*, 66 Law and Contemporary Problems (1-2) 263 (2003).

Georg Nolte, *Zur Forderung der Presseverleger nach Einführung eines speziellen Leistungsschutzrechts. Eine kritische Auseinandersetzung*, Zeitschrift für Geistiges Eigentum (2) 165 (2010).

Georg Nolte & Jörg Wimmers, *Wer stört? Gedanken zur Haftung von Intermediären im Internet – von praktischer Konkordanz, richtigen Anreizen und offenen Fragen*, GRUR-Beil. (1) 58 (2014).

Jan B. Nordemann, *Liability for Copyright Infringements on the Internet: Host Providers (Content Providers) – The German Approach*, JIPITEC 37 (1) 46 (2011).

Ansgar Ohly, *Zwölf Thesen zur Einwilligung im Internet*, GRUR (10) 983 (2012).

Ansgar Ohly, *Urheberrecht in der digitalen Welt – Brauchen wir neue Regelungen zum Urheberrecht und zu dessen Durchsetzung?*, NJW-Beilage (2) 47 (2014).

Ansgar Ohly, *Die Verantwortlichkeit von Intermediären*, ZUM (4) 308 (2015).

Pieter-Jan Ombelet, Aleksandra Kuczerawy & Peggy Valcke, *Supervising Automated Journalists in the Newsroom: Liability for Algorithmically Produced News Stories*, CiTiP Working Paper 25/2016.

Maria Pallante, *The Next Great Copyright Act*, 36 Columbia Journal of Law & the Arts 315 (2013).

Frank Pasquale, *Beyond Innovation and Competition: The Need for Qualified Transparency in Internet Intermediaries*, 104 Northwestern University Law Review 105 (2010).

Frank Pasquale, *Platform Neutrality: Enhancing Freedom of Expression in Spheres of Private Power*, 17 Theoretical Inquiries in Law 487 (2016).

Graham Pearce & Nicholas Platten, *Promoting the Information Society: The EU Directive on Electronic Commerce*, European Law Journal (4) 363 (2000).

Karl-Nikolaus Peifer, *Leistungsschutzrecht für Presseverleger – "Zombie im Paragrafen-Dschungel" oder Retter in der Not?*, GRUR-Prax (7) 149 (2013).

Clement Petersen & Thomas Riis, *Private Enforcement of IP Law by Internet Service Providers: Notice and Action Procedures* (T. Riis ed., 2016).

Alexander Peukert, *The Fundamental Right to (Intellectual) Property* 145 (Christophe Geiger ed. 2015).

Miquel Peguera, *Copyright Issues Regarding Google Images and Google Cache*, 169 (Aurelio Lopez-Tarruella ed., 2012).

Maayan Perel & Niva Elkin-Koren, *Accountability in Algorithmic Copyright Enforcement*, 19 Stanford Technology Law Review (3) 473 (2016).

Rupprecht Podszun & Stephan Kreifels, *Digital Platforms and Competition Law* 5 Journal European Consumers and Market Law 33 (2016).

Anne Prentice, *Copyright, WIPO and User Interests: Achieving Balance among the Shareholders*, The Journal of Academic Librarianship (4) 309 (1997).

Corien Prins, *Normering, regulering en rechtshandhaving door technologie: over de implicaties van techno-regulering voor het privaatrecht*, Weekblad voor Privaatrecht, Notariaat en Registratie 1075 (2011).

Antoon Quaedvlieg, *Een modern citaatrecht belemmert niet de uitingsvrijheid*, AMI 197 (2006).

Michelle Ravn, *Navigating Terra Incognita: Why the Digital Millennium Copyright Act Was Needed to Chart the Course of Online Service Provider Liability for Copyright Infringement*, Ohio State Law Journal (2) 755 (1999).

Chris Reed, *Taking Sides on Technology Neutrality*, 3 SCRIPT-ed 263 (2007).

Anthony Reese, *Copyrightable Subject Matter in the 'Next Great Copyright Act'*, 29 Berkeley Technology Law Journal 1489 (2014).

Jorg Reinbothe & Silke von Lewinski, *The WIPO Treaties on Copyright* (2015).

Tito Rendas, *How Playboy Photos Compromised EU Copyright Law: The GS Media Judgment*, Journal of Internet Law (5) 11 (2017).

Thomas Riis & Jens Schovsbo, *Users' Rights: Reconstruction Copyright Policy on Utilitarian Grounds*, 29 European Intellectual Property Review 1 (2007).

Sam Ricketson, *Berne Convention for the Protection of Literary and Artistic Works: 1886-1986* (1987).

Allard Ringnalda, *Orphan Works, Mass Rights Clearance, and Online Libraries: The Flaws of the Draft Orphan Works Directive and Extended Collective Licensing as a Solution*, 8 Medien und Recht International 3 (2011).

Jean-Charles Rochet & Jean Tirole, *Platform Competition in Two-sided Markets*, 1 Journal of the European Economic Association 990 (2003).

Felipe Romero-Moreno, *'Notice and Staydown' and Social Media: Amending Article 13 of the Proposed Directive on Copyright*, International Review of Law, Computers & Technology (2) 187 (2019).

Eleonora Rosati, *Judge-Made EU Copyright Harmonization: The Case of Originality* 187 (2012).

Eleonara Rosati, *GS Media and its Implications for the Construction of the Right of Communication to the Public within EU Copyright Architecture*, Common Market Law Review (4) 1221 (2017).

Mark Rose, *Authors and Owners: The Invention of Copyright* 3 (1993).

Jennifer Rothman, *Best Intentions: Reconsidering Best Practices Statements in the Context of Fair Use and Copyright Law*, 57 Journal of the Copyright Society of the U.S.A. (3) 371 (2010).

Matthew Sag, 73 *Predicting Fair Use*, Ohio State Law Journal (1) 47 (2012).

Pamela Samuelson, *The U.S. Digital Agenda at WIPO*, Virginia Journal of International Law (2) 369 (1997).

Pamela Samuelson, *Copyright and Freedom of Expression in Historical Perspective*, 10 Journal of Intellectual Property Law 319 (2003).

Pamela Samuelson, *Unbundling Fair Uses*, 77 Fordham Law Review (5) 2537 (2009).

Pamela Samuelson, *Possible Futures of Fair Use*, 90 Washington Law Review (2) 815 (2015).

Pekka Savola, *Blocking Injunctions and Website Operators' Liability for Copyright Infringement for User-Generated Links*, European Intellectual Property Review (5) 279 (2014).

Frederick Schauer, *Playing by the Rules: A Philosophical Examination of Rule-Based Decision-Making in Law and in Life* 140 (1991).

Maurice H.M. Schellekens & Gijsbert Brunt, *Auteursrecht in Digiworld* (Wolter Wefers Bettink ed., 1996)

Maurice Schellekens, *Aansprakelijkheid van internetaanbieders* 203 (2001).

Maurice Schellekens, *The Internet Access Provider: Unwilling or Unable?*, International Journal of Law and Information Technology (3) 310 (2015).

Henry Schermers & Denis Waelbroeck, *Judicial Protection in the European Union* (2001).

Martin Schippan, *Der Schutz von kurzen Textwerken im digitalen Zeitalter*, ZUM (5) 358 (2013).

Gregor Schmid, *BestWater: Framing No 'Communication to the Public'*, Journal of Intellectual Property Law & Practice (2) 82 (2015).

Sandra Schmitz, *The RedTube Copyright Infringement Affair in Germany: Shame on Who?*, International Review of Law, Computers & Technology (1) 33 (2015).

John Schulman, *Fair Use and the Revision of the Copyright Act*, 53 Iowa Law Review 832 (1967).

Robert Schweizer, *Schutz der Leistungen von Presse und Journalisten*, ZUM (1) 7 (2010).

Jacqueline Seignette, *Napster en de controle van de rechthebbende over de distributie van zijn werk*, AMI (2) 29 (2001).

Wendy Seltzer, *Free Speech Unmoored in Copyright's Safe Harbor: Chilling Effects on the DMCA on the First Amendment*, 24 Harvard Journal of Law & Technology (1) 171 (2010).

Martin Senftleben, *Copyright, Limitations, and the Three-Step Test: An Analysis of the Three-Step Test in International and EC Copyright Law* (2004).

Martin Senftleben, *The International Three-Step Test*, JIPITEC (2) 67 (2012).

Martin Senftleben, *Quotations, Parody and Fair Use* 360 (Bernt Hugenholtz, Antoon Quaedvlieg & Dirk Visser eds, 2012).

Martin Senftleben, *Internet Search Results – A Permissible Quotation?*, Revue Internationale du Droit d'Auteur (1) 3 (2013).

Martin Senftleben, *Breathing Space for Cloud-Based Business Models – Exploring the Matrix of Copyright Limitations, Safe Harbours and Injunctions*, JIPITEC (2) 87 (2013).

Martin Senftleben, *Comparative Approaches to Fair Use: An Important Impulse for Reforms in EU Copyright Law* 63 (Graeme Dinwoodie ed., 2013).

Martin Senftleben, *Copyright Reform, GS Media and Innovation Climate in the EU – Euphonious Chord or Dissonant Cacophony?*, AMI (5) 130 (2016).

Martin Senftleben, *The Perfect Match – Civil Law Judges and Open-Ended Fair Use Provisions*, 33 American University International Law Review 231 (2017).

Martin Senftleben, *User-Generated Content – Towards a New Use Privilege in EU Copyright Law* (Tanya Aplin ed., 2019).

Martin Senftleben et al., *The Recommendation on Measures to Safeguard Fundamental Rights and the Open Internet in the Framework of the EU Copyright Reform*, European Intellectual Property Review (3) 149 (2018).

Julie Sheinblatt, *The WIPO Copyright Treaty*, Berkeley Technology Law Journal (1) 535 (1998).

Ulrich Sieber & Marc Liesching, *Die Verantwortlichkeit der Suchmaschinenbetreiber nach dem Telemediengesetz*, MMR-Beil. (8) 1 (2007).

Leonie Siemerink, *IE(-rechten), P2P en ISP: handhaving van auteursrechten op internet nog mogelijk?*, Maandblad voor Vermogensrecht (7/8) 179 (2008).

Bart van der Sloot, *De verantwoordelijkheid voorbij: de ISP op de stoel van de rechter*, Tijdschrift voor Internetrecht (5) 136 (2011).

Henry Smith, *Property and Property Rules*, 79 New York University Law Review 1719 (2004).

Henry Smith, *Intellectual Property as Property: Delineating Entitlements in information*, 116 Yale Law Journal 1742 (2007).

Jan Smits, *The Mind and Method of the Legal Academic* (2012).

Gerald Spindler, *Europäisches Urheberrecht in der Informationgesellschaft*, GRUR (2) 105 (2002).

Gerald Spindler, *Der Auskunftsanspruch gegen Verletzer und Dritte im Urheberrecht nach neuem Recht*, ZUM (8/9) 640 (2008).

Gerald Spindler, *Bildersuchmaschinen, Schranken und konkludente Einwilligung im Urheberrecht Besprechung der BGH-Entscheidung 'Vorschaubilder'*, GRUR (9) 785 (2010).

Gerald Spindler, *Die Reform des Urheberrecht*, NJW (35) 2550 (2014).

Gerald Spindler, *Zivilrechtliche Sperrverfügungen gegen Access Provider nach dem EuGH-Urteil 'UPC Telekabel'*, GRUR (9) 826 (2014).

Gerald Spindler & Matthias Leistner, 37 *Secondary Copyright Infringement – New Perspectives in Germany and Europe*, IIC 788 (2016).

Gerald Spindler, *Das Ende der Links: Framing und Hyperlinks auf rechtswidrige Inhalte als eigenständige Veröffentlichung?*, GRUR 157 (2016).

Gerald Spindler, *Sperrverfügungen gegen Access-Provider – Klarheit aus Karlsruhe?*, GRUR (5) 451 (2016).

Jaap Spoor, Feer Verkade & Dirk Visser, *Auteursrecht. Auteursrecht, naburige rechten en databankenrecht* (2011).

Joachim Sternberg, *Die Rechtsprechung des EuGH und des BGH zum Urheberrecht und zu den verwandten Schutzrechten im Jahre 2014*, GRUR (3) 205 (2015).

Malte Stieper, *Das Leistungsschutzrecht für Presseverleger nach dem Regierungsentwurf zum 7 . UrhRÄndG*, ZUM (1) 10 (2013).

Alain Strowel, *Introduction: Peer-to-Peer File Sharing and Secondary Liability in Copyright Law* (Alain Strowel ed., 2009).

Alain Strowel & Nicolas Ide, *Liability with Regard to Hyperlinks*, Columbia Journal of Law & the Arts (4) 403 (2001).

Maurice Stucke & Alan Grunes, *Big Data and Competition Policy* (2016).

Cass Sunstein, *Problems with Rules*, 83 California Law Review 953 (1995).

Tatiana-Eleni Synodinou, *The Lawful User and a Balancing of Interests in European Copyright Law*, 41 International Review of Industrial Property and Copyright Law 819 (2010).

Roosa Tarkiainen, *Tipping the Scale in GS Media: A Proposal to Restore the Balance Between Rightholders and Internet Users*, Journal of Intellectual Property Law & Practice (6) 502 (2017).

Ivan Taylor, *Video Games, Fair Use and the Internet: The Plight of the Let's Play*, University of Illinois Journal of Law, Technology & Policy (1) 247 (2015).

Eric Tjong Tjin Tai, *Zorgplichten en zorgethiek* (2006).

Eric Tjong Tjin Tai, *Zorg, Privaatrecht en publiekrecht: van ondersteuning naar handhaving, en terug*, Recht der Werkelijkheid (3) 6 (2010).

Eric Tjong Tjin Tai, *Aansprakelijkheid voor robots en algoritmes*, 14 Nederlands Tijdschrift voor Handelsrecht 123 (2017).

Takis Tridimas, *The General Principles of EU Law* (2006).

Alexander Tsoutsanis, *Why Copyright and Linking Can Tango*, Journal of Intellectual Property Law & Practice (6) 495 (2014).

Rebecca Tushnet, *Legal Fictions: Copyright, Fan Fiction, and a New Common Law*, 17 Loyola of Los Angeles Law Review 651 (1997).

Rebecca Tushnet, *Fair Use's Unfinished Business*, 15 Chicago-Kent Journal of Intellectual Property (2) 399 (2016).

Jennifer Urban, Joe Karaganis & Brianna Schofield, *Notice and Takedown in Everyday Practice* 96 (2016).

Jennifer Urban & Laura Quilter, *Efficient process or 'Chilling Effects'? Takedown Notices under Section 512 of the Digital Millenium Copyright Act*, 22 Santa Clara Computer & High Technology Law Journal (4) 621 (2005).

Andrea Usai, *The Freedom to Conduct a Business in the EU, Its Limitations and Its Role in the European Legal Order: A New Engine for Deeper and Stronger Economic, Social and Political Integration*, 14 German Law Journal 1867 (2013).

Nancy Van House & Elizabeth Churchill, *Technologies of Memory: Key Issues and Critical Perspectives*, 1 Memory Studies 295 (2008).

Agnieszka Vetulani-Cęgiel, *EU Copyright Law, Lobbying and Transparency of Policy-Making: The Cases of Sound Recordings Term Extension and Orphan Works Provisions*, 2 JIPITEC 146 (2015).

Luc Verhey & Charald Aal, *Delegatie van regelgevende bevoegdheid in Nederland: tijd voor herbezinning*, 32 RegelMaat: Kwartaalblad voor Wetgevingsvraagstukken 241 (2017).

Feer Verkade, *100 jaar 'Oneerlijke concurrentie' in Nederland – Molengraaff en de onbetamelijke mededinging*, Bijblad Industriële Eigendom (7) 155 (1987).

Jullian Villanueva & Philip Seager, *Marketing in a New Media World* 55 (Mark Rosenberg & Philip Seager eds, 2017).

Dirk Visser, *The Economic Rights Involved: Report on the Netherlands* (Marcel Dellebeke ed., 1997).

Dirk Visser, *'Napsteren', 'Gnutellen' en de afwezigheid van legale muziek op Internet*, Computerrecht (3) 131 (2001).

Dirk Visser, *De Auteurswet gewijzigd: Artikel 15 Aw (citaatrecht)*, AMI (5) 132 (2005).

Dirk Visser, *Openbaar maken: Communication to the Public* 228 (Bernt Hugenholtz, Antoon Quaedvlieg & Dirk Visser eds, 2012).

Dirk Visser, *Openbaar maken met ketchup*, AMI (2) 41 (2013).

Caroline de Vries, *Subjectieve verwijtbaarheid. Een toets om de aansprakelijkheid van internettussenpersonen voor het faciliteren van auteursrechtinbreuken te beoordelen*, AMI (1) 1 (2012).

Edward Walterscheid, *To Promote the Progress of Science and Useful Arts: The Anatomy of a Congressional Power*, 2 (1) 1 (2003).

Artur-Axel Wandtke, *Zum Leistungsschutzrecht der Presseverleger und dem Beteiligungsanspruch der Urheber*, *ZUM* (11) 847 (2014)

A.P. de Wit, *De civielrechtelijke aansprakelijkheid van internetproviders (Deel I)*, Tijdschrift voor Internetrecht (2) 37 (2009).

Lutz-Christian Wolff, *Law and Flexibility – Rule of Law Limits of a Rhetorical Silver Bullet*, 11 The Journal Jurisprudence 549 (2011).

Tim Wu, *When Code Isn't Law*, 89 Virginia Law Review 103 (2003).

Tim Wu, *Tolerated Use*, 31 Columbia Journal of Law & the Arts 617 (2008).

Raquel Xalabarder, *Google News and Copyright*' (Aurelio Lopez-Tarruella ed., 2012).

Sonya Yan Song & Steven Wildman, *Evolution of Strategy and Commercial Relationships for Social Media Platforms: The Case of YouTube* (Mike Friedrichsen & Wolfgang Mühl-Benninghaus eds, 2013).

Leon Yankwich, *What Is Fair Use*, 22 University of Chicago Law Review (1) 203 (1945).

Alfred Yen, *Torts and the Construction of Inducement and Contributory Liability in Amazon and Visa*, 34 Columbia Journal of Law & the Arts (4) 513 (2009).

Lior Zemer, *The Making of a New Copyright Lockean*, 29 Harvard Journal of Law & Public Policy 891 (2005).

Nicolo Zingales, *Internet Intermediary Liability: Identifying Best Practices for Africa* (2013).

Jonathan Zittrain, *Internet Points of Control*, 44 Boston College Law Review 653 (2002).

Jonathan Zittrain, *A History of Online Gatekeeping*, 19 Harvard Journal of Law and Technology 253 (2006).

Frederik Zuiderveen Borgesius et al., *Should We Worry about Filter Bubbles?*, 5 Internet Policy Review 1 (2016).

Table of Cases

European Union

European Court of Human Rights

The Netherlands

Dutch Supreme Court

Court of Appeals

Germany

German Federal Constitutional Court

German Federal Court of Justice

Circuit Court of Appeals

District Courts

Other jurisdictions

Index

G

J

K

L

Q

R

S

www.ingramcontent.com/pod-product-compliance
Lightning Source LLC
LaVergne TN
LVHW020644300926
849161LV00004B/808